CITY POLITICS

The Political Economy of Urban America

Seventh Edition

DENNIS R. JUDD
University of Illinois at Chicago

TODD SWANSTROM
Saint Louis University

Longman
New York San Francisco Boston
London Toronto Sydney Tokyo Singapore Madrid
Mexico City Munich Paris Cape Town Hong Kong Montreal

Editor-in-Chief: Eric Stano
Marketing Manager: Lindsey Prudhomme
Production Coordinator: Scarlett Lindsay
Project Coordination, Text Design, and Electronic Page Makeup: S4Carlisle Publishing Services
Senior Cover Design Manager: Nancy Danahy
Cover Photos: From back to front: Ford Assembly Line, © Hulton Collection/
    Getty Images, Inc.; Students on Their Way to Desegregate Clinton High School, © Howard
    Sochurek/Getty Images, Inc.; Immigrants Demand Reform in New Jersey, © Chris Hondros/
    Getty Images, Inc.
Senior Manufacturing Buyer: Roy L. Pickering, Jr.
Printer and Binder: RR Donnelley & Sons Company/Harrisonburg
Cover Printer: RR Donnelley & Sons Company/Harrisonburg

Library of Congress Cataloging-in-Publication Data

Judd, Dennis R.
  City politics : the political economy of urban america/Dennis R. Judd, Todd Swanstrom.
—7th ed.
    p. cm.
  Includes bibliographical references and index.
  ISBN 978-0-205-73697-3
  1. Municipal government—United States. 2. Urban policy—United States. 3. United States—
Economic policy. 4. Sociology, Urban—United States. I. Swanstrom, Todd. II.
Title.
JS331.J78 2010
320.8'50973—dc22   2009017277

Longman
is an imprint of

2 3 4 5 6 7 8 9 10—DOH—12 11 10

www.pearsonhighered.com

ISBN-13: 978-0-205-73697-3
ISBN-10:   0-205-73697-1

CONTENTS

iii

PREFACE

The seventh edition of *City Politics* is based upon an understanding that the politics of American cities in the global era can be fully understood only by placing it into historical context. Some features of contemporary urban politics are unique to this period. But the historical continuities far outweigh the differences. From the nation's founding, a devotion to the private marketplace and to democratic governance have been the twin pillars of American culture. The tension between the pursuit of local economic prosperity and the need to negotiate the political differences among contending groups has been displayed repeatedly, and often dramatically, in the cities. This dynamic is the thread that allows us to dissolve the past and the present into a singular, continuous narrative.

We divide that narrative into three parts. Part I is composed of four chapters that trace the history of urban America in the first long century, from the nation's founding in 1789 through the Great Depression of the 1930s. The "long century" spans a period of time in which the cities of the expanding nation competed fiercely for a place in the nation's rapidly evolving economic system. At the same time, cities were forced to cope with the social tensions and disruptions caused by wave after wave of immigration. These tensions played out in a struggle to control local democratic institutions, but by the late nineteenth century some urban residents began to leave the cities altogether by moving into the first suburban enclaves, a process that has continued to unfold up to the present day.

The urban crisis of the twentieth century erupted onto the national political agenda in the years after World War II, and it continued to dominate discourse about American cities until the 1990s. The crisis can be understood through the lens of the three imperatives of urban politics. First, older central cities were plunged into economic crisis by the massive suburbanization of the postwar period, and metropolitan areas in the North began losing population and investment to the new cities of the Sunbelt. In the past, cities had tried to solve their economic problems by pursing local strategies of growth. After World War II, the cities entered into a different kind of competition, this time for a share of the rapidly expanding array of urban and social programs being funded by the federal government. But the preoccupation with urban decline played out against the social tensions that threatened to engulf the cities. In the years after World War II, millions of southern blacks poured into northern cities, a process that incited a protected period of social unrest and racial animosity. Affluent whites fled the cities, carving out suburban enclaves in an attempt to escape the problems of the metropolis. The imperative of governance—the need to find ways of brokering among the contending racial, ethnic, and other interests making up the urban polity—became a driving force in city politics, just as it had been in the previous century.

For contemporary urban politics, though specific issues may have changed, the broad outlines are familiar. As in the past, the three imperatives of urban politics continue to define the political struggles of the global era. Especially when combined with the drying up of federal programs, the deindustrialization that began in the 1980s threw cities into a competitive race for survival that harkened back to the intense interurban competition of the nineteenth century. Another parallel with that period is the massive immigration that picked up speed in the 1990s, with all the conflicts and tensions that accompany such rapid social change. When these developments are considered against the historical background, a powerful narrative emerges that situates urban politics firmly within the contours of our national history. We have crafted our text to be read through the lens of that narrative.

Over the years we have been pleased that this book has been widely used in college courses at all levels. We are equally pleased that, over the years, it has been copiously cited in the scholarly literature of our field. Textbooks do not ordinarily make substantial scholarly contributions because they frequently rely excessively upon a secondary literature. In this edition, as in the past, we have worked very hard to avoid that shortcoming by incorporating three elements: a strong and original thematic structure with a blending of the vast secondary literature with primary sources, new data, and our own research. We have provided notes at the end of each chapter to encourage students to supplement the text by conducting their own research.

City Politics is useful to advanced scholars and graduate students as well as to students taking their first courses in urban politics, urban sociology, urban planning, urban geography, and urban history. To enrich the classroom and research opportunities for scholars and students alike, we have incorporated new research and data in every chapter of the book. The several new features incorporated into this seventh edition include:

- A comprehensive discussion throughout the text of the impact of the global economic recession of 2008/2009
- Research that incorporates the urban policies of the Obama Administration
- A thorough recasting of the chapter on the fiscal politics of cities to take into account the dramatic effects of the recession of 2008/2009 on city budgets and spending
- A reorganization of chapters to make the linkage between central cities and suburbs more explicit

We are pleased to be able to thank, in print, the following reviewers who made insightful comments and suggestions: Kathryn Brice, Georgia State University; Stefanie Chambers, Trinity College; Joseph Frank, Washington University—St. Louis; Ron Hayduk, Borough of Manhattan Community College; Roxanne Ezzet, University of Texas at Dallas; Charlie Tyler, University of South Carolina; Robert Blair, Univeristy of Nebraska at Omaha; Cynthia H. Kramer, William Woods University; and Susan E. Clarke, University of Colorado—Boulder. Dennis Judd would like to thank Daniel Bliss for his valuable research assistance. We also wish to thank Eric Stano, our experienced and perceptive editor at Longman Publishers, for keeping the book on track.

DENNIS R. JUDD
TODD SWANSTROM

CHAPTER 1

THE EVOLUTION OF CITY POLITICS IN AMERICA: AN INTRODUCTION

CITIES IN THE GLOBAL ERA

Cities and urban regions are at the center of the globalization processes of the twenty-first century. Two streams of movement have transformed large and small cities alike in the space of a remarkably few years. One stream has been made up of highly educated white-collar professionals—for example, corporate managers, management consultants, legal experts, accountants, computer specialists, financial analysts, media and public relations specialists. Especially in larger cities, these affluent professionals have moved into downtown condominium towers and gentrified nearby neighborhoods. Another stream has been composed of service workers in search of jobs and opportunity. Maintenance, clerical, and personal services jobs required in high-rise office buildings and the low-wage, often seasonal work available in restaurants, entertainment venues, tourism, and associated businesses have drawn large numbers of immigrants and ethnic minorities. One of the results of these two movements is that cities have become both prosperous and divided, a development with far-reaching consequences that are difficult to foresee because of the global economic crisis that began to unfold in 2008. Since the early 1990s most inner cities have experienced a stunning revival,[1] but it is probable that some cities, including the largest global cities, will become less prosperous but even more divided because of the economic downturn. If this transpires, then the inner-city renaissance could be put on hold or even reversed, at least in the most troubled places.

For much of the twentieth century, cities occupied secure economic niches—Detroit made automobiles; St. Louis made beer, automobiles, airplanes, and chemicals; Pittsburgh was a steelmaking center; Chicago relied on meatpacking and steel and machine parts, and a complex mix of manufacturing. But in the years after World War II, the fortunes of these urban centers changed very quickly. In the 1950s, millions of white families began leaving for the suburbs. Manufacturing, retailing, and other economic sectors soon followed. Meanwhile, in one of the largest population movements in U.S. history, millions of blacks began a historic exodus from the South to northern industrial cities. These momentous demographic upheavals opened a chasm between the suburbs and the central cities. Most suburbs prospered, but the cities located at the center of metropolitan regions became increasingly segregated, dilapidated, economically stagnant, and poor. The prospects for the cities became even dimmer in the 1970s when manufacturing began moving to sites with lower labor costs in southern or southwestern states, or left the country entirely. In older cities, unemployment rates climbed rapidly, and it became clear that if cities were to survive, they would have to find ways to attract new investment. Cities began to turn around only when local governments recognized that they could turn some aspects of these economic changes to their advantage.

Public leadership and public money have been essential for making the transition to a global economy revolving around services, tourism, and culture. In recent decades cities everywhere have devoted huge energies and financial resources to attract these sectors. Their efforts are visible in such projects as downtown malls, sports stadiums, convention centers, and a host of other projects subsidized by taxpayers' dollars. Politicians and civic elites have been so enthusiastically engaged in the cause of promoting the local economy that it sometimes has seemed as if they are incapable of paying attention to anything else. At such times, city politics appears to revolve around one singular imperative, *growth*.

However, another imperative, *governance* also drives urban politics. Cities are arenas in which contending interests work out their differences. Democratic norms and procedures give citizens a means of holding their leaders to account for their use of public resources. In the global era, conflicts over priorities and policies are often heated and contentious because there are claimants representing an extraordinarily diverse array of interests.

International migration is transforming societies around the globe, and the United States is no exception. More immigrants came to the United States in the 1990s than in any previous decade in the nation's history, and the flow has continued into the twenty-first century. The social and political effects of large-scale population movements are dramatically evident in big global cities such as Miami, New York, Chicago, and San Francisco, and in many other places as well. In such cities, politics pivots around issues of racial and ethnic identity at least as much as around issues of economic development.

Local governments often find it difficult to walk the fine line between the imperatives of growth and governance. In even the most prosperous cities, symbols of corporate power, personal wealth, and luxury consumption typically stand in sharp contrast to neighborhoods exhibiting high rates of poverty, violence, and physical dereliction. Sometimes the inequalities occur on the same block, when office workers walk by homeless people or stop to eat at a fast-food restaurant staffed by minimum-wage employees. Affluent professionals drive up the price of downtown real estate to stratospheric levels and lead the gentrification of nearby neighborhoods, but slums can be found close by. As long as these contrasts exist, policies that appear to be weighted in favor of affluent residents, downtown business, and tourists will often provoke opposition.

To fully trace the contours of urban politics in the global era, we must, finally, add a third imperative, the *politics of defended space*. Metropolitan landscapes are fractured into a complex geography that reflects the inequalities and demographic processes of the global era. Political fragmentation facilitates a pattern of segregation that separates people according to racial and ethnic identity and social class differences. All through the twentieth century, the white middle class escaped the cities by moving to the suburbs. Patterns of segregation arising from city-suburban divide are now augmented by the rise of privatized gated communities. The proliferation of walled and gated residential developments adds an important new dimension to the fragmentation of metropolitan areas because it allows some urban residents to escape from the democratic politics of the public realm altogether.

It is essential to recognize that the politics of growth, governance, and defended space are not new to the global era. In some form these imperatives have acted as the driving forces in urban politics throughout the nation's history. To understand city politics today, it is important to understand how much the past still reverberates in the global era. In the remainder of this chapter, we attempt to clarify this point by tracing some of the continuities that knit the history of urban politics into a coherent historical narrative.

THE POLITICS OF GROWTH

Throughout America's national history the most fundamental goal of urban residents and their civic leaders has generally been local economic prosperity. Founded originally as centers of trade and commerce, the nation's cities and towns came into being as places where people could make money. This was true for the oldest colonial cities and, later, for cities on the expanding American frontier. The nineteenth-century movement across the continent placed towns at the leading edge of territorial expansion:

> America was settled as a long, thin line of urban places, scattering outward and westward from the Atlantic seaboard. The popular imagination has it that farmers came first and villages later. The historian's truth is that villages and towns came first, pulling farmers along to settle the land around and between urban settlements.[2]

Each town was its own capitalist system in miniature, held together by the independent actions of individuals in search of profit and fortune. The restless pursuit of new opportunities encouraged the formation of what urban historian Sam Bass Warner has called a national "culture of privatism," which stressed individual efforts and aspirations over collective or public purposes: "[The] local politics of American cities have depended for their actors, and for a good deal of their subject matter, on the changing focus of men's private economic activities."[3]

Attempts to promote local prosperity have been a constant feature in the history of urban politics in America. On the frontier, the founders of cities and the entrepreneurs who made their money in them recognized that in order to ensure their mutual success, they had to take steps to promote their city and region. Boosters went to some pains to advertise their city's supposed advantages—a harbor or strategic location on a river, for example, or proximity to rich farming and mining areas. They also boasted about local culture: music societies, libraries, and universities. And they went further than boasting; they used the powers of city governments to promote local growth. Municipalities were corporations that could be used to help finance a variety of local undertakings, from subscriptions in railroad stock to improvements in harbors and docks. Cities still play that role today, even though the particular economic development strategies have changed. In the global era, investors and business leaders fight for lower taxes and public subsidies for developers who build office towers, luxury hotels, and tourism and entertainment facilities.

The only reason such efforts often generate controversy is that they do not benefit everyone; there are always winners and losers. For renters and low-income residents, a booming economy with rising land values may put affordable housing out of reach. Growth in the downtown corporate and financial sectors may create some high-paying jobs for educated professionals but leave many central-city residents in low-paying jobs or on the unemployment rolls. A downtown that encroaches on nearby neighborhoods may benefit the businesses located in the new office towers but may also compromise the quality of life for nearby residents. People who do not care about sports may resent helping to pay for a new football stadium. Different perspectives such as these explain why there is a politics of growth at all instead of a reliable consensus around the idea that governments should do everything necessary to promote it.

The use of eminent domain by local governments illustrates the kinds of disputes that break out over a city's employment of public powers to promote economic development. Recently, the widespread use of eminent domain to take property to make way for big-box stores, malls, condominium projects, and other projects has provoked heated controversy. For most of the nation's history, local governments have possessed the authority to take property without the owners' consent if it serves a legitimate public purpose.[4] The power of eminent domain has been used to assemble land for public infrastructure, such as highways, parks, and airports. A significant change occurred in the public housing and urban renewal programs of the 1950s, when eminent domain became tied to the goal of revitalizing the inner cities. To make it possible to replace "lesser" with "higher" uses of urban land, local governments were empowered to declare entire neighborhoods "blighted." The clearance of neighborhoods for urban renewal projects reached such proportions in the 1950s that it ignited massive protest that spread to many cities.

Recently, conflicts over the eminent domain powers of local government have once again swept the nation. In a bid to attract development, public officials have made liberal use of eminent domain to promote for a wide range of economic development projects, ranging from the redevelopment of deteriorated neighborhoods to the building of entertainment centers in downtown areas to the construction of shopping mall complexes and multiplex theaters in the suburbs. As part of the development process, governments have often even assigned their eminent domain authority to private corporations engaged in redevelopment.

Public officials tend to regard these steps as useful tools for improving their communities, but the owners of private property regard it through a much more skeptical eye, especially when the result has been to increase profits for developers. On December 20, 2000, a group of homeowners led by Sussette Kelo filed suit to challenge a decision by the city of New London, Connecticut, to cede its eminent domain authority to a private corporation that wanted to raze their homes. Things came to a head on June 23, 2005, when the U.S. Supreme Court upheld lower-court rulings against the homeowners. The Court's decision provoked a nationwide reaction from the advocates of property rights. In response to the public furor, by the fall of 2006 state legislatures in 30 states had enacted restrictions on the use of eminent domain and hundreds of towns and cities had done likewise. In the fall elections of 2006, voters in 12 states passed referendums prohibiting the taking of property for private development.[5]

The lesson from the *Kelo v. New London* case is that despite the fact that almost everyone embraces the goal of prosperity and realizes that economic development is necessary for achieving it (nobody likes the opposite!), other values are also at stake. The process of governance involves the arbitration among contending interests when clashes like these occur over basic values.

THE POLITICS OF GOVERNANCE

Although American cities often seem preoccupied with promoting prosperity, they are not plutocracies that cede political power to wealthy elites. American city governments are run according to rules that reflect a long tradition of local democracy that cuts against the grain of the culture of privatism and private gain.[6] Individuals have a right to pursue their own private interests, but they do so within a political system based on democratic principles.[7] City charters and the formal rules of city politics emphasize votes, not money. Just as the currency of the economic marketplace is money, votes are the currency of the political system. To assemble a winning electoral coalition, politicians must spread the benefits of city government broadly enough to gain a minimum level of satisfaction from a variety of political interests and groups.

City governments are mechanisms for arbitrating among the groups and factions that make up the local polity, a task as difficult today as it ever was in the past. Democratic procedures invest those who govern with the legitimacy to act in the name of citizens collectively. Governmental authority springs from the right to "make and apply decisions that are binding upon any and all segments of society."[8] At the same time that city officials must satisfy investors, they must also satisfy voters. To remain in office, at least over the long run, they must seem sufficiently responsive to a large enough proportion of the electorate.

Until the mid-nineteenth century, when cities were still small and colonial-era values still prevailed, men of social standing and wealth held most of the political authority. In the cities, "leadership fell to those who exercised economic leadership. All leadership, political, social, economic, tended to collect in the same set of hands."[9] Business owners, professionals, and aristocrats ran municipal affairs without challenge, deriving their authority primarily from their social standing. Obviously, the governance of cities is much more complicated today, for two reasons: Cities have taken on a greater range of responsibilities, and a complex mix of interests expect to have a voice in the democratic system.

The powers and responsibilities of cities have grown because of the problems that arise in densely populated environments, and also because, over time, urban residents have come to expect more from government. As cities grew from the colonial period to the end of the century, sometimes exploding within a few years from small settlements to densely packed industrial cities, citizens saw they were powerless to correct or to escape from collective problems such as crime, fire, and disease. City services were created to address such problems, and they have continued to evolve ever since. Cities today provide a remarkable array of services. They build and maintain a public infrastructure—roads, bridges, sewer lines, sewage treatment plants, water mains, parks, zoos, hospitals, and sometimes even universities. They provide police and fire protection. They collect garbage (or pay someone who does). They run public health services that inspect restaurants, vaccinate children, and test for the HIV (AIDS) virus. Through city zoning ordinances, they influence the location of homes, factories, office buildings, restaurants, and parking lots. Through local building codes, they regulate such matters as plumbing, wiring, building materials, the height of structures, and architectural styles. Cities poison rats and sometimes try to scare away pigeons. These public undertakings, and a long list more, are essential to the safety and well-being of people living in cities. Without them, life in most cities would quickly become not only dangerous but intolerable.

But just what should cities do, and who should benefit from their activities? These questions take on a sense of urgency because the demands and needs of the interests operating in the political sphere differ sharply. The needs of one group—say, business—cannot always win because so many other groups make political claims. In a democratic system, politicians must take care to distribute the rewards of public policies widely enough to construct governing coalitions. If only a few benefit, opposition will arise, and political leaders may find themselves replaced. If enough people begin to feel that their interests or needs are ignored, two things may happen: Other politicians may step into the fray and depose those in office, or unrest and even violence may erupt as an expression of pent-up grievances.

In the history of American cities, ethnic and racial divisions have always been the most enduring fault line in the politics of governance. During the nineteenth and the early twentieth centuries, cities attracted waves of immigrants, first from England, Ireland, and Germany, then from Italy and Eastern Europe. In the twentieth century, they received millions of new migrants, this time African Americans from the South and destitute whites from rural pockets of poverty, plus Mexicans escaping violence and poverty in their own country. In the global era, cities have attracted waves of immigrants from all over the world. These movements have made cities culturally and socially dynamic places, but they have also meant that the politics of governance often revolves around issues of race and ethnicity, as in the past.

Throughout its history, America has been a nation of immigrants. As a result, racial and ethnic divisions have always been important dimensions of its political life. Recurring riots directed against Irish and other immigrants in the nineteenth century; the rise of the Ku Klux Klan and violence against blacks in the first decades of the twentieth century; race riots that swept cities from coast to coast in the 1960s; the Rodney King incident and the Los Angeles riots of 1992: These episodes demonstrate that race has long been a prominent feature of politics in American cities. Race continues to be a fundamental dividing line in the voting booth. Perhaps the most vivid example of the continuing power of race in city politics came in New Orleans in 2005. When the storm surge from Hurricane Katrina breached the dikes surrounding New Orleans on August 29, 2005, 80 percent of the city was flooded and nearly 100,000 people were left to deal with the consequences. Wrenching images of human suffering filled television news programs: 25,000 people trying to live under impossible conditions in the Superdome; 20,000 more in the Convention Center; residents walking on bridges and overpasses and desperately waving from rooftops. More than 1.5 million people were displaced, 60,000 homes were destroyed, and 1,300 people died.[10] The catastrophe exposed glaring weaknesses in America's intergovernmental system, but no interpretation of the disaster can avoid the fact that black neighborhoods located on the lowest and least desirable land bore the brunt of the destruction. The racial inequalities that made this possible are a legacy of New Orleans' past, and they will not be easily addressed.

THE POLITICS OF DEFENDED SPACE

A deeply ingrained distrust of cities bias has long been a important feature of American culture. Only a few years after the Constitution was ratified, Thomas Jefferson wrote, "I view great cities as pestilential to the morals, the health, and the liberties of man."[11] In the 1970s John V. Lindsay, the former mayor of New York, observed that "in the American psychology, the city has been a basically suspect institution."[12] These attitudes have persisted despite the fact that, according to the 2000 census, 80 percent of Americans now live in metropolitan areas.[13] But it is unclear what it means to observe that America is an urban nation. Residents of Phoenix or Dallas may feel they have little in common with residents of New York City or Boston, and the people living in the suburbs of these cities may feel only distantly related to their central cities, or to one another.

Because America has always been a land of immigrants and movers, it has sometimes been said that Americans have a tendency to pick up and leave whenever they feel dissatisfied. First was the move to America, and then—or so goes the standard narrative—came the restless migration across the continent. The story of westward expansion fills the history books, but in the same years, the demographic geography of cities was being fundamentally changed by the flight of the wealthy and the middle classes from the densely crowded neighborhoods close to the waterfront. Throughout the nineteenth and twentieth centuries, the development of new forms of transportation, first the omnibus, the horsecar, the streetcar, and finally the automobile, enabled the well-to-do to move farther and farther from the inconvenience and problems of the congested city.

The proliferation of suburban communities became only the latest chapter in this long-term trend. Today's metropolitan regions are fragmented into hundreds of governmental jurisdictions. By 2002 there were 87,900 governments in the United States.

In addition to the federal government and the 50 states, there were 38,971 local governments: 3,034 counties and 35,937 subcounty governments, including 19,431 municipalities and 16,506 townships. The remainder, which comprises over one-half of the total, are special-purpose local governments, including 13,522 school districts and 35,356 special districts.[14] Special districts and authorities set up with taxing and spending powers that serve special purposes, such as running toll bridges or building sewer systems, are the fastest growing types of local government in the United States. Many of the services previously supplied by city governments are now provided by special districts, which are run more like private corporations than governments.[15]

In addition to these public governments, in recent decades thousands of privatized communities have sprung up, each governed by a neighborhood association that assesses fees for maintenance, services, and amenities. These communities are often "gated," separated from surrounding neighborhoods by walls or other physical barriers. These developments, which sometimes sprawl over large areas, allow affluent homeowners to achieve an almost pure segregation from the less well-off. Those who lack the resources to move to desirable suburbs or gated communities are forced to live in jurisdictions that have fewer resources for providing adequate public services and amenities.

The terrorist attacks on September 11, 2001, added still another element to the mix. A prominent urban scholar, Peter Marcuse, has predicted that the events of 9/11 would have the effect of increasing the fortification and close surveillance of urban space, thus emphasizing a trend that was already in process.[16] Security cameras have become ubiquitous on urban streets, and metal detectors are increasingly used in public buildings and in schools. Will the result of these developments be the erosion of social and political life, as Marcuse asserts?[17] The answer is not obvious, but it is an important question to ponder.

THE UNFINISHED TASK

In recent years two developments have become clear: Central cities are reviving, and a panoply of income and ethnic groups are moving to the suburbs. Waves of immigration from all over the world have created the multiethnic metropolis. A question posed at many places in this text is how this development will be managed. It is possible that the new metropolis will be as fragmented as in the twentieth century. There is much evidence, however, that the patterns of segregation inherited from the past are breaking down. Ethnic and racial groups are becoming widely distributed throughout metropolitan areas. The 2000 census showed that more than half of all Latinos, almost 40 percent of blacks, and 55 percent of Asians lived in suburbs, and in many urban regions, the proportions were much higher.[18] Many more suburbs than before are ethnically diverse. Even so, it can accurately be said that there is no metropolitan community. America's urban areas are still fractured into many governments, communities, and enclaves. Whether they can learn to live in harmony with one another is one of the great unfinished challenges of this century.

NOTES

1. Saskia Sassen, *The Global City: New York, London, Tokyo,* 2nd ed. (Princeton, N.J.: Princeton University Press, 2001).
2. Lawrence J. R. Herson and John M. Bolland, *The Urban Web: Politics, Policy, and Theory* (Chicago: Nelson-Hall, 1990), p. 43.
3. Sam Bass Warner Jr., *The Private City: Philadelphia in Three Periods of Its Growth* (Philadelphia: University of Pennsylvania Press, 1968), p. 4.
4. For a history and full discussion, see Wikipedia *(http://en.wikipedia.orgn/wiki/Eminent_domain).*
5. See Institute of Justice *(http://www.ij.org/private_property/connecticut/index);* William Yardley, "Anger Drives Property Rights Measures," *New York Times,* October 8, 2006 *(http://www.nytimes.com).*
6. Robert Bellah et al., *Habits of the Heart: Individualism and Commitment in American Life* (Berkeley: University of California Press, 1985).
7. For a theoretical analysis of the popular democratic theory of American local government, see Anwar Syed, *The Political Theory of Local Government* (New York: Random House, 1966).
8. Eric Nordlinger, *On the Autonomy of the Democratic State* (Cambridge, Mass.: Harvard University Press, 1981).
9. Herson and Bolland, *The Urban Web,* p. 46.
10. Louise Comfort, "Cities at Risk: Hurricane Katrina and the Drowning of New Orleans," *Urban Affairs Review* 41 (March 2006): 501–506.
11. Quoted in James A. Clapp, *The City: A Dictionary of Quotable Thoughts on Cities and Urban Life* (New Brunswick, N.J.: Center for Urban Policy Research, Rutgers University, 1984), pp. 128–129.
12. Quoted in ibid., p. 148.
13. U.S. Bureau of the Census, *Census 2000 (http://www.census.gov/cens2000).*
14. U.S. Bureau of the Census, *2002 Census of Governments,* July 2002 *(http://www.census.gov/govs/ www/cog2002).*
15. Nancy Burns, *The Formation of American Local Governments: Private Values in Public Institutions* (New York: Oxford University Press, 1994).
16. Peter Marcuse, "The 'War on Terrorism' and Life in Cities After September 11, 2001," in *Cities, War, and Terrorism: Towards an Urban Geopolitics,* ed. Stephen Graham (New York: Blackwell, 2005), p. 271.
17. Ibid., pp. 274–275.
18. John Logan, "The New Ethnic Enclaves," in William H. Frey, *Melting Pot Suburbs: A Census 2000 Study of Suburban Diversity* (Washington, D.C.: Center for Urban and Metropolitan Policy, Brookings Institution Press, June 2001), p. 2.

PART I

THE CHANGING DYNAMICS OF URBAN POLITICS: THE FIRST CENTURY

CHAPTER 2

THE POLITICAL LEGACY
OF AMERICA'S URBAN PAST

NATIONAL DEVELOPMENT AND THE CITIES

When the U.S. Constitution was ratified in 1789, the cities of the new nation were scattered along the eastern coastline of a vast, mostly unexplored continent. Only five of these cities—Boston, New York, Philadelphia, Baltimore, and Charleston—exceeded 10,000 in population. In the decades to follow, the nation's social and economic development went hand in hand with the growth of cities. By the beginning of the twentieth century, a culture that had defined its character by reference to rural life and a western frontier had been transformed. The frontier had closed; 40 percent of Americans lived in towns and cities; and the nation's economy had become more industrial than agricultural. Urbanization occurred at such an incredible pace and scale that it threatened to rend the fabric that held American culture together. The symbols and the reality of the industrial age—belching smokestacks, wave after wave of foreign immigrants, social disorder, and racial and ethnic strife—all were concentrated in the cities. Americans, though all descended from immigrants themselves, developed a fear and distrust of cities and urban life. The antiurban attitudes formed in this period became a feature of American culture that has endured right up to the present day.

The industrial economy required a steady supply of cheap and plentiful labor. A flood of foreign immigration began to surge into the country in the 1840s, and it did not ebb until Congress passed legislation to curb it, in the 1920s. Most of the immigrants settled in crowded urban neighborhoods close to the factories. Right from the start tensions arose between the newcomers and the people who had come earlier, as dramatically portrayed in the 2002 film release *Gangs of New York*. Cultural and religious conflict became an everyday occurrence, and sometimes it escalated into violence. Successive waves of immigrants—poor, often illiterate, unfamiliar with the language and customs of their new country, and unaccustomed to city life—struggled to cope with miserable conditions in overcrowded slums. Those who had come to

OUTTAKE

CITY-BUILDING HAS ALWAYS REQUIRED PUBLIC EFFORTS

All through American history, civic leaders have used public resources to promote local economic prosperity. In the nineteenth century, the intense competition among cities ignited a "struggle for primacy and power" in which "like imperial states, cities carved out extensive dependencies, extended their influence over the economic and political life of the hinterland, and fought with contending places over strategic trade routes." In the American West the job of marketing new towns was often daunting because many of them were, in fact, hard, isolated places in which to live. In such circumstances local promoters played up the positive features of their town or, frequently, made up fantastical tales: "Questioning a place's promise affected not just those doing the questioning but also all who had put stock, mental and material, in the place." Everyone in a locality, from town councils to realtors and chambers of commerce, were vigilant in discouraging any negative information from leaking out. Instead, promoters made the smallest towns seem like centers of high culture and made the most desolate deserts sound like fertile land waiting for the plow.

But civic leaders did not rely upon marketing alone. It became obvious after midcentury that to prosper or even survive, cities would have to tie into the emerging national railroad network. In an attempt to gain advantage in the urban sweepstakes, civic boosters raised private subscriptions and used the public resources of city government to induce railroad companies to make connections to their city, and often the municipality paid for local stations and offloading facilities. The railroads received huge subsidies from the national and state governments, but cities contributed the most of all. Eventually the competition for rail connections became so frenzied the companies were building new lines just to obtain subsidies. The expectation that these subsidies would guarantee local prosperity was dashed when hundreds of rail companies went belly up in the 1870s, leaving towns and cities with big debts but no way to pay them.

The parallel with the politics of growth in today's cities is striking. In recent decades, huge public resources have again been devoted to boosting local economic vitality. As in the nineteenth century, civic boosters are fired with the conviction that the fate of their cities hangs in the balance. This time, cities have expended great resources on building an infrastructure to lure tourist and suburban visitors. Since the 1980s cities have been engaged in a virtual arms race to build stadiums, convention centers, malls and entertainment centers, and other facilities. Cities also compete to host such events as auto races, music festivals, and special museum exhibits.

Most supporters of public subsidies believe the expenditures are worthy of public support because, they argue, the public investment will help contribute to the local economy and therefore benefit everyone. But vigorous disagreement often ensues about what should be built and who should pay for it. In the nineteenth century and still today, when taxpayers foot the bill, the question always arises: Who benefits?

Source: The two quotations are from Richard C. Wade, *The Urban Frontier: Pioneer Life in Early Pittsburgh, Cincinnati, Lexington, Louisville, and St. Louis* (Chicago: University of Chicago Press, 1959), p. 103; David M. Wrobel, *Promised Lands: Promotion, Memory, and the Creation of the American West* (Lawrence: University Press of Kansas, 2002), p. 71.

America first generally viewed the most recently arrived not only as inferior but threatening and morally deficient.

The basic outlines of this historical narrative are relevant to the contemporary American city because long after the waves of foreign immigration of the industrial age, many Americans continued to associate cities with images of poverty, crime, racial conflict, social disorder, and moral decline.[1] In the years after World War II, southern blacks poured into the cities while whites fled to the suburbs. By the 1990s, a different backlash, this one against immigrants from Latin America, began to take the form of legislation to curb immigration and to reduce social spending on illegal immigrants and laws requiring English-only instruction in the schools. It is remarkable how similar the reactions against newcomers in earlier periods were to today's cultural backlash. For this reason, to understand the contemporary contours of urban politics in the United States, the best place to start is with the cities of the past.

A CENTURY OF URBAN GROWTH

In the nineteenth century, cities of the industrializing nations grew at a pace unprecedented in history. In 1800 London was the only city in the world to approach one million in population.[2] Paris ranked second among European cities with a population of 547,000. Just over 60,000 people lived in New York, which was the largest city in America by far. But only 100 years later, 11 Western cities had topped the million-person mark: London had 6,586,000, Paris 2,714,000,[3] and New York 3,437,000. In England and Wales, the percentage of the population living in towns[4] and cities increased from 25 to 77 percent in the same period. Never before in world history had cities grown so large or so fast, and never before had such a high proportion of the population lived in cities. The urban historian Eric Lampard has said, "the period c. A.D. 1750–1850 [is] one of the crucial disjunctions in the history of human society. Whatever constraints had hitherto checked or moderated the growth and re-distribution of population were suddenly relaxed."[5] Commenting on the growth of cities in 1895, the *Atlantic Monthly* noted, "The great fact in . . . social development . . . at the close of the nineteenth century is the tendency all over the world to concentrate in great cities. This tendency is seen everywhere."[6]

The American experience paralleled these developments. As shown by the data in Table 2.1, from the first national census of 1790 to the census of 1920, the urban population (defined by the Census Bureau as people living in cities and towns of 2,500 or more) increased in most decades more than twice as fast as the U.S. population as a whole. The only significant exception to this trend showed up between 1810 and 1820, when homesteaders and farmers streamed across the Appalachian Mountains to settle the Old Northwest (now western Pennsylvania, Ohio, and Indiana). Soon, however, even the expanding frontier could not absorb enough people to keep pace with urban growth. From 1790 to 1860, the U.S. population increased by 30 percent or more each decade; it continued to climb by 20 percent per decade in the half century from 1860 to 1910 (before falling to a 15 percent rate of growth from 1910 to 1920). The cities grew much faster, however, they added more than 60 percent to their populations

Table 2.1   The Pace of Urbanization in the United States, 1790–1920

Year	Total Population	Percentage Increase over Preceding Census	Urban Population	Percentage Increase over Preceding Population	Percentage Total Population in Cities[a]
1790	3,929,214	—	201,655	—	5%
1800	5,308,483	35%	322,371	60%	6
1810	7,239,881	36	525,459	63	7
1820	9,638,453	33	693,255	32	7
1830	12,866,020	33.5	1,127,247	63	9
1840	17,069,453	33	1,845,055	64	11
1850	23,191,876	36	3,543,716	92	15
1860	31,443,321	36	6,216,518	75	20
1870	39,818,449	27	9,902,361	59	26
1880	50,155,783	26	14,129,735	43	28
1890	62,947,714	25.5	22,106,265	56.5	35
1900	75,994,575	21	30,214,832	37	40
1910	91,972,266	21	42,064,001	39	46
1920	105,710,620	15	54,253,280	29	51

[a]Cities and towns of 2,500 or more.

Sources: U.S. Department of Commerce, Bureau of the Census, *Historical Statistics of the United States, Colonial Times to 1970,* pt. 1, Bicentennial ed. (Washington, D.C.: U.S. Government Printing Office, 1975), p. 8; U.S. Department of Commerce, Bureau of the Census, *1970 Census of Population,* vol. 1, *Characteristics of the Population,* pt. 1 (Washington, D.C.: U.S. Government Printing Office, 1973), p. 42.

from 1790 to 1820, and 32 percent during the 1820s. These numbers were but a prelude to the explosive growth to follow, with cities growing by more than 40 percent between most national census tallies.

Urban life on this scale was an entirely new and often shocking experience. Even as late as the census of 1840, a full half century after the nation's founding, only one American in ten lived in cities and towns of 2,500 or more. In the years leading up to the Civil War, however, cities began growing at breakneck speed. Foreign immigrants began pouring into the cities in search of jobs in the factories; at the same time a steady migration from farm to city was unfolding for the same reason. By 1860 the Census Bureau classified 20 percent of the American population as urban. By century's end the urban proportion had doubled again to almost 40 percent. When the 1920 census was taken, more than half—51 percent—of Americans lived in cities and towns. In less than a century, the United States had become more urban than rural.

Because of their importance as financial and commercial (and later as industrial) centers, the old cities on the eastern seaboard benefited from national development. New York maintained its supremacy as the hub of finance and trade. Its continued status as the nation's premier city was ensured in 1825, the year the Erie Canal was completed. The canal linked the city directly to the Great Lakes, turning New York into a giant funnel gathering the resources of a vast continent into a worldwide trading system. After the Civil War, it consolidated its position by becoming a great manufacturing city. Huge throngs of immigrants passed through the port of New York, and many of them settled there. From a population of 369,000 in 1840, New York exploded to over 3.4 million people by 1900—nearly a tenfold increase in 60 years! By 1920, when its population reached 5.6 million, it had consolidated its position as a leading global center of finance, trade, and manufacturing.

Despite its incredible growth, New York's share of the nation's urban population fell steadily throughout the nineteenth century. Thousands of new towns and cities sprang up as the nation expanded westward, and these places often grew even faster than New York—although none were destined to challenge its supremacy. In 1800, 18 percent of the nation's urban population lived in New York City, but by 1890 this proportion had fallen to 7 percent.[7] New York remained the largest city, but as the century progressed, other cities assumed prominent places in an increasingly integrated national and international network of cities. The data in Table 2.2 help tell this story. New York grew from a city of 137,388 in 1820 to more than 1 million by 1860, and to 5.6 million by 1920, but over the same period other cities grew just as rapidly. Philadelphia had a population of 64,000 in 1820, topped 565,000 by 1860, and grew to a city of more than 1.8 million by 1920. Boston increased its population from 43,000 in 1820 to nearly 178,000 in 1860, and to almost 750,000 by 1920.

Meanwhile, cities in the interior grew at almost unbelievable rates, typically changing from small frontier towns to busy urban centers in only a few years. St. Louis, the old French settlement where Lewis and Clark outfitted their expedition in 1805, exploded from a town of only 16,000 people in 1840 to a city of over 160,000 by 1860, and to more than 772,000 by 1920. But Chicago's growth was even more startling. In the 20 years from 1840 to 1860 it was transformed from a swampy frontier village of 4,500 to a city of more than 112,000. But this was only the beginning. By 1880 Chicago had left St. Louis in the dust, and by 1920 its population had soared to 2.7 million people, putting it second only to New York. Smaller urban settlements dotted the landscape between cities like St. Louis and Chicago. Few of these places had any prospects of challenging their larger rivals, though their promoters never gave up trying. Places like St. Louis, New Orleans (on the Mississippi River), Chicago (at the foot of Lake Michigan), and Cincinnati (on the Ohio River) had got a head start as major trading centers, transferring goods through the Great Lakes or the inland river system to the eastern seaboard cities or directly to Europe. Smaller cities and towns prospered by finding a specialized niche in an emerging urban hierarchy. At the top of the pyramid, the largest cities drew the largest number of immigrants, produced the greatest range of goods, and asserted command over vast hinterlands. Second-tier cities had more specialized economies, and they served as transfer points to the larger urban centers. The bottom of the hierarchy was composed of the multitude of small towns that shipped agricultural and extractive resources gathered from mines, forests, and farms to the larger cities, which entered them into international commerce or transformed them into manufactured goods. This expanding network of cities, was the key element in opening the American frontier.

Table 2.2 Population and Rate of Growth in Five Large Cities, 1820–1920[a]

	New York City[b]	Percentage Increase	Chicago	Percentage Increase	Philadelphia	Percentage Increase	St. Louis	Percentage Increase	Boston	Percentage Increase	Percentage Increase in U.S. Population
1820	137,388		—		63,802		4,598		43,298		
1830	220,471	60%	—		80,462	26%	5,847	27%	61,392	42%	33%
1840	369,305	67	4,470		93,665	16	16,469	182	93,383	52	33
1850	660,803	79	29,963	570%	121,376	30	77,860	373	136,881	47	36
1860	1,183,148	79	112,172	274	565,529	366	160,773	107	177,840	30	36
1870	1,546,293	31	298,977	167	674,022	19	310,864	93	250,526	41	27
1880	2,061,191	33	503,185	68	847,170	26	350,522	13	362,839	45	26
1890	2,507,474	22	1,099,850	119	1,046,964	24	451,770	29	448,477	24	26
1900	3,437,202	37	1,698,575	54	1,293,697	24	575,000	27	560,892	25	21
1910	4,766,883	39	2,185,283	29	1,549,008	20	687,029	20	670,585	20	21
1920	5,620,048	18	2,701,705	24	1,823,779	18	772,897	13	748,060	12	15

[a]These five cities were ranked as the five largest in the 1910 census.
[b]Using the consolidated borough boundaries of 1898.

Sources: Glen E. Holt, personal files; U.S. Department of Commerce, Bureau of the Census, *The Growth of Metropolitan Districts in the United States: 1900–1940*, by Warren S. Thompson (Washington, D.C.: U.S. Government Printing Office, 1947); Blake McKelvey, *American Urbanization: A Comparative History* (Glenview, Ill.: Scott Foresman, 1973), pp. 24, 37, 73.

INTER-URBAN RIVALRY AND THE POLITICS OF GROWTH

Individual cities did not spring up merely by happenstance and chance. Town promotion and civic boosterism became a way of life as local promoters competed for the settlers and investors who swept across the continent. The fortunes of cities were only partially determined by locational advantages—what might be called "place luck." Transportation connections—turnpikes, canals, and, later, railroads—were also crucial in determining a city's destiny. Links to the national transportation network could instantly secure a city's future by expanding its reach into the hinterland surrounding it and by tying it into national and international trade networks. Because such connections were so important to a city's prospects, promoters freely used the fiscal resources and powers of local governments to secure them. In the early century, canal-building reached a fever pitch, but within a few years railroads provided better links to other cities and to broader markets. Cities scrambled to offer subsidies to railroad corporations in the form of free land and terminal facilities and stock purchases. The logic was simple: Rising real estate values were expected to provide more than enough additional revenues to pay off the debts. These hopes did not always pan out, but any city that failed to make the effort to secure good rail links would surely die on the vine.

The battle for rail connections was fought with white-hot intensity. Before the railroads, corn could be transported by wagon only 125 miles and wheat, 250 miles before the cost made it unmarketable.[8] Beyond that distance, agricultural land was almost worthless for anything except subsistence farming because there was no way of getting crops to market. The cost and inconvenience of hauling goods on horse-drawn wooden wagons guaranteed that settlements without access to water transportation could not amount to much. In the first decade of the nineteenth century, a ton of goods could be shipped all the way from Europe for the same amount it cost to haul it 9 miles over roads.[9] Inland cities without waterfronts could not conceivably compete with port and river cities as centers of trade. Railroads opened up huge areas of farmland to commercial agriculture, which not only allowed the countryside to fill in but also resulted in soaring land values and population growth for the cities able to capture the increased trade in agricultural goods. Thus, rather than depending on luck and circumstance, civic leaders tried to shape patterns of trade and economic development. Local entrepreneurs were keenly aware they were involved in a competition in which some cities would grow while others would stagnate or even die.

The building of the Erie Canal had already demonstrated how individual cities could gain control over their own destinies. In 1817, after being prodded by the civic elite of New York City, the New York State legislature authorized money for the construction of a 364-mile waterway to connect the Hudson River with Lake Erie. When the canal opened in 1825, it became possible to ship huge volumes of agricultural and extractive goods from the continental interior through the Great Lakes to Buffalo, down the canal, and on to the port at New York, where they could be distributed along the eastern seaboard, used in factories, or shipped to Europe. Many producers and shippers abandoned the long, circuitous, and hazardous journey down the Ohio, Missouri, and Mississippi rivers to the port at New Orleans. New York's direct connection to the heartland via the canal quickly vaulted it past all the other eastern seaboard cities in population and volume of trade. By 1860, 62 percent of the nation's foreign trade passed through New York's harbor.[10]

The lesson was not lost on city boosters elsewhere. Civic leaders lobbied their state capitals for financial assistance to build canals. Pennsylvania, Maryland, Virginia, North Carolina, and South Carolina financed canal projects designed to cut through the Appalachians. Between 1824 and 1840, more than 3,000 miles of canals were completed, most of them run by state governments.[11] About 30 percent of the costs were raised through private sources, but the capacity of the states to sell bonds was essential for financing such ambitious undertakings.[12]

Canal building was so expensive, the engineering so complicated, and the natural barriers often so formidable that most cities could not hope to build them unless state legislatures helped out. Natural topographic barriers left many cities out of the competition altogether. The railroads opened the way to an era of intensified inter-urban competition that almost any city might join. Until the railroad, water was the singularly critical ingredient determining a city's fate; canals were just a means of trying to make up for what nature had not endowed. In the first decades of the nineteenth century, for the river towns like St. Louis, Pittsburgh, Cincinnati, and New Orleans, the steamboat had been "an enchanter's wand transforming an almost raw country-side of scattered farms and towns into a settled region of cultivated landscapes and burgeoning cities."[13] In the 1850s, the railroads became the new enchanter's wand. The rail lines became rivers of commerce, capable of carrying huge volumes at amazing speeds over long distances. The railroads guaranteed that America's frontier would eventually vanish and a network of cities, towns, and villages would spread over the entire continent.

In 1840 only 2,800 miles of track existed, most of it in the urban East. No connection reached even as far west as Pittsburgh. The early steam locomotives were hazardous and unreliable contraptions, blowing up with a regularity that provoked opposition to their use in urban areas. Lacking the capital to take on bigger projects, railway companies built short lines. Because each company used its own particular gauge (width between the rails), at the end of each line goods had to be unloaded from one company's cars and put onto cars that fit the next company's rails. Even with these limitations, however, the early rail system was vastly superior to the only alternative, horse-drawn wooden wagons.

Rail lines were built at astonishing speed, and by the 1880s the adoption of standard gauge sizes made the system much more efficient. In 1857 the newly consolidated Pennsylvania Railroad first connected Pittsburgh to Chicago. Three years later, 11 trunk lines ended in Chicago and 20 branch and feeder lines passed through it, making the city the nation's largest rail center terminus. By 1869 and with much fanfare, the symbolic Golden Spike was pounded in at Promontory Point, Utah. It completed the first cross-continental route by joining the Union Pacific line originating on the East Coast to the Central Pacific line starting in San Francisco. Within a few years, the outline of the modern rail system was almost complete, a spider's web with strands reaching into every section of the country. In just the half century between 1850 and 1900, the network expanded from 9,021 miles of track in 1850 to 258,784 miles.[14]

More miles of track were laid more quickly than in any other nation in the world. The main reason for this rapid growth was the huge public subsidies that were pumped into railroad building. Relying strictly on private investment, the railroads would have expanded much more slowly than they did. Until the 1890s most private corporations lacked the ability to raise the huge amounts of capital that would later become routine for them. Subsidies from governments at all levels helped make the railroads "America's first big business."[15] In the Pacific Railways Acts of 1862 and 1864, the federal government gave massive amounts of land to railroad corporations, which the companies sold to raise capital. The most generous subsidies, however, were provided by cities. To a considerable degree, the cities' pivotal role could be traced to a loss of nerve by state legislators to take on financial risk. Historically, the national government had also steered clear of involvement. Treasury Secretary Albert Gallatin's 1808 plan for a federal system of turnpike and harbor improvements had failed to gain congressional approval because of regional rivalries.[16] Following President Andrew Jackson's veto of a federal turnpike bill in 1830, transportation became viewed mainly as a state responsibility. States rushed into the vacuum and began feverishly subsidizing canal and railroad construction. The Panic of 1837 bankrupted scores of companies involved in these enterprises, causing private investors and the states alike to lose their capital. Taxpayers and politicians were up in arms, inciting a "revulsion against internal improvements"[17] financed by state governments. In the 1840s many states wrote prohibitions against loaning money or buying stock in private corporations. Facing restrictions at the state level, railroad promoters quickly shifted their efforts to cities, which raced to outbid one another for railroad stock.

The anarchic competition imposed many costs, including overbuilding and redundancies that resulted in bond defaults and bankruptcies. Up to 1861, 25 to 30 percent of all direct investment in railroad building was supplied by state and local governments. The cities were the biggest spenders; they contributed an estimated $300 million in subsidies; the states spent $229 million and the federal government $65 million.[18] In addition, state and federal subsidies came in the form of land grants, which the railroad companies then converted to cash by selling the land to settlers. In the post–Civil War period, the railroads accumulated so much land that they sent agents to the Scandinavian countries, Germany, and elsewhere to recruit immigrants to buy and settle it. Partly because the railroad companies recruited heavily there (and also because of hardships in their homeland), one-sixth of all Swedish citizens left for the United States in the last half of the nineteenth century, many of them settling in a broad swath of territory paralleling rail routes from the Great Lakes through the Dakotas and Montana.

Railroad owners became adept at playing cities against one another in an attempt to secure lucrative subsidies. By the 1850s cities along the eastern seaboard were floating bond issues so they could invest in railroad stock, clear rights-of-way, and build terminal facilities—actions intended to ensure rail connections. The competition quickly spread west. In the 1860s the business leaders of Kansas City, Kansas, sold bond issues to private investors, gave the proceeds to a railroad company, and persuaded Congress to approve a federal land grant to the company. As a result of its success in this venture, Kansas City prospered while its nearby rival Leavenworth stagnated (today, Leavenworth is known mainly for its federal prison).[19] Denver's board of trade raised $280,000 to finance a 100-mile spur line to obtain access to the intercontinental track that ran through Cheyenne, Wyoming.[20] Some of Denver's businesses had already moved to Cheyenne in the expectation that its position astride the intercontinental line would make it the premier city of the Rocky Mountain West. The convergence of rail lines from all directions at Denver, however, secured its status as the dominant city of the Rocky Mountain region.

No city benefited from railroad building as dramatically as Chicago, whose phenomenal growth was founded on its access to agricultural and extractive products gathered from a vast region. Corn and grain, cattle and hogs, iron ore and coal poured into Chicago through the Great Lakes and over the rails. The city became a center for steelmaking; the manufacture of agricultural implements, tools, and machines; slaughtering and meatpacking; and trade. By the mid-1870s Chicago eclipsed St. Louis as the Midwest's premier city, a feat accomplished partly through the success of its local business community in securing rail links. Chicago built its first railroad in 1852 and then helped finance feeder lines into the city. The city also invested in grain elevators, warehouses, switching yards, and stockyards. By contrast, for too long St. Louis's business community held fast to a faith that the steamboats would be enough to guarantee the city's continued prosperity. By the time St. Louis began seeking rail connections, Chicago's lead was overwhelming. Although Chicago also enjoyed the considerable benefits of being located on the Great Lakes and it was closer to the great farming regions of the Midwest than St. Louis, its aggressive leadership reinforced its locational advantage.

For many years the question of whether cities should go into debt to secure rail connections remained beyond dispute. Most urban voters enthusiastically supported the issuance of city bonds to finance railroad subsidy schemes. As long as everyone's attention was riveted on external threats to local prosperity, a politics of consensus prevailed. Local promoters were encouraged to think that virtually any scheme that benefited them personally was also in the public interest: "Developmental policy was almost wholly a product of consensus-building among groups of merchant elites to support particular canal, turnpike, rail and other projects in response to merchant elites in nearby communities."[21] From 1866 to 1873, the legislatures of 29 states granted over 800 authorizations for aid by local governments to railroad projects.[22] A study of governmental aid to railroads in New York found that no community ever voted against subscribing to railroad stock.[23] The votes were usually so lopsided as to be a foregone conclusion.[24]

The fight for rail connections brought prosperity to many cities, but the overheated competition brought disaster to some. Railroad promoters played one town against another in search of better subsidies (a process akin to the competition today among state and local governments for footloose businesses such as sports franchises). The competition among cities was often so fierce that they often bid up the subsidies beyond what was economically rational; cities incurred huge debts on a hope and a promise. In New York State, for example, 50 towns bypassed by a major rail line joined in a $5.7 million stock subscription to the New York and Oswego Railroad. Zigzagging across the state to link the towns, the company went bankrupt shortly after completing the line in 1873 because the areas it served had too few people and products to sustain a healthy business. Most of the investments made by the towns were wiped out, with taxpayers left holding the bag.[25]

Promoters exaggerated the positive effects expected of public subsidies, predicting rapid town growth, rising real estate values, and overflowing municipal treasuries. Profits on railroad stocks, they often promised, would eliminate the need for local taxes altogether. For most cities, however, "the direct effect on government finances was on the whole unfavorable."[26] Too many cities bought stock that went bust, or the new lines brought far less prosperity than promised. Cities that had heavily invested in speculative railroad ventures often found themselves dragged into fiscal crisis. Some cities defaulted on their debts in the 1860s, but it was merely a harbinger of things to come. During the three-year economic depression that began in 1873, which was initially brought on by the overbuilding of railroads and the overvaluing of railroad stock and local real estate, hundreds of towns and cities were forced into default. In 1873 an astounding $100 million to $150 million of municipal debt was involved in railroad bond defaults—one-fifth of all the municipal debt in the nation.[27]

Municipal defaults on railroad bonds and revelations of political corruption associated with railroad building affected politics at all levels. Citizens rebelled against paying back eastern financiers for bonds that had become worthless. In some cases the lines had not even been built. When federal marshals came to towns to collect the debts, they were sometimes run off by shotgun-wielding mobs. Cries of debt repudiation filled the air, and some cities and states did manage to repudiate their debts.[28] From 1864 to 1888, the most common type of case before the U.S. Supreme Court involved railroad bonds.[29] Many states adopted restrictions on local debt and limited the aid that could be given to private corporations.[30] Financial and political abuses by railroad barons fueled a populist rebellion against big business that shook the national political system in the late nineteenth century.[31]

INDUSTRIALIZATION AND THE DECLINE OF COMMUNITY

At the nation's founding and for the decades to follow, American city politics reflected a culture of consensus enforced by an aristocratic and merchant governing class. Over time, however, the pace and scale of urban growth and the economic and technological changes brought about by industrialization led to an abrupt break from the past. Cities changed from relatively compact communities held together by informal community norms to sprawling industrial cities characterized by social stratification and segregation, constant population change, and social and political conflict. By degrees, urban elites lost their hold on the processes of governance. Increasingly, urban politics became a battleground revolving around social class and ethnic identity.

Before the emergence of the industrial city, trading cities sprang up along navigable waterways and harbors. The economy of the merchant cities revolved around trade and commerce: the importation and distribution of European goods; the regulation of docks and farmers' markets; the financing and insuring of ships and goods; and the printing of accounting ledgers, handbills, and newspapers. Educated aristocrats, importers, bankers, wholesalers, and shopkeepers were among a city's most prominent citizens. Craft workers, artisans engaged in services, and small manufacturing were a notch down in the social hierarchy: shoemakers, hatters, bakers, carpenters, blacksmiths, potters, butchers, wheelwrights, saddle and harness makers, and shipwrights. At the bottom were sailors, domestic workers, servants, and the unskilled workers who moved goods from docks to warehouses. Overall, in colonial New England the inequality in wealth was about the same as in the slaveholding South.[32] At the time of the Revolution, about three out of four white persons in Pennsylvania, Maryland, and Virginia had come to America as indentured servants, and most of them remained at the bottom.[33]

People at all places of the social spectrum generally accepted the rigidly enforced class relationships, in part because they shared the same spaces on a daily basis. The lifeblood of these cities flowed along the waterfront. Wharves and docks, warehouses, clerks' offices, banks, newspapers and printing establishments, taverns and breweries, and private homes all clustered close to the harbor or riverfront. Urban historians have labeled the mercantile city "the walking city" because the area of urban settlement was bounded by the distance the inhabitants could walk within an hour or two. Typically, the city spread about 2 miles from the center, but the area of dense settlement was only a few blocks deep. The small size of the merchant cities (so-called because social, economic, and political affairs were dominated by the merchant class) moderated the effects of inequality by fostering "a sense of community identification similar to that of traditional societies."[34] Production was located mostly in small shops typically run by skilled artisans who employed one or two apprentices, who often lived on the premises. A close relationship and interdependence between employer and employee was common. People of all classes often lived within the same neighborhoods. Workers clustered together in shanties or back alleys, still within shouting distance of the better homes of wealthy merchants.

In his study of colonial Philadelphia, the historian Sam Bass Warner found that various occupational groups were highly segregated in 1774, but it was a proximate segregation: "It was the unity of everyday life, from tavern, to street, to workplace, to housing which held the town together in the eighteenth century."[35] Class conflict was moderated by this proximity as well as a sense that everyone's welfare depended on the commercial success of the city. The merchant elites expected to run the city's affairs, and they did. With few exceptions, they held the mayor's office and dominated city councils without opposition.[36] Consistent with their view that the scope of local government should be limited, they spent very little on the poor or on public services for public health, sanitation, parks, and libraries. In 1810 prosperous New York City spent only $1 per capita on all public services combined.[37]

All this began to change in the second half of the nineteenth century. In 1850 not much more than 10 percent of all workers were engaged in manufacturing, and they produced less than 20 percent of the nation's economic output. But by 1870 industrial production exceeded the commercial and agricultural sectors in value added to the economy, and by the turn of the century, manufacturing accounted for more than both sectors combined.[38] Industrialization moved economic production from small shops and homes into factories. Before the Civil War, manufacturing establishments rarely employed more than 50 workers, and even in large cities they ranged between 8 and

20 workers. In 1832, for example, the average-sized manufacturing establishment in Boston employed 8.5 workers.[39] In the years following the Civil War, manufacturing firms grew quickly in size. In agricultural implements and machinery, the number of employees per establishment increased from 7.5 in 1860 to 79 in 1910. In malt liquor breweries, the number of workers increased from 5 to 39, and in iron and steel establishments, from 54 to 426.[40]

The rapid growth of big corporations spawned a class of industrial magnates who flaunted their wealth by building mansions and estates, throwing lavish parties, and constructing monuments to themselves.[41] Capital became concentrated in large firms. Limited-risk corporations[42] were relatively rare before the Civil War, but by the turn of the century 40,000 such firms existed, and although they amounted to only one-tenth of all companies, they produced 60 percent of value in manufacturing.[43] (Such corporations raised capital by selling stocks to investors who risked their investment but not their personal assets if the company failed.) In 1896 12 firms were valued over $10 million, but by 1903 50 firms were worth more than $50 million.[44] Several giant corporations formed between 1896 and 1905, including U.S. Steel, International Harvester, General Electric, and American Telephone and Telegraph, became models of the corporate form in the twentieth century.

The relationships between employers and workers became increasingly estranged and hostile. In the small shops of the merchant cities, relations between owners and workers tended to be highly personal and informal. By contrast, a vast chasm separated factory owners from their workers. The workplace became impersonal, hierarchical, and rigid. Most workers did not even know the owner of the business that employed them. Machine-tooled, standardized parts replaced handcrafted goods. Standardized production began in 1798, when Eli Whitney designed a musket that was built and repaired with interchangeable parts. Before long, standardized components made it possible to make a variety of goods rapidly and cheaply, so clocks, sewing machines, and farm machinery, for example, soon were assembled by factory workers rather than by craft workers. Huge military orders during the Civil War led to mass-produced shoes and clothing. As a result of these new processes, work became regimented and closely monitored. Factory methods of production required specialized, repetitive work and a rigid distinction between management and workers.

Class differences became expressed in segregated residential patterns. A series of transportation improvements allowed people to commute farther to work and residence; accordingly, cities began to increase in size and urban populations began a process of spatial segmentation that continues to the present day. While immigrant working-class tenement slums crowded close to the downtown business districts or in bottomlands near the docks and factories, middle-class neighborhoods tended to be located away from the crowded center. The wealthy claimed such exclusive areas as Park Avenue in New York and Beacon Hill in Boston, and spent their weekends and holidays on bucolic suburban estates.

When the omnibus was introduced to the streets of New York City in 1828, it represented a genuine breakthrough in urban transportation. The way that people commuted to work had changed little for hundreds of years. The wealthy owned or rented carriages; everyone else walked or, rarely, rode a horse. From the 1830s until the Civil War, dozens of omnibuses careened down the streets of the larger cities. Basically an enlarged version of the long-distance stagecoach, the omnibus was pulled by a team of two to four horses and typically carried up to a dozen people. Omnibuses were crowded and uncomfortable, cold in the winter, hot in the summer, and slow, barely moving faster than a person could walk. The coaches swayed and lurched over cobblestones and rutted unpaved streets.[45] A newspaper of the time complained that "during certain periods of the day or evening and always during inclement weather, passengers are packed in these vehicles, without regard to comfort or even decency."[46]

Despite such discomforts, those who could afford the fares—merchants, traders, lawyers, artisans, managers, junior partners—crowded into these crude conveyances. The omnibus ran on a fixed schedule and route, and it picked up and dropped off passengers at frequent intervals. The fixed fare, typically a nickel, was a small fraction of the cost of renting a hackney coach. The omnibus was thus more convenient and less expensive than any alternative mode of traveling, except walking. By encouraging in some urban residents the "riding habit,"[47] the omnibus signaled the beginning of the end of the walking city. For the first time, the workplace could be located at some distance from the home. Almost immediately, the American city began fragmenting into distinct neighborhoods and enclaves.

Other transportation innovations also contributed to the process. Steam railroad lines, for example, were constructed in Boston in the late 1830s and in several other large cities over the next 20 years. Steam engines were suited for constant speed rather than for frequent stops and starts, they were expensive to build and operate, and they were fearfully loud and prone to blowing up. They did not therefore compete with omnibuses on crowded urban streets but instead facilitated the commute from the area of dense settlement in the city center to smaller towns and villages a few miles away. The 40- to 75-cent fares were out of reach of all but the wealthy (the average laborer made about $1 a day; sometimes skilled workers made as much as $2 a day).[48] Even so, by 1848 one-fifth of Boston's businessmen commuted daily by steam railway,[49] although in cities less hemmed in by water the proportion was much lower.

After 1852, with the development of a steel rail that could be laid level with the surface of the street, horse-drawn streetcars quickly replaced the omnibuses on main thoroughfares. Because they were pulled on rails rather than over potholed streets, the horsecars were able to carry twice as many passengers and travel almost twice as fast as the omnibuses. The lower cost of the horsecars "contributed to the development of the world's first integrated transportation systems."[50] In the bigger cities, the lines radiated from the center like spokes on a wheel. Because horsecars could travel 6 to 8 miles in an hour, middle-class residential settlements spread that far and more from the city center. (The rule of thumb, then as now, was that most people were willing to commute up to an hour, but not much more.) In addition, the horsecar lines sometimes extended well beyond built-up areas, serving hospitals, parks, cemeteries, and independent villages.[51] Wherever they reached, land speculators and builders bought up property in the expectation that development would follow and real estate values would rise.

In 1888 Frank Julian Sprague revolutionized urban transit when he installed the first electric streetcar system in Richmond, Virginia.[52] The motive force driving the electric streetcar came from a wheeled carriage that moved atop an overhead cable. This device trolled along the wires, pulling the car as it went. The "troller" gave the trolley car its name.[53] Trolley cars had so many advantages over horsecars that despite the expense of installing overhead wires, traction companies and cities rushed to install them. In 1890, 60 percent of the nation's streetcars were still pulled by horses, but 12 years later the figure was less than 1 percent.[54] Trolleys traveled almost twice as fast as horsecars. Areas 6 to 8 miles from the city center could now be reached in half an hour, making it possible for people to live 10 miles or more from work. And electric streetcars were infinitely cleaner than the horsecars they replaced. City residents had always complained about "an atmosphere heavy with the odors of death and decay and animal filth and steaming nastiness."[55] The trolley allowed cities to remove thousands of horses, together with their tons of manure, from the streets.

The horse-drawn streetcars and then the electric trolleys (and later, the automobile) facilitated an increasingly finer-grained segmentation of activities. Until the 1870s crowded financial and retailing districts were located close by and even mixed in with warehouses and factories.[56] In the last third of the nineteenth century, well-defined downtown shopping and financial districts became separated from industrial and warehouse areas. The middle class developed a new shopping habit, riding the streetcars downtown to shop in the chain and department stores that were popping up. The first chain retail company, the Great Atlantic and Pacific Tea Company, was organized in 1864, and in the 1870s the A&P stores expanded to several cities. Frank W. Woolworth opened his five-and-dime store in Lancaster, Pennsylvania, in 1879, and by the 1880s Woolworth's became a familiar marquee in downtown areas.[57] The middle-class habit of shopping in downtown stores for major purchases persisted right up until the end of the 1950s, by which time the streetcar system had been dismantled in most cities.[58]

While separate residential and business zones were evolving within the cities, new residential communities were springing up just beyond the city limits. Between 1890 and 1910, America experienced its first significant period of suburban development. In most large metropolitan areas, suburban growth kept pace with the central cities in the 1890s, and after the turn of the century, in many urban areas the suburbs grew at a faster rate than the cities at the center. Chicago's population grew by 29 percent between 1900 and 1910, but the population of its suburbs increased by 88 percent. In the St. Louis, Philadelphia, Boston, Pittsburgh, and New York urban areas, suburban growth outpaced the central cities.[59]

The development of social and ethnic segregation among neighborhoods, cities, and suburbs eroded the sense that everyone lived cooperatively in a mutually beneficial urban community. If the term "community" once evoked images of a diverse assortment of people rubbing shoulders in their daily lives, it gradually came to refer to the patterns of interaction among people living within homogeneous neighborhoods. The poor began to inhabit distinct enclaves, as did the middle class and the wealthy. The kind of community that existed in the merchant cities became a thing of the past, little more than a nostalgic remembrance.

THE IMMIGRANT TIDE AND THE POLITICS OF GOVERNANCE

The final blow to the consensus politics of the preindustrial city was delivered by the floodtide of immigration that swept over the cities in the latter half of the nineteenth century. The industrial economy depended on a constantly expanding pool of cheap labor. Millions of foreign immigrants were pushed out of their homelands by war, civil unrest, and hardship and pulled to American shores by opportunity. They worked on the railroads, in meatpacking, in steelmaking, in coal and lead mining, and in factories of every kind. Simultaneously, an unprecedented migration from farm to city was set in motion. Between 1830 and 1896, developments in farm machinery cut in half the average time and labor required to produce agricultural crops. During this period, the time required to harvest wheat was reduced by 95 percent and labor costs for farming fell by one-fifth.[60] The new machinery drove up the capital investment required for starting and running a farm. Unemployed farm laborers and young people streamed into the cities.

Between 1820 and 1919, 33.5 million foreign immigrants came to America. The Irish and then the Germans set off the first big surge of nineteenth-century immigration. Beginning in the mid-1840s, famine and disease pushed the Irish to American cities. Irish peasants subsisted primarily on potatoes and vegetables grown on tiny rocky plots of ground and in strips of soil along the roads, the only usable land not claimed by English landlords. When a potato blight swept through Europe in the 1840s, its effects were more devastating in Ireland than elsewhere. Between 1845 and the mid-1850s, up to a fourth of Ireland's peasants starved to death. Many of the survivors streamed into Liverpool and bought or bartered passage on ships heading for America. In the late 1840s, years of civil war drove Germans to America. As shown by the data in Table 2.3, all through the 1840s and 1850s, the Irish and Germans made up more than 70 percent of all the newly arriving immigrants.

After the depression of 1873–1879, immigration surged to unprecedented levels. The flow doubled from 2.7 million in the 1870s to 5.2 million in the 1880s. After falling slightly because of a major depression in the 1890s, the number of new arrivals in the first decade of the twentieth century soared to the highest level in American history, to over 8 million people, with an additional 6.5 million coming in the years between 1910 and 1920. These astonishing numbers were driven by people coming from countries not much represented in the American population up to that point. Irish and Germans kept coming, but by the 1880s they accounted for just 40 percent of the immigrant flow, and after the turn of the century they made up only about 8 percent. Likewise, immigration from the United Kingdom declined decade by decade before plummeting after the turn of the century. They were replaced by Italians, Greeks, immigrants from several eastern European nations (Bohemians, Czechs, Slavs, Lithuanians, Poles), and Jews. In the 1890s Jews from Russia and Austria-Hungary, together with Catholics from Italy, made up 42 percent of immigrants, and their proportion of all immigrants rose to more than 60 percent from 1900 to 1920. In just the two decades between 1900 and 1920, 14.5 million immigrants entered the country.[61] The flow would have continued if Congress had not enacted restrictive immigration laws in 1921 and 1924.

Table 2.3 Decennial Immigration to the United States, 1820–1919

	1820–1829	1830–1839	1840–1849	1850–1859	1860–1869	1870–1879	1880–1889	1890–1899	1900–1909	1910–1919
Total in millions	0.1	0.5	1.4	2.7	2.1	2.7	5.2	3.7	8.2	6.3
Percentage of total from:										
Ireland	40.2%	31.7%	46.0%	36.9%	24.4%	15.4%	12.8%	11.0%	4.2%	2.6%
Germany	4.5	23.2	27.0	34.8	35.2	27.4	27.5	15.7	4.0	2.7
United Kingdom	19.5	13.8	15.3	13.5	14.9	21.1	15.5	8.9	5.7	5.8
Scandinavia	0.2	0.4	0.9	0.9	5.5	7.6	12.7	10.5	5.9	3.8
Canada	1.8	2.2	2.4	2.2	4.9	11.8	9.4	0.1	1.5	11.2
Russia					0.2	1.3	3.5	12.2	18.3	17.4
Austria-Hungary					0.2	2.2	6.0	14.5	24.4	18.2
Italy					0.5	1.7	5.1	16.3	23.5	19.4

Sources: From N. Carpenter, "Immigrants and Their Children," *U.S. Bureau of the Census Monograph,* no. 7 (Washington, D.C.: U.S. Government Printing Office, 1927), pp. 324–325.

Wherever the newcomers were headed, for most of them the Statue of Liberty gave them their first view of America. Sixty percent of all the European immigrants between 1820 and 1919 passed through New York harbor. Between the turn of the century and World War I, approximately two-thirds of all U.S.-bound immigrants were processed through New York's Ellis Island, making it (together with the Statue of Liberty) an enduring symbol of America's immigrant history. Almost three-fourths of the new arrivals, 24 million in all, settled in the cities. By 1870 more than half the population of at least 20 American cities were foreign-born or children of parents who had immigrated. In some cities the proportions were much higher. As shown in Table 2.4, by 1870, first- and second-generation immigrants accounted for at least 72 percent of the populations

Table 2.4 Proportion of Immigrant Population in Cities of 500,000 or More, 1870 and 1910

		Percentage Foreign-Born	Percentage Foreign-Born or Native-Born with at Least One Foreign Parent[a]
New York	1870	44%	80%
	1910	40	79
Chicago	1870	48	87
	1910	36	78
Philadelphia	1870	28	51
	1910	25	57
St. Louis	1870	36	65
	1910	18	54
Boston	1870	35	63
	1910	36	74
Cleveland	1870	42	75
	1910	35	75
Baltimore	1870	21	38
	1910	14	38
Pittsburgh	1870	32	58
	1910	26	62
Mean for all 8 cities	1870	40	72
(each counted equally)	1910	32	72

[a]Native-born with foreign parents is unavailable in the 1870 census. The figures for 1870 are estimated by adding 80 percent to the number of foreign-born. In all cases, this should yield a safely conservative estimate.

Sources: U.S. Department of the Interior, Superintendent of Census, *The Ninth Census* (June 1, 1870), vol. 1, *Population and Social Statistics* (Washington, D.C.: U.S. Government Printing Office, 1872), p. 386; U.S. Department of Commerce, Bureau of the Census, *Thirteenth Census of the United States Taken in the Year 1910*, vol. 1, *Population 1910* (Washington, D.C.: U.S. Government Printing Office, 1913), p. 178.

of eight cities of more than 500,000 people. In New York City, immigrants made up almost 80 percent of the population. In Chicago, an astounding 87 percent of the population was composed of the foreign-born and their American-born children.

And the immigrants kept coming. Despite a huge migration from rural areas to the cities in the latter years of the nineteenth century, by 1910 the proportion of first- and second-generation foreign-born in most cities was about the same as it had been 40 years before. In 1920 more than 80 percent of the Italians, Irish, Russian, and Polish immigrants were urban, as were 75 percent of the immigrants from the United Kingdom.[62] By the census of 1920, just before Congress passed legislation restricting immigration, 58 percent of the population of all cities with over 100,000 people was first- or second-generation immigrant.[63]

Although clustered in large numbers in a few northeastern and midwestern cities, immigrants spread out to all the cities that supplied industrial jobs, and large numbers fanned out to the growing cities in the interior, went on to mining camps, or joined railroad construction gangs. About one-third of the German immigrants lived outside towns and cities, reflecting the fact that in the middle decades of the century many of them had settled in rural areas of the Midwest. A smaller proportion of Scandinavians moved to cities than any other group, many of them lured into immigration by railroad agents sent to the Scandinavian countries in search of buyers for land secured through government land grants. Enough Scandinavians settled in rural areas in Wisconsin, Minnesota, the Dakotas, and throughout the Midwest that only 55 percent were classified as urban in the census of 1920.

As soon as they arrived, immigrants encountered hostility and sometimes violence. But special enmity was reserved for the Irish because they were raggedly poor and Catholic. Irish workers could rarely read or claim a skilled occupation. They took menial, temporary, low-paying jobs—moving goods on the waterfront, building streets and roads, working in slaughterhouses and packinghouses. Because of their poverty and their religion and their peasant origins as well, they became etched in the public mind as dangerous, alcoholic, criminal, and dirty. As portrayed in the 2002 film *Gangs of New York*, anti-Catholic and anti-Irish riots broke out from time to time. Irish churches, taverns, and neighborhoods were attacked by mobs whipped up by a rhetoric that spoke of "an invasion of venomous reptiles . . . , long-haired, wild-eyed, bad-smelling, atheistic, reckless foreign wretches."[64] Protestant Yankees were in a position to hire, promote, and fire. Even as late as the 1920s, want ads in Boston frequently added "Protestant" as a qualification for employment.[65] The Irish clustered on the lowest rungs of the social and economic ladder well into the twentieth century.

The Germans encountered far less antipathy because a large proportion of them were wealthy or from middle-class origins. They were escaping war and political turmoil, not poverty and starvation. They brought with them music and literary societies and a commitment to formal education. Although the Germans nominally faced a greater language barrier than did the Irish, the Irish brogue and the widely used Gaelic sounded just as foreign to American ears as the German language did.

Important variations existed among the different immigrant groups as they strove to catch up to the native Yankee Protestants. In late-nineteenth-century Boston, for example, an immigrant "pecking order favored some groups over others."[66] The

Irish and Italians competed for the lowest wages and lowest-skill jobs. Only blacks were positioned below them. German and recent British immigrants frequently entered middle-class occupations right away. A few with exceptional education or a needed skill achieved real success quickly. The Russian and eastern European Jews, who came in the 1890s and later, placed emphasis on formal education and business. Although discrimination kept them out of corporations and larger business enterprises, they carved out their own niche as job brokers, middlemen, and shopkeepers.

Most of the immigrants crowded into densely packed communities near the waterfront and factories. In the 1840s and 1850s, real estate speculators and landlords shoehorned them into deteriorated houses, attics and basements, and unused warehouses and factories. Housing was so scarce and rents so high that a large proportion of property owners made money by renting extra space in their own living quarters.[67] Narrow three- and four-story buildings divided into tiny living quarters sprang up in alleyways and on back lots. On vacant lots and behind and between buildings, immigrants crowded into sheds and shanties.

In New York as early as the 1850s and in other cities somewhat later, the first tenement districts began to spread. With the middle class beginning to leave the city center, it became cost-efficient to raze older structures and replace them with buildings designed to crowd as many people as possible into the available space. The tenement—the name given to any low-cost multiple-family rental building—became a universal symbol for urban slums. Indeed, by the twentieth century, multistory buildings of any kind came to represent city living, and the suburbs became identified with freestanding houses and low-density subdivisions. The dumbbell—so named because of two 28-inch-wide air shafts that provided the only light and air to the interior rooms—became the most notorious tenement structure. Based on an award-winning 1879 design, the dumbbell maximized economic return but not ventilation and sanitation. Tenants on the upper floors would pitch their garbage down the shafts, where it was left to rot. On each floor, located next to the foul air shafts, were one or two public toilets and a sink. By 1893, 70 percent of the population of New York City lived in tenements, most of them dumbbells.[68]

In spite of the obvious problems caused by overcrowding, the concentration of the immigrant groups into densely packed enclaves was crucially important for assimilating them into city life. A variety of religious and social institutions sprang up to nurture ethnic traditions and a sense of solidarity and shared identity. The immigrant neighborhoods also facilitated the rise of a politics that firmly brought ethnic issues into the local political systems. By the 1880s, urban party machines began to emerge based on the close relationship forged between ethnic voters and a new breed of politicians skilled at mobilizing their followers. In Chapter 3 we describe this historic development.

THE CAPACITY TO GOVERN

As the industrial cities grew, the capacity of local governments to respond to the needs of urban residents came into question. For many city residents in the latter half of the nineteenth century, the conditions of life ranged from squalid to barely tolerable. Epidemics periodically swept through, sometimes killing several hundred people in a summer. Streets turned to seas of mud in winter and to dust bowls in summer, and in every season they were littered with refuse and piles of steaming horse manure. A Swedish novelist commented that Chicago in 1850 (when it still had only 30,000 people) was "one of the most miserable and ugly cities," where people had come "to trade, to make money, and not to live."[69]

Urban residents complained about the conditions of daily life, but no one was sure what municipal governments should do about the situation. In the American political tradition, government was considered a necessary evil; there was far more concern about its potential dangers than about the ways it might be put to positive use. The suspicion of government was reinforced by a culture of privatism—the idea that progress comes through individual, not collective, endeavors. Although urban leaders could persuade their fellow citizens to use local government to support schemes promoting the local economy, it was much more difficult to persuade them to tax themselves to support the services that might improve the local quality of life.

In the compact merchant cities, volunteers had provided most services. Volunteer night watchmen, for instance, tried to enforce the law; even in the larger cities (New York had 369,000 people by 1840), full-time, paid, uniformed police forces were rare until the mid-nineteenth century. Volunteer fire gangs answered the fire alarm. Individual property owners swept the streets and collected refuse. Even when city life became increasingly unpleasant, city residents were reluctant to acknowledge that municipal government might do better than the community's volunteer efforts. Nevertheless, the responsibilities of municipal governments vastly increased in the latter half of the nineteenth century. In New York City, for example, per capita city expenditures increased from $6.53 in 1850 to $27.31 in 1900.[70] During this half century, cities spent more money and employed more people than either the state governments or the national government. When governmental spending was cataloged for the first time in the federal census of governments in 1902, local governments accounted for half of all governmental expenditures in the United States.[71]

Despite a national culture that preferred minimal government, over the course of a century municipal responsibilities had vastly increased. At least three reasons account for this expansion. First, new services were provided in cases when urban residents of all classes felt threatened by imminent catastrophe or crisis. Second, local boosters assumed the lead in organizing public services when their absence threatened local economic vitality. And third, by the late nineteenth century, the growing middle class became intolerant of urban conditions that had previously been considered normal or inevitable.

In the early postcolonial period, urban services had been minimal. Essential as they were to basic health, water systems, for instance, were chronically inadequate. In the early nineteenth century, most city residents got their water from wells, and these were often contaminated by waste. As a result, outbreaks of contagious diseases occurred with regularity. In the summer of 1793, 10 percent of Philadelphia's population died from yellow fever.[72] The city's economy came to a standstill, and a third of the population and virtually all wealthy families fled for the summer months. Outbreaks of yellow fever or cholera occurred in Philadelphia, Baltimore, and New

Haven (Connecticut) in 1793; in New York City, Baltimore, and Norfolk (Virginia) in 1795; and in Newburyport (Massachusetts), Boston, and Charleston (South Carolina) the next year.[73] Nearly a dozen cities were hit in 1797; three-fourths of Philadelphia's population fled and 4,000 people died (about 7 percent of the population).[74]

Such catastrophes prompted cities to invest in waterworks, drain swamps, and to regulate the keeping of animals and the dumping of refuse. Philadelphia was goaded by its epidemics to construct the first municipal waterworks in the nation's history. Begun in 1799 and operational by 1801, it piped water to the city from the upper Schuylkill River. Philadelphia's system was constantly improved by the merchant elites that ran the Watering Committee. By the 1840s, however, these elites began to withdraw from political activities, partly because competition for political office had become more intense. Without their guiding hand on the committee, the water supply system became less and less adequate.[75] Only slowly did the city take over the responsibilities given up by the Watering Committee.

Despite the manifest need, municipal services tended to lag because they always constituted a minimal response to a crisis; "municipal authorities, loath to increase taxes, usually shouldered new responsibilities only at the prod of grim necessity."[76] Devastating outbreaks of yellow fever, typhoid, and cholera periodically made their rounds, especially in the cities such as New Orleans and Memphis that lagged furthest behind in providing uncontaminated water. Several urban water systems were built in the 1850s, and by the Civil War 70 towns had waterworks, which were owned by 80 private companies.[77] Most people, however, had to fetch the water from street hydrants and hand pumps. Only wealthy people, who could afford to pay for the service, had water piped into their homes. In 1860 about one-tenth of Boston's residents had access to a bathtub, and only 5 percent of the homes had indoor water closets.[78]

Urban water supplies were polluted by human and animal waste. Sewage was generally not drained away from the cities but instead was collected in huge community cesspools, which had to be dug out frequently. Even when sewer pipes carried waste away from the city, the main result was merely to move the pollution somewhere else. Serious typhoid epidemics broke out in the cities along the Merrimac River in Massachusetts in the 1880s because residents were drinking water polluted by cities located upstream. Because of Boston's habit of dumping wastes directly into it, by 1877 Boston Harbor had become "one vast cesspool."[79] Until the 1920s, crowded residential districts were dotted with outdoor privies, and water, bearing a burden of horse manure and other refuse, flowed in open gutters along the edges of the streets. The sources of contamination were so numerous, only those cities that piped their water from isolated watersheds far away from urban settlement could avoid a contaminated water supply.

Ultimately, the water supply problem could be solved only through the development of adequate technology. Even Philadelphia's relatively sophisticated system delivered its water with just the heaviest silt filtered out.[80] Pumps frequently failed; in the winter, pipes froze. People found dirt, insects, and even small fish in their water. During the first decade of the twentieth century, when modern filtration techniques were developed, death rates in New York, Boston, Philadelphia, and New Orleans fell by one-fifth.[81]

Epidemics also prompted cities to build sewers. In 1823 Boston began installing the nation's first sanitary sewers. Other large cities followed suit, but slowly. By 1857 New York City, with a population of nearly a million people, had built sewers under only one-fourth of its streets, and most of these were storm rather than sanitary sewers.[82] Taxpayers resisted the high cost of laying underground pipes and installing costly pumps. Although most of the big cities had constructed sewers by the 1870s, these were usually paid for by the property owners who subscribed, leaving vast areas—always the neighborhoods inhabited by the poor—without service.

A perceived crisis of a different sort forced cities to begin financing and organizing professional police forces. As cities grew in size and complexity, violence, crime, and disorder threatened to disrupt the lives of every urban resident. The informal methods of the preindustrial cities, where social control had been based on face-to-face relations within the household and the community, became increasingly inadequate. In the early years of the century, most cities remained "a community in which every citizen was closely bound to other members of the community by familial, recreational, economic, and social ties. The social hierarchy was clear; a series of institutions supported that hierarchy; and the community was so compact that it was difficult to escape the vigilance of the dominant class."[83] Accordingly, until at least midcentury the law was enforced in most cities by part-time or volunteer night watches and constables.

The constant influx of immigrants provoked high levels of ethnic conflict, pushed up crime rates, and broke apart the bonds of community. For example, in the 1830s and 1840s, rioting directed against Irish immigrants and free blacks broke out regularly in Philadelphia. Almost all cities experienced rising levels of violence. In frontier cities, the connection between rapid population growth and social instability was especially obvious. In the early years, more than half the residents of San Francisco, St. Louis, and New Orleans were transients. A constant stream of river men, wagon drivers, and traders moved in and out of these cities. Saloons proliferated; gambling and prostitution flourished. In San Francisco during the gold rush years of the 1850s, violent crimes became such a fact of everyday life that merchants funded vigilante committees. The vigilantes soon organized their own crime rings and became almost as dangerous as the criminals they were supposed to catch.[84]

In 1845 Boston became the first city to provide uniforms for its officers. The same year, when its population numbered more than 400,000, New York replaced its force of part-time police with full-time officers. The police went about their jobs in street clothes, completely untrained and without supervision.[85] Eight years later, the city's police finally received uniforms and some modest training. Until the late 1830s, Philadelphia relied on posses, militia, and night watches to enforce the law. They worked part time and did not wear uniforms.[86]

New York's police forces were in constant turmoil for many years. There was considerable resistance to the idea of creating a professional police force because the two political parties that contended for power in the city regarded the police as an important source of patronage. Following the 1857 mayoral election, the new mayor fired everyone on the police force and installed officers loyal to his own party. The former officers refused to quit their jobs, and so for several months the city had two competing police forces. In June of that year, a full-scale riot broke out between the two groups.[87] Similar confusion repeated itself in 1868, when the newly elected Democratic governor removed all of the city's police commissioners because they were Republicans. The commissioners refused to vacate their offices. Finally, the state legislature resolved the dispute by assuming the power to appoint them.

These events illustrate why it took so long to build modern, fully professionalized police forces. Many people feared that, as a quasi-military organization, the police might be used by one political faction against another. This fear was well founded. Far into the twentieth century, police departments were prolific sources of patronage, and their political loyalties and political debts, as well as their ethnic and racial prejudices, often affected their work. A presidential commission investigating the urban riots of the 1960s found that police conduct was the most common provocation for rioting.[88] Police conduct was a contentious issue as soon as professionalized police forces were organized in the nineteenth century, and it remains so even today.

If it seems that crisis goaded governing elites into organizing and financing municipal services, this fact still begs an important question: What provoked a sense of crisis? Objective conditions, however dire, may be adjusted to, considered normal, or seem beyond anyone's control. The answer to the question is that urban elites held ambitious aspirations for their cities and for themselves. Chronic problems like crime, poor sanitation, and impassable streets threatened the quality of life of all urban residents, and even threatened the economic vitality and very existence of the cities in which they lived. Faced with this reality, civic elites and business leaders preferred to support public services rather than abandon the city.

Once provided, urban services became institutionalized; they quickly seemed normal and routine; there could be no going back to a time when they were not provided. This was especially the case with services such as water systems and fire departments that required the construction of permanent infrastructure and investment in expensive equipment. In this way, the responsibilities of city governments grew step by step. In the early nineteenth century, when confronted with a new problem, the cities' merchants, landowners, and other civic leaders would typically organize a committee to decide what to do. Over time, such informal arrangements gave way to services provided by full-time paid employees. This is exactly what happened with Philadelphia's waterworks. At first, the Watering Committee raised money through private donations and individual subscriptions to the water service. Prominent merchants led the committee until 1837.[89] But over the next few decades, the system expanded until it provided water to all citizens, and it became necessary to impose taxes to support it.

The origins of modern government can be found in the breakdown of informal community norms as a means of governance. Part-time politicians could not organize and supervise complex urban services. Increasingly, paid employees, organized into bureaucratic hierarchies, provided public services. As the scope of municipal services broadened, the number of employees on the city payroll multiplied. Where volunteers once joined firehouse gangs and scavengers picked garbage off the streets, salaried employees took their place.

Milwaukee's volunteer fire department gave way to paid professionals in the 1850s when new steam pumps proved too complicated for volunteers to maintain and operate.[90] Public works employees were hired to maintain the streets when it became too difficult to find volunteers for the task. In the same decade, the provision of health services became too complex for volunteers when the Milwaukee city council required vaccination for smallpox and when it provided funds to build a sewer system. Gradually, the day-to-day administration of services was put in the hands of paid employees. "Politics became a full-time business and professionals moved in to make careers of public office."[91]

In the last third of the nineteenth century, a growing middle class began to demand improved water and sewer systems,[92] and by the 1890s there was popular pressure to upgrade services of all kinds. From the 1850s to the 1870s, assistance to railroads had been the largest single cause of municipal debt. In striking contrast, during the last 30 years of the century, the cities went into debt mainly to finance the expansion of new services and to build infrastructure.[93] Because of rising standards of public health, new technologies, even when very expensive, were quickly adopted. The construction of integrated sewerage systems is instructive. Systems of separate sanitary and storm sewers were not completed in most cities until very late in the nineteenth century. Laying sewer pipe was a huge public works project for any city. Nevertheless, the number of miles of sewer pipe laid increased fourfold from 1890 to 1909.[94]

By the turn of the century, American cities, in general, provided more and better services than their European counterparts, with more miles of sewer and water mains, more miles of paved streets, more street lamps, better mass transportation, and more fire departments with better equipment.[95] Urban residents in the United States used more than twice as much water per capita as their counterparts in England and many times more than city dwellers in Germany,[96] probably because flush toilets and bathtubs were far more widespread in American cities.[97] The cities also vastly expanded public health efforts. Using the new science of bacteriology, health inspectors examined children in schools, checked buildings for ventilation and faulty plumbing, and inspected food and milk.[98] Such public health measures, when combined with the completion of integrated sewer systems and installation of new water filtration technology, dramatically reduced typhoid mortality rates.[99] Overall death rates fell sharply in the big cities, by 20 percent or more in New York, Chicago, Cleveland, Buffalo, and other cities in the 1890s,[100] and just as sharply again in the first decade of the twentieth century.[101]

The late nineteenth century was the golden age of American city-building. The massive investment in physical infrastructure placed city governments at the cutting edge of technology, resulting in such engineering marvels as the Brooklyn Bridge and New York's Croton aqueduct system, with its thousands of miles of pipes and reservoirs. The Parks Movement and the City Beautiful Movement, both supported by urban elites and the middle class, swept the country, resulting in urban amenities such as parks, ponds, formal gardens, bandstands, ball fields, broad tree-lined avenues, and ornate public buildings. Urban residents came to expect a level of municipal services that was not conceivable in an earlier time. The squalor of the nineteenth-century industrial city began to yield to the relative safety, cleanliness, and health of the twentieth-century metropolis.

THE LIMITED POWERS OF CITIES

The ability of American cities to adapt to changing circumstances by developing the capacity to govern in an increasingly complex environment is a remarkable story. More so than in any European nation, cities in the United States were truly left on their own to devise solutions to the problems that faced them. The national government was distant and indifferent: only in the twentieth century would the federal government establish any relationship to the cities. States were alternatively hostile and indifferent. For the most part, state legislatures—made up as they were by part-time politicians who met for a few weeks or months every other year—paid little attention. More than all else, the rural constituencies that controlled state politics wanted to keep the cities from intruding into their domain. This fact led Alexis de Tocqueville, in his classic work *Democracy in America* (1835), to emphasize that local governments in the United States were sovereign. He compared them to independent nations: "Municipal independence is . . . a natural consequence of the principle of the sovereignty of the people in the United States: all the American republics recognize it more or less."[102] But his assessment was not quite accurate. The autonomy of cities substantially relied upon indifference to how they governed themselves. Although the states possessed the legal authority to control them in almost every detail, they exercised that right unpredictably and sometimes capriciously.

Advocates for the right of cities to govern themselves continued to plead their cause in articles, books, and court rulings.[103] However, the courts consistently upheld the powers of the states to define the powers and obligations of local governments. In 1819, in the *Dartmouth College* case, the U.S. Supreme Court held that cities were created by the states and their charters could therefore be amended or rescinded at will. (By contrast, private corporations were protected from interference by the constitutional provision against "impairing the obligation of contract.")[104] A second definitive case was handed down in 1868, when the chief justice of the Iowa Supreme Court, John F. Dillon, declared that states could rightfully exert total control over their cities, with no restrictions whatsoever:

> Municipal corporations owe their origin to, and derive their powers and rights wholly from, the legislature. It breathes into them the breath of life without which they cannot exist. As it creates so it may destroy. . . . Unless there is some constitutional limitation on the right, the legislature might, by a single act, if we can suppose it capable of so great a folly and so great a wrong, sweep from existence all of the municipal corporations of the state, and the corporations could not prevent it. . . . They are, so to phrase it, the mere tenants at will of the legislature.[105]

Judge Dillon was motivated by the fact that cities had been active in providing subsidies to railroads, and he reasoned that if they could help private corporations so directly, they could regulate them as well. Dillon's missionary zeal was also fired by a conviction that riffraff governed the cities: "men the best fitted by their intelligence, business experience, capacity and moral character, for local governors and counsellors are not always, it is feared—it might be added, are not generally—chosen."[106] His solution was for state governments and courts to supervise cities and strictly limit their powers. In 1872 Dillon published his *Treatise on the Law of Municipal Corporations*. Originally 800 pages long, by the time the fifth edition was published in 1911, it had grown to five thick volumes.[107] Dillon's treatise became the bible on municipal law. By 1924 William Munro, the author of a leading textbook *The Government of American Cities*, wrote that Dillon's rule was "so well recognized that it is not nowadays open to question."[108]

Inspired by a similar distrust of cities—or, rather, of immigrant voters—state legislators took steps to ensure that no matter how fast and big cities grew, their representatives to the statehouse would never be able to gain a majority of seats in state legislatures. Most rural legislators would probably have agreed with the delegate to the New York State constitutional convention of 1894 who said, "the average citizen in the rural district is superior in intelligence, superior in morality, superior in self-government to the average citizen of the great cities."[109] The distrust of cities was hardly new. Decades earlier, Maine's constitutional convention of 1819 had established a ceiling on the number of representatives who could represent towns in the state legislature. In 1845 the Louisiana legislature limited New Orleans to 12.5 percent of the state's senators and 10 percent of the state's assemblymen. (The population of New Orleans then accounted for 20 percent of the state's total.)[110] By the end of the century, every state had ensured that no matter how large cities became, representatives from rural legislative districts would continue to hold a controlling majority in state legislatures.

By the end of the nineteenth century, more people lived in the cities of some states than lived outside them. If their influence in state legislatures had grown in step with their populations, cities would have been able to secure state financial support for the expansion of city services. In fact, however, cities received practically no help at all. If urban voters had been able to gain more influence in state politics and in state governments, they also could have asserted a political voice in national politics. Rural elites firmly controlled the state party caucuses that nominated governors, members of Congress, senators, and presidents. Immigrants and labor unions had no effective means of influencing governmental policies at the state or national levels. The underrepresentation of the cities resulted in indifference to the problems faced by big cities in state legislatures, governors' offices, Congress, and the White House. Traffic congestion, slum housing, orphaned children, contagious diseases, poverty—none of these problems interested rural and small-town legislators or a Congress and president beholden to state party leaders who answered to rural constituents.

Underrepresentation of cities throughout the federal system exerted profound and lasting consequences, for it allowed governmental leaders at all levels to wash their hands of the devastating effects of industrialization and urbanization. In the late nineteenth century, powerful populist movements pushed for the recognition of the right of labor unions to organize. In the first 20 years of the twentieth century, reformers lobbied state legislatures to adopt universal health insurance, workers' compensation, and relief programs for widows, children, and the elderly. A groundswell of opposition to child labor swept the country; nevertheless, the federal government did not adopt child labor legislation until 1916, and it was struck down by the Supreme Court two years later.[111] Partially because urban residents had so little political voice, these and other reforms were delayed until the New Deal of the 1930s, and some reforms, such as national health care, have never been adopted.

The federal courts finally moved against legislative malapportionment in the 1960s, more than 40 years after the 1920 census showed that a majority of Americans lived in urban places. In *Baker v. Carr* (1962), a group of Knoxville residents challenged the fact that the Tennessee legislature had not been reapportioned since 1901.[112] Their lawyers argued that citizens living in urban areas were being deprived of "equal protection of the law," as guaranteed by the Fourteenth Amendment to the U.S. Constitution. The important court decision that decided this case, as well as others, came on June 15, 1964, when the U.S. Supreme Court, in *Reynolds v. Sims*, ruled that state legislative apportionments must follow a "one man, one vote" principle.[113] Within a few years, for the first time in the nation's history, state legislative and congressional districts were apportioned to give city residents equal representation.

By the time the courts imposed the one-man, one-vote remedy, it was too late. Older industrial cities were rapidly losing population to the suburbs and to the Sunbelt. These demographic changes meant also that the balance of power in national politics was also shifting. If cities had gained equal representation in state legislatures and in Congress decades earlier, the influence of urban voters would have virtually guaranteed that they could have secured from the federal government as well as from many states funding for such urban priorities as mass transit, public housing, urban revitalization, and public health programs. Financial assistance for cities and for urban infrastructure would have been similar to the support provided to cities by European countries. But the American political system was biased against the urban electorate—a circumstance that arose because the people who lived in the cities of America had long been regarded as "strangers in the land."[114] In light of this background, the ability of American cities to respond to their problems as well as they did must be regarded as a notable success.

NOTES

1. Robert A. Beauregard, *Voices of Decline: The Postwar Fate of U.S. Cities* (New York: Blackwell, 1993).
2. London proper had 957,000, but the greater London area had 1,117,000 people.
3. Brian R. Mitchell, *European Historical Statistics, 1750–1970* (New York: Columbia University Press, 1975), p. 76.
4. Defined as settlements with at least 5,000 population.
5. Eric Lampard, "Historical Aspects of Urbanization," in *The Study of Urbanization*, ed. Philip M. Hauser and Leo F. Schnore (New York: Wiley, 1965), p. 523.
6. "The Inevitability of City Growth," reprinted from *Atlantic Monthly*, April 1985, in *City Life, 1865–1900: Views of Urban America*, ed. Ann Cook, Marilyn Gittell, and Herb Mack (New York: Praeger, 1973), p. 17.
7. Eric H. Monkkonen, *America Becomes Urban: The Development of U.S. Cities and Towns, 1780–1980* (Berkeley: University of California Press, 1988), p. 78.

8. D. Philip Locklin, *Economics of Transportation*, 7th ed. (Homewood, Ill.: Irwin, 1972).

9. Allan R. Pred, *The Spatial Dynamics of Urban–Industrial Growth, 1800–1914* (Cambridge, Mass.: MIT Press, 1966), p. 103.

10. David M. Gordon, "Class Struggle and the Stages of American Urban Development," in *The Rise of the Sunbelt Cities*, ed. David C. Perry and Alfred J. Watkins (Beverly Hills, Calif.: Sage, 1977), p. 64.

11. George Rogers Taylor, *The Transportation Revolution, 1815–1860* (New York: Holt, Rinehart & Winston, 1951), p. 52.

12. Carter Goodrich, *Government Promotion of American Canals and Railroads, 1800–1890* (New York: Columbia University Press, 1960), pp. 266–267.

13. Richard C. Wade, *The Urban Frontier: Pioneer Life in Early Pittsburgh, Cincinnati, Lexington, Louisville, and St. Louis* (Chicago: University of Chicago Press, 1959), p. 70.

14. U.S. Department of Commerce, *Historical Statistics of the United States, Colonial Times to 1970*, pt. 2, pp. 728, 731.

15. Alfred D. Chandler, *The Railroads: The Nation's First Big Business* (New York: Harcourt Brace Jovanovich, 1965).

16. Paul Kantor, *The Dependent City Revisited: The Political Economy of Urban Development and Social Policy* (Boulder, Colo.: Westview, 1995), p. 24.

17. Carter Goodrich, "The Revulsion Against Internal Improvements," *Journal of Economic History* 10, no. 2 (November 1950): 145–169.

18. David Chalmers, *Neither Socialism nor Monopoly* (Philadelphia: Lippincott, 1976), p. 4.

19. Blake McKelvey, *American Urbanization: A Comparative History* (Glenview, Ill.: Scott Foresman, 1973), pp. 25–26.

20. Ibid.

21. Paul Kantor with Stephen David, *The Dependent City: The Changing Political Economy of Urban America* (Glenview, Ill.: Scott Foresman, 1987), pp. 499–500.

22. Goodrich, *Government Promotion*, p. 241. Goodrich estimates that until 1860 local governments provided 29 percent of total public subsidies (p. 268). The proportion of local contributions increased significantly after the Civil War. In his study of New York from 1826 to 1875, Harry Pierce concludes that three-quarters of the subsidy came from local governments and one-quarter from the state. See Harry H. Pierce, *The Railroads of New York: A Study of Government Aid, 1826–1875* (Cambridge, Mass.: Harvard University Press, 1953).

23. Ibid.

24. In 1849, for example, the voters of Cleveland approved a $100,000 subscription to stock in the Cleveland and Pittsburgh Railroad by a vote of 1,157 to 27. Despite the enthusiasm of the voters, the stock never paid any dividends and eventually sold at far below par. Charles C. Williamson, *The Finances of Cleveland* (New York: Columbia University Press, 1907), pp. 218–220.

25. Goodrich, *Government Promotion*, p. 42.

26. Ibid., p. 272. One study gave the following figures for New York: "Only 52 of the 297 municipalities that bought stock in a railroad disposed of their securities at par or better, 162 held stock with no market value" (Pierce, *The Railroads of New York*), p. 273.

27. A. M. Hillhouse, *Municipal Bonds: A Century of Experience* (Upper Saddle River, N.J.: Prentice Hall, 1936), p. 39.

28. Goodrich, *Government Promotion*, pp. 268–271. Repudiation goes beyond default, which is simply a failure to pay the debt on time. Repudiation declares an unwillingness to ever repay the debt.

29. Alberta M. Sbragia, *Debt Wish: Entrepreneurial Cities, U.S. Federalism and Economic Development* (Pittsburgh: University of Pittsburgh Press, 1996), p. 91.

30. Goodrich, "Revulsion Against Internal Improvements"; see also Sbragia, *Debt Wish*, Chapter 5.

31. Lawrence Goodwyn, *The Populist Movement* (New York: Oxford University Press, 1978).

32. Edwin J. Perkins, *The Economy of Colonial America* (New York: Columbia University Press, 1980), p. 157.

33. Philip Foner, *History of the Labor Movement in the United States* (New York: International, 1975), pp. 13–18.
34. Howard P. Chudacoff, *The Evolution of American Urban Society* (N.J.: Prentice Hall, 1975), p. 26.
35. Sam Bass Warner Jr., *The Private City: Philadelphia in Three Periods of Its Growth* (Philadelphia: University of Pennsylvania Press, 1968), p. 21.
36. Kantor, *The Dependent City*, p. 22.
37. Ibid., p. 33.
38. Pred, *The Spatial Dynamics*, p. 16.
39. Ibid., p. 170.
40. Ibid., pp. 68–69.
41. The skyscraper boom on Fifth Avenue between 1900 and 1915 was largely fueled by the desire of rich individuals to outdo one another in pretentious architecture. See Seymour I. Toll, *Zoned American* (New York: Grossman, 1969), Chapter 2.
42. Chartered by the states, limited-risk corporations allowed the selling of shares to investors whose liability in case of corporate failure was limited to their direct investment. In partnerships, the partners were liable for all debts incurred by the company, and these could easily exceed the partners' own assets. The corporate form of business organization thus made it easier to raise capital, for investors risked less than in other forms of business investment.
43. U.S. Department of the Interior, Census Office, *Census Reports of 1900*, vol. 7, *Manufacturers*, pt. 1: "United States by Industries" (Washington, D.C.: U.S. Government Printing Office, 1902), pp. 503–509.
44. William Miller, "American Historians and the Business Elite," *Journal of Economic History* 9 (1949): 184–208.
45. Kenneth Jackson, *Crabgrass Frontier: The Suburbanization of the United States* (New York: Oxford University Press, 1985), p. 35.
46. George Rogers Taylor, "Building an Intra-Urban Transportation System," in *The Urbanization of America: An Historical Anthology*, ed. Allen M. Wakstein (Boston: Houghton Mifflin, 1970), p. 137.
47. Glen E. Holt, "The Changing Perception of Urban Pathology: An Essay on the Development of Mass Transit in the United States," in *Cities in American History*, ed. Kenneth T. Jackson and Stanley K. Schultz (New York: Knopf, 1972), p. 327.
48. Taylor, "Building an Intra-Urban Transportation System," p. 139.
49. C. G. Kennedy, "Commuter Services in the Boston Area, 1835–1860," *Business History Review* 26 (1962): 277–287.
50. Jackson, *Crabgrass Frontier*, p. 41.
51. David Ward, *Cities and Immigrants: A Geography of Change in Nineteenth-Century America* (New York: Oxford University Press, 1971), p. 4.
52. Jackson, *Crabgrass Frontier*, p. 108.
53. Ibid.
54. Gary A. Tobin, "Suburbanization and the Development of Motor Transportation: Transportation and Technology and the Suburbanization Process," in *The Changing Face of the Suburbs*, ed. Barry Schwartz (Chicago: University of Chicago Press, 1975), p. 99.
55. "The Smell of Cincinnati," *Enquirer* (Richmond, Va.), November 15, 1874, in *City Life*, ed. Cook, Gittell, and Mack, p. 143.
56. Ward, *Cities and Immigrants*, Chapter 3.
57. Blake McKelvey, *The Urbanization of America, 1860–1915* (New Brunswick, N.J.: Rutgers University Press, 1963), p. 54.
58. For an excellent history of America's downtowns, see Robert M. Fogelson, *Downtown: Its Rise and Fall, 1880–1950* (New Haven, Conn.: Yale University Press, 2001).
59. U.S. Bureau of the Census, *The Growth of Metropolitan Districts in the United States: 1900–1940*, by Warren S. Thompson (Washington, D.C.: U.S. Government Printing Office, 1947).

60. Samuel P. Hays, *The Response to Industrialism, 1885–1914* (Chicago: University of Chicago Press, 1957), p. 14.
61. Thomas Monroe Pitkin, *Keepers of the Gate: A History of Ellis Island* (New York: New York University Press, 1975), p. ix.
62. Ward, *Cities and Immigrants*, p. 56.
63. Ibid., p. 52.
64. John Higham, *Strangers in the Land: Patterns of American Nativism, 1860–1925* (New Brunswick, N.J.: Rutgers University Press, 1955), pp. 54–55.
65. Stephen Thernstrom, *The Other Bostonians: Poverty and Progress in the American Metropolis, 1880–1970* (Cambridge, Mass.: Harvard University Press, 1973), p. 160.
66. Ibid.
67. Charles N. Glaab and A. Theodore Brown, *A History of Urban America* (New York: Macmillan, 1967), p. 160.
68. Gwendolyn Wright, *Building the American Dream: A Social History of Housing in America* (Cambridge, Mass.: MIT Press, 1983), p. 123. Dumbbell waiters are rope-pulley devices used to move small items up and down a shaft in multistory buildings.
69. Glaab and Brown, *A History of Urban America*, p. 86.
70. Ibid., p. 180.
71. Terrence J. MacDonald and Sally K. Ward, eds., *The Politics of Urban Fiscal Policy* (Beverly Hills, Calif.: Sage, 1984), p. 14.
72. Nelson M. Blake, *Water for the Cities: A History of the Urban Water Supply Problem in the United States* (Syracuse, N.Y.: Syracuse University Press, 1956), p. 6.
73. Ibid., pp. 102–103.
74. Ibid., p. 6.
75. Warner, *The Private City*, pp. 107–109.
76. Arthur N. Schlesinger, "A Panoramic View: The City in American Life," in *The City in American Life*, ed. Kramer and Holborn, p. 23.
77. McKelvey, *The Urbanization of America*, p. 13.
78. Edgar W. Martin, *The Standard of Living in 1860* (Chicago: University of Chicago Press, 1942), pp. 44–47, 89–112.
79. McKelvey, *The Urbanization of America*, p. 90.
80. Ibid., p. 13.
81. Ibid., p. 90.
82. McKelvey, *American Urbanization*, p. 44.
83. Stephen Thernstrom, *Poverty and Progress: Social Mobility in a Nineteenth-Century City* (Cambridge, Mass.: Harvard University Press, 1964), p. 39.
84. Fred M. Wirt, *Power in the City* (Berkeley: University of California Press, 1974), p. 110.
85. James F. Richardson, "To Control the City: The New York Police in Historical Perspective," in *Cities in American History*, ed. Kenneth T. Jackson and Stanley K. Schultz (New York: Knopf, 1972), pp. 272–289.
86. Warner, *The Private City*, Chapter 7.
87. Richardson, "To Control the City," p. 278.
88. *Report of the National Advisory Commission on Civil Disorders* (New York: Bantam Books, 1968).
89. Warner, *The Private City*.
90. Bayrd Still, *Milwaukee: The History of a City* (Madison: State Historical Society of Wisconsin, 1984), Chapter 10.
91. Warner, *The Private City*, p. 86.
92. Sbragia, *Debt Wish*, p. 76.
93. Ibid.
94. Ibid.
95. Jon Teaford, *The Unheralded Triumph: City Government in America, 1870–1900* (Baltimore: Johns Hopkins University Press, 1984), Chapter 8.

96. Ibid., p. 222.
97. Ibid., p. 221.
98. Ibid., p. 247.
99. Stanley K. Schultz, *Constructing Urban Culture: American Cities and City Planning, 1800–1920* (Philadelphia: Temple University Press, 1989), p. 174.
100. Ibid., p. 246.
101. McKelvey, *The Urbanization of America*, p. 90.
102. Alexis de Tocqueville, *Democracy in America*, vol. 1 (New York: Shocken Books, 1961), p. 60.
103. For citations, see Gerald Frug, "The City as a Legal Concept," *Harvard Law Review* 93, no. 6 (April 1980): 1113–1117.
104. See *Dartmouth College v. Woodward*, 4 Wheat. 518 (1819).
105. *City of Clinton v. Cedar Rapids and Missouri River Railroad Co.*, 24 Iowa 455–475 (1868).
106. Schultz, *Constructing Urban Culture*, p. 73.
107. Ibid., p. 69.
108. William Munro, *The Government of the American Cities*, 3rd ed. (New York: Macmillan, 1924), p. 53.
109. Mark I. Gelfand, *A Nation of Cities: The Federal Government and Urban America, 1933–1965* (New York: Oxford University Press, 1975), p. 11.
110. Ibid.
111. *Hammer v. Dagenhart et al.*, 247 U.S. 251 (1918).
112. *Baker v. Carr*, 369 U.S. 189 (1962).
113. *Reynolds v. Sims*, 377 U.S. 533 (1964). "One man, one vote" was the term used in the Court's decision.
114. Higham, *Strangers in the Land*.

CHAPTER 3

PARTY MACHINES
AND THE IMMIGRANTS

MACHINES AND MACHINE-STYLE POLITICS

The image of the rotund, cigar-smoking machine politician handing out buckets of coal to poor widows and cutting deals in smoke-filled rooms in the back of taverns holds a sacred place in the lore of American politics. What continues to make the image fascinating is its colorful, larger-than-life aspect: the politician who is free-wheeling, generous, and who manages to parley this quality into political support. But there is a darker side, too. The television series *The Sopranos* or Francis Ford Coppola's film *The Godfather* come to mind as an apt comparison, all the more because they serve as a reminder that machine politicians and the Mafia shared a general style, though they rarely utilized the same means. The cases when machine politicians crossed the line into thuggish violence are probably the exceptions, but not enough for comfort. Recall, for example, *The Untouchables* television series and movie, based on the heyday of the Chicago machine of the 1920s and 1930s, when politicians, judges, and police officers were bought off by Al Capone, and Elliott Ness arrived on the scene to take on not only Capone, but an entire system of criminal and political corruption. In a few instances, information fed by machines to criminal gangs was used to kill informants, and on occasion investigative reporters were killed.[1] Happily, however, the day-to-day operations of most of the party machines were far more prosaic.

The impressions from the era of machine politics are still very much alive, but they are misleading in key respects. It is true that the machines thrived on corruption, some spectacularly so. But it is also true that machine politicians provided a path by which ethnic voters could gain a measure of access to a political system that had previously excluded them. Looked at in this way, it is possible to see the machines as classic mechanisms of assimilation and, for some, a means of personal advancement. For decades, the battle over who would control the apparatus of local government pitted machines against reformers. Over time the reformers might have prevailed, but a study of the machines still provides a timely and often entertaining glimpse into a struggle for power that has helped shape the contemporary American city.

Some degree of machine-style politics—a style that relies on material incentives to nurture loyalty—is present in every political system. A clique of silver-haired "suits" who help their favored developers obtain zoning variances for a suburban mall are acting as much like machine politicians as a ward boss who provides assistance to a constituent dealing with a rat inspector who wants to close down a restaurant or apartment building. In politics, material incentives come in many forms: a patronage job, a government contract, a zoning variance, a fixed parking ticket, an expedited business license. In all political systems, claims to lofty ideals are often little more than fig leaves covering naked self-interest. For this reason, something more than machine-style politics is necessary if we are to accurately apply the term "machine" to a political organization.[2] A machine is a hierarchical organization controlled by a single leader, a "boss," or a tightly organized clique. In some local governments a hierarchical structure centralizes power into the hands of a few individuals. A full-fledged political machine is characterized by both machine-style politics and a well-defined hierarchy of command, coordination, and control.

A majority of America's big industrial cities once were governed by machines organized in this fashion. Between 1870 and 1945, 17 of the nation's 30 cities with populations of more than 500,000 had boss rule and a disciplined, hierarchical party organization at some point.[3] In most of these cities, factional machine-style politics existed for some time before the actual machines emerged. With only two or three exceptions in the big cities, the classic machines flowered in the last years of the nineteenth century and the first few years of the twentieth century. Boss rule peaked sometime in the 1920s. In 1932, the year Democratic candidate Franklin D. Roosevelt won the presidency, 10 of America's 30 biggest cities were ruled by machine bosses. Today, the urban political machine is pretty much extinct. The death of Chicago boss Richard J. Daley in 1976 marked the end of the era of the classic party machines, which relied on patronage and material incentives to keep their organizations intact.[4]

Despite the demise of the machines, any serious discussion of city politics in America must take them into account because their legacy still reverberates throughout the political system. Early in the twentieth century, the machines became the object of a furious campaign designed to clean up politics and reduce the influence of immigrant voters. The reforms they sponsored undeniably cleaned up politics, but they also changed the rules of the game to the disadvantage of people at the lower end of the social spectrum. Battles continue to be fought in the courts over voter registration rules that make it harder for less educated people to register and at-large electoral systems that dilute the electoral influence of minority voters. Battles over the rules of the game are timeless because these rules are important in determining access to the political system. The skirmishes pitting machine politicians against the reformers illustrate what is at stake.

OUTTAKE

MACHINES HAD TWO SIDES

The careers of two machine politicians, James and Tom Pendergast of Kansas City, Missouri, illustrate both the positive and the negative sides of machine politics.

In 1876 James Pendergast, an Irishman with a short, thick neck and massive arms and shoulders, moved to Kansas City. Just 20 years old and with only a few dollars in his pocket, he rented a room in the West Bottoms ward, an industrial section on the floodplain of the Missouri River. The residents of West Bottoms worked in the meat packinghouses, machine shops, railroad yards, factories, and warehouses of the area. Blacks, Irish, Germans, and rural migrants lived in crowded four- and five-story tenements and tiny shanties. Overlooking this squalid area of dirt streets and open sewers was Quality Hill, from which the wealthy elite presided over the town. Pendergast held jobs in the packinghouses and in an iron foundry until 1881, when he used racetrack winnings to buy a hotel and a saloon.

He named the saloon Climax in honor of his lucky horse. The Climax Saloon became a social center of the ward, which put Pendergast in a position to meet the people of his ward. And he was generous. On payday, he cashed payroll checks and settled credit agreements; he posted bonds for men who had been arrested for gambling. His generosity cost money, but his business flourished: "Men learned that he had an interest in humanity outside of business and that he could be trusted, and they returned the favor by patronizing his saloon and giving him their confidence." In this way Pendergast's politics and his everyday life became one and the same. He soon found himself being promoted for an alderman's seat, which he won in 1892.

The same year, Pendergast opened another saloon in the Second Ward, located in the city's North End. In that saloon he employed 22 men to run gambling tables, and in his West Bottoms ward he continued to employ a large gambling staff. Gambling was run on a large scale in Kansas City. Opening his own operations in the North End enabled Pendergast to forge close relationships with the politicians of that ward, and he soon became as influential in the Second Ward as he was in the First. He was able to secure police protection for gambling and liquor operations by paying off police officers and by influencing the choice of a police chief in 1895.

Pendergast could have run for mayor, but he preferred to stay behind the scenes. By 1900 he was so powerful that he was able to select the mayoral candidate personally. In return, the newly elected mayor gave Pendergast control over hundreds of patronage jobs and appointed Pendergast's brother, Tom, to the position of superintendent of streets. More than two hundred men were employed by the streets department, which placed orders for gravel and cement with suppliers and contractors loyal to the machine. James Pendergast also gained control over positions in the fire department and also named the city's deputy license inspector, an important job because saloons and other business establishments needed licenses to operate. Finally, and perhaps most important of all, by 1902 he had personally selected 123 of the 173 patrolmen on the police force. Although he never was mayor, he soon became Kansas City's most powerful politician.

Like the party machines in other cities, the Pendergast machine operated on the basis of mutually beneficial relationships. The boss distributed material rewards and expected loyalty in return. Some machine politicians made this relationship explicit, but the most effective ones never had to. A politician could get a lot of mileage out of only a modest amount of help; the word spread. James Pendergast expressed the principle in this way: "I've been called a boss. All there is to it is having friends, doing things for people, and then later on they'll do things for you." Pendergast's ward always elected him by at least a 3-to-1 margin, and without discernible vote fraud. It never occurred to him that he would need to steal an election.

Jim Pendergast's style contrasted starkly with his brother Tom's. Tom, who inherited the Kansas City Democratic organization after James died, regularly resorted to a mixture of fraud and coercion. In the summer of 1914, Tom Pendergast's organization "used money, repeat voters, and toughs to produce North Side majorities" to gain approval of a proposed railway franchise. Machine workers distributed liquor and money in black and Italian neighborhoods. They "paid men to vote under assumed names; and election judges who questioned some of those dragged off the streets and out of flop houses to vote were intimidated and abused, both verbally and physically." On Election Day in 1934, four persons were killed by thugs. Two years later, an attempted assassination and massive voter fraud led to an investigation that eventually resulted in 259 convictions for election fraud and criminal behavior.

James Pendergast succeeded in politics because he went out of his way to ascertain the needs of his constituents. By building a powerful political organization, he was able to provide them with jobs and other benefits. However, when his brother Tom took over the organization, corruption and intimidation became the order of the day. The story of the two Pendergasts highlights a question often asked about the classic party machines: Were they vehicles for democracy, or were they inherently flawed by the concentration of power they facilitated?

Source: Lyle W. Dorsett, *The Pendergast Machine* (New York: Oxford University Press, 1968). Quotations are from pp. 14, 26, 59, 60.

THE ORIGINS OF MACHINE POLITICS

The confluence of two factors made the rise of the machines possible: the emergence of a mass electorate, and industrialization.[5] When the Constitution was ratified in 1789, only about 5 percent of adult white males were eligible to vote. The political systems of American cities became democratic only slowly. Property qualifications for voting began to be eased after 1776, and by 1850 almost all free white males were eligible to vote.[6] Until the 1820s almost all mayors were appointed by governors or city councils. Beginning with Boston and St. Louis in 1822, charter revisions gradually transformed the office into a popularly elected post, and by 1840 this practice had become nearly universal.[7] In the presidential election of 1840, 80 percent of adult white males went to the polls, the highest rate in any major democracy.[8] The spread of universal male suffrage coincided with the explosive growth of cities. From the 1830s to the 1920s, more than 30 million immigrants came to the United States, most of them pouring into the cities. As soon as they were citizens, if they were male, they could vote. A new breed of enterprising politician took advantage of this circumstance.

In most large American cities, a "friends and neighbors" or "local followings" style of politics evolved that reflected the decentralized nature of their political systems. Aldermen were elected from wards, and because these electoral units were quite small, politicians were able to enter politics by taking advantage of their social connections. No one benefited from this arrangement more than pub owners. Saloons were central to day-to-day life in working-class wards and, more than any other institution, they served as neighborhood centers. Especially in Irish neighborhoods, pub owners were considered reliable sources of information and advice. The density of pubs in immigrant neighborhoods was astonishing. In 1915, for example, there was a saloon for every 515 residents in New York, and the ratio was greater in Chicago, with a saloon for every 335 persons, and in San Francisco, with a saloon for every 218 residents.[9] In working-class districts, the ratio in most cities was at least one pub for every 50 males.[10] In late-nineteenth-century Chicago, half the city's total population entered a saloon every day.[11] A large proportion of machine politicians got their start as pub owners. Of New York City's 24 aldermen in 1890, 11 were pub owners. Pub owners made up a third of Milwaukee's city council members in 1902 and a third of Detroit's aldermen at the turn of the century.[12]

Party machines combined two seemingly incompatible qualities: the absence of formal rules and a disciplined organization. Machine politicians were not "hired" into party organizations, and they did not have a job description. Their ability to deliver votes and their skill at forging alliances with other politicians determined their standing in the organization. Normally, a machine politician started at the bottom and worked his way up. Precinct captains, who were responsible for getting out the vote in the smallest and most basic political unit of the city, knew each voter personally, often as a friend and neighbor. To secure a following at this level, a politician had to be known not only as a person involved in politics but as someone who participated in local community life. Politicians climbed the political ladder only if they demonstrated they could reliably deliver the vote. If they did, the next rung they reached for was alderman.

Most machine politicians came from backgrounds that offended silk-stocking elements. Schooled in rough-and-tumble political competition, they generally were men of incredible energy, quick temper, and rough manners. At the least, they loved what they were doing; they felt no alienation from their job. Politics was everything the machine politicians knew and did—it was their social life, their profession, their first love. They pursued political power, not social standing.[13] George Washington Plunkitt, a member of the Tammany Hall organization in New York, advised against what he called the "dangers of the dress suit in politics." "Live like your neighbors," Plunkitt admonished aspiring politicians, "even if you have the means to live better. Make the poorest man in your district feel that he is your equal, or even a bit superior to you."[14]

Disciplined political organizations emerged when skillful leaders succeeded in persuading other politicians that everyone would benefit if they cooperated. When this happened, a military-style hierarchy evolved, with those lower in the organization waiting for their chance to move up. This structure was once described by Frank Hague, the Jersey City boss, to columnist Joseph Alsop, who wrote, "He [Hague] was

Figure 3.1   The Organization of Machine Politics

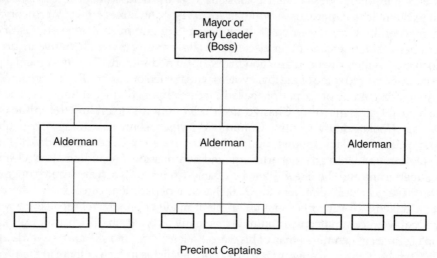

Precinct Captains

The organization of local political machines, or parties, parallels the formal structures of government but is also separate from them. Like the mayor, the party leader or boss controls the entire city, or perhaps county. The alderman represents a ward in the city council or board of aldermen. The alderman may or may not serve as ward leader of the party. Each ward consists of many precincts or election districts. Precinct captains are responsible for delivering the vote in their precinct.

   In principle, power flows from the bottom up: Precinct captains elect the ward leaders, and the ward leaders elect the party boss. But in fact, power flows from the top.

talking in the dining room of one of the local hotels. He took the squares on the table-cloth to illustrate precincts and wards, tracing them out with his finger, and he explained the feudal system of American politics, whereby the precinct captain is governed by a ward lieutenant, the lieutenant by a ward leader, and each ward leader by the boss."[15]

   As shown in Figure 3.1, precincts and precinct captains constituted the foundation of the machine organization. The typical precinct had 400 to 600 voters, and precinct captains were expected to know most of them by name. Thirty to forty precincts were generally included within a ward. The captains of the precincts were chosen by and worked for the ward's alderman. The alderman served as the chair of the ward's party committee, unless he selected a committeeman to supervise the precinct captains on his behalf. Finally, the aldermen reported to the machine boss, who was usually but not always the mayor.

   The whole structure held together because everyone gained by cooperating in what was, in essence, a "system of organized bribery."[16] Bosses and individual aldermen had at their disposal patronage jobs in police, fire, sanitation, and streets departments—and sometimes even in private industry. Construction projects, such as levee construction or road building, could give a boss control over hundreds of permanent and temporary jobs. Precinct captains usually held low-level jobs arranged through the machine, perhaps serving as supervisors on street crews. Ward committeemen generally were rewarded with higher-paying administrative positions in city government. Aldermen and other elected officials typically owned lucrative insurance companies, ran their own construction firms, or owned saloons. The most menial jobs were passed along to some of the loyal voters who turned out faithfully on Election Day.

An understanding of the patronage ladder can be gained by examining the machine of Richard J. Daley, mayor of Chicago from 1953 until his death in 1976. In the early 1970s, the Cook County Central Committee (which contains Chicago) had about 30,000 positions available for distribution. Most of these jobs were unskilled; 8,000 were available through Chicago's departments and commissions, including street cleaners, park supervisors, and the like.[17] The jobs ranged from $3,600-a-year elevator operators and $6,000-a-year stenographers to $25,000-a-year department directors (in the early 1970s, a skilled factory worker in a union plant made approximately $9,000 per year). Individual ward committeemen controlled as many as 2,000 jobs. (Richard J. Daley had begun his career as committeeman of his ward.) There were (and still are) 50 wards in the city of Chicago, with an average of 500 to 600 jobs available in each of them in the 1970s.[18]

The Election Day result determined the number of jobs available for distribution by individual precinct captains and ward committeemen. A precinct captain in Chicago was expected to know all the voters in the precinct and to be known by them. "When a man is given a precinct, it is his to cover, and it is up to him to produce for the party. If he cannot produce for the party, he cannot expect to be rewarded by the party. 'Let's put it this way,' [one alderman said] 'if your boss has a salesman who can't deliver, who can't sell his product, wouldn't he put in someone else who can?'"[19]

Alderman Vito Marzullo was a successful salesman for the Chicago organization. Every week he scheduled a formal audience with his constituents. Flanked on each side by a precinct captain, he heard their complaints:

> A precinct captain ushered in a black husband and wife. "We got a letter here from the city," the man said. "They want to charge us twenty dollars for rodent control in our building." "Give me the letter, I'll look into it," Marzullo replied. The captain spoke up. "Your daughter didn't vote on November fifth. Look into it. The alderman is running again in February. Any help we can get, we can use."[20]

In the course of hearing his constituents, Marzullo exclaimed, "Some of those liberal independents in the city council, they can't get a dog out of a dog pound with a ten-dollar bill. Who's next?" Marzullo then arranged to have a traffic ticket fixed, agreed to recommend someone for a job at an electric company, refused to donate money to the Illinois Right to Life Committee ("Nothing doing. . . . I don't want to get into any of those controversies. People for it and people against it."), agreed to try to find a job for an unemployed truck driver, and gave $50 to a welfare mother. Responding to several more requests, he offered to "see what I can do."[21]

During the Richard J. Daley years, the Chicago machine was structured like a political pyramid. Committeemen and the aldermen directed the captains of the precincts within their wards; in turn, they reported to the Cook County Central

Committee. Although most of the city machines at the turn of the century were similarly organized, some were directed from the top with an iron hand, as in Daley's Chicago; others were little more than loose confederations of politicians. However tightly run the individual machines were, they all showed these qualities: They were rooted in neighborhoods, and a combination of material incentives and ethnic and community attachments held them together.

Being close to constituents did not mean the machines were democratic. Although all machines provided something to their supporters, many of them engaged in corrupt practices that undermined elections, such as vote buying and even intimidation of voters. Machine politicians often enriched themselves by taking bribes and making backroom deals. Positive assessments of the machines advanced by historians and social scientists have relied on three major claims: The machines (1) centralized power and "got the job done," (2) served as vehicles of upward mobility for immigrants, and (3) helped assimilate the immigrants into American life. In the next three sections, we examine these claims.

DID MACHINES "GET THE JOB DONE"?

It has generally been assumed that political machines arose in the late nineteenth century to fill a void left by the absence of effective local governments. City governments were characterized by an extreme, often chaotic division of responsibilities among a multitude of separate officials, boards, and departments. The mayor generally wielded little authority. The city council or board of aldermen typically controlled the budget and made most decisions. Day-to-day administrative responsibilities were generally assumed by committees whose members were appointed by the city council, or sometimes by the mayor, state legislature, governor, or other state or local officials. When committee or board members were elected by the voters, a long list of names on the ballot made it impossible to know anything about the candidates (much like today, in states where judges are elected). Edward Sait wrote in 1933 that "when the people or particular groups among them demanded positive action, no one had adequate authority to act. The machine provided an antidote."[22] In other words, he was saying, machines were necessary if anything was to get done.

If it is true that machines arose mainly to fill a void left by disorganized and inefficient government, then we would expect to find that machines prospered especially in cities where governments were the most politically and administratively fragmented. As it turns out, however, by the time most machines came into being, municipal reformers had achieved their goal of concentrating more power in the hands of mayors and civil service administrators.[23] The reformers thought such reforms would persuade voters to keep office holders more accountable, but in this respect they failed. It turns out that it was easier to build disciplined organizations where local government had been streamlined and reformed than where government was fragmented and chaotic. In 1913, for example, reformers in Jersey City, New Jersey, persuaded the voters to fuse legislative and executive functions into one five-member commission. When the machine mayor, Frank Hague, gained control of the city commission, he was able to accomplish something he had not been able to do before: consolidate his power over a faction-ridden Democratic Party and become the uncontested boss of Jersey City.[24]

Control of municipal government was a prize worth pursuing. Between 1870 and 1900, municipal workforces grew even faster than the population of cities.[25] During this period, local governments spent more money than either the federal government or the state governments.[26] Cities ran up debts at a feverish pace to finance water systems, lay sewers lines, pave streets, build parks and public buildings, improve harbors, and improve public health.[27] Even cities with factionalized politics, such as Los Angeles, made huge investments in infrastructure.[28] The political support for reducing disease rates through better water and sewer services, for better roads and public transit, and for new public utilities and better parks was sufficiently strong that these services were bound to expand, regardless of how a city was run.[29] A study of cities from 1890 to 1940 found no difference between machine and nonmachine cities in the overall level of public expenditures.[30]

Without question, corruption often diverted resources from important municipal services. Corruption could make the price of "getting the job done" astonishingly high. Probably the most notoriously corrupt machine in American history was led by William Marcy "Boss" Tweed, who ran the infamous Tweed Ring in New York City from 1868 to 1871. In three years, Tweed took $30 million to $100 million of public funds for himself and his cronies. Under his regime, the machine's traditional take of 10 percent on construction contracts ratcheted upward. A courthouse project originally estimated to cost $250,000 ended up costing taxpayers $14 million. At least 90 percent of this cost overrun went to pay payoffs, bribes, and fake contracts.[31] Tweed's rule has been called the politics of "rapacious individualism" because everyone in the machine seemed to be after personal wealth. Because Tweed was not able to count on the loyalty of his fellow politicians, he was forced to buy it directly, and therefore his authority was fragile and short-lived.[32] In 1869 and 1870, the city's debt increased from $36 million to $97 million. By 1871, when Tweed was arrested, the city was bankrupt.

Machine bosses frequently resorted to corruption to build and maintain their organizations. Machine politicians were in a position to use the powers of cities to help businesses make money; in return, bribes were there for the taking. Cities awarded multiyear contracts for streetcar operations and utility services (such as electricity, gas, and telephone). Cities issued tavern and liquor licenses and regulated gambling and prostitution (or had the option of looking the other way when they were illegal). They engaged in a continuous stream of public works projects, including the building of roads, bridges, public buildings, sewer and water systems, streetlights, and parks. There was money to be made on both sides of these transactions.

Control over the police force opened an avenue for bribes to Abraham Reuf's regime, which ruled San Francisco just after the turn of the century.[33] Soon after his handpicked candidate for mayor entered city hall in October 1901 (Reuf himself was an attorney who never held public office), Reuf let it be known that the city's laws against prostitution would be strictly enforced. He advised the brothel owners that it would be wise to have an attorney—himself—who could effectively represent their interests. The owners agreed to pay him a fourth of their profits, half of which Reuf shared with the mayor. This arrangement allowed the brothels to continue their operations without fear of prosecution. Reuf also "advised" saloons in the red-light district to pay premium prices for a low-quality whiskey supplied by one of Reuf's legal clients. In return, the saloon owners were protected from police raids.

San Francisco invested huge resources in municipal services, and business leaders competed for the contracts. A lot was at stake. The mayor, the city council, or a utilities commission could, in a single stroke of a pen, enrich a business owner by awarding a contract to build trolley lines, install streetlights, supply gas, or install telephones. The temptation to make decisions secretly in smoke-filled rooms was overwhelming. The chair of the public utilities committee of the San Francisco Board of Supervisors reminded a group of business leaders in January 1906,

> It must be borne in mind that without the city fathers there can be no public service corporations. The street cars cannot run, lights cannot be furnished, telephones cannot exist. And all the public service corporations want to understand that we, the city fathers, enjoy the best of health and that we are not in business for our health. The question at this banquet board is: "How much money is in it for us?"[34]

There seemed to be plenty of money for everyone. When two telephone companies submitted competing bids to supply service to the citizens of San Francisco, Reuf collected a $1,200 monthly "attorney's fee" from one company while secretly accepting a $125,000 bribe from the other. Reuf persuaded the board of supervisors to award the contract to the company that paid the biggest bribe. Keeping $63,000 for himself, he used a loyalty test to distribute the remainder of the $125,000 to the individual supervisors: $6,000 each to those who had taken no independent bribes (showing they were not trying to compete with Reuf), $3,500 to those voting correctly despite bribes to do the opposite, and nothing to those who did not cooperate.

Reuf's position as the power behind the mayor's throne ended when he was indicted and tried for corruption. His downfall was precipitated by too much success. After seeing how lucrative politics in the city could be, other members of the city administration struck out on their own in search of bribes, and before long the feeding frenzy attracted attention.

Reuf's behavior was perhaps more reckless than usual, but in almost all cities, machines forged alliances with illicit business owners. The relationship benefited both parties: The businesses were free to operate without having to worry about the law, and the politicians could count on a steady flow of bribes. One of the reasons that machines flourished in the 1920s is that the national prohibition of liquor sales opened unprecedented opportunities for selling police protection to speakeasies and bootleggers. Prohibition facilitated a cooperative arrangement between machines and organized crime not only in Chicago, where the arrangement was especially notorious, but elsewhere as well. In many cases, the level of flagrant corruption and rising levels of violence brought a reaction that brought the machines down for good.

Machines took bribes from legitimate enterprises as well. The temptation was enormous. The machines governed the cities during a period of explosive growth in population, services, and construction. Even if the politicians tried to be honest, business tycoons eager to expand their empires were eager to spread their money around to get what they wanted. They found it convenient to work with politicians who could make decisions expeditiously behind the scenes. Big business paid bigger bribes than anyone else, and this put them in a position to negotiate monopoly contracts on favorable terms. The franchises typically were granted for periods of 50 to 100 years, and some specified no terminal dates at all.[35] In the 1880s and 1890s, national financial syndicates made millions of dollars by gaining control of street railway franchises. In 1890 there were 39 street railway companies in Philadelphia, 19 in New York City, 24 in Pittsburgh, 19 in St. Louis, and 16 in San Francisco.[36] By the turn of the century, only one or two major street railway companies operated in most cities.

It needs to be said that then, as now, corruption was not confined to machines—it was virtually everywhere. In any case, the extent and style of corruption varied from one machine to the next, as did the apparent benefits. During the 1930s Boss George Cox was credited with bringing "positive and moderate reform government to Cincinnati."[37] In the years when Richard J. Daley was boss (1955–1976), Chicago was known as "the city that works." Daley was popular with voters because they felt he was responsible for the efficient delivery of city services, and no evidence indicates he ever took money for himself.[38]

WERE MACHINES VEHICLES OF UPWARD MOBILITY?

An influential scholar has argued that the machines succeeded partly because they provided "alternative channels of social mobility for those otherwise excluded from the more conventional avenues of 'advancement.'"[39] In the nineteenth century, many employers refused to hire the Irish; "Irish need not apply" was written on many an employment notice. Local politics was "like a rope dangling down the formidable slope of the socioeconomic system" that poor immigrants could use to pull themselves up.[40]

Ample evidence supports the thesis that machines aided the upward mobility of immigrants. Although of course it is an exceptional story, politics was pivotal to the rise of the Kennedy clan in Boston from poverty to wealth and national power. President John F. Kennedy's grandfather on his mother's side, John "Honey Fitz" Fitzgerald, rose from a ward heeler running errands for an alderman to the office of mayor of Boston. Kennedy's grandfather on his father's side was a respected ward politician and saloonkeeper whose contacts helped the early career of the president's millionaire father, Joseph P. Kennedy, who made a fortune in bootleg liquor.[41]

The idea that the machines enhanced the upward mobility of immigrants is based on the notion that machines had to work tirelessly to incorporate new groups of voters into their coalitions by offering jobs and other favors. In their early years, machine politicians typically worked hard to attract voters so they could gain access to the patronage jobs in city government.[42] Once they had built a winning coalition, however, machine politicians often became complacent. They continued to reward their loyal supporters but stopped reaching out to new groups.

Most of the big-city machines built in the nineteenth century were dominated by Irish politicians, and they stayed that way for a long time. In a study of six machines, Steven Erie concluded they were consistently biased in favor of Irish constituents.

Machine leaders "turned their backs on later-arriving immigrants."[43] Between 1900 and 1930, for example, the machines in New York City, Jersey City, and Albany, New York, added nearly 100,000 municipal jobs. Close to two-thirds of the new jobs went to Irish constituents, even though they made up only about one-third of the population in these cities. The Irish were especially careful to maintain their control over police forces. As late as 1970, for instance, 65 percent of police officers in Albany were of Irish descent, even though no more than 25 percent of the city's population could trace their ancestry to Ireland.[44]

Later-arriving immigrants found themselves shut out of the benefits of machine rule. In New York City, for example, the machine organization called Tammany Hall was run by and for the Irish. Although Jews and Italians represented 43 percent of New York's population by 1920, only 15 percent of the city's aldermen and assemblymen were Jewish and only 3 percent were Italian in 1921.[45] Fiorello LaGuardia, elected mayor in 1933, was able to smash the Tammany machine by assembling a coalition of disgruntled Jews, Italians, and other excluded groups. LaGuardia was a master at ethnic politics, perhaps because "half Jewish and half Italian, married first to a Catholic and then to a Lutheran of German descent, himself a Mason and an Episcopalian, he was practically a balanced ticket all by himself."[46]

It perhaps goes without saying that blacks were excluded from nearly all urban machines. In Chicago, however, a "submachine" run by black politicians evolved, but they were subordinate in every way to the white machine organization.[47] William Dawson, a member of Congress from 1942 until his death in 1970, ran a submachine in Chicago's South Side ghetto, but white politicians kept him carefully in check. Dawson reliably delivered huge pluralities for machine candidates from the black wards, but black voters received relatively little in return.[48] Throughout Chicago's history, weak and inexperienced black politicians who accepted a devil's bargain were recruited into the machine: In exchange for a few favors, they delivered the vote and kept a more militant black leadership from emerging.[49] The legacy of such practices was still apparent in the Daley years. Although blacks made up 40 percent of Chicago's population in 1970, they held only 20 percent of the government jobs in the city, and most of those jobs were the least desirable.[50] A study of a typical ward in Chicago in the 1970s found that the machine consistently over-rewarded middle-class voters and under-rewarded loyal working-class voters.[51]

Disaffected groups finally challenged the Chicago machine. In 1983 a charismatic black politician, Harold Washington, assembled a coalition of poor people, blacks, Hispanics, and white liberals to defeat the machine's mayoral candidate.[52] But the victory was short-lived. Two years after Washington suffered an unexpected heart attack in his office in 1987, Richard M. Daley, Richard J.'s son, won the mayor's race in 1989 by successfully reassembling the remnants of his father's organization and forging alliances with African American and Latino politicians, and with the downtown business establishment.

It made perfect sense for machine politicians to keep their coalitions from expanding any more than necessary.[53] The more ethnic groups joined together in a coalition, the greater the interethnic squabbles over the distribution of patronage and the thinner the distribution of rewards. As a consequence, "once minimal winning coalitions had been constructed, the machines had little incentive to naturalize, register, and mobilize the votes of later ethnic arrivals."[54] For entrenched machines, expanding the electoral base past the coalition needed for winning just complicated things.

Even for the Irish, who benefited most from machine rule, the machines did not generally provide many opportunities for upward mobility. Although city governments grew rapidly in the late nineteenth century, the number of public jobs was pitifully small compared to the jobs available in the private economy. In 1900 Tammany's vaunted patronage army made up 5 percent of New York City's workforce. It is true that from 1900 to 1920 local governments grew so fast that public employment accounted for 20 percent of all urban job growth.[55] But for most people, including immigrants, private industry rather than patronage provided the best opportunities for upward mobility.

Although for decades the Irish laid claim to a disproportionate share of the jobs in city government, it took a long time for them to catch up to other ethnic groups in the broader economy. Scandinavians, Germans, and Jews, for example, participated relatively little in machine politics. Yet they assimilated into the American middle class faster than the Irish, who achieved economic parity with these groups only in the 1960s and 1970s. Ironically, the preoccupation of the Irish with public-sector employment may have slowed their entry into middle-class occupations. Especially at the bottom of the patronage ladder, jobs were deliberately kept low paying in order to maximize the number that politicians could distribute. Most patronage jobs were blue collar, and they were distributed not to further the upward mobility of immigrants but to maintain machine organizations.

DID THE MACHINES HELP IMMIGRANTS ASSIMILATE?

Although the machines did not appreciably contribute to the economic success or upward mobility of their constituents, they nevertheless were instrumental in assimilating millions of impoverished immigrants into a culture that was generally fearful of and hostile to every new immigrant group. The machines helped nurture a sense of community and belonging for the immigrants. Machine organizations organized picnics, patriotic gatherings (always Fourth of July celebrations), baseball teams, choirs, and youth clubs. Machines were important community institutions: The Democratic Club was a place where men played cards and checkers or just talked.[56]

With the material resources at their disposal already devoted to their core constituency, machine politicians learned to satisfy immigrants who arrived later with largely symbolic benefits. In New York City, Tammany leader "Big Tim" Sullivan, an Irishman, ruled the Lower East Side even though as early as 1910 it was 85 percent Jewish and Italian. He retained the loyalty of his constituents by doing favors:

> He and his Irish lieutenants distributed coal, food, and rent money to needy Jews and Italians on the Lower East Side. Tammany's police department opened up station houses as temporary shelters for the homeless. Sullivan expedited business licenses for ethnic shopkeepers and pushcart peddlers. He shamelessly "recognized" the new immigrants with symbolic gestures and donned a yarmulke to solicit Jewish votes. Sullivan solicited Italian votes by sponsoring legislation to make Columbus Day a holiday.[57]

Many immigrants felt like outsiders in the dominant Protestant and middle-class culture of the United States. One of the secrets of the machines' appeal was that they tolerated the immigrants' "strange" practices and defended them from the dominant culture.[58] This was a benefit that machine politicians could deliver at little cost. Although working-class communities in American cities were not economically independent, they were, to a remarkable degree, socially independent. Immigrants built their own churches, mutual aid societies, and clubs for drinking and gambling. Machine politicians supported such activities because they could use them for campaigning and political organizing.[59]

Machine politicians appealed to and were supported by immigrant voters because they represented the possibility of success in this strange new country. Almost all machine politicians came from lower-class immigrant origins. One study of 20 bosses found that 15 were first- or second-generation immigrants; 13 had never finished grammar school; and most had gone into politics at a young age, serving as messenger or detail boys at rallies and meetings.[60] Machine leaders, therefore, became symbols of success. Immigrants may not have read the Horatio Alger stories, but in machine bosses they could see men who had risen out of poverty. Aspiring politicians often accepted this interpretation of themselves, too; they viewed themselves as examples of what could be done with hard work and a little luck along the way. These real-world symbols of upward mobility were sources of pride and hope for the masses of immigrants who lived and worked under incredibly difficult conditions. However, symbol exceeded substance, especially for later-arriving southern and Eastern European immigrants. Irish politicians would shrewdly pick a handful of men from other immigrant groups and place them in lesser positions on the ballot to demonstrate their generosity. Meanwhile, the bread-and-butter patronage stayed home.

The immigrants paid a high price for assimilation on these terms. Machines never attempted to address the collective aspirations of ethnic groups. The immigrants were encouraged to "cast their ballots on the basis of ethnicity rather than policy considerations."[61] Immigrants gave their votes to party politicians not as an act of consciousness about group goals but because it was easy to do and plausible alternatives were rare. The vote was a minimal commitment for the immigrant but a sufficient one for the machine. Constituents could hardly expect miracles in return.

The operating principles and structures of the urban machines ensured that the politicians who ran them steered clear of ideological battles. To deal with constituents' requests effectively, machine politicians had to learn the art of manipulating power within the framework of the existing political system. A special premium was placed on effective pragmatism, the ability to pull strings to get things done. Idealism was scorned. If a constituent came to complain about a building inspector, the politician's job was to make things nice with the inspector. Changing the building code was irrelevant and even counterproductive because it might reduce the need for the politician's services.

Machines were hostile to political movements that tried to reform the system because such movements threatened their control of the immigrant vote. Until the 1930s, most machines vigorously opposed labor unions. In the first years of the twentieth century, Irish machine politicians ordered the police to attack labor organizers in Lawrence, Massachusetts, and in New York City.[62] In Pittsburgh's 1919 steel strike, the machine likewise ordered police to harass strikers.[63] After Franklin D. Roosevelt's landslide victory in the presidential election of 1932, some of the big-city machines forged alliances with the moderate trade unions, but the relationship was never easy to maintain. The machines expected the unions to respect their turf by keeping out of local politics and focusing mainly on state and national politics and on labor–business relations.

On balance, the machines stunted the immigrants' potential as a political force. Working-class immigrants desperately needed reforms such as widows' pensions, better working conditions, laws regulating hours and wages (especially for women and children), and workers' compensation. On occasion, machine politicians supported these reforms as well as the regulation of utilities, the legal recognition of labor unions, and the regulation of insurance companies.[64] But the selective and often halfhearted support for a few reform measures did not exactly transform machine politicians into crusading reformers. Machine politicians were willing to offer support for reform legislation at the state level if it made them look good, but they never became active advocates for progressive causes. Machine politicians could be quite capricious, for immediate political circumstances always took precedence over principle.

Machine politicians rarely considered how things could be changed. They often referred to reformers as "goody-goodies" or "goo-goos" who presumably were in politics for a few thrills. ("Goo-goo" was derived from "good government," often the reformers' rallying cry.) Much of their disdain was rooted in the social differences between themselves and upper-class reformers. As a result, they had an excessive respect for the pragmatic fix.

THE SOCIAL REFORM ALTERNATIVE

Defenders of political machines have argued that few alternatives to the machines' style of politics existed, that in the face of the vast economic and political resources held by corporations and wealthy elites, machine politicians milked the system on behalf of their constituents as effectively as they could, and that to criticize them is to engage in wishful thinking about what might have been.

A look at the political movements of the time, however, shows that practical alternatives were available. In the first two decades of the twentieth century, social reformers won elections in cities all across the country. The social reformers were intent on improving the quality of life for immigrants and workers, and they campaigned for support from both working-class immigrant and middle-class voters.[65] Mayors Tom L. Johnson of Cleveland, Ohio (1901–1909), Samuel "Golden Rule" Jones of Toledo, Ohio (1897–1903), and Brand Whitlock of Toledo (1906–1913) all won election by fighting against high streetcar and utility rates and for fair taxation and better social services. Their campaigns became models for like-minded reformers elsewhere. Reform-oriented mayors in Jersey City, Philadelphia, and Cincinnati attempted to increase municipal revenue by raising taxes for businesses and wealthy property owners and by renegotiating streetcar and utility franchises. Machine politicians and the business community bitterly fought reform in these cities, just as they had a few years earlier in Cleveland and Toledo.[66]

The career of Hazen S. Pingree, who served as Detroit's mayor from 1890 to 1898, revealed the enormous possibilities of reform. Born in Maine to a poor farmer and itinerant cobbler, Pingree did not seem destined to become a political reformer. After fighting in the Civil War, Pingree moved to Detroit, where he worked as a leather cutter in a shoe factory. After a few years, he and a partner pooled their savings to purchase the outdated factory. By modernizing the machinery and producing a new line of shoes that fit current fashions, Pingree became independently wealthy. He was picked as the Republican candidate for mayor in 1889, mostly because he was the only member of the exclusive Michigan Club who could be persuaded by its members to run. The business leaders who controlled Republican politics trusted him, as a member of the club, to advocate a program of low taxes and a minimal number of municipal services. In any case, few of them imagined he would win, and they had grown accustomed to working with the Irish-dominated Democratic machine.

But unlike the typical business candidate, Pingree campaigned in the ethnic wards, and in fact kicked off his campaign by drinking whiskey in an Irish saloon. Pingree was a big hit with German and Polish voters, who had long been ignored by the Irish politicians. He called attention to the corruption of the machine and advocated an eight-hour workday for city employees. His willingness to seek the ethnic vote was the foundation on which he built his subsequent political success.

Pingree's programs, and the strategies he used to implement them, reveal how much could have been accomplished in other cities. When Pingree took over city hall, Detroit had one of the worst street systems in the nation. Many of the streets were made of wooden blocks, which caught fire in the summer and sank into the mire in the winter. The paved streets were pocked with ruts and potholes. Pingree quickly realized that collusion between paving contractors and machine politicians was at the heart of the street problem. He launched an aggressive campaign against this arrangement, appealing to his business supporters by pointing out that the prosperity of the city depended on good streets. His insistent efforts led the city council to adopt strict paving specifications for the city, and as a result, by 1895 Detroit had one of the best street systems in the United States.

It was not long before Pingree understood that the local business establishment was as much a problem as the machine. He challenged the high fare charged for a ferry ride across the Detroit River to Belle Isle Park. The company dropped its rate from 10 cents to 5 cents after the mayor threatened to revoke its franchise or put into operation a municipal ferry service. Pingree also found that private companies had located along the Detroit River waterfront, often on municipal property, which choked off public access to water and recreation. He took action to open up waterfront areas for public use.

Above all, it was Pingree's fight with the Detroit City Railway Company that turned him into a true social reformer willing to use public authority to curb private power to benefit the city as a whole. At a time when streetcar companies in other cities were converting from horses to electric power, Detroit's company refused to make the change. In April 1891 the company's employees went on strike, presenting a perfect opportunity for Pingree to begin a battle for modernization and lower fares. The three-day strike culminated in a riot in which workers and citizens tore up the tracks, stoned the streetcars, and drove off the horses. Pingree ignored the company's request to call in the state militia and instead took the position that privately owned public services were "the chief source of corruption in city governments."[67] Pingree's stance initiated a protracted, bitter fight to regulate the streetcars. This conflict vaulted him to national prominence.

Many business leaders had supported the strike, believing the street railway was so badly run that it was hurting local business. The business community was mainly interested in more reliable service, but Pingree pressed further for lower fares and municipal ownership. Such a position ran afoul of business leaders when the company passed into the hands of an eastern business mogul. The new owner's first action was to pack the company's board of directors with prominent business leaders from Detroit. The company then demanded that the city negotiate a more favorable franchise. Pingree countered with a lawsuit meant to terminate the existing company in favor of municipal ownership. At that point, the company bought Pingree's own attorney away from him and proceeded to offer bribes to city council members, including a $75,000 bribe to Pingree himself. The Preston National Bank dropped Pingree from its board of directors; he lost his family pew in the Baptist church; and he and his friends were shunned in public. For Pingree, the lesson he learned in all this was that business supported reform only on its own terms. And he also began to form his own analysis about what was wrong with America's cities.

In 1891 Pingree began attacking the tax privileges of the city's corporations. The railroad, he observed, owned more than one-fifth of the property value in the city but paid no taxes at all because of the tax-free status granted to it by the state legislature. Shipping companies, docks and warehouses, and other businesses escaped local taxation by claiming that their principal places of business existed outside the city. The city's biggest employer, the Michigan-Peninsula Car Company, paid only nominal taxes. Although he was unsuccessful in equalizing the tax burden, Pingree was able to modify some of its worst features, especially the practice of assessing, for tax purposes, real estate owned by wealthy people at rates far below its value. Pingree earned the special enmity of the city's elite by successfully campaigning for a personal property tax on home furnishings, art objects, and other luxury items.

On April 1, 1895, Detroit began operating a municipal electric plant to supply power for its streetlights. This ended a five-year running battle between Pingree and the private lighting company. Pingree had used two issues to win his battle. His main argument against the private control of electricity was that it cost too much. Pingree gathered voluminous information to show that Detroit's service was more expensive and less reliable than service in other cities. Despite the merits of his case he would have lost, but a scandal tipped the scales in his favor. In April 1892 Pingree walked into a city council meeting waving a roll of bills and dramatically accused the Detroit Electric Light and Power Company of bribing council members. The mayor had been sure to pack the room with his working-class supporters. With Pingree's followers whipped into a dangerous mood, the council members hastily capitulated.

Pingree used similar tactics in his fights with the gas and telephone interests. To force the Detroit Gas Company to lower its rates for natural gas, he initiated a campaign to inform the public about the high price of Detroit's gas. When his attempt to force lower prices stalled in the courts, he got the public works board to deny permits to excavate streets for the purpose of laying gas lines. When the gas company attempted to excavate anyway, Pingree saw to it that the owners were arrested. "Possession is a great point," argued Pingree. "Let them get their gas systems connected and then they could float their $8,000,000 of stock in New York City and become too powerful for the city to control. Detroit would be helpless in the hands of corporations as never before in her history."[68]

Pingree continued his battle, encouraging users not to pay their gas bills. As public resistance against the Detroit Gas Company mounted, investors' confidence in the company plummeted, initiating a plunge in the company's stock values. Even after Southern Pacific Railroad magnate Samuel Huntington became the company's principal investor, stock prices continued to fall, and Huntington negotiated an agreement to lower the price of gas from $1.50 per cubic foot to $0.80.

In his fourth term, Pingree took on the Bell Telephone Company. Again, the issue was high prices and inadequate service. This time he helped organize a competing phone company that charged less than half Bell's rate. The new Detroit Telephone Company soon attracted twice as many customers as Bell. In response, Bell initiated a rate war and began to improve its equipment and service. By 1900, when Michigan Bell bought out Detroit Telephone, Detroit had the lowest telephone rates and the most extensive residential use among large American cities.

No other mayor in America accomplished such a broad program of social reform. During his last two terms, Pingree traveled around the country making speeches and gathering information. He wrote prolifically. He inspired reformers elsewhere, and his national prominence helped him bring reform to his own city. After winning four terms as the mayor of Detroit, Pingree went on to serve two terms as the governor of Michigan, where he continued to fight for reform.

Pingree recognized the necessity of building a broad-based political coalition. He so assiduously courted ethnic voters that by his fourth term he had even won the dependable Irish away from the Democratic machine. In effect, Pingree pieced together his own machine, filling patronage jobs with his own supporters and firing his opponents. However, "he absolutely refused to tolerate dishonesty or theft."[69] Unlike Detroit's machine politicians, who regularly exploited ethnic hostilities to win votes in their wards, Pingree tried to unify working-class Poles, Germans, Irish, and the middle class. In short, he was aware that to accomplish reform it was necessary to "recruit a coalition of power sufficient for his purpose."[70] A great many political machines had likewise constructed powerful electoral coalitions, but the politicians who built them were more interested in furthering their own careers than in making the economic and political system more just.

MACHINE POLITICS IN TODAY'S CITIES

Cities are once again magnets for millions of immigrants and minorities. Despite their shortcomings, the machines showed respect for the newcomers and distributed highly valued resources. Considered in this light, an intriguing question arises: Would recent immigrants and ethnic and racial minorities benefit if they built political machines much like those that ruled a century ago? The historical record indicates that the answer is "not much."

The urban machines brokered a deal in which poor immigrants and economic elites each gave up something and got something in return. Business elites ceded control over local governments to working-class ethnic politicians who controlled armies of patronage workers, supported in part by income from bribes and contributions paid by the wealthy. In return, machine politicians essentially promised to leave business alone. In effect, each side struck a bargain by recognizing a sharp separation between the market and the public sphere. This compromise was important in managing the tension between capitalism, with its attendant inequalities, and popular democracy.[71]

Machine politicians and their ethnic supporters gave up a great deal and got little in return. Rather than passing out favors and low-paying jobs, machine politicians could have emulated Pingree by attacking the practices that inflated the cost of urban services and infrastructure. They could have forged alliances with labor unions to pursue programs designed to modify dangerous working conditions, long hours, child labor, and low pay. Instead, the machines discouraged immigrants from organizing around their common interests.

There is reason to believe that today's city residents can expect even less from any machines that might arise. The machines prospered in rapidly growing industrial cities that required massive expenditures on roads, bridges, sewers, streetcar systems, schools, and parks.[72] The resulting government jobs, contracts, and franchises were traded for the political support necessary to maintain the party organizations. By contrast, in today's cities it would be extremely difficult for today's politicians to assemble the patronage and other material rewards necessary to build and maintain machine organizations. City services are now administered through civil service bureaucracies, and merit employment systems have been put in place so patronage can no longer be regularly delivered on the basis of personal or political relationships. And in any case, federal prosecutors would quickly sniff out patronage and vote-buying arrangements, which have been outlawed.

The last of the old-style machines, held together by Chicago's Mayor Richard J. Daley, died along with him in 1976. Today his son, Richard M. Daley, presides over the last party machine in a big city, and in some respects it looks similar to his father's. Like his father, Richard M. presides over a disciplined political organization. The "rubber stamp" city council almost always endorses his proposals; even on controversial issues, few aldermen dare to vote no.[73] Nevertheless, the political style and policy priorities of the machine run by the younger Daley are utterly different from his father's. Richard J. ran campaigns primarily through aldermen and precinct captains; for his son, the most effective techniques involve direct mail and television ads crafted by the best political consultants in the country. To pay for media campaigns, new sources of money have been tapped. Significant contributions now come from the sectors making up the new global economy—lawyers, bankers, insurance agencies, and the conventions, tourism, and entertainment industry. For the 1999 mayoral campaign the financial services industry contributed roughly 10 percent of the cost of Daley's campaign and the legal community produced 5.5 percent. The tourism, entertainment, and hospitality industry, which had given very few dollars to previous mayors, has emerged as a significant supporter for Daley, accounting for 4 percent of his campaign contributions in 1999. The owner of the Chicago Blackhawks hockey team threw in $10,000, and another $10,000 came from a livery firm from Frankfort, Illinois (which sponsors carriage rides in tourist areas of the city). The union representing hotel employees gave Daley's campaign $30,000. By contrast, government officials produced less than 2 percent of Daley's financial support.[74]

A new kind of white-collar patronage is now distributed to lawyers, brokers, financial consultants, advertising and public relations firms, and lobbyists. The big volumes of money required for Daley's campaigns go more to media advertising than to grassroots campaigning. Media-centered campaigns have replaced door-to-door and face-to-face campaigns at all levels of the American political system. The election of media mogul Michael Bloomberg as mayor of New York City in 2002 suggests that media-based politics has become common in the larger cities of the United States. National issues such as abortion rights, gay rights, and social welfare spending have also become important in local politics almost everywhere.[75] Because voters care about many national issues, it is difficult to imagine how an old-style party machine oriented to ethnic voters or to a politics of immediate material rewards would again emerge in any city.

Only in Chicago has the political culture necessary to sustain a party-based machine lingered on. Richard M. Daley runs a tight-knit political organization, but whether it should be called a "new machine"[76] or not is subject to debate.[77] Even though it clearly has key elements of machine politics, it is difficult to keep those aspects of its operation together. As a way of securing the machine's support among a new generation of ethnic voters, City Hall has attempted to distribute as many jobs as possible to pro-Daley groups. The problem with the long-standing practice of fixing job applications for favored applicants was revealed late in 2005, when federal prosecutors began looking into the city's hiring practices. On July 6, 2006, the former director of the mayor's Office of Intergovernmental Affairs and three other former employees of the mayor's office were convicted in federal court of doctoring job applications, which violated a 1969 court decree forbidding the city from making patronage appointments. (The so-called Shakman decree carried the name of Michael Shakman, a Chicago lawyer who had filed suit against the city to stop patronage hiring.) Although Mayor Daley denied any knowledge of the practices, the corruption investigation threatened to spread out of control when the convicted employees and others fearing they might be prosecuted began talking to investigators. Federal prosecutors and the FBI promised that more was to come. Some people thought it might even bring the mayor down.[78] By the end of 2007, two of the mayor's aids were serving terms in federal prison, and the investigation was still going on in 2009. Even in a city famed for its special style of politics, the long era of machine politics, old and new, may be numbered.

If so, it is certain that many Chicago residents will miss the machine. Under the leadership of Mayor Daley the city has been transformed into a magnet for tourists all over the world, and it has become the center of culture, leisure, and entertainment for the region. The extraordinary public amenities all along the lakefront, the downtown, and in neighborhoods owe much to the mayor's ability to provide sustained leadership over a long period. This success story illustrates precisely the conundrum posed by machine politics: Are the benefits of strong leadership worth the price paid?

NOTES

1. Jessica Trounstine, "Challenging the Machine-Reform Dichotomy," in Richardson Dilworth, *The City in American Political Development* (New York: Routledge, 2009), pp. 77–97.

2. Raymond Wolfinger, "Why Political Machines Have Not Withered Away and Other Revisionist Thoughts," in *Readings in Urban Politics: Past, Present, and Future*, ed. Harlan Hahn and Charles H. Levine (New York: Longman, 1984), p. 79. Wolfinger makes the distinction that we draw here between machine politics and a centralized machine. See also Roger W. Lotchin, "Power and Policy: American City Politics Between the Two World Wars," in *Ethnics, Machines, and the American Urban Future,* ed. Scott Greer (Cambridge, Mass.: Schenkman, 1981), p. 9.

3. M. Craig Brown and Charles N. Halaby, "Machine Politics in America, 1870–1945," *Journal of Interdisciplinary History* 17, no. 3 (Winter 1987): 598. To qualify as a dominant political machine, a machine-style party had to control both the executive and the legislative branches of the city for an uninterrupted series of three elections.

4. One of the last classic machines, the O'Connell machine in Albany, New York, lost its grip in the 1980s. See Todd Swanstrom and Sharon Ward, "Albany's O'Connell Organization: The Survival of an Entrenched Machine" (paper delivered at the American Political Science Association Convention, Chicago, September 1987). In Chicago, Richard M. Daley, the son of Richard J., still presides over a disciplined machine, but it relies on well-funded media campaigns and a high level of amenities and services rather than on patronage and spoils for its support. For a comprehensive history of machine politics in Chicago, see Dick Simpson, *Rogues, Rebels, and Rubber Stamps: The Politics of the Chicago City Council, 1863 to the Present* (Boulder, Colo.: Westview Press, 2001).

5. Amy Bridges, *A City in the Republic* (Cambridge, U.K.: Cambridge University Press, 1984), p. 8.

6. Donald S. Lutz, *Popular Consent and Popular Control: Whig Political Theory in the Early State Constitutions* (Baton Rouge: Louisiana State University Press, 1980), p. 105; Advisory Commission on Intergovernmental Relations, *Citizen Participation in the American Federal System* (Washington, D.C.: U.S. Government Printing Office, 1979), p. 41.

7. William Bennett Munro, *Municipal Government and Administration* (New York: Macmillan, 1923), p. 94.

8. William N. Chambers, "Party Development and the American Mainstream," in *The American Party System: Stages of Political Development*, 2nd ed., ed. William Nisbet Chambers and Walter Dean Burnham (New York: Oxford University Press, 1975), p. 12.

9. Jon M. Kingsdale, "The 'Poor Man's Club': Social Functions of the Urban Working-Class Saloon," in *The Making of Urban America*, ed. Raymond A. Mohl (Wilmington, Del.: Scholarly Resources, 1988), p. 123.

10. Ibid.

11. Ibid.

12. Ibid., p. 130.

13. "He [the boss] does not seek social honor; the 'professional' is despised in 'respectable society.' He seeks power alone, power as a source of money, but also power for power's sake." Max Weber, "Politics as a Vocation," in *From Max Weber: Essays in Sociology*, ed. H. H. Gerth and C. Wright Mills (New York: Oxford University Press, 1946), p. 109.

14. William L. Riordan, *Plunkitt of Tammany Hall* (New York: Dutton, 1963), p. 50.

15. Quoted in Dayton McKean, *The Boss* (Boston: Houghton Mifflin, 1940), p. 132.

16. Edward C. Banfield and James Q. Wilson, *City Politics* (New York: Vintage Books, 1963), p. 125.

17. Milton Rakove, *Don't Make No Waves . . . Don't Back No Losers: An Insider's Analysis of the Daley Machine* (Bloomington: Indiana University Press, 1975). The following material on Daley's machine is drawn from Rakove.

18. Ibid., pp. 114–115.

19. Ibid., p. 115.

20. Ibid., p. 120.

21. Ibid., p. 122.

22. Edward McChesney Sait, "Political Machines," in *Encyclopedia of the Social Sciences*, ed. Edwin R. A. Seligman (New York: Macmillan, 1933), p. 658. See also Robert M. Merton, *Social Theory and Social Structure* (New York: Free Press, 1949), pp. 126–127. For decades, Merton's functional analysis of political machines was widely accepted, but it has been seriously challenged in recent years. See Steven P. Erie, *Rainbow's End: Irish-Americans and the Dilemmas of Urban Machine Politics, 1840–1985* (Berkeley: University of California Press, 1988); Alan DiGaetano, "The Rise and Development of Urban Political Machines," *Urban Affairs Quarterly* 24, no. 2 (December 1988): 247, Table 3; M. Craig Brown and Charles N. Halaby, "Functional Sociology, Urban History, and the Urban Political Machine: The Outlines and Foundations of Machine Politics, 1870–1945" (Albany: Department of Sociology, State University of New York at Albany, n.d.).

23. A. DiGaetano, "The Rise and Development of Urban Political Machines," pp. 257–262. See also M. Craig Brown and Charles N. Halaby, "Bosses, Reform, and the Socioeconomic Bases of Urban Expenditure, 1890–1940," in *The Politics of Urban Fiscal Policy*, ed. Terrence S. McDonald and Sally K. Ward (Beverly Hills, Calif.: Sage), p. 90.

24. A. DiGaetano, "The Rise and Development of Urban Political Machines," p. 261. Urban politics is often portrayed as a morality play in which reformers are pitted against machine politicians. In fact, machines often used reforms to consolidate their power and put reformers on the ballot in order to legitimate their rule. On the other side, reformers often created their own type of political machines. For a critique of the dichotomy between bosses and reformers, see David P. Thelen, "Urban Politics: Beyond Bosses and Reformers," *Reviews in American History* 7 (September 1979): 406–412. For an example of a reformer who created a new type of political machine, see Robert Caro's masterful biography of Robert Moses, *The Power Broker: Robert Moses and the Fall of New York* (New York: Vintage Books, 1974).

25. A. DiGaetano, "The Rise and Development of Urban Political Machines," p. 247, Table 3. For more information on the expansion of city governments in the late nineteenth century, see Jon C. Teaford, *The Unheralded Triumph: City Government in America, 1870–1900* (Baltimore: Johns Hopkins University Press, 1984); Eric H. Monkkonen, *America Becomes Urban: The Development of U.S. Cities and Towns, 1780–1980* (Berkeley: University of California Press, 1988).

26. Terrence J. McDonald and Sally K. Ward, eds., *The Politics of Urban Fiscal Policy* (Beverly Hills, Calif.: Sage, 1984), Introduction, p. 14.

27. Ibid.

28. Lotchin, "Power and Policy," p. 11.

29. Stanley K. Schultz, *Constructing Urban Culture: American Cities and City Planning, 1800–1920* (Philadelphia: Temple University Press, 1989).

30. Brown and Halaby, "Bosses, Reform, and the Socioeconomic Bases of Urban Expenditure, 1890–1940," p. 87. Interestingly, the authors found that machine cities, after reform—such as the establishment of a city manager form of government—spent more than other cities (p. 89).

31. Many sources of information are available on the Tweed Ring. The two books used here are Alexander Callow Jr., *The Tweed Ring* (New York: Oxford University Press, 1966), and Seymour J. Mandelbaum, *Boss Tweed's New York* (New York: Wiley, 1965). For a provocative, yet ultimately unpersuasive, defense of Tweed, see Leo Hershkowitz, *Tweed's New York: Another Look* (Garden City, N.Y.: Anchor Books, 1977).

32. Martin Shefter, "The Emergence of the Political Machine: An Alternative View," in *Theoretical Perspectives on Urban Politics*, ed. Willis D. Hawley et al. (Upper Saddle River, N.J.: Prentice Hall, 1976), p. 21.

33. The information presented here on Abraham Reuf's machine is taken from Walter Bean, *Boss Reuf's San Francisco* (Berkeley: University of California Press, 1952; reprinted 1972). Only direct quotations from Bean are cited by page in subsequent notes.

34. Ibid., pp. 93–94.

35. Paul Kantor, with Stephen David, *The Dependent City: The Changing Political Economy of Urban America* (Glenview, Ill.: Scott Foresman, 1988), p. 104.

36. Ernest S. Griffith, *A History of American City Government: The Conspicuous Failure, 1870–1900* (New York: Praeger, 1974), p. 183.

37. Zane Miller, *The Urbanization of Modern America: A Brief History* (New York: Harcourt Brace Jovanovich, 1973), p. 121.

38. Ester R. Fuchs and Robert Y. Shapiro, "Government Performance as a Basis for Machine Support," *Urban Affairs Quarterly* 18, no. 4 (June 1983): 537–550.

39. Merton, *Social Theory and Social Structure*, p. 130.

40. Robert A. Dahl, *Who Governs? Democracy and Power in an American City* (New Haven, Conn.: Yale University Press, 1961), p. 34.

41. See Doris Kearns Goodwin, *The Fitzgeralds and the Kennedys: An American Saga* (New York: Simon & Schuster, 1987).

42. The discussion of mobilizing versus entrenched machines relies heavily on Erie's "life cycle" theory of political machines in *Rainbow's End*.

43. Erie, *Rainbow's End*, p. 69.

44. Terry Nichols Clark, "The Irish Ethic and the Spirit of Patronage," *Ethnicity* 2 (1975): 341–342.

45. Martin Shefter, "Political Incorporation and the Extrusion of the Left: Party Politics and Social Forces in New York City," in *Studies in American Political Development*, vol. 1, ed. Karen Orren and Stephen Skowronek (New Haven, Conn.: Yale University Press, 1986), p. 55.

46. Caro, *The Power Broker*, p. 354.

47. For a useful review of the relationships between African Americans and political machines, see Hanes Walton Jr., *Black Politics: A Theoretical and Structural Analysis* (Philadelphia: Lippincott, 1972), Chapter 4.

48. William J. Grimshaw, *Bitter Fruit: Black Politics and the Chicago Machine, 1931–1991* (Chicago: University of Chicago Press, 1992).

49. Ibid.

50. Erie, *Rainbow's End*, p. 165.

51. Thomas M. Guterbock, *Machine Politics in Transition: Party and Community in Chicago* (Chicago: University of Chicago Press, 1980).

52. See Paul Kleppner, *Chicago Divided: The Making of a Black Mayor* (DeKalb: Northern Illinois University Press, 1985).

53. Michael Johnston, "Patrons and Clients, Jobs and Machines: A Case Study of the Uses of Patronage," *American Political Science Review* 73, no. 2 (June 1979): 385–398.

54. Erie, *Rainbow's End*, p. 218.

55. Ibid., pp. 48, 242.

56. For a discussion of the role of political clubs in the evolution of Tammany Hall, see Shefter, "The Emergence of the Political Machine," p. 35.

57. Erie, *Rainbow's End*, pp. 102–103.

58. Kenneth D. Wald argues that ethnics supported machines not so much in response to socioeconomic disadvantage but out of an awareness of their social marginality and in the belief that machines would defend them from external pressures; see his "The Electoral Base of Political Machines: A Deviant Case Analysis," *Urban Affairs Quarterly* 16, no. 1 (September 1980): 3–29.

59. It would be misleading to say that such practices simply reflected the desires of poor immigrants. Irish family life was disrupted by the easy availability of illicit entertainment. Catholic priests and a significant proportion of the immigrant population opposed vice activities.

60. Harold Zink, *City Bosses in the United States* (Durham, N.C.: Duke University Press, 1930).

61. Wolfinger, "Why Political Machines Have Not Withered Away," p. 70.

62. Allan Rosenbaum, "Machine Politics: Class Interest and the Urban Poor," paper delivered at the annual meeting of the American Political Science Association (September 4–8, 1973), pp. 25–26.

63. Ibid., p. 26.

64. John D. Buenker, *Urban Liberalism and Progressive Reform* (New York: Scribner, 1973). Joseph J. Huthmacher also provides evidence of machine legislators' support for reform; see his "Urban Liberalism and the Age of Reform," *Mississippi Valley Historical Review* 44 (September 1962): 231–241.

65. For the distinction between social and structural reformers, see Melvin G. Holli, *Reform in Detroit: Hazen S. Pingree and Urban Politics* (New York: Oxford University Press, 1969), Chapter 8. We discuss the social reformers in this chapter; in Chapter 4 we discuss the structural reformers.

66. Martin J. Schiesl, *The Politics of Efficiency: Municipal Administration and Reform in America, 1880–1920* (Berkeley: University of California Press, 1977), pp. 80ff.

67. Quoted in Holli, *Reform in Detroit*, p. 42.

68. Quoted in ibid., p. 92.

69. Ibid., p. 195.

70. Peter Marris and Martin Rein, *Dilemmas of Social Reform* (New York: Atherton Press, 1967), p. 7.

71. Kantor, *The Dependent City*, pp. 117–118. Machine politicians appealed to voters on the basis of where they lived (their ethnic identification), not on the basis of where they worked (their class identification). Thus machine politics reflected the "city trenches" that have divided the American political landscape into community politics and workplace politics and blunted political action by the working class. See Ira Katznelson, *City Trenches: Urban Politics and the Patterning of Class in the United States* (New York: Pantheon, 1981).

72. See James C. Scott, "Corruption, Machine Politics, and Political Change," *American Political Science Review* 63 (December 1969): 1142–1158; Clarence N. Stone, Robert K. Whelan, and William J. Murin, *Urban Policy and Politics in a Bureaucratic Age*, 2nd ed. (Upper Saddle River, N.J.: Prentice Hall, 1986), Chapter 7.

73. Simpson, *Rogues, Rebels, and Rubber Stamps*, p. 280.

74. Ibid., pp. 280–290.

75. Elaine Sharp, ed., *Culture Wars and Urban Politics* (Lawrence: University Press of Kansas, 1999).

76. Ibid., pp. 287–290.

77. Larry Bennett, "The Mayor Among His Peers: Interpreting Richard M. Daley," unpublished paper (June 2008).

78. Rudolph Bush and Dan Mihalopoulos, "Daley Jobs Chief Guilty"; Dan Mihalopoulos and Charles Sheehan, "Jurors Kept Focus on Case"; Gary Washburn, "Daley's Plans for Re-election Turn Murky"; and John Chase, "Things Are Not Over, FBI Boss Here Says," *Chicago Tribune*, July 7, 2006, pp. 1, 6.

THE REFORM CRUSADES

THE MOTIVE FOR REFORM

In 1902 George Washington Plunkitt of Tammany Hall pontificated that reformers "were mornin' glories—looked lovely in the mornin' and withered up in a short time, while the regular machines went on flourishin' forever, like fine old oaks."[1] At the time Plunkitt delivered himself of that poetic homily, he was essentially correct. Through the last quarter of the nineteenth century, reform movements sprang up in cities all across the country. The reformers aimed to dismantle the party organizations that thrived on immigrant votes, but these movements tended to be short-lived, exactly as Plunkitt observed. Reformers were often successful in persuading state legislatures to take budgeting and the administration of some services out of the hands of aldermen and city councilors and put them under the control of boards dominated by a so-called better class of people. But they were not able to undercut the political influence of immigrant voters. Aldermen elected from individual wards still decided such matters as streetcar and utility franchises, construction contracts, and the provision of city services. Plenty of patronage and money, the lifeblood of machine politics, were bound up in these decisions.

To many middle- and upper-class Americans, the cities seemed to be in the hands of criminals who plundered the public purse for personal gain. Although reformers in Cleveland, New York, Chicago, and other cities sometimes succeeded at throwing machine politicians out of office and getting some of them prosecuted in the courts for corruption, the offending politicians were easily replaced by men cut from the same cloth. Commenting on this fact of life, Englishman James Bryce expressed the view that "the government of cities is the one conspicuous failure of the United States."[2] Many middle- and upper-class voters shared his opinion. As stated at the time in a pro-reform textbook on municipal government,

The privilege seeker has pervaded our political life. For his own profit he has willfully befouled the sources of political power. Politics, which should offer a career inspiring to the noblest thoughts and calling for the most patriotic efforts of which man is capable, he has . . . transformed into a series of sordid transactions between those who buy and those who sell governmental action.[3]

The concern about political corruption in the cities was closely connected to a rising fear of foreign immigrants—the so-called Great Unwashed. The reaction against immigrants had been building for a long time. As early as 1851, an article in the *Massachusetts Teacher* asked,

The constantly increasing influx of foreigners . . . continues to be a cause of serious alarm to the most intelligent of our people. What will be the ultimate effect of this vast and unexampled immigration . . . ? Will it, like the muddy Missouri, as it pours its waters into the clear Mississippi and contaminates the whole united mass, spread ignorance and vice, crime and disease, through our native population?[4]

Protestants descended from the older immigrant groups were scandalized by lurid newspaper accounts of prostitution, gambling, and public drunkenness in the immigrant wards. Protestant moralists secured city and state statutes abolishing prostitution, gambling, and Sunday liquor sales. To teach immigrant children middle-class versions of dress, speech, manners, and discipline, reformers passed laws requiring school attendance and raised the upper age limit for mandatory schooling. Truant officers were hired to search for wayward youth.

The vicious reaction against immigrants aggravated class, racial, and religious tensions. Immigrants were compared to the Goths and Vandals who invaded the Roman Empire in the second century A.D. In his book *Our Country*, the Reverend Josiah Strong accused the immigrants of defiling the Sabbath, spreading illiteracy and crime, and corrupting American culture and morals. Gathered into the cities, he said, the immigrants provided "a very paradise for demagogues" who ruled by manipulating the "appetites and prejudices" of the rabble.[5]

The spatial segregation of social classes within the cities exacerbated middle- and upper-class fears about the immigrants. By the turn of the century, all large cities contained sprawling, overcrowded immigrant ghettos near the waterfronts and factories, with middle- and upper-class neighborhoods located farther from the urban center. Jobs were still concentrated in downtown districts, so affluent city residents could hardly escape seeing, on their way to work and to shop, the drab tenements, dirty streets, and littered alleys where the immigrants lived.

The fight to reform the urban political system involved a broad-based coalition that included wealthy industrialists and other members of the upper class, well-educated members of the middle class, and middle-class voters. Andrew Carnegie and John D. Rockefeller initially financed the New York City Bureau of Municipal Research, founded in 1906. The U.S. Chamber of Commerce provided office space and paid the executive secretary of the City Managers Association for several years. Civic clubs and voters' leagues generally contained names from elite social directories, and the professionals involved in reform tended to be the most prestigious members of

OUTTAKE

MUNICIPAL REFORM WAS AIMED AT THE IMMIGRANTS

The municipal reforms of the early nineteenth century were designed to undercut the electoral influence of the working-class and immigrant voters. Nearly all machine politicians were from lower-class, immigrant origins. Most machine bosses, like their followers, had little formal education; typically they had started out in politics by carrying messages and working on Election Day. Reformers were at the other end of the social spectrum. Most of the prominent reformers of the Progressive Era were upper-class people, and many, in fact, were wealthy industrialists, with names like McCormick, du Pont, Pinchot, Morgenthau, and Dodge. Most of them had a college education in a day when this fact marked a very select social stratum; even more telling, most of the women and social workers had gone to college.

Machine politicians, ethnic voters, and working-class groups usually opposed reform proposals because they correctly perceived that these were designed to make it more difficult for working-class candidates to win public office. Because immigrants accounted for a disproportionate share of the working class and poor within cities, class and ethnicity were important factors determining attitudes toward reform. In the big cities, immigrant and working-class voters were generally successful in opposing key features of the reform agenda. In smaller cities and cities outside the northern industrial belt, however, these groups were generally outvoted. When reformers won these battles, they quickly moved to make their gains permanent. A dramatic illustration of the effects of reform occurred in the 1938 municipal elections in Jackson, Michigan. The local chamber of commerce persuaded voters to approve a council-manager charter with at-large elections. After the charter was adopted, the new slate of chamber-sponsored candidates swept into office. The new mayor and council members celebrated with a reception in the Masonic hall (the Masons were a virilent anti-Catholic organization) and, once in power, they dismissed most of the Roman Catholic city employees.

The two-sided nature of reform makes most people ambivalent about its effects. On the one hand, it helped reduce widespread corruption in city politics. On the other hand, it made it harder for immigrants to gain a voice in the policy decisions of government. Whatever one's views about reform, it is important to recognize that it represented a battle over the most essential question in politics: "Who governs?"

Sources: George Mowry, *The Era of Theodore Roosevelt, 1900–1912* (New York: Harper & Row, 1958); James Weinstein, *The Corporate Ideal in the Liberal State, 1900–1918* (Boston: Beacon Press, 1968).

their professions. They were able to sell their message to growing numbers of middle-class voters. Between 1870 and 1910, the number of clerical workers, salespersons, government employees, technicians, and salaried professionals multiplied 7.5 times, from 756,000 to 5,609,000.[6] It was an unstoppable political force, and within a few years the reformers had accomplished most of their major aims. The way Americans elect their leaders, hire public employees, and administer public services still reflects the politics of the reform era.

THE REFORM ENVIRONMENT

The reform impulse that swept the country in the first decades of the twentieth century energized the municipal reform movement. Several developments ushered in the Progressive Era. Excesses of wealth existed side by side with the grinding poverty of the immigrant wards. Newly developed mass media brought a heightened awareness about these conditions to upper-class and educated middle-class readers. By the turn of the century, falling paper prices and technical advances in rapid printing made it possible to produce high-quality mass-circulation newspapers and magazines. During the 1890s newspaper circulation doubled and then tripled. A multitude of new periodicals appeared. All that was required to develop a mass audience was a way to popularize the press. Muckraking was such a technique. Crusading journalists investigated and reported "inside stories" exposing organized vice and the corruption of the urban machines. They also wrote about pervasive corruption in the national government, big business, the stock market, and the drug and meatpacking industries.

Beginning with its September 1902 issue, *McClure's* magazine printed a series of seven articles by Lincoln Steffens that told lurid stories of municipal corruption in the nation's big cities. In October *McClure's* carried an article by Ida Tarbell exposing corporate corruption and profiteering by John D. Rockefeller's Standard Oil Company. The stories were an instant success, revealing an insatiable appetite in the public for sensational accounts of wrongdoing in business and government. A new mass-circulation formula was thus born. Over the next few years, *Munsey's, Everybody's, Success, Collier's, Saturday Evening Post, Ladies' Home Journal, Hampton's, Pearson's, Cosmopolitan*, and dozens of daily newspapers carried stories that appealed to the popular feeling that political, economic, and social institutions had become corrupt. Big business was accused of producing unsafe and shoddy goods, fixing prices, and crushing competition. There were exposés of fraudulent practices in banking; heartrending accounts of women and children working at long, tedious, and dangerous jobs in factories and sweatshops; and stories about urban poverty, prostitution, white slavery, and business–government collusion to protect vice.

An outpouring of popular books played on the same themes. In 1904 Steffens gathered his *McClure's* articles together into a best-selling book, *The Shame of the Cities*. Other popular titles included *The Greatest Trust in the World*, an exposé of price-fixing and collusion in the steel industry; *The Story of Life Insurance*; and *The Treason of the Senate*, which detailed systematic bribery of U.S. senators. Several novelists entered the field. In *An American Tragedy*, Theodore Dreiser described the corrupting influence of greed on a self-made small-town boy. Dreiser's *Sister Carrie* and David Graham Phillip's *Susan Lenox* both played on the theme of how the impersonal forces of urban life victimized young women. In *The Financier*, Dreiser's theme revolved around the ruthless drive for power and wealth, using the Chicago streetcar magnate Charles Yerkes as his model. Upton Sinclair's *The Jungle* dealt with a Lithuanian immigrant's fight to survive in a corrupt and chaotic Chicago. Beaten down by destitution and poverty, eventually his wife becomes a prostitute, his children die, and he becomes a socialist revolutionary. By vividly portraying the nauseating conditions in Chicago's meatpacking industry (with rats, feces, and spoiled meat being swept into sausage vats, for example), Sinclair catalyzed a national crusade that resulted in congressional legislation creating the U.S. Food and Drug Administration in 1905. The literature produced by the muckrakers—an epithet applied to them in 1906 by President Theodore Roosevelt, referring to a character in John Bunyan's 1645 book *Pilgrim's Progress* who was too busy raking muck to look up and see the stars—was influential in building popular interest in reform. Although the details of reform were often dull and unexciting to the average citizen, the muckrakers' stories provided a feeling of drama and urgency.

This environment spawned the formation of organizations dedicated to the goals of regulating business practices, improving working conditions, imposing standards on the professions, and reforming government. Business leaders organized the National Civic Federation in 1900. By advocating workers' compensation and other minor social insurance schemes, the founders of the federation hoped to undermine more militant demands proposed by union organizers.[7] The National Child Labor Committee was organized in 1904 to fight for child labor legislation. In 1910 the National Housing Association brought together housing reform groups from many cities to agitate for building codes. A large number of public officials' associations and municipal research bureaus came into existence specifically to promote municipal reform: the National Association of Port Authorities, the Municipal Finance Officers Association, the American Association of Park Superintendents, the Conference of City Managers, and the National Short Ballot Association.

Although government corruption had provoked campaigns to "throw the rascals out" in a few cities during the 1870s and 1880s, the issues had usually been local and the remedies specific to an immediate situation. Several developments in the 1890s transformed reform into a national movement aimed at promoting systematic change in local government structures. In response to widespread government corruption, citizens' groups sprang up all across the country to lobby for improved public services and honesty in government. The problems faced by the reformers varied little from one city to another. Like-minded reformers from different cities soon began to exchange advice and information about their efforts. These informational networks subsequently led to the formation of national reform organizations.

In 1894 delegates to the First Annual Conference for Good City Government met in Philadelphia to found the first national municipal reform organization, the National Municipal League. The delegates to the conference were united in the belief that machine politicians and their immigrant constituents had corrupted democratic institutions in the cities. But they disagreed about the measures that should be taken to change this situation. "We are not unlike patients assembled in a hospital," one of the participants put it, "examining together and describing to each other our sore places."[8] After the formation of the National Municipal League, the nationalization of reform proceeded quickly. Within two years, 180 local chapters were affiliated with the league, and, by the turn of the century, all large cities had member organizations. In their annual meetings, reformers from all over the country got a chance to compare notes. By its November 1899 meeting, the members of the National Municipal League reached agreement on a model municipal chapter meant to serve as a blueprint for bringing fundamental change to local government.

In an attempt to undermine the foundation of machine politics—the close relationship between politicians and their immigrant constituents—the model charter recommended that electoral wards be abolished, instead, each city council member should be elected "at-large," that is, by all the voters of the city. It also recommended that nonpartisan elections replace the party label on election ballots. The charter urged reformers to fight for civil service appointment procedures so that party officials would not be able to use public jobs for patronage. The league also said that local elections should be held in different years than national and state elections, so that the national political parties would find it more difficult to influence local affairs.[9]

In addition to eliminating the machines, the reformers wanted to thoroughly reorganize local government. The league's model charter urged reformers to lobby for new city charters that would give the mayor the power to appoint top administrators and to veto legislation. The assumption behind this reform—called "strong mayor government"—was that with authority centralized in the hands of the mayor, voters would be able to hold the mayor accountable for the city's overall governance. At the same time, the reformers thought this change might help end the style of politics in which city council members or aldermen cut deals with one another behind the scenes. Finally, the league urged city reformers to seek so-called home rule charters from their state legislatures, reasoning that this reform would free cities from state party leaders and reduce meddling by the legislatures in local affairs.

The municipal reformers shared the conviction that it was their responsibility to educate and instruct the public about the principle of what they called "good government." They placed their faith in rule by educated upper- and middle-class Americans and, increasingly, in administration by trained administrators and professionals. In this way, the municipal reform movement began to build a style of government by bureaucratic agencies that Americans have often complained about up to the present day.

THE CAMPAIGNS AGAINST MACHINE RULE

The urban machines and their immigrant constituents were the reformers' principal targets. In their zeal to undermine the machines, some reformers went so far as to question the wisdom of universal suffrage, using the argument that immigrants were too ignorant and illiterate to vote intelligently. The Tilden Commission, appointed by the New York legislature to investigate the Tweed Ring scandals in New York City, recommended in 1878 that suffrage be restricted to those who owned property.[10] The commission's report was reprinted in an 1899 issue of *Municipal Affairs,* the National Municipal League's magazine, and those reformers who shared the view that an ignorant electorate accounted for the city's problems read it with approval. Andrew D. White, the first president of Cornell University, stated the rationale for disenfranchising the immigrants in an 1890 issue of *Forum:*

> A city is a corporation; . . . as a city it has nothing whatever to do with general political interests. . . . The questions in a city are not political questions. . . . The work of a city being the creation and control of the city property, it should logically be managed as a piece of property by those who have created it, who have a title to it, or a real substantial part in

it, . . . [and not by] a crowd of illiterate peasants, freshly raked in from the Irish bogs, or Bohemian mines, or Italian robber nests.[11]

Although taking the vote from the non-property-owning immigrants appealed to some reformers, it was hardly feasible to attempt such a drastic remedy. To wage an all-out campaign on this issue would surely have invited a negative reaction even from groups that supported reform causes. From the constitutional period until the Jacksonian voting reforms of the 1820s and 1830s, most states had restricted the vote to owners of property. The abolition of these restrictions had been hailed as a triumph for popular democracy. It seemed unlikely that property qualifications could ever again be attached to the vote. The 1912 charter of Phoenix, in the new state of Arizona, restricted voting in municipal elections to taxpayers, but the state courts invalidated this restriction as unconstitutional.[12] Even before Phoenix's attempt, it was clear the reformers would have to find less direct and more creative methods to reduce the influence of the Great Unwashed.

Most reformers did not oppose voting participation by immigrants per se. They were convinced the real problem with elections was that they were run in a corrupt fashion by machine politicians who victimized their immigrant constituents. They were not entirely wrong: Without doubt, municipal elections were chaotic and corrupt, conducted in the absence of well-established rules and regulations. Because the political parties were considered private organizations, their nominating procedures were not regulated at all. To select candidates for public office, political parties held city conventions or ward caucuses according to their own changeable or unwritten rules, often on short notice and at locations known only to insiders. It was not unusual for caucuses to be held in the back rooms of saloons owned by ward bosses. According to one scholar,

> This was the period of massive voting frauds. In the elections of 1868 and 1872, 8 percent more people voted in New York state than were registered. In 1910, when the New York City vote was challenged and recounted, half of the votes were found to be fraudulent. In New Jersey, the stuffing of ballot boxes was so common that the state legislature replaced the wooden boxes with glass ballot jars. In Pennsylvania and Michigan, gangs of thugs moved from polling place to polling place beating up the opposition and voting at will. Fictitious and repeat voters, false counting, and stuffed ballot boxes were such regular features of city elections that voting statistics from this period are suspect.[13]

A Philadelphia politician once boasted that the signers of the Declaration of Independence were machine loyalists: "'These men,' he said, 'the fathers of American liberty, voted down here once. And,' he added with a sly grin, 'they vote here yet.'"[14]

Politicians sometimes completed the ballot for voters or accompanied them into the voting booth. "Farmer Jones," a member of the Chicago machine in the 1890s, revealed to an inquiring reformer how he guaranteed voter loyalty:

> [The reformer asked,] "When you got the polling stations in your hands, what did you do?"
> "Voted our men, of course."
> "And the negroes, how did they vote?"
> "They voted as they ought to have voted. They had to."
> ". . . how could you compel those people to vote against their will?"

"They understood, and besides," said he, "there was not a man voted in that booth that I did not know how he voted before he put the paper in the judges' hands."[15]

Buying the vote was the most direct and effective means of guaranteeing Election Day results. The 1896 election in the First Ward of Chicago provides a good example:

> The bars were open all night and the brothels were jammed. By ten o'clock the next morning, though, the saloons were shut down, not in concession to the reformers, but because many of the bartenders and owners were needed to staff the First Ward field organization. The Bath, Hinky Dink and their aides ran busily from polling place to polling place, silver bulging in their pockets into which they dug frequently and deeply. The effort was not in vain, and the outcome was gratifying.[16]

Not content with mere fraud, machine politicians sometimes resorted to intimidation and violence. The Chicago ward boss John Powers threatened voters and told business owners they would lose their business licenses unless they supported him in his 1898 campaign for alderman.[17] "Hinky Dink" Kenna and "Bathhouse John" Coughlin of Chicago's First Ward defended their loyal constituents but routinely harassed opponents. During the 1920s organized crime and machine politics in Chicago became closely connected. Gangland hits were visited on meddling politicians who stood outside the inner circle of men controlling and protecting illegal liquor, speakeasies, prostitution, and gambling.

There was soon a reaction to such practices. Ed Crump, the boss of Memphis, Tennessee, won his first mayoral election in 1909 by watching the polls himself. He personally stopped the use of marked ballots by a machine organization he was opposing, in one case by hitting a voter in the face.[18] In Pittsburgh's state and city elections of 1933, the Democrats and Republicans—both rightly fearing fraud by the other party—mobilized opposing armies of poll watchers. The state police were called in to keep the peace, and lawyers and judges stood by to provide quick court action.[19]

In the late 1890s, reformers introduced several measures to reduce election fraud. The key reforms included:

- *Voter registration and literacy requirements.* These requirements reduced repeat voting and stopped the practice of importing voters for an election. By 1920 almost all states had imposed registration laws.
- *Australian ballot.* This was a ballot that could be marked only by the voter, and it was cast in secrecy. Before the Australian ballot was introduced in the 1880s, the parties printed the ballots and often marked and placed them in a ballot box in front of observers. The ballots were even handed to voters already marked. Use of the Australian ballot became universal after the turn of the century.
- *Nonpartisan elections.* Reformers fought hard to remove party labels of any kind from many state, and most municipal, election ballots. Where they succeeded, voters had only one clue as to how they should vote: the printed name of the individual candidate.

Although these reforms helped clean up elections, they also had the effect of reducing voting participation by immigrants and less educated voters. Large numbers of voters were effectively disenfranchised by reforms adopted in the cities that lacked machine organizations, where there were no precinct captains and ward committeemen to help voters register or look over a sample ballot. Twenty-five percent of the white males of voting age in the United States in 1900 were first-generation immigrants, and two-thirds of them had come from non-English-speaking countries. In the cities, the proportion of foreign-born immigrants was much higher—typically more than two-thirds of the voters in the big cities. Illiterate voters often asked for help in reading and filling out the ballot, or requested a premarked one. When they showed up at the polling place, no one questioned their right to vote. After reforms were adopted, they had to register to vote in writing, often months before an election. And when they went to the polling station they now faced an election judge, a secret voting booth, and a printed ballot they could not read. Machine politicians were frequently able to get around the problems of the secret ballot by controlling the polling places, but these actions exposed them to the possibility of criminal prosecution.

By 1905 voter registration laws had been placed on the books in most of the states.[20] Between 1905 and 1920, states and localities set up election boards, made it illegal to vote more than once, and tried to define the legitimate uses of campaign funds. Although enforcement of these laws was uneven, especially in the cities—the machines continued to control prosecutors and the courts in many places—the existence of new laws provided the basis for investigations and prosecutions when the middle- and upper-class public became disturbed about corruption.

Once electoral reform was adopted, the reformers focused their attention on the machine organizations. It was obvious that machine politicians derived their strength from the ethnic neighborhoods and that the machines greatly benefited from the immigrants' ability to identify a party label on the election ballot. By voting a straight party ticket, the voter did not have to read the candidates' names. To make it harder for the voters to support machine candidates in this way, the reformers fought hard for two reforms—nonpartisan ballots and at-large elections.

Municipal reformers argued that party labels encouraged bloc voting and blind loyalty to a political organization. They wanted a more "rational," informed voter with the ability to "accumulate and carry in his head the brief list of personal preferences and do without the guidance of party names and symbols on the ballot."[21] The reformers asserted it was the responsibility of citizens to educate themselves and to vote for the best candidates strictly on their merits, not on the basis of party loyalty or ethnic solidarity.

The proposal to remove the party label from election ballots reflected the reformers' conviction that an overall public interest overrode the preferences of particular ethnic groups or political factions. Reformers generally agreed with the principle that public services should be provided as cheaply and efficiently as possible, and that this required cities to be run by educated professionals. Just as business firms produce a product as cheaply and efficiently as possible, cities should, they maintained, do the same. Party symbols created the impression of political differences when, according to the reformers, everyone shared the same fundamental interest. The public interest was defined very narrowly. Voters were supposed to ask only one question: Which candidate is most qualified to help the city provide services at lowest cost? Brand Whitlock, the famous reform mayor of Toledo, Ohio, observed,

It seems almost incredible now that men's minds were ever so clouded, strange that they did not earlier discover how absurd was a system which, in order to enable them the more readily to subjugate themselves, actually printed little woodcuts of birds—roosters and eagles—at the heads of the tickets, so that they might be more easily and readily recognize their masters and deliver their suffrages over to them.[22]

Just as the reformers intended, the nonpartisan ballot made it harder for immigrants to vote as a bloc. Reading their alderman's printed name could be hard for illiterate voters. Recognizing the party symbol on the ballot was infinitely easier than reading the names of candidates.

Nonpartisan elections were also intended as a measure to change the kinds of candidates who would seek public office. The party organization supplied campaign money and workers and freed working-class candidates from the necessity of holding a normal job, which would have denied them time to participate in politics. Few politicians in the cities could have started or stayed in politics without a party organization's help. Party organizations pooled resources and built cooperative relationships among politicians; without them, people of wealth and social standing tended to hold an overwhelming advantage. This result was, in fact, the objective of the nonpartisanship crusade—to make politics once again a calling appropriate to the educated and cultured classes.[23]

The proposal to replace wards with at-large elections was also designed to break the link between neighborhoods and machine politicians. Andrew White complained that "wards largely controlled by thieves and robbers can send thieves and robbers" into public office, and "the vote of a single tenement house, managed by a professional politician, will neutralize the vote of an entire street of well-to-do citizens."[24] The remedy was to require every candidate for the city council or board of aldermen to seek the votes of all city residents. By constituting the entire city as the one and only election district, no particular neighborhood or ethnic group could elect a candidate. Gone would be the politics of trade-offs, logrolling, and compromise among legislators representing their own neighborhoods, ethnic groups, and wards. "Special interest" politics would supposedly give way to "public interest" politics. To the reformers, honest politics was virtually impossible as long as elections were decided by the voters in individual wards:

> For decades the election of councils by wards had superimposed a network of search for parochial favors, of units devoted to partisan spoils, and of catering to ethnic groups that time and again had either defeated comprehensive city programs or loaded them with irrelevant spoils and ill-conceived ward projects. The ward and precinct were the heart of machine control, and the councils so elected were usually also infested with corruption, however acceptable the councilors may have been to the voters of their wards.[25]

Wards potentially gave even relatively small ethnic and racial groups leverage at the ballot box. Lithuanian voters, for example, might be able to send a Lithuanian alderman to the city council, even if they constituted a tiny proportion of a city's total population. Wards multiplied the points of access through which groups and individuals could influence public officials. Citywide, at-large elections exerted an opposite effect. If the city is one big electoral district, candidates representing ethnic and racial groups clustered in specific neighborhoods are handicapped; in order to be elected, they are forced to appeal to a variety of groups distributed over many neighborhoods.

Because campaigns covering a city are costly and time-consuming, wealthier candidates have a built-in advantage. In such a system, personal wealth and social status become the ingredients of political success. These effects were well known to reformers, which explains why the National Municipal League's model city charter of 1899 recommended at-large elections and nonpartisan ballots. Every subsequent model charter of the league contained these two features, and over the years the league compiled annual statistics to track the adoption of these reforms across the nation.

Civil service hiring systems constituted the last big plank in the reform platform. Reformers considered civil service crucial because it was aimed at the machines' practice of rewarding loyal supporters with patronage jobs. Under civil service reform, written and oral civil service examinations were to become the sole basis for hiring municipal employees, and a system of tenure and seniority was supposed to make employees safe from political firings. Reformers thought of civil service as the silver bullet because without patronage, they expected the machines to quickly wither away.

Within the first two decades of the twentieth century, nonpartisan, at-large elections and civil service reforms were implemented in cities from coast to coast. Reformers were least successful in the big industrial cities with large numbers of immigrant voters. In smaller cities, however, and in the newer cities in the West and Southwest, working-class voters tended to be outnumbered, discouraged from voting, or divided along ethnic lines. As a consequence, when reform measures were put before the voters, they usually passed. In the cases when local electorates balked, the reformers were sometimes able to bypass them altogether by persuading state legislatures to abolish ward elections and require nonpartisan elections, civil service, and other reforms for all cities in the state.

A melodramatic rhetoric that recounted lurid tales of corruption energized campaigns to adopt nonpartisan, at-large elections and civil service. Such stories could just as well be, and often were, imported from cities hundreds of miles away. In this fashion, reformers were able to persuade voters to adopt reform even in cities where machines had never existed. Reformers made machines into a scary bogeyman hiding just around the corner, ready to pounce at the first opportunity.[26] In smaller towns and cities, where the machine threat did not seem plausible, reformers said they just wanted to streamline government and make it efficient. This was an easy sell because the residents of smaller places tended to view government, at best, as a necessary evil that should do little else but provide such essential public services as water, sewage disposal, streets, and perhaps libraries and community centers. "Consensus" politics—which tended to ignore the ethnic and racial minorities that might be present—characterized politics in small towns then as it often does now.

The electoral rules preferred by the municipal reformers are much in evidence in contemporary cities. Before 1910 nonpartisan elections were almost unknown, but by 1929 they were utilized in 57 percent of the cities with populations of more than 30,000.[27] By the 1960s many states required their cities to use nonpartisan elections; these included Minnesota, California, Alaska, and most of the western states. In ten more states, nonpartisan ballots were used in 90 percent or more of the cities (the exceptions usually being cities above a specified size). In the West, 94 percent of cities used nonpartisan elections. The eastern seaboard was the only region of the country where more cities used partisan than nonpartisan elections. The only places where partisan elections are still common are the big cities. Among those with of more than 500,000 people, 85 percent still print party labels on the ballot. Reforms generally go together; most cities with nonpartisan elections also use at-large rather than district or ward elections.

Reformed electoral systems were originally designed to reduce the influence of working-class ethnic voters, and plenty of evidence indicates that they accomplished this purpose. Before the adoption of nonpartisan and at-large elections, working-class candidates, some of them socialists, were elected to city offices in dozens of cities.[28] At-large elections made it much more difficult for these kinds of candidates to win. In the 1909 elections in Dayton, Ohio, socialists elected two aldermen and three assessors from wards. Without the ward system, these candidates could not have won. Before the 1913 election, Dayton implemented citywide elections and abolished ward boundaries. In 1913 the socialists received 35 percent of the popular vote and, in 1917, 44 percent, but because all candidates were elected at-large, in neither year were the socialists able to elect a single candidate. Similarly, in 1911 Pittsburgh adopted at-large elections, with the result that upper-class business leaders and professionals pushed lower- and middle-class groups out of their previous places on the city council and the school board.[29]

St. Louis provides a graphic example of these two electoral systems at work. The members of the city's board of aldermen are elected to office through partisan elections in each of the city's 28 wards (see Figure 4.1). In a city that was 41 percent African American in 1970, race had become a hotly contested terrain. Because of St. Louis's ward system, 10 blacks were elected to the city's board of aldermen in the 1977 municipal elections (and 11 by 2000). All of them represented predominantly African American wards located in the northern half of the city. All of the 18 wards with a majority of white voters elected white aldermen. (As in many cities, *alderman* is an official term in the St. Louis city charter and does not refer exclusively to males.)

Because all school board candidates must run at-large, the composition of the school board was entirely different from the makeup of the Board of Aldermen. In the 1977 election, in a city where 70 percent of the public school enrollment was African American, not a single black candidate was elected to the school board. All five of the seats on the ballot went to white middle-class candidates because white voters, who represented a majority of the citywide electorate, rejected the three African American candidates. The St. Louis case illustrates the dramatic effect that at-large elections can have on the representation of racial and ethnic minorities. In the St. Louis of the late 1970s, the African American minority, which was heavily concentrated on the city's north side, was excluded from any participation in the governing of the local schools, even though more than two-thirds of the students in the city school system were African American. By contrast, the ward system ensured that blacks would be represented in City Hall.

The combination of nonpartisan and at-large elections was adopted by virtually all cities throughout the Southwest. Partially as a result, a style of politics evolved that was tilted heavily in favor of business elites. Most cities provided a minimal level of services, but they took strong measures to promote economic development. "Frugality, efficiency, and professionalism in public administration" have always been the themes

Figure 4.1   Racial Composition of Municipal Wards in the City of St. Louis, 1977

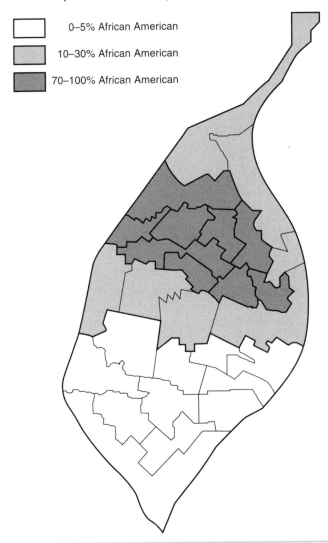

guiding government in southwestern cities, but frugality has rarely been applied to what business has wanted government to do.[30] For decades, legions of bureaucrats and professionals have found employment in special districts and authorities devoted to developing land, providing water, dredging harbors, supplying electricity, and lobbying the federal government so that business could grow.[31] Until the 1960s candidates for public office tended to be selected by business groups. In effect, these groups constituted a kind of political machine that controlled local politics. Turnout for elections was generally much lower than for elections in the industrial cities of the North.[32] This state of affairs began to change in the 1960s only when civil rights and neighborhood groups mobilized in several Sunbelt cities to challenge regimes that had long been dominated by business interests.

"EFFICIENCY AND ECONOMY" IN MUNICIPAL AFFAIRS

In the early years of municipal reform, "efficiency and economy" became code words for good government. When Theodore Roosevelt addressed the delegates to the First Annual Conference for Good City Government in 1894, he urged them to go beyond their moral outrage at the way things were being run to find ways of streamlining and improving government: "There are two gospels I always want to preach to reformers. . . . The first is the gospel of morality; the next is the gospel of efficiency. . . . I don't think I have to tell you to be upright, but I do think I have to tell you to be practical and efficient."[33] Actually, it is doubtful the reformers needed such advice. Municipal reformers were hard at work searching for guidelines that would show them how to govern cities. If they succeeded at "kicking the rascals out," they needed to know what to do with their inheritance.

The extreme disorganization of city governments gave the reformers a big target. All through the nineteenth century, cities had tended to add new responsibilities and services piecemeal, one at a time. By the late nineteenth century, every city had a multitude of independent boards and commissions administering water, police, health, and other services. No organization charts existed, so it would have been impossible to make sense of how an individual city ran. This state of affairs was a perfect recipe for chaos and corruption. Typically, a city was governed by a board of aldermen or a city council, with each alderman representing a separate ward. A politics of trade-offs, logrolling, and partisan wrangling could, and often did, result in a free-for-all, with each alderman looking for a way to trade his vote for some personal favor. Individual aldermen often sold their votes to paving contractors, restaurant or brothel owners, or utility companies in exchange for contracts, licenses, and franchises. Aldermen also got in the habit of filling the multitude of independent committees, boards, and commissions with their political cronies, who also took bribes when the opportunity arose.

The widespread graft and corruption incensed civic and business elites and middle- and upper-class voters, but what was to be done? One remedy was to approach state legislators with requests for special legislation designed to enhance the power of mayors and curtail the powers of aldermanic councils. In contrast to the aldermen, mayors generally came from prominent, even upper-class, backgrounds. Rather than running for election in only one ward, they were required to win citywide elections, and thus they were forced to appeal to a broad cross section of the urban electorate. Campaigns covering an entire city were expensive, and in the late nineteenth century candidates for mayor paid most of their own campaign costs.[34] What was an advantage, even a requirement, for an alderman—to come from the neighborhood, meet people in saloons and beer halls, speak the language of immigrants, accentuate ethnic identity, be one of the people—became a liability for someone running for citywide office.

State legislatures intervened to take budgetary and supervisory authority from elected councils and to give these powers to mayors or to full-time boards and commissions whose members were appointed by the mayor. In 1891 the Indiana legislature gave the Indianapolis comptroller the authority to draft the budget; the council retained the authority to lower but could not increase appropriations. New charters granted the mayors of Cleveland and Indianapolis the right to remove executive officials, a feature that was also adopted in charters approved in other states: New Orleans in 1896 and Baltimore in 1898.[35] In 1892 New York's legislature mandated a Board of Estimate and Apportionment, modeled on New York City's, for all cities over 50,000 in population. In the 1870s and 1880s, state legislative committees assumed financial or administrative control of the police departments of Detroit, Baltimore, Boston, St. Louis, Kansas City, and New York. In other states, boards and commissions were created to take over functions such as public parks, education, libraries, health, and public works.

Reformers became accustomed to trying to persuade legislatures to pass special legislation favoring their cause. Legislatures became, in effect, referees among the contending interests that were trying to control politics within the cities. Even if they had wanted to, state legislatures could not have stayed aloof from the political battles occurring in the cities. Local governments provided key public services, and representatives to state legislatures answered to local constituents; therefore local and state affairs were closely entwined: "The ordinary work of state politics was local affairs, and an ordinary branch of local government was the state legislature."[36] Most legislators were not inclined to interfere actively in issues arising from local governments outside their legislative districts. In a sample drawn from a large number of states, two scholars have shown that "virtually all bills affecting big cities were introduced by representatives from those cities."[37] Nonlocal representatives "routinely deferred to local governments."[38] Therefore the important question became: Who spoke for local governments?

Ordinarily, the big-city representatives to the state legislature came from the upper strata of society. Whereas aldermen and city council members came from and represented neighborhoods, the members of boards and commissions often were "bastions of the city's elite."[39] They were business leaders, bankers, lawyers, and other men of professional and social standing. The men of wealth and social prestige, who had deserted electoral politics in the industrial city, now found a new niche. They refused to run for office against the new breed of immigrant saloonkeepers and party loyalists. Instead, governors, legislative committees, and mayors appointed them to sit on boards and commissions. These boards were "protected from popular control, insulated from the undue influence of the city's aldermen, and dominated by those perched proudly on the top rung of the urban social ladder."[40]

But this method of reform was flawed. Even if the reformers managed to persuade state legislatures to change city charters by special legislation, this piecemeal approach caused as many problems as it solved. If anything, city government was becoming even more disorganized. The various boards and commissions often went their separate ways, and political appointment by a mayor, governor, or even legislative committee was not a guarantee of good government. What the reformers felt they needed was a consistent, comprehensive approach.

By the late 1890s, the advocates of municipal reform managed to develop a theory of governance. The reformers advanced the position that a public interest could be defined that would benefit all citizens equally. Their version of the public interest was based on four sacred principles: (1) there must be strict budgetary controls to ensure taxes would be kept as low as possible and public services delivered at the lowest possible cost; (2) the day-to-day administration of city government should be strictly separated from "politics"; (3) experts with training, experience, and ability should run city services; and (4) government should be run like a business and the principles of scientific management, then being applied in business organizations, should also be applied to government. The reformers derived their ideas about how to run government from the scientific management movement that was then sweeping the country. As businesses became larger, accountants, engineers, and corporate managers were busily inventing the structure of the modern corporation. What emerged from this search for efficiency was a quasi-military model of hierarchical administrative control.

In 1911 Frederick Winslow Taylor became world famous with the publication of his book *The Principles of Scientific Management*.[41] Basically, Taylor wanted to apply military discipline and hierarchy to the factory. He said the movements of individual workers could be studied to discover how to organize work tasks and thus achieve the maximum output with a minimum expenditure of each worker's energy. Taylor promised that his efficiency principles would bring progress, prosperity, and happiness to society by increasing material wealth to all. By applying the new science of management, Taylor said, it would be possible to achieve harmony and cooperation between owners and workers because both had the same interest in maximizing output. There was even a spiritual side; principles of efficiency would allow each worker to develop "his greatest efficiency and prosperity."[42] The essence of the Taylor catechism was that "In the past, the man has been first; in the future the system must be first."[43] Taylor and his disciples spread an urgent message: "Soldiering" (slow work) and inefficiency should be stamped out at home as well as at work. Popular magazines featured articles on efficient housework—describing, for instance, how a homemaker could sequence her daily chores and arrange appliances and furniture to minimize wasted movement while doing household work. The efficiency movement quickly achieved the status of a secular religion; its gospel of progress through efficiency swept the country.

To its advocates, scientific management seemed to be a bloodless revolution, a perfect solution to hostile employer–worker relations, disastrous economic panics, and poverty and want. Efficiency societies sprang up in cities all over the country, and efficiency experts were in great demand as speakers.[44] Taylor's disciples invaded the factories to implement the gospel of efficiency. They also applied the principles of scientific management to the governmental realm. Efficiency and scientific management— "business methods"—soon became the model for municipal reform. To the municipal reformers, the advantages of applying efficiency principles to the workings of government seemed obvious: "The rising prestige of technicians in industry and the increasing demand for new public works and municipal services strengthened the desire for more technical efficiency in local government."[45]

In 1912 Henry Brueré, the first director of the privately funded New York Bureau of Municipal Research, published a book applying efficiency principles to municipal management.[46] Brueré took the position that much of the mismanagement in New York City "formerly attributed to official corruption and to popular indifference was really due to official and popular ignorance of . . . orderly and scientific procedures."[47] What these procedures amounted to were elaborate accounting and reporting devices designed to codify the responsibilities of city officials, the actions taken by them to carry out their duties, the costs of equipment and personnel, and other details. Brueré invented a scoring system whereby the efficiency of cities could be rated and compared, and reduced to a number. Cities were to be rated on the basis of such items as: "Is a record kept of all city property?" "How often are the treasurer's books audited?" "Twenty questions on the protection of milk supply." "Is the location of houses of prostitution known and recorded?"[48] In all, Brueré and his aides used a list of 1,300 standardized questions to rate cities from the "worst governed" to the "best."

In 1913 Brueré was given the opportunity to make New York City efficient. In November of that year, John Purroy Mitchell, one of Brueré's closest confidants, was elected New York's mayor. Mitchell appointed Brueré to the office of city chamberlain (the mayor's policy adviser). Brueré immediately launched an attack on Tammany Hall's patronage system and managed to push through the first large civil service system in the nation. Brueré assigned the task of designing the details of the civil service system to Robert Moses, a young staff member at the New York Bureau of Municipal Research. Moses carried out his assignment with the enthusiasm of a Taylorite zealot. He proposed a system in which all municipal employees would be closely and constantly monitored at work by efficiency experts trained to rate each worker's efficiency by applying an elaborate mathematical formula. The responsibilities of employees were codified and "given a precise mathematical grade. These grades would . . . be used as a basis for salary increase and promotion."[49] To implement his system, Moses instructed his assistants to draw up rating forms, which he then distributed to supervisors. The idea was that each day, the supervisors would hand a scorecard containing a mathematical rating to every employee. City workers would be paid, promoted, or fired on the basis of the scores.

Such a system, if implemented, would have fallen of its own weight. There was no way to ensure objective ratings. The amount of time required to rate employees would have resulted in a truly enormous civil service administrative staff. Instead of spending the prodigious amounts of money required to hire hundreds of specially trained supervisors, Moses tried to rely on existing city employees. The 50,000 city employees steadfastly refused to use the reporting forms, objecting that the system was hopelessly time consuming and unwieldy, and arbitrary and capricious to boot.

The civil service reform attempted during Mitchell's mayoral tenure illuminates the values, assumptions, and foibles of the municipal reformers. As Taylor had put it, "The natural laziness in men is serious, but by far the greatest evil from which both workmen and employers are suffering is the systematic soldiering which is almost universal."[50] Reformers were taking on the formidable task of remaking human beings. Such an ambition could only be based on a distrust of people as they were. An essential human element was lacking. Mayor Mitchell, while trying to reorganize city departments and implement civil service procedures, tried to reduce all "unnecessary" programs and expenditures. He instituted cutbacks in school expenditures, asked teachers to work without salaries in the summers, tried to close down special schools for persons with mental disabilities, and reduced park and recreational expenditures.[51]

New York's civil service proposals proved too draconian even for most reformers. Suitably modified, however, some of the reform agenda made sense. Streamlined administration and better-trained city workers clearly could save money and improve services. Cities across the country adopted civil service systems but omitted New York City's elaborate reporting system. Not only the cities but the federal government and the states entered the field. President Taft appointed a Commission on Economy and Efficiency, and President Wilson later created the Bureau of Efficiency. Between 1911 and 1917, 16 states established efficiency commissions. These commissions generally recommended streamlining budgeting procedures, centralizing more power in the governor, consolidating state agencies, and establishing civil service.[52]

THE BUSINESS MODEL

With efficiency and scientific management supplying the rationale, it was predictable that municipal government would be modeled as close as possible on the business corporation. Reformers pointed out that the municipal governments inherited from the past were terribly inefficient. A history of reform written by scholars sympathetic with this view described the problem in these terms: "The reformers, who tried to get good men into office, found . . . that, even if they elected a mayor or council, they were intolerably handicapped by the existing systems of municipal government. [Due to] the principles of separation of powers and of checks and balances . . . there was no single elective official or governing body that could be held responsible for effecting reform."[53] Reformers claimed that the "weak mayor" form of government, which existed in most cities, left too much authority in the hands of a multitude of politicians—aldermen or council members as well as specialized boards and commissions. They employed organizational charts like the one shown in Figure 4.2 to demonstrate this fact. In this "weak mayor" organizational chart, the mayor presides over meetings of the city council, but the council presides over the departments that provide city services. The question being asked was, who could the voters blame if they were dissatisfied with the way the city was being run?

It was supposed that businesses, in contrast, operated efficiently because of the clear separation between policy making, located in a board of directors, and day-to-day administration, left in the hands of professional executive officers. Applied to cities, this model would still leave policymaking to elected officials, who represented their constituents, just as a board of directors in a business were supposed to represent the interests of the stockholders. The policies they enacted, however, would be implemented by professional administrators who were guided by principles of cost accounting and personnel management.

The business model required an executive with sufficient authority to run the company. Applying this insight to city government, advocates of reform lobbied for

Figure 4.2 Weak Mayor Government

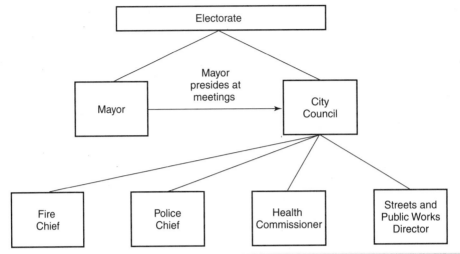

charter reforms designed to reduce the number of elected officials and create a "strong mayor" with authority to appoint most city officials and to veto legislation passed by the council. A model city charter published in 1899 by the National Municipal League represented this principle in charts much like those shown in Figure 4.3. In this scheme, the mayor presides at the top of a hierarchical chain of command with clear lines of authority and accountability. A small city council of five to nine members, each elected at-large, replaces the large boards of aldermen that were typical at the time. According to the reformers, with this arrangement in place, voters would be able to clearly understand who was in charge of the affairs of the city, and thus hold them accountable for how well they did their jobs.

Now that the reformers felt confident they knew what to do if they managed to gain control of the cities, they launched a crusade to persuade state legislatures to grant the cities broad "home rule" charters. In contrast to the latter decades of the nineteenth century, when municipal reformers often went to state legislatures to request special legislation in an effort to bypass elected officials, they now wanted cities to possess full authority to set their own tax rates, regulate their internal affairs, and decide how and where to provide services. In this way the cities would be free to realize the full potential offered by their new and efficient governmental structures. At its state constitutional convention in 1875, Missouri became the first state to write a general home rule charter for its cities, although the legislature retained control of St. Louis's police budget. The state still retained ultimate legal power, but Missouri's cities would not have to seek approval for their every action, as long as they stayed within their broad charter authority. Cities were now permitted to hire new sanitation workers and firefighters, for example, or build a new street without consulting the legislature. The general charter spelled out the range of services to be provided, but

Figure 4.3   Strong Mayor Government

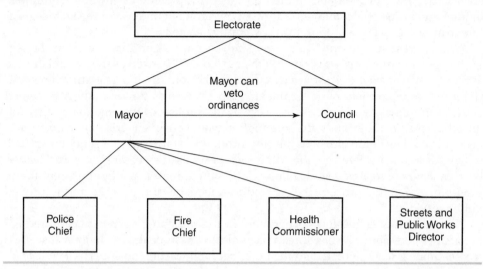

not such details as salary levels, the location of firehouses and streets, and the number of city employees. The home rule movement, pushed hard by the National Municipal League and other organizations, quickly spread to other states. By 1925 14 states had granted home rule charters to their cities, and today virtually all cities are governed by such charters.

COMMISSION AND MANAGER GOVERNMENT

Galveston, Texas, set up the first municipal government derived explicitly from the business model. In 1894 Galveston's business and professional leaders organized a campaign to elect business leaders to the most significant positions in the city government. The following year, a coalition of city council members and business leaders secured a charter amendment from the Texas legislature that abolished wards and created at-large elections. To the reformers' great disappointment, however, this new election procedure did not result in the sweeping changes its sponsors had hoped for. Over the next few years, some business leaders were elected to the city council, but on important matters they were regularly outvoted by a nonbusiness faction.[54]

A natural disaster provided the pretext for business and corporate leaders to assert themselves decisively. On September 8, 1900, hurricane-driven waves breached the seawall protecting Galveston, and the inrushing sea washed over the town, killing 6,000 of the town's 37,000 residents. Half of the property in the city was destroyed. In an effort to rebuild the city, prominent business leaders organized the Deepwater Committee and set out to gain control of local government. Civic leaders argued that if "a municipality is largely a business corporation,"[55] then it follows that it should be run as such, with the voters being viewed as stockholders and a board of directors responsible to the stockholders. Guided by this principle, the Deepwater Committee drafted an outline of a commission form of government and asked the state legislature to approve it. Their proposal was promptly enacted.

The Galveston Plan created a five-member commission that exercised the legislative powers previously assigned to the city council, as well as the administrative authority to oversee the city's services. Each of the commissioners assumed responsibility for a department of government. Such a concentration of authority seemed entirely appropriate, and even necessary, in the context of the emergency that followed the hurricane. Initially, the commission was even given jurisdiction over criminal and civil law enforcement in the city, although a state court subsequently struck down this authority. Even so, the commission exercised sweeping powers. Headed by five aggressive business leaders, Galveston initiated a vigorous rebuilding program, and, in the process, the city reduced its debts and restored and improved public services.

The success of Galveston's experiment in commission government captured national attention. The new idea spread like wildfire. Its appeal was obvious: It seemed to streamline government; it held the potential for attracting business and civic leaders back into active government service; and it was a straightforward plan around which reformers could rally in challenging machine politics and the urban party bosses. Galveston's performance so impressed business leaders in other Texas cities that they pressed the Texas legislature to allow them to follow Galveston's example and install commission government. By 1907 seven major cities in the state had imitated Galveston's charter, including Houston, Dallas, and Fort Worth.

In 1908 voters in Des Moines, Iowa, gave the commission concept a shot in the arm by placing it into an entire package of reform. In addition to a five-member commission, Des Moines adopted the initiative, referendum, and recall; nonpartisan and at-large elections; and a civil service system. This package of items, which reformers labeled the Des Moines Plan, caught on rapidly. The Plan was adopted by 23 cities in 1909 and by 66 cities in 1910.[56] By September 1915, at least 465 cities were governed by a commission, and by 1920 about 20 percent of all cities with populations of more than 5,000 had adopted the model.[57] During these years, a few states made commission government compulsory for their cities, and in most states it became an option for cities that wanted to adopt it.

Reformers promoted the Des Moines Plan as a cure-all for every ill, sure to bring less taxation, more efficient public services, and a "better class of men" to government. In city after city, it was promoted as a means of making government more businesslike. Accordingly, chambers of commerce and other organized business groups became the strongest backers. The Commercial Club succeeded in pushing through Des Moines's new charter in 1907, although, interestingly, the first commissioners voted into office represented a working-class slate—much to the dismay of the business group.[58] In Pennsylvania, the Pittsburgh Chamber of Commerce organized a statewide convention of business organizations to persuade the state legislature to require cities above a minimum size to adopt commission government. The coalition of bankers, merchants, and manufacturers secured the legislation in 1913.[59] A similar scenario played out elsewhere: business leaders trying to transform government into a businesslike operation.

Commission government was not without its problems, however. To its critics, its worst feature was that it did not fit the business model faithfully enough. A commission was not truly like a board of directors because commissioners engaged in both policy making and administration. Because each of the commissioners headed a separate department, leadership was fragmented, with the commissioners often refusing to cooperate with one another. Sometimes they built personal empires by adroitly handing out jobs and contracts, thereby acting a lot like machine politicians. It was hard for the mayor to prevent such practices because each of the commissioners was a "first among equals." This feature was the chief complaint of the secretary of the National Short Ballot Association, Richard S. Childs. Noting that commission government was "an accident, not a plan" (referring to the Galveston emergency that brought it into being), he addressed the problem of having five coequal executives: "The theory that the commission as a whole controlled its members in their departmental activities became neglected—the commission could not discipline a recalcitrant member."[60] Childs noted that commissioners would typically ignore one another's performance ("You attend to your department and quit criticizing mine") or exchange favors and support ("I'll vote for your appropriation if you'll vote for mine").[61] This was not exactly the model of efficiency that reformers like Childs had in mind.

The crusaders for governmental reform responded to these criticisms with a new idea: place all administrative authority in the hands of a single appointed, trained administrator—a city manager. This plan would make the mayor and the council responsible for making policy, but a professional city manager specifically trained for the job would assume responsibility for policy implementation and the day-to-day running of government. "The reform leaders realized that technical ability could not be expected of elected officials, and they hoped that a strong mayor could appoint trained technicians and administrators as department heads."[62] In this way, the reformers hoped, the city manager would bring to local government administrative unity, expertise, accountability, and formal training in management.[63]

This time, the reformers intended to get the business model right. In 1913 the National Municipal League issued a report (written by Childs) recommending that commission government be abandoned in favor of the city manager plan. Only six years later, in 1919, the league amended its model charter to recommend the city manager form. Because of its persuasive logic and "pure" business analogy, the city manager structure quickly replaced commission government almost everywhere, and by the 1920s the commission form was regarded as a failed experiment.

Between 1908 and 1912, several midwestern cities hired city managers. The idea caught on in earnest when Dayton, Ohio, changed its city charter, although the ward system remained. As in Galveston, a natural disaster served as the catalyst for a new government form. In 1913 John H. Patterson, president of the National Cash Register Company, persuaded the Dayton Chamber of Commerce to draft a new city charter. The chamber established the Bureau of Municipal Research to promote the idea, and the Committee of One Hundred, a group funded by the business community, sponsored a slate of candidates for the coming election who were pledged to changing the charter. By organizing a campaign ward by ward, the business slate put several Republican candidates on the city council, but Democratic machine politicians still outnumbered them. Charter reform seemed to be stymied. Two months later, however, the Miami River flooded the town, and the municipal government was slow in organizing emergency services. Patterson turned his factory into a shelter for flood victims. Overnight, he became the town's leading citizen. When requested by local business leaders, the state governor appointed Patterson to head a new charter reform commission. The commission successfully persuaded the voters to adopt its recommended charter.[64]

The results were spectacular. The new government improved public services, retired most of the city debt, instituted new budget-making procedures, enforced a uniform eight-hour day for city employees, and established civil service. The Dayton Plan soon became the nation's most popular "good reform" reform model. Although rarely instituted in the big industrial cities, it became the most common form of government in smaller cities around the country. In the five years before 1918, some 87 cities adopted manager charters, and 153 did so between 1918 and 1923. During the next five years, 84 more cities were added to the list.[65]

The commission and, after that, the manager plans became popular because they seemed able to fulfill the reformers' desire to find an objective, nonpolitical, efficient way to run government. Analogies to business organizations almost always supplied the principal supporting arguments for reform. The *Dallas News* promoted the manager plan in 1930 by asking, "Why not run Dallas itself on a business schedule by business methods under businessmen? . . . The city manager plan is after all only a business management plan. The city manager is the executive of a corporation under a board of directors. Dallas is the corporation. It is as simple as that. Vote for it."[66]

Despite such references to the business model, like all reforms the city manager model was political in both intent and effect. It was intended not merely to achieve efficient government but also to ensure the election of a different class of people who would insulate government from the influence of the Great Unwashed. A few participants in the reform crusades recognized the issue this raised about democratic processes. A delegate to the 1913 meeting of the League of Kansas Municipalities, after listening to his colleagues orate about the necessity of treating the city as a business, protested that "a city is more than a business corporation" and "good health is more important than a low tax rate."[67] The vast social chasm dividing municipal reformers from the rest of the urban populace, however, made such utterances anathema to most reformers.

Reformers made ambitious claims about the efficiencies to be realized by adopting businesslike models of government. But evidence indicates these claims were overblown. The adoption of city manager government had little, if any, effect on the level of city expenditures.[68] Machine and reform cities taxed at about the same rate and spent similar amounts on key public services. The major difference between them was that they distributed services and other valuable governmental benefits to different political groups. Reform governments tended to neglect lower-income neighborhoods so that they could reward their supporters in more affluent parts of the city. They built libraries; increased services to homeowners (such as free refuse collection); and zoned land to maximize new housing developments. Above all, they promoted policies that directly benefited downtown businesses and corporations. Bureaucratic rules made it easy to control the distribution of rewards, as well. In the 1980s in the city of New Haven, "acquiring delivery of some services like tree pruning or waste disposal required attaining a series of permits from offices open at irregular, infrequent times."[69] It is certain that such a system makes things more difficult for less educated workers, and those who find it hard to get off work. Wouldn't if be easier if everyone could just pick up their phone and call their alderman? As convenient as that sounds, there are costs for that system, too. Political appointees tend to be less professional, and groups outside the orbit of the machine are probably more thoroughly neglected than they are in a bureaucratic system, whatever its frustrations.[70] The bottom line is that it is impossible to take politics out of government. It is only possible to choose who wins, and who loses.

DID REFORM KILL THE MACHINES?

It has often been assumed the party machines died out because the reformers were successful in changing the rules of the game under which local politics was conducted. A large number of machines had short lives, only a decade or so, before they went into slow decline or the machine politicians suddenly lost their grip on elective offices. Between 1909 and 1918, machines fell apart in Dayton, Ohio; Detroit and Grand Rapids, Michigan; Los Angeles; Portland, Oregon; Milwaukee; Minneapolis; San Francisco; and Seattle. In each case, a variety of reforms was put through; in each case, civil service systems changed hiring rules.[71] Most of the machines that survived this era of reform died by the mid-1950s, if not before, including New York's Tammany Hall. By World War II, it would have been impossible to find a city left completely untouched by reform. Voter registration was universal and civil service hiring was nearly so; at-large, nonpartisan elections were used in most cities. Even in the big industrial cities, where reform was generally less successful, election rules were at least partially reformed. Boston, New Orleans, and Pittsburgh had switched to at-large elections; Memphis and Detroit had adopted both at-large and nonpartisan elections. Denver, New Orleans, Philadelphia, Cleveland, and Pittsburgh also became nonpartisan before World War II.[72]

However, these reforms did not lead inexorably to the demise of the machines, and they did not invariably restructure politics so ethnic voters lost influence. "The adoption of structural reform was not sufficient to eliminate or preclude the appearance of machine politics."[73] Machines were often adept at adjusting to the new rules and institutions. In 15 cities, they actually seem to have been helped by the reformers' centralization of power in the hands of mayors or city managers.[74] The reformers accomplished their goal of making someone accountable to voters, but the voters did not always use their power as the reformers hoped. After the adoption of city manager government in Cleveland in the 1920s, the city's machine was able to appoint a party hack as city manager because it still controlled the council, which was elected by wards.[75] Richard J. Daley built his powerful machine in Chicago, beginning with his election in 1955, despite the fact that the city's elections were nonpartisan and the vast majority of its employees were civil servants.

The machines died, in most cases, because they were unable to adapt to the large-scale population and economic transformations that were changing the cities. Two developments were particularly important. First, the immigrant base of the machines began to erode. After the turn of the century, Irish and German immigration dropped sharply; the bulk of new immigrants came from Italy and Eastern Europe. The Irish and, secondarily, the Germans had been the mainstay groups for most machines, and, as their numbers declined, machines found that their support gradually eroded. In Boston, for example, the Irish and Germans accounted for 32 percent of ethnics in 1890 but only 20 percent by 1930; in New York City, their share of the total ethnic population fell even more. In New York City, Fiorello LaGuardia put together a coalition of Italian and Jewish voters to defeat Tammany Hall's candidate in 1933. James Michael Curley, Boston's longtime boss, lasted longer than most other bosses but was finally defeated for reelection in 1949.[76]

The second devastating blow to the machines occurred when their immigrant constituents began to move up the economic ladder. As the immigrants joined the ranks of the middle class, the petty favors and patronage offered by the machines carried less weight, both in material and symbolic terms. After World War II, the immigrants and the children of immigrants joined the mass movement to the suburbs. Precinct captains saw their constituents moving out of the city, and sometimes they moved, too. Machines were not generally successful in reaching out to immigrants or to blacks and poor whites who moved into the cities during and after World War II.[77]

After the war, a new generation of politicians came to power by mobilizing the business community, labor, and the middle class behind programs of urban revitalization. In this cause they were helped by the federal government, which supplied the funds for public housing and slum clearance programs. Richard J. Daley rebuilt the Chicago machine by adding the middle class, business, and African Americans to the machine's base in the old immigrant neighborhoods. Daley aggressively sought federal funds for the city. Machine leaders in other cities, however, had neither the vision nor the political ability to follow his example.

THE REFORM LEGACY

Today, as in the era of municipal reform, rules governing elections and representation are crucial battlegrounds because they determine the balance of power among competing groups and interests. Battles over the "rules of the game" have been rekindled in recent decades because of clear evidence that racial and ethnic minorities have been consistently underrepresented at all levels of the American political system. These conflicts are enduring legacy of the era of municipal reform. Since the 1970s, actions have brought in the federal courts challenging electoral rules on the ground that they violated the Fourteenth Amendment guarantees of equal protection of the laws for all citizens. Groups such as the National Association for the Advancement of Colored People (NAACP) and the United Latin American Citizens have challenged the at-large elections systems of local governments and the boundaries of state legislative and congressional districts, claiming they were drawn to place hurdles in the way of minority candidates. The courts have sometimes upheld challenges to at-large elections but struck down the drawing of legislative boundaries expressly to increase minority representation (a practice known as racial gerrymandering)[78] of legislative districts. The intensity of the battles fought in and out of the courts serves as a reminder that the rules of representation are still as crucial as they were during the reform crusades 100 years ago.

Research has consistently shown that at-large elections result in the underrepresentation of racial and ethnic minorities.[79] In response to the accumulating evidence and over the strenuous objections of the Reagan administration, in 1982 Congress amended the 1965 Voting Rights Act to make it easier for minorities to challenge local election practices. Congress passed the amendments, contained in Section 2 of the new act, in reaction to a 1980 U.S. Supreme Court decision that required litigants to demonstrate an *intent* to discriminate before an election rule could be declared invalid.[80] In Section 2, Congress specified that challenges to local election rules could meet a much easier standard than before: They would be considered illegal if they merely had the *effect* of underrepresenting minorities in elected positions.

On June 30, 1986, the Supreme Court handed down a landmark decision, *Thornburg v. Gingles,* interpreting the 1982 amendments.[81] This case came to the Court after the U.S. Justice Department brought suit against the state of North Carolina, arguing that several multimember state legislative districts in North Carolina violated the voting rights of blacks because in those districts white candidates invariably won all seats.[82] The Court ordered North Carolina to create single-member districts and laid down standards for deciding when at-large and multimember district systems would be considered suspect: (1) when litigants could show it would be possible to create at least one single-member electoral district that would give a minority group an electoral majority; (2) when it could also be demonstrated the minority group seeking more representation was politically cohesive; and (3) when it could be shown that whites had previously voted as a bloc to prevent minority candidates from being elected.[83]

At-large district systems have since been successfully challenged throughout the United States. In 1986, after finding that at-large elections made it impossible for African American candidates to win, a federal court ordered several Alabama counties to institute single-member districts for electing county commissioners.[84] In a 1987 lawsuit filed against the city of Springfield, Illinois, a federal judge ordered the city to expand the number of its electoral districts from five to ten. Because only 10.8 percent of the city's population was African American, the expansion to ten districts was necessary if any one of them was to contain a majority of black voters.[85] (Interestingly, a different federal judge did not require this solution in a similar suit against the Springfield Park District.[86]) In the same year, the city of Danville, Illinois, expanded its city council to 14 members elected from seven wards after a federal judge threw out its previous system in which a three-member commission and a mayor were all elected at-large.[87]

The numerous court decisions arising from the 1982 amendments to the Voting Rights Act produced an extraordinary amount of confusion about local election rules. All through the 1980s and into the 1990s, court decisions called into question the electoral systems of hundreds of cities, counties, townships, and special districts. To preempt court action, some local governments voluntarily redrew district and ward boundaries to facilitate minority representation. Frequently, this required devising districts with tortuously meandering boundaries.[88] The attempt to redraw boundaries, however, is not a solution available to every city. It may, in fact, be available only to those whose minority populations live in rather segregated circumstances rather than in several distinct but unconnected neighborhoods because in segregated cities it is easier to draw boundaries that seem coherent. In a series of decisions beginning in 1993, the U.S. Supreme Court invalidated congressional district boundaries that did not meet standards of "compactness, contiguity, and respect for political subdivisions."[89]

Although the courts seemed to be enforcing this standard quite strictly for a time, it did not necessarily signal an end to all redistricting meant to achieve representation for particular racial or ethnic groups.[90] One way to meet the Court's standards would be to increase the number of legislative districts to ensure that even small minority neighborhoods would make up a compact legislative district. For several years, it was unclear whether there was some upper limit to the number of districts a local government might have to draw to achieve the equitable representation of minorities. By 1987, however, it seemed likely (despite the city of Springfield case) that, under normal circumstances, the number of districts already existing would be left alone.[91]

Another question that arose was whether the entire minority population or the voting-age minority population would be counted in the districts drawn to give minorities better representation. Most courts decided that a majority voting-age population was required.[92] Could two or more minority groups be combined to constitute a district if the combined minorities would make up the majority of voters in a district? Only, the courts have said, if it could be shown the groups were politically cohesive—and research makes it clear, for example, that blacks and Latinos do not generally vote similarly.[93]

Proponents of the principle that electoral districts should be drawn to maximize the representation of ethnic and racial minorities also took their fight to the state and federal levels. In 1991 minority representation was at the forefront of the political infighting over congressional reapportionment required as a result of the decennial census of 1990. Because state legislatures approve the boundaries for congressional districts, party control at the state level was crucial. In 1990 there were 37 blacks and Latinos in Congress. In 1992, as a result of redistricting, 19 additional blacks and Latinos were elected to Congress. In many states, it was Republicans, working with the Congressional Black Caucus, who promoted the formation of districts safe for minority candidates. This move increased the number of minorities in Congress, but by locating minorities into fewer districts, it reduced the number of districts favorable for white Democratic candidates.[94]

In June 1991 the Supreme Court ruled that judicial elections in Louisiana and Texas violated the 1982 Voting Rights Act because at-large election districts diluted the electoral strength of minorities. A flurry of lawsuits followed that challenged election procedures for state and local judges. Traditionally, nearly all state and local judges have been elected at-large—that is, multiple positions were filled in each electoral district. This perhaps explains why, as of 1985, only 3.8 percent of judges in state courts were African American and only 1.2 percent were Latino.[95]

The court challenges resulted in a revolution in local electoral practices. In 1981, 66.5 percent of cities used at-large electoral systems. By 1986, in a space of only five years, the proportion had fallen to 60.4 percent.[96] This very significant change can be traced to research demonstrating that changing from at-large to district elections did, as anticipated, improve the representation of blacks and Latinos.[97] Cities almost everywhere came under pressure to institute a ward system or to redraw existing ward and district boundaries. In 1991, for example, African American leaders in St. Louis threatened to go to court to force a redrawing of the boundaries of the city's 28 wards. At the time, 11 of the 28 aldermen were African American, but a new ward map would have made it mathematically possible to give half of the wards a majority of African American voters.[98]

Court cases in the 1990s seemed to signal that the courts wanted to get out of the business of telling state and local governments how to draw their districts, except in extreme circumstances. In an interesting twist, the courts also indicated that electoral districts that were gerrymandered to excessively increase or decrease minority representation now would be treated as suspect. In *Shaw v. Reno* (1993), the U.S. Supreme Court ruled that a very oddly shaped district in North Carolina made up almost entirely of blacks was illegally gerrymandered, calling such districts "political apartheid." Speaking for the majority, Sandra Day O'Connor wrote, "when a district obviously is created solely to effectuate the perceived common interests of one racial group, elected officials are more likely to believe that their primary obligation is to represent only the members of that group, rather than the constituency as a whole."[99] The Court left the door open for modest attempts to take race into account in redistricting by declaring that race could not be the "predominant factor" in drawing district boundaries, and in 1996 it declared that each case would be decided on its own merits and that minority districting might be permissible if the boundaries were sufficiently compact and coherent.[100] These rulings had the effect of discouraging the drawing of tortured boundaries but otherwise did not change the status quo greatly.

After the municipal reforms of the Progressive Era, it took more than half a century for questions about representation and local democracy to resurface as a contentious political issue. The years since the Voting Rights Act of 1965 may be properly regarded, therefore, as the first reform period since the Progressive Era aimed specifically at local electoral politics. This latter period of reform focused on undoing some key reforms of that period precisely because they had placed roadblocks in the way of equitable representation. The new era of reform has increased representation for African Americans and for Latinos. It has also resulted in increases in the volume of state aid received by state legislative districts that were reapportioned by court order because they were underrepresented in state legislatures.[101]

Intense conflicts over the rules of the game still go on, though the primary battleground has shifted from electoral districts to voter registration rules. Especially since the razor-thin presidential election decision in 2000, Republicans and Democrats have become locked in a protracted struggle over voter registration requirements. Both parties have a lot at stake. As in the Progressive Era, strict voter registration rules tend to reduce participation for minorities, the poor, and others who find it more difficult to negotiate the bureaucratic labyrinth. The outcome of the presidential election of 2000 was decided before Election Day in the state of Florida, when the Republican secretary of state invalidated the registration of more than 70,000 black voters because of technical problems with their applications, such as a misspelled name or failure to change address. Several hundred were invalidated mistakenly because their names matched a list of convicted felons. These actions proved to be decisive; ultimately, the election was determined by a little more than 500 voters.

Both parties took the lesson to heart. Democrats redoubled efforts to make it easier to register and to mobilize voter registration drives. The Republican Party fought such reforms in state after state. When immigration became a contentious national issue, their attempts to impose more rules of registration began to bear fruit. In 2008, a major battle erupted over whether states should impose proof of citizenship as a condition of registration, and a photo ID as a condition to vote. Previously, in most of the 25 states that required a form of identification at the polls, identification could come in several forms, including utility bills, paychecks, driver's licenses, or student or military IDs. The wave of new reforms would require passports, birth certificates, or naturalization papers as a condition of voting. Democrats charged that these proposals were thinly veiled attempts to discourage low-income and minority voters from coming to the polls; Republicans countered by asserting they were merely measures to reduce voting fraud.[102]

It is hazardous to take such claims at face value. It is clear that these conflicts reflect the political interests of the antagonists, a point driven home by controversies over the registration of college students. In September 2008, a local elections registrar in Virginia (a Republican) announced that Virginia Tech students who registered to vote in Blacksburg might lose scholarships or become subject to Virginia state taxes if they listed their campus as their voting address. His announcement clearly contradicted a U.S. Supreme Court decision granting students the right to vote where they go to school, but it nevertheless provoked confusion on the VPI campus. As it turns out, the Virginia case was not an exception. Eleven states discourage student voting by refusing to treat P.O. boxes and dormitories as legitimate addresses, or by requiring that out-of-state driver's licenses cannot be used to vote. All these cases virtually invite election officials to throw out votes in close elections, as occurred in Florida in 2000.[103]

How can it be, more than a century after voter registration and polling rules were first enacted, that these issues continue to be so controversial? The era of municipal reform, as well as our own, suggests the answer. Reform is never without politics, however lofty the stated principles may be. In politics, the rules of the game matter more than almost anything else because they determine who will govern. Accordingly, they will always be the object of contest and contention.

NOTES

1. William L. Riordon, *Plunkitt of Tammany Hall* (New York: Dutton, 1963), p. 17.
2. James Bryce, *The American Commonwealth*, 3rd ed., vol. 1 (New York: Macmillan, 1924), p. 642.
3. H. E. Deming, *The Government of American Cities: A Program of Democracy* (London and New York: Putnam, 1909), p. 194.
4. Quoted in Michael B. Katz, *School Reform: Past and Present* (Boston: Little, Brown, 1971).
5. Josiah Strong, *Our Country*, ed. Jurgen Herbst (Cambridge, Mass.: Belknap Press, Harvard University Press, 1963; first published in 1886), p. 55.
6. Samuel P. Hays, *The Response to Industrialism, 1885–1914* (Chicago: University of Chicago Press, 1957), p. 73.
7. James Weinstein, *The Corporate Ideal in the Liberal State, 1900–1918* (Boston: Beacon Press, 1968).
8. Melvin G. Holli, "Urban Reform in the Progressive Era," in *The Progressive Era*, ed. Louis L. Gould (Syracuse, N.Y.: Syracuse University Press, 1974), p. 137.
9. Frank Mann Stewart, *A Half Century of Municipal Reform: The History of the National Municipal League* (Berkeley: University of California Press, 1950), Chapter 1.
10. Samuel Haber, *Efficiency and Uplift: Scientific Management in the Progressive Era, 1890–1920* (Chicago: University of Chicago Press, 1964), p. 99.
11. Andrew D. White, "City Affairs Are Not Political," originally titled "The Government of American Cities," *Forum*, (December, 1890): pp. 213–216; reprinted in Dennis Judd and Paul Kantor, eds., *The Politics of Urban America*, 2nd ed. (New York: Addison Wesley Longman, 2002).
12. Amy Bridges, "Winning the West to Municipal Reform," *Urban Affairs Quarterly* 27, no. 4 (June 1992): 511.
13. Arthur T. Hadley, *The Empty Polling Booth* (Upper Saddle River, N.J.: Prentice Hall, 1978), p. 61.
14. Alexander B. Callow Jr., ed., *The City Boss in America* (New York: Oxford University Press, 1976), p. 158.
15. William T. Stead, *If Christ Came to Chicago* (Chicago: Laird and Lee, 1894), pp. 56–57.
16. Lloyd Wendt and Herman Kogan, *Bosses in Lusty Chicago* (Bloomington: Indiana University Press, 1967), p. 169.
17. Allan F. Davis, *Spearheads for Reform* (New York: Oxford University Press, 1967), pp. 156–162.
18. William D. Miller, *Mr. Crump of Memphis* (Baton Rouge: Louisiana State University Press, 1964), p. 74.
19. Bruce M. Stave, *The New Deal and the Last Hurrah: Pittsburgh Machine Politics* (Pittsburgh: University of Pittsburgh Press, 1970), p. 77.
20. Ernest S. Griffith, *A History of American City Government: The Conspicuous Failure, 1870–1900* (New York: Praeger, 1974), p.71.
21. Richard S. Childs, *Civic Victories: The Story of an Unfinished Revolution* (New York: Harper and Brothers, 1952), p. 299. In this passage, Childs was referring to the short ballot reform in conjunction with nonpartisanship. The short ballot reformers advocated fewer elected officials so voters would not be confused and elected officials would be held accountable to voters.
22. Edward C. Banfield, ed., *Urban Government: A Reader in Administration and Politics* (New York: Free Press, 1969), p. 275. Selection from Brand Whitlock, *Forty Years of It*, preface by Allen White (New York and London: Appleton, 1925; first published in 1914).
23. Haber, *Efficiency and Uplift*, pp. 99–101.
24. White, "City Affairs Are Not Political," pp. 213–216.
25. Griffith, *A History of American City Government*, p. 130.
26. Amy Bridges, *Morning Glories: Municipal Reform in the Southwest* (Princeton, N.J.: Princeton University Press, 1997), Chapter 8.
27. Willis D. Hawley, *Nonpartisan Elections and the Case for Party Politics* (New York: Wiley, 1973), p. 14. Subsequent information on the use of nonpartisan elections is from Hawley, pp. 15–18.

28. Weinstein, *The Corporate Ideal,* p. 109. Subsequent information on the Dayton election is from Weinstein.
29. Samuel P. Hays, "The Politics of Reform in Municipal Government in the Progressive Era," in *Social Change and Urban Politics: Readings,* ed. Daniel N. Gordon (Englewood Cliffs, N.J.: Prentice Hall, 1973), pp.107–127.
30. Bridges, *Morning Glories,* p. 146.
31. Ibid., Chapter 7.
32. Ibid., pp. 144–145.
33. Quoted in Holli, "Urban Reform in the Progressive Era," p. 144.
34. Ibid., p. 47.
35. Ibid., p. 45.
36. Nancy Burns and Gerald Gamm, "Creatures of the State: State Politics and Local Government 1871–1921," *Urban Affairs Review* 33, no. 1 (September 1997): 90.
37. Ibid., p. 86.
38. Scott Allard, Nancy Burns, and Gerald Gamm, "Representing Urban Interests: The Local Politics of State Legislatures," *Studies in American Political Development* 12 (Fall 1998): 294; see also Nancy Burns, Laura Evans, Gerald Gamm, and Corrine McGonnaughy, "The Local Politics of State Legislatures," paper delivered at the annual meeting of the Midwest Political Science Association, April 25, 2002.
39. Allard, Burns, and Gamm, "Representing Urban Interests," p. 68.
40. Ibid., p. 76.
41. Frederick Winslow Taylor, *The Principles of Scientific Management* (New York: Harper and Brothers, 1919; first published in 1911).
42. Ibid., p. 140.
43. Ibid., p. 7.
44. Haber, *Efficiency and Uplift,* p. 56.
45. Harold A. Stone, Don K. Price, Kathryn H. Stone, *City Manager Government in the United States: A Review After Twenty-Five Years* (Chicago: Public Administration Service, 1940), p. 5.
46. Henry Brueré, *The New City Government: A Discussion of Municipal Administration Based on a Survey of Ten Commission-Governed Cities* (Upper Saddle River, N.J.: Prentice Hall, 1912).
47. Ibid., p. v.
48. Ibid., pp. 27–29.
49. Robert A. Caro, *The Power Broker: Robert Moses and the Fall of New York* (New York: Oxford University Press, 1969), p. 75.
50. Taylor, *The Principles of Scientific Management,* p. 20.
51. Melvin B. Holli, *Reform in Detroit: Hazen S. Pingree and Urban Politics* (New York: Oxford University Press, 1969), p. 167.
52. Haber, *Efficiency and Uplift,* p. 115.
53. Stone, Price, and Stone, *City Manager Government,* p. 4.
54. Martin J. Schiesl, *The Politics of Municipal Reform: Municipal Administration and Reform in America, 1880–1920* (Berkeley: University of California Press, 1977), pp. 134–135.
55. Quoted in Weinstein, *The Corporate Ideal,* p. 96.
56. Clinton R. Woodruff, ed., *City Government by Commission* (Upper Saddle River, N.J.: Prentice Hall, 1911), pp. 293–294.
57. Childs, *Civic Victories,* p. 138.
58. Hays, "The Politics of Reform," p. 116.
59. Weinstein, *The Corporate Ideal,* p. 99.
60. Childs, *Civic Victories,* p. 137.
61. Ibid.
62. Stone, Price, and Stone, *City Manager Government,* p. 5.
63. Griffith, *A History of American City Government,* p. 167.

64. Ibid., p. 166; Schiesl, *The Politics of Municipal Reform*, pp. 175–176.

65. Weinstein, *The Corporate Ideal*, pp. 115–116.

66. Quoted in Stone, Price, and Stone, *City Manager Government*, p. 27.

67. Quoted in Weinstein, *The Corporate Ideal*, pp. 106, 107.

68. Anirudh V. S. Ruhil, "Structural Change and Fiscal Flows: A Framework for Analyzing the Effects of Urban Events," *Urban Affairs Review* 38, no. 3 (January 2003): 396–416.

69. Jessica Trounstine, *Political Monopolies in American Cities: The Rise and Fall of Bosses and Reformers* (Chicago: University of Chicago Press, 2008), pp. 162–163.

70. Ibid., p. 163.

71. Alan DiGaetano, "Urban Political Reform: Did It Kill the Machine?" *Journal of Urban History* 18, no. 1 (November 1991): 37–67.

72. Ibid.

73. Ibid.

74. Ibid.

75. Ibid., p. 67.

76. Ibid.

77. Steven P. Erie, *Rainbow's End: Irish-Americans and the Dilemmas of Urban Machine Politics, 1840–1985* (Berkeley: University of California Press, 1988).

78. Jay M. Shafritz, *The Dorsey Dictionary of American Government and Politics* (Homewood, Ill.: Dorsey Press, 1988), pp. 244–246. A legislative district is considered gerrymandered when it is drawn with tortuously meandering boundaries as a means of advancing the interests of a party or group. The term comes from a district drawn in Massachusetts in 1811 and signed into law by Governor Elbridge Gerry.

79. Robert L. Lineberry and Edmond P. Fowler, "Reformism and Public Policies in American Cities," *American Political Science Review* 61 (September 1967): 701–716; Chandler Davidson and George Korbel, "At-Large Elections and Minority Group Representation: A Re-examination of Historical and Contemporary Evidence," *Journal of Politics* 43 (November 1981): 982–1005; Jerry L. Polinard, Robert D. Wrinkle, and Thomàs Longoria Jr., "The Impact of District Elections on the Mexican American Community: The Electoral Perspective," *Social Science Quarterly* 71, no. 3 (September 1991): 608–614; Richard L. Engstrom and Michael D. McDonald, "The Effect of At-Large Versus District Elections on Racial Representation in U.S. Municipalities," in *Electoral Laws and Their Political Consequences*, eds. Bernard Grofman and Arend Liphart (New York: Agathon, 1986), pp. 203–225; W. E. Lyons and Malcolm E. Jewell, "Minority Representation and the Drawing of City Council Districts," *Urban Affairs Quarterly* 23 (1988): 432–447; Delbert Taebel, "Minority Representation on City Councils: The Impact of Structure on Blacks and Hispanics," *Social Science Quarterly* 59 (1982): 729–736; Jeffrey S. Zax, "Election Methods, Black and Hispanic City Council Membership," *Social Science Quarterly* 71 (1990): 339–355.

80. *City of Mobile v. Bolden*, 446 U.S. 55 (1980).

81. *Thornburg v. Gingles*, 106 S. Ct. 2752 (1986).

82. A multimember legislative district is just like an at-large system that covers an entire city. All candidates for city council seats must run in the same district; by contrast, in a ward system, a single alderman or council member represents each ward.

83. C. Robert Heath, "*Thornburg v. Gingles*: The Unresolved Issues," *National Civic Review* 79, no. 1 (January–February 1990): 50–71.

84. *Dillard v. Crenshaw County*, 649 F.Supp. at 289 (C.O. Ala. 1986).

85. *McNeal v. Springfield*, 658 F.Supp. at 1015, 1022 (C.D. Ill. 1987).

86. *McNeal v. Springfield Park District*, 851 F.2d at 937 (7th Cir. 1988).

87. *Derrickson v. City of Danville*, 87–2007 (C.D. Ill. 1987).

88. Joseph F. Zimmerman, "Alternative Local Electoral Systems," *National Civic Review* 79, no. 1 (January–February 1990): 23–36.

89. The quotation is from *Shaw v. Reno* 509 U.S. 630 (1993), commonly known as Shaw I. Other cases are *Miller v. Johnson*, 63 U.S.L.W. 4726 (1995); *Shaw v. Hunt*, 64 U.S.L.W. 4437 (known as Shaw II); *King v. Illinois Board of Elections*, 65 U.S.L.W. 3353 (1996); *Abrams v. Johnson*, 65 U.S.L.W. 4478.

90. Carmen Cirincione, Thomas Darling, and Timothy O'Rourke, "Does the Supreme Court Have It Right?" Paper delivered at the 1997 annual meeting of the American Political Science Association, Washington, D.C., August 28–31, 1997.

91. Heath, "*Thornburg v. Gingles*," pp. 51–53.

92. Ibid., pp. 54–55.

93. Ibid., pp. 55–59; Charles S. Bullock III, "Symbolics or Substance: A Critique of the At-Large Election Controversy," *State and Local Government Review* 21, no. 3 (Fall 1989): 91–99.

94. Edward Blum and Roger Clegg, "The GOP's 2002 Racial Redistricting Dilemma," *Weekly Standard*, October 17, 1992 (*http://www.ceousa.org/html/redistarticle1.htm*).

95. Scott Armstrong, "Minorities Seek More Clout on the Bench," *Christian Science Monitor*, October 1, 1991, pp. 1–2.

96. International City Management Association, *Baseline Data Report: Municipal Election Processes: The Impact on Minority Representation* 19, no. 6 (November–December 1987): 3–4.

97. Ibid., pp. 6–9; Polinard, Wrinkle, and Longoria, "The Impact of District Elections," pp. 608–614.

98. Tim O'Neil, "Blacks Want Half of City's Wards in Redistricting," *St. Louis Post-Dispatch*, June 8, 1991, p. 3A.

99. *Shaw v. Reno*, 92 357 (1993). In 1996 the Court rejected a somewhat redrawn 12th congressional district in North Carolina yet again.

100. *Miller v. Johnson*, 515 U.S. 900 (94 631), 1995; *Bush v. Vera*, 571 U.S. 900 (94 805), 1996.

101. Stephen Ansolabehere, Alan Gerber, and James Snyder, "Equal Votes, Equal Money: Court-Order Redistricting and Public Expenditures in the American States," *American Political Science Review* 96, no. 4 (December 2002): 767–777.

102. Ian Urbina, "Voter ID Battle Shifts to Proof of Citizenship," *New York Times*, May 12, 2008 (*http://www.nytimes.com/2008/05/12/us/politics/12vote.html*).

103. Nikki Schwab, "Confusing Voter Registration Laws Could Affect Presidential Election," *U.S. News and World Report*, September 24, 2008 (*http://www.usnews.com/articles/campaign-2008/09/2008/09/24*).

URBAN VOTERS AND THE RESHAPING OF NATIONAL POLITICS

CITY AND NATION IN THE TWENTIETH CENTURY

From the perspective of the early twenty-first century, it may be difficult to recall a time when there was political support for programs to help the cities. But the explanation is straightforward: Attention to the problems of the cities emerged when both of the national political parties began to win or lose elections on the basis of urban votes. With Franklin D. Roosevelt's landslide victory in the presidential election of 1932, voters in the industrial cities became crucial to the electoral prospects of the Democratic Party. The nation's 11 largest cities provided 27 percent of the popular vote in 1932 and a commanding majority in several of the industrial states with the largest numbers of electoral college votes.[1] For the first time in the nation's history, the politicians representing urban voters began to wield influence in national politics. Their loyalty to the national Democratic Party fundamentally shaped American politics until the election of Republican Ronald Reagan in 1980.

Modern American liberalism, as expressed in the New Deal programs of the 1930s and the Great Society programs of the 1960s (both terms were borrowed from the campaign slogans of Presidents Roosevelt and Johnson), can be traced to the mobilization of the urban electorate in the 1930s. The alliance that provided the foundation for the Democratic Party's ascendancy was made up of two wings, the urban North and the solid South. Urban voters learned to vote Democratic because of the programs enacted during the New Deal years. For the first time in the nation's history, federal agencies were granted powers to regulate the economy and to assist citizens during times of need. Urban working-class people were benefited by labor legislation such as Section 7a of the National Industrial Recovery Act and the Wagner Labor Act, which implemented workers' compensation for death or injury, safety and workplace regulations, and the right of workers to organize unions. As a result,

OUTTAKE

URBAN ETHNICS BECAME A MAINSTAY OF THE DEMOCRATIC PARTY

In the first years of the twentieth century, ethnic voters in the cities did not reliably vote Democratic. About half the urban party machines were Republican, but whatever their partisan affiliation, machine leaders were not well connected to the national or even the state party organizations. In most states, party leaders came out of the governor's mansion and state legislature, which tended to be dominated by rural, not city, interests. Machine politicians had gotten into politics through their local precincts and wards, and they paid little attention to national candidates and issues. They specialized in a politics of ethnicity and trade-offs, not of abstract principles. The machines were strictly local organizations, a product of the segregation of ethnic voters from the rest of American society.

Urban ethnic politicians elected to the state legislature received little pay and even less respect. It was often a kiss of political death to be sent away to small upstate or downstate towns like Albany, New York, or Springfield, Illinois, away from friends, family, and the local community. When the machine organization Tammany Hall sent Al Smith to the state legislature at the age of 30, he had scarcely been outside New York City. He felt exiled:

> Al Smith went to Albany unprepared to be legislator—or even to sleep away from home. . . . [O]vercome by the intricacies of the legislative process, he sat day after day in the high-ceilinged chamber in silence.
>
> As he sat there staring down at the desk, a page boy would deposit another pile of bills on it. The wording was difficult enough for the expert. It might have been designed to mock a man whose schooling had ended in the eighth grade, who had never liked to read even the simple books of childhood, who, he had once said, had in his entire life read only one book cover to cover: *The Life of John L. Sullivan.*

Before Al Smith, who was later elected governor of New York and nominated for the presidency in 1928, Tammany politicians had never prospered in Albany.

Their personal loyalties and their pocketbooks, more than political issues, also motivated urban ethnic voters. When precinct captains took them to the polls, they voted for the local party organization, not for a cause. What in their background would excite them about abstract national issues like tariff policy or child labor legislation? The upshot was that although powerful party machines dominated many cities, the leaders of these organizations and their loyal constituents had only occasionally become important in gubernatorial contests and had never figured at all in presidential contests.

This would all change when urban ethnic and labor union workers became an important constituency of the New Deal coalition of the 1930s.

Source: Robert A. Caro, *The Power Broker: Robert Moses and the Fall of New York* (New York: Knopf, 1974), pp. 118–119. John L. Sullivan was a famous boxing champion.

union members became reliable Democratic voters. The black electorate also became important to the northern wing of the party. Even in the 1930s, long before civil rights legislation became politically possible, the Roosevelt administration took steps to ensure that blacks received some appointments to federal posts and a share of the benefits from job and relief programs. The legacy of these New Deal loyalties only began to weaken in the 1960s and later, when racial animosities drove a wedge between inner-city blacks and white working-class and southern voters.

A NEW POLITICAL CONSCIOUSNESS

In 1912 a Harvard political scientist wrote, "before many years have passed, the urban population of the United States will have gained numerical mastery."[2] He based his judgment on a simple calculation of demographic change.[3] In the 30 years from 1890 to 1920, more than 18 million immigrants poured into America's cities. These new immigrants came mainly from Italy, Poland, Russia, Greece, and Eastern Europe. They were overwhelmingly Roman Catholic and Jewish. They made up the preponderance of the workforces in the iron and steel, meatpacking, mining, and textile industries. Few spoke English when they arrived, and many were illiterate even in their own language.

The ever-present nineteenth-century nervousness about the "strangers in the land" escalated into a national phobia in the twentieth century. The rise of the cities in national politics began when nativist Protestants launched a carefully coordinated assault on the city machines and their immigrant constituents. In the past, immigrant voters were brought into politics by the urban party machines, which were strictly local organizations that stayed away from big issues. But the nativist assaults on the immigrants gradually made them aware that they had a stake in national politics.

The campaigns for prohibition were aimed squarely at immigrants and their cultural values. Proposed to the states by Congress in 1917 and ratified in 1919, the Eighteenth Amendment prohibited the sale and distribution of alcoholic beverages. Small-town Methodists and Baptists—joined in their crusade by upper- and middle-class Protestants in the cities and in the new suburbs—said they wanted to reduce poverty, improve workers' efficiency and family life, and end immorality and crime by forcing the immigrants to abstain from alcohol. Prohibition became the most compelling political issue of the 1920s because it gave middle-class Protestants and rural voters, a way to attack the cultural values and customs of the immigrants:

> [Drinking] was associated with the saloonkeepers who ran the city machines and who used the votes of the whiskey-loving immigrant . . . with the German brewers and their "disloyal" compatriots who drank beer and ale. . . . The cities, which resisted the idea that "thou shalt not" was the fundamental precept of living, were always hostile to prohibition. The prohibitionists, in turn, regarded the city as their chief enemy, and prohibitionism and a pervasive antiurbanism went hand-in-hand.[4]

To rural and urban Protestants, the sins of liquor were indistinguishable from the sins of the immigrants. Southern and western newspapers reflexively connected crime, national origin, and liquor. When it was not legitimate to attack foreigners directly, it was easy to attack them through the surrogate liquor issue, allowing "prohibition partisans to talk about morality when in reality they were worried about cultural dominance and political supremacy."[5]

Prohibition was intimately connected to religious conflict. To Protestant Americans, the Roman Catholic Church was evil incarnate. It signified ostentatious authority—the robes, the ceremony, and the architecture of Catholic cathedrals bespeaking a menace to the simplicity and informality of small-town life. Like the right-wing groups of the 1950s obsessed by the idea that an international communist conspiracy was poised to subvert the American system, religious fundamentalists of the early twentieth century were convinced the Roman Catholic Church was intent on subverting civil authority around the world.

Feeding on such fears, the Ku Klux Klan attracted millions of members. Revived in Atlanta in 1915, for a few years the Klan enjoyed spectacular growth in both the North and the South. Klan membership skyrocketed in California, Oregon, Indiana, Illinois, Ohio, Oklahoma, Texas, Arkansas, and throughout the South. In 1924, at its peak, 40 percent of the Klan's membership resided in Ohio, Indiana, and Illinois. Half of its membership was located in cities of more than 50,000, with chapters of hundreds of members in such cities as Chicago, Detroit, Indianapolis, Pittsburgh, Baltimore, and Buffalo.[6] The Klan was a powerful political force until at least the mid-1920s. It helped elect a member of the Senate; governors in Georgia, Alabama, Oregon, and California; and 75 members of the House of Representatives.

Although the Klan found its strongest support among lower-middle-class fundamentalist Christians, its basic message reached a broad audience. In 1916 Madison Grant, curator of New York City's Museum of National History, published *The Passing of the Great Race,* in which he worried that Aryans might someday be overwhelmed by dark-skinned races. His book was elevated to the status of a scientific work, along with Lothrop Stoddard's *The Rising Tide of Color Against the White World-Supremacy* (1921).

Congress responded to the rising xenophobia with the Emergency Quota Act of 1921 and the National Origins Act of 1924. Both laws drew support from intellectuals, labor leaders, rural people from all sections of the country, and anxious middle-class voters. The Emergency Quota Act reaffirmed the total exclusion of Asians and established a national origins quota of 3 percent of each nationality's proportion of the U.S. population as recorded in the 1910 census. The law succeeded in cutting immigration from 805,228 in 1920 to 309,556 in 1921–1922.[7] Three years later, the National Origins Act reduced the origins quota to 2 percent and established the 1890 census as the new baseline. By changing the baseline census used for calculating the percentage of each ethnic group allowed into the country, Congress was able to drastically reduce the numbers for nationality groups flooding into the country. Italian immigration was reduced by 90 percent; British and Irish immigration, by contrast, declined by just 19 percent.[8] The total number of immigrants fell sharply, from 357,803 in 1923–1924 to 164,667 in 1924–1925.

In debates on these two bills, members of Congress reviled the foreign-born of the cities in language that seemed to be lifted from Ku Klux Klan pamphlets. This assault helped make immigrants aware of how deeply national politics could affect them, and in the 1920s they began to express their new understanding. Before long, it became apparent they "were not going to support candidates who wanted them to stop drinking, Protestantize their schools, or tell them as often as possible that they were inferior."[9] Before long, they made their presence felt in national politics.

THE CHANGING POLITICAL BALANCE

Before the 1930s neither the Republicans nor the Democrats paid much attention to the cities. For their part, the Republicans, the triumphant party of Abraham Lincoln, emerged from the Civil War as the dominant party controlling Congress and the presidency. Between 1860 and 1928, the Republicans won 14 of 18 presidential contests and controlled both houses of Congress the majority of the time. Because the party's main base of support came from the financial, industrial, and commercial interests, it opposed taxes on business, enacted high tariffs on foreign imports, encouraged private exploitation (mineral, grazing, homesteading) of federal lands in the West, and used federal troops to quell strikes. At the same time, the Republicans were popular in the middle- and working-class electorates in the North because of the outcome of the Civil War and because it presided during a period of general economic expansion tied closely to frontier development and industrial growth.

For several decades after the Civil War, the Democratic Party tried to hold together a loose alliance made up of groups opposed to economic domination by eastern banks and corporations, the railroads, and "big money." The party's presidential candidates tried to appeal for support from urban workers, but a lot of other interests jostled for attention too. The worst problem with the Democrats' coalition was its fragility, for its major issues arose from the abiding enmity of Southerners to the party of Lincoln, the insecurities of small farmers about credit and prices, and the tensions between business and industrial workers. The party did better during hard times but lost support when the economy improved.

The cleavages within the Democratic Party mirrored the conflicts that obsessed the nation. Composed as it was of an unlikely combination of urban ethnics, western farmers, prohibitionists, southerners, and racist religious fundamentalists, the party had been held together mainly with the glue of shared grievances. The fragile nature of this alliance was revealed at the 1924 Democratic convention, held in Madison Square Garden in New York City. The Democrats treated the first radio audience of a national convention to a futile 16-day, 103-ballot marathon. The galleries booed the speeches of Southerners and Westerners, especially when William Jennings Bryan, a three-time failed candidate for president, asked the convention to reject a proposed resolution condemning the Ku Klux Klan by name. The resolution to condemn the Klan brought forth such heated oratory that police were brought onto the convention floor in case a free-for-all broke out. Delegates shouted at and cursed one another. When the final vote on the resolution to condemn the Klan was taken, it lost by one vote, 542 ³⁄₂₀ to 541 ³⁄₂₀. Demands for a recount were drowned out when the band struck up "Marching Through Georgia," which incited the southern delegates to paroxysms of anger. After 16 days, the convention finally nominated a presidential candidate almost nobody wanted.

The crowds and the din of New York City confused and frightened the delegates from the towns and farms of the South and West. They found New Yorkers unfriendly and rude, and the city seemed all too easy to get lost in. Delegates who "wandered downtown to Fourteenth Street to gawk at Tammany Hall with its ancient Indian above the door reacted as if they expected to see an ogre come popping out. Almost all delegates were dismayed by the New York traffic, the noise and hustle."[10] Their antagonism toward the city was reaffirmed every day the convention dragged on through the muggy July heat. Small-town reporters filled their hometown newspapers with vivid accounts of the horrors of the city.[11]

Despite these divisions, only four years later the Democrats named Al Smith, the four-term governor of New York, as their presidential candidate. Smith represented everything that was anathema to the city haters. He was a self-made Catholic member of the nation's most notorious machine, Tammany Hall. He said "foist" instead of "first" and wore a brown derby, which only accentuated his bulbous nose and ruddy complexion. He proudly reminisced about his past: swimming in the East River and working at the Fulton Fish Market as an errand boy. Considering the divisive conflicts within the party, how could he have been nominated? Once he was nominated, why did the party not simply come apart?

The southern and western factions had little choice but to stay within the fold. In spite of their differences, the Democrats had come to share, however crudely, a class interest. The party had symbolically become—mostly by default because the Republicans took an uncompromising probusiness stand—the "little man's" party. Those who opposed Republican policies could never hope to have a voice in national politics unless they aligned with the Democrats.

The time was ripe for compromise. Few Democrats thought Smith could win, but no candidate was available who was capable of bridging the gap between the factions. Smith had acquired broader political support than anyone else. As the four-term governor of New York, he had gained national prominence as a progressive leader who had created state parks and beaches, sponsored workers' safety legislation, and financed public improvements throughout the state. He had reorganized state government, making New York the model for progressives who believed in efficiency principles. Admired by progressives for his record as governor and supported by Democratic organizations with ethnic constituencies, his nomination could be denied by rural delegates, but only at the cost of another fiasco like 1924—multiple ballots and a guaranteed loss for the presidential nominee. There was even reason to believe Smith might have a chance. In his victorious gubernatorial run in 1924, he had received 100,000 more votes than the losing Democratic presidential ticket in New York.

In 1928 the Democrats gave the nomination to Al Smith. Although he lost the election, his candidacy marked the beginning of the party's political ascendancy in the big cities. The election of 1928 marked a significant change in the attitude of the urban masses. Both in 1920 and 1924, the 12 largest cities in the United States had, taken together, given a decisive majority to the Republicans; now the tables were turned, and the Democrats came out ahead. As later elections were to prove, this marked the beginning of a long-term trend in which voters in the cities cast most of their ballots for Democrats.[12]

For the Roman Catholic ethnics in the cities, Smith's campaign educated them about the national issues of Prohibition, ethnicity, and religion. Smith campaigned with his brown derby and his theme song, "The Sidewalks of New York." Protestants shuddered at the idea of a Catholic in the White House. Smith's equivocal stand on Prohibition made drink the main issue of the campaign. Blue-blood upper-class Protestants found him beneath them. The campaign highlighted the issues of race,

Table 5.1   The Revolt of the City: Voting in the 12 Largest Cities

Year	Net Party	Plurality
1920	1,540,000	Republican
1924	1,308,000	Republican
1928	210,000	Democratic
1932	1,791,000	Democratic
1936	3,479,000	Democratic
1940	2,112,000	Democratic
1944	2,230,000	Democratic
1948	1,481,000	Democratic

Note: The cities in this table include New York, Chicago, Philadelphia, Pittsburgh, Detroit, Cleveland, Baltimore, St. Louis, Boston, San Francisco, Milwaukee, and Los Angeles.

Source: Reprinted from the table on page 49 in *The Future of American Politics,* 3rd revised edition, by Samuel Lubell. © 1951, 1952, 1956, 1965 by Samuel Lubell. Reprinted by permission of Harper & Row Publishers, Inc.

religion, culture, and social class so clearly that never again would the ethnics be unmindful of their stake in national politics.

The election of 1928 brought a Democratic electoral plurality to the cities of the nation (see Table 5.1). In 1920 the Republican presidential ticket carried the 12 largest cities by more than 1.5 million votes, and in 1924 the ticket did almost as well. But in 1928, with Al Smith as the Democratic candidate, the Republican margin shrank to a narrow 210,000 votes. In the 1932 election, the Democrats beat the Republicans in the big cities for the first time, and decisively, by a margin of almost 1.8 million votes. Four years later, Franklin Delano Roosevelt's landslide demonstrated the Democrats now had a firm lock on the urban constituency. Since then, the major cities have voted heavily Democratic, and this fact proved to be the decisive difference in two presidential elections. In 1948 Harry S. Truman barely won the national popular vote, but he carried the cities by nearly 1.5 million votes. City voters provided the winning margins again in the 1960 election when they put John F. Kennedy over the top.

THE DEPRESSION AND THE CITIES

The Great Depression came as a shock to Americans and to their public leaders. The 1920s had been a decade of prosperity and optimism, especially for the rapidly growing middle class. Business leaders and politicians promoted the idea that the potential for sustained economic growth was limitless. A strong undertow of poverty ran below the surface, in the immigrant slums and on farms alike, but on the surface the signs of prosperity prevailed. It was an age that extolled mass consumption and complacency. For the middle classes, the discontent of the industrial age seemed long past.

October 24, 1929, is the symbolic beginning of the Great Depression. On that day—Black Thursday—disorder, panic, and confusion reigned on the New York Stock

Exchange. Stock prices virtually collapsed. For several months prices had sagged, then rallied, then sagged again, with each trough lower than the previous one and each peak less convincing. When the bottom fell out, "the Market . . . degenerated into a wild, mad scramble to sell, . . . the Market . . . surrendered to blind, relentless fear."[13] In one morning, 11 well-known speculators committed suicide. From Wall Street the economic catastrophe rippled outward, with consequences that fundamentally reshaped American politics.

Over the next three years, the nation sank steadily deeper into economic stagnation. In the spring of 1929, the unemployment rate stood at 3.2 percent. Within a few months, the number of unemployed exceeded 4 million, representing 8.7 percent of the labor force.[14] By 1932, 24 percent of all workers—more than 12 million in all—could not find jobs. In the depths of the depression, during the spring of 1933, the number of unemployed reached 13 million workers, fully one-fourth of the labor force.[15]

The depression dragged on for a decade. Unemployment levels remained above 20 percent in both 1934 and 1935 and dropped below 15 percent only in 1937. Most of those who managed to find work made less than before. From 1929 to 1933, the average income of workers fell by 42.5 percent.[16] Weekly wages dropped from an average of $28 in 1929 to $17 by 1934, and workers faced the ever-present threat of layoffs. Many jobs were reduced from full-time to part-time status, and employers cut wages and hours to meet payrolls. For example, the payroll of the nation's largest steel company, U.S. Steel, was cut in half from 1929 to 1933, and in 1933 the company had no full-time workers at all.[17] Steel mills operated at only 12 percent of capacity by 1932.[18]

The productive capacity of business seemed irreparably damaged. In the three years following the stock market collapse, national income fell by 44.5 percent. By the summer of 1932, stocks had fallen 83 percent below their value in September 1929.[19] By the end of 1932, 5,096 commercial banks had failed. Farm income declined from $7 billion in 1929 to $2.5 billion in 1932.[20] For many farmers whose incomes had been sharply dropping throughout the 1920s, the depression was the final blow.

The statistics of disaster suggested the extent of human suffering. Between 1 million and 2 million men rode the rails and gathered in hobo jungles or camped in thickets and railroad cars. Others lived in "Hoovervilles," clusters of cardboard, scrap wood, and scrap metal shacks in empty lots and city parks. Those who had been chronically poor in the 1920s were now hungry and destitute. They stood in bread lines, ate from garbage cans, or went begging from door to door. One-quarter of all homeowners lost their homes in 1932, and more than 1,000 mortgages a day were foreclosed in the first half of 1933.[21] By March 1933, when Franklin D. Roosevelt was inaugurated as president, 9 million savings accounts had been lost.[22]

Never before had the nation faced an economic catastrophe of this magnitude, nor was there a tradition of federal government assistance for the unemployed and destitute.[23] Unemployment and poverty were certainly not new. In the period from 1897 to 1926, unemployment levels in four major industries fluctuated around the 10 percent level,[24] and poverty was a chronic condition of industrialization and immigration. What made this depression unique was its depth, persistence, and broad reach. In earlier depressions, including the panics of the 1870s and 1890s, production and employment declined much less severely, and the recovery began within a year or two.[25] The depression of the 1930s lasted for over a decade, it touched all classes, and people at all income levels felt its effects. The measure of the crisis of the 1930s was not just unemployment and poverty but also the breakdown of economic institutions.

No one knew how to respond. President Herbert Hoover firmly resisted intervention by the federal government and instead launched two national drives to encourage private relief. Late in 1930 he appointed the President's Emergency Committee for Employment. Its main task was to encourage state and local committees to expedite public construction and coordinate public and private funding for relief efforts. In August 1931 he formed the President's Organization on Unemployment Relief, whose job was to help organize private unemployment committees in states and communities.

Despite Hoover's adament opposition to federal assistance, two programs were funded during his administration. First, the Federal Home Loan Bank Act supplied capital advances to a small number of mortgage institutions so they could forbear rather than foreclose on mortgages in default. This program saved a few banks. Second, the Emergency Relief and Construction Act extended $300 million in loans to state and local governments so they could continue to provide relief to indigent people.

Hoover was hardly alone in opposing aggressive federal action. Until 1932 most governors took a "we'll do it ourselves" attitude toward solving unemployment and its associated problems.[26] Two governors refused to work with the President's Organization on Unemployment Relief, even though federal funds were not involved.[27] The officials of financially strapped local governments were also skeptical of federal aid. In July 1931 the socialist mayor of Milwaukee wrote to the mayors of the largest 100 cities asking them to come to a conference to discuss a joint request for a national relief program. He got no response at all from many of the major cities, and several mayors criticized the idea, arguing that federal aid would constitute "an invasion of community rights."[28]

In the 1932 campaign, the Democrats accused Hoover of doing too much rather than too little. Their nominee, Roosevelt, promised to balance the budget while accusing Hoover of having presided over "the greatest spending administration in peace times in all our history."[29] It was apparent that the weight of the past lay heavily on both political parties. Against a cultural tradition that extolled individualism and free enterprise, there was great reluctance to expand the powers of government— especially the federal government—to meet the crisis. Nevertheless, when Roosevelt was inaugurated on March 4, 1933, he set in motion a concentrated period of reform that vastly increased the powers of the federal government in areas of business regulation, farm policy, and social insurance. Why did Roosevelt break so thoroughly from the tradition of a limited national government?

Roosevelt's change of heart was motivated by the overwhelming sense of crisis that ushered him into the White House. Between his election in November and his inauguration in March, the nation passed through the worst months of the depression.[30] The economy teetered on the brink of utter collapse. In February 1933 some of the nation's biggest banks failed. "People stood in long queues with satchels and paper bags to take gold and currency away from the banks to store in mattresses and old shoe boxes. It seemed safer to put one's life's savings in the attic than to trust the financial institutions in the country."[31] Roosevelt wondered if anything would be left to salvage by the time he assumed office. By Inauguration Day, 38 states had closed their banks, and on that day the governors of New York and Illinois closed the nation's biggest banks.[32] The New York Stock Exchange stopped trading. The Kansas City and Chicago Boards of Trade closed their doors. "In the once-busy grain pits of Chicago, in the canyons of Wall Street, all was silent."[33]

It was also one of the harshest winters on record. In desperation, people overran relief offices and rioted at bank closings. Relief marchers invaded state legislative chambers. Farmers tried to stop foreclosure proceedings and blockaded roads. Amid marches, riots, arrests, and jailings, many people feared there might be a revolution against the capitalist system.

In its first 100 days, Roosevelt's administration presented Congress with a flood of legislative proposals.[34] On March 9 Roosevelt signed the Emergency Banking Act. The act extended financial assistance to bankers so they could reopen their doors and gave the government authority to reorganize banks and to control bank credit policies. It received a unanimous vote from a panicked Congress, sight unseen. A flurry of legislation followed: the Civilian Conservation Corps (March 31), the Agricultural Adjustment Act and the Federal Emergency Relief Act (May 12), the Tennessee Valley Authority (May 18), the Federal "Truth in Securities" Act (May 27), the Home Owners' Loan Act (June 13), the National Industrial Recovery Act (June 16), and more than a score of other bills.

Most of the legislative onslaught was designed to stimulate, regulate, and stabilize the most important economic institutions of the economy. But the benefits filtered down. After the Emergency Banking Act was passed, depositors gained confidence and redeposited their savings. Under the National Housing Act (adopted in 1934), home buyers could secure long-term mortgages from banks whose loans were guaranteed by the federal government. Foreclosures on farms and homes were sharply reduced when the government, through the Farm Credit Administration and Home Owners' Loan Corporation, agreed to buy up defaulted mortgages. New Deal programs affected many people's lives by salvaging their savings, houses, and farms. Nevertheless, the New Deal's attempts to reform the economy were designed more to bring stability to financial institutions than to fight poverty and destitution. Home lending and farm credit programs primarily helped the nation's important economic institutions and secondarily aided the heavily mortgaged middle class.

The other side of the New Deal included its public works and relief programs. Between 1933 and 1937, the federal government administered public works programs for several million people and supplied direct relief to millions more. The earliest of the public works programs was the Civilian Conservation Corps (CCC). Overall, the CCC employed more than 2.5 million boys and young men. In 1935 alone, 500,000 men were living in CCC camps. They planted trees, built dams, fought fires, stocked fish, built lookout towers, dug ditches and canals, strung telephone lines, and built and improved bridges, roads, and trails. Their contribution to conservation was enormous; the CCC was responsible for more than half of all the forest planted in the United States up to the 1960s.[35]

The Civil Works Administration (CWA) was much larger and broader in scope. Established in November 1933, it employed 4.1 million by the third week of January 1934.[36] In a few months, it employed almost a third of the unemployed labor force. Although the CWA lasted for less than a year—Roosevelt ended it in the spring of 1934 because he thought it was too costly—it enabled many families to survive the bitter winter of 1934. The CWA was "immensely popular—with merchants, with local officials, and with workers," and its demise was resisted in Congress.[37] The Public Works Administration (PWA) enjoyed a longer run, and its impact was more lasting. In six years, from 1933 to 1939, the PWA built 70 percent of the new school buildings in the nation and 35 percent of the hospitals and public health facilities.[38]

The Federal Emergency Relief Act (FERA), signed into law on May 12, 1933, was never as popular as public works legislation, for it undercut the cherished principles of work and independence by making relief money directly available to the destitute. Roosevelt himself viewed the Federal Emergency Relief Administration with distaste, thinking it would sap the moral strength of the poor. Roosevelt constantly sought ways to cut its budget, but the destitution and the civil disorder that prevailed in Roosevelt's first term made the program necessary. In the winter of 1934, 20 million people received FERA funds.[39]

The FERA was treated as an embarrassing necessity. The government's response was understood to be an emergency measure, comparable to helping victims of catastrophes such as floods, earthquakes, and tornadoes. Congressional debate on the FERA received little coverage by the media. When the act was passed on May 9, 1933, the *New York Times* only mentioned it on page 3 in a column listing legislation passed by Congress. When President Roosevelt signed it on May 12, it made page 21 of the *Times* but only in reference to the appointment of the administrator. In a culture that extolled individualism, competition, and hard work, people were uncomfortable with the idea of relief.

Roosevelt often expressed doubts about relief and public works programs. He preferred economic recovery to government spending. But his response to the economic emergency vastly broadened the base of the Democratic Party. Public works and relief created a loyal following among middle- and working-class people who benefited. By the 1936 election, and for decades thereafter, voting in small towns split between the Republicans on the right side of the tracks and the working class and poor on the other. The most reliable new Democratic following, however, could be found in the cities. Urban ethnics, especially if they were union members, learned to vote Democratic. The New Deal programs also broke black voters away from the Republican Party. Before the 1936 election, a prominent black publisher counseled, "My friends, go turn Lincoln's picture to the wall. That debt has been paid in full."[40] In that election, blacks gave Roosevelt 75 percent of their votes, and they have voted heavily for the Democrats ever since.

The Great Depression revolutionized the group composition of the party system in the United States. In addition to their traditional base in the South, the Democrats now claimed solid support among workers, blacks, and the poor in the northern cities, where large numbers of the working class and the poor were concentrated. Additionally, so many people benefited through New Deal programs that the electoral coalition supporting the party broadened sufficiently to ensure the Democrats would become the ascendant national party for some time. In 1936 the Gallup poll found that 59 percent of farmers favored Roosevelt (Agricultural Adjustment Act, Farm Credit Administration, Farm Mortgage Corporation, abolition of the gold standard); 61 percent of white-collar workers (bank regulation, Federal Housing Administration, savings deposit insurance); 80 percent of organized labor (government recognition of collective bargaining, unemployment insurance, work relief); and 68 percent of people under age 25 (Civilian Conservation Corps, National Youth Administration). Among lower-income groups, 76 percent favored Roosevelt, compared with 60 percent of the middle class.[41] By contrast, upper-income groups identified overwhelmingly with the Republican Party, and they do so to this day.

CITIES GAIN A VOICE

The depression years marked a turning point in American politics. Presidential candidates and a large number of senators and House members knew they needed to campaign for the votes of people living in cities. To secure the votes of urban ethnics, they supported the New Deal's initiatives. These links were reinforced by another development: the forging of a direct relationship between the federal government and the cities. Three elements stand out as key factors in this development: (1) a fiscal and social crisis in the cities; (2) indifference by the states; and (3) the forging of an alliance among city officials for the purpose of securing a federal response to their problems.

Even before Roosevelt took office, the cities had exhausted their resources. In the 1920s they had borrowed heavily to finance public improvements and capital construction. They were already seriously in debt when the onset of the depression confronted them with rising unemployment and poverty. Local officials could not avoid seeing the misery and want on their streets. Faced with a manifest emergency, they provided relief funds as rapidly as they could, but it was not enough. Municipal governments simply lacked the financial resources to cope with the emergency.

During the 1920s counties and municipalities financed a multitude of new public improvement programs. The government activity represented a response to the automobile, to middle-class demands for improved public education, and to public demands for parks and recreational facilities. The auto imposed heavy new costs on local governments. Cities invested in traffic signals, police cars, garbage trucks, school buses, snowplows, roads, and bus and airline terminals. The cities increased spending for education, built new school buildings and public libraries, and invested heavily in improving parks and recreational facilities.

Local governments made heavier investments in these areas than did either the state or the federal governments. During the 1920s counties and municipalities spent 55 to 60 percent of all public funds in the nation, and their total debts mounted to $9 billion.[42] From 1923 to 1927, while the states increased expenditures by 43 percent, spending by the largest 145 cities rose by 79 percent, and cities of 100,000 or more increased their budgets by 82 percent.[43] In these latter cities expenditures for work relief and welfare shot up by 391 percent from 1923 to 1932; during the same period, states increased their relief and welfare budgets by only 63 percent. In the last year of the Hoover administration, the 13 cities with populations above 100,000 spent $53 million more than all the states combined for public welfare. Federal grants as a percentage of all public expenditures actually declined from 2 to 1.3 percent over the decade of the 1920s.[44] The 13 biggest cities incurred 50 percent more debt in the 1920s, and many of them were hard pressed, even at the beginning of the depression, to pay for government services and public improvements.[45]

The depression placed unprecedented responsibilities on city officials at the very time that fiscal resources were drying up. Cities were unable to increase tax revenues to keep pace with their additional responsibilities. Two-thirds of the revenue for city budgets came from property taxes. As property values plummeted, property tax revenues fell by 20 percent from 1929 to 1933.[46] At the same time, the rate of tax delinquency increased from 10 to 26 percent in cities of over 50,000 in population.[47] Between 1931 and 1933, tax losses resulted in a reduction in the budgets of the largest 13 cities from $1.8 to $1.6 billion.[48] State-imposed debt limitations did not allow cities to borrow for day-to-day services. Cities were allowed, in principle, to borrow for capital improvements, but this option soon evaporated. By 1932, because of their high debt loads, cities found it impossible to sell long-term bond issues to investors. In 1932 and 1933, many states and municipalities, including Mississippi, Montana, Buffalo, Philadelphia, Cleveland, and Toledo, were unable to market any bond issues at all.[49] Temporary loans with high interest rates replaced long-term notes.

When the cities financed public works programs to help the unemployed, their budgets quickly ran dry. Municipal governments lacked sufficient resources to treat the depression's symptoms, yet many mayors saw this as their principal mission. Detroit's experience revealed the impossibility of the task. In the fall of 1930, Frank Murphy won a surprise victory in a special mayoral election on a campaign promising unemployment relief.[50] His efforts to provide relief by expanding public jobs and welfare in Detroit attracted national attention. He appointed an unemployment committee, operated an employment bureau, sponsored public works projects, raised private donations for poor relief, and consulted with private firms about rehiring workers. Detroit did more than any other city for its unemployed, but its compassion was costly. With over 40,000 families receiving relief and one-third of the workforce unemployed, it was spending $2 million a month for relief in 1931, far more than second-place Boston.[51]

The burden soon brought financial disaster to the city, and by the spring of 1931, Detroit faced municipal bankruptcy. To avoid default on its debts and payroll, Murphy curtailed the city's health and recreational services and slashed the fire and police department budgets. Only an emergency bank loan allowed Murphy to meet the June 1931 payroll, but even this measure was insufficient. Under pressure from the New York banks that held most of Detroit's bonds, Murphy was forced to cut relief expenditures in half during 1932. Thousands of families were dropped from the relief rolls as it became obvious that Detroit could not single-handedly solve the local problems caused by a national economic calamity.

The mayors of other cities were learning the same lesson. Finally, their sense of desperation galvanized them to take action. In the spring of 1932, Murphy invited the mayors of the major cities to a conference. In June, representatives from 29 cities met in Detroit with a single purpose in mind. Murphy stated the cities' case succinctly: "We have done everything humanly possible to do, and it has not been enough. The hour is at hand for the federal government to cooperate."[52] New York City's mayor likewise pleaded for assistance:

> The municipal government is the maternal, the intimate side of government; the side with heart. The Federal Government doesn't have to wander through darkened hallways of our hospitals, to witness the pain and suffering there. It doesn't have to stand in the bread lines, but the time has come when it must face the facts and its responsibility.
>
> We of the cities have diagnosed and thus far met the problem; but we have come to the end of our resources. It is now up to the Federal Government to assume its share. We can't cure conditions by ourselves.[53]

The mayors' demands for federal assistance marked a turning point in federal–local relations. Historically, there had been no direct relationship between cities and the federal government. Many local officials felt it was illegitimate to ask the federal government for help, and others feared any aid, thinking it might cause their cities to lose their independence. Only a few months before, most of the mayors had declined to attend a similar mayors' conference suggested by the mayor of Milwaukee.[54] Desperation finally brought about a change of heart.

The situation was made worse by the fact that state governments refused to respond to the cities' plight. While municipal governments' expenditures for jobs and relief skyrocketed, the states sharply cut back; "As tax revenues dwindled and unemployment increased, economy in government became a magic word."[55] Beginning in 1932, several states slashed their budgets: Arizona by 35 percent; Texas, Illinois, and Vermont by 25 percent; South Carolina by 33 percent. As state tax revenues declined, public works and construction programs were curtailed. In 1928 the states had spent $1.35 billion for public works projects, mainly in the form of road building, but this amount was reduced to $630 million by 1932 and to $290 million for the first eight months of 1933.[56] Per capita spending for highways and education fell only slightly from 1927 to 1932,[57] but in some states budgets were cut drastically. Tennessee, for example, failed to provide funds for its rural schools for much of 1931.[58] State educational institutions, especially universities, were hard hit. During 1933 education budgets dropped by 40 percent in Maryland, 53 percent in Wyoming, and more than 30 percent in several other states.[59] All of these cutbacks reduced public payroll and thus aggravated the unemployment crisis.

Relief spending by the states went up in the early years of the depression, from $1.00 per capita in 1927 to $3.50 four years later.[60] But the overall amount of welfare spending was small and failed to come close to what was needed. The overall statistics, in any case, masked a tremendous variation among the states. From mid-1931 to the end of 1932, welfare spending by the states increased from $500,000 to $100 million, but almost all of the money was provided by a few states, principally New York, New Jersey, and Pennsylvania. When the New Deal began, only eight states provided any money at all for relief.[61]

Local officials petitioned the states for help, and their pleas sounded increasingly desperate as the depression wore on.[62] Except for the very few states that provided relief payments to the unemployed, no response was forthcoming. State governments were slow to respond to the needs of their cities because rural representatives controlled their legislatures. In state after state, legislative districts were drawn up to ensure that rural counties would outvote cities in the state legislative chambers. In Georgia, each county was represented equally in the legislature, regardless of its population.[63] Louisiana likewise provided that each parish would have at least one representative in the state senate and house. Rhode Island applied this standard to each town.[64] Without exception, all the states made sure representatives from rural areas would continue to hold legislative majorities, no matter how much a state's population became concentrated in the cities.

There were important political stakes in this pattern of underrepresentation. If cities were allowed to gain majorities in legislatures because of their growing populations, political alignments and party structures would fundamentally change. Incumbent rural legislators would lose their positions, and a shift in legislative power would inevitably result in new governmental policies. The persistent underrepresentation of urban areas resulted in indifference to urban problems. Traffic congestion, slums, inadequate park space, and smoke pollution did not interest rural and small-town legislators. Governors, too, tended to be insensitive to urban problems. Governors' and legislators' national conferences studiously ignored the depression. At the 1930 governors' conference in Salt Lake City, for example, the major topics of discussion included such items as the essentials of a model state constitution, the need for constitutional revisions, constitutional versus legislative home rule for cities, and the extent of legislative control of city governments.[65] The 1931 conference likewise ignored the economic crisis. In the face of such indifference, the cities had nowhere to go but to the federal government.

Urban leaders could not necessarily expect a favorable response from the federal government either. Conditions in many rural areas were even worse than in the cities. Grinding poverty was pervasive in the Appalachian region and throughout the South; families lived in one-room hovels, children walked around with bellies distended by malnutrition, and some parents could not afford to clothe their children to send them to school. A drought from the Midwest to the Rockies turned much of the Plains into a vast dust bowl; in the winter of 1934, New England's snow turned red from the huge billowing clouds of dust blowing from Texas, Kansas, and Oklahoma. Families left the ravaged land by the thousands. The experiences of those heading for California provided the grist for John Steinbeck's moving novel *The Grapes of Wrath*.

In addition to the compelling need in rural areas, Roosevelt and his advisers distrusted city politics and culture. Roosevelt's first public works program, the Civilian Conservation Corps, was based on his feeling that the moral character of unemployed youth in the cities would be improved by living in the country.[66] Roosevelt felt "small love for the city."[67] One of the president's closest advisers confessed that "since my graduate school days, I have always been able to excite myself more about the wrongs of farmers than those of urban workers."[68] In its first two years, the New Deal accomplished a comprehensive farm policy of guaranteed price supports, crop allotments to reduce supplies and increase prices, and federally guaranteed mortgages. By contrast, in 1937 it produced its first program specifically for the cities. The Public Housing Act (also called the Wagner-Steagall Public Housing Act after the names of its legislative sponsors) provided slum clearance and public housing on a very limited scale.

Despite the initial indifference to the plight of the cities, city officials succeeded in forging productive relationships with politicians and administrators in Washington, D.C. The New Deal's first relief and recovery programs were administered through the states, but federal programs were later enacted that put local officials in charge. Federal officials administered the three largest public works programs—the Public Works Administration, Civilian Works Administration, and the Works Progress Administration—in cooperation with both state and local officials. The Federal Emergency Relief funds were channeled through the states, but local relief agencies actually administered the funds. In several cities, such as New York, Pittsburgh, and Kansas City, local Democratic machines found that the new federal resources allowed them to rebuild their strength.[69] Local officials found themselves testifying to congressional committees about programs that affected the cities. By 1934 a southern mayor observed, "Mayors are a familiar sight in Washington these days. Whether we like it or not, the destinies of our cities are clearly tied in with national politics."[70]

THE URBAN PROGRAMS OF THE NEW DEAL

The first hint of any national concern about the problems of urban America came in 1892, when Congress appropriated $20,000 to investigate slum conditions in cities with more than 200,000 people.[71] In his subsequent report to the Congress, the commissioner of labor noted, among other observations, that all of the nation's big cities contained block after block of rundown tenement districts that packed immigrants together into often unsafe and unsanitary conditions. The commissioner made much of the fact that these areas had a higher incidence of arrests and saloons than anywhere else in the country. In effect, the report amounted to a moral condemnation of city life.

Federal assistance for the construction of urban housing can be traced to the entry of the United States into World War I. In 1918 Congress authorized direct federal loans to local realty companies.[72] At a cost of $69.3 million, 8 hotels, 19 dormitories, 1,100 apartment units, and approximately 9,000 houses were constructed to house wartime shipyard workers in 27 cities and towns.[73] Later in the same year, Congress approved the nation's first public housing program, designed to accommodate defense plant workers who needed housing near wartime factories. The U.S. Housing Corporation was created to manage the program. In the brief three months of the program's existence, the Housing Corporation built about 6,000 single-family dwellings, plus accommodations for 7,200 single men, on 140 project sites scattered around the country.[74] At the conclusion of the war, all of these federally owned housing units were sold to private owners, and in this way the government removed itself from the housing business.

The first significant federal intervention into housing came during the Great Depression. Even after the prosperous 1920s, all the nation's cities contained rundown business districts and residential slums. As the depression wore on, the situation deteriorated; landlords and owners invested little or no money in repairs and renovation, and the construction of new housing slowed to a crawl. The solutions to the problems of housing and slums lay beyond the financial capacity of local governments. The slums that plagued the nation's cities slowly became defined as a national problem, and local officials and business elites who were concerned about deteriorating business and residential districts looked to the national government for help.

In 1932, the last year of Herbert Hoover's presidency, Congress created the Reconstruction Finance Corporation (RFC) and authorized it to extend loans to private developers for the construction of low-income housing in slum areas.[75] Only two projects were actually ever undertaken, with over 98 percent of the money spent in three slum blocks of Manhattan to construct Knickerbocker Village, with its 1,573 apartments.[76] This program had two contradictory purposes. On the one hand, it was supposed to help revive the construction industry; on the other hand, it was supposed to increase the supply of low-income housing in New York. In the case of Knickerbocker Village, the first goal won out. Eighty-two percent of the slum families who initially moved into the apartments were soon forced to move back to the slums they had left because of the escalating rents charged by the owners.[77]

Franklin D. Roosevelt introduced a long list of national programs designed to stimulate the economy and end the depression. One of the first of these, the National Industrial Recovery Act of 1933, included a minor provision authorizing "construction, reconstruction, alteration, or repair, under public regulation or control, of low-rent housing and slum clearance projects."[78] The Housing Division of the Public Works Administration (PWA) was charged with implementing this provision. At first, the PWA tried to entice private developers into constructing low-income housing by offering them low-interest federal loans. This strategy conformed with one of the major purposes of the program, which was "to deal with the unemployment situation by giving employment to workers . . . [and] to demonstrate to private builders the practicability of large-scale community planning."[79] But contractors and home builders did not find low-interest loans sufficiently attractive, and only seven projects ever met specifications and were approved. As a result, the PWA decided to bypass the housing industry altogether and finance and construct its own federally owned housing. The U.S. Emergency Housing Corporation was created for this purpose in 1933, and it claimed the right of eminent domain to force the owners of slum property to sell so that the land could be prepared for construction.

Federal court decisions in Kentucky and Michigan stopped federal administrators from using eminent domain to take over slum land for clearance,[80] so they tried another tack. The Emergency Housing Corporation decided to make low-income housing grants to local public housing authorities. States could legally charter local authorities, and previous court cases made it clear that the states could use eminent domain to accomplish a variety of public purposes. With the offer of federal money dangled before them, city officials lobbied their state legislatures to allow them to create local housing authorities to receive the funds. In 1937, by the end of the PWA public housing program, 29 states had passed enabling legislation allowing local governments to create and operate local public housing authorities, and 46 local housing agencies had come into existence.[81] These authorities built almost 22,000 public low-income housing units in 37 cities.[82]

For all the effort to get the PWA program off the ground, the eventual results were mixed, at best. More low-income units were torn down through slum clearance than were ever built. Local public housing authorities were closely tied to the housing industry in their communities, with the result that a substantial proportion of PWA funds was used to help owners sell their properties at inflated prices.[83] These properties were then slated for clearance, even though no new housing units were planned to replace them. In all these respects, the PWA experience provided a warning for the future: Program goals were easily subverted if local communities were allowed to make all of the consequential decisions. Unfortunately, the warning was ignored.

The PWA experience provided the administrative model for future housing programs. It was accepted that if federal grants were made available for public housing in the future, local public housing agencies would become the recipients of the funds and federal agencies would not try to build public housing units themselves. The Public Housing Act of 1937 replaced the PWA program. The act was based on the principle that housing programs would be implemented through federal grants-in-aid to local housing authorities. Under the legislation, public housing would be built and administered by local agencies, not by the federal government, and real estate agents and contractors would handle land sales and construction. Its stated purposes were:

> To provide financial assistance to the states and political subdivisions thereof for the elimination of unsafe and unsanitary housing conditions, for the eradication of slums, for the provision of decent, safe, and sanitary dwellings for families of low-income and for the reduction of unemployment and the stimulation of business activity, to create a United States Housing Authority, and for other purposes.[84]

The Public Housing Act of 1937 was "designed to serve the needs of low-income families who otherwise would be unable to afford decent, safe, and sanitary dwellings."[85] The absence of substantial profits for real estate agents, builders, and banks for constructing public housing projects, however, meant that they steadfastly opposed the program. As far as they were concerned, government-owned housing competed with the private housing market, and its only redeeming virtue was that public housing provided jobs in the construction industry. But this benefit failed to outweigh the unpopularity of providing housing subsidies to the bottom third of the population. As explained by the president of the National Association of Real Estate Boards, the housing industry's philosophy was that low-income housing should become available through a filter-down process:

> Housing should remain a matter of private enterprise and private ownership. It is contrary to the genius of the American people and the ideals they have established that government become landlord to its citizens. There is a sound logic in the continuance of the practice under which those who have the initiative and the will to save acquire better living facilities and yield their former quarters at modest rents to the group below.[86]

Senator Robert F. Wagner of New York, one of the cosponsors of the 1937 housing bill, defended the legislation by pointing out it was not intended as a program that would interfere with the private housing market:

> The object of public housing, in a nutshell, is not to invade the field of home building for the middle class or the well-to-do which has been the only profitable area for private enterprise in the past. Nor is it even to exclude private enterprise from major participation in a low-cost housing program. It is merely to supplement what private industry will do, by subsidies which will make up the difference between what the poor can afford to pay and what is necessary to assure decent living quarters.[87]

To make sure middle-class families could not opt out of the private housing market by moving into public housing, the legislation contained specific limitations on the costs and quality of rental units and a restriction that occupancy be strictly limited to low-income families. A requirement was also added that the number of new housing units constructed could not exceed the number of slum dwellings torn down.[88]

The 1937 act authorized the U.S. Housing Administration (USHA) to extend low-interest loans to local public housing agencies. The loans could cover up to 100 percent of the cost of financing slum clearance and the construction of low-income housing units. The USHA was also authorized to make grants and annual subsidies to local housing agencies for the operation and maintenance of housing units after they were built. The USHA and its successor agencies, the Federal Public Housing Authority (1942–1946) and the Public Housing Administration (1946–the present), completed a total of 169,451 low-income public housing units under the authority of the 1937 housing act.[89]

World War II was the third national emergency (the others were World War I and the Great Depression) that Congress recognized as requiring the production of publicly built and financed housing. In addition to 50,000 units built during the war through the 1937 housing act authorizations, 2 million more housing units were provided through temporary and emergency programs to house workers who streamed into cities to take jobs in defense industry plants. Of these, around a million units were privately built with federal financial assistance.[90] Another million units were completed under programs that left ownership in the hands of the federal government. As soon as the war was over, these government-owned units were sold on the private market.

THE NEW DEAL LEGACY

The New Deal transformed American politics. Local officials learned to petition the federal government for help. This learning process took two forms. First, it became legitimate to seek federal assistance. Second, local officials formed an enduring urban lobby organized specifically to represent cities in the federal system. Through the United States Conference of Mayors (USCM), formed in 1932, mayors met annually to discuss their mutual problems. The USCM financed a permanent office in Washington to lobby for urban programs. Together with the International City Management Association (now the International City and County Management Association), the National Municipal League, the American Municipal League, and other organizations representing local public officials, cities developed the capacity to lobby federal administrators, Congress, and the White House.

The nation's first urban programs were implemented because of the newfound capacity to bring political pressure to bear on Washington. Through the 1937 Housing Act, the federal government undertook slum clearance and built public housing. In the late 1930s, federal policy makers expressed a concern about urban problems. The National Resources Committee, composed of federal administrators and experts appointed by the president, published a report in 1937 titled *Our Cities: Their Role in the National Economy.*[91] The committee asserted that slums and urban blight threatened a hoped-for economic recovery and recommended federal action to improve the economic performance of cities. In 1941 the National Resources Planning Board prepared a report titled *Action for Cities: A Guide for Community Planning.* The report recommended that cities devise local plans to combat blight and the federal government provide assistance for this purpose.[92] In 1944 a federally assisted highways bill was enacted; unlike previous highway legislation, this time the cities got their fair share of construction money. Five years later, in 1949, Congress passed a massive program to build public housing and clear slums in the inner cities.

Between 1953 and 1961, when a Republican president, Dwight Eisenhower, served in the White House, urban interests were able to push through only one significant new program, the Interstate Highway Act of 1956, and only because nonurban interests wanted it too. From 1959 to 1961, President Eisenhower even eliminated public housing requests from the federal budget. But in the wake of the election of John F. Kennedy in 1960, the urban lobby found a receptive environment, and it did not take long for them to exploit it. The New Deal experience had convinced city officials they had a right to lobby for their interests in Washington. Democrats in the White House and the Congress would ignore the concerns of the urban lobby, and the voters they spoke for, at their peril.

NOTES

1. Samuel J. Eldersveld, "The Influence of Metropolitan Party Pluralities in Presidential Elections Since 1920: A Study of Twelve Key Cities," *American Political Science Review* 43, no. 6 (December 1949): 1200.
2. W. B. Munro, *The Government of American Cities* (New York: Macmillan, 1913), p. 27.
3. In the first significant suburban movement of the twentieth century, which lasted from the late 1890s to about 1914 (the outbreak of World War I), the rate of growth in the suburbs exceeded the rate of growth in many central cities, but the total population gains in those cities were much larger than the population gains in suburbs. Growth rates can be deceptive when expressed as percentage increases on a small original population base.
4. William E. Leuchtenburg, *The Perils of Prosperity, 1914–1932* (Chicago: University of Chicago Press, 1958), pp. 213–214.
5. Robert K. Murray, *The 103rd Ballot: Democrats and the Disaster in Madison Square Garden* (New York: Harper & Row, 1976), p. 9.
6. Kenneth T. Jackson, *The Ku Klux Klan in the City, 1915–1930* (New York: Oxford University Press, 1967).
7. Murray, *The 103rd Ballot,* p. 7.
8. Ibid.
9. Kenneth Finegold, *Experts and Politicians: Reform Challenges to Machine Politics in New York, Cleveland, and Chicago* (Princeton, N.J.: Princeton University Press, 1995), p. 174.
10. Ibid., p. 103.
11. For good accounts of the 1924 convention, see Murray, *The 103rd Ballot;* Edmund A. Moore, *A Catholic Runs for President: The Campaign of 1928* (New York: Ronald Press, 1956); and Arthur M. Schlesinger Jr., *The Crisis of the Old Order, 1919–1933* (Boston: Houghton Mifflin, 1956).
12. John D. Hicks, *Republican Ascendancy, 1921–1933* (New York: Harper, 1960), p. 212.
13. John Kenneth Galbraith, *The Great Crash, 1929,* rev. ed. (Boston: Houghton Mifflin, 1979; first published in 1961), p. 99.

14. Lester V. Chandler, *America's Greatest Depression, 1929–1941* (New York: HarperCollins, 1970), p. 5.
15. Ibid.
16. Ibid., p. 35.
17. William E. Leuchtenburg, *Franklin D. Roosevelt and the New Deal, 1932–1940* (New York: Harper & Row, 1963), p. 19.
18. Ibid., p. 1.
19. Chandler, *America's Greatest Depression*, p. 19.
20. Ibid., p. 57.
21. Arthur M. Schlesinger Jr., *The Coming of the New Deal* (Boston: Houghton Mifflin, 1957), p. 3.
22. Leuchtenburg, *Franklin D. Roosevelt*, p. 18.
23. Most relief was given by local public and private agencies. Although many states had programs for relief to designated categories of people—dependent children, people who are blind or disabled—few of these were actually funded.
24. Arthur E. Burns and Edward A. Williams, *Federal Work, Security, and Relief Programs* (New York: Da Capo Press, 1971), pp. 1–2; first published as *Research Monograph 24* (Washington, D.C.: Works Progress Administration, Division of Social Research, 1941).
25. James T. Patterson, *The New Deal and the States: Federalism in Transition* (Princeton, N.J.: Princeton University Press, 1969), p. 30.
26. Ibid., p. 15.
27. Ibid.
28. Mark I. Gelfand, *A Nation of Cities: The Federal Government and Urban America, 1933–1965,* Urban Life in America Series (New York: Oxford University Press, 1975), p. 35.
29. Leuchtenburg, *Franklin D. Roosevelt*, p. 11.
30. Inauguration Day was changed to January by the Twentieth Amendment to the Constitution, ratified in 1933.
31. Leuchtenburg, *Franklin D. Roosevelt*, p. 39.
32. Ibid.
33. Ibid., p. 40.
34. For a thorough account of New Deal programs, see Burns and Williams, *Federal Work*.
35. Leuchtenburg, *Franklin D. Roosevelt*, p. 174.
36. Burns and Williams, *Federal Work*, pp. 29–36.
37. Leuchtenburg, *Franklin D. Roosevelt*, pp. 122–123.
38. Ibid., p. 133.
39. Josephine Chapin Brown, *Public Relief, 1929–1939* (New York: Holt, Rinehart & Winston, 1940), p. 249.
40. Quoted in William E. Binkley, *American Political Parties: Their Natural History* (New York: Knopf, 1943), p. 284.
41. Ibid., pp. 380–381.
42. Patterson, *The New Deal and the States*, p. 26.
43. Calculated from James A. Maxwell, *Federal Grants and the Business Cycle* (New York: National Bureau of Economic Research, 1952), p. 23, Table 7.
44. Ibid.
45. Gelfand, *A Nation of Cities*, p. 49.
46. U.S. Department of Commerce, Bureau of the Census, *Historical Statistics on State and Local Government Revenues, 1902–1953* (Washington, D.C.: U.S. Government Printing Office, 1955), p. 12.
47. Maxwell, *Federal Grants and the Business Cycle*, p. 27, Table 11.
48. Ibid., p. 24, Table 8.
49. Ibid., p. 29.
50. Gelfand, *A Nation of Cities*, p. 31.
51. Ibid., p. 32.
52. Ibid., p. 36.

53. Ibid.

54. Ibid., p. 34.

55. Patterson, *The New Deal and the States,* p. 39.

56. Ibid., p. 40.

57. Ibid.

58. Ibid., p. 44.

59. Ibid., p. 47.

60. Ibid., p. 40.

61. Brown, *Public Relief,* pp. 72–96.

62. George C. S. Benson, *The New Centralization: A Study in Intergovernmental Relationships in the United States* (New York: Holt, Rinehart & Winston, 1941), pp. 104–105.

63. Robert G. Dixon Jr., *Democratic Representation: Reapportionment in Law and Politics* (New York: Oxford University Press, 1968), p. 174.

64. Ibid., pp. 71–75, 80, 86–87.

65. Patterson, *The New Deal and the States,* p. 45.

66. Leuchtenburg, *Franklin D. Roosevelt,* p. 52.

67. Ibid., p. 136.

68. Guy Rexford Tugwell, quoted in ibid., p. 35.

69. Finegold, *Experts and Politicians,* p. 12; Bruce M. Stave, *The New Deal and the Last Hurrah: Pittsburgh Machine Politics* (Pittsburgh: University of Pittsburgh Press, 1970); Lyle W. Dorsett, *Franklin D. Roosevelt and the City Bosses* (Port Washington, N.Y.: Kennikat, 1977); Dorsett, *The Pendergast Machine* (New York: Oxford University Press, 1968).

70. Quoted in Gelfand, *A Nation of Cities,* p. 66.

71. Public Law 65–102, 65th Cong. (1918); refer to Congressional Quarterly Service, *Housing a Nation* (Washington, D.C.: author), p. 166; Edith and Elmer Wood, *Recent Trends in American Housing* (New York: Macmillan, 1931), p. 79.

72. Congressional Quarterly Service, *Housing a Nation,* pp. xiii.

73. Joint Resolution 52–22, 52d Cong. (1892); refer also to U.S. Congress, House, *Your Congress and American Housing—The Actions of Congress on Housing,* 82d Cong., 2d sess., 1952, H. Doc. 82–532, p. 1.

74. Public Laws 65–149 and 65–164, 65th Cong. (1918); refer also to Twentieth Century Fund, *Housing for Defense* (New York: Twentieth Century Fund, 1940), pp. 156–157; Congressional Quarterly Service, *Housing a Nation,* p. 18.

75. Refer to the Emergency Relief and Reconstruction Act, Public Law 72–302, 72d Cong. (1932).

76. The only other loan made under this authorization was $155,000 for rural housing in Ford County, Kansas.

77. Edwin L. Scanton, "Public Housing Trends in New York City" (Ph.D. diss., Graduate School of Banking, Rutgers University, 1952), p. 5.

78. Public Law 73–67, 72d Cong. (1933).

79. From a statement by Harold L. Ickes, Secretary of Interior and Public Works Administrator, quoted in Bert Swanson, "The Public Policy of Urban Renewal: Its Goals, Trends, and Conditions in New York City," paper delivered at the American Political Science Association Meeting, New York, September 1963, p. 10.

80. *U.S. v. Certain Lands in City of Louisville,* Jefferson County, Ky., et al., 78 F.2d 64 (1935); *U.S. v. Certain Lands in City of Detroit* et al., 12 F.Supp. 345 (1935).

81. Refer to Glen H. Boyer, *Housing: A Factual Analysis* (New York: Macmillan, 1958), p. 247.

82. Richard D. Bingham, *Public Housing and Urban Renewal: An Analysis of Federal-Local Relations,* Praeger Special Studies in U.S. Economics, Social, and Political Issues (New York: Praeger, 1975), p. 30.

83. Nathaniel S. Keith, *Politics and the Housing Crisis Since 1930* (New York: Universe Books, 1973), p. 29.

84. Public Law 75–412, 75th Cong. (1937). Also found in U.S. Congress, House Committee on Banking and Currency, *Basic Laws and Authorizations on Urban Housing,* 91st Cong., 1st sess., 1969, p. 225.

85. Roscoe Martin, "The Expended Partnership," in *The New Urban Politics: Cities and the Federal Government,* ed. Douglas Fox (Pacific Palisades, Calif.: Goodyear, 1972), p. 51.

86. Keith, *Politics and the Housing Crisis,* p. 33.

87. Speech delivered before the Fourth Annual Meeting of the National Public Housing Conference, New York, December 1935, cited in ibid., pp. 32–33.

88. The restriction limiting participation to low-income families, seen from a comparative perspective, is a root cause of the failure of public housing in America. See Arnold J. Heidenheimer, Hugh Heclo, and Carolyn Teich Adams, *Comparative Public Policy: The Politics of Social Choice in Europe and America* (New York: St. Martin's Press, 1975), pp. 69–96.

89. Public Law 76–671, 76th Cong. (1940), relating to defense housing needs; Public Law 80–301, 80th Cong. (1946), suspended cost limitations for some low-income housing projects.

90. U.S. Housing and Home Finance Agency, *Fourteenth Annual Report* (Washington, D.C.: U.S. Government Printing Office, 1961), p. 380.

91. U.S. Department of the Interior, National Resources Committee, Urbanism Committee, *Our Cities: Their Role in the National Economy* (Washington, D.C.: U.S. Government Printing Office, 1937).

92. Philip J. Funigiello, "City Planning in World War II: The Experience of the National Resources Planning Board," *Social Science Quarterly* 53 (June 1972): 91–104.

PART II

THE URBAN CRISIS
OF THE TWENTIETH
CENTURY

THE CITY–SUBURBAN DIVIDE

A CENTURY OF DEMOGRAPHIC CHANGE

The movement of millions of white affluent families from the central cities to low-density suburbs constitutes one of the "great population migrations in American history"[1] (another author used similar words to describe the post–World War II exodus of blacks from the South to northern cities).[2] It did not take long for these side-by-side streams to create a sharp divide between the central cities and the suburbs. A new phrase, "the urban crisis," was coined as a way of referring to stark images of "the black ghetto," which stood out in bold relief when juxtaposed against a powerful cultural stereotype: the American dream in the suburbs. Although the actual residential patterns were more complex than this portrait in black and white, the contrasting images accurately captured a fundamental fact: Racial segregation, which had always been present in American social life, had become the transcendent issue in national politics and culture, in the North as well as in the South. Although the era of the urban crisis appears to be passing, many of its effects continue to ripple through the American political system.

All through the twentieth century, as in the previous one, the cities served as magnets for people escaping oppression and poverty and searching for jobs and opportunity. Before and again after the Great Depression of the 1930s, blacks left the South by the millions and poured into the cities of the North, Mexicans made their way to cities of the Southwest, and poverty-stricken white families fled depressed rural areas for industrial cities. After World War II, these population movements accelerated. Mexican immigration increased. White families trying to escape the grinding poverty of Appalachia and other pockets of rural poverty headed for the cities. In the same years African Americans headed for the industrial cities of the North. Between 1940 and 1970, 5 million blacks moved from the South to northern cities.

At the same time, middle-class white families were fleeing the cities to low-density, single-family homes in suburban subdivisions. In the 1920s, for the first time in the nation's history, the suburbs had grown faster than the central cities.[3] After a brief pause in the years of the Great Depression, the suburban movement turned into a stampede. By the 1970 census, for the first time, more Americans lived in suburbs than in either rural areas or the central cities of metropolitan areas. All through the 1980s and 1990s, suburban population continued to sprawl in ever-widening arcs around the urban core.

The movements into and out of the cities created an almost unbridgeable social chasm. Americans became accustomed to thinking in dichotomies—city–suburban, black–white, ghetto–subdivision, poor–affluent—and these habits of thought consistently cast cities in a dismal light.[4] The rapidly growing suburbs became identified, in the popular imagination, with tranquil subdivisions with cul-de-sacs and green expanses of lawn; at the same time, images of race, poverty, crime, and slums came to symbolize the inner cities. By the 1970s stories of murder, mayhem, and drugs in inner-city neighborhoods became the way that local news stations kept their ratings up. For suburban residents, crime became a signifier of the inner city and the people who lived there.[5]

Since the mid-1980s, the United States has been experiencing still another demographic transformation. Millions of immigrants have been making their way to the United States from countries all over the world. But unlike any previous period, many are bypassing the cities and going directly to the suburbs. In the process they are transforming urban politics in unexpected ways. The tensions of urban society are no longer located primarily in central cities; instead, they are spread throughout metropolitan areas. Urban politics has become increasingly complex because ethnic and racial groups are jostling for political influence. As of 2004, the 37.5 million Latinos almost equaled the 41.3 million African Americans in the United States, and another 10 percent of the population were immigrants or their children.[6] By midcentury, Latinos are expected to outnumber blacks by more than two to one.[7] Already, these trends are causing profound social and political changes. Within urban areas, the city–suburban dichotomy is rapidly being replaced by metropolitan areas fractured into a complex racial and ethnic mosaic. The political landscape of cities and suburbs is becoming as complex as this new metropolitan geography.

STREAMS OF MIGRATION

Three periods of migration and immigration created the crisis of segregation, race, and poverty that beset America's cities in the twentieth century.[8] As shown in Table 6.1, the first wave crested in the two decades before the Great Depression. Between 1910 and 1930, some 700,000 Mexicans moved into Texas, New Mexico, Arizona, and California, and more than a million blacks left the southern states for Chicago, Detroit, Cleveland, New York City, Pittsburgh, Philadelphia, and other cities of the industrial Midwest and Northeast. The second, bigger wave washed over the cities during World War II and did not ebb until the late 1960s. From 1940 to 1970, up to 5 million blacks and 700,000 Mexicans moved into America's inner cities. During this same period, more than a million and a half impoverished whites also streamed into the cities, although their migration received little attention.

Table 6.1   Rural to Urban Migrant Streams in Twentieth-Century America

Migrant Group	Principal Migration Period	Approximate Number of Migrants[a]	Origin	Destination
Appalachian whites	1940–1970	1,600,000	Southern Appalachian Mountains (Kentucky and West Virginia)	North central states
Mexicans	1910–1930	700,000	Mesa Central primarily, also Mesa del Norte	Texas and south-western states
	1950–1970	700,000	Mesa Central primarily, also Mesa del Norte	Texas and California
Blacks	1910–1930	1,250,000[b]	Mississippi delta, Atlantic black belt, coastal plain	Illinois, Ohio, Michigan, New York, and Pennsylvania
	1940–1970	5,000,000[b]	Mississippi delta, Atlantic black belt, coastal plain	Cities everywhere

[a]These figures are approximate. The data for the Mexican migration, for example, are obscured by contract labor, two-way migration, and illegal entrants.

[b]U.S. Bureau of the Census, *Historical Statistics of the United States: Colonial Times to 1970* (Washington, D.C.: U.S. Government Printing Office, 2002). Greenberg's original table lists 1 million blacks, 1910–1930, and 3.5 million blacks, 1940–1965.

Source: Adapted from Stanley B. Greenberg, *Politics and Poverty: Modernization and Response in Five Poor Neighborhoods* (New York: Wiley, 1974), p. 19.

Between 1910 and 1926, the bloody and protracted violence of the Mexican Revolution drove Mexicans into the southwestern states. Although the revolution released millions of peasants from their feudal relationship with landholders, it left many of them without a way to make a living. Bloody confrontations between the Mexican government and landowners drove the newly liberated peasants into Texas, Arizona, and California. During World War II and its aftermath, employment opportunities in the southwestern states induced still more Mexicans to cross the border. By 1970, 5.5 million Mexican Americans were living in the American Southwest, accounting for more than 90 percent of all the people of Mexican descent in the United States.[9] By 2000, 17.9 million Mexican Americans were spread out in the South and throughout the western states, about 87 percent of the nation's total.[10] Latino immigrants from several other Latin American countries streamed into the southwestern states in even larger numbers in the 1980s and 1990s, pushed by political repression and poverty and pulled by the availability of jobs.

The decline of the coal industry in the southern Appalachian Mountains and the Cumberland Plateau of Virginia, West Virginia, and Kentucky from the 1930s to the 1960s prompted a massive movement of desperately poor rural white families. The exodus reached such proportions after World War II that some counties in Appalachia

OUTTAKE

IMMIGRANTS ARE MOVING NEARLY EVERYWHERE

Unlike any period in the past, immigrants are now moving nearly everywhere in the United States. It was once assumed, correctly, that most immigrants moved to a few gateway cities, and that this pattern contributed to sharp differences between central cities and suburbs. But suburbs are becoming ethnically diverse. In the 1990s, for example, immigrants from an impressive number of countries moved to the suburbs of Long Island: Japanese, Koreans, Vietnamese, Indians, Pakistanis, and Iranians from Asia, and Guatemalans, Cubans, Haitians, and Salvadorans from the Caribbean and Latin America. Most of these immigrants were poor and unaccustomed to American culture, which caused anxiety among the current residents. One of the complaints was that the newcomers did not conform to the suburban norm of retreating into the shelter of home (presumably with the television as a constant companion). Instead, men gathered on street corners and played music until all hours of the night. This brought street life to the suburbs for the first time but annoyed the residents who drove by. As one resident complained, "Suburbia does not like the idea of people congregating fifteen to twenty of them on suburban street corners, sitting on top of their cars blaring their big radios." Immigrants also sent their children to the local schools, thus breaching the most sacred ground held by those residents who had moved to Long Island to escape signs of the city.

Immigrants are also moving to cities of all sizes and small towns and rural areas in almost every region of the country. Some rural areas have been changed almost overnight as immigrant workers moved near large employers of low-skilled labor, such as meatpacking plants, poultry operations, and agribusinesses devoted to raising livestock or processing agricultural products. Within a few years, Beardstown, Illinois, located in downstate Illinois near the Mississippi River, was transformed from a sleepy hamlet to a town bustling with Mexican immigrants, who were attracted by the jobs in a nearby meat processing plant. Because most of the new immigrants arrived unable to speak English, schools, churches, hospitals, and local businesses were suddenly forced to adapt by employing translators and providing new programs. But for the first time in decades, a renewed prosperity came to the local economy.

However, such massive changes, multiplied in cities and towns across the United States, spawned fear and resentment. Hundreds of measures were introduced into state legislatures to curb and regulate immigration. In 2007, state legislatures considered 1,562 immigration-related measures and enacted 240 of them, a threefold increase over 2006. Among other things, these laws made it a felony for an employer to hire an illegal immigrant, even unknowingly, or for illegal immigrant to hold a job; made it harder for illegal immigrants to get state ID papers or driver's licenses; and barred illegal immigrants from receiving unemployment insurance or other public services. Over the next two years local governments adopted literally thousands of anti-immigrant ordinances, any of them of doubtful legality, and police departments took measures to rid their communities of illegal immigrants—and, critics charged, of all Hispanics. As a pretext for deportation, local police departments targeted Hispanic people they thought might be immigrants by arresting them for minor crimes, or detained Hispanics merely on the suspicion that they may be in the country illegally. If anything, hostility toward immigrants has been further inflamed by the economic crisis that began to unfold in 2008. The nation has not seen this level of anti-immigrant sentiment for almost 100 years, and that period ended in a national legislation intended to drastically reduce immigrant flows.

Sources: Rosalyn Baxandall and Elizabeth Ewen, *Picture Windows: How the Suburbs Happened* (New York: Basic Books, 2000); Dan Anderson, "Times Topics: Immigration and Refuges," *New York Times,* June 9, p. 20 *(http://www.nytimes.com/2008/immig.html).*

were almost depopulated in just a few years. In his moving book, *Night Comes to the Cumberlands*, Harry Caudill describes the abject poverty that forced families and entire communities to pick up and leave their marginal farm plots and shabby towns. Many of the families could trace their roots in Appalachia several generations back. An entire genre of country music—bluegrass—was inspired by homesickness for the hills and hollows left behind. In the 1950s alone, a quarter of the population deserted the Cumberland plateau, settling in cities and towns of Kentucky, Tennessee, Maryland, Virginia, and the industrial belt of the upper Midwest.[11] Joining them were a steady stream of impoverished white families who were leaving the border areas of southern Illinois, Kentucky, and Arkansas. Regardless of where they actually came from, the new migrants were derisively called Hoosiers, Okies, and Arkies.

But the movement of African Americans was much larger and it lasted longer. It constituted "one of the largest and most rapid mass internal movements of people in history—perhaps the greatest not caused by the immediate threat of execution or starvation."[12] From 1910 to 1920, 450,000 blacks moved out of the South, followed by another 750,000 in the 1920s.[13] In the 20 years between 1910 and 1930, about a million blacks—one-tenth of all blacks living in the South—moved to cities in the Northeast and Midwest. In just 20 years, the black population living outside the South shot up by 134 percent, and the proportion of the nation's black population residing in the South dropped from 89 to 79 percent.[14] The depression of the 1930s slowed the northward migration, but it became virtually a flood tide during and after World War II. Between 1940 and 1970, an estimated 5 million blacks left the South.

Like the generations of European immigrants who preceded them, African Americans were pushed by crisis and pulled by opportunity. Poverty and unemployment in the South provided the push, jobs in the North the pull. Beginning in southern Texas in the late 1890s and sweeping eastward through Georgia by 1921, boll weevil infestations wiped out cotton crops, forcing black sharecroppers off the land. In the same period, an abrupt decline in European immigration occasioned by World War I, combined with the rapid expansion of armaments industries, produced labor shortages in the northern industrial cities.

Almost all the African Americans leaving the South left poverty-stricken rural areas and settled into densely packed neighborhoods in northern cities. Only 10 percent of the nation's blacks lived in cities of 100,000 or more in 1910; this percentage increased to 16 percent in 1920 and to 24 percent by 1930.[15] The biggest cities lured most of the migrants. The proportion of blacks living in cities smaller than 100,000 declined from 1910 to 1930, but the proportion increased substantially in cities of over 100,000.[16] Thus the Great Migration, as it came to be labeled by historians, had two principal components: Blacks were becoming northern, and they were becoming urban.

African Americans made up more than 2 percent of the population in only a handful of northern cities in 1910. By 1930, however, they accounted for 18 percent of the population of Gary, Indiana, and 16 percent in East St. Louis, Illinois, with its stockyards, rail yards, and heavy industry. As shown in Table 6.2, in the same two decades black populations had grown by two to three times or more in the big cities. By 1930 percentages ranged from almost 5 percent in New York City to 7 percent in Chicago and 8 percent in Cleveland, to just over 11 percent in St. Louis and Philadelphia.

Table 6.2   Growth of Black Population in Several Cities, 1910–1930

City	Total Population			Percentage Increase		
	1910	1920	1930	1910–1930	1910	1930
New York	91,709	152,467	327,706	257.3%	2%	5%
Chicago	44,103	109,458	233,903	429.3	2	7
Philadelphia	84,459	134,229	219,599	160.0	5.5	11
St. Louis	43,960	69,854	93,580	112.9	6	11
Cleveland	8,448	34,451	71,889	751.0	1.5	8

Source: U.S. Bureau of the Census, *Negroes in the United States, 1920–1932* (Washington, D.C.: U.S. Government Printing Office, 1935), p. 55.

African Americans became concentrated in well-defined ghettos. In north Harlem in New York City, about one-third (36 percent) of the population was African American in 1920, but this proportion increased to 81 percent by the 1930 census.[17]

Three factors prompted the African American exodus: the absence of employment opportunities, the intense poverty of southern agricultural life, and dissatisfaction with the racial caste system in the South. The North was a "promised land" that offered an escape from the violent racism of the South and the opportunity for economic advancement. With the onset of the Great Depression of the 1930s, which brought destitution and unemployment to northern cities as well as to the South, the migration from the farms to the cities slowed abruptly and did not pick up again until after World War II.

Southern blacks began to stream to northern cities and states as a means of escaping the shackles of the southern system of race relations. The migration northward had already commenced when, in May 1917, the publisher of the *Chicago Defender* launched "The Great Northern Drive" to persuade blacks to move. Founded in 1905, by World War I the *Defender* already had reached a circulation of 100,000, and blacks read it avidly throughout the South. The *Defender*'s editorials exhorted blacks to come north to the land of opportunity, where they could find employment and, if not equality, at least an escape from harassment and violence. Its columns of job advertisements added substance to the promised land vision. At the same time, the *Defender* attacked conditions in the South. Lynchings and incidents of discrimination were regularly highlighted in lurid detail. Moving out of the South was portrayed as a way to advance the cause of racial equality for all blacks.[18]

The *Defender* was only one of many voices encouraging African Americans to leave the South. Those who had already moved wrote letters to relatives and friends describing their new life in glowing terms. Despite job and housing discrimination in the North, they found conditions preferable to those they had left behind. Throughout the South, blacks lived under a cloud of terror. From 1882 to 1930, there were 1,663 lynchings in the five states of the Cotton Belt alone—Alabama, Georgia, Louisiana,

Mississippi, and South Carolina—and 1,299 blacks were legally executed.[19] In the ten southern states, more than 2,500 blacks—an average of about one person per week—were lynched between 1880 and 1930.[20] The legal systems of the southern states were so completely rigged that the difference between lynching and legalized murder by police and the courts was not much more than a technicality. Blacks who failed to obey the racial caste system, even inadvertently, could expect immediate retribution in the form of beatings or worse. Failing to step off the sidewalk, forgetting to say "sir" or "ma'am," or looking a white person in the eye could be cause for violent retribution. Lynchings frequently descended into orgies of depravity, the victims slowly tortured to death with blowtorches or other devices, and the mobs carrying off clothing and body parts as souvenirs.[21]

The opportunities for leaving such conditions improved in proportion to labor shortages in northern factories. After war broke out in Europe in 1914, factory owners found themselves with lucrative armaments contracts but too few workers. They sent labor agents into the South with free train tickets in hand, which could be exchanged for a labor agreement. Southern white employers and planters took steps to prevent the exodus of their cheap labor. Magazines, newspapers, and business organizations decried the movement, as in this October 5, 1916, editorial in the Memphis *Commercial Appeal*:

> The enormous demand for labor and the changing conditions brought about by the boll weevil in certain parts of the South have caused an exodus of negroes which may be serious. Great colonies of negroes have gone north to work in factories, in packing houses and on the railroads. . . .
>
> The South needs every able-bodied negro that is now south of the line, and every negro who remains south of the line will in the end do better than he will do in the North. . . .
>
> The negroes who are in the South should be encouraged to remain there, and those white people who are in the boll weevil territory should make every sacrifice to keep their negro labor until there can be adjustments to the new and quickly prosperous conditions that will later exist.[22]

States and communities went to considerable lengths to discourage migration. Jacksonville, Florida, passed an ordinance in 1916 levying heavy fines on unlicensed labor agents from the North. Macon, Georgia, made it impossible for labor agents to get licenses and then outlawed unlicensed agents. The mayor of Atlanta talked to blacks about the "dreadfully cold" northern winters.[23] In some communities, police were sent to railroad stations to harass blacks near the stations, keep them from boarding trains, or even drive them off the trains.

But the promised land beckoned, and the exodus continued. What the new arrivals found was opportunity—but not equal opportunity—and persistent discrimination. Whenever blacks attempted to move into white neighborhoods, they were harassed or violently assaulted. In the workplace, they were the last hired and the first fired. They were kept in the most menial occupations. Job opportunities were limited not only by employers but even more so by labor unions, which generally prohibited blacks from membership. Because the North was more heavily unionized than the South, there were actually fewer opportunities in some occupations, especially for skilled laborers.[24]

In both union and nonunion shops, white workers often refused to work alongside blacks. To avoid trouble, employers assigned blacks to the least desirable jobs.

African Americans found it difficult to adjust to urban life. Hardly any of them had previously lived in a city. Many had never even participated directly in the cash economy. Sharecroppers had often worked under contracts with provisions that they buy only from the planters' stores and then with scrip and credit rather than cash. Some of them had never seen U.S. currency. As was the case with previous immigrant groups, they were often cheated and overcharged.

These conditions, when amplified by the intense segregation into dilapidated, overcrowded ghettos, led to astonishing levels of social pathology. The arrest rate for blacks in Detroit in 1926 was four times that for whites. Blacks constituted 31 percent of the nation's prison population in 1923, although they made up only 9 percent of the total population. The death rate in Harlem between 1923 and 1927 was 42 percent higher than in New York City as a whole, even though Harlem's population was much younger than the overall city population. Harlem's infant mortality rate was 111 per 1,000 births, compared with the city's rate of 64 per 1,000. Tuberculosis, heart disease, and other illnesses also far exceeded the rates for the city's general population.[25]

Blacks moving into northern cities were often surprised when they encountered hostility, racism, and discrimination nearly as bad as in the South. Restaurants and stores refused to serve them; banks typically refused them loans. Cemeteries, parks, bathing beaches, and other facilities were put off limits or divided into "white" and "colored" sections. Many dentists, doctors, and hospitals refused to treat blacks. Worse, the violence that had plagued them in the South followed them everywhere they went. On July 2, 1917, 39 blacks and 5 whites died in a race riot in East St. Louis, Illinois.[26] In the infamous "Red Summer" of 1919, more than 20 cities experienced race riots, all of them involving attacks by white mobs on blacks. Chicago's riot of that summer started when a black teenager inadvertently swam across the strip of water separating the beach designated "For Coloreds Only" from the beach reserved for whites only. A white crowd stoned the boy to death and then terrorized blacks throughout the city for days. From July 1, 1917, to March 1, 1921, Chicago experienced 58 racial bombings.[27] Unemployed blacks were forced out of Buffalo by city police in 1920. That same year, in perhaps the worst mass murder of blacks in U.S. history, more than 300 blacks were killed by white mobs in Tulsa, Oklahoma—an incident covered up for almost 80 years.[28] In 1925 blacks who attempted to move into white neighborhoods in Detroit were terrorized by cross burnings, vandalism, and mob violence.

In all cities, restrictive covenants were attached to property deeds to keep African Americans from buying into white neighborhoods. Deeds with these restrictions were filed in the office of the county clerk or the register of deeds and enforced by the courts. Chicago, with more than 11 square miles covered by restricted deeds in 1944, was typical of northern cities.[29] Neighborhood improvement associations sprung up in new subdivisions and, by legal prosecution and social persuasion, they forced homeowners to accept and abide by restrictive covenants. The result was that racial segregation in northern cities had become firmly fixed even before the great wave of black migration.

RACIAL CONFLICT IN THE CITIES: THE POSTWAR ERA

Although the movement to the North slowed to a crawl during the Great Depression, it picked up momentum again during and after World War II. As before, factory jobs pulled blacks into northern cities, and conditions in the South provided a push. The mechanization of southern agriculture, in particular the widespread adoption of the mechanized cotton picker, threw hundreds of thousands of sharecroppers and farm laborers out of work. From Texas, Louisiana, and Arkansas, blacks streamed into cities of the West, especially in California; from the middle South, they moved to St. Louis, Chicago, Detroit, Cleveland, and other cities of the Midwest; and from Mississippi and eastward in the Deep South, they moved to Washington, D.C., New York, Boston, and other cities in the East. In 1940, 77 percent of the nation's blacks still lived in the southern states (compared with 87 percent in 1910). By 1950 only 60 percent lived in the South, and in the next two decades the South's share declined to 56 percent (1960) and to 53 percent (1970).[30] Nearly all the northward-bound migrants ended up in cities.

As blacks continued their northward trek, the pressure on existing housing stock intensified. Black families living in the ghetto expressed resentment about the ghetto walls that kept them out of the more desirable neighborhoods inhabited by whites.[31] At the other end of the scale, nearly all whites felt that their neighborhoods should remain segregated.[32] Realtors engaged in steering to keep blacks out of favored neighborhoods and block-busting to create panic among white homeowners and to reap the profits from the resulting sales.[33]

The resistance to black movement into white neighborhoods assumed some of the aspects of war. In Detroit, for example, a homeowners' movement swept through neighborhoods in the 1950s, dedicated to the goal of keeping blacks out. These organizations held meetings, often with real estate agents in attendance, to urge their neighbors not to sell to blacks and to discuss strategies of resistance. An interview subject in one study gave a typical response when she said that blacks "just destroy the whole neighborhood" because "They neglect everything. Their way of life is so different from ours."[34]

When combined with fear that property values would fall, attitudes like this often fueled violent reactions. At night, when they could most effectively terrorize their victims, white crowds gathered in front of houses newly purchased by black families, shouting racial epithets and insults; strewing garbage on the lawn; breaking windows with stones, bricks, and bottles; tearing down fences; breaking car windshields; and, if everything else failed, setting fire to the house.[35] Racial change in the neighborhoods occurred in block-by-block skirmishes, with whites making a slow retreat until panic set in. By the mid-1960s, "white flight" had become a generalized phenomenon.

The dislocations for both blacks and whites shattered lives and left an enduring legacy of bitterness. Whites who fled in panic sold out cheap to real estate agents. Blacks who had to abandon their houses in the face of white intimidation often lost their investments and any hope of moving out of the slums. The scale of the dislocations can only be compared to natural disasters like Hurricane Katrina, which struck New Orleans in August 2005. The results were just as long-lasting, too. Many neighborhoods never recovered; for others, it would take decades, if it happened at all. In 2005 Detroit was a city in which 11 percent of the population was white and 82 percent was

African American. The contrast with Detroit's suburbs could hardly be more stark: There, African Americans comprised less than 10 percent of the population.[36]

As a result of the twin migrations—blacks moving into the cities, whites fleeing to the suburbs—the racial composition of the cities changed quickly. In the wake of urban riots in 1965 and 1966, a series of presidential commissions gave expression to the rising concern that the extreme racial segregation of cities and suburbs had developed into a national urban crisis. The National Commission on Civil Disorders of 1967 (called the Kerner Commission after its chair, Illinois governor Otto B. Kerner) warned of "two nations, one black, one white—separate and unequal."[37]

The relentless stream of newcomers and the white flight to the suburbs combined to sharpen racial fears and antagonisms. Within a few years the racial divide that began to open after World War II quickly widened into a chasm. As shown in Table 6.3,

Table 6.3 Percentage of Blacks in Central Cities and Suburban Rings in 12 Selected SMSAs, 1940, 1970, 2000[a]

	Central City			Suburban Ring		
	1940	1970	2000	1940	1970	2000
New York[b]	6%	23%	29.5%	5%	6%	10%
Los Angeles–Long Beach	6	21	12	2	7	6
Chicago	8	34	37	2	4	11
Philadelphia	13	34	45	7	7	12
Detroit	9	44	83	3	4	9
San Francisco–Oakland	5	33	12	4	9	6
Boston	3	18	28	1	2	3.5
Pittsburgh	9	27	28	4	4	5
St. Louis	13	41	52	7	8	13
Washington, D.C.	28.5	72	61	14	9	23
Cleveland	10	39	52	1	1	11
Baltimore	19	47	65	12	6	14.5
All 12 SMSAs	9	31	33.5	4	6	10

[a]Except for St. Louis, Baltimore, and Washington, D.C., figures refer to the Consolidated Metropolitan Statistical Areas (CMSAs), which are not strictly comparable to the Standard Metropolitan Statistical Areas (SMSAs) used in earlier years. For 2000 additional central cities are included for some urban areas: Oakland for San Francisco–Oakland; Bridgeport (Connecticut), Newark, Jersey City, and New Haven for New York. As of 2000 Washington, D.C., and Baltimore were considered central cities of a single metropolitan area, but they are kept separate to facilitate accurate comparisons with earlier censuses. Camden has also been deleted as a separate central city for the Philadelphia region. Calculated from U.S. Bureau of the Census, *Census of 2000* (http://www.census.gov).

[b]Includes data from the Nassau–Suffolk SMSA, which was deleted from the New York City SMSA in 1971. They are included to maintain comparability across time periods.

Source: Data for 1940 and 1970 adapted from Leo F. Schnore, Carolyn D. André, and Harry Sharp, "Black Suburbanization, 1930–1970," in *The Changing Face of the Suburbs*, ed. Barry Schwartz (Chicago: University of Chicago Press, 1976), p. 80. Reprinted by permission. The figures here were transposed to yield data on black percentages.

in 1940 blacks constituted more than 10 percent of the population in only 4 of 12 big cities that became magnets for black migrants after World War II; on average, the proportion was 9 percent in these cities. But by the census of 1970, blacks accounted for more than 72 percent of the population of Washington, D.C., 47 percent in Baltimore, 44 percent in Detroit, 39 percent in Cleveland, and 41 percent in St. Louis. The African American proportion of the population in 9 of the 12 cities continued to increase after the 1970s so that, for example, by the 2000 census Baltimore's population was 65 percent black, Detroit's 83 percent, and St. Louis's 52 percent.

The suburbs, meanwhile, remained mostly white. In none of the metropolitan areas shown in Table 6.3 did blacks make up as much as 10 percent of the suburban population in 1970; in most cases the proportions were much lower: 4 percent in Chicago's, Detroit's, and Pittsburgh's suburbs; 2 percent in Boston's, and 1 percent in Cleveland's (at a time when 39 percent of Cleveland's population was black). But in the 1970s a significant number of blacks began moving to the suburbs, a trend that has continued to the present day.[38] As a consequence, by the 2000 census the African American proportion of suburban populations had increased in most metropolitan areas, to 23 percent in the suburbs of Washington, D.C., 14.5 percent in Baltimore, 13 percent in St. Louis, and more than 10 percent in the suburbs of New York, Chicago, Philadelphia, and Cleveland.

The postwar movement of millions of poverty-stricken, mostly rural blacks to the inner cities and their concentration into densely packed neighborhoods inevitably created intractable social problems. Blacks were not only crowded into segregated slums; their plight was aggravated by the constant influx of new arrivals, by the ever-present threat of the urban renewal bulldozer, and by their high rate of poverty. A large proportion of blacks lived in neighborhoods in which almost everyone was poor. Ironically, the problem of concentrated poverty became even worse when the housing opportunities for middle-class blacks improved in the 1970s. As more affluent blacks left the ghetto, the poverty level of many neighborhoods rose sharply. In 1970 the Census Bureau classified more than one-fourth (27 percent) of the census tracts in the 100 largest cities as "poverty" tracts, defined as areas where at least 20 percent of the residents were poor. Of these census tracts, 6 percent were classified as "extreme poverty" areas, where the census found that at least 40 percent of residents lived in poverty. By the 1990 census the percentage of poverty tracts had increased sharply, to 39 percent of all census tracts, and the proportion of extreme poverty tracts had more than doubled, to 14 percent.[39] In 2000 the poverty rate in central cities was more than double the poverty rate in the suburbs, as it had been for decades.[40]

An analysis of 60 metropolitan areas found that in 1980 blacks were twice as segregated as Latinos and Asians.[41] Over the next decade, the concentration of poor blacks into poverty census tracts intensified.[42] When the 1990 census was taken, 71 percent of low-income, black, central-city residents lived in poverty neighborhoods, compared with 40 percent of low-income, white, central-city residents.[43] Low-income whites were often able to escape the ghetto and move into working-class or even middle-class neighborhoods, but low-income blacks found it very difficult or impossible to find affordable housing outside racially segregated areas. The intense segregation of the poor interacted with the segregation of minorities to create a hypersegregation of the minority poor.[44]

Most children living in impoverished areas attend racially segregated schools. In 1996 about 8 percent of U.S. schools had 90 percent or higher enrollment of African American and Latino students, and nearly all of them were located in central cities. In most of these schools, half or more of the students came from families in poverty. By contrast, only 8 percent of the students in schools with 10 percent or less black and Latino enrollment lived in poverty.[45]

In the 1980s the sociologist William Julius Wilson used the term *underclass* to refer to people who were concentrated in low-income areas and who were chronically out of work and out of the social mainstream.[46] The media, politicians, and social scientists quickly appropriated the term, using it to refer loosely to "a constellation of behaviors or conditions, including being poor and living in the inner city, being chronically unemployed, on welfare, homeless, residing in a single-parent family (especially with illegitimate children), having a criminal record, or using drugs (especially crack cocaine)."[47] Although this list clearly included behaviors that might be exhibited throughout society or by poor people regardless of where they lived, the term was normally used to refer to African Americans exclusively. Frequently, "underclass" was defined so broadly that it included blacks not living in poverty areas at all but who allegedly exhibited a single characteristic (such as unemployment or single parenthood) that was thought of as "underclass." In short, the underclass concept became a way of speaking about race without actually admitting that race was the topic of conversation.[48]

Because the underclass concept was widely exploited for ideological purposes and as a media stereotype, most scholars have abandoned it. Wilson stopped using the term and began instead to refer to the harmful effects that result from segregating the poor together as "concentration effects."[49] Later, he used the term *the new urban poverty*, and his main focus turned to the high proportion of unemployed males in particular areas: "poor, segregated neighborhoods in which a substantial majority of individual adults are either unemployed or have dropped out of the labor force altogether."[50] Without work, he said, a necessary structure for daily life was eroded, and the activities that replaced work—such as hanging out on the corner, engaging in petty crime, becoming involved with drugs—often undermined family life.[51] The persistent joblessness among African Americans could be traced to a steep decline of manufacturing jobs in the 1970s and 1980s. In the past, African Americans held a disproportionate share of blue-collar jobs, and even though their employment in the service sector rose sharply in the period of deindustrialization, full-employment wages declined by 25 to 30 percent by the mid-1990s.[52] Wilson's research was alarming because it appeared that the conditions of life in the inner-city ghettos were getting worse, with no end in sight. It was a dismal prospect, fully a quarter century after the civil rights legislation and the programs of the Great Society.

The outpouring of research revealed the startling dimensions of the unresolved problems. More than two-thirds of African American families were headed by single women. By itself this would not have seemed so bad, except that in 1993 families headed by divorced women made 40 percent as much as households headed by a husband and a wife.[53] Households headed by women who had never been married made only 21 percent as much, and *two-thirds* of all children in such families lived in poverty (compared to one-tenth of children in married-couple families).[54] Since the mid-1970s, middle-class families had been able to maintain high living standards because there are typically two wage earners. Increasingly, many African American women were forced to work in low-paying and seasonal jobs. When combined with the rising unemployment levels among African American men, the pathways out of poverty seemed few indeed.

Health and health care in inner-city poverty areas continued to deteriorate after the 1970s. The poor generally lacked health insurance, and so were forced into over-crowded health clinics and emergency rooms. For these reasons, in 1990 the United States had among the highest infant mortality rates in the industrialized world.[55] The overall national rate was about 10 deaths for every 1,000 live births in the late 1980s, but the rate for inner-city poverty neighborhoods approached that of developing countries. In 1988–1989, for example, the infant mortality rate in central Harlem was 23 per 1,000 births, about the same as in Malaysia.[56] The interaction between health and poverty was equally obvious in the case of the AIDS epidemic. Ten metropolitan areas with one-eighth of the nation's population had five-eighths of the nation's case-load in 1988, and these were concentrated in poverty areas.[57]

In the 1980s the drug epidemic began to devastate inner-city neighborhoods. The murder rate among young black males tripled between 1984 and 1991, in part because of crack cocaine and heroin use.[58] Young men in well-armed gangs fought one another to control the lucrative business. The connection between crack and violence went be-yond the gangs, however. Because crack was so addictive, users resorted to robbery, burglary, car theft, and prostitution to feed their habit.

Fueled by turf fights between gangs and by the drug trade, violent crime soared in American cities in the late 1980s and early 1990s.[59] In 1990 New York City set a record with 2,262 murders, yet its per capita homicide rate ranked it only slightly above aver-age for the country's 25 largest cities.[60] Violent death reached pandemic proportions among young black and Latino males in inner-city areas. Citing the fact that homicide was the leading cause of death for black males aged 15 to 24 in 1990, the federal Centers for Disease Control and Prevention (CDC) stated the casualty rate was approaching that of war. According to a study in the *New England Journal of Medicine,* young men in Harlem, primarily because of high homicide rates, were less likely to survive to the age of 40 than their counterparts in Bangladesh.[61] A late 1980s survey of schoolchildren in Chicago found that an astonishing 24 percent of them had personally witnessed a murder.[62] Despite the fact that overall crime rates in the 1990s fell, the level of random violent crime in low-income minority areas has continued. Gang warfare is more or less a constant, and innocent bystanders frequently get caught up in street-level violence.

The problems in the urban ghetto bred a national obsession with crime and violence. Sensationalized accounts of crime had become a staple of local newspaper and television news. Approximately 20 percent of front-page news stories and local news broadcasts focused on violent crime.[63] Live footage of crime scenes became a standard feature of local news stations. A reporter typically stood at a crime scene in front of a minicam, the talking head soon giving way to a video collage of a bloodstained street or sidewalk, shocked spectators, and perhaps grief-stricken friends and relatives. The discourse about the inner cities became "our . . . national morality play," a perfor-mance made up of sensationalized and exaggerated narratives of good and evil.[64]

If the urban crisis is defined as the great divide between cities and suburbs, then it would be accurate to say that it has pretty much come to an end. Other issues in our national life, such as the economic crisis, immigration, and the environment, have largely displaced concern about the cities and their problems. Nevertheless, it is important to emphasize that most of the problems previously associated with the urban crisis have not disappeared. Blacks still remain more highly segregated than any other racial or ethnic group in American society, and poverty and violence remain as intractable problems.

THE SUBURBAN EXODUS

To understand how the urban crisis evolved and why it has begun to run its course, it is not sufficient to focus solely on the condition of the central cities and the people who lived in them. The waves of migration to the cities occurred at the same time that they were being abandoned by the wealthy and the white middle class. The exodus took place in a series of movements that have turned America's urban areas into the sprawled metropolitan landscapes we see today. In the latest chapter of this century-long process, it has become harder to tell the cities and the suburbs apart, a trend that is gradually making the old city/suburban dichotomy less relevant than it was in the twentieth century.

Over the course of the twentieth century, the movement to the suburbs has come in four great bursts, each fueled by some combination of middle-class prosperity, transportation innovations, a desire for a larger house and a higher standard of living—and a rejection of the city. Although some suburbs date from the mid-nineteenth century, when railroads began to radiate out from the densely settled cities, the first big wave of suburban development came in the late nineteenth and early twentieth centuries, with the growth of the streetcar suburbs. The second surge was prompted by middle-class prosperity, the adoption of the automobile, and the building of paved roads in the 1920s. But the suburban movement that truly altered the geography of urban America and redefined its national politics came in the years after World War II, with the full-scale flight of middle- and working-class white families from inner-city neighborhoods. These were the years when the urban crisis became the central drama of American political life. We will consider these great population movements, in turn.

The Romantic Suburban Ideal: 1815–1918

Early traces of the city–suburban split began to appear in the nineteenth century. The impulse to escape the city goes a long way back in American history, and it had often been energized by a deep distrust of cities and the people who lived within them. The American habit of wanting to escape the cities can be traced not only to the conditions in the crowded cities of nineteenth-century America, but also to a deeply ingrained hostility to urban life that dates to the nation's founding. Thomas Jefferson is well known for his suspicion that cities undermined the democratic impulse. "The mobs of great cities," he wrote, "add just so much to the support of pure government, as sores do to the strength of the human body."[65] In the 1830s and 1840s, the tendency to dislike cities was given specific form by the romantic movement, whose writers admired nature and abhorred cities and technology. Despite such attitudes, however, the opportunities offered in cities made them an irresistible lure.

As soon as they were able, wealthy people began leaving the industrial cities to escape from what they perceived to be the inconvenience, and anarchy of urban life. As soon as new forms of transportation made it possible, some families of the upper and upper-middle classes began fleeing the congestion of downtown. In 1814 Robert Fulton began the first steam ferry service between Manhattan and Brooklyn, providing a chance for those who could afford it to live apart from the dirt and din of Manhattan. Brooklyn thus became the first commuter suburb.[66] The nineteenth century witnessed a succession of transportation innovations that made it possible for more upper- and upper-middle-class people to escape the crowded urban center. Railroad lines gave wealthy people the opportunity to leap-frog several miles beyond the area of contiguous urban settlement. Horse-drawn streetcars became widespread after 1850, providing less expensive transportation for urban residents and expanding the commuting distance for workers up to 3 miles from downtown.[67] The electric trolley began to revolutionize urban transportation in the 1890s. It was the breakthrough that caused a sudden jump in the rate of suburban development, and trolleys continued to run until the 1960s, many decades after autos had made their entrance. By tripling the radius of cities, the trolley increased the amount of land that could be developed for residential use by 900 percent.

In the years after the Civil War, railroad connections enabled a small elite to live in pristine isolation from the problems of industrial society. In a pattern repeated in every stage of urban history, transportation improvements were planned not so much for moving people as for capturing the increased land values that resulted from opening up new suburban land for development. Some railroads lost money on day-to-day operations, but that did not prevent railroad entrepreneurs from amassing fabulous fortunes through suburban land speculation.[68] Commuter tickets on railroads were far too expensive for ordinary workers; thus the railroad suburbs were restricted to the wealthiest classes. The first suburb inspired by the ideals of the romantic era, Llewellyn Park, 13 miles from New York City, was founded in 1853 by a wealthy entrepreneur who thought that placing people in a natural setting would revive religious and moral values. Lake Forest, a few miles north of Chicago, was founded in 1857 with a picturesque village square surrounded by lanes winding among the hills and bluffs along Lake Michigan. After the Civil War, the romantic suburbs multiplied, all built on the same principles: "gracefully-curved lines, generous spaces, and the absence of sharp corners, the idea being to suggest and imply leisure, contemplativeness and happy tranquility."[69] Even today, most of the suburbs built on this model retain their exclusive character: In contrast to the grid-patterned streets of cities, these suburbs look like "scattered buildings in a park," the homes integrated with nature, with no hint of the grimy factory on which this suburban wealth was based.[70]

The image of the suburb as a romantic idyll entered the popular press and the public imagination. At the turn of the century, a back-to-nature movement, built on a romanticized version of nature and rural environments, swept the country. Boy

Scouts, Campfire Girls, Woodcraft Indians, and other organizations sought to expose children to the healthy influence of nature study. Children's literature was filled with stories of adventure in "natural" settings. Adults, too, were thought to be purified and rejuvenated by visits to the countryside. Bird-watching and nature photography became major pastimes. Tourism to national parks boomed, especially after automobiles became more widely available to the middle classes.

Although the suburban ideal was intimately linked with a yearning for a romanticized version of nature, suburban residents had no intention of giving up the amenities and advantages of the cities they had left behind. Instead, they attempted a fusion of both worlds—the urban and the rural—in the suburbs. Magazines and newspapers of the day were filled with articles on the advantages of suburban life as an amalgam of city conveniences and rural charm. In 1902 one magazine writer claimed that suburban living could "offer the best of chances for individualism and social cooperation."[71] The next year, *Cosmopolitan* carried an article hailing the "new era" of suburban living:

> The woeful inadequacy of facilities of communication and transportation which formerly rendered every suburbanite a martyr to his faith have, in great measure, been remedied; and moreover, residents in the environs have now reached the happy point where they consider as necessities the innumerable modern conveniences of the city house which were little short of luxuries in the suburban residence of yesterday.[72]

Advertisements for suburban property just after the turn of the century stressed the presence of springs, orchards, and forests; activities such as bathing, fishing, and shooting; the healthfulness of the environment; and houses that had such modern conveniences as hot water, gas lighting, and telephones.[73] "A Country Home with All City Comforts," promised one advertisement, alongside another that talked of crops of oats and hay, orchards, trees and shrubbery, fruit trees, and other accompaniments of the rural environment.[74] Most of the advertisements carried drawings or photographs of wide expanses of lawn, trees, and meticulously tended gardens.

By the 1890s the electric streetcar had quickened the pace of suburban development. New suburbs sprang up along the boundaries of the older cities, such places as University City, Missouri, just outside St. Louis, and Oak Park, 8 miles west of Chicago. These suburbs tried to capture pieces of the romantic ideal with landscaped yards, large free-standing homes, tree-lined streets, and ample parks, but they were basically upper-middle subdivisions located on grid streets. But the romantic ideal persisted. It was only one side of a two-sided coin; the other side was not so attractive. Popular literature exuded an intellectual and sentimental reaction against the city. Cities had few defenders and a host of critics. Academic writers promoted the idea that "our great cities, as those who have studied them have learned, are full of junk, much of it human."[75] A Boston University professor called city life "a self-chosen enslavement" and indicated that "the psychological causes of urban drift are socially most sinister."[76] Already, a presentiment of the attitudes that would later be directed at African Americans in the postwar era was clearly evident. Cities were thought to nurture every conceivable sort of evil, as evidenced by such titles of sociological research as *The Social Evil in Chicago; Five Hundred Criminal Careers; The City Where Crime Is Play; Family Disorganization; Sex, Freedom and Social Control;* and *The Ghetto.*[77]

The Automobile Suburbs: 1918–1945

For several decades the quickening pace of suburban development seemed to pose no threat to the vitality of the old urban centers. For the industrial cities, overcrowding, not emptying out, was their biggest problem. In hindsight, of course, it is clear that this would eventually change. As shown in Table 6.4, even before the automobile, the suburbs of several big cities grew at a much faster pace than their core cities. Between 1900 and 1910, New York City's population increased by 39 percent, but in the same decade its suburbs grew by 61 percent. Meanwhile, Chicago's suburbs skyrocketed, growing by 88 percent in the first decade of the century. St. Louis's suburbs grew even faster, by 91 percent. As more people took to the streetcars and the first automobiles, the trend continued; between 1910 and 1920, the suburbs of Los Angeles grew by 108 percent and Cleveland's by an astonishing 140 percent.

Even so, the day when this might become a problem seemed to be a long way off. The rates of growth in the suburbs were fast, but the total population base was very small. Between 1900 and 1920, for instance, New York City grew by 2.2 million people, compared to a population increase of just 190,000 in its surrounding area. By the census of 1920 New York City's population had reached 5.6 million people, but only 379,000 lived in its suburbs. Likewise, in all urban areas the vast majority of people still lived within the city limits. Likewise, industrial and manufacturing facilities

Table 6.4   Metropolitan Area Population, 1900–1940 (Increases in Population Expressed as Percentage Growth and Number of People Added)

	1900–1910		1910–1920		1920–1930		1930–1940	
Districts	Central City	Outside Central City	Central City	Outside Central City	Central City	Outside Central City	Central City	Outside Central City
Boston	20%	23%	9%	21%	4%	21%	−1%	3%
Chicago	29	88	23	79	25	74	0.6	10
Cleveland	46	46.5	40	140	12	126	−1	13
Los Angeles	206	553	81	108	115	158	−3	30
New York City[a]	39	61	18	35	23	67	8	18
St. Louis	19	91	12.5	26	7	71	−1	16
Mean for all metro districts (nation)	34	38	25	32	21	47	4	14

[a]Includes growth of population in New York City proper and in satellite areas of New York State. New Jersey population is excluded.

Source: U.S. Bureau of the Census, *The Growth of Metropolitan Districts in the United States, 1900–1940,* by Warren S. Thompson (Washington, D.C.: U.S. Government Printing Office, 1947), especially Table 2.

remained near water and rail transportation links in the city centers. Between 1904 and 1914, St. Louis lost some industry to its suburbs (its share of industrial employment fell from 95 to 90 percent of the area's manufacturing establishments), as did Baltimore (96 to 93 percent) and Philadelphia (91 to 87 percent), but these cities were the exception rather than the rule.[78] The industrial cities overwhelmingly dominated the economies of their urban areas. Men left the suburbs in the morning to commute to their jobs downtown, and at night they returned home. Railroad and streetcar suburbs prospered, but the people who lived in them were still completely dependent on downtown jobs. As a result, downtown streets were jammed with traffic.

Though it took a few decades for the process to fully unfold, the automobile brought a fundamental change in the relationship between cities and suburbs. When it made its appearance in the late nineteenth century, the car was mainly an expensive toy for the rich. Henry Ford soon made it affordable. In 1908 Ford introduced the Model T, a car for the masses that was dependable and easy to operate. Through the introduction of the moving assembly line in 1913, Ford was able to reduce the cost of a Model T from $950 in 1910 to $290 in 1924. Car ownership skyrocketed. American car production increased from 63,000 automobiles in 1908 to 550,000 by 1914. After World War I, car production really took off, reaching 2.27 million in 1922 and 4.45 million in 1929.[79] The construction of adequate roads lagged seriously behind car ownership, but this problem was eventually solved when automobile owners successfully pressed for massive state and federal funding, mainly through gasoline taxes.

The automobile provided the opportunity for the rapidly expanding middle class to begin to move in big numbers to the suburbs. Whereas streetcar suburbs had sprung up along the rail tracks like the spokes on a wheel, the automobile made it possible to develop the areas in between. Vast new tracts of land were opened to land speculation and suburban development, and the upper-middle class invested much of its newfound wealth in suburban real estate. Total national wealth doubled in the ten years from 1912 to 1922, and from 1915 to 1925 average hourly wages climbed from 32 to 70 cents.[80] The value of residential land and improvements doubled in the 1920s.[81]

The combination of middle-class prosperity and the mass ownership of the automobile conspired to push suburban development to new levels. In the prosperous 1920s, the cities of Boston, St. Louis, and Cleveland grew more slowly than ever in their history, but their suburbs boomed, both in total population and rates of growth. The truck and the automobile began to change well-established economic patterns as well. The proportion of factory employment in the cities of more than 100,000 residents declined between 1920 and 1930, and this trend was likely to continue because the new assembly-line production techniques required lots of land rather than vertical buildings, and this land was located in the suburbs. Still, it would take decades for the process of decentralization to fully work itself out. Almost all white-collar people worked and shopped in the old downtowns. Downtown office space tripled in the 1920s, and employment continued to soar in most central cities.[82] For the central cities the day of reckoning had not yet arrived, but it was not far off.

The Great Depression of the 1930s signaled the twilight of the city-building era. As the data in Table 6.4 reveal, Boston, Los Angeles, St. Louis, and Cleveland all lost population in the 1930s; so did Philadelphia, Kansas City, and the New Jersey cities—Elizabeth, Paterson, Jersey City, and Newark (not shown in the table). San Francisco, which had added 27 percent to its population in the 1920s, suddenly stopped growing. Small manufacturing cities of New England and the Midwest slid into decline—Akron and Youngstown, Ohio; Albany, Schenectady, and Troy, New York; Joplin, Missouri; and New Bedford, Massachusetts.

The depression hit the suburbs hard, too, because most upper-middle- and middle-class people lacked the means to buy a new home. The growth rate of New York's suburbs fell from 67 percent in the 1920s to only 18 percent in the 1930s. In the same decade, Chicago's suburban expansion slowed from 74 percent in the 1920s to 10 percent in the 1930s; Cleveland's dropped from 74 to 13 percent, and Los Angeles's from 158 to 30 percent. All through the 1930s, the effects of the depression lingered. With the coming of World War II, materials needed for housing construction were commandeered for the war effort. Suburban growth came to a standstill.

The Bedroom Suburbs: 1946–1970s

The slowdown in housing construction during the depression and the war would have caused a serious housing shortage all by itself, but the postwar baby boom made the situation worse. After reaching a low point during the Great Depression, the birthrate began to rise in 1943 and then took off in the postwar years, when 16 million GIs returned to civilian life.[83] By 1947, 6 million families were doubling up with relatives or friends because they could not find a home of their own.[84] The housing industry geared up to meet the demand, pushing single-family housing starts from only 114,000 in 1944 to 1,692,000 by 1950.[85] Virtually all of this new construction occurred in the suburbs.

Utilizing mass production methods and sophisticated marketing techniques, big companies began to dominate the housing industry. The big firms accounted for only 5 percent of all houses built in 1938, but increased their share of the market to 24 percent by 1949. A decade later, they produced 64 percent of all new homes.[86] Their preferred method was to buy tracts of land on the outskirts of cities and to create entire new subdivisions by bulldozing everything to an even surface and constructing houses quickly using standardized production techniques. The emergence of cookie-cutter residential developments stimulated a boom in suburban construction. In the ten years between 1940 and 1950 the suburbs experienced a 36 percent increase; in the same decade, the core cities they surrounded grew by only 14 percent. In fact, however, suburban growth right after the war had occurred much faster than these statistics suggest because no subdivisions at all were built until 1946, when wartime conditions finally ended. After the war, the pent-up demand for housing ignited a virtual gold rush to the new suburban subdivisions. In earlier decades, suburban development had been mainly an upper- and middle-class phenomenon, but now it filtered down to embrace working-class families, too. Federally insured home loans, cheap energy, and new, efficient building technologies made it less expensive to build a new house in the suburbs than to rehabilitate a home or rent an apartment in the city. The nation's homeownership rate increased from 44 percent in 1940 to 63 percent by 1970.[87]

The suburban boom accelerated in the prosperous years of the 1950s. While their satellite cities grew by 49 percent, the average population growth in central cities was

11 percent. But these statistics understate the scope of the real problem because they lump together newer, healthier cities with older industrial cities that had slipped into serious decline. Virtually all the old industrial cities, wherever they were located, were losing population, some of them at a dramatic pace. The big cities all through the industrial belt that stretched from New England through the Great Lakes states were hemorrhaging population; for instance, between 1950 and 1960 Boston's population shrunk by 13 percent, St. Louis's by 12.5 percent, and Cleveland's by 4 percent. Things only got worse in the 1960s: St. Louis lost 17 percent of its population in the 1960s and an extraordinary 27 percent in the 1980s. Against this dismal record, the city's 16 percent loss in the 1990s was an improvement. In 1950, when it started its long slide, it had held 857,000 people, but by century's end only 335,000 people were left in the city.[88]

Likewise, other industrial cities also slipped into decline. In the 40 years from 1950 to 1990, most older cities bled population: Boston's fell by 13 percent in the 1950s, 12 percent in the 1960s, and 3 percent in the 1980s. New York, Chicago, and Cleveland also declined. The 1990s were kinder, but only marginally: 20 major cities continued to slide.[89] And for several cities, the trend has continued into the new millennium. Even though downtowns and many inner-city neighborhoods have been on the rebound, the population of many cities has continued to sag. Between the 2000 census and 2003, Cleveland, Baltimore, Flint (Michigan), Detroit, and Cincinnati all shrank by 3.5 percent or more, an experience shared by 30 other older cities.

Table 6.5 shows the effects of more than a half century of population losses in the central cities and rapid growth in the suburbs. Already by 1940 only 29 percent of the

Table 6.5 Share of Metropolitan Population Living in Selected Central Cities, 1940–2000[a]

	Percentage Living in Central City			
	1940	**1960**	**1980**	**2000**
Boston	29.0%	21.8%	11.0%	10.1%
Chicago	70.4	51.5	37.0	31.6
Cleveland	64.1	32.1	19.5	16.2
Los Angeles	51.6	32.0	25.8	22.6
New York	64.3	50.5	37.8	37.8
St. Louis	57.0	35.0	18.8	13.4

[a]It is difficult to calculate precise figures over time of city–suburban ratio because the Census Bureau's definition of metropolitan areas has changed from time to time. Corrections have been made to minimize this problem. Although Lorain–Elyria counties were not included in the 1940 Cleveland metropolitan area, they have been added because these counties were included from 1960 and thereafter. For Boston, the four major counties are included for 1940 and 1960, which is comparable to the regional definition from 1970 to 2000.

Sources: U.S. Bureau of the Census, *Statistical Abstract of the United States* (Washington, D.C.: U.S. Government Printing Office, various years): 1987, pp. 29–31, Table 34; 1993, pp. 37–39, Table 42; 2003, p. 32, Table 27.

population in Boston's metropolitan area resided in the city—a reflection of the fact that suburbanization had begun there as early as the 1840s. In the Chicago region 70 percent of the population lived in the city in 1940, compared to 64 percent for Cleveland and New York and 57 percent for St. Louis. Even in the Los Angeles metropolitan area, which had begun sprawling since the early years of the century, more than half of the region's population still lived within the city limits in 1940. But the post–war suburban exodus changed regional geographies very quickly. As an example, by the 2000 census only 10 percent of the people living in Boston's metropolitan were still residing in the city of Boston. For St. Louis the figure had dropped to 13 percent, and for Cleveland, 16 percent. Among older industrial cities, New York and Chicago stood out because they still captured about a third of their region's population in 2000.

The suburbs of the 1950s and 1960s were by no means all cut from the same cloth. The legacy of the past was plain to see, with middle-class housing tracts, a sprinkling of working-class blue-collar subdivisions, a few isolated areas populated by blacks, and, of course, enclaves inhabited by the wealthy. But most of the housing tracts built in the postwar years were marketed to white middle-class families. Individual suburbs tended to be remarkably uniform, with row after endless row of houses that looked as if they had been produced by a giant cookie cutter. Suburbia came to be portrayed in the popular media as a place of look-alike streets and people, where bored couples with small children spent their free time watching television and picking crabgrass out of their lawns, where the men commuted to office jobs leaving behind frustrated housewives to care for the children in culturally sterile environments. This image of suburbia was captured in three best-selling novels published during the period: *The Man in the Gray Flannel Suit* (1955), *The Crack in the Picture Window* (1956), and *The Split Level Trap* (1960). Although the cultural images of suburbia undoubtedly traded on stereotypes, they struck a responsive chord.[90]

Civic leaders in the cities were now thoroughly alarmed that the suburbs threatened the vitality and even viability of the urban core. It was not only that the suburbs were growing so fast. As affluent white families deserted the cities, they were leaving behind a population made up of blacks and poor people. Increasingly, suburbanization was understood in racial terms; the phrase "white flight" started to be heard, suggesting that suburban development was motivated in part by racism, a suggestion for which there is abundant evidence.[91] The riots of the mid-1960s heightened the fears connected to race. In 1967, when the National Commission on Civil Disorders called attention to the stark dichotomy between the cities and suburbs, the suburbs had become far removed from life in the inner cities. Increasingly, suburbanites regarded the cities as reservations for blacks, and many blacks had become completely estranged from the rest of America.[92] At that point, all the ingredients that defined the twentieth-century urban crisis had come together.

THE MULTIETHNIC METROPOLIS

By the end of the 1960s, the momentous movement that had brought millions of southern blacks to northern cities had pretty much spent itself. Indeed, a modest reverse migration of blacks back to the South began; in the 1990s black migration in the opposite direction, back to the South, totaled 579,000.[93] Fair housing and antidis-crimination laws, as well as a swelling middle class, allowed African Americans to begin their own suburban movement, at the very time that white flight slowed. A surge of foreign immigration added still more complexity to the picture. Immigrants began streaming into the nation, at first from Latin America and Asia, then from al-most everywhere in the world. By the twenty-first century, the segregation of blacks and whites was being supplanted by a new reality: America was becoming a mul-tiracial and multiethnic society, a trend that has changed the suburbs at least as dra-matically as the central cities. Unlike previous periods of immigration, this time the newcomers were settling in the suburbs more than anywhere else. All through met-ropolitan areas, ethnic enclaves began springing up, sometimes in unlikely places.

The volume of immigration in the 1990s was second only to the teens, and in both periods the immigrant tide prompted national legislation to regulate the flow. The movement has continued into the twenty-first century. Nationally, the number of im-migrants increased 16 percent from 2000 to 2005, and the rise was much faster in some states that had not received as many of them as in the past: a 34 percent increase in Indiana, 44 percent in South Dakota, 32 percent in Delaware, 31 percent in Missouri, and 26 percent in New Hampshire.[94] According to census estimates, in September 2004 there were 11.6 million Legal Permanent Residents in the United States, with 8 million of them eligible to be naturalized; in addition, more than 5 million illegal aliens were thought to reside within the nation's borders.[95]

The number of immigrants entering the country has increased steadily since 1950, and during this period the sources of immigration have shifted from Europe to Asia, Latin America, and the Caribbean. Table 6.6 reveals that in the decade of the 1950s, Europe was the largest source of immigration (57 percent). Just 22.5 percent came

Table 6.6   Immigrants by Place of Origin, 1951–2000

Year	*Percentage of Total Immigration*					Total Number (Thousands)
	Europe	Asia[a]	Canada[a]	Other Western Hemisphere[b]	All Other[c]	
1951–1960	57%	6%	11%	22.5%	3%	2,515.5
1961–1970	37	13	9	39	2	3,321.7
1971–1980	18	36	3	40	3	4,493.3
1981–1990	10	38	2	47	3	7,338.1
1991–2000	14	32	1.5	48	5	9,092.9

[a]Cambodia, China, Taiwan, Hong Kong, India, Iran, Israel, Japan, Korea, Philippines, Thailand, Vietnam, and "other Asia."

[b]Mexico, Caribbean, Central America, South America.

[c]Africa, Australia, New Zealand.

Sources: U.S. Department of Justice, Immigration and Naturalization Service, *Statistical Yearbook of the Immigration and Naturalization Service, 1989* (Washington, D.C.: Government Printing Office, 1990), pp. 2–5; and U.S. Bureau of the Census, The Official Statistics, *Statistical Abstract of the United States, 2003* (Washington, D.C.: U.S. Government Printing Office, 2004).

from the Western Hemisphere south of the United States, and 6 percent came from Asia. However, the composition of immigrant flows changed dramatically in the following decades. The proportion of immigrants from Europe fell sharply, finally accounting for less than 10 percent of the total numbers of arrivals in the 1980s before rebounding to about 14 percent by 2000 because of a movement from Russia and from the formerly communist countries of Eastern Europe. Asian immigrants shot up from 6 percent to more than 38 percent of the total in the 1980s and still accounted for more than 30 percent up to 2000. Immigrants from the Western Hemisphere south of the United States, mostly from Mexico and Latin America, increased in every decade, and since 2000 they have constituted nearly half of the flow.

The immigration laws in effect from the 1920s to the mid-1960s were adopted in a climate of xenophobic fear and resentment. The National Origins Immigration Act of 1924 allowed 2 percent of the base population of foreign-born nationality groups, as recorded in the census of 1890, to immigrate into the United States. This quota accomplished its intended goal of drastically reducing immigration by all groups except those from northern Europe. Immigration by Slavs, Jews, Italians, Greeks, and other supposedly "inferior" peoples, most of whom entered the country after 1890, was cut by more than 90 percent.

By the 1960s such a blatantly racist formula became politically controversial. In the Hart-Cellar Act of 1965, Congress essentially put immigrants from all countries on an equal footing and granted a high priority to family reunification. Expanded by special provisions for political refugees from socialist and communist countries, immigration soared well beyond expectations, and the ethnic composition of the immigrant flow changed radically. After the 1960s between 80 and 85 percent of the new immigrants entering the United States were Latino or Asian. (As of the 2000 census, the U.S. Census Bureau used the terms *Latino* and *Hispanic* interchangeably; we follow that practice here.) Both groups came from many nations and ethnic groups—Latinos from a vast area from the Caribbean to the tip of South America; Asians from a great arc of countries from Japan to India.

In 1990 Congress again reformed the immigration laws, as a result of the legislation, the number of legal immigrants allowed into the country increased by 40 percent. The law more than doubled the number of visas granted to foreigners with job skills needed in the United States, and it allowed the highest percentage of European-origin groups into the country since Hart-Cellar.[96] Immigration from Eastern Europe, Russia, and the nations that broke from the former Soviet Union increased sharply. By the mid-1990s, the United States was admitting more legal immigrants than all the rest of the nations of the world combined.[97]

In the 1980s Asians were the fastest-growing ethnic group, with the metropolitan areas of Los Angeles, San Francisco, and New York having the largest Asian communities. The number of people coming from Asia in the 1980s almost equaled the number from all countries of the Western Hemisphere south of the U.S. border. But in the 1990s Asian immigration slowed while Latino immigration increased.[98] As a result of the rising volume of immigration and the relatively large size of Latino families, in 2005 Latinos outnumbered blacks for the first time in the nation's history.

The flow from the Caribbean, Latin America, Central America, and South America reveals a complex mixture of languages, cultures, and nationalities. A significant proportion of immigrants from the Caribbean are black, which thoroughly confuses census categories (nearly all other Latinos filling out the census forms fit the "white" racial category). In 2000 nearly 8 percent of blacks in the United States were foreign-born, with the figure over 20 percent in New York, Florida, and New Jersey. Most of these people came from the Caribbean.[99] The Census Bureau has found it difficult to identify ethnic categories accurately in New Mexico (where 42 percent of the population is officially classified as Hispanic) because many families are descended from American citizens who lived in the region generations before most settlers arrived; as a consequence, even if they were once citizens of Mexico (before New Mexico was ceded to the United States in 1846), they cannot accurately be classified as coming from there.

The data in Figure 6.1 reveal that the racial and ethnic composition of the immigration stream differs remarkably among the seven metropolitan areas that received

Figure 6.1   Seven U.S. Metropolitan Areas with Largest Immigrant Flows (One Year), Fiscal Year 2004

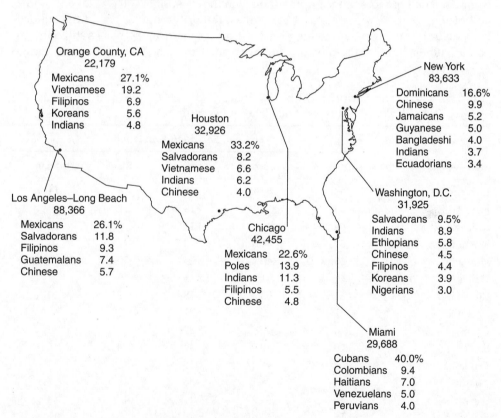

Orange County, CA
22,179

Mexicans	27.1%
Vietnamese	19.2
Filipinos	6.9
Koreans	5.6
Indians	4.8

Houston
32,926

Mexicans	33.2%
Salvadorans	8.2
Vietnamese	6.6
Indians	6.2
Chinese	4.0

New York
83,633

Dominicans	16.6%
Chinese	9.9
Jamaicans	5.2
Guyanese	5.0
Bangladeshi	4.0
Indians	3.7
Ecuadorians	3.4

Los Angeles–Long Beach
88,366

Mexicans	26.1%
Salvadorans	11.8
Filipinos	9.3
Guatemalans	7.4
Chinese	5.7

Chicago
42,455

Mexicans	22.6%
Poles	13.9
Indians	11.3
Filipinos	5.5
Chinese	4.8

Washington, D.C.
31,925

Salvadorans	9.5%
Indians	8.9
Ethiopians	5.8
Chinese	4.5
Filipinos	4.4
Koreans	3.9
Nigerians	3.0

Miami
29,688

Cubans	40.0%
Colombians	9.4
Haitians	7.0
Venezuelans	5.0
Peruvians	4.0

Note: "Chinese" includes imigrants from mainland China only.

Source: Department of Homeland Security (*http://www.uscis.gov/graphics/shared/statistics/yearbook/2005/ImmSupTable2fy04D.xls*).

the largest numbers of immigrants in 2004. In Orange County, California, which is composed of numerous interlocking cities, Mexicans and Vietnamese are the largest immigrant groups, followed by Filipinos, Koreans, and Indians. By contrast, Cubans were the most numerous group to arrive in Miami in the same year, and nearly all the rest were from other Caribbean and Latin American countries. Mexicans easily led the list in Los Angeles and Houston, but a significant number also came from Asia and elsewhere in Latin America. The immigrant flow to the New York region is so diverse that only Dominicans account for more than 10 percent of the total; the other leading groups are Chinese, Jamaicans, Guyanese, Bangladeshi, Indians, and Ecuadorians. Washington, D.C., attracted a complex mixture of Asian and Latino immigrants, with a significant number of Ethiopians added to the mix. In the Chicago region, Mexicans led all groups, with Poles and Indians next.

In 1987 more than 93 percent of legal immigrants settled in urban areas, and more than half of them moved into just seven metropolitan areas in the United States. The data in Table 6.7 show recent trends for the nation's 14 most diverse metropolitan areas (for areas of more than 500,000). In all of the 14 central cities listed, minorities comprised half or more of the population when the census of 2000 was taken—and in all but four of these same metropolitan areas, minority populations in the suburbs exceeded 40 percent. In the Washington, D.C., and Newark areas, blacks still outnumbered Latinos, but the differences were much smaller in the New York and Chicago

Table 6.7 City and Suburban Minority Shares, Year 2000 Metropolitan Areas with Populations over 500,000 (in Percentages)

			Share of Suburban Population		
Metro Area	**City**	**Suburban**	**Latino**	**Black**	**Asian**
Los Angeles	69%	69%	45%	8%	14%
New York	65	32	13	12	4
Chicago	65	26	11	8.5	5
Washington, D.C.	61	40.5	8.5	22	7
Houston	68	40	23	10	5
Dallas	62	31	15	9	4
Riverside	51	53	38	7	4
Phoenix	37	30	21	3	2
Orange County	70	40	22	1	14
San Diego	50	40	27	4	6
Oakland	67	48	19	8	17
Miami	82	78.5	56	19.5	1.5
Newark	86	34	11	17	4.5
San Francisco	56	43	19	3	17

Source: Adapted from William H. Frey, *Melting Pot Suburbs: A Census 2000 Study of Suburban Diversity* (Washington, D.C.: Center on Urban and Metropolitan Policy, Brookings Institution Press, June 2001), p. 14.

metropolitan regions. In the other urban regions shown in Table 6.7—all located in the Sunbelt—Latinos constituted the largest minority group by far. Asians constituted less than 10 percent in all areas of the Sunbelt except the California metropolitan areas of Los Angeles, Orange County, Oakland, and San Francisco. Clearly, the distribution of immigrant groups is extremely even.

The census of 2000 showed that more than three-fourths of the nation's Hispanics lived in five southwestern states, plus Florida. Half of the Latinos residing in the United States lived in California and Texas, despite the fact that all but two of the cities with the largest Latino populations, Chicago and New York, are located in other states (the other three leading cities are Los Angeles, Houston, and San Antonio).[100] Approximately 80 percent of the Latinos in the southwestern states came originally from Mexico, compared to 60 percent for the United States as a whole. But beginning in the 1990s, these patterns began to change in important ways. The largest percentage increases in Latino population in the decade of the 1990s were in North Carolina (479 percent increase), Arkansas (388 percent), Georgia (374 percent), Tennessee (327 percent), and Nevada (271 percent).[101] What was once mainly a regional phenomenon has become a truly national trend.

Adverse economic conditions and political repression pushed most of the Latino immigrants to American shores. Economic opportunity in the United States exerted the necessary pull. The minimum wage in the United States, for example, was approximately six times the prevailing wage in Mexico in 1990, where wages were higher than in most other Latin American countries.[102] Illegal immigration helps account for persistently low wages and low levels of education among Latinos. Undocumented aliens are willing to take (or are coerced into taking) jobs paying less than the minimum wage, and they often end up in sweatshops, meat-processing plants, or in agricultural jobs working under abysmal conditions. Frequently led across the border by professional smugglers, called *coyotes* for their predatory habits, illegal aliens remain at the bottom of U.S. society. Because they live in constant fear of detection by the United States Citizenship and Immigration Services (USCIS), a bureau of the Department of Homeland Security, they are in no position to bargain with employers.

To deal with the problem of illegal immigration, Congress enacted the Immigration Reform and Control Act (IRCA) in 1986, which established stiff penalties for employers who knowingly hired them. At the same time, the law made it possible for illegals who had already entered the country to achieve citizenship by registering with the Immigration and Naturalization Service (INS). After passage of IRCA, approximately 2.5 million formerly illegal aliens attained legal status by 1990,[103] and the INS stepped up efforts to find employers who violated the law. One of the unintended effects of the 1986 reform is that many employers began to discriminate against anyone who looked or sounded like they came from anywhere south of the U.S. border.[104] Reflecting a growing national anxiety about illegal immigration, the successor agency to the INS, the USCIS, began to round up illegal immigrants in spectacular, well-publicized raids. After the U.S. Senate failed to pass an immigration bill in 2006, several states adopted legislation requiring employers to check the backgrounds of employees; in addition, 15 states have passed laws with criminal penalties for smugglers who bring immigrants into the country.[105] Towns and cities across the nation adopted an extraordinary variety of laws signaling the reaction to immigrants—for example, laws requiring business owners to check the identity of potential employees, property owners to check the backgrounds of renters, public buildings to post "English only" public signs, and other measures. Local police departments rounded up anyone looking like immigrants for minor violations, such as, in Georgia, fishing without a license.[106] These actions, many of doubtful legality, gave police the pretext for beginning deportation orders. Of course the furious reaction against immigrants have frayed the social bonds of many communities.

HAS THE URBAN CRISIS DISAPPEARED?

The twentieth-century urban crisis of city versus suburb, black versus white, is coming to an end. In the past, most immigrants have settled in central cities, often moving into neighborhoods already occupied by the same group, but the pattern of settlement within urban areas is becoming more complex and less predictable. Many of the recent immigrants have been bypassing the central cities entirely and moving directly into suburbs. By 2000, 55 percent of Asians, 50 percent of Latinos, and 39 percent of blacks lived in suburbs, and the proportions were much higher in many Sunbelt metropolitan urban regions.[107] The ethnic and racial movement to the suburbs continues. In the seven-county area surrounding Chicago, for instance, non-Hispanic whites accounted for 58 percent of the population in 2000, but only 55 percent by 2005.[108] Several of the communities that minorities moved into are now ethnically diverse, which reduces the extreme polarization between central city and suburb that characterized urban areas only a few years ago.

The movement to the suburbs has had the effect of moderating the extremely rigid racial and ethnic segregation that was a defining feature of the urban crisis. Research shows that in the 1990s the level of segregation declined in 272 metropolitan statistical areas (MSAs) and increased in only 19 MSAs.[109] Most of the metropolitan areas where segregation increased were located in second-tier older industrial cities in the Northeast and Midwest, which tend to be less diverse than the faster-growing metropolitan areas elsewhere. In one study, the authors found that between 1970 and 2000 all ethnic groups had become more spatially assimilated, although blacks remained more segregated than Asians or Latinos.[110] The dismal findings from earlier studies of segregation based on data from the 1970s, which justified a book title *American Apartheid*,[111] no longer seem to describe most urban areas in the United States accurately.

Recent research on urban poverty also offers evidence that other aspects of the urban crisis may be moderating. In the 1990s the number of people living in neighborhoods of concentrated poverty—which researchers define as neighborhoods where 40 percent or more of the residents are under the poverty line—fell dramatically in the 1990s, by 24 percent, or 2.4 million people.[112] The proportion of people living in high-poverty neighborhoods fell among all racial and ethnic groups, and the sharpest declines were in cities in the Midwest and South, such as Detroit, Chicago, St. Louis, Milwaukee, Memphis, New Orleans, Houston, San Antonio, and Dallas. Researchers referred to the decline in concentrated poverty as "stunning progress."[113]

There is also evidence that the social ills that gave rise to the label "the urban underclass" have become much less concentrated. In the 1970s and 1980s, four indicators of underclass social ills—female-headed households, high-school dropouts, male unemployment, and welfare dependence—were highly concentrated in areas of high poverty. The clustering of these social ills in a few areas fell so dramatically in the 1990s that the scholars conducting the research called the trend "nothing short of profound." The researchers drew the conclusion that "many fewer neighborhoods now resemble the depressing descriptions of the inner city that were commonplace in journalistic and scholarly accounts of previous years."[114]

One of the most dramatic and persistent elements of the urban crisis, the crime rate, also fell, though the decline may prove to be temporary. In the 1990s rates of violent crime went into a steep, and surprising, decline. For the nation as a whole, violent crime per 100,000 persons decreased by 29 percent from 1990 to 2000 (after an increase of 20 percent from 1987 to 1990), and the murder rate fell by 41 percent (after a 13 percent increase).[115] The drop in crime was even more dramatic in big cities than elsewhere; homicide rates, for example, fell by 75 percent in New York City from 1990 to 2003 (from more than 2,200 in 1990 to 597 in 2003).[116] There has been a rise in crime rates in some cities since 2005, but the overall incidence of crime still remains lower than in the past.

Despite such evidence, it would be premature to conclude the urban problems of the twentieth century—high levels of segregation, inequality and poverty, and racial and ethnic tensions—are disappearing. The urban crisis of the twentieth century was defined by reference to the great city–suburban divide. That pattern is now slowly disappearing, and in that important sense the old urban crisis is mostly a thing of the past. But some of the problems previously associated with broad swatches of central-city ghetto neighborhoods are now cropping up all over the place. Although concentrated poverty has declined somewhat in central cities, it has not fallen in the suburbs or in rural areas.[117] In metropolitan areas with the highest rates of suburban growth, economic segregation dropped the least in the 1990s.[118]

What does the changing urban pattern mean? All we can say for certain is that the spatial geography of urban development is different than in the past. The politics of urban areas, and in the nation, will no longer be defined as black versus white or city versus suburb. Urban areas, and urban problems, will be multiethnic and more spatially complex. What meaning we should attach to this difference is in the eye of the beholder.

The prospects for the central cities have changed, but all groups have not benefited. By many measures, downtowns and residential areas in the central cities have been on the rebound since sometime in the 1990s. Fifteen large older industrial cities—including, for example, St. Louis, Gary, Baltimore, Buffalo, Pittsburgh, Cincinnati, and Detroit—continued to lose population in the 1990s, but the rate of loss slowed. In any case, declining population could no longer automatically be interpreted as a measure of decline. Many cities were becoming less dense, and single and childless households were replacing larger families. The picture was decidedly mixed, both between and within cities. In some places, the continued flight of married-couple households created a patchwork in which some neighborhoods experienced rapid gentrification by single, affluent professionals, while others continued to grow poorer.[119]

The inequalities between the downtown professional class and the residents of minority neighborhoods have become transparently obvious in cities tied closely to the global economy. Global cities have attracted a more diverse profile of immigrants than any other cities.[120] Jobs are the lure. The concentration of multinational businesses, financial services corporations, and the businesses connected to them draw highly educated workers from all over the globe. But the greatest demand for jobs (at least expressed in numbers) is found at the other end of the job market. Lower-status service workers are indispensable to the working of a global city. Clerical workers; janitors and cashiers; nannies; cooks and busboys; maintenance and security workers; hotel maids; and a multitude of personal-service specialists from masseuses, personal shoppers, and dog walkers: These kinds of jobs are taken disproportionately by immigrants and minorities. The jobs generally paid little, with the result that inequality escalated upward. New York's experience is revealing. In the late 1980s, the poorest 20 percent of the population in the New York metropolitan region accounted for 5 percent of incomes, but the top 20 percent of wage earners had a 45 percent share. By 1997 the percentage of earnings claimed by the poorest quintile had fallen to just above 2 percent whereas the richest quintile received 56 percent of all earnings. In the 1990s the poverty rate in New York rose from 29 to 32 percent of households.[121]

Rising inequality is occurring not only in global cities but also throughout American society. In 1980 the bottom one-fifth of the population earned 4.3 percent of all earned income, but only a few years later, in 1998, the poorest fifth of wage earners accounted for just 3.6 percent. Meanwhile, from 1980 to 1998 the richest fifth increased its share from 44 to 49 percent. Perhaps even more telling, the top 5 percent of wage earners had increased its share of earnings in the same period from 16 to 21.4 percent.[122]

Minorities continue to lag behind significantly. Indicators of economic well-being show that Latinos, as a group, have a long way to go to catch up with the general U.S. population. The median income for Hispanic families in 2006 was 72 percent of the average earnings for non-Hispanic white families (down from 75 percent in 2001) but above the average earnings of black families, which was 61 percent of white family income.[123] Latinos lagged far behind on educational attainment; 86 percent of all non-Hispanic whites had completed high school in 2007, compared with 60 percent of Hispanics and 82 percent of blacks. Only 13 percent of Hispanics had earned a college degree by 2005, but 30 percent of whites and 17 percent of blacks had done so.[124]

The lag in educational qualifications, plus a measure of discrimination, has meant that Latinos have occupied lower rungs on the job ladder. Even though Hispanics held 12 percent of all jobs in 2000, only 6 percent of them were in managerial or professional positions.[125] The economic crisis that began in 2008 has affected Hispanics and blacks disproportionately. As of February 2009, the unemployment rate for Hispanics was 12.9, an increase in one year from 6.9 percent. During the same period black unemployment levels rose from 8.4 percent to 13.8 percent. For whites, the levels were much lower; from March 2008 to March 2009, they increased from 4.8 percent to 7.3 percent.[126] With differences of this magnitude, the ethnic and racial tensions that have long plagued America's urban areas are certain to persist, and possibly grow worse.

It is unrealistic to suppose that persistent inequality can occur without a simultaneous increase in social problems. Within urban areas, extreme inequality has always been expressed in two ways: social disorder (in the form of crime, riots, and family disorganization, for instance), and residential patterns of segregation. No one knows whether the falling crime rates of recent years will continue or whether the incidence of concentrated poverty will continue to fall, but increasing inequality ensures that these and other social problems will persist in some form. These problems may assume a different spatial geography than in the past, but whether this amounts to a difference without a difference is hard to tell. The distinction between city and suburb may be disappearing, but the problems associated with the old urban crisis are likely to persist.

NOTES

1. Barry Checkoway, "Large Builders, Federal Housing Programs, and Postwar Suburbanization," in *Marxism and the Metropolis: New Perspectives in Political Economy,* ed. William K. Tabb and Larry Sawers (New York: Oxford University Press), p. 156.
2. Nicolas Lemann, *The Promised Land: The Great Migration and How It Changed America* (New York: Vintage Books, 1991), p. 6.
3. Population growth on the outskirts probably exceeded population growth in the center before the 1920s. However, before 1920, annexation of suburban land by central cities obscured the statistical trend. See John D. Kasarda and George V. Redfearn, "Differential Patterns of City and Suburban Growth in the United States," *Journal of Urban History* 2, no. 1 (November 1975): 53.
4. Robert A. Beauregard, *Voices of Decline: The Postwar Fate of U.S. Cities* (Cambridge, Mass.: Blackwell, 1993).
5. Dennis Judd, "Urban Violence and Enclave Politics: Crime as Text, Race as Subtext," in *Managing Divided Cities,* ed. Seamus Dunn (Keele, Staffordshire, U.K.: Ryburn Publishing, Keele University Press, 1994), pp. 160–175.
6. U.S. Bureau of the Census, *Statistical Abstract of the United States,* 2005 (*http://www.census.gov/prod/2005pubs/06statab/pop.pdf*).
7. Pew Research Center, *Social and Demographic Trends,* 2008 (*http://pewsocialtrends.org/topics/raceandethnicity/*).
8. A brief but excellent account of these movements may be found in Stanley B. Greenberg, *Politics and Poverty: Modernization and Response in Five Poor Neighborhoods* (New York: Wiley, 1974), pp. 15–27.
9. See Ibid., pp. 15–27; and Leo Grebler, Joan W. Moore, and Ralph C. Guzman, *The Mexican-American People* (New York: Free Press, 1970), p. 113.
10. U.S. Bureau of the Census, *Statistical Abstract of the United States,* 2005.
11. Harry M. Caudill, *Night Comes to the Cumberlands* (Boston: Little, Brown, 1962).
12. Nicholas Lemann, *The Promised Land: The Great Migration and How It Changed America* (New York: Vintage Books, 1991), p. 6.
13. Stewart E. Tolnay and E. M. Beck, "Rethinking the Role of Racial Violence in the Great Migration," in *Black Exodus: The Great Migration from the American South,* ed. Afrerdteen Harrison (Jackson: University Press of Mississippi, 1991), p. 20.
14. Robert B. Grant, ed., *The Black Man Comes to the City: A Documentary Account from the Great Migration to the Great Depression, 1915–1930* (Chicago: Nelson-Hall, 1972), p. 27; see pp. 16–30 for a complete set of statistics on black migration from 1890 to 1930. These data are used throughout this section.
15. Ibid., p. 22.
16. Ibid., p. 23.
17. Winfred P. Nathan, *Health Conditions in North Harlem, 1923–1927,* Social Research Series No. 2 (New York: National Tuberculosis Association, 1932), pp. 44–45, excerpted in Grant, *The Black Man Comes to the City,* pp. 59–61.

18. *Chicago Defender,* reprinted in Grant, *The Black Man Comes to the City,* pp. 31–40.

19. Tolnay and Beck, "Rethinking the Role of Racial Violence," p. 27.

20. Philip Dray, *At the Hands of Persons Unknown: The Lynching of Black America* (New York: Random House, 2002).

21. A collective amnesia has erased much of this past from America's consciousness. A recent book of photographs from the period is shocking but an effective antidote to cultural denial. See James Allen, *Without Sanctuary: Lynching Photography in America* (Sante Fe, N.M.: Twin Palms Publishers, 2000).

22. Memphis *Commercial Appeal,* October 5, 1916, reprinted in Grant, *The Black Man Comes to the City,* pp. 43–44.

23. *Chicago Defender,* August 12, 1916, reprinted in Grant, *The Black Man Comes to the City,* p. 45.

24. Herbert Northrup, *Organized Labor and the Negro* (New York: Kraus Reprint, 1971).

25. These statistics are from several sources excerpted in Grant, *The Black Man Comes to the City,* pp. 58–61.

26. See Elliott M. Rudwick, *Race Riot at East St. Louis, July 2, 1917* (Carbondale: Southern Illinois Press, 1964), for a discussion of this event.

27. Chicago Commission on Race Relations, *The Negro in Chicago: A Study of Race Relations and a Race Riot* (Chicago: University of Chicago Press, 1922), p. 122.

28. Tom Kenworthy, "Okla. Starts to Face up to, '21 Massacre," *USA Today,* February 18, 2000, p. 4A.

29. Grant, *The Black Man Comes to the City,* p. 71.

30. U.S. Department of Commerce, Bureau of the Census, *Census of Population 1970: General Social and Economic Characteristics* (Washington, D.C.: U.S. Government Printing Office, 1972), pp. 448–449, Table 3.

31. Douglas Massey and Nancy Denton, *American Apartheid: Segregation and the Making of the Underclass* (Cambridge, MA: Harvard University Press, 1993), pp. 89, 91.

32. Ibid., p. 91.

33. Rosalyn Baxandall and Elizabeth Ewen, *Picture Windows: How the Suburbs Happened* (New York: Basic Books, 2000), p. 202; Ray Suarez, *The Old Neighborhood: How We Lost in the Great Suburban Migration, 1966–1999* (New York: Free Press, 1999), pp. 40–41.

34. Quoted in Thomas J. Sugrue, *The Origins of the Urban Crisis: Race and Inequality in Postwar Detroit* (Princeton, N.J.: Princeton University Press, 1996).

35. Quoted in ibid., pp. 252–253.

36. U.S. Bureau of the Census, *American FactFinder,* 2005 (*http://factfinder.census.gov/home/saff/main. html?_lang=en*).

37. *Report of the National Advisory Commission on Civil Disorders* (New York: Bantam Books, 1968), p. 1.

38. U.S. Bureau of the Census, *1990 to 1998 Annual Time Series of Population Estimates by Age, Race, Sex, and Hispanic Origin,* January 2000 (*http://www.census.gov/population/estimates/countypop .html*).

39. John Kasarda, "Inner-City Concentrated Poverty and Neighborhood Distress: 1970 to 1990," *Housing Policy Debate* 4, no. 3 (1993): 253–302.

40. Poverty in the United States: 2000 (Joseph Dalaker, September 2001), *Current Population Reports* (Washington, D.C.: U.S. Bureau of the Census), pp. 60–214.

41. Douglas S. Massey and Nancy Denton, "Trends in the Residential Segregation of Blacks, Hispanics, and Asians: 1970–1980," *American Sociological Review* 52 (1987): 802–825.

42. Ibid.; see also Douglas Massey and Mitchell Eggers, "The Ecology of Inequality: Minorities and the Concentration of Poverty, 1970–1980," *American Journal of Sociology* 95 (March 1990): 1153–1189; Douglas Massey, "American Apartheid: Segregation and the Making of the Underclass," *American Journal of Sociology* (June 1990): 329–357; William Julius Wilson, *The Truly Disadvantaged: The Inner City, the Underclass, and Public Policy* (Chicago: University of Chicago Press, 1987); William Julius Wilson, *When Work Disappears: The World of the New Urban Poor* (New York: Knopf, 1996).

43. William W. Goldsmith and Edward J. Blakely, *Separate Societies: Poverty and Inequality in U.S. Cities* (Philadelphia: Temple University Press, 1992), p. 48.

44. Douglas Massey and Nancy Denton, *American Apartheid* (Cambridge, Mass.: Harvard University Press, 1993), pp. 74–78.

45. Myron Orfield, *American Metro Politics: The New Suburban Reality* (Washington, D.C.: Brookings Institution Press, 2002).

46. Wilson, *The Truly Disadvantaged*.

47. Michaela di Leonardo, "White Lies/Black Myths: Rape, Race, and the Black Underclass," *The Village Voice*, September 22, 1992, p. 31.

48. Norman Fainstein, "Race, Class, and Segregation: Discourses About African-Americans," *International Journal of Urban and Regional Research* 17, no. 3 (1993): 384–403.

49. Wilson, *The Truly Disadvantaged*.

50. Wilson, *When Work Disappears*, p. 19.

51. Wilson, *When Work Disappears*, pp. 25–88.

52. Ibid., p. 31.

53. Ibid., p. 92.

54. Ibid., p. 93.

55. Lisa W. Foderaro, "In Harlem, Children Reflect the Ravages U.N. Seeks to Relieve," *New York Times*, September 30, 1990, p. 1.

56. Walter J. Jones and James E. Johnson, "AIDS: The Urban Policymaking Challenge," *Journal of Urban Affairs* 11, no. 1 (1989): 85.

57. *Confronting AIDS: Update 1988* (Washington, D.C.: National Academy Press, 1988), p. 52.

58. Joel A. Devine and James D. Wright, *The Greatest of Evils: Urban Poverty and the American Underclass* (New York: De Gruyter, 1993), p. 167.

59. Robert D. McFadden, "New York Leads Cities in Robbery Rate, But Drops in Murders," *New York Times*, August 11, 1991, p. 1.

60. See James Diego Vigil, *Barrio Gangs: Street Life and Identity in Southern California* (Austin: University of Texas Press, 1988).

61. Ronald Kotulak, "Study Finds Inner-City Kids Live with Violence," *Chicago Tribune*, September 28, 1990, p. 1.

62. Jonathan Kozol, *Rachel and Her Children: Homeless Families in America* (New York: Crown, 1988), p. 9.

63. Margaret T. Gordon and Claudette Guzan Artwick, "Urban Images in the Mass Media" (research proposal, Urban University Research Consortium, June 17, 1991), p. 2.

64. di Leonardo, "White Lies/Black Myths," p. 31.

65. Quoted in James A. Clapp, ed., *The City: A Dictionary of Quotable Thoughts on Cities and Urban Life* (New Brunswick, N.J.: Center for Urban Policy Research, Rutgers University, 1984), p. 129.

66. Ibid., pp. 25–30. Robert Fishman dates the first true suburb somewhat earlier, in the 1790s in Clapham and other villages outside London; see Robert Fishman, *Bourgeois Utopias: The Rise and Fall of Suburbia* (New York: Basic Books, 1987), p. 53.

67. Peter O. Muller, *Contemporary Suburban America* (Upper Saddle River, N.J.: Prentice Hall, 1981), p. 28.

68. For accounts of railroad suburbs and land speculation, see Jackson, *Crabgrass Frontier*, Chapter 5; Fishman, *Bourgeois Utopias*, Chapter 5; and Harry C. Binford, *The First Suburbs: Residential Communities on the Boston Periphery, 1815–1860* (Chicago: University of Chicago Press, 1985).

69. John W. Reps, *The Making of Urban America: A History of City Planning in the United States* (Princeton, N.J.: Princeton University Press, 1965), p. 344.

70. The phrase "scattered buildings in a park" is Lewis Mumford's; see his *The City in History: Its Origins, Its Transformations, and Its Prospects* (New York: Harcourt, Brace and World, 1961), p. 489.

71. Editorial, (New York) *Independent,* February 27, 1902, p. 52.

72. Weldon Fawcett, "Suburban Life in America," *Cosmopolitan* (July 1903): 309.

73. Advertisement in *Country Life in America* (November 1906): 3.

74. Advertisement in *Country Life in America* (March 1908): 474.

75. Robert Park, Ernest W. Burgess, and Roderick D. McKenzie, *The City* (Chicago: University of Chicago Press, 1925), p. 109.

76. Quoted in Peter J. Schmitt, *Back to Nature: The Arcadian Myth in Urban America* (New York: Oxford University Press, 1969), p. 180; original quotation found in Ernest Groves, "The Urban Complex," *Sociological Review* 12 (Fall 1920): 74, 76.

77. A more complete list of titles can be found in Schmitt, *Back to Nature,* pp. 180–182.

78. Gary A. Tobin, "Suburbanization and the Development of Motor Transportation: Transportation Technology and the Suburbanization Process," in *The Changing Face of the Suburbs,* ed. Barry Schwartz (Chicago: University of Chicago Press, 1976), p. 100. See also U.S. Bureau of the Census, *Industrial Districts: 1905, Manufactures and Population,* Bulletin 101 (Washington, D.C.: U.S. Government Printing Office, 1909), pp. 9–80; and U.S. Bureau of the Census, *Census of Manufactures: 1914,* vol. 1, *Reports by States with Statistics for Principal Cities and Metropolitan Districts* (Washington, D.C.: U.S. Government Printing Office, 1918), pp. 564, 787, 1292.

79. These data are cited in Tobin, "Suburbanization and the Development of Motor Transportation," pp. 102, 103, and are also available in National Industrial Conference Board (NICB), *The Economic Almanac 1956: A Handbook of Useful Facts About Business, Labor and Government in the United States and Other Areas* (New York: Crowell for the Conference Board, 1956).

80. Tobin, "Suburbanization and the Development of Motor Transportation," pp. 102, 103.

81. Ibid.

82. Jackson, *Crabgrass Frontier,* pp. 174, 184.

83. The birthrate (the number of live births per 1,000 population) increased from 18.4 in 1936 to 26.6 in 1947. U.S. Bureau of the Census, *Historical Statistics of the United States, Colonial Times to 1970,* Bicentennial edition, pt. 2 (Washington, D.C.: U.S. Government Printing Office, 1975), p. 49.

84. Jackson, *Crabgrass Frontier,* p. 232.

85. Ibid., p. 233.

86. Barry Checkoway, "Large Builders, Federal Housing Programs, and Postwar Suburbanization," pp. 155–156.

87. U.S. Bureau of the Census, *Historical Statistics of the United States, Colonial Times to 1970,* Bicentennial edition, pt. 1 (Washington, D.C.: U.S. Government Printing Office, 1975), p. 646.

88. U.S. Department of Commerce, Bureau of the Census, *Census of Population, 1950,* vol. 1 (Washington, D.C.: U.S. Government Printing Office, 1952), p. 69, Table 17; *Census of Population, 1970,* vol. 1, *Characteristics of the Population,* pt. A, p. 180, Table 34; *Census of Population, 1980,* suppl. reports, *Standard Metropolitan Statistical Areas and Standard Consolidated Statistical Areas,* p. 2, Table B, p. 6, Table 1, and p. 49, Table 1; *State and Metropolitan Areas Data Book,* 1991, Table D; Bruce Katz and Robert Lang, ed., *Redefining Urban and Suburban America: Evidence From Census 2000* (Washington, D.C.: Brookings Institution Press, 2003), pp. 47–50.

89. Katz and Lang, ibid.

90. For criticisms of the 1950s stereotype of suburbia, see Bennett M. Berger, *Working-Class Suburb: A Study of Auto Workers in Suburbia* (Berkeley: University of California Press, 1968); and Herbert J. Gans, *The Levittowners: Ways of Life and Politics in a New Suburban Community* (New York: Pantheon Books, 1967).

91. Thomas M. Guterbock, "The Push Hypothesis: Minority Presence, Crime, and Urban Decon-centration," in *The Changing Face of the Suburbs,* ed. Barry Schwartz (Chicago: University of Chicago Press, 1976), p. 26.

92. National Advisory Commission on Civil Disorders, *Report of the National Advisory Commission on Civil Disorders* (New York: Bantam Books, 1968), p. 1.

93. William H. Frey, "Census 2000 Shows Large Black Return to the South, Reinforcing the Region's 'White-Black' Demographic Profile," U.S. Bureau of the Census, PSC Research Report No. 02-473, May 2001.

94. Rick Lyman, "Census Shows Growth of Immigrants," *New York Times*, August 15, 2006 (*http://www.nytimes.com*).

95. Department of Homeland Security, Office of Immigration Statistics (*http://www.uscis.gov/graphics/shared/statistics/publications/LPRest2004.pdf*).

96. Robert Pear, "Major Immigration Bill Is Sent to Bush," *New York Times*, October 29, 1990, p. A1; see also Stephen Castles and Mark J. Miller, *The Age of Migration: International Population Movements in the Modern World* (New York: Guilford Press, 1993), p. 249.

97. Rodman D. Griffin, "Illegal Immigration," *CQ Researcher* 2, no. 16 (1992): 364.

98. U.S. Bureau of the Census, *1990 to 1998 Annual Time Series of Population Estimates by Age, Race, Sex, and Hispanic Origin*, January 2000 (*http://www.census.gov/population/estimates/countypop.html*).

99. Frey, op. cit., May 2001.

100. U.S. Census Bureau News, "Census 2000 Paints Statistical Portrait of the Nation's Hispanic Population" (*http://www.census.gov/press-release/www/releases/archives/population/00434/html*).

101. Ibid.

102. Alejandro Portes and Ruben Rumbaut, *Immigrant America: A Portrait* (Berkeley: University of California Press, 1990), p. 10.

103. "Immigration Reform; Recent Trends and Legislative Responses," *The Urban Institute Policy and Research Report* (Winter/Spring 1991), p. 13.

104. Reported in Charles Kamasaki and Paul Yzaguirre, "Black-Hispanic Tensions: One Perspective," paper delivered at the annual meeting of the American Political Science Association, Washington, D.C., August 29–September 1, 1991, p. 5. See also Castles and Miller, *The Age of Migration*.

105. Julia Preston, "Surge in Immigration Laws Around the U.S.," *New York Times*, June 23, 2008 (*http://www.nytimes.com/2007/08/06/washington/06immig.html*).

106. Dan Anderson, "Times Topics: Immigration and Refugees," *New York Times*, June 9, 2008 (*http://www.nytimes.com*).

107. Logan, "The New Ethnic Enclaves in America's Suburbs," a report by the Lewis Mumford Center for Comparative Urban and Regional Research (Albany, N.Y.: 2002)," p. 2; William H. Frey, *Melting Pot Suburbs: A Census 2000 Study of Suburban Diversity* (Washington, D.C.: Center for Urban and Metropolitan Policy, Brookings Institution Press, June 2001).

108. John McCormick and Jo Napolitano, "Hispanics Propel Growth in Suburbs," *Chicago Tribune*, August 4, 2006, pp. 1, 23.

109. Edward L. Glaeser and Jacob L Vigdor, "Racial Segregation: Promising News," in Katz and Lang, *Redefining Urban & Suburban America*, pp. 211–234.

110. Jeffrey M. Timberlake and John Iceland, "Change in Racial and Ethnic Residential Inequality in American Cities, 1970–2000," *City & Community* 6, no. 4 (December 2007): 335–365.

111. Massey and Denton, *American Apartheid*.

112. Paul Jargowsky, *Stunning Progress, Hidden Problems: The Dramatic Decline of Concentrated Poverty in the 1990s* (Washington, D.C.: Brookings Institution Press, 2004), pp. 1–2.

113. Ibid., p. 1.

114. Paul A. Jargowsky and Rebecca Yang, "The 'Underclass' Revisited: A Social Problem in Decline," *Journal of Urban Affairs* 28, no. 1 (2006): 76.

115. Federal Bureau of Investigation, *Uniform Crime Reports*, January–December 2003 (preliminary; *http://fbi.gov/ucr/htm*). See also U.S. Bureau of the Census, *Statistical Abstract of the United States 2003*, Table 305, Crimes and Crime Rates, by Type of Offense: 1980 to 2001, p. 199.

116. Federal Bureau of Investigation, *Uniform Crime Reports*, January–December 2003 (preliminary; *http://fbi.gov/ucr/htm*).

117. Ibid.

118. Rebecca Yang and Paul A. Jargowsky, "Suburban Development and Economic Segregation in the 1990s," *Journal of Urban Affairs* 28, no. 3 (2006): 253–273.

119. William H. Frey and Alan Berubé, "City Families and Suburban Singles: An Emerging Household Story," in Katz and Lang, *Redefining Urban & Suburban America*, p. 265.

120. Mark Abrahamson, *Global Cities* (New York: Oxford University Press, 2004), pp. 99–100.

121. Ibid., p. 101.

122. U.S. Bureau of the Census, *The Changing Shape of the Nation's Income Distribution, 1947–1998*, p. 3, Table 1 (published June 2000; *http://www.census.gov/prod/2000*).

123. U.S. Bureau of the Census, *The 2009 Statistical Abstract of the United States*, Table 669 (*http://www.census/gov/compendia/statab*).

124. Ibid., Table 221.

125. U.S. Bureau of the Census, Table 11, Employment Status of Civilian Population, Sex, Race, and Hispanic Origin: 2005 (*http://www.bls.gov/html*).

126. Ibid., Table A-2.

NATIONAL POLICY AND THE CITY–SUBURBAN DIVIDE

THE UNINTENDED CONSEQUENCES OF NATIONAL POLICIES

By the end of World War II, there was a growing national concern about the condition of the inner cities. The neglect of basic infrastructure brought about by the Great Depression and then by war could be observed in the decay of business districts, the dilapidation of older housing stock, and the tattered state of roads, bridges, parks, and urban amenities. These problems seemed all the more urgent because of over-crowding. The wartime boom had brought a crush of new residents to cities, but housing was hard to find. At first, the suburban subdivisions seemed like a welcome safety valve, but while they grew the cities slid ever deeper into decline. This was alarming because cities had always been pivotal to America's social and economic development, and thus their fate seemed inextricably tied to the nation's well-being.

In the postwar period, congressional leaders from both political parties worked with mayors and urban lobby, groups to push the cause of inner-city revitalization. In 1949 Congress made available massive volumes of public funding for urban renewal and public housing programs. These programs also leveraged an astonishing amount of private investment—$35.8 billion by 1968.[1] But even while funds were pro-vided to revitalize the cities, a variety of federal policies also helped fuel the suburban boom. Millions of white middle-class homeowners borrowed federally insured loans. Highway systems paid for by the federal government cut broad swaths through central-city neighborhoods in order to open up access to suburban subdivisions.

Within metropolitan areas, federal programs created a pernicious dynamic. Within the cities, slum clearance and public housing policies sharply reduced the sup-ply of housing available to African American homebuyers and renters. But because they were denied access to the suburbs by discriminatory policies administered by the real estate industry and by federal administrators, many low-income blacks were forced into the high-rise public housing projects being constructed through federal

OUTTAKE

HIGHWAY PROGRAMS CONTRIBUTED TO THE DECLINE OF THE CITIES

It is inaccurate to use the phrase "national urban policy" when referring to all the policies that have influenced urban development in the United States. There has never been a national policy for the cities. Instead, a very mixed bag of policies have been adopted at various times. Sometimes they work at cross-purposes because they have been enacted at different times, are located in dozens of departments and agencies, and are virtually never coordinated. Even when they have profound impacts on urban development, the urban dimension is often not considered at all. Considering the political forces at work and the complexity of the governmental system in the United States, it is doubtful that a comprehensive and well-coordinated urban policy would ever be possible.

Highway programs serve as an enlightening example. Though federally assisted highway building has exerted a huge impact on metropolitan spatial development, national policies have been aimed at many goals, with scant attention paid to their influence on cities. Early in the twentieth century, the federal government began supplying aid for state-constructed roadways as a way of connecting farmers to the national economic system and for opening up new areas for settlement. By the 1930s, federal aid became focused on a more abstract objective of promoting the use of the automobile. The political muscle of the automobile industry expanded in step with its economic importance. The states established trust funds that relied primarily upon gasoline taxes, and federal legislation in 1934 established penalties for any state that used any auto taxes for other purposes than building and maintaining highways.

In 1956 the federal role expanded enormously when Congress declared the intention to create a 42,000-mile national system of interstate highways. As in previous years, the taxes used to finance the system were "disproportionately collected in cities and disproportionately spent outside of cities," which reflected the power of rural interests and state legislatures and the aims of the highway engineers. It also accorded with the thinking of President Eisenhower, who thought that a national system of highways was important to the national defense: In times of war, it would make it easier to move troops and equipment. There was another consideration as well. It was widely thought that the concentration of populations and economic activity in cities made the United States vulnerable if atomic warfare broke out. An influential city planner warned that urban areas had to decentralize or face disaster: "If we delay too long, we may wake up some morning and find that we haven't any country, that is, if we wake up at all that morning." With so many purposes folded into one program, it should come as no surprise that highway builders did not watch out for the interests of the central city.

Sources: Quotations are from Owen D. Gutfreund, *20th Century Sprawl: Highways and the Reshaping of the American Landscape* (New York: Oxford University Press, 2004), p. 56; Robert M. Fogelson, *Downtown: Its Rise and Fall, 1880–1950* (New Haven, Conn.: Yale University Press, 2001), p. 392.

funding, and both low-income and middle-class blacks were forced into an intense competition for housing in neighborhoods left behind when whites fled for the suburbs.

Although the federal government shifted course in the 1960s, the changes came too little and too late. The patterns of residential segregation that separated the central cities from the suburbs continued to evolve for decades. The cities and their inner-ring suburbs became increasingly differentiated from the new subdivisions, which kept spreading inexorably outward. The metropolitan pattern of rigid racial segregation became firmly fixed, and the national government had helped put it in place. Later, in the 1960s and beyond, governments at all levels would be forced to devote huge resources trying to address an urban crisis of city versus suburb, black versus white, that national policies had helped create.

THE POLITICS OF URBAN REDEVELOPMENT

The concerns about inner-city slums that had been expressed in the depression years were voiced again following World War II. Local public officials and business leaders were alarmed by the condition of downtown business districts and nearby residential areas. Public housing administrators, labor unions, social workers, and liberal Democrats were concerned about the plight of the poor and argued that slum residents had a moral right to adequate housing. In addition, they said, slums bred disease, crime, and delinquency and were therefore detrimental to the moral fiber and social fabric of the city. It was noted, for example, that although Cleveland's slum areas contained only 3 percent of the city's population, they accounted for 8 percent of the juvenile delinquency arrests and 21 percent of the city's murders in 1932.[2] Improving the physical environment of slum residents, it was argued, was a good thing to do not only because it gave poor people immediate aid but also because it would help families and individuals living in the slums join the mainstream of society by improving their lives.

Realtors, developers, financial institutions, and local business elites had entirely different reasons for favoring slum clearance. They were not concerned so much about the conditions of life for slum dwellers as for their own investments in inner-city property. Dilapidated commercial and residential areas, they maintained, threatened the economic vitality of the central cities. Even the very conservative National Association of Real Estate Boards (NAREB) favored federally funded urban redevelopment, but the issue remained subordinated to their venomous opposition to public housing programs, in large part because of the real estate industry's interest in preventing government competition with private developers and landlords.[3]

A broad coalition of groups important to the Democratic Party fought for public housing. Organized labor led the way in criticizing the real estate industry's proposals for redevelopment without public housing. Local government officials represented by the U.S. Conference of Mayors, the National League of Cities, and the American Municipal Association all lined up behind a program of federally subsidized development. They were instrumental in knitting together a coalition sufficiently broad that the legislation before Congress would not be sabotaged by bickering over details. After the general elections of 1948 returned Democratic majorities to both houses of Congress, the Housing Act passed in the spring of 1949. Despite intensive lobbying efforts by the real estate agents and their allies, the public housing title was retained by a razor-thin five-vote margin, and the entire bill was then passed by a bipartisan majority of northern Democrats, urban Republicans, and a few southern Democrats.[4]

In the Housing Act, Congress declared a national commitment to rebuild the cities, eliminate slums and blight, and provide decent housing for the nation's citizens. The preamble to the act, titled a "Declaration of National Housing Policy," made a sweeping statement about the need for a housing program:

> The general welfare and security of the Nation and the health and living standards of its people require housing production and relating community development sufficient to remedy the serious housing shortage, eliminate substandard and other inadequate housing through the clearance of slums and blighted areas, and the realization as soon as feasible of the goal of a decent home and suitable living environment for every American family.[5]

The housing industry got most of what it wanted in the bill, but to win federal subsidies for slum clearance, it was forced to accept public housing. In the end the housing bill received the endorsement of key business, real estate, and housing interests because of the important provisions that allowed local authorities to supervise and profit from redevelopment. Title I of the act empowered the Housing and Home Finance Agency (HHFA) to assist local efforts at blight and slum removal. Through this agency, the federal government offered grants-in-aid to help local urban renewal agencies absorb the cost of a write-down on the sales price for land that had been cleared of slum buildings. The write-down was the difference between the local agency's cost of assembling and clearing the site and a negotiated below-market price subsequently paid by private developers.

In addition to the money authorized for the write-down subsidies, the HHFA was authorized to extend loans to local urban renewal or public housing agencies for land assembly and site clearance. The act gave private developers preference over local governments in redeveloping the clearance sites. Tenants and slum dwellers displaced by renewal programs were supposed to be supplied with "decent, safe and sanitary dwellings." The redevelopment effort was required to be "predominantly residential" in character. Amendments to the legislation, adopted in 1954, allowed communities to use 10 percent of project funds for nonresidential, commercial revitalization. In 1960 this proportion was raised to 30 percent.

Title III, Low-Rent Public Housing, authorized (but did not appropriate money for) the production of 810,000 government-subsidized housing units over a six-year period. This amounted to 10 percent of the estimated national need for new low-cost dwellings. Occupancy preferences were given for veterans and families displaced by Title I (clearance) activities. Per-room and per-unit cost limitations were imposed to prevent "extravagance and unnecessary" amenities. Rent levels and tenant eligibility requirements were regulated to minimize competition with the private housing market and to ensure that public housing benefited only the neediest families.

URBAN RENEWAL AS "GOOD POLITICS"

Local political and economic elites were far more concerned about the economic decline of central business districts (CBDs) than they were about slum residents. Business leaders and politicians were convinced that slums were responsible for the steady decline in downtown property values and retail activity. Right from the beginning, low-income housing was sacrificed to commercial development, a practice made possible by the way federal administrators interpreted the legislation. Any renewal project that allocated 51 percent or more of its funds to housing was classified by federal administrators as a "100 percent housing" project. By taking advantage of such misleading definitions or by ignoring program guidelines altogether, local authorities often were able to allocate as much as two-thirds of their funds for commercial projects, despite the "predominantly residential" language contained in the original legislation.

Public housing immediately ran into trouble. In the abstract, housing for low-income people might seem worthwhile, but few local politicians felt they could afford to tolerate it in their own neighborhoods. Site selection was of paramount concern, for example, to Chicago's white politicians in the 1950s, who saw to it that public housing would not be built in their wards.[6] Any attempts to locate public housing in or near white neighborhoods were bound to incite protests and even violence. As early as December 1946, when the Chicago Housing Authority tried to move a few families of African American veterans into a public housing project built with funds from the 1937 housing act, white mobs jeered and threw stones. In August 1947, white mobs gathered to keep blacks from moving into a project on the city's southwest side. A contingent of police were assigned to protect the black families, and they stayed six months.[7] The CHA learned its lesson well, and was very careful about its proposal for building public housing under the 1949 act.

The Chicago experience was duplicated in cities across the country. Local chapters of the National Association of Real Estate Boards organized opposition to public housing projects in city after city. In vitriolic campaigns, the opponents of subsidized housing played on fears that public housing might be used to promote racial integration. Between 1949 and the end of 1952, public housing programs were rejected by referenda, many of them sponsored by local chapters of NAREB, in Akron, Houston, Los Angeles, and almost 40 other cities. Social and political realities at the local level made public housing a volatile issue. Local officials were acutely aware "there could hardly be many votes to be gained in championing the cause—and perhaps a great many lost."[8]

By contrast, slum clearance and economic redevelopment added up to good politics. Seizing on redevelopment as a way to secure federal funds, enterprising mayors could simultaneously advance their political fortunes and improve the public image of the city. To implement big clearance and redevelopment projects, an alliance had to be forged between the mayor and other local officials on the one hand and the business community on the other. In most cities, the most important members of the alliance were corporate executives, but other crucial participants were involved as well. Real estate and business interests in central business districts, metropolitan newspapers, and the construction trades unions lent their support. For many years, this political alliance constituted a "new convergence of power" that completely dominated the politics of most large cities.[9]

The programs financed by the 1949 housing act were perfect vehicles for mayors who wished to secure their personal political futures. Richard J. Daley, first elected mayor of Chicago in 1955, rebuilt the Democratic machine in that city by using urban renewal funds to launch an ambitious program to revitalize Chicago's downtown Loop and lakefront. In Boston, the candidate selected by the business-sponsored New Boston Committee defeated longtime machine boss James Michael Curley in the 1951 mayoral race, then backed the massive clearance of Boston's Italian West End and the construction of a large government center. Ultimately, Boston's renewal program took 10 percent of the city's land area.[10] In 1950 St. Louis's mayor, Joseph Darst, received widespread national publicity when his city became the nation's first to secure federal funding for a massive urban renewal program. Raymond Tucker, who replaced him in 1953, was even more aggressive in pushing clearance projects. A former St. Louis mayor recalled that renewal united political and business leaders behind a common cause:

> About a year ago, a group of distinguished citizens of our community were called into the Mayor's office and there charged by Mayor Darst with the responsibility of giving leadership to a program. . . . It was suggested that an urban redevelopment corporation be organized. There was much fine publicity on the part of the metropolitan press—they not only gave considerable space but they also subscribed to the extent of better than a quarter of a million dollars to the debentures and stock of that corporation. So, we salute the press on this occasion. I should add that many other fine business institutions, 69 in number, subscribed a total in excess of $2,000,000 toward the capital structure of the corporation. It is a distinguished list. There's the May Department Stores, Stix, Baer and Fuller, Scruggs, Vandervoort and Barney, the Anheuser Busch Company, Ely Walker Company, the Falstaff Company, the First National Bank, . . . and others.[11]

A similar alliance came together in New Haven, Connecticut, where the young Democrat Richard Lee won several terms by leading a broad coalition that sponsored federally funded redevelopment. Lee's political capital derived from an alliance between government officials and local notables, particularly business leaders. Mayor Lee referred to this coalition as

> the biggest set of muscles in New Haven. . . . They're muscular because they control wealth, they're muscular because they control industries, represent banks. They're muscular because they head up labor. They're muscular because they represent the intellectual portions of the community. They're muscular because they're articulate, because they're respectable, because of their financial power, and because of the accumulation of prestige they have built up over the years as individuals in all kinds of causes.[12]

Mayors and business leaders tended to share the view that the economic fortunes of their cities depended on the health of the central business district. The flight of the middle class to the suburbs was seriously undermining the economic viability of inner cities. Because the central business district was the center of activity where the local business establishment held heavy real estate and business investments, it was only logical that businesses would seek to protect their investments through revitalization of their immediate environment. The need for political visibility and campaign contributions from wealthy donors ensured that elected officials would favor downtown sites. Those areas were generally the oldest in the cities and therefore easily designated as officially "blighted" by the local urban renewal authority, the first step in a process that led to condemning and clearing property.

The members of the urban renewal coalition needed one another. Local officials coveted the investment capital and the public prestige the business community possessed. In turn, the business community depended on the resources of the public sector. Governmental authority was a necessary ingredient for a successful redevelopment effort. Public authority was, in the first instance, called on to apply for federal funds through an officially constituted urban renewal agency. The government's power of eminent domain, which allowed it to condemn "blighted" property for a "higher" public use, was crucial for land assembly because individual property owners could not otherwise be compelled to sell. Finally, the unique ability of local renewal agencies to receive the necessary write-down subsidies and loans from the federal government made local officials and agencies indispensable to business leaders who wanted urban redevelopment. "This strange coalition"[13] was thus a mutually reinforcing alliance of formidable power.

The urban renewal program "engineered a massive allocation of private and social resources" in the cities.[14] Public funds were used to make downtown areas more desirable to investors. By 1968 private institutions had committed $35.8 billion in 524 renewal projects across the nation.[15] From 1953 to 1986, when the last money left in the pipeline was finally exhausted, over $13 billion in direct federal spending had been committed to urban renewal.[16] In addition, the huge federal expenditures on the interstate highway program, funded through the National Defense Highway Act of 1956, provided hundreds of thousands of jobs and considerable profits to construction firms building limited-access highways through urban neighborhoods.

The clearance of neighborhoods associated with urban renewal and highway building soon ignited resistance and controversy. Although business leaders talked glibly about benefiting all the residents of the city through the provision of jobs and increases in business investment, it became painfully apparent that viable neighborhoods were often destroyed in the process. In Boston, block after block of well-kept bungalows and row houses, grocery stores, barber shops, bakeries, and taverns—all the elements making up historic, safe, thriving Italian neighborhoods in Boston's West End—were leveled. *Blight* was such a loose term that it could be, and often was, applied even to healthy neighborhoods.[17]

All across the country, community protests were directed at the destruction of neighborhoods caused by urban renewal and highway construction projects. According to one scholar, "development issues . . . dominated the neighborhoods" in the 1950s and 1960s in the four cities he studied.[18] Considering the intensity and frequency of protest, it seems surprising that neighborhoods won few victories. The reason for this poor record was that the groups opposing renewal were small and often divided from one another on the basis of race and ethnicity. Neighborhoods basically tried to protect their own turf; it was difficult for them to make common cause with other neighborhoods. By astutely selecting renewal and redevelopment sites, urban renewal administrators found it easy to pursue a politics of divide and conquer.

Atlanta provides an excellent example of this process. Beginning in 1952 Atlanta's Metropolitan Planning Commission became concerned about the movement of blacks into neighborhoods close to the central business district. In its report of that year, *Up Ahead*, the commission maintained that "from the viewpoint of planning the wise thing is to find outlying areas to be developed for new colored housing." The commission recommended "public policies to reduce existing densities, wipe out blighted areas, improve the racial pattern of population distribution, and make the best possible use of central planned areas."[19] The actual goal, thinly disguised by this rhetoric, was to move blacks into areas farther from the downtown area and to secure land near the CBD for redevelopment.

Atlanta's organization of big corporations, the Central Atlanta Improvement Association, backed faithfully by the white-owned newspapers, energetically promoted clearance. Special care was taken to obtain the support of the Chamber of Commerce, which represented smaller businesses. The Atlanta Real Estate Board was brought on board by promises that renewal would help maintain segregated housing patterns and no public housing would be constructed on urban renewal land. Support from some leaders of the black community was obtained by promises to make land available for the construction of black housing subdivisions farther from the CBD and by a commitment to build single-family, owner-occupied housing for blacks, which was to be subsidized by federal funds available under Section 221 of the 1949 housing act. Years after the area was cleared, downtown Atlanta was still undergoing massive clearance and reconstruction, and a huge enclosed mall called the Peachtree Center was slowly replacing the historic downtown.

The local renewal coalitions born in the 1950s used their political muscle to crush opponents. Although almost any city could be used as an example, San Francisco's single-minded pursuit of downtown renewal is especially revealing.[20] In 1953 the San Francisco Board of Supervisors approved a plan to clear several blocks of land adjacent to the financial district and south of Market Street. This area, with its market stalls, narrow passageways, and constant bustling activity, concerned business and political leaders, who worried about the impact it might have on the future downtown, which they envisioned as an expanding agglomeration of corporate, cultural, and tourist facilities. By the late 1950s, a plan for redevelopment had taken shape. The city planned to build a huge sports arena and convention center on the site, to be named the Yerba Buena Center. It was thought that Yerba Buena would act as a magnet for the expansion of the city's financial center.

This vision appealed to the scores of corporate giants located in the heart of the city, including Standard Oil of California, Southern Pacific, Transamerica Corporation, Levi Strauss, Crown Zellerbach, Del Monte, Pacific Telephone and Telegraph, Bethlehem Steel, and Pacific Gas and Electric. Among the many financial institutions located in downtown San Francisco were Bank of America, Wells Fargo, Crocker National Bank, Bank of California, Aetna Life, John Hancock, and Hartford Insurance. During the 1960s the buildings that housed these institutions changed San Francisco's skyline. Twenty-three high-rises were constructed in downtown San Francisco between 1960 and 1972.[21]

The director of the San Francisco Redevelopment Agency, M. Justin Herman, became the "chief architect, major spokesman, and operations commander" for the massive renewal project. Under his leadership, the redevelopment agency hired several hundred professionals and dozens of consultants and applied for millions of dollars in federal urban renewal subsidies. Herman believed in his mission so zealously that he interpreted any criticism of his project as an attempt by parochial interests to stand in the way of progress. In 1970 he was quoted as saying, "This land is too valuable to permit poor people to park on it."[22] He was cited in a major publication in 1970 as "one of the men responsible for getting urban renewal" renamed "the federal bulldozer" and "Negro removal":

> He was absolutely confident that he was doing what the power structure wanted insofar as the poor and the minorities were concerned. That's why San Francisco has mostly luxury housing and business district projects—that's what white, middle-class planners and businessmen envision as ideal urban renewal.[23]

Federal administrators turned a blind eye to the fact that the Yerba Buena Center project was being planned with no thought to building replacement housing for the people who lived in the area being cleared. During the summer of 1969, the residents living in the proposed clearance area challenged the project in federal court, arguing it violated the 1949 housing act's requirement that residents in clearance projects be relocated into safe and suitable housing. The judge who heard the case concluded that the secretary of the Department of Housing and Urban Development "had not been provided with any creditable evidence at all" in regard to the redevelopment agency's plan to relocate residents.[24] Temporarily stopped in its tracks, the redevelopment agency eventually agreed to increase the hotel tax in San Francisco in order to finance the construction of low-income housing for tenants who would be displaced by the Yerba Buena Center. Court battles over this plan, however, plus the escalating costs of the center, eventually doomed it, and it was not built.

National-level opposition to federally assisted urban renewal emerged in the early 1960s. Liberal critics viewed urban renewal as a "federally financed gimmick to provide relatively cheap land for a miscellany of profitable, prestigious [private] enterprises."[25] Conservatives were also appalled by the results of the program. At its inception and through its early years, business leaders and politicians expected a miraculous reversal of central-city decline. The optimism soon turned into frustration. Redevelopment took too long. By the late 1960s, it took an estimated four years to plan a clearance and renewal project and then an additional six years to complete it. Often, by the time a project was finished, the original plans had long been abandoned.[26] Blighted neighborhoods and slums grew faster than the renewal projects could eliminate them.

RACIAL SEGREGATION AND "THE PROJECTS"

In the core areas of the cities, poverty and race were inextricably linked; as a result, most urban renewal programs had racial (or racist) overtones. The blacks who moved to the cities in the twentieth century were housed in the most rundown areas of the inner cities. The oldest and most dilapidated housing generally was located near central business districts, which meant clearance projects frequently displaced black populations.

The "black residents of the inner cities [and] black businesses were among the prime victims of federally-sponsored urban renewal programs" referred to as "black removal."[27] The program was derisively referred to by critics as "Negro clearance," a phrase that derived from the fact that over three-fourths of the people displaced by urban renewal in the first eight years of the program were black.[28] African American tenants were forced into other parts of the city by clearance projects—usually to dilapidated housing in a slightly more distant slum or to public housing constructed on cleared land still surrounded by slums. Economic and racial barriers left them no choice other than to move to another area much like the slum they had left behind: "Given the realities of the low-income housing market . . . it is likely that, for many families, relocation [meant] no more than keeping one step ahead of the bulldozer."[29] Thus a new game was added to the harsh realities of urban life—"musical slums."

Black families who were displaced by urban renewal found their options to be few. Their status as slum dwellers gave blacks "the dubious privilege of eligibility for public housing."[30] Nationwide, nonwhites accounted for 38 percent of all public housing tenants in 1952, but by 1961 this percentage had risen to 46 percent. In big cities the proportions were much higher, and segregation was the norm. Whites who were eligible for public housing or who had been victims of slum clearance had housing options in the private market that were unavailable to blacks. Blacks, therefore, tended to take over public housing by default.

Not only were the poor displaced but they also were forced to pay higher rents when the supply of low-rent housing units dwindled. By the end of 1961, clearance projects had eliminated 126,000 housing units. The 28,000 new units that replaced them could house less than one-fifth of the 113,000 families and 36,000 individuals displaced by clearance.[31] There was a 90 percent decline in the supply of low-income housing within redevelopment areas during the first ten years of the program's operation.[32] Only $34.8 million of the urban renewal funds—less than 1 percent—was used for relocation assistance, placing a disproportionate share of the cost of the program on the slum residents who were forced to move.[33]

Public housing was designed to fail. Three nearly fatal restrictions were built into the program. The first and perhaps most important problem was that eligibility was restricted to those who could not afford any other kind of housing. The real estate lobby would have tolerated no other policy. The insidious result of such a policy was to concentrate those poor families together that, for whatever reasons, were unable to improve their circumstances. Tenants who got jobs and increased their incomes were evicted. Already, in the 1950s, the concentration of families in poverty meant that public housing projects were prone to high levels of violence and juvenile crime. Over the years, public housing tenants were increasingly made up of "broken families, dependent families, and welfare families."[34] If the families whose incomes went up had been able to stay in their apartments by paying higher rents, the rise in social pathologies might have been moderated,[35] and the rental income they paid would have helped make public housing more economically viable.

A second flaw was related to the fact that public housing projects almost always were built on slum land that had been cleared for that purpose; almost never were they built outside ghetto areas and never in the suburbs. This meant that nearly all projects were surrounded by slums, and most of these areas were inhabited by blacks.

From the beginning, most public housing projects were segregated by explicit policy in all but a few northern states. A significant portion of the buildings were occupied by whites and were, for a time, considered desirable by young families headed by veterans, who received first priority.[36] But by the time President John F. Kennedy signed an executive order forbidding the racial segregation of public housing projects in 1962, it could have little practical effect because by then the overwhelming majority of public housing tenants in large cities were African American anyway; white families found it easy to find other housing, but black families did not. Thus public housing policy had the perverse effect of reinforcing and intensifying the racial segregation that already existed in the cities.

A third fundamental problem flowed from cost and design restrictions that guaranteed most of the units would be undesirable, especially as they aged. Public housing served as a constant reminder to its tenants and to everyone else that this was a grudging welfare program. To save money on site preparation and construction costs, cities built clusters of high-density high-rise buildings. The African American writer James Baldwin might have been describing almost any of these projects when he referred to those in Harlem as "colorless, bleak, high and revolting."[37] Of course, big American and European cities are full of high-rises that command steep rents from affluent clientele, but such structures, especially when built cheaply, "were not suitable for poor people with big families."[38] It was difficult for parents to supervise children even when play facilities were available. The architecture was a virtual invitation to vandalism and crime; elevators were often broken and stuck, laundry rooms were many floors removed from tenants' apartments, dark hallways and stairwells were poorly lighted even when bulbs were available.

The Cabrini-Green projects north of Chicago's Loop began as two-story brick row houses built to house war workers in World War II. All of the occupants were white. In 1958 these houses were replaced by 15 high-rise buildings, and another 8 were constructed in 1962. These 19-story rectangular monstrosities loomed over the surrounding neighborhoods. Almost all the tenants were black. The same situation existed in New York City, where public housing often rose to more than 20 stories. The Pruitt-Igoe project in St. Louis, completed between 1954 and 1959, was composed of 2,762 apartments in 33 eleven-story buildings on a 57-acre site. By the time the last building was completed, the project was already a community scandal.[39] By 1973 it had become an international symbol for the failure of American public housing. In that year, photographs that made *Life* magazine's "The Year in Review" showed the shocking spectacle of one of the buildings imploding from hundreds of charges of carefully placed dynamite. As a monument to a policy failure, the episode could hardly have been more dramatic and fitting: Explosives experts got the opportunity to hone their demolition skills on buildings that had been built, complete with awards to the architectural firm, just 15 years before.

In 1965 rent supplement programs were enacted as an alternative to public housing for the poor. Through direct housing aid, the poor would presumably be able to choose their own housing on the private market. The Housing and Urban Development Act of 1968 required that a majority of housing units constructed on redevelopment sites be for low- and moderate-income families.[40] Such tinkering with the urban renewal and public housing programs came too late to make much of a difference.

Low-income housing continued to be replaced at far less than a one-to-one basis; indeed, only 51 percent of the new units built in urban renewal areas after 1968 were reserved for people of low or moderate incomes.[41]

Both public housing and urban renewal met their effective demise in the 1970s. In 1974 urban renewal was merged into the Community Development Block Grant program. Public housing was allowed to wither away during the Nixon administration, from 104,000 starts in 1970 to only 19,000 starts by 1974.[42] A few years later, it was essentially abandoned when the Reagan administration eliminated low-income housing built by the government in favor of programs to subsidize landlords and a few experiments in housing vouchers.

Slum clearance and public housing were always defended as socially beneficial to slum residents. The promise was that instead of living in dilapidated, unsafe properties, the poor would have the opportunity to move into safe and adequate housing constructed by the government. The politics of urban renewal and public housing programs, however, undercut their announced social objectives. For blacks, these programs turned into a cruel hoax. Local politicians and businesses used slum clearance to protect the property values of downtown business districts. Slum clearance became a means of moving blacks from potentially valuable real estate.

Perhaps the most enduring legacy from this period of public housing is that "the projects" became cultural symbols of blacks on welfare. Dense clusters of high-rise fortresses became the worst of slums that segregated the poorest of blacks even more than before. Ironically, racist stereotypes were also encouraged when middle-class blacks tried to break out of the slums. Shut off from the new housing in the suburbs, middle-class black families inherited the housing left by whites fleeing the cities. In the typical scenario, they displaced whites who lived in areas near all-black neighborhoods or bought into neighborhoods targeted by real estate agents for blockbusting. Because this process was so often repeated again and again, the white middle class developed the habit of associating declining property values with an "invasion" by blacks.

One way to understand the effect of this dynamic is to imagine the difference it might have made if middle-class blacks had been as free as the white middle class to leapfrog to suburban housing tracts. No doubt a high degree of racial segregation would have continued to exist. Even if it had, however, some black homeowners would have been able to (1) find affordable and desirable housing by buying new homes, instead of moving into neighborhoods already occupied by whites, and (2) benefit from the dynamics of the housing market, just as white homeowners did. With this dynamic in operation, the presence of blacks in a neighborhood would not have become so automatically equated, in the white imagination, with dilapidated housing or with declining property values.

NATIONAL POLICY AND THE SUBURBS

In the decades after World War II, millions of white families moved from the cities to the suburbs. Suburban growth would have occurred with or without governmental policies to hurry the process along, but it would have been far slower and more unpredictable if it had depended on the housing market alone. Two federally funded programs accelerated suburban development: the Federal Housing Administration (FHA) loans established by the National Housing Act of 1934 and the Veterans Administration (VA) loans made available to returning GIs by the Serviceman's Readjustment Act of 1944. Millions of Americans were able to purchase their first suburban home because of the liberal financing features of the FHA and VA programs.

Until the depression of the 1930s, the government played little direct role in housing provision. The notable exception was that the federal and state courts enforced restrictive covenants attached to property deeds; usually, such attachments restricted the sale of homes in urban neighborhoods to whites only. Restrictive covenants exerted a huge impact on the housing market, but the role of the courts was not considered to be a matter of government policy; rather, enforcement of the covenants was considered a private contractual matter between buyer and seller that the courts were occasionally called upon to mediate.

During the Great Depression the federal government was prompted to intervene in the nation's housing market because it constituted a significant sector of the national economy. Second only to agriculture as an employer, the housing industry experienced a sudden, devastating retrenchment during the depression. Before the stock market crash of October 1929, 900,000 new housing units were being built each year. In 1934 only one-tenth of this number, 90,000 units, was constructed. Throughout the 1930s, housing starts lagged far behind the demand for new housing.[43] In Chicago, only 131 new housing units were constructed in all of 1933, compared with 18,837 in 1929 and 41,416 in 1926.[44] Across the nation, 63 percent of the workers in the housing industry were unemployed in 1933. Foreclosures on millions of mortgages brought hardship to homeowners and drove thousands of banks out of business. The banks looked to the federal government for assistance.

The National Housing Act of 1934 created both the FHA and the Federal Savings and Loan Insurance Corporation (FSLIC). The FSLIC insured individual accounts up to $5,000 (this level has since risen in a series of steps to more than $100,000). It was hoped such insurance would inspire confidence by potential savers and investors, so people would put their savings into banks instead of under their mattresses. These savings accounts would enable savings and loan institutions to invest more capital in the floundering housing market.

The most important provision of the housing act is Section 203, the basic home mortgage insurance program under which the bulk of FHA insurance has been written up to the present day. Fully 79 percent of all FHA-insured units from 1934 to 1975, about 9.5 million units representing a face value of more than $109 billion, were insured under Section 203.[45] The purpose of the program was to finance the acquisition of proposed, under construction, or existing one- to four-family units. The act provided for FHA insurance of 80 percent of the value of the property. (Through the Housing and Urban Development Act of 1974, this share was increased to 97 percent of the first $25,000 and 80 percent of the remaining value, and since then the formula has been changed from time to time.) The low risk involved for the lending institution permits the borrower to pay a low down payment, with the remaining principal and interest spread over a period of up to 30 years.

There were many different expectations about the 1934 housing act. Title I of the act provided FHA insurance for loans used for "permanent repairs that add to the basic livability and usefulness of the property."[46] Social welfare liberals saw Title I as a means of eliminating substandard living conditions in the central cities by providing low-interest, low-risk loans. City officials hoped Title I would entice affluent people to stay within the city limits and remodel their homes rather than move to new homes in the suburbs. Downtown business interests had a different goal in mind: They favored it because they thought it could shore up the value of the central business districts. Most banks, savings and loan institutions, real estate agents, and contractors saw Section 203 as a way to finance new construction beyond the city. In lobbying for the housing act, they had agreed to Title I only as a compromise to facilitate quick congressional action.

Despite the impression one might get from reading the legislation, new construction under FHA came to mean housing outside the cities. Very little money was ever appropriated to finance Title I repairs. Section 203, by contrast, was used to assist millions of people to move to the suburbs in the years after World War II. The VA loans had much the same impact as the FHA. Together with the FHA, the no-down-payment policy of the VA helped increase the federally insured share of the mortgage market from 15 percent in 1945 to 41 percent by 1954.[47]

Table 7.1 shows how much more difficult it was to buy a home before the FHA program. In the 1920s, down payments of 30 to 50 percent were standard, and savings and loan institutions normally allowed a maximum of 11 years for loans to be repaid. Banks were not so generous; 5 years was the norm, often with a balloon payment (the entire loan) due at the end. In the 1960s conventional mortgage loans typically required 25 percent down and were amortized over a 20-year period (since then, loans with 10 to 20 percent down became the norm, with amortization periods of 30 years). Under the FHA, a home buyer could get a 30-year mortgage with only 5 percent down

Table 7.1   Relative Burden of Loan Terms, 1920s and 1960s[a]

Decade and Lender	Terms
1920s	
Savings and loan association	60 percent of house value loaned for 11 years fully amortized
Bank or insurance company	50 percent of house value loaned for 5 years unamortized (balance due at end)
1960s	
Conventional lender	75 percent of house value loaned for 20 years fully amortized
FHA	95 percent of house value loaned for 30 years fully amortized

[a]For a house equal to approximately 2.5 times the purchaser's annual salary.

Source: Adapted from Henry J. Aaron, *Shelter and Subsidies: Who Benefits from Federal Housing Policies,* Studies in Social Economics (Washington, D.C.: Brookings Institution Press, 1972), p. 77. Copyright © 1972 by the Brookings Institution.

and could obtain a much larger loan. The VA allowed banks to finance a mortgage with no down payment at all.

The FHA loan guarantee program fundamentally changed the home credit market. Between 1935 and 1974, more than three-fourths of the FHA-insured home mortgages financed new (as opposed to existing) housing.[48] The proportion of all homes that were owner occupied increased from 44 percent in 1940 to 63 percent in 1970, and to 68 percent in 2002.[49] As shown in Table 7.2, more than one-third of all homes purchased in 1950 and 1955 were financed through the FHA or VA programs, and the proportion of new single-family home sales financed under these programs varied from a low of 26 percent (in 1960 and 1990) to a high of 50 percent (in 1970). In 1995 FHA/VA financed 19 percent of mortgages, and the proportion fell to 14 percent in 2002.[50] The declining reliance on FHA and VA loans in the 1990s occurred mainly because lending institutions began offering variable-rate and other creative forms of mortgage financing.

Almost all of the new homes bought with FHA/VA loans were built in the suburbs. Throughout the 1940s and 1950s, the FHA exhibited an overwhelming bias in favor of the suburbs; for instance, in its first 12 years it did not insure a single dwelling in Manhattan. In part, the FHA's suburban bias reflected a preference for less dense, single-family neighborhoods, as found in the suburbs, over more dense, multiunit neighborhoods, as found in the cities. But the FHA suburban preference went far beyond

Table 7.2 Use of FHA- and VA-Insured Loans in the United States, 1950–2002

Year	Percentage of Private Housing Financed Through FHA or VA[a]
1950	35%
1955	41
1960	26
1965	30
1970	50
1980	36
1990	26
1995	19
2002	14

[a]Data from 1950, 1955, and 1960 for all private-sector housing. Data from 1965 to 2002 for newly built, private-sector, single-family homes that are actually built and sold within the reporting year. These new methods are not strictly comparable; the percentages for all private-sector housing will tend to be somewhat smaller than for private-sector, single-family housing built and sold within the reporting year. This bias will tend to understate FHA/VHA financing for 1950, 1955, and 1960.

Sources: U.S. Bureau of the Census, *Historical Statistics of the United States to 1970, Colonial Times to 1970*, pt. 2 (Washington, D.C.: U.S. Government Printing Office, 1975), pp. 369, 641 (for 1950, 1955, 1960); *Historical Statistics of the United States* (Washington, D.C.: U.S. Government Printing Office, various years) 2003: pp. 611–612, Tables 943–945; 2002: pp. 591–592, Tables 921–923; 1999: pp. 724–725, Tables 1201–1202; 1998: pp. 718–719, Tables 1199–1201; 1993: pp. 718–719, Tables 1221, 1224; 1989: p. 715, Tables 1262–1263; 1987: p. 706, Tables 1273–1274; 1982–1983: p. 748, Tables 1341–1342; 1973: pp. 684–685, Tables 1156–1158; 1969: pp. 697, 698, Tables 1071, 1075.

a simple matter of geography; FHA administrators actively promoted the idea that housing, and therefore neighborhoods, should be racially and ethnically segregated.

FHA mortgage insurance programs depended on private-sector lending institutions, which made the actual loans. From the beginning, the FHA absorbed the values, policies, and goals of the real estate and banking industries.[51] Indeed, the staff of the FHA was drawn from the ranks of those industries, and it was only logical that the FHA's philosophy would parallel theirs. Thus "FHA's interests went no farther than the safety of the mortgage it secured."[52] Mortgages were typically made available only in "economically sound" areas, where depreciating housing values seemed unlikely.

FHA administrators shared the real estate and banking industry's view that racially segregated neighborhoods were the soundest investments. When it issued its underwriting manual to banks in 1938, one of the guidelines instructed loan officers to steer clear of changing or racially mixed areas:

> Areas surrounding a location are [to be] investigated to determine whether incompatible racial and social groups are present, for the purpose of making a prediction regarding the probability of the location being invaded by such groups. If a neighborhood is to retain stability, it is necessary that properties shall continue to be occupied by the same social and racial classes. A change in social or racial occupancy generally contributes to instability and a decline in values.[53]

A revealing glimpse into how sensitive FHA administrators were to the issue of race can be gained by reading the language of a 1933 report submitted to the agency by one of its consultants, Homer Hoyt, a well-known sociologist and demographer at the time. He offered his view that land values and the racial composition of a neighborhood were closely linked:

> If the entrance of a colored family into a white neighborhood causes a general exodus of the white people it is reflected in property values. Except in the case of Negroes and Mexicans, however, these racial and national barriers disappear when the individuals of the foreign nationality groups rise in the economic scale or conform to the American standards of living.... While the ranking may be scientifically wrong from the standpoint of inherent racial characteristics, it registers an opinion or prejudice that is reflected in land values; it is the ranking of races and nationalities with respect to their beneficial effect upon land values. Those having the most favorable effect come first in the list and those exerting the most detrimental effect appear last:
>
> 1. English, Germans, Scotch, Irish, Scandinavians
> 2. North Italians
> 3. Bohemians or Czechoslovakians
> 4. Poles
> 5. Lithuanians
> 6. Greeks
> 7. Russian Jews of lower class
> 8. South Italians
> 9. Negroes
> 10. Mexicans[54]

FHA administrators advised the developers of residential projects to draw up restrictive covenants barring sales to nonwhites before they applied for FHA-insured financing.[55] Banks were made to understand that even "a single house occupied by a black family in an urban neighborhood, even one tucked away on an inconspicuous side street, was enough for the FHA to label a predominantly white neighborhood as unfit for mortgage insurance."[56] Through such policies, the federal government, in effect, required that new subdivisions be segregated. Thus federal policy acted as a powerful instrument to establish the social and racial patterns that emerged in urban America in the postwar years.[57] Between 1946 and 1959, blacks purchased less than 2 percent of all the housing financed with the assistance of federal mortgage insurance.[58] In the Miami area, only one black family received FHA backing for a home loan between 1934 and 1949, and there is "evidence that he [the man who secured the loan] was not recognized as a black" at the time the transaction took place.[59]

When the U.S. Supreme Court ruled in 1948 that racial covenants attached to property deeds could not be enforced in courts of law, the FHA was forced to amend its official policies. In 1950 the FHA revised its underwriting manual so it no longer openly recommended racial segregation or restrictive covenants. It did nothing to reverse the effects of its previous policies, however, and took no actions to discourage real estate agents, developers, or lending institutions from discriminating against blacks. Until the passage of the Housing Act of 1968, it was still legal for real estate agents and mortgage institutions to discriminate on the basis of race.

Under Title VIII of the Civil Rights Act of 1968,[60] Congress outlawed racial discrimination in housing. Its provisions were sweeping, barring discrimination in rentals and sales and in the provision of information about cost and availability, advertising, purchasing, construction and repair, and real estate services and practices. The statute mandated that each of the federal regulatory agencies involved with the real estate industry take affirmative steps to enforce both the spirit and the letter of the law.[61]

The 1968 legislation helped open the suburban housing market to African Americans. Between 1970 and 1980, the number of blacks who lived in suburbs grew by almost 50 percent, an increase of 1.8 million persons.[62] One in ten blacks living in the central cities in 1970 moved to the suburbs during this period, and the percentage of urban blacks living in the suburbs increased from 16 to 21 percent.[63] In the 1980s the trend continued. By the 1990 census, about 25 percent of urban black families lived in the suburbs; about 85 percent of white families did so.

Blacks who moved to the suburbs tended to have higher incomes than those who stayed behind.[64] Suburbanization undoubtedly expanded housing choice for blacks, but those who moved to the suburbs in the 1970s and 1980s remained about as segregated from whites as they were before.[65] Blacks moved mostly into older inner-ring suburbs, where they displaced white residents, much as they had previously in central cities.[66] These older suburbs tended to have many of the same problems as central-city neighborhoods. In general, the suburbs to which blacks moved had lower tax bases, higher debts, poorer municipal services, lower socioeconomic status, and higher population densities than did suburbs that were mostly white.[67]

Most suburban whites continued to have little contact with suburban blacks. In the mid-1980s, 86 percent of suburban whites lived in suburbs with a black population of less than 1 percent.[68] Even those suburbs that were racially mixed tended to be segregated internally, and it appeared that racial segregation intensified during the

1980s.[69] Why was the racial segregation characteristic of the cities being replicated in the suburbs? Research indicated that discrimination, not social class or income, determined residential location.[70] Socioeconomic differences between blacks and whites accounted for less than 15 percent of the segregation among suburbs in 1980.[71] Research conducted in the St. Louis area indicated that in the 1980s, nonracial factors such as housing cost and economic factors seemed to be less important in explaining patterns of residential segregation than in any previous decade,[72] and this pattern appeared to persist into the 1990s.[73]

Racial discrimination in housing continued even though legislation had outlawed it, in part because the enforcement provisions of the 1968 legislation were weak. Rather than being granted positive responsibilities for identifying discrimination, the Department of Housing and Urban Development (HUD) was limited to receiving complaints initiated by individual citizens. By thus assuming a passive rather than an active enforcement role, it was easy for HUD to avoid controversy by treating each case as an isolated occurrence rather than as part of a pattern. For citizens, the time and red tape involved in initiating a complaint was daunting, and thus all through the 1970s the volume of HUD-processed complaints remained low. Interestingly, enforcement improved somewhat under a Republican president, Ronald Reagan, when HUD took steps to publicize the remedies available under the 1968 civil rights legislation. Partially as a result, the number of complaints that HUD received rose sharply in the 1980s. Still, most citizens bypassed HUD and state and local civil rights agencies and went directly to the courts.[74] By focusing on individual remedies rather than on large-scale efforts to enforce compliance, the governmental role in fair housing enforcement remained small and inconsequential.

Some efforts by the federal government to eliminate housing discrimination benefited blacks, but in very limited ways. The Equal Credit Opportunity Act of 1974, the Mortgage Disclosure Act of 1975, and the Community Reinvestment Act of 1977 (CRA)[75] were intended to ensure that blacks receive equal consideration for home loans and that banks stop redlining areas where blacks lived. (Redlining derives its name from the red line drawn on maps to designate neighborhoods considered poor investment risks.) In the past, banks generally refused to make home loans in certain areas regardless of the qualifications of individual loan applicants. Since the 1977 legislation, banks have been subjected to repeated protests and a substantial amount of litigation from community groups challenging apparent redlining practices. Rather than engage in extensive litigation and respond to investigations by federal regulators, banks often have been willing to enter into negotiations with community groups. According to one estimate, by 1991 approximately $18 billion in urban reinvestment commitments had been negotiated in more than 70 cities across the country.[76] Just as it would be premature to conclude that all redlining has stopped, however, it would be inaccurate to assume all individual loan applications are judged strictly on their merits. A 1992 study by the Federal Reserve Bank of Boston found that minorities were roughly 60 percent more likely to be turned down for a mortgage, even after controlling for 38 factors affecting creditworthiness, such as credit history and total debt.[77]

To change the patterns of residential segregation that exist in urban areas, the federal government would have to implement housing policies with the strength and effect of the policies once used to promote segregation. Such policies would change the dynamics of the housing market. Rather than merely regulating lending institutions, for instance, the government could, conceivably, become a primary lender. It could also, in principle, seek reparations and damages from landlords and homeowners who violate antidiscrimination laws. It could challenge local zoning laws that have the effect of maintaining segregated housing patterns. Perhaps it should go without saying that no such policies are likely to be adopted.

SUBURBS, HIGHWAYS, AND THE AUTOMOBILE

As we have seen, housing and urban renewal policies sponsored by the federal government have powerfully shaped the patterns of racial and socioeconomic segregation that exists in America's urban areas. National transportation policies also encouraged suburban growth and central-city decline. In a few years and at great expense, the U.S. government ensured the triumph of the automobile over mass transit. In doing so, the poor were left stranded in the central cities, ever more distant from suburban jobs, and with few affordable ways to get to them. "Automobility" enabled Americans to implement Henry Ford's solution to urban problems: "We shall solve the problems of the city by leaving the city."[78] Only in the last decade have the policies favoring the automobile been somewhat modified, but so far they are having little effect.

Americans depend on the automobile for urban travel more than people in any other nation. Although other advanced industrial nations such as Germany, Britain, and Japan embraced the automobile, they also maintained modern systems of mass transit as workable alternatives, despite the fact that automobile use has gone up in those countries. In West Germany, for example, between 1950 and 1974, at the same time that automobile travel increased 15 times, public transit use more than doubled.[79] In the United States, by contrast, between 1950 and 1977, as the volume of automobile traffic on urban roads more than tripled, urban mass transit ridership declined by over half, and it has not rebounded since. For the United States as a whole, only 4 percent of workers used public transit to commute to work in 2000—a decline from a peak of 5.4 percentage in 1983.[80] In all but a handful of cities in the Northeast, notably New York City, less than 5 percent of workers use mass transit.

As its title implies, the 1956 National Defense Highway Act was justified partly on military grounds—two of its stated purposes were to aid the movement of troops and supplies and to help evacuate American cities in case of a nuclear attack. The main rationale, however, was that freeways would stimulate the economy by creating a national system of superhighways linking all the major metropolitan areas in the nation. Within urban areas, the new expressways were expected to solve the growing problem of traffic congestion. A committee appointed by President Eisenhower asserted that suburbs were superior to cities and recommended that the new freeway system be used to decentralize American urban areas.[81] That is exactly what the new freeways eventually did.

The 1956 legislation placed federal gasoline taxes and new excise taxes on tires and heavy vehicles into a Federal Highway Trust Fund. Congress established a grant-in-aid formula of a 90 percent federal and a 10 percent state share for construction.

The federal government agreed to distribute the funds for the 42,500-mile system on the basis of need. Because costs in built-up urban areas were greater, urban areas would get the most funds.

In the years leading up to the legislation, urban planners debated with highway engineers about how a national highway system should be built. Urban planners wanted to design highways in the context of larger efforts to shape regional development and revitalize declining central cities. Highway engineers, however, believed the new interstate system should be designed with one goal in mind: to move people and goods in the most efficient manner from point A to point B. This meant, in effect, that freeways would go directly from the suburbs to the central cities and whatever got in the way would have to go. The engineers got their way. The 1956 act was written so that the funds allocated by the federal government would be administered by state highway departments. As one historian put it, "Since federal and state road engineers controlled the program, they had few incentives to include urban renewal, social regeneration, and broader transportation objectives in the programming."[82] When highways were built through urban areas, state highway planners chose routes without reference to their effects on existing neighborhoods.

Laying wide swaths of concrete had different effects in crowded cities than in the open countryside. As the highway builder Robert Moses said in a speech before the National Highway Users Conference in 1964, "You can draw any kind of picture you like on a clean slate . . . but when you operate in an overbuilt metropolis, you have to hack your way with a meat axe."[83] The meat axe approach turned out to be the main method Moses used to build his highways, displacing 250,000 people in the New York City area alone.[84] Because the highway engineers wanted to cause the least disruption to private commercial land values, highways were routed through neighborhoods, especially those with the cheapest housing occupied by poor people and minorities.[85] The program was justified not only as highway building but also as slum clearance. According to one estimate, the uncompensated loss to city residents who were displaced averaged 20 to 30 percent of one year's income.[86]

The way the interstate highways were rammed through neighborhoods left a damaging imprint that lingers to the present day. The highways took land off the tax rolls, but the most enduring impact was that some neighborhoods became so isolated, they could not avoid deterioration, and downtown areas were cut off from their waterfronts. In St. Louis, Interstate 70 divides the Mississippi River waterfront from the downtown, a separation that has made downtown revitalization difficult, a problem repeated in cities across the nation. By separating the South Bronx from the rest of the city, the Cross-Bronx Expressway in New York helped turn the South Bronx into an infamous ghetto. Scholars estimate that the unsightliness of the Fitzgerald Expressway in Boston reduced surrounding property values by about $300 million.[87] In 2004, after more than 15 years of work and more than $15 billion in funding, Boston completed a massive project to tear down the expressway and replace it with an underground tunnel. The land once occupied by the freeway is being turned into a park.

In response to the meat axe approach, "freeway revolts" began to proliferate.[88] One of the first successes came in 1959 when San Franciscans successfully prevented the completion of the Embarcadero Freeway. If their protests had failed, a freeway would today run along the shores of the San Francisco Bay, making the development of such tourist attractions as Ghirardelli Square and the Wharf almost impossible. Protests forced highway planners to become more sensitive to aesthetic and social considerations, but not before irreversible harm had been done to hundreds of urban neighborhoods and waterfronts.

By the 1980s the price tag for building the interstate system exceeded $100 billion. Although highway building received huge subsidies year in and year out, urban mass transit was starved. Unlike Europe, where gasoline taxes had always been used to help support mass transit, federal gas taxes in the United States could not be allocated for that purpose until 1975. Funding for urban mass transit gradually increased after that but remained small. Senator Gaylord Nelson of Wisconsin estimated that up to the 1980s, 75 percent of government expenditures for transportation in the United States in the postwar period had been spent on highways and roads, but only 1 percent went for urban mass transit (most of the rest was spent for railroads and shipping).[89] The inadequate state of mass transit discourages most people from trying it.

In the 1990s, concerns about urban air pollution and long commuting patterns emerged on the national policy agenda, in considerable part because Democrats enjoyed majorities in Congress. In 1992 Congress passed the Intermodal Surface Transportation Efficiency Act (ISTEA, commonly referred to as "ice tea").[90] The significance of ISTEA is that it took substantial authority over interstate highway funds from politically insulated state transportation departments, which had always been dominated by highway engineers, and put decisions about urban transportation systems into the hands of Metropolitan Planning Organizations (MPOs). Governed by delegates representing municipal governments within urban regions, MPOs assumed authority over funding categories designed to reduce auto congestion and improve air quality.

The ISTEA legislation encouraged regional transportation planning by "flexing" federal highway funds, a process that allowed a portion of motor vehicle taxes to be spent on mass transit and even bicycle and pedestrian uses, if local transportation planners chose to. Between fiscal year 1992 and fiscal year 1999, $33.8 billion was available for transfer from transportation programs to transit projects, but local planners decided to transfer only 12.5 percent, or $4.2 billion, of this amount. Some states, such as New York, Massachusetts, California, and Oregon, transferred more than one-third of highway funds available to them to transit use; others transferred little or none.[91]

The precedent set for local flexibility was carried over in the 1998 Transportation Equity Act for the 21st Century (TEA 21), which replaced ISTEA. Under this legislation, highway builders were required to submit studies of the air quality effects for major new federally funded projects. But despite the new efforts to encourage the funding of public transportation, as shown in Table 7.3, the proportion of commuters using automobiles increased very slightly in most cases from 1990 to 2006, and for most metropolitan areas, less than 4 percent of commuters used mass transit. Improvements in mass transit systems might improve these numbers, but even after the 1998 legislation, adequate funding for that purpose would not be available to most transit authorities. On average, state and local governments still provided 90 percent of the funds for mass transit systems.

Table 7.3 Commuting Patterns 1990–2000, Selected Metropolitan Areas

	Percentage Public Transit 1990	Percentage Public Transit 2006
Boston	10.6%	8.9%
Chicago	13.7	10.8
Dallas	2.4	1.6
Denver	4.2	4.2
Los Angeles	4.6	4.9
New York	26.6	26.2
St. Louis	3.0	2.4
San Francisco	9.3	9.2

Note: Urban Area Definitions in 2006 are slightly larger than those previously used, and therefore include more low-transit ex-urban areas than before. However, this method does not change ridership statistics significantly.

Source: 1990 data, U.S. Bureau of the Census, Summary File 3, *Transit Ridership Share 1990,* July 2004 (*http://www.census.gov*).

In 2008, sharply rising gasoline prices provided incentives for people to reduce the use of their cars. As gas prices climbed to a national average of more than $4 for regular during that summer, buses, interurban trains, and light-rail systems became packed with riders. Cities such as New York and Boston, with their well-developed transit systems, showed an increase of 5 percent or more, but by far the largest increases in ridership, in the 10 to 15 percent range, occurred in urban areas that have been the most dependent on the automobile. However, in most metropolitan areas it will be difficult to significantly change transit patterns. In almost all urban areas, mass transit systems are not developed well enough to conceivably absorb more than a very small fracture of commuters, even if they run full all the time. In places like Denver, St. Louis, and any number of other cities, light-rail systems are important for transporting visitors to and from airports and for bringing fans to downtown ball games and other events, but they do not, and cannot, carry a large proportion of daily commuters. As a result of decades of investment in highway systems, urban transportation systems are well established and commuting habits are basically fixed. Any significant changes will require very costly infrastructure investments that will take years to complete.

Mass transit systems tend to be chronically underfunded. During the financial crisis of 2008–2009, several metropolitan areas reduced service on their transit systems in order to avoid drastic service cuts and layoffs. The irony is that fiscal problems were occurring at the same time that ridership had increased. This was because only about one-fifth of the revenues from mass transit systems come from fares; the remaining portion comes from state and local taxes, and these were sharply declining. In early 2009, the Metropolitan Transit Authority of New York City was trying to close a $1.2 billion budget gap. In the St. Louis area, officials were temporarily closing 2,300 bus stops, a move that threatened to raise unemployment levels by stranding workers who relied on the system. Transit authorities almost everywhere were considering fare increases and service cuts.[92]

Local officials looked to the federal government with high expectations that help was on the way. The American Recovery and Reinvestment Act of 2009, signed into law by President Obama on February 17, made $27.5 billion available for surface transportation, highways, roads, and bridges. As part of the administration's "green" initiative, about $12 billion was reserved for mass transit. Because the program was regarded mainly as a jobs initiative, federal administrators indicated that it had to be spent only on infrastructure projects such as new train cars, track repair, and station renovations.[93] These measures were likely to improve the quality of service, but they would do nothing for the most basic long-term problem for mass transit in the United States: a funding system that worked against basic investments in systems that might appreciably alter transit patterns in metropolitan areas.

THE DAMAGING EFFECTS OF NATIONAL POLICIES

It is a tragic irony that the urban programs initiated after World War II contributed to racial segregation and discrimination. While urban renewal clearance programs bull-dozed slum housing, public housing projects segregated blacks more than ever. Meanwhile, white middle-class Americans were paid, in essence, to move to the suburbs, and expensive new freeway systems eased their commute to their jobs in the center city. These programs powerfully shaped metropolitan development in the United States. For decades, millions of white middle-class families were able to secure loans guaranteed by the federal government. It allowed them to move into new suburban developments, where housing values appreciated. For white middle-class America in the postwar period, the home became the principal source of family worth and savings, money that could be invested in a child's education, in a bigger or newer house, or saved for retirement. Until the late 1940s, federal policy excluded African Americans from federal home loan programs, and it took until the late 1960s, when open-housing legislation was passed, for African American families to be able to enter the real estate market in any meaningful sense.

With or without federal programs, a high degree of residential segregation would have existed in metropolitan areas. But if federal housing programs had encouraged banks to loan to blacks as well as to whites, some middle-class black homeowners would have been able to find affordable and desirable housing by buying new homes, instead of moving into neighborhoods already occupied by whites. With this dynamic in operation, the presence of blacks in a neighborhood would not have become so automatically equated, in the white imagination, with neighborhood changes and declining property values. Equally important, if blacks had been able to buy homes wherever they chose much sooner, they also would have been able to invest in the future. Most African Americans were denied this crucial means of life savings and upward mobility.

Despite significant progress in breaking down racial barriers in recent decades, family wealth remains as one of the enduring differences between black and white American families. In 1995 the median net worth (assets minus debts) for white households was $49,030, compared to $7,073 for black households—a ratio of 1 to 7.[94]

The median net financial assets (cash that is immediately available) in the early 1990s was $6,999 for white families but *zero* for black families.[95] This gap, which measures the ability of families to pass on life chances from generation to generation, was created in substantial measure by the federal government. Many of the effects of these policies may have been unintended, but they were no less powerful because of that fact.

NOTES

1. John H. Mollenkopf, "The Post-War Politics of Urban Development," in *Marxism and the Metropolis: New Perspectives on Urban Political Economy,* eds. William K. Tabb and Larry Sawers (New York: Oxford University Press, 1978), p. 140.
2. U.S. Congress, Senate Special Committee on Post-War Economic Policy and Planning, *Housing and Urban Development: Hearings Pursuant to S. Res. 102,* Senate, 79th Cong., 1st sess., 1945, pp. 1228–1237.
3. Mark Gelfand, *A Nation of Cities: The Federal Government and Urban America, 1933–1965,* Urban Life in America Series (New York: Oxford University Press, 1975), p. 14.
4. See Nathaniel S. Keith, *Politics and the Housing Crisis Since 1930* (New York: Universe Books, 1973), pp. 41–100.
5. Housing Act of 1949, Public Law 81–171, Preamble, sec. 2, 81st Cong. (1949).
6. Martin Meyerson and Edward C. Banfield, *Politics, Planning, and the Public Interest* (New York: Free Press, 1955).
7. Ibid.
8. Leonard Freedman, *Public Housing: The Politics of Poverty* (New York: Holt, Rinehart and Winston, 1969), p. 55.
9. Robert H. Salisbury, "The New Convergence of Power in Urban Politics," *Journal of Politics* 26 (November 1964): 775–797.
10. Mollenkopf, "The Post-War Politics of Urban Development," p. 138.
11. Quoted in Institute of Housing, "Proceedings" (University College, Washington University, St. Louis, March 21–22, 1952, Mimeograph), p. 18. For studies of the coalition in other cities, see Harold Kaplan, *Urban Renewal Politics: Slum Clearance in Newark* (New York: Columbia University Press, 1963); Meyerson and Banfield, *Politics, Planning, and the Public Interest;* Peter H. Rossi and Robert A. Dentler, *The Politics of Urban Renewal—The Chicago Findings* (New York: Free Press, 1961). Refer also to Jewel Bellush and Murray Hausknecht, "Entrepreneurs and Urban Renewal: The New Mean of Power," *Journal of the American Planning Institute* 32 (September 1961); George S. Duggar, "The Relation of Local Government Structure to Urban Renewal," in *Urban Renewal: People, Politics and Planning,* eds. Jewel Bellush and Murray Hausknecht (Garden City, N.Y.: Doubleday, Anchor Books, 1967), pp. 179–187, 200–208, as reprinted from *Law and Contemporary Problems* 26 (Winter 1961); Herbert Kay, "The Third Force in Urban Renewal," *Fortune,* October 1964.
12. Quoted in Robert A. Dahl, *Who Governs: Democracy and Power in an American City* (New Haven, Conn.: Yale University Press, 1961), p. 136. For another insightful example of the use of urban renewal by political entrepreneurs, see Jewel Bellush and Murray Hausknecht, "Urban Renewal and the Reformer," in *Urban Renewal: People, Politics and Planning,* ed. Jewel Bellush and Murray Hausknecht (Garden City, N.Y.: Doubleday, Anchor Books, 1967), pp. 189–197.
13. Gelfand, *A Nation of Cities,* p. 161.
14. Mollenkopf, "The Post-War Politics of Urban Development," p. 140.
15. Ibid., p. 138.
16. Williamson, Imbroscio, and Alperovitz, *Making a Place for Community,* p. 76.
17. Herbert J. Gans, *The Urban Villagers: Group and Class in the Life of Italian-Americans* (New York: Free Press, 1962), Chapter 13.

18. John H. Mollenkopf, "On the Causes and Consequences of Neighborhood Political Mobilization," paper delivered at the annual meeting of the American Political Science Association, New Orleans, September 4–8, 1973.

19. Quoted in Clarence N. Stone, *Economic Growth and Neighborhood Discontent: System Bias in the Urban Renewal Program of Atlanta* (Chapel Hill: University of North Carolina Press, 1976), pp. 48–49.

20. See Chester Hartman et al., *Yerba Buena: Land Grab and Community Resistance in San Francisco* (San Francisco: Glide, 1974). The following material on the Yerba Buena controversy draws on this excellent book. In most cases, citations are limited to quotations or specific data.

21. Ibid., p. 31.

22. Ibid., p. 19.

23. Ibid., p. 190.

24. Ibid., p. 128.

25. National Commission on Urban Problems, *Building the American City* (New York: Praeger, 1969), p. 153. This commission, appointed by the president, was established in January 1967 and headed by former Illinois senator and longtime urban policy advocate Paul H. Douglas.

26. Ibid., pp. 164–165.

27. Arthur I. Blaustein and Geoffrey Faux, *The Star-Spangled Hustle*, foreword by Ronald V. Dellums (Garden City, N.Y.: Doubleday, Anchor Books, 1973), p. 71.

28. See Martin Anderson, *The Federal Bulldozer: A Critical Analysis of Urban Renewal, 1949–1962* (Cambridge, Mass.: MIT Press, 1964), p. 65; compare Rossi and Dentler, *The Politics of Urban Renewal*, p. 224.

29. Chester Hartman, "The Housing of Relocated Families," in *Urban Renewal: The Record and the Controversy*, ed. James Q. Wilson (Cambridge, Mass.: MIT Press, 1966), p. 322, as reprinted from *Journal of the American Institute of Planners* 30 (November 1964): 266–286.

30. Freedman, *Public Housing*, p. 140.

31. Anderson, *The Federal Bulldozer*, pp. 65–66; see also Bellush and Hausknecht, "Urban Renewal and the Reformer," p. 13.

32. Anderson, *The Federal Bulldozer*, p. 65.

33. Mollenkopf, "The Post-War Politics of Urban Development," p. 140.

34. Lawrence M. Friedman, *Government and Slum Housing: A Century of Frustration* (Chicago: Rand McNally, 1968), p. 121.

35. Freedman, *Public Housing*, p. 111.

36. Friedman, *Government and Slum Housing*, p. 123.

37. James Baldwin, *Nobody Knows My Name* (New York: Dial Press, 1961), p. 63, quoted in Freedman, *Public Housing*, p. 117.

38. Friedman, *Government and Slum Housing*, p. 121.

39. Lee Rainwater, *Behind Ghetto Walls: Black Families in a Federal Slum* (Chicago: Aldine, 1970).

40. Housing and Urban Development Act of 1968, Public Law 90–448, 90th Cong. (1968).

41. John C. Weicher, *Urban Renewal: National Program for Local Problems*, Evaluative Studies Series (Washington, D.C.: American Enterprise Institute for Public Policy Research, 1972), p. 6, citing unpublished HUD statistics: 538,044 housing units had been demolished as a result of urban renewal activities through 1971.

42. U.S. Department of Housing and Urban Development, *1974 Statistical Yearbook of the U.S. Department of Housing and Urban Development* (Washington, D.C.: U.S. Government Printing Office, 1976), p. 104.

43. Stephen David and Paul Peterson, eds., *Urban Politics and Public Policy: The City in Crisis* (New York: Praeger, 1973), p. 94.

44. Charles Abrams, *The Future of Housing* (New York: HarperCollins, 1946), p. 213.

45. Bureau of National Affairs, *The Housing and Development Reporter* (Washington, D.C.: Bureau of National Affairs, 1976).

46. Ibid.

47. Calculated from data in Congressional Quarterly Service, *Housing a Nation*, p. 6.

48. U.S. Department of Housing and Urban Development, *1974 Statistical Yearbook of the Department of Housing and Urban Development*, pp. 116–117.

49. U.S. Bureau of the Census, *Historical Statistics of the United States, Colonial Times to 1970*, pt. 1, Bicentennial ed. (Washington, D.C.: U.S. Government Printing Office, 1975), p. 646; for 2002 data, Danter Company (*http://www.danter.com/statistics/homeown.htm*).

50. Compiling reliable statistics on FHA/VA loans is difficult because of inconsistent data over time. The most accessible source is the *Statistical Abstract of the United States* (Washington, D.C.: U.S. Government Printing Office) for various years.

51. For a discussion of this phenomenon, see Murray Edelman, *The Symbolic Uses of Politics*, 7th ed. (Champaign: University of Illinois Press, 1976), pp. 44–76. We are indebted to Jeffrey Gilbert for several of the ideas contained in this section.

52. Michael Stone, "Reconstructing American Housing" (unpublished manuscript), quoted in Chester W. Hartman, *Housing and Social Policy*, Prentice Hall Series in Social Policy (Upper Saddle River, N.J.: Prentice Hall, 1975), p. 30.

53. Quoted in Brian J. L. Berry, *The Open Housing Question: Race and Housing in Chicago, 1966–1976* (Cambridge, Mass.: Ballinger, 1979), p. 9.

54. Quoted in ibid., pp. 9, 11.

55. Luigi M. Laurenti, "Theories of Race and Property Value," in *Urban Analysis: Readings in Housing and Urban Development*, eds. Alfred N. Page and Warren R. Seyfried (Glenview, Ill.: Scott Foresman, 1970), p. 274.

56. Richard Moe and Carter Wilkie, *Changing Places* (New York: Henry Holt, 1997), p. 48.

57. Charles Abrams, quoted in Norman N. Bradburn, Seymour Sudman, and Galen L. Gockel, *Side by Side: Integrated Neighborhoods in America* (Chicago: Quadrangle Books, 1971), p. 104.

58. Gelfand, *A Nation of Cities*, p. 221.

59. Nathan Glazer and David McEntire, eds., *Housing and Minority Groups* (Berkeley: University of California Press, 1960), p. 140.

60. Public Law 90–284, 90th Cong. (1968), Title VIII ("Fair Housing"), sec. 805.

61. D.C. Public Interest Research Group (DCPIRG), Institute for Self-Reliance, and Institute for Policy Studies, *Redlining: Mortgage Disinvestment in the District of Columbia* (Washington, D.C.: Authors, 1975), p. 3.

62. U.S. Department of Housing and Urban Development, *1974 Statistical Yearbook of the Department of Housing and Urban Development*, pp. 116–117.

63. Thomas A. Clark, "The Suburbanization Process and Residential Segregation," in *Divided Neighborhoods: Changing Patterns of Racial Segregation*, ed. Gary A. Tobin (Newbury Park, Calif.: Sage, 1987), p. 115; Larry Long and Diane Deare, "The Suburbanization of Blacks," *American Demographics* 3 (1981), cited in Douglas S. Massey and Nancy A. Denton, "Suburbanization and Segregation in U.S. Metropolitan Areas," *American Journal of Sociology* 3 (November 1988): 592–626.

64. Kenneth T. Jackson, *Crabgrass Frontier: The Suburbanization of the United States* (New York: Oxford University Press, 1985), p. 205.

65. John R. Logan and Harvey L. Molotch, *Urban Fortunes: The Political Economy of Place* (Berkeley: University of California Press, 1987), p. 195.

66. Clark, "The Suburbanization Process and Residential Segregation," pp. 115–137.

67. Massey and Denton, "Suburbanization and Segregation in U.S. Metropolitan Areas," pp. 592–626.

68. Logan and Molotch, *Urban Fortunes*, p. 194.

69. Douglas S. Massey and Mitchell L. Eggers, "The Spatial Concentration of Affluence and Poverty During the 1970s," *Urban Affairs Quarterly* 29, no. 2 (December 1990). See also S. Roberts, "Shifts in 80's Failed to Ease Segregation," *New York Times*, July 15, 1992, pp. B1–B3.

70. John F. Kain, "Housing Market Discrimination and Black Suburbanization in the 1980's," in *Divided Neighborhoods: Changing Patterns of Racial Segregation*, ed. Gary A. Tobin (Newbury Park, Calif.: Sage, 1987), p. 68.

71. John Farley, *Segregated City, Segregated Suburbs: Are They the Products of Black-White Socioeconomic Differentials?* (Edwardsville: Southern Illinois University, 1983), cited in Joe T. Darden, "Choosing Neighbors and Neighborhoods: The Role of Race in Housing Preference," in *Divided Neighborhoods: Changing Patterns of Racial Segregation,* ed. Gary A. Tobin (Newbury Park, Calif.: Sage, 1987), p. 16.

72. John F. Farley, "Race Still Matters: The Minimal Role of Income and Housing Cost as Causes of Housing Segregation in St. Louis, 1990," *Urban Affairs Review* 31, no. 2 (November 1995): 244–254.

73. Public Policy Research Centers, University of Missouri–St. Louis, *Analysis of Impediments to Fair Housing: St. Louis County* (St. Louis: Author, 1995).

74. William E. Nelson and Michael S. Bailey, "The Weakening of State Participation in Civil Rights Enforcement," in *Public Policy Across States and Communities,* ed. Dennis R. Judd (Greenwich, Conn.: JAI Press, 1985), p. 160.

75. Public Law 94–200, 94th Cong. (1975), Title III, and Public Law 95–128, 95th Cong. (1977), Title VIII.

76. Calvin Bradford, *Community Reinvestment Agreement Library* (Des Plaines, Ill.: Community Reinvestment Associates, 1992), as cited in *From Redlining to Reinvestment: Community Responses to Urban Disinvestment,* ed. Gregory D. Squires (Philadelphia: Temple University Press, 1992), p. 2.

77. Mitchell Zuckoff, "Study Shows Racial Bias in Lending," *Boston Globe,* October 9, 1992, p. B1.

78. Henry Ford, quoted in J. Allen Whitt and Glenn Yago, "Corporate Strategies and the Decline of Transit in U.S. Cities," *Urban Affairs Quarterly* 21, no. 1 (September 1985): 61.

79. James A. Dunn Jr., *Miles to Go: European and American Transportation Policies* (Cambridge, Mass.: MIT Press, 1981), p. 59.

80. U.S. Federal Transportation Administration (USFTA), *Summary of Travel Trends, 1995 National Personal Transportation Survey,* December 1999; USFTA and U.S. Bureau of Transportation Statistics, *National Household Travel Survey,* 2001.

81. Alan Lupo, Frank Colcord, and Edmund P. Fowler, *Rites of Way: The Politics of Transportation in Boston and the U.S. City* (Boston: Little, Brown, 1971), p. 184.

82. Mark Rose, *Interstate Express Highway Politics, 1941–1956* (Lawrence: Regents Press of Kansas, 1979), p. 97.

83. Quoted in Helen Leavitt, *Superhighway—Superhoax* (Garden City, N.Y.: Doubleday, 1970), p. 53.

84. Robert A. Caro, *The Power Broker: Robert Moses and the Fall of New York* (New York: Random House, 1974), p. 19.

85. Between 1951 and 1974, for example, 89 percent of the 10,000 households displaced by public projects in Baltimore were black. See Anthony Downs, *Urban Problems and Prospects* (Chicago: Marsham, 1970), pp. 204–205.

86. Ibid., p. 223.

87. John R. Meyer and Jose A. Gomez-Ibanez, *Auto Transit and Cities* (Cambridge, Mass.: Harvard University Press, 1981), p. 177.

88. By 1970 there were 400 struggles under way by community groups to oppose highway construction. Harry C. Boyte, *The Backyard Revolution: Understanding the New Citizen Movement* (Philadelphia: Temple University Press, 1980), p. 11.

89. Jackson, *Crabgrass Frontier,* p. 250.

90. This account of ISTEA relies on Paul G. Lewis, "The Politics of Structure in Transportation Policy: Resuscitating Metropolitan Planning Organizations Under ISTEA," paper delivered at the annual meeting of the Urban Affairs Association, Toronto, Canada, April 17, 1997.

91. Pietro S. Nivola, *Laws of the Landscape: How Policies Shape Cities in Europe and America* (Washington, D.C.: Brookings Institution Press, 1999), p. 15.

92. Michael Cooper, "Rider Paradox: Surge in Mass, Drop in Transit," *New York Times,* February 3, 2009 (*http://www.nytimes.com/2009/02/04/us/04trans.html*).

93. Ibid.

94. Melvin Oliver and Thomas Shapiro, *Black Wealth/White Wealth: A New Perspective on Racial Inequality* (New York: Routledge, 1997), pp. 85–87.

95. Ibid.

CHAPTER 8

URBAN POLICY AND THE POLITICS OF RACE

THE BRIEF LIFE SPAN OF INNER-CITY PROGRAMS

The problems of racial segregation and discrimination, poverty, and inner-city decline burst onto the nation's political agenda in the 1960s amid a growing recognition that previous programs were not doing the job. Especially within the Democratic Party, there was a consensus that a comprehensive strategy was needed to address social and urban problems. For a brief time urban problems became the main focus of national policy. The National Commission on Urban Problems (1958), the National Commission on Civil Disorders (1967), the President's Task Force on Suburban Problems (1967), President Nixon's Commission on Population Growth and the American Future (1972), and a host of state and city task forces decried the segregation of blacks and the poor in ghetto areas of the central cities. A great deal of hope was invested in the social and urban policies of the 1960s. But the political support for effective programs proved to be short-lived, and therefore it is difficult, perhaps impossible, to assess their potential for success.

Most of the programs of the Great Society (Lyndon Johnson's campaign slogan in the 1964 presidential race) were passed in a two-year period from 1965 to 1967. By the 1968 election, spending for the Vietnam War had already begun to undermine support for new policies, but racial divisions proved to be even more decisive. The landslide win by the Democrats in 1964 masked a development that would soon undermine the party's ability to win presidential elections. The issue of race was tearing apart the coalition the Democrats had fashioned in the 1930s. Johnson, the Democratic candidate, lost throughout the Deep South. The Republican standard-bearer, Barry Goldwater, received 87 percent of the popular vote in Mississippi, almost 70 percent in Alabama, and substantially more than 50 percent in Louisiana, Georgia, and South Carolina. After 1964 Republican candidates began to win elections in the South for the first time since the carpetbagger governments imposed on southern states after the Civil War.

Richard Nixon's victory in the 1968 election made it clear that it was impossible to divorce the issue of race from social welfare and urban programs. This had become obvious as early as the 1930s, when southern Democrats in Congress often expressed their concern that New Deal programs might be used to upset traditional racial relationships in the South. In the postwar years, they successfully fought to ensure that public housing would not be used to promote racial integration. As long as the programs advanced by Democratic liberals did not challenge race relations in the South, southern Democrats were willing to go along. But this tacit bargain ended with the civil rights legislation and the social programs of the 1960s.

In the public's imagination, the Great Society became identified as a constellation of programs that primarily benefited inner-city blacks. The truth is that very few programs had this character; funds for Head Start and the War on Poverty, for example, were spread broadly across the country, to urban and rural areas alike, and social programs such as Medicare and Medicaid benefited people regardless of where they lived. But impressions mattered. From 1969 to 1976, when Republican presidents Richard Nixon and Gerald Ford occupied the White House, many of the Democratic-sponsored programs came under attack, and Ronald Reagan's victory in the 1980 presidential election quickly brought an end to most urban programs. Urban programs vanished along with the alliance the Democrats had inherited from the New Deal years in the 1930s. Most of the Great Society programs lasted for 20 years or less, a life span too brief to effectively remedy the problems they were meant to address.

OUTTAKE

RACIAL DIVISIONS EVENTUALLY DOOMED URBAN PROGRAMS

The federal urban programs of the 1960s were adopted in response to civil disorders in the cities and the serious social problems highlighted by the racial turmoil. The federal response deeply divided the Democratic Party, which relied upon both urban voters and the Solid South. The urban vote had been essential to the Democrats for decades. Time after time, overwhelming Democratic majorities in the big cities balanced out Republican pluralities in the suburbs and small towns, providing the margin of victory in key states holding large blocs of electoral votes. The Democrats would have lost the presidency in 1940, 1944, and 1948 without the overwhelming margins delivered in 12 big cities in the nation. The urban electorate was essential to John F. Kennedy's victory in the close election of 1960. Kennedy beat Nixon by 112,000 votes, a margin of less than one-tenth of 1 percent, but he carried 27 out of the 39 largest cities in the nation. In 1964 Lyndon Johnson won by an unprecedented landslide, with the cities topping the national Democratic margins by 10 percent or more.

But the attempt to address the long-standing grievances of African Americans alienated white southerners and white working-class voters in almost everywhere. In 1968 the Republicans capitalized on resentment provoked by the successes of the civil rights movement. The

(continued on next page)

Democratic presidential candidate, Hubert Humphrey, carried only one southern state, Texas. Across the South, he won just 31 percent of the vote, running behind both Republican Richard Nixon (34.5 percent) and Alabama governor and third-party candidate George Wallace (34.6 percent), who ran as an avowed segregationist. In 1968 the Nixon campaign adopted law and order as its main theme. This had also been the campaign slogan of the Republican nominee in 1964, Barry Goldwater, but he had handled it crudely and ineptly. Goldwater's television ads tried to convey an impression that America's cities were in ruins by showing scenes of blacks rioting. In the scenes meant to portray Goldwater's vision of the American past he would like to restore, blacks were shown picking cotton. The spot ads that Nixon aired four years later were less blatant, although they were not subtle either. One of his television spots showed scenes of urban riots, with a Nixon voice-over calling for "some honest talk about the problem of order." At least blacks were not shown in a rendition of a bucolic agricultural past.

Richard Nixon won 32 percent of the African American vote in 1960, but his share fell to 12 percent in 1968. One of the president's closest advisers, John Erlichman, told civil rights administrators that "blacks are not where the votes are, so why antagonize the people who can be helpful to us politically?" After the 1960s the Republican Party mostly wrote off the African American vote. The Republican base became increasingly conservative, embracing working-class whites, a (now) solid Republican South, suburban and Sunbelt Republican voters, and the religious right. The razor-thin margin that decided the 2000 presidential election suggested that the Republican coalition was losing some of its force, an impression confirmed by the 2006 congressional elections. Even so, Democrats are not likely to propose policies intended primarily for the central cities. The votes simply are not there.

Sources: Statistics and quotations from Theodore H. White, *The Making of the President, 1960* (New York: Atheneum, 1961), p. 1201; John Mollenkopf, *The Contested City* (Princeton, N.J.: Princeton University Press, 1983), p. 83; Kathleen Hall Jamieson, *Packaging the Presidency: A History and Criticism of Presidential Campaign Advertising* (New York: Oxford University Press, 1984), pp. 202–203; Joseph McGinniss, *Selling the President, 1968* (New York: Trident Press, 1969); Numan V. Barley and Hugh D. Graham, *Southern Politics and the Second Reconstruction* (Baltimore: Johns Hopkins University Press, 1975), pp. 126–127; Everett Carl Ladd Jr., "The Shifting Party Coalitions, 1932–1976," in *Emerging Coalitions in American Politics,* ed. Seymour Martin Lipset (San Francisco: Institute for Contemporary Studies, 1978), p. 98; A. James Reichley, *Conservatives in an Age of Change: The Nixon and Ford Administrations* (Washington, D.C.: Brookings Institution Press, 1981), pp. 145, 186.

THE DEMOCRATS AND THE CITIES

When President Kennedy took office on January 20, 1961, his administration was already committed to helping the cities. Even before his campaign, Kennedy had concluded that the problem of the cities was "the great unspoken issue in the 1960 election."[1] During the campaign, the Democrats talked about doing something about the urban crisis whereas the Republicans tried to avoid such issues. "If you ever let them campaign only on domestic issues," confided presidential nominee Richard M. Nixon to his aides, "they'll beat us."[2] President Kennedy "emerged as an eloquent spokesman for a new political generation. In presidential message after message Kennedy spelled out in more detail than the Congress or the country could easily digest the most complete programs of domestic reforms in a quarter century."[3]

The Kennedy administration mapped out an ambitious agenda. Poverty, racial segregation, juvenile delinquency and crime, bad schools, and a host of other social problems were discovered in the 1960s only in the sense that they were no longer "out of sight, out of mind." They had existed for a long time and were no worse and little different by the advent of the Kennedy administration than they had been under Presidents Roosevelt, Truman, and Eisenhower. What made them seem worse was their greater visibility. Martin Luther King Jr. understood the task of creating visibility during the civil rights demonstrations in 1963. "I saw no way," he later commented, "of dealing with things without bringing the indignation to the attention of the nation."[4]

King turned the civil rights issue into a national crisis in Birmingham, Alabama, in the summer of 1963. What started in Birmingham spread across the South and even filtered into northern cities. During the summer, there were 13,786 arrests of demonstrators in 75 cities of the 11 southern states.[5] In the ten weeks that followed nationally publicized police attacks on demonstrators in Birmingham, the Justice Department counted 758 demonstrations across the nation. It quickly became clear that the administration could no longer avoid dealing with civil rights. The brutal treatment of civil rights demonstrators throughout the South was being televised in the living rooms of millions of American homes. By mid-June 127 civil rights bills had been introduced in the House of Representatives. The Kennedy administration, like it or not, was being drawn into the nation's most significant and divisive internal conflict since the Civil War.

The political pressures applied by the civil rights movement were reinforced by the influence of the black electorate. As John C. Donovan observed in his book *The Politics of Poverty,* "The greatest strength of the Negro communities lies in its voting power, in its numbers, and in their strategic location."[6] In the South, the black population was geographically diffused and systematically denied the right to the vote. When they moved to northern cities, blacks gained the franchise. Their votes were concentrated in the cities of the states holding a majority of the electoral college votes—Illinois, California, Massachusetts, Ohio, Michigan, New Jersey, New York, Texas, and Pennsylvania. Kennedy targeted his campaign on these key states, and the 68 percent plurality that black voters gave him was crucial to his razor-thin victories in Illinois, Missouri, and other states. In 1956 Adlai Stevenson, the liberal Democratic candidate from Illinois, had received 61 percent of the black vote.[7] If Kennedy had not done better, he would have lost the election: "It is difficult to see how Illinois, New Jersey, Michigan, South Carolina, or Delaware (with 74 electoral votes) could have been won had the Republican Democratic split of the Negro wards and precincts remained as it was, unchanged from the Eisenhower charm of 1956."[8]

On June 11, 1963, Kennedy overruled his advisers and announced he would propose a civil rights bill. When Kennedy was assassinated on November 22, the bill had just reached the House Rules Committee. The assassination created an emotionally charged atmosphere that the new president, Lyndon Baines Johnson, adroitly exploited. Opinion polls indicated overwhelming public support for civil rights legislation. Seizing the moment, Johnson added new provisions to the legislation and harried Congress into acting quickly. When Republicans joined with northern Democrats to move the bill out of the House Rules Committee, the bill was sent to the floor, where it passed by a vote of 290 to 130. On June 6, 1964, the Senate mustered the necessary two-thirds vote to overcome a filibuster mounted by southerners, and the legislation passed.

The Civil Rights Act of 1964 was far reaching. It outlawed discrimination in public accommodations, thus effectively striking down the South's Jim Crow laws, which denied blacks equal access to bus stations, restaurants, lunch counters, theaters, sports arenas, gasoline stations, motels, hotels, and lodging houses. It outlawed racial discrimination in the hiring, firing, training, and promoting of workers. It barred discrimination in the administration of federal grants. A year later, Congress passed the Voting Rights Act, which not only outlawed literacy tests and other discriminatory voting restrictions but also provided that federal registrars could replace local registrars in counties where there had been a history of discrimination against black voters.

Taking advantage of the post-assassination atmosphere, President Johnson also pressed for a program to redress economic inequalities.[9] Kennedy's advisers had persuaded him that the time had come for his administration to devise a program to attack poverty and unemployment. In June 1963 Kennedy had told Walter Heller, the chair of his Council of Economic Advisors, to appoint a task force of officials who would be responsible for proposing a program to attack poverty. Although Kennedy's commitment to a program was almost certain by the time of his assassination, it was not clear how hard he would have fought for it.

President Johnson was told about the proposed antipoverty program only two days after assuming office, but he quickly responded, "That's my kind of program. It will help people. I want you to move full speed ahead."[10] The idea of an ambitious, highly visible program appealed to Johnson's desire to be perceived as a second Roosevelt, as a president who would go down in history as the one who completed the social agenda left unfinished in the 1930s. In his first State of the Union address, on January 10, 1964, President Johnson announced he would seek a "total effort" to end poverty in the United States. Using a grandiose military analogy, he said, "This Administration here and now declares unconditional war on poverty in America, and I urge this Congress and all Americans to join me in that effort."[11] When Johnson signed the Economic Opportunity Act on August 8, he had two big legislative victories, the civil rights act and his "war on poverty," to carry into the presidential campaign.

The 1964 campaign provided the setting for a contentious national debate over the federal government's role and responsibilities. The Republican nominee, Barry Goldwater, was one of the few nonsoutherners to vote against the civil rights act in the Senate. He attacked the welfare programs funded through the Social Security Act of 1935 and even questioned the immensely popular old-age insurance program established through that legislation. The Republican Party's platform warned that "individual freedom retreats under the mounting assault of expanding centralized power."[12] Lyndon Johnson, by contrast, called for a Great Society that would eliminate poverty and treat other social ills through federal action on civil rights, the cities, health care, welfare, education, and employment.

Johnson won the election by a landslide, receiving 61 percent of the popular vote and picking up 486 electoral college votes to Goldwater's 53. The dimensions of the landslide allowed the Democrats to ignore the fact that Goldwater had won nearly all of his electoral college votes in the South, where Democrats had always won. The president's coattails were long; Democrats commanded a 289 to 146 majority in the House to go along with a 67 to 33 majority in the Senate.

The Democrats' overwhelming victory set the stage for a period of legislative activism not seen since Roosevelt's fabled One Hundred Days in 1933. Between 1964 and 1966, Congress authorized 219 new programs, which included some of the most important and enduring social initiatives of the 1960s. In 1965 Congress approved Medicare for the elderly and Medicaid for welfare recipients. The Elementary and Secondary Education Act provided federal grants to schools. Food stamps, an experimental program tried during the Kennedy years, became permanent in 1966. New and expanded educational and job-training assistance was made available for individuals with mental and physical disabilities. The public housing and urban renewal programs were expanded, and a new "model cities" program to treat the problems of cities was initiated. In 1966 Congress also created a new cabinet-level department, the Department of Housing and Urban Development (HUD), to administer urban programs.

Figure 8.1 shows that spending on federal regional and community programs rose sharply from 1962 to 1980, then fell almost as rapidly until 2005; since then, spending

Figure 8.1   Federal Spending on Regional and Community Development, 1962–2008 (in 2008 Dollars)

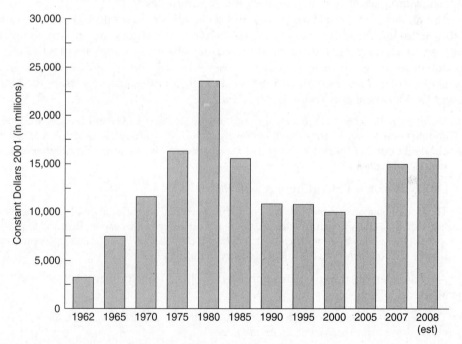

Note: Figures exclude spending on disaster relief.

Sources: U.S. Office of Management and Budget, *Budget of the United States Government, Fiscal Year 2009, Historical Tables* (Washington, D.C.: U.S. Government Printing Office, 2008), pp. 62–71, Table 3.2, Function 450, Community and regional development; Federal Spending on Regional and Community Development, 1962–2002 (in 2001 Dollars).

has spiked to about the same level that it was in 1985, at the beginning of President Reagan's second term. In 1962 the federal government spent $3.8 billion on these programs (in constant 2008 dollars; the actual figure that year was $445 million) to $24.2 billion in 1980 (2008 dollars; $9.2 billion in actual dollars). Local governments became increasingly dependent on intergovernmental transfers from federal and state governments. In 1950 grants from states and from the federal government accounted for only 10 percent of the revenues making up local budgets, but this proportion rose to over 26 percent of municipal revenues by 1978. By the end of the 1990s, cities received only about 7 percent of their income from intergovernmental revenues; the figure was about 10 percent in 2008.

The explosion in federal spending was energized by the conviction that the national government should take the nation in a new direction. Not since the closing of the frontier in the 1870s had the federal government attempted so forcefully to chart a course for the nation. The Louisiana Purchase of 1803, a succession of township and homestead acts, generous land grants to railroad companies, and an aggressive military policy toward the Indians supported the federal government's intention to open up the West in the nineteenth century.[13] In the 1960s the President and Congress pursued a national agenda of comparable ambition. This time, the national government set out to eliminate poverty, erase racial discrimination, provide equal opportunity in education and jobs, and revitalize cities and communities.

The national emphasis on equality and social justice was reflected in clear terms in the case of the Civil Rights Act of 1964, when the federal government served notice that its new civil rights statutes would override state and local racial practices. The preambles to the grant programs of Kennedy's New Frontier and Johnson's Great Society articulated a variety of national goals. Consider this example, from the Manpower Development and Training Act of 1962:

> It is in the national interest that current and prospective manpower shortages be identified and that persons who can be qualified for these positions through education and training be sought out and trained, *in order that the nation may meet the staffing requirements of the struggle for freedom.*[14]

Or the Economic Opportunity Act of 1964:

> The United States can achieve its full economic and social potential as a nation only if every individual has the opportunity to contribute the full extent of his capabilities and to participate in the workings of our society. *It is, therefore, the policy of the United States* to eliminate the paradox of poverty in the midst of plenty in this nation.[15]

And the Demonstration Cities and Metropolitan Development Act of 1966 (the so-called Model Cities legislation):

> The Congress hereby finds and declares that *improving the quality of urban life is the most critical domestic problem facing the United States.*[16]

Imagine such statements of intention introducing hundreds of pieces of legislation, ranging from rent supplements to federal school aid to crime control, and the complexity of the new system of grants becomes readily apparent. Hardly an economic or a social problem escaped attention, and each program specified its own complicated methods of implementation. Recipient institutions were subjected to complex rules and close scrutiny. After all, it makes no sense to fund a national priority unless the money is going to be used carefully, according to prescribed guidelines and standards.[17]

The War on Poverty and Model Cities programs attracted great public attention because they were sold with grandiose promises about what they would accomplish. In 1964, when Lyndon Johnson proposed the War on Poverty, he announced his objective was "total victory."[18] Such a promise could not possibly be fulfilled no matter how well the program might be implemented. As it turned out, the War on Poverty became a lightning rod for controversy, as did the Model Cities program, which was funded through the Demonstration Cities and Metropolitan Development Act of 1966. Under the terms of the War on Poverty, community action agencies were instructed to operate with the "maximum feasible participation" of the poor. Likewise, Model Cities agencies were supposed to galvanize participation by local residents. City Hall and other agencies of local government were cut out of the loop. The idea was to create new institutions in the cities capable of mobilizing the energies of people outside the established power structure. An early program guide distributed by the Office of Economic Opportunity said that to qualify for funding, local antipoverty programs should involve the poor from the very first "in planning, policy-making, and operation."[19]

These programs were, in effect, a means of fomenting a revolution in local politics. According to two scholars, Frances Fox Piven and Richard A. Cloward, many of the Great Society programs were formulated to preserve and strengthen the Democratic Party's electoral advantage in the industrialized states holding the largest blocs of votes in the electoral college.[20] Rather than work through local politicians who had repeatedly shown an unwillingness to mobilize the votes of inner-city blacks, federal administrators tried to work directly with organizations and leaders in black communities. The expectation was that blacks would vote Democratic in return.

A multitude of new agencies was established to receive and spend federal dollars. Of all the community action funds the Office of Economic Opportunity spent by 1968, only 25 percent of the funds was given to public agencies. The remainder went to organizations such as universities, churches, civil rights groups, settlement houses, family services agencies, United Way programs, and newly established nonprofit groups.[21] Likewise, only 10 percent of the funds distributed through programs administered by the Department of Health, Education and Welfare were administered by state and local governments.[22]

A handful of programs became controversial when political activists associated with them became embroiled in political fights with mayors and local government officials. In Syracuse, San Francisco, and the state of Mississippi, local administrators of antipoverty programs led protest actions against mayors, welfare departments, and school boards, demanding the implementation of programs that responded to complaints from the black community. Although such protests happened in only a few places, local authorities were upset when they saw federal monies flowing into their jurisdictions to groups and organizations that regularly opposed City Hall. Such organizations encouraged complaints about all sorts of things—police brutality, the hiring of teachers, welfare policies, public housing maintenance, the list could be endless.

Despite such controversies, the War on Poverty and the Model Cities programs continued to receive congressional support mainly because the funds ended up in a large number of states and congressional districts. Thus politicians of both parties were able to take credit for bringing federal spending to their states and districts. To broaden the base of support in Congress, the Johnson administration abandoned its original intention to restrict the antipoverty and Model Cities programs to a few "demonstration" projects. Instead, the available federal dollars were spread thin so that programs could be located in as many states and congressional districts as possible. The effect was to dilute the impact of each of the programs.

THE REPUBLICANS AND THE NEW FEDERALISM

When Richard Nixon assumed the presidency in January of 1969, it seemed likely that the programs sponsored by the Democrats would be dismantled. But somewhat surprisingly, from 1969 through 1976, when Republicans held the presidency, aid to state and local governments actually climbed, from $20 to $59 billion, staying well ahead of inflation.[23] Funding continued to rise because the Democrats controlled Congress and a powerful constellation of interest groups rallied to the cause. Even some Republican congressional representatives, governors, and local officials wanted the flow of funds to continue. After a failed attempt to kill the War on Poverty in 1969, President Nixon bowed to political realities and set a middle course by trying to reform rather than eliminate urban programs.

Nixon signaled his desire to change how federal programs were administered. He spoke of the grant programs as producing a "gathering of the reins of power in Washington," which he saw as "a radical departure from the vision of federal-state relations the nation's founders had in mind." He proposed a New Federalism, meant to restore "a rightful balance between the state capital and the national capital."[24] To change the system, Nixon wanted to take the decisions about how to spend money out of the hands of federal bureaucrats and give the authority to local governments. A revenue-sharing program was the first major initiative of the New Federalism. Revenue sharing gave local officials extraordinary latitude in deciding how to spend federal money. Because of the lack of detailed federal oversight, revenue-sharing dollars were intermingled with other monies that flowed into the treasuries of the more than 39,000 state, county, township, and municipal governments across the nation. As a consequence, they could not be traced beyond the reports filed with the Treasury Department by local officials.

Revenue-sharing monies constituted a small supplement to the tax revenues of state and local governments. In 1974 the $4.5 billion apportioned among 35,077 local governments accounted for an average of 3.1 percent of their revenues for that year.[25] Financially strapped big cities were under the greatest pressure to use revenue-sharing funds just to keep things going; as a consequence, they spent nearly all of their revenue-sharing dollars on day-to-day operations and maintenance.[26] Congressional Democrats complained that the programs ignored the needs of disadvantaged populations, but for Republicans that was the whole point. The program continued at a low level until 1986, when President Reagan killed it without much protest.

The Community Development Block Grant (CDBG) program, enacted by Congress in 1974 and signed into law by President Gerald Ford in January 1975, is the only significant survivor of the major urban policies enacted in the pre-Reagan era. It has survived so long because it has been useful to so many people. For local officials, it is a source of much-needed funding. It has enjoyed broad bipartisan support because CDBG funds go to thousands of communities. Unlike for general revenue sharing, cities were required to submit an annual application for CDBG funds even though they were automatically eligible. But the process was quite painless. By the end of the program's first year, Secretary Carla Hills reported that HUD had reduced the average review period from two years for the programs that the CDA replaced to 49 days, and that applications averaged 50 pages, compared with an average of 1,400 pages for the old urban renewal applications alone.[27]

In the first few years, the recurring issue was raised that communities were spending their CDBG money in violation of program guidelines. The original legislation included a requirement that cities give "maximum feasible priority" to low- and moderate-income areas.[28] Communities were often accused of ignoring this requirement, a fact documented by the Department of Housing and Urban Development.[29] That community development funds would be spent in affluent areas was hardly a surprising turn of events because local political elites exerted a controlling voice in the allocation process. In most local communities, poorer residents had little influence. As a result of this circumstance, Little Rock, Arkansas, for example, spent $150,000 of the city's block grant funds to construct a tennis court in an affluent section of town. When questioned about this use of funds, the director of the local Department of Human Resources unpersuasively claimed that "ninety-nine percent of this money is going to low and moderate income areas." But he revealingly continued, "You cannot divorce politics from that much money. We remember the needs of the people who vote because they hold us accountable. Poor people don't vote."[30]

PRESIDENT CARTER AND THE DEMOCRATS' LAST HURRAH

In the four years that he was in office, Democratic president Jimmy Carter attempted to give urban programs some of the attention they had received in the past, but his difficulties showed just how much national politics had changed since the heyday of the cities. Carter could have been expected to respond favorably to the cities of the northern industrial states. Voters in these cities had remained faithful to the Democrats for decades, and they helped give Carter his margin of victory in several states in the 1976 presidential election. Accordingly, the administration tried to develop policies that would shore up support among urban voters. The president persuaded Congress to pass an amendment to the revenue-sharing program that added an "excess unemployment" factor to the distribution formula.[31] Cities with high unemployment levels received all the money. He successfully sought increases in CDBG funding and significantly amended the program in 1978 to help the big cities. Large increases were legislated for Comprehensive Employment and Training Act (CETA) programs, which gave money to local training centers and to local governments to put people to work repairing parks and public facilities. Despite these accomplishments, however, by the time Carter left office he seemed to be abandoning urban policy altogether, a process that would reach its logical conclusion under his Republican successor, Ronald Reagan.

Soon after Carter assumed office in January 1977, his administration began efforts to reward his electoral base in the cities. A significant effort was initiated to amend the Community Development Act with the objective of increasing aid to older industrial cities. As it happened, the original formula for distributing CDBG funds to cities actually discriminated against the worst-off cities of the Northeast and Midwest. The older industrial cities were destined to receive a declining share of CDBG funds over time, whereas fast-growing Sunbelt cities were going to receive more.[32] This was mostly because the formula for distributing the money was partially tied to population. The older cities were going to receive fewer funds over time simply because they were rapidly losing population; by contrast, Sunbelt cities were growing fast.

The administration initiated efforts to persuade Congress to revise the formula to take into account population *loss* in a city, which would increase funding for the Frostbelt cities.[33] As soon as the legislation was introduced, a bitter feud broke out between representatives from the Northeast and Midwest and the congressional delegations from southern and western states. Ultimately, the new formula won in a vote that divided along regional, not party, lines: Representatives from the East and Midwest voted overwhelmingly in favor, while almost all of those from the South and West voted against. Although the legislation passed the house in May 1977, the battle with Congress showed that in the future, regional divisions were likely to become fundamentally important factors in national political life.

The fight over the block grant program marked a watershed. In the Great Society years, urban programs had placed a heavy emphasis on social purposes. But in the Carter administration, new programs began to stress a different goal: leveraging private investments in troubled cities and neighborhoods. Because it relied upon the private market, it attracted support from local officials in the Sunbelt, and cut across party lines. The first test of this bipartisan strategy came in 1978, when Congress approved the Urban Development Action Grants (UDAG) program. Over the years, UDAG grants were used to build festival malls such as Union Station in St. Louis and Harborplace in Baltimore; to expand convention centers; to build public infrastructure (such as improved streets, new lighting, landscaping, and fountains) that might leverage private investment; to repair historic buildings; and to support neighborhood improvements.

As time went on it became apparent that the administration was retreating from any emphasis at all on social, as opposed to economic development, goals. On March 28, 1978, President Carter announced, with great fanfare, a comprehensive new urban policy that emphasized private investment. Asserting "the deterioration of urban life in the United States is one of the most complex and deeply rooted problems of our age," the president stated that "the federal government has the clear duty to lead the effort to reverse that deterioration."[34] The centerpiece of the president's proposal was a national development bank, which would be authorized to guarantee loans to businesses in depressed urban and rural areas; in addition, the administration wanted to offer tax credits for businesses hiring ghetto youths, a labor-intensive public works program, and more money for housing rehabilitation. The amount of additional money requested was relatively modest (about $4.4 billion), but this did not deter the president from promising a "new Partnership involving all levels of government, the private sector and neighborhood and voluntary organizations."[35]

Carter's ringing call for a comprehensive urban policy raised hopes in city halls, but it quickly turned into an abject political failure. The only major legislative proposal enacted into law was the Targeted Employment Tax Credit. The timing was bad for any new legislative initiative.[36] In 1978 California voters passed Proposition 13, which sharply reduced local property taxes. The gathering strength of a tax revolt across the nation helped shape a mood of fiscal conservatism in Congress and a go-slow approach in the White House.[37] Perhaps sensing a changing political climate, Carter did an about-face in the last two years of his term, turning his attention away from urban policy toward the problems of the national economy and the cost and availability of energy. A sharp decline in manufacturing jobs and an acceleration in foreign investment by American companies, together with an increase in imports, became the leading domestic issues of the 1980 presidential campaign.

After Carter's election in 1976, Mayor Kenneth A. Gibson of Newark had spoken for many Democratic mayors when he remarked "we have every reason to believe that this is the beginning of a new relationship between the White House and the nation's mayors."[38] The new relationship, however, proved to be short-lived. Even if Carter had won the 1980 presidential race, it is doubtful any significant urban programs would have emerged in a second term.

REPUBLICANS AND THE END OF FEDERAL ASSISTANCE

In the campaigns of 1980 and 1984, the Republicans virtually wrote off the African American vote. Richard Wirthlin, Ronald Reagan's campaign strategist, advised before the 1980 election that the "Reagan for President 1980 campaign must convert into Reagan votes the disappointment felt by Southern white and rural voters."[39] Reagan won only 10 percent of the black vote in 1980 and slightly less in 1984. In 1984, however, three out of four southern whites supported him. The Reagan White House actively worked to undo civil rights guarantees, slashing the budgets of civil rights enforcement units and slowing or stopping enforcement.[40] The Reagan administration also set out to dismantle federal programs designed to help the cities, and over the course of eight years it largely succeeded.

President Reagan's approach marked a radical departure. Philosophically, Reagan believed that the federal government should stop helping the cities altogether. Instead, he thought, they, and the people who lived within them, should help themselves. In a press conference held in October 1981, President Reagan suggested the residents of cities where unemployment was high should "vote with their feet" and move to more prosperous areas of the country.[41] His remark ignited an instant political controversy, but, in fact, it was consistent with the recommendations of a presidential commission appointed by his predecessor, Jimmy Carter. In a report issued only a few weeks after Reagan took office, the Presidential Commission on the National Agenda for the Eighties urged that the national government stop helping cities. The commission emphasized that federal policies should be used to promote national economic growth, but these policies should be neutral about where that growth occurred:

> It may be in the best interest of the nation to commit itself to the promotion of locationally neutral economic and social policies rather than spatially sensitive urban policies that either explicitly or inadvertently seek to preserve cities in their historical roles.[42]

Recommending that the federal government let the process of decay in some areas and growth in others take its natural course, the commission noted that cities adapt and change in response to economic and social forces. This process of adaptation, said the commission, should be facilitated, not altered, by governmental policy:

> Ultimately, the federal government's concern for national economic vitality should take precedence over the competition for advantage among communities and regions.[43]
>
> To attempt to restrict or reverse the processes of change—for whatever noble intentions—is to deny the benefits that the future may hold for us as a nation.[44]

The recommendations by Carter's commission and the policies subsequently pursued by the Reagan administration constituted a revolutionary change in philosophy. For the first time since national urban policy was first enacted in the 1930s, the judgment was made that individual cities were not valuable cultural, social, or economic entities except to the degree to which they contributed to a healthy national economy. Three University of Delaware researchers characterized the new policy as "a form of Social Darwinism applied to cities."[45] Cities would survive if they could manage to regenerate their local economies. Otherwise, they would be allowed to wither away.

The Reagan administration began to sharply reduce federal urban aid, proclaiming "the private market is more efficient than federal program administrators in allocating dollars."[46] Cities were instructed to improve their ability to compete in a struggle for survival in which "state and local governments will find it is in their interests to concentrate on increasing their attractiveness to potential investors, residents, and visitors."[47] The assumption was that free enterprise would provide a bounty of jobs, incomes, and neighborhood renewal, and such local prosperity would make federal programs unnecessary. The Community Development Block Grant (CDBG) and Urban Development Action Grant (UDAG) programs won a reprieve from being drastically reduced in the 1983 budget, and so did revenue sharing. The administration, bending to a weakened but still viable urban lobby—represented principally by governors and mayors, quite a few of them Republican—backed off. Local government representatives came away relieved the budget cuts were less severe than they had feared. Only two years later, however, the administration realized its goal of eliminating most urban programs.

Urban programs gave way to a new priority: tax cuts. On February 18, 1981, President Reagan proposed a massive tax cut to stimulate the economy. Reagan signed the Economic Recovery Tax Act of 1981 on August 13, 1981, asserting it was "a turnaround of almost a half a century of . . . excessive growth in government bu-reaucracy, government spending, government taxing."[48] In its final version the act reduced individual tax rates by 25 percent over three years and also substantially reduced business tax liability. The revenue losses were huge. In just the first two years, $128 billion in revenue was lost to the federal treasury, and the total losses by 1987 amounted to more than $1 trillion.[49] The 1981 tax cuts, in combination with massive increases in military spending, created huge budget deficits into the late 1990s.

The Tax Reform Act of 1986 added to the effects of the legislation adopted five years earlier. Tax rates fell only modestly or not at all for most taxpayers, but they were cut drastically for the rich. In subsequent years, a perception that tax burdens fell unfairly on the middle class helped fuel a tax revolt. George H. W. Bush won the presidency in 1988 partly with the promise, "Read my lips: no new taxes." As a follow-up, the administration cut spending for programs for education, housing, health, and welfare.

President Reagan's cuts were the first reductions of consequence in grants-in-aid expenditures since the 1940s. Broad entitlement programs with middle-class recipients, such as the old-age and survivors' benefits funded through the Social Security Act of 1935, veterans' benefits, and Medicare, were affected only marginally. By contrast, deep cuts and new eligibility restrictions were imposed on public assistance programs for the poor. Medicaid, which was available through the states to welfare recipients, was subjected to tighter eligibility requirements, but Medicaid outlays soared anyway because of rising medical costs. Enrollment in Aid to Families with Dependent Children (AFDC) fell by half a million. A million people lost food stamps. It became harder to get unemployment benefits; whereas 75 percent of the unemployed received benefits during the recession of 1975, only 45 percent were able to qualify during the 1982–1983 recession.[50]

Several urban programs were also killed off by the end of Reagan's first term, including revenue sharing and federally assisted local public works. The Urban Development Action Grants were cut in 1986, although a trickle of money continued to flow in the administrative pipeline for several years (the total spending fell from an annual level of between $400 and $500 million for the first ten years of the program [fiscal years 1978 to 1987] to $200 million in fiscal 1988 and dried up to a nominal $3 million by fiscal 1994).[51] Other budget cuts also affected the cities. Most subsidies for the construction of public housing were eliminated. Only 10,000 new units a year were authorized after 1983, compared with the 111,600 new or rehabilitated units authorized for 1981.[52]

Despite his opposition to urban programs of almost any kind, President Reagan moved to put his stamp on the "Republican" approach to the cities by pushing legislation meant to stimulate investment in troubled inner-city neighborhoods. On March 7, 1983, the president sent the proposed Urban Enterprise Zone Act to Congress, claiming the legislation represented a sharp break from past policy:

> Enterprise zones are a fresh approach for promoting economic growth in the inner cities. The old approach relied on heavy government subsidies and central planning. A prime example was the model cities program in the 1960s, which concentrated government programs, subsidies and regulations in distressed urban areas. The enterprise zone approach is to remove government barriers, bring individuals to create, produce and earn their own wages and profits.[53]

No matter what claims the president made, the legislation was not a "fresh approach" but a logical extension of past policies. Since the latter years of the Carter administration, federal policy had stressed the role of government in subsidizing private investment. Throughout the Reagan years, the enterprise zones idea surfaced from time to time, but the administration never gave it priority. After George Bush's election to the presidency in 1988, the idea continued to receive an occasional nudge from the president or from HUD, but urban policy of any kind did not surface as a meaningful item on the president's legislative agenda until very late in his term.

The administration of George H. W. Bush was not motivated by its electoral base or its ideology to propose urban legislation. In the 1988 presidential election, Bush used race issues to mobilize voters. Republicans ran an attack ad that featured a police photograph of Willie Horton, who had raped a woman in Maryland and stabbed her fiancé while on a weekend pass from a Massachusetts prison. The Democratic candidate, Michael Dukakis, had been the governor of Massachusetts at the time. According to Bush's campaign director, Lee Atwater, the fact that Willie Horton was black was the key element explaining the ad's emotional impact.

In the 1992 election, the Bush campaign refined its racial appeals by resorting to a code language that used attacks on cities as a signifier of race and welfare-state liberalism. In one of the opening salvos of the campaign, Vice President Dan Quayle attacked New York City by saying, "The liberal vision of a happy, productive and content welfare state hasn't even worked on 22 square miles of the most valuable real estate in the world."[54] A later Quayle attack prompted a *New York Post* headline: "City to Dan Quayle: DON'T DIS' US!"[55] An editorial in the *New York Times* called Quayle's attacks an attempt to make New York City "The Willie Horton of 1992."[56]

Nevertheless, late in his term President Bush made some gestures, mostly symbolic, in the direction of urban policy. The pressure to do so came on April 29–May 3, 1992, when serious rioting broke out in Los Angeles. Measured by the number of deaths (53), injuries (2,383), property damage (over $700 million), and the response required to reestablish order, the Los Angeles riot was the country's worst episode of civil disorder in the twentieth century.[57] Many people thought the riot could be used as an opportunity to call attention to the problems of urban America. Two weeks after the riots, 150,000 people descended on Washington for a Save Our Cities/Save Our Children rally. As the crisis atmosphere faded, however, urban issues got lost in election-year politics. Democratic candidate Bill Clinton initially blamed the riots on "twelve years of denial and neglect" by Presidents Bush and Reagan, but fearing he might be accused of advocating new spending programs, Clinton soon muted his criticisms.[58] On Monday, May 5, Bush's press secretary, Marlin Fitzwater, said the Great Society's programs of the 1960s were to blame for the rioting. Nevertheless, in an attempt to look like he was responding positively, President Bush proposed an emergency aid package. In June Congress passed $1.3 billion in emergency aid that allocated $500 million for summer jobs, $382 million for loans to businesses damaged or destroyed in the riot areas, and some flood relief for the city of Chicago.

Through the summer and early fall of 1992, Congress worked on a larger permanent urban aid bill. A version was finally approved by the House on October 6 and the Senate on October 8. The legislation would have created 25 urban and 25 rural enterprise zones and financed so-called weed and seed programs that combined enhanced law enforcement with job training and education programs. The bulk of the legislation, however, was made up of an array of items that had nothing to do with cities, including liberalized (tax-free) retirement accounts for upper-income people and a provision for the repeal of luxury taxes on yachts, furs, jewels, and planes (Democrats backed this amendment as enthusiastically as Republicans). It was estimated that of the $30 billion the bill would cost over five years, about $6 billion would be used to help depressed areas in cities.[59] By the time the legislation was passed and sent to the White House for President Bush's signature, the election was over. Bush vetoed it, claiming it was contaminated by pork-barrel amendments.

Among urban programs, the only real survivor of the Reagan cuts was the Community Development Block Grant program. CDBG spending fell from $4 billion in the 1981 fiscal year to $2.8 billion in fiscal 1990 before rebounding slightly in fiscal 1992, the year the Democrats reclaimed the White House. Under President Clinton, CDBG spending rose modestly to $4.6 billion by the 1996 fiscal year,[60] and to $5.1 billion by Clinton's last budget, the 2001 fiscal year (however, when adjusted for inflation, funding for the program stayed even). Under President George W. Bush, the level of funding fell, but the program was not eliminated entirely.[61]

POLITICAL REALITY AND URBAN POLICY

As a self-styled "new Democrat" who wanted to project an image as a friend of the "forgotten middle class," Bill Clinton could not be expected to place aid to cities or to the poor on the front burner. In the 1992 presidential election the Clinton campaign decided to concentrate on appealing to the white suburban middle class and to assume that inner-city voters would support him anyway because they had no place else to go. Clinton's electoral strategy succeeded in making him the first Democrat to be elected to two full terms since Franklin D. Roosevelt. Clinton succeeded by winning back many of the white suburban voters who had deserted the party in 1980. Even so, he still lost the overall white vote by a 39 to 41 percent margin. He carried huge pluralities in the cities, coming out of New York City, for example, with almost a million-vote lead. His ability to capture 82 percent of the African American vote was crucial to his victory.

The logic behind Clinton's suburban strategy was compelling. By the 1990 census, 48 percent of the nation's population lived in suburbs. Because they tended to turn out for elections at a relatively high rate, it seemed certain they would cast a majority of the votes in the 1992 election.[62] In addition, a large proportion of suburban voters were so-called Reagan Democrats, blue-collar and middle-class voters who had abandoned the party to vote Republican in the three previous presidential elections. They were heavily concentrated in the older suburbs in key states such as New Jersey, Michigan, and California, which could deliver the big blocs of Electoral College votes coveted by every presidential candidate. To bring them back to the fold, Clinton wanted to avoid identifying himself with policies that were targeted to cities, and especially to blacks.

In developing this strategy, Clinton followed the advice of a well-known African American sociologist, William Julius Wilson, whose 1987 book, *The Truly Disadvantaged*, warned against race-specific policies. Wilson, who was a friend and adviser of the president, recommended a "hidden agenda" in which inner-city minorities might be helped "by emphasizing programs to which the more advantaged groups of all races and classes can positively relate."[63] In an interview before the election, Wilson praised Clinton's programs for targeting "all low- to moderate-income groups, not just minorities."[64]

Clinton ended up developing what two scholars called a "stealth urban policy" composed of programs that were not specifically targeted to cities but would help them.[65] In their campaign book, *Putting People First*, Bill Clinton and Al Gore advocated so-called cross-cutting policies designed to help both the middle class and the disadvantaged. Clinton's highly successful campaign bus tours avoided the inner cities and provided the media with ample opportunities to photograph the candidate against small town and rural backdrops. After winning the nomination, Clinton did attend a meeting of the United States Conference of Mayors (USCM) and lent his support to a public works initiative. Clinton stressed, however, that the primary goal was to stimulate the economy and that aiding cities would be a secondary effect.

Clinton began his presidency with the intention of rewarding the cities that had voted lopsidedly for him. To accomplish this, he put together a $19.5 billion economic stimulus bill that included $4.4 billion for public works (mostly in cities), $2.5 billion for community development grants, and $735 million for inner-city schools and jobs. Led by minority leader Bob Dole (R.-Kans.), Senate Republicans filibustered the bill, refusing to let it come up for a vote. Lacking the 60 votes necessary to end the filibuster, the Democrats were forced to back down. Eventually, all that was passed was a $4 billion extension of unemployment benefits for the chronically unemployed.[66]

The only significant new urban initiative that the Clinton administration could claim was the Empowerment Zones/Enterprise Communities (EZ/EC) program, which was included as Title XIII of the Omnibus Budget Reconciliation Act of 1993. Republicans and even many conservatives had pushed for enterprise zones during the Reagan and Bush administrations because it was based on the strategy of cutting taxes and regulations in inner cities, with the intention of stimulating investment in depressed neighborhoods. The Clinton administration adopted this same free-market approach. To promote investment in EZ/EC zones, tax credits were provided for employers who hired workers who lived in the zone, and businesses located within the zones became eligible for accelerated depreciation on business property and tax-exempt bond financing for new construction. Grant money was also made available to assist zone residents in obtaining education, job training, and child care so that they could work. Ultimately, 31 Empowerment Zones were created across the country, and 74 additional distressed areas (33 in rural areas) also won grants, but these were small in comparison to the full-fledged Empowerment Zones.

Empowerment Zones proved to be the only politically viable urban program. The midterm 1994 elections dealt a deathblow to those who supported urban and social welfare policies. Led by House Speaker Newt Gingrich and his Contract with America (labeled Contract on America by detractors), the Republicans won control of both houses of Congress for the first time in 40 years. The Republicans were openly hostile to what remained of federal urban programs. Speaker Gingrich called for the complete elimination of the Department of Housing and Urban Development, asserting, "You could abolish HUD tomorrow morning and improve life in most of America." He was blunt about why HUD was being singled out for especially harsh treatment: Its "weak constituency," he said, "makes it a prime candidate for cuts."[67]

In a desperate attempt to stave off disaster, HUD secretary Henry Cisneros proposed to "reinvent" his department in ways satisfying to conservatives. Announced a month and a half after the 1994 election, HUD's *Reinvention Blueprint* called for consolidating HUD's 60 programs into three flexible block grants that cities and states would administer, and it proposed converting all public housing aid to vouchers, which would allow recipients to find housing wherever private landlords would take them. Reinventing HUD became the centerpiece of Clinton's National Urban Policy Report, issued in July 1995.[68]

The long-term decline in public housing and urban programs predated the Clinton administration, but having a Democrat in the White House again did not bring about a revival. In the Reagan and Bush years, HUD experienced the largest cuts of any cabinet-level department in the federal government. HUD budget authority (what Congress authorizes it to spend) fell from 7.5 percent of the total federal budget in 1978 to 1.3 percent by 1990. During the Clinton administration, annual HUD spending recovered slightly, but this only enabled HUD to meet past commitments for housing subsidies. Four programs of special interest to city governments, General Revenue Sharing, Urban Development Action Grants, Local Public Works, and Antirecession Fiscal Assistance, were zeroed out—eliminated entirely.

The welfare reform bill Clinton signed in August 1996 also hurt the cities. Ending the 61-year federal entitlement to welfare, the Personal Responsibility Act of 1996 converted Aid to Families with Dependent Children to a block grant run by the states. In addition to a 64 percent decline in welfare spending from 1990 to 1998, food stamps and community services programs were cut sharply. Three programs—child nutrition, supplemental (infant) feeding, and housing assistance—increased somewhat because they were linked to welfare reform efforts. Medicaid costs went up substantially (by 146 percent), but the big winner was justice assistance, which skyrocketed 1,250 percent in less than a decade! Although some of this money went to cities, the states used most of it to build prisons. Obviously, crime control trumped any other social purpose.

THE POLITICAL INFLUENCE OF THE CITIES

Until the election of Barack Obama to the presidency in November 2008, both political parties had largely abandoned the cities. It was a matter of making a political calculus. In the case of the Republicans, party leaders had long sought to capitalize on white suburbanites' disaffection from the Democratic-sponsored civil rights and antipoverty policies of the 1960s. What is more interesting is the way the past friend of the cities, the Democratic Party, has shied away from urban issues. In 1968 the Democrats used the word *city* 23 times in the party platform adopted at their presidential nominating convention. It did not appear even once in the 1988 platform. The substitute term, which signaled a recognition of the political importance of the suburbs, was *hometown America*. In 1992 and 1996, Clinton avoided policies targeted to cities and concentrated his appeals on the suburban middle class. Notably, in the 2000 campaign, Democratic candidate Al Gore mentioned urban sprawl as a significant national issue. By the new century, urban policy no longer referred to central cities but to urban regions.

The near-invisibility of cities in national politics by the twenty-first century can be explained by a simple fact: by then, central-city voters accounted for a very small percentage of the national electorate. The central cities of the 32 largest metropolitan areas reached a high-water mark of 27 percent of the electorate in 1944, but by 1992 they accounted for just 14 percent of the national vote[69] and 12 percent by the 2000 election. As shown in Figure 8.2, the share of their states' votes cast by their largest central cities has fallen steadily for half a century in New York, Illinois, Pennsylvania, Michigan, and Massachusetts.[70] In 1952, New York City voters represented 48 percent

Figure 8.2 City Proportion of Actual State Electorate, 1952–2000

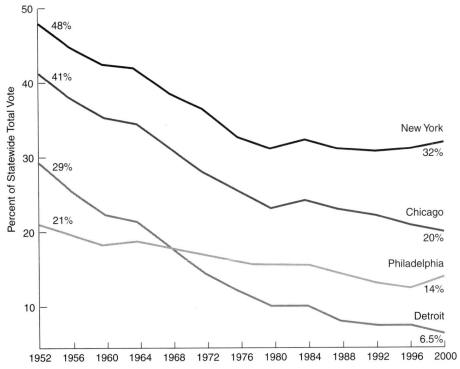

Sources: Richard Scammon, *America Votes* (various issues); U.S. Bureau of the Census, *Census of Population and Housing,* various years; and reports of actual city votes from county boards of elections (and newspapers for 1996 election). Data compiled by Richard Sauerzopf. Data from 2000 from Peter Dreier, John Mollenkopf, and Todd Swanstrom, *Place Matters,* 2nd ed. (Lawrence: University Press of Kansas, 2004), p. 282.

of the statewide electorate, but by the 2000 presidential election their proportion of the statewide vote had fallen to 32 percent. Chicago claimed 41 percent of the Illinois presidential vote in 1952 but only 20 percent by 2000.

Cities also lost representation in the U.S. House of Representatives. Between 1963 and 1994, the number of congressional districts with a majority of the population coming from central cities fell from 94 to 84; in the same period, the number of districts with a majority of suburban voters increased from 94 to 214. In 1994, after the Republicans took control of the House, the proportion of leadership positions held by representatives from districts with a sizable proportion of central-city voters fell precipitously, from 30 to 10 percent.[71] Similar trends reduced the power of central cities in state governments as well.[72] The number of states with suburban electoral majorities increased from 3 in 1980 to 14 in 1990 and increased again when seats were reapportioned as a result of the 2000 census.

It is generally assumed the suburbs now hold the key to winning national elections. Suburban votes were critical to the presidential victories of Presidents Ronald Reagan and George H. W. Bush; Reagan won huge landslides in 1980 and 1984 even though he only carried about a third of the central-city vote. In the 1988 election, suburban voters gave Bush such a comfortable cushion that he could have carried almost all of the northern industrial states without a single vote from the big cities in those states. By contrast, the central-city electorate was an important part of Bill Clinton's winning coalition in 1992 and 1996. In 1992 New York City provided Clinton with 92 percent of his nearly one-million statewide vote margin, and Clinton lost to Bush in suburban Long Island (Nassau and Suffolk counties). In 1996 Clinton did even better in the cities, winning 67 percent of the vote in Milwaukee, 74 percent in Boston, 76 percent in St. Louis and New York, and 80 percent in Chicago.[73] In the 2000 presidential election Al Gore won similar pluralities in the cities, but it was not enough to overcome George W. Bush's near-sweep of southern and less urban, less populated states of the Plains and the West. Gore won the national popular vote by more than 500,000 votes, but Bush was able to win the election by commanding a bare majority of votes in the electoral college.

Although President Clinton owed a great deal to central-city voters for his two election victories, he did not make urban issues a priority. During his presidency, federal spending for the cities continued to fall. Clearly, Clinton felt he could take his urban base for granted; city voters had no other place to go. This strategy did impose a potential cost on the Democrats, however; as the federal government turned away from the cities, voter turnout in them went into a steep slide. Indeed, in the past half century, 40 percent of the loss in the proportion of votes cast in the 32 largest cities can be traced to falling turnout and not to shrinking population.[74]

A NEW DAY FOR URBAN POLICY

It would appear that Barack Obama's election put the voters of central cities and their constituency groups into a more favorable position than they had enjoyed for decades. For the first time since the Carter administration, the president announced he would pay attention to urban problems. However, it is important to note that this did not mean that urban policies would be like those of an earlier era, when city voters and the urban lobby held a commanding position. Contemporary urban policies will be less divisive than in the past because "urban" now means regional. In this sense, policies have come to reflect the changes within metropolitan areas themselves, in which the old division between cities and suburbs has been replaced by a complex urban geography. The new reality is that the problems faced by older central cities are also shared by a great many suburbs, and by smaller towns and cities outside urban areas. This is the context for understanding how the urban policies of the Obama administration are likely to evolve.

More than at any time in decades, programs initiated by the Obama administration will significantly influence metropolitan development and the fiscal condition of states and cities. The American Recovery and Reinvestment Act, which authorizes the expenditure of $787 billion over the ten-year period, is already having an important effect. The act allocates $79 billion to provide fiscal assistance to states, an important initiative because the states were in the process of imposing deep budget cuts that would make the economic crisis worse. In addition, legislation authorizes $144 billion for infrastructure projects, which includes $32 billion for transportation projects, $10 billion for rail and mass transit, and $2 billion for airports.[75] School districts are slated to receive $41 billion in grants for construction projects and other activities. The legislation sets aside money for a wide array of activities to promote clean energy and conservation. Among other initiatives, the administration also announced a $1 billion program to put 5,500 more police officers on the streets.[76]

Organizations representing urban interests, broadly defined, have been invigorated by the new initiatives. On March 14–18, 2009, the National League of Cities convened its Annual Congressional City Conference, a gathering of local officials from across the country. By contrast to previous years, the conference revolved around a wide-ranging agenda featuring discussions of new federal initiatives in many areas, including infrastructure investment, jobs programs, green energy, and transportation. Without doubt, state and local governments will find themselves involved in administering a broader variety of new federal programs than they have since the 1960s. In recognition of the importance it gives to its relations with state and local officials, in February the Obama administration announced the appointment of Adolfo Carrion, the president of Borough of the Bronx, as its "urban czar," charged with coordinating its urban-related programs. The appointment represented a stunning revival of federal–local relations.

NOTES

1. Reported in the *New York Times*, December 1, 1959, p. 27, quoted in Mark I. Gelfand, *A Nation of Cities: The Federal Government and Urban America*, Urban Life in America Series (New York: Oxford University Press, 1975), p. 295. See also John F. Kennedy, "The Great Unspoken Issue," *Proceedings, American Municipal Congress 1959* (Washington, D.C.: American Municipal League, n.d.), pp. 23–28; and John F. Kennedy, "The Shame of the States," *New York Times Magazine*, May 18, 1958.

2. Quoted in Theodore H. White, *The Making of the President, 1960* (New York: Atheneum, 1961), p. 206. Nixon's strategy, which White contends was no strategy at all, was a "national" one, in which he committed himself to visit all 50 states; Kennedy, in contrast, used an urban strategy centered on the industrial states with large blocs of electoral votes (see pp. 267–352).

3. John C. Donovan, *The Politics of Poverty,* 2nd ed. (New York: Bobbs-Merrill, Pegasus, 1973), p. 19.

4. Quoted in White, *The Making of the President,* p. 165.

5. Donovan, *The Politics of Poverty,* p. 225.

6. Ibid., p. 104.

7. Nelson W. Polsby and Aaron Wildavsky, *Presidential Elections: Contemporary Strategies of American Electoral Politics,* 7th ed. (New York: Free Press, 1988). The statistics given are for "nonwhite" voters.

8. White, *The Making of the President,* p. 354.

9. For good recent summary accounts, see ibid.; also James A. Morone, *The Democratic Wish: Popular Participation and the Limits of American Government* (New York: Basic Books, 1990), Chapter 6.

10. Quoted in Richard Blumenthal, "The Bureaucracy: Antipoverty and the Community Action Programs," in *American Political Institutions and Public Policy,* ed. Allan P. Sindler (Boston: Little, Brown, 1969), p. 149.

11. *Message of the President to Congress,* reprinted in *Congressional Quarterly Weekly Report* 32, no. 2 (January 11, 1964).

12. *Congress and the Nation, 1945–1964* (Washington, D.C.: Congressional Quarterly Service, 1965), p. 1379.

13. Refer to Daniel J. Elazar, *The American Partnership: Intergovernmental Cooperation in the Nineteenth Century United States* (Chicago: University of Chicago Press, 1962).

14. Manpower Development and Training Act of 1962, Public Law 87–415, 87th Cong. (1962); emphasis added.

15. Economic Opportunity Act of 1964, Public Law 88–452, 88th Cong. (1964); emphasis added.

16. Demonstration Cities and Metropolitan Development Act of 1966, Public Law 89–754, 89th Cong. (1966); emphasis added.

17. See James L. Sundquist and David W. Davis, *Making Federalism Work: A Study of Program Coordination at the Community Level* (Washington, D.C.: Brookings Institution Press, 1969), pp. 3–5.

18. Lyndon B. Johnson, "Total Victory over Poverty," Message to Congress, March 15, 1964, reprinted in *The Failure of American Liberalism: After the Great Society,* ed. Marvin E. Gettleman and David Mermelstein (New York: Vintage Books, 1970), p. 181.

19. U.S. Office of Economic Opportunity, *Community Action Program Guide* (Washington, D.C.: U.S. Government Printing Office, 1965).

20. Frances Fox Piven and Richard A. Cloward, *Regulating the Poor: The Functions of Public Welfare* (New York: Pantheon, 1971).

21. Ibid., p. 295.

22. U.S. Advisory Commission on Intergovernmental Relations, *Fiscal Balance in the American Federal System,* vol. 1 (Washington, D.C.: U.S. Government Printing Office, 1967), p. 169.

23. U.S. Office of Management and Budget, *Special Analyses: Budget of the United States Government: Fiscal Year 1981* (Washington, D.C.: U.S. Government Printing Office, 1982), p. 254.

24. Reagan, *The New Federalism* (New York: Oxford University Press, 1972), p. 97.

25. U.S. Department of the Treasury, Office of Revenue Sharing, *Reported Uses of General Revenue Sharing Funds, 1974–1975: A Tabulation and Analysis of Data from Actual Use,* Report 5 (Washington, D.C.: U.S. Government Printing Office, 1966), p. 5.

26. Ibid., p. 25.

27. "New Directions Cited in First Annual Block Grant Reports," *Housing and Development Reporter,* January 12, 1976, p. 761.

28. Housing and Community Development Act of 1974, sec. 104(a).

29. Reported in *Housing and Development Reporter,* January 10, 1977, p. 684.

30. Interview by Sharon Cribbs (investigator for the Southern Governmental Monitoring Project) with Nathaniel Hill, Director, Department of Human Resources, Little Rock, Arkansas (Summer 1975), quoted in Southern Governmental Monitoring Project, *A Time for Accounting: The Housing and Community Development Act in the South: A Monitoring Report,* by Raymond Brown with Ann Coil and Carol Rose (Atlanta: Southern Regional Council, 1976), p. 53.

31. Ann R. Markusen and David Wilmoth, "The Political Economy of National Urban Policy in the U.S.A.: 1976–81," *Canadian Journal of Regional Science* (Summer 1982): 145–163.

32. Rochelle L. Stansfield, "Federalism Report: Government Seeks the Right Formula for Community Development Funds," *National Journal,* February 12, 1977, p. 242.

33. Ann R. Markusen, "The Urban Impact Analysis: A Critical Forecast," in *The Urban Impact of Federal Policies,* ed. Norman Glickman (Baltimore: Johns Hopkins University Press, 1979); see also discussion by Ann R. Markusen, Annalee Saxenian, and Marc A. Weiss, "Who Benefits from Intergovernmental Transfers?" in *Cities Under Stress: The Fiscal Crises of Urban America,* ed. Robert W. Burchell and David Listokin (New Brunswick, N.J.: Center for Urban Research, 1981), p. 656; and Stansfield, "Federalism Report."

34. Quoted in Robert Reihold, "President Proposes a Broad New Policy for Urban Recovery," *New York Times,* March 28, 1978.

35. "Excerpts from the President's Message to Congress Outlining His Urban Policy," *New York Times,* March 28, 1978.

36. F. J. James, "President Carter's Comprehensive National Urban Policy: Achievements and Lessons Learned," *Environment and Planning C: Government and Policy* 8 (1990): 34.

37. Markusen and Wilmoth, "The Political Economy of National Urban Policy," p. 15.

38. "Washington Update: Administration Officials, Mayors Have Love Fest," *National Journal,* January 29, 1977, p. 189.

39. Quoted in Theodore H. White, *America in Search of Itself: The Making of the President, 1956–1980* (New York: Harper & Row, 1982), p. 381.

40. D. Lee Bawden and John L. Palmer, "Social Policy: Challenging the Welfare State," in *The Reagan Record,* ed. John L. Palmer and Isabel V. Sawhill (Cambridge, Mass.: Ballinger, 1992), p. 200.

41. *New York Times,* October 23, 1981, p. 1.

42. President's Commission for a National Agenda for the Eighties, *A National Agenda for the Eighties* (Washington, D.C.: U.S. Government Printing Office, 1980), p. 66.

43. Ibid., p. 4.

44. Ibid., p. 66.

45. Timothy K. Barnekov, Daniel Rich, and Robert Warren, "The New Privatism, Federalism, and the Future of Urban Governance: National Urban Policy in the 1980s," *Journal of Urban Affairs* 3, no. 4 (Fall 1981): 3.

46. U.S. Department of Housing and Urban Development, *The President's National Urban Policy Report* (Washington, D.C.: U.S. Government Printing Office, 1982), pp. 2, 23.

47. Ibid., p. 14.

48. Ibid., p. 135.

49. Ibid., p. 138.

50. Robertson and Judd, *The Development of American Public Policy,* p. 233.

51. U.S. Office of Management and Budget, *Budget of the United States Government, Fiscal Year 1996, Historical Tables* (Washington, D.C.: U.S. Government Printing Office, 1996), Table 12.3.

52. Henry J. Aaron and Associates, "Nondefense Programs," in *Setting National Priorities: The 1983 Budget,* ed. Joseph A. Pechman (Washington, D.C.: Brookings Institution Press, 1982), p. 119.

53. White House press release, March 7, 1983.

54. Quoted in Robert Pear, "Quayle Criticizes New York as Proof of Welfare's Ills," *New York Times,* February 28, 1992, p. 1.

55. *New York Post,* April 28, 1992, p. 1.

56. "The Willie Horton of 1992," *New York Times,* March 3, 1992, p. 3.

57. James H. Johnson Jr., Cloyzelle K. Jones, Walter C. Farrell Jr., and Melvin L. Oliver, "The Los Angeles Rebellion: A Retrospective View," *Economic Development Quarterly* 6, no. 4 (November 1992): 356–372.

58. Robert Pear, "Clinton, in Attack on President, Ties Riots to 'Neglect,'" *New York Times,* May 6, 1992, p. 1.

59. Clifford Krauss, "Congress Passes Aid to Cities," *New York Times,* June 9, 1992, p. A20.

60. U.S. Office of Management and Budget, *Budget of the United States Government, Fiscal Year 1996, Historical Tables,* Table 12.3.

61. U.S. Office of Management and Budget, *Budget of the United States Government, Fiscal Year 2003* (Washington, D.C.: U.S. Government Printing Office, 2003), Appendix, p. 485.

62. William Schneider, "The Suburban Century Begins," *Atlantic Monthly,* July 1992, pp. 33–44.

63. William Julius Wilson, *The Truly Disadvantaged: The Inner City, the Underclass, and Public Policy* (Chicago: University of Chicago Press, 1987), p. 155.

64. "A Visit with Bill Clinton," *Atlantic Monthly,* October 1992; and William Julius Wilson, "The Right Message," *New York Times,* March 17, 1992.

65. Bernard H. Ross and Myron A. Levine, *Urban Politics: Power in Metropolitan America,* 5th ed. (Itasca, Ill.: F. E. Peacock, 1996), p. 434.

66. Adam Clymer, "G.O.P. Senators Prevail, Sinking Clinton's Economic Stimulus Bill," *New York Times,* April 22, 1993, p. 1.

67. Quoted in Kenneth J. Cooper, "Gingrich Pledges a Major Package of Spending Cuts Early Next Year," *Washington Post,* December 13, 1994, p. 1.

68. U.S. Department of Housing and Urban Development, *Empowerment: A New Covenant with America's Communities* (Rockville, Md.: HUD USER, July 1995).

69. Peter F. Nardulli, Jon K. Dalager, and Donald E. Greco, "Voter Turnout in U.S. Presidential Elections: An Historical View and Some Speculation," *PS: Political Science and Politics* (September 1996): 484.

70. Calculations are from Richard Sauerzopf and Todd Swanstrom, "The Urban Electorate in Presidential Elections, 1920–1992: Challenging the Conventional Wisdom," paper delivered at the annual meeting of the Urban Affairs Association, Indianapolis, April 22–25, 1993. Updated by authors.

71. Hal Wolman and Lisa Marckini, "Changes in Central City Representation and Influence in Congress," paper prepared for delivery at the annual meeting of the Urban Affairs Association, Toronto, Canada, April 17, 1997. See also Demetrios Caraley, "Washington Abandons the Cities," *Political Science Quarterly* 107, no. 1 (1992): 20.

72. Margaret Weir, "Central Cities' Loss of Power in State Politics," *Cityscape: A Journal of Policy Development and Research* 2, no. 2 (May 1996): 23–40.

73. From CNN.com (*http://www.cnn.com/ELECTION/1996*).

74. Nardulli, Dalager, and Greco, "Voter Turnout in U.S. Presidential Elections," p. 484.

75. *Wall Street Journal,* "Stimulus Package Unveiled" (*http://online.wsj.com/article/ SB123202946622485595. html*).

76. National League of Cities, "NLC Applauds Announcement of COPS Hiring Recovery Program" (*http://www.nlc.org/PRESSROOM/PRESSRELEASEITEMS/*).

THE RISE OF THE SUNBELT

A REVOLUTIONARY SHIFT

Over the last half century, regional population shifts have wrought radical changes in the nation's politics, economics, and culture. Historically, the center of gravity for the nation's politics had been centered in the big industrial states and cities of the Northeast and the heartland. The South remained marginalized by its Civil War and slave-owning past; Democratic politicians from the South could influence national politics only by voting as a bloc in the House and Senate, and by maintaining a tenuous alliance with northern Democrats. Most northerners regarded southern culture as a curious relic of a faded past. But at least the South exerted a visible presence in national politics. By contrast, the Southwest was almost invisible, its population small and dispersed, still defined largely by its frontier legacy. Except for Los Angeles, there were no other cities of significant size in the vast region stretching from New Mexico to the Southern California coast. Just over 1.5 million people lived in Los Angeles in 1940, compared to San Diego, with a population of 203,000, Phoenix, with 65,000, and tiny Las Vegas, with its 8,500 residents. But over the next few decades, population growth would be so rapid in cities of the South and the Southwest that these two regions would become fused into something called the Sunbelt.

The redistribution of national population has brought with it enormous political consequences. The rise of the Sunbelt largely accounts for the conservative shift in American politics in the last quarter century. For decades, corporations moved South and West to escape higher labor costs in the North and to take advantage of a vast pool of low-wage, nonunionized labor. Twelve out of 15 Sunbelt states have right-to-work laws that allow employers to hire workers in a plant even if they refuse to join the plant's union. By contrast, none of the 14 Frostbelt states, which transect an arc through the industrial Midwest and up through New England, has a right-to-work law. These laws have discouraged unionization and kept wages lower than states where unions

OUTTAKE

THE SUNBELT'S CONSERVATIVE BENT MAY NOT LAST MUCH LONGER

The term *Sunbelt* was popularized in the mid-1970s, and it quickly became almost indispensable in everyday discourse about national development and politics. Even though the geographic boundaries of the Sunbelt are rather vague in most people's minds, the term conveys a distinctly positive image of a part of the country that is prosperous and growing: "When a person hears the term on radio or on television, or reads it in a magazine or book, or sees it in the telephone book or on a firm's letterhead, it is likely to conjure up an image of growing cities and booming economies in Southern or Southwestern cities with pleasant climates." It would be possible to regard the term as merely a "rhetorical ruse," as one scholar called it, or a "public relations coup," as the president of a corporation helping other companies move to the Sunbelt labeled it, were it not for the fact that the long-term population growth in the region has resulted in a fundamental realignment of political power in the nation. Until Barack Obama, all the winning presidents since John F. Kennedy came from the South. Over the past half century, the reapportionment that follows each decennial census has shifted the balance of power in Congress decisively toward the congressional delegations that represent southern and western states. Without doubt, this realignment of power helps account for the decline in federal aid to the cities since the late 1970s and the shift toward conservative social policies.

Over time, the Sunbelt was able to flex its muscles in Washington because population equals votes. Politicians could scarcely ignore this reality. The Republicans were strongest in the suburbs, the West, and, after 1964, the South, all of which were booming. Each decennial census was followed by a reapportionment of seats in the House of Representatives, which, together with the two senators from each state, determines the number of Electoral college votes each state casts in a presidential election. The Sunbelt states increased the number of their votes in the Electoral College every time the country was reapportioned after 1928; over the same period the Frostbelt states steadily lost Electoral College votes. In 1928 the 15 Sunbelt states were able to cast 146 Electoral College votes, compared to the 237 cast by electors representing the 14 Frostbelt states. By the 2000 presidential election, the situation was reversed: The Sunbelt states held 222 votes, compared to 180 for the Frostbelt states. If Al Gore had won the same states but run for the presidency in 1960 instead of 2000, he would have won the election by 275 to 262 Electoral College votes; likewise, John Kerry, the Democratic candidate in 2004, would have won.

Sources: Bradley R. Rice, "Searching for the Sunbelt," in *Searching for the Sunbelt: Historical Perspectives on a Region,* ed. Raymond A. Mohl (Knoxville: University of Tennessee Press, 1990), p. 217: David R. Goldfield, *Cotton Fields and Skyscrapers: Southern City and Region, 1706–1980* (Baton Rouge: Louisiana State University Press, 1982), p. 192, cited in Rice, "Searching for the Sunbelt," p. 218; Sam Allis, "Regions," *Wall Street Journal,* April 14, 1981, cited in Rice, "Searching for the Sunbelt," p. 218. Data are from the *Federal Register* (http://www.archives.gov/federalregister/electoralcollege/).

are stronger.[1] In the Sunbelt, these policies have reflected a political culture that is highly individualistic and generally hostile to governmental action, unless that action is geared toward helping business, supporting military bases, or financing water and other federal projects that promote economic development. Due in part to the rising influence of Sunbelt politicians in both parties who promoted such values, the nation's political culture was transformed in the second half of the twentieth century.

Recently, however, the politics of the Sunbelt is changing. Blacks have been moving back into the South from northern states, and millions of immigrants have been moving into southern metropolitan regions and into smaller towns. The new demographic realities have created a shifting political landscape. Since 1990 Hispanics have accounted for almost 40 percent of the population growth in the United States, and Sunbelt cities and suburbs have attracted the largest numbers. Twelve of the 18 U.S. cities whose populations changed from a majority of whites to a majority of minority residents during the 1990s were located in the Sunbelt.[2] In addition, the fast-growing Sunbelt suburbs with large numbers of highly educated professionals are not nearly as conservative as other groups of Sunbelt voters.[3] These changes are transforming the politics of cities and urban areas within the Sunbelt, and are also bringing about a realignment in national politics. In only 20 years Democratic and independent-leaning voters have turned Florida and Arizona from solidly Republican into swing states, and California from a Republican to a solidly Democratic state, as the 2000, 2004, and 2008 presidential elections revealed. With Florida peeling away in the presidential vote of 2008, the South is no longer as solidly Republican as it once was, and the South and Southwest are going in distinctly separate directions. Barack Obama is the first elected president since John F. Kennedy to come from outside the South, Southwest, or a border state. The Sunbelt ascendancy may be coming to a close. Indeed, the Sunbelt itself may be losing its identity altogether. This would surely bring a political realignment on a scale not seen since the 1960s.

THE CONCEPT OF THE SUNBELT

Kevin Phillips, the chief political analyst for the 1968 Republican presidential campaign, is generally credited as the person who coined the term *Sunbelt*. In his book *The Emerging Republican Majority*, published in 1969, Phillips asserted the United States was going through a historic electoral realignment that was transforming the Republican Party into the nation's majority party. The basis of this national political realignment, he said, was the movement of millions of Americans out of the old industrial cities of the North to the suburbs and to the South and West. Phillips sometimes lumped the South and the West into an area he called the Sunbelt, although he never actually defined its boundaries; indeed, of 47 maps in his book, none portrays such a region.[4]

Phillips's prediction that regionalism would become an ascendant influence in national politics turned out to be correct. In 1973 an embargo on the sale of oil by the Arab oil-producing nations drove the world price of oil sharply upward. The economies of oil-producing states such as Texas, Louisiana, Oklahoma, and Colorado boomed, and new jobs were created throughout the southern and western states. At the same time, energy-dependent industries and consumers in the northern states were hit hard. In 1974 and 1975, northern states went through an economic depression that saw hundreds of thousands of layoffs in industrial jobs. By the spring of 1975, New York City was facing bankruptcy and had to ask the federal government for loan guarantees. President Gerald Ford initially refused to help.[5] Congressional legislative battles began to reflect sharply divided regional politics pitting a prosperous South and West against a declining North.

In this atmosphere, Kirkpatrick Sale's book *Power Shift*, published in 1975, quickly became a national best seller.[6] Sale wrote that the states of the South and West—a region he called the Southern Rim—were gaining national political power at the expense of the older industrial states. Trying to find a way to report on the political issues raised by the new regional antagonisms, the media revived Phillips's notion of the Sunbelt, and the term soon came into common use. In February 1976 the *New York Times* published a five-part series documenting the demographic and political trends favoring the Sunbelt. In May *BusinessWeek* devoted its feature article to "The Second War Between the States."[7] The regional war became one of the hot topics helping sell newspapers and magazines in 1976 and 1977.

Although the concept of the Sunbelt has entered the everyday language of Americans (the term has been included in dictionaries since the late 1970s), the precise boundaries of the region are hard to pin down. In a letter to a scholar researching the politics of the Sunbelt, Kevin Phillips defined it as the "territory stretching from the eastern Carolina lowlands down around (and excluding) Appalachia, picking up only the Greater Memphis area of Tennessee, omitting the Ozarks and moving west to Oklahoma, thence virtually due west," possibly also including Colorado.[8] It is understandable that Phillips would want to draw his boundaries to exclude pockets of poverty in the border states, but his description is extremely imprecise. In this chapter, we adopt Sale's definition, as shown in Figure 9.1. Sale's Sunbelt encompasses the entire portion of the United States below the 37th parallel, extending across the country from North Carolina to the West Coast, including Southern California and part of southern Nevada.[9] (For statistical purposes, we include all of California and Nevada.) Thus there are 15 states in the Sunbelt. The 14 states of the Northeast and the upper Midwest constitute what is sometimes called the *Frostbelt*.

A significant number of scholars have considered the concept of the Sunbelt to be suspect. For one thing, the huge area encompassed by Sale's definition is far from uniformly prosperous. The most rapid economic and population growth has occurred in Florida, parts of Texas, Arizona, southern Nevada, and Southern California. Rural areas all across the Sunbelt and many urban areas of the South have remained untouched by the prosperity that is proclaimed as the Sunbelt's principal defining feature, a fact that led two scholars to note that the Sunbelt "has collapsed into only a few 'sunspots.'"[10]

A second problem with the Sunbelt concept is that it assumes the South and the Southwest are similar enough to be lumped together under a single label. Until its image was burnished by its inclusion in the prosperous Sunbelt, the South was often thought of as a backward, poverty-ridden, violent region with a peculiar caste system. Most political studies of the South focused on issues of race, the enduring effects of the Civil War and Reconstruction, and the dominance of a single, authoritarian

Figure 9.1   The American Sunbelt and Frostbelt

Source: Adapted from Richard M. Bernard and Bradley R. Rice, eds., *Sunbelt Cities: Politics and Growth Since World War II* (Austin: University of Texas Press, 1985), p. 7.

party (until the 1960s, the Republican Party rarely ran candidates in most southern states)—the elements making up a conservative political culture that had changed little since the Civil War. The main industries that had located in the South were those associated with low-wage labor. In the 1930s Franklin Roosevelt and the New Deal administrators looked at federal programs as a way to bring economic development to this backward region.[11]

The image of the West, by contrast, tended to be "urban, opulent, energetic, mobile, and individualistic, a region of economic growth and openness to continual change which matched America's self-image."[12] If the image of perpetual sunshine gave the Sunbelt its name, then certainly this image fit the West better than the South. Because Los Angeles was the home of the movie and television industries, America's popular culture became increasingly identified with western images. Los Angeles served as a vision of America's future, with its sprawling suburbs, freeways, shopping centers, and even its smog.

Some observers claimed that the idea of the Sunbelt was nearly dead and its brief existence was overplayed anyway. Nicholas Lemann, who edited the *Texas Monthly* in the 1980s, observed that "millions of people were living in the Sunbelt without one of them realizing it. They thought of themselves as Southerners or Texans, or Los Angelenos."[13] The concept of the Sunbelt was regarded with suspicion not only because there were so many differences within it but also because all regions of the United States seemed to be becoming more alike. The old industrial states were becoming less industrial, urban populations were spreading out into suburbs in all parts of the country, and a media-based national culture was replacing regional cultural differences. "Just try to find a town anywhere in the United States without a McDonald's or a television happy-news format featuring an anchorperson with an unidentifiable accent."[14]

Despite the shortcomings of the Sunbelt–Frostbelt dichotomy, it remains useful as a starting point for understanding the national political realignments of the past half century. Without these realignments, the older cities and their voters would have been able to demand a much larger share of the nation's resources. Programs to treat urban decay, joblessness, and poverty in the cities and to build mass transit systems and other infrastructure would be funded at more generous levels than they are today. The 2008 presidential election signaled a realignment that once again favors urban interests, though it is important to note that these are now broadly defined to include all residents of metropolitan regions and even smaller towns and cities, and not only those who live within central cities.

THE RISE OF THE SUNBELT

For the past half century, population and economic activities in the United States have been moving away from older urban areas. This population movement contrasts sharply with the historic pattern of national growth. Since the early years of the nineteenth century, the industrial cities had acted as magnets, drawing millions of immigrants from abroad and luring migrants from the countryside. The industrial cities were the engines of the nation's economy, and patterns of settlement reflected this fact. In 1950, 65 percent of the nation's metropolitan population lived in or near the industrial belt that reached from Boston and New York in the Northeast across to the Great Lakes and down to St. Louis.[15] More than two-thirds of the manufacturing jobs and 10 of the nation's 14 urban areas of more than a million people were stretched across this industrial zone. Over the next half century, however, a historic shift in the regional distribution of population occurred.

In the five decades between 1940 and 1990, the population of the 15 Sunbelt states increased 163 percent (to 103,868,000), compared to a population gain in the 14 Frostbelt states of 48 percent (to 92,818,000).[16] Over this half century, the fastest-growing states were Nevada (+50 percent), Arizona (+35 percent), Florida (+33 percent), and California (+26 percent). The only Frostbelt state to show a significant gain was New Hampshire (+20.5 percent), which was attracting commuters from elsewhere in the Northeast urban corridor.[17] As shown in Figure 9.2, these trends continued right into the twenty-first century. Every state with a growth rate faster than 13.2 percent for the decade (the national average) was located in the West or in the Sunbelt, with the addition of Virginia. Three of the states that gained more than 25 percent in population—Colorado, Utah, and Idaho—were located outside the Sunbelt, as were two other rapidly growing states, Oregon and Washington.

Most metropolitan areas in the Sunbelt have grown so rapidly since World War II that it has been difficult to build infrastructure fast enough. Table 9.1 compares the growth rates for seven Sunbelt metropolitan areas with population growth in six

Figure 9.2   Population Growth in States, 1990–2000

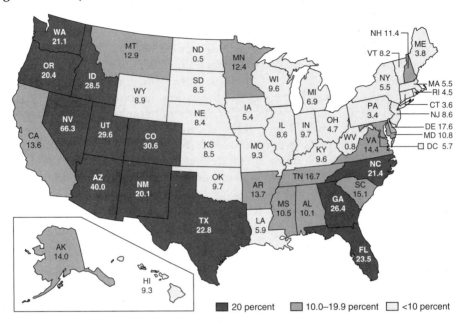

Source: U.S. Bureau of the Census, *Statistical Abstract of the United States, 2001* (Washington, D.C.: U.S. Government Printing Office, 2001), p. 7.

Frostbelt urban regions from 1950 to 2000. All seven of the Sunbelt metropolitan areas boomed in the half century from 1950 to 2000, in many cases growing by more than 40 percent per decade. Phoenix had a population of 107,000 in 1950 but grew to a metropolitan region of more than 3 million people in half a century. Las Vegas was transformed from a dusty, seedy gambling town of 24,000 in 1950 to a major metropolis (and entertainment city) of 1.4 million by 2000. Several smaller metropolitan areas in the Sunbelt grew even faster than the larger urban areas. For example, Fort Myers, Cape Coral, Ocala, Sarasota, and Naples (all in Florida) attracted large numbers of retirees. Other smaller cities in the Sunbelt and West, such as Austin, Texas; San Diego and San Jose, California; Boise, Idaho; and Provo, Utah, boomed because of an influx of high-tech industries.

Meanwhile, the six Frostbelt metropolitan areas listed in Table 9.1 went in exactly the opposite direction. Until the late 1960s, the Chicago, Detroit, and St. Louis regions continued to prosper as industrial centers, but the bottom fell out during the deindustrialization of the 1970s and 1980s. Modest growth in the 1950s and 1960s was followed by stagnation or population losses; indeed, five of the six Frostbelt cities shown in Table 9.1 lost population in the 1970s. Manufacturing firms picked up and moved abroad or to cheaper sites in the Sunbelt, where labor unions were weak. Older metropolitan areas began to revive their economies by the 1990s by attracting service or

Table 9.1   Population Growth of Selected Metropolitan Areas, 1950–2000

Metropolitan Area (Ranked by % Growth in 1970s)	*Percentage Increase in Population*				
	1950–1960	1960–1970	1970–1980	1980–1990	1990–2000
Sunbelt and West					
Denver–Boulder	52%	32%	31%	44%	32%
Houston	52	40	45	21	25
Las Vegas	123	115	69	61	85.5
Los Angeles–Long Beach	45.5	16	6	18.5	10
Phoenix	100	46	55	40	45
San Diego	85.5	32	37	34	12.6
Frostbelt					
Boston	7.5%	6%	–5%	6.5%	6%
Chicago	20	12	2	0.2	11
Detroit	28	12	–2	–2	5
New York City	12	8	–4.5	3	9
Pittsburgh	9	20	–5	–7	–1.5
St. Louis	20	12	–2	3	4.6

Sources: U.S. Bureau of the Census, *1970 Census of Population,* vol. 1, *Characteristics of the Population,* pt. A (Washington, D.C.: U.S. Government Printing Office, 1973), p. 171, Table 32; *1980 Census of Population, Supplementary Reports, Standard Metropolitan Statistical Areas and Standard Consolidated Statistical Areas* (Washington, D.C.: U.S. Government Printing Office, 1981), p. 3, Table 1; U.S. Bureau of the Census, *State and Metropolitan Area Data Book: 1991* (Washington, D.C.: U.S. Government Printing Office, 1991), Table A; U.S. Bureau of the Census, *Standard Metropolitan Area Data Book: 1997–98* (Washington, D.C.: U.S. Government Printing Office, 1999), pp. 60–65, Table B-1.

other high-growth industries. The Chicago region grew by 11 percent in the 1990s, New York by 9 percent, and the Boston area by 6 percent.

The old manufacturing cities did much worse than these metropolitan-wide population summaries might suggest. In the 1970s, as deindustrialization reached its zenith, St. Louis lost 27 percent of its population but the St. Louis region shrunk just 2 percent because the suburbs were growing significantly, by more than 6 percent. All of the cities in the industrial belt were undergoing a similar experience; for example, in the 1970s Chicago's population fell by 11 percent, Detroit's by 20.5 percent, and Cleveland's by 24 percent, but the suburbs in each of these urban regions continued to grow (although slowly). Most of these cities hemorrhaged population in the 1980s, but in most cases the rate of loss slowed in the 1990s. In fact, New York, Chicago, and a few other older industrial cities held their own or even added population for the first time in 20 or 30 years.

In the Sunbelt, most central cities grew in step with their metropolitan regions. One reason Sunbelt cities did well was that many of them were newer and less built up than the cities in the North. Another is that they were usually not completely encircled by suburbs. David Rusk has categorized cities according to their degree of "elasticity"—their ability to grow either by filling in undeveloped land or by annexing new territory. Of the 52 metropolitan areas of more than 200,000 population that Rusk rated as having "high" or "hyper" elasticity in 1990, 49 were located in the Sunbelt. No Frostbelt city made the list.[18]

Older cities found it impossible to change their boundaries, mostly because they had become surrounded by independent suburban municipalities able to resist annexation or merger. Even in the Sunbelt, the older cities fit this profile; Atlanta, for instance, lost 14 percent of its population during the 1970s, but its regional population grew by 46 percent. Denver likewise lost population (−4.5 percent) while its suburbs grew (by 60 percent). By contrast, many Sunbelt cities were able to annex large tracts of land before they became land-locked. Oklahoma City, for example, grew from about 51 square miles in 1950 to 636 square miles by 1970, and Phoenix expanded from just 17 square miles in 1950 to 469 square miles by 1996.[19] Sunbelt cities gobbled up a substantial amount of surrounding land in the 1950s and 1960s and at least some additional territory after that.[20]

WHY THE SUNBELT BOOMED

The movement of people to the Sunbelt has been matched by a redistribution of the nation's economic resources. In recent decades, job growth has heavily favored the South and West. Table 9.2 shows that in 1960, 58 percent of the nation's workforce was located in the Northeast and Midwest. The West was relatively underdeveloped, with only 15 percent of U.S. employment. But by the 1980s, the share of jobs located

Table 9.2 Comparison of Regional[a] Shares of U.S. Employment and Shares of U.S. Job Growth 1960–2000 (in Percentages)

	Share of U.S. Employment			Share of Job Growth	
	1960	**1980**	**2000**	**1960–1980**	**1980–2000**
Northeast	29%	23%	21%	13.5%	12%
Midwest	29	26	25	21.5	20
South	27	32	34	39.5	42
West	15	19	20	25.5	26

[a]Regions defined according to Bureau of the Census definition; North Central changed to Midwest in 1989.

Sources: Adapted from U.S. Bureau of the Census, *Statistical Abstract of the United States, 1973* using 1960 and 1970 census data, p. 227; *U.S. Statistical Abstract of the United States, 2001,* using 1990 and 2000 census data; *Statistical Abstract of the United States, 1996,* using 1980 census data.

in the Northeast and Midwest had slipped to 49 percent, and by 2000 it was down to 46 percent. Big gains occurred in the South and West, which together accounted for 56 percent of U.S. employment by 2000 (21 percent in the West). The number of jobs in the South rose by 39.5 percent from 1960 to 1980 and by even more, 42 percent, from 1980 to 2000. Meanwhile, the West experienced a 25.5 percent job growth from 1960 to 1980 and a 26 percent growth over the next 20 years. The rate of growth outside the Sunbelt was much slower.

The reasons for the Sunbelt's economic success are many and complex. Economic and technological factors played a major role.[21] The urban infrastructure of the older Frostbelt cities was geared to the high-density patterns of production of the industrial period. Sunbelt cities had an advantage because they could start afresh to build infrastructure suited to the postindustrial economy. The building of the interstate highways network provided the foundation for a national economy that favored the decentralization of economic activities. The adoption of air conditioning made the Sunbelt more attractive both for living and for white-collar work.[22] The materials used in manufacturing shifted from heavy metals such as iron and steel to lighter materials such as aluminum and plastic, and the newer manufacturing plants could be located on relatively cheap, easily available land in Sunbelt metropolitan areas. Most importantly, the source of energy for industry and for homes shifted from Frostbelt coal to Sunbelt oil. Oil jumped from meeting less than half of the nation's energy needs in 1940 to almost 78 percent by 1975. By the mid-1970s, coal met no more than 17 percent of the nation's energy needs.[23]

Changing demographics and lifestyles favored the Sunbelt as well. More leisure time and a greater emphasis on recreation lured people to warmer climates. After World War II, tourism became an increasingly important component of the national economy. Major recreational and tourist facilities developed in Florida and California (homes of Disney theme parks) and in New Orleans and Las Vegas. Whole communities, such as Lake Havasu, Arizona, arose to serve the needs of an expanding class of retired people who preferred Sunbelt lifestyles and the lower cost of living found there.

However, demographic and economic trends do not explain solely the Sunbelt boom. Governmental policies played a pivotal role in redistributing national resources. The powerful role of governments in promoting regional economic growth can be appreciated by looking at the experience of other advanced industrial countries. Largely because they have different national policies, no European country has experienced the extraordinary degree of redistribution of population and production that the United States has undergone in the last half century. Like the United States, European countries have their own "sunbelts": in Britain, employment has shifted from the industrial north to the south of England, where a high-technology economy has emerged along the M-4 motorway between London and Bristol; in Germany, growth has shifted from the traditional centers of industry in the Ruhr and Saar regions to new centers of high-technology engineering and electronics in the southern states of Hesse, Baden-Württemberg, and Bavaria.

However, populations have moved less in Europe than in the United States partly because the European countries have enacted explicit regional development policies designed to counteract uneven development. Britain adopted regional policies in the

1930s to restrain the growth of London and to aid the economies of the industrial north to employ laid-off miners and industrial workers. Britain's regional policies were supported by both Labour and Conservative governments, until the accession of Margaret Thatcher in 1979.[24] Support for regional development policies was even stronger in continental Europe, where programs to move jobs to declining regions were inaugurated in Italy (1950), West Germany (1951), the Netherlands (1951), Ireland (1952), France (mid-1950s), Denmark (1958), and Belgium (1959).[25] The effects of these policies are difficult to evaluate, but in a country like France, which made regional development policy an integral part of national economic planning, there is little doubt that national planners wielding construction controls and powerful incentives were able to disperse jobs and population from Paris to "growth poles" in languishing regions.

The United States has always lagged far behind European democracies in enacting policies to promote economic development in depressed regions. Some regional development policies were begun in the 1960s (such as the Appalachian Regional Commission in 1962), but these policies did nothing but provide some federal assistance for local economic development efforts. Overall, the United States has never enacted comprehensive regional development policies; "Indeed, in treating the geographical distribution of economic activity and population as a matter of market forces, rather than national planning . . . the United States stands alone among advanced democratic countries."[26]

Although regional development planning has been absent in the United States, public spending has exerted a powerful impact. In particular, the Pentagon budget has induced military-dependent sectors to migrate to the Sunbelt. No other major industrialized nation used military spending so forcefully to relocate economic activity from one region to another.[27] The Great Depression ended in the United States when government spending for military procurement climbed sharply in 1940 in response to the stunning success of the Nazi blitzkrieg in Europe. As military contracting soared, the War Production Board made a policy decision to spread out defense installations and productive capacity to make bombing and a potential invasion more difficult. The South and West possessed the advantage of favorable weather for aircraft training facilities. Overall, an estimated 60 percent of the $74 billion wartime expenditures went into the 15 states of the Sunbelt at a time when those states contained less than 40 percent of the national population.[28]

The metropolitan areas of the South experienced the most rapid growth of any region. World War II pulled the rural poor into the cities in search of relatively well-paid industrial employment, which contributed to the rapid urbanization of the South. The beginning of a decades-long process began in the three years between 1940 and 1943, when the population of the metropolitan counties of the South grew by 4 percent and those of the West by 3 percent; by contrast, the metropolitan counties in the upper Midwest grew by only 2 percent and the northeastern metropolitan areas contracted by 0.6 percent.[29] Some cities, most of them located in the South and West, experienced phenomenal growth when people migrated in search of jobs in defense plants. Between April 1940 and October 1941, 150,000 people poured into Los Angeles, increasing the city's population by about a third. During the war years, San Diego grew by

27 percent and Wichita, Kansas, by 20 percent.[30] The wartime boom taxed the housing stock, infrastructure, and public services in these cities to the breaking point.

Near the end of World War II, war production began to shift from heavy industry (tanks and guns) to high-tech weaponry such as missiles, jet airplanes, and sophisticated communications systems. During the Cold War, military spending remained high, and most of it went to the Sunbelt. One study showed a "definite regional shift" from the Northeast to the Sunbelt between 1950 and 1976 in the awarding of defense contracts.[31] During that period, the number of defense employees in the nation increased by more than 35 percent but fell by 3 percent in the 16 northeastern and upper Midwestern states.[32] By 1975 the defense budget contributed only 4 percent to personal incomes in the Northeast, compared to 9 percent in the Sunbelt.[33]

Defense spending shifted to the Sunbelt not just because the region was an efficient location for some kinds of military production. For a long time, Democratic senators and representatives from the South were so secure in their seats because of uncontested one-party elections that they were able to control key committees in Congress through the seniority system. The southerners used their powerful positions as committee chairs to steer defense spending and major infrastructure investments, such as dams and water projects, to their states and districts. Perhaps the best example is Mendell Rivers, who represented Charleston, South Carolina, for 40 years, from 1930 to 1970. As chair of the powerful House Armed Services Committee, Rivers succeeded in getting the federal government to build in his hometown "an Army depot, a Marine Corps air base, a Marine boot camp, two Navy hospitals, a Navy shipyard, a Navy base, a Navy supply center, a Navy weapons center, a Navy submarine base, a Polaris missile base, two Air Force bases, and a federal housing development."[34] Because senators and representatives from more pluralistic and diverse Frostbelt districts usually served fewer terms in Congress before being defeated for reelection, they were not able to accumulate comparable seniority and congressional clout.[35]

Other federal spending programs also disproportionately benefited the Sunbelt. Extensive federal subsidies for highways favored Sunbelt growth over the Frostbelt, which relied more heavily on railroads and mass transit. Federal grants for new sewer and water systems and for large dams and water projects tended to favor the Sunbelt. Of course, some federal spending programs, such as public employment programs and social welfare spending, were biased toward the older industrial cities. The difference is that federal spending oriented to the Frostbelt often came in the form of infusions of urban aid or welfare grants that did little to create sustained economic development. By contrast, federal spending in the Sunbelt created permanent federal payrolls and infrastructure to support whole new industries, such as microelectronics. One of the most important ingredients of economic growth is a skilled labor force. The military actively recruited highly trained white-collar workers, engineers, and scientists to areas near Sunbelt military installations. "Every year the Department of Defense pays a number of companies a large sum of money to move college-educated (often at the public expense) engineers and scientists from the Midwest and other regions to the Southwest."[36]

Besides spending, provisions in the federal tax code favored the Sunbelt over the Frostbelt. In 1954 accelerated depreciation allowances deducted from corporate income taxes provided tax breaks for constructing new commercial and industrial structures but not for rehabilitating old buildings. Accelerated depreciation thus speeded up the flow of capital out of older industrial cities to suburban and Sunbelt locations.[37] Between 1954 and 1980, this subsidy was worth $30 billion in reduced taxes. The investment tax credit, which President Kennedy introduced in 1962, granted a dollar-for-dollar reduction in corporate taxes for investments in new plants and equipment. Thus the federal tax code encouraged companies to abandon older plants in the Frostbelt and build new plants in the Sunbelt. Between 1962 and 1981, this subsidy was worth $90 billion,[38] and in 1982 alone it was worth $20 billion.[39] A study conducted in the early 1980s of nine tax subsidies that promoted the mobility of investment (such as accelerated depreciation allowances on old plant and equipment and allowances for new equipment) found they were worth more than twice the total budget of the U.S. Department of Housing and Urban Development.[40]

Regional inequities in federal policy brought about a proliferation of lobbying groups. In June 1976 the Coalition of Northeast Governors was organized, and in September 1976 congressional representatives from 16 states formed the Northeast-Midwest Economic Advancement Coalition (today called the Northeast Midwest Institute). To counter the lobbying of the Frostbelt politicians, the Southern Growth Policy Board, which had been formed in 1971, stepped up its efforts.[41] Regional disparities in federal spending narrowed somewhat between 1975 and 1979,[42] but Ronald Reagan's election in 1980 decisively shifted the momentum.[43] Once in office, Reagan sharply cut programs targeted to older central cities.[44] Between 1980 and 1987, grant programs of special importance to cities, such as mass transit, public housing, social welfare, and job training, were cut by 47 percent.[45] At the same time, his administration increased defense and highway programs that disproportionately benefited the Sunbelt.

The federal budget became a way to redistribute national resources from other regions of the country, in the process rewarding the constituencies that favored Republicans the most. Between 1983 and 1998, the citizens of just two states, New York and New Jersey, paid $500 billion more into the federal treasury than was returned in benefits.[46] In 1997 the citizens of nine southern and border states paid $45 billion less in federal taxes than those states received back; in the same year, eight northern states paid an $82 billion surplus into the federal treasury. Put simply, northern taxpayers have helped pay for much of the economic prosperity of the Sunbelt.

THE NEW POLITICS OF SUNBELT CITIES

Since the 1980s, the culture and politics of Sunbelt cities have been undergoing a sea of change. Only half a century ago, the South was an economically backward, generally poor region mired in a racist political tradition. The Southwest was an area of the country heavily dependent on military installations and agriculture, with a politics mainly devoted to securing more federal spending for water projects and military bases. Today, from Florida to Southern California, cities that have been growing rapidly since the 1950s are still on an upward trajectory. The population increases have been driven by the growth of services and high-tech industries, and the workers drawn to them; retirees; and a huge influx of immigrants, mainly from the Western Hemisphere. The politics of the Sunbelt have changed in step with these historic processes.

Before World War II, most Sunbelt cities were governed by caretaker governments presided over by politicians from long-established, sometimes prominent, families. The leadership structures looked a lot like party machines led by bosses or cliques that had been around for a long while, but in other respects they bore little resemblance to the turn-of-the-century machines of the northern cities. Immigrants and poor voters might deliver the vote, but they were manipulated by scare-mongering about race and the alleged influence of outsiders. The political leadership of these cities wanted, above all, to protect local culture against change. Such organizations governed Tampa, Florida; San Antonio, Texas; and many other cities until well after World War II. New Orleans was run by a longtime machine, the Regular Democratic Organization, until de Lesseps S. Morrison was elected mayor in 1946.[47]

These machines were ill prepared for the changes set in motion by the defense buildup during World War II. After the war, a new generation of political activists appeared on the scene. In city after city, "G.I. revolts" sprang up in which "bright young candidates marched against corrupt or inept city hall cliques under the banner of progress."[48] They appealed to middle-class voters who had few ties to the old ways. Coalitions of white-collar professionals, business leaders, and growth-oriented city managers and bureaucrats came together to form business-dominated reform governments committed to modernization, new infrastructure, and growth.

This wave of reform transformed the political landscape throughout the Sunbelt, especially in southwestern cities. Between 1945 and 1955, San Antonio, Houston, Dallas, Oklahoma City, Albuquerque, Phoenix, and San Jose all adopted significant reforms, usually installing nonpartisan city-manager systems with at-large electoral arrangements.[49] These movements, instigated by such organizations as the Phoenix Charter Government Committee, the Albuquerque Citizens Committee, and San Antonio's Good Government League, were led by middle- and upper-class Anglo professionals and business leaders.

San Antonio produced a typical example of the Sunbelt version of municipal reform. In 1949 A. C. "Jack" White won the mayoralty with the support of good government reformers and the business community. It was not until 1951, however, that reformers put aside their disagreements and voted in a council-manager charter. Subsequently, the Good Government League began endorsing candidates. From 1955 to 1971, the league endorsed and recruited 77 out of San Antonio's 81 city council members. The Good Government League became the functional equivalent of a political party, a "sort of upper-middle-class political machine, officing not in Tammany Hall, but in a savings and loan association, whose electoral wonders are impressive to behold."[50]

The Good Government League succeeded in passing a series of bond referenda to finance infrastructure improvements to facilitate San Antonio's growth; for example, by 1986 the league had built a massive 98-mile freeway system within the city limits. It also sponsored urban renewal clearance and revitalization of the central business district and facilitated the construction of the HemisFair tourism and shopping project on 149 acres southeast of the Alamo. The HemisFair was a classic example of civic boosterism, with local government providing subsidies to a project that the private sector largely planned and operated.[51]

These postwar business-dominated organizations campaigned for support from middle-class voters. Their attitudes toward issues of race and ethnicity were little different from the machines they had replaced. Over the years, whites had used various methods, both legal and extralegal, to keep African Americans and Latinos from voting. One of the most effective devices was the white primary, which kept blacks from casting ballots in the Democratic primaries used to nominate the party's candidates. In the southern states, where Democratic candidates ran unopposed, this was tantamount to disenfranchisement. In 1944 the U.S. Supreme Court struck down the white primary as a violation of the Fifteenth Amendment of the Constitution.[52]

Other methods continued to be used to dilute the electoral influence of blacks and Latinos. Many cities used at-large election districts to ensure that minority neighborhoods would be outvoted in the citywide totals. The 1965 Voting Rights Act, however, gave federal judges the power to strike down voting systems that systematically reduced minority representation. In 1975 the act was extended to Latinos. Both Houston and Dallas were forced to modify their at-large systems by adopting wards that would maximize representation for blacks and Latinos. Likewise, Los Angeles was forced to redraw its ward boundaries. Minority voters helped pass new city charters that provided for ward-based representation in San Antonio, Fort Worth, Albuquerque, San Francisco, Atlanta, Richmond, and several other cities.[53]

These measures began opening up politics all across the Sunbelt, but even without reform the growing populations of African Americans and Latinos would have made political change impossible to resist. By 1990 blacks and Latinos made up a majority of the population in many cities in Florida and in a belt stretching from Texas to California, with Latinos outnumbering blacks about two to one. In Miami, more than 90 percent of the population was minority, compared to 60 percent in Los Angeles, Houston, and San Antonio. Minorities constituted more than 50 percent in most Sunbelt cities with populations of more than 500,000. Minority populations continued to grow in the central cities during the 1990s, but they went up much faster in the suburbs.

Minority populations in the suburbs of Sunbelt metropolitan areas shot upward in the 1990s—by more than 18 percent in the Fort Lauderdale area and by more than 11 percent in the Oakland, Las Vegas, Atlanta, San Jose, Houston, Orange County (California), Miami, and Dallas areas, among others.[54] Within Sunbelt areas, the biggest increases were in the suburbs. As a result of three decades of immigration, by the census of 2000 minorities made up at least 40 percent of the population of the suburbs in 20 metropolitan areas in the Sunbelt. Table 9.3 shows that the urban areas with the highest proportions of minorities in the suburbs are located in the Sunbelt. Latinos accounted for 69 percent of the suburban population in the Los Angeles urban region by 2000, nearly 80 percent of the suburban population in the Miami and Honolulu areas, and 90 percent or more of the suburban populations of El Paso and McAllen, Texas.

By contrast, fewer minorities live in the suburbs of Frostbelt regions. In fact, in the middle-sized urban areas in the industrial belt—anchored by such cities as Scranton, Allentown, and Harrisburg, Pennsylvania; Youngstown, Akron, Toledo, and Columbus,

Table 9.3   Suburban Minority Populations in Metro Areas[a] with Population over 500,000 (Census of 2000)

	Highest Suburban Minority Percentage		Lowest Suburban Minority Percentage	
Rank	Metro Area	Percentage	Metro Area	Percentage
1	McAllen, TX	92%	Scranton, PA	3%
2	El Paso, TX	90	Fort Wayne, IN	4
3	Honolulu, HI	79	Knoxville, TN	5
4	Miami, FL	78.5	Syracuse, NY	5
5	Los Angeles, CA	69	Youngstown, PA	5.5
6	Jersey City, NJ	62.5	Indianapolis, IN	6
7	Albuquerque, NM	56	Akron, OH	6
8	Fresno, CA	55	Milwaukee, WI	6
9	Riverside, CA	53	Buffalo, NY	6
10	Bakersfield, CA	51.5	Albany, NY	6
11	Oakland, CA	48	Allentown, PA	6
12	Ventura, CA	45	Toledo, OH	7

[a]Several of the metropolitan areas list two or more central cities. In this table, they are identified only by the name of the first central city, as listed in alphabetical order by the Census Bureau.

Source: Adapted from William Frey, *Melting Pot Suburbs: A Census 2000 Study of Suburban Diversity* (Washington, D.C.: Center on Urban and Metropolitan Policy, Brookings Institution Press, June 2001), p. 5, Table 1.

Ohio; and Buffalo, Albany, and Rochester, New York—minority suburban populations are in the single digits. Clearly, the metropolitan areas of the Sunbelt owe much of their recent growth to a continuing stream of immigrants; by contrast, lower immigration rates partially explain the slow growth of some of the urban regions in the Frostbelt.

The number of African American and Latinos winning public office has kept pace with the population changes. Nationwide, the number of black elected officials increased from 1,469 in February 1970 to 9,040 in January 2000.[55] African Americans were elected mayors in some of the largest Sunbelt cities, including Los Angeles, New Orleans, Atlanta, and Birmingham, as well as in suburban and nonmetropolitan cities and counties. With about 20,000 Latino immigrants gaining citizenship and the right to vote each year, Latino gains have been especially dramatic. Nationwide, the number of Latino public officials increased from 3,147 in September 1985 to 5,205 in September 2000.[56] Latinos were elected mayor in Miami, Denver, San Antonio, and many smaller cities.

The incorporation of minorities into the politics of Sunbelt cities has brought about significant policy changes. Atlanta is a good example. Black mayors have governed Atlanta since 1973. The majority of the city council and of the school board is black, and blacks hold a majority of the key appointed and civil service positions in the city government. Under the city's first African American mayor, Maynard Jackson, the African American proportion of the police department rose from 19 to 35 percent in only four years, and complaints about police brutality fell.[57] The city established 24 neighborhood councils, each with professional staff, so that neighborhoods could influence city planning and development decisions. A preferential program begun under Jackson's first term raised the percentage of minority firms holding city contracts from one-tenth of 1 percent to 35 percent by 1988.[58]

Similar gains have been achieved in Birmingham, Alabama, and New Orleans, which have had black mayors since 1979 and 1977, respectively. In both cities, political participation by minorities has increased significantly, and community organizations have become active. In both cities, police brutality, a major concern to blacks, has become less important as a policy issue.[59]

Latinos have experienced political gains as well. In Miami, Latinos have become the most important electoral constituency because they are the largest population group and have become successful economically. In the 1990s Latinos succeeded in overturning at-large election systems that disadvantaged them in Miami and surrounding counties. As a result, Latinos have been able to win public offices at all levels, and Latinos and blacks have become well represented on boards and commissions and in public employment.[60] Similarly, blacks and Latinos have become incorporated into the political system of Denver (a city with many Sunbelt characteristics). In 1983, with the election of Frederico Peña, Denver became the first city without a Latino majority to elect a Latino mayor (at the time, 18 percent of Denver's population was Latino). After Peña's two terms, Wellington Webb became the city's first black mayor at a time when blacks made up 11 percent of the city's population. Latinos and blacks have become well represented on the city council and on city boards and commissions, in public employment, and on the civilian police board.[61]

REGIONAL CONVERGENCE AND NATIONAL POLITICS

A number of scholars have predicted a Sunbelt–Frostbelt economic and political convergence.[62] Economic forces are diversifying the economies as well as changing the demographic profiles of cities all over the nation. In the Frostbelt, corporate white-collar employment, services, and tourism have become increasingly important to urban regions and to downtown economies. Frostbelt metropolitan regions are less heavily blue collar and union than in the past, and central cities in the North have been attracting a significant proportion of affluent households. At the same time, many of the characteristics traditionally associated with older industrial cities—rapid immigration, concentrated poverty, and racial and ethnic conflict—have come to the cities of the Sunbelt. Cities all over the country are now multiracial and multiethnic.

Reflecting this convergence in demographics and politics, the public policies of cities are becoming more alike. Older industrial cities of all sizes have moved aggressively to become more "entrepreneurial" in their pursuit of business investment.[63] Accordingly, many of them have shifted resources away from social services and toward developmental programs that subsidize investment.[64] Large volumes of public money have been invested in facilities such as sports stadiums, convention centers, and redevelopment districts.[65] By investing in high-tech and corporate services and developing an infrastructure to support tourism and recreation, Frostbelt cities have become more like the cities of the Sunbelt.

The regional differences in voting behavior and party identification may be disappearing as well. In the past, the Sunbelt favored the Republican Party and pulled the country in a conservative direction. Recent research shows, however, that Democrats are gaining in metropolitan areas in both the North and the South, and in suburbs as well as central cities.[66] This trend is fueled, in part, by immigration; African Americans, Latinos, and Asians, when combined, are about 75 percent Democratic. They now constitute more than 20 percent of the U.S. population and a much higher percentage in several Sunbelt states and metropolitan areas. White-collar professionals, heavily concentrated in suburbs and in central cities with high-tech sectors, made up 21 percent of the electorate in 2000. They tend to be moderate on social issues and to support environmental protection, civil rights, and women's rights, and their numbers are rapidly growing throughout the Sunbelt. Notably, 54 percent of voters in the fastest-growing 50 counties in the nation—nearly all located in the Sunbelt—supported Al Gore in the 2000 election. In 2002 two scholars argued that these trends sum up to an "emerging Democratic majority" in national politics.[67]

Their predictions seemed to come to fruition in the 2008 presidential election. A tier of southern states still went heavily Republican, but the electoral map showed big gains for the Democratic Party almost everywhere else. Four southern, four Midwestern, and three Western states supported John McCain by more than 55 percent margins, while California, Nevada, Colorado, New Mexico, and Florida voted as blue states. Whatever utility the Sunbelt concept had in the past, in 2008 it seemed to explain very little of the election result.

The recent economic meltdown has even put into question the vaunted economic advantages of the Sunbelt. More than anywhere else, much of the wealth of Sunbelt cities had been based on real estate and construction. These sectors have been hit the hardest in the economic downturn, and as a result, the nation's highest home foreclosure rates and declines in housing values have occurred in metropolitan areas of the South and Southwest: in the year from October 2007 to October 2008, housing values in Phoenix and Las Vegas fell by a third, compared to a decline in the New York region of 7.5 percent.[68] People in the Sunbelt must be startled to see that after years of feeling sorry for those left behind in the frozen North, the shoe is now on the other foot.

NOTES

1. Robert Goodman, *The Last Entrepreneurs: America's Regional Wars for Jobs and Dollars* (New York: Simon & Schuster, 1979), p. 42.
2. Alan Berube, "Racial and Ethnic Change in the Nation's Largest Cities," in *Redefining Urban & Suburban America: Evidence from Census 2000,* ed. Bruce Katz and Robert E. Lang (Washington, D.C.: Brookings Institution Press, 2003), p. 142.
3. John B. Judis and Ruy Teixeira, *The Emerging Democratic Majority* (New York: Scribner/A Lisa Drew Book, 2002).

4. Kevin P. Phillips, *The Emerging Republican Majority* (New Rochelle, N.Y.: Arlington House, 1969).

5. Prompting the famous headline, "Ford to City: Drop Dead!" *New York Daily News*, October 29, 1975, p. 1.

6. Kirkpatrick Sale, *Power Shift: The Rise of the Southern Rim and Its Challenge to the Eastern Establishment* (New York: Random House, 1975).

7. "The Second War Between the States," *BusinessWeek*, May 17, 1976.

8. Quoted in Carl Abbott, *The New Urban America: Growth and Politics in Sunbelt Cities* (Chapel Hill: University of North Carolina Press, 1987), p. 6.

9. Sale, *Power Shift*, p. 11.

10. Bernard Weinstein and Harold Gross, interview quoted in Abbott, *The New Urban America*, p. 4.

11. Bruce J. Schulman, *From Cotton Belt to Sunbelt: Federal Policy, Economic Development, and the Transformation of the South, 1938–1980* (New York: Oxford University Press, 1991), Chapter 2.

12. Abbott, *The New Urban America*, p. 22.

13. Quoted in David R. Goldfield and Howard N. Rabinowitz, "The Vanishing Sunbelt," in *Searching for the Sunbelt: Historical Perspectives on a Region*, ed. Raymond A. Mohl (Knoxville: University of Tennessee Press, 1990), p. 224.

14. Ibid., p. 231.

15. William H. Frey, "Metropolitan America: Beyond the Transition," *Population Bulletin* 45, no. 2 (July 1990): 14.

16. U.S. Bureau of the Census, *Statistical Abstract of the United States, 1980*, 101st ed. (Washington, D.C.: U.S. Government Printing Office, 1981), p. 10; U.S. Bureau of the Census, *Statistical Abstract of the United States, 1992*, 112th ed. (Washington, D.C.: U.S. Government Printing Office, 1992), p. 22.

17. U.S. Bureau of the Census, *Statistical Abstract of the United States, 1992*, p. 22.

18. David Rusk, *Cities Without Suburbs* (Washington, D.C.: Woodrow Wilson Center Press, 1993).

19. Timothy Egan, "Urban Sprawl Strains Western States," *New York Times*, December 29, 1996, p. 6.

20. Rusk, *Cities Without Suburbs*.

21. For a thorough analysis of the growth of the Sunbelt that emphasizes economic and technological factors, see John D. Kasarda, "The Implications of Contemporary Redistribution Trends for National Urban Policy," *Social Science Quarterly* 61, no. 3 (December 1980): 373–400.

22. Raymond Arsenault, "The End of the Long Hot Summer: The Air Conditioner and Southern Culture," in *Searching for the Sunbelt*, ed. Mohl, pp. 176–211.

23. Kirkpatrick Sale, "Six Pillars of the Southern Rim," in *The Fiscal Crisis of American Cities*, ed. Roger E. Alcaly and David Mermelstein (New York: Random House, Vintage Books, 1977), p. 174.

24. For a brief discussion of British regional policies, see James L. Sundquist, *Dispersing Population: What America Can Learn from Europe* (Washington, D.C.: Brookings Institution Press, 1975), Chapter 2.

25. David Pinder, *Regional Economic Development and Policy: Theory and Practice in the European Community* (London: Allen and Unwin, 1983), pp. 13–14.

26. Sundquist, *Dispersing Population*, p. 241.

27. Ann R. Markusen, *Regions: The Economics and Politics of Territory* (Totowa, N.J.: Rowman and Littlefield, 1987), p. 113.

28. Sale, "Six Pillars of the Southern Rim," p. 170.

29. Funigiello, *The Challenge to Urban Liberalism, Federal-City Relations During World War II* (Knoxville: University of Tennessee Press, 1978), pp. 12–13.

30. Abbott, *The New Urban America*, p. 103.

31. Maureen McBreen, "Regional Trends in Federal Defense Expenditures: 1950–76," in *Selected Essays on Patterns of Regional Change: The Changes, the Federal Role, and the Federal Response*, submitted by Senator Henry Bellmon to the Senate Committee on Appropriations (Washington, D.C.: U.S. Government Printing Office, 1977), p. 527.

32. A report issued by the Northeast-Midwest Economic Advancement Coalition, cited in Edward C. Burks, "16 Northeast and Midwest States Find Inequities in Defense Outlays," *New York Times*, September 22, 1977.

33. Richard S. Morris, *Bum Rap on America's Cities: The Real Causes of Urban Decline* (Upper Saddle River, N.J.: Prentice Hall, 1978), pp. 148–149.

34. Sale, *Power Shift*, p. 149.

35. Since the early 1970s, both parties have permitted exceptions to the seniority rule, and the power of committee chairs has been reduced.

36. Ann R. Markusen, "Regional Planning and Policy: An Essay on the American Exception," Working Paper No. 9 (Brunswick, N.J.: Center for Urban Policy Research, Rutgers University, July 1989).

37. See George Peterson, "Federal Tax Policy and Urban Development," in *Central City Economic Development*, ed. Benjamin Chinitz (Cambridge, Mass.: Abt Books, 1979), pp. 67–78.

38. Michael I. Luger, "Federal Tax Incentives as Industrial and Urban Policy," in *Sunbelt/Snowbelt: Urban Development and Regional Restructuring*, ed. Larry Sawers and William K. Tabb (New York: Oxford University Press, 1984), pp. 204–205.

39. John F. Witte, "The Growth and Distribution of Tax Expenditures," in *The Distributional Impacts of Public Policies*, ed. Sheldon H. Danziger and Kent E. Portney (New York: St. Martin's Press, 1988), p. 179.

40. Peter Marcuse, "The Targeted Crisis: On the Ideology of the Urban Fiscal Crisis and Its Causes," *International Journal of Urban and Regional Research* 5, no. 3 (1981): 339.

41. See Markusen, *Regions*, Chapter 8. The Southern Growth Policy Board relinquished its federal monitoring activities to the Congressional Sunbelt Council in January 1981.

42. "Neutral Federal Policies Are Reducing Frostbelt-Sunbelt Spending Imbalances," *National Journal*, February 7, 1981, pp. 233–236.

43. For evidence on the Sunbelt bias of direct federal military expenditures during the Reagan administration, see the data compiled in the *New York Times*, December 20, 1983, cited in Michael Peter Smith, *City, State, and Market: The Political Economy of Urban Society* (New York: Blackwell, 1988), p. 57.

44. Harold Wolman, "The Reagan Urban Policy and Its Impacts," *Urban Affairs Quarterly* 21, no. 3 (March 1986): 311–336.

45. Peggy L. Cuciti, "A Nonurban Policy: Recent Public Policy Shifts Affecting Cities," in *The Future of National Urban Policy*, ed. Marshall Kaplan and Franklin James (Durham, N.C.: Duke University Press, 1990), p. 243.

46. Thad Williamson, David Imroscio, and Gar Alparovitz, *Making a Place for Community: Local Democracy in a Global Era* (New York: Routledge, 2002), p. 56.

47. See Gary Mormino, "Tampa: From Hell Hole to the Good Life," in *Sunbelt Cities: Politics and Growth Since World War II*, ed. Richard M. Bernard and Bradley R. Rice (Austin: University of Texas Press, 1983), pp. 138–161; and Abbott, *The New Urban America*.

48. Abbott, *The New Urban America*, p. 247.

49. Amy Bridges, "Politics and Growth in Sunbelt Cities," in *Searching for the Sunbelt*, ed. Mohl, p. 2.

50. Robert L. Lineberry, *Equality and Urban Policy: The Distribution of Municipal Public Services* (Beverly Hills, Calif.: Sage, 1977), pp. 55–56, quoting Abbott, *The New Urban America*, p. 139.

51. Our account of San Antonio's business-dominated reform movement relies on Abbott, *The New Urban America*.

52. *Smith v. Allwright*, 321 U.S. 649 (1944). See the discussion in V. O. Key, *Politics, Parties, and Pressure Groups*, 5th ed. (New York: Crowell, 1964), p. 607.

53. Abbott, *The New Urban America*, p. 217.

54. William Frey, *Melting Pot Suburbs: A Census 2000 Study of Suburban Diversity* (Washington, D.C.: Center for Urban and Metropolitan Policy, Brookings Institution Press, June 2001), p. 8.

55. Joint Center for Political and Economic Studies, *Black Elected Officials: A Statistical Summary, 2001*, April 2001, p. 250 (*http://www.jointcenter.org/databank/graphs/99beo.pdf*).

56. Ibid., citing original source as *National Roster of Latino Elected Officials* (Washington, D.C.: National Association of Hispanic Elected and Appointed Officials, annual).

57. Michael Leo Owens and Michael J. Rich, "Is Strong Incorporation Enough? Black Empowerment and the Fate of Atlanta's Low-Income Blacks," in *Racial Politics in American Cities*, 3rd ed., ed. Rufus P. Browning, Dale Rogers Marshall, and David H. Tabb (New York: Longman, 2003), pp. 209–210.

58. Timothy Bates and Darrell Williams, "Preferential Procurement Programs and Minority-Owned Business," *Journal of Urban Affairs* 17, no. 1 (1995): 1.

59. Huey L. Perry, "The Evolution and Impact of Biracial Coalition and Black Mayors in Birmingham and New Orleans," in Browning, Marshall, and Tabb, *Racial Politics*, pp. 228–254.

60. Christopher L. Warren and Dario V. Moreno, "Power Without a Program: Hispanic Incorporation in Miami," in Browning, Marshall, and Tabb, *Racial Politics*, pp. 281–306.

61. Rodney E. Hero and Susan E. Clarke, "Latinos, Blacks, and Multiethnic Politics in Denver: Realigning Power and Influence in the Struggle for Equality," in Browning, Marshall, and Tabb, *Racial Politics*, pp. 309–330.

62. Theodore J. Lowi, "The State of Cities in the Second Republic," *Fiscal Retrenchment and Urban Policy*, ed. J. P. Blair and D. Nachmias (Beverly Hills, Calif.: Sage, 1979), pp. 43–54; John H. Mollenkopf, *The Contested City* (Princeton, N.J.: Princeton University Press, 1983); Paul Kantor, *The Dependent City Revisited: The Political Economy of Urban Development and Social Policy* (Boulder, Colo.: Westview Press, 1995).

63. Peter K. Eisinger, *The Rise of the Entrepreneurial State: State and Local Economic Development Policy in the United States* (Madison: University of Wisconsin Press, 1988).

64. For evidence of this shift, see Kenneth K. Wong, *City Choices: Education and Housing* (Albany: State University of New York Press, 1990), p. 16.

65. Dennis R. Judd, ed., *The Infrastructure of Play: Building the Tourist City* (Armonk, N.Y.: M. E. Sharpe, 2003).

66. John B. Judis and Ruy Teixeira, *The Emerging Democratic Majority* (New York: Scribner/A Lisa Drew Book, 2002).

67. Ibid.

68. Richard Florida, "How the Crash Will Reshape America," *The Atlantic*, March 2009, p. 54.

PART III

THE FRACTURED
METROPOLIS

CHAPTER 10

THE POLITICS OF SUBURBAN DEVELOPMENT

METROPOLITAN TURF WARS

Even before the successive waves of suburban development in the twentieth century, upper-status native-born Americans had tried to separate themselves from recently arrived immigrants. Over time, the cities became fragmented into distinct neighborhoods, often with sharply defined boundaries. Suburbanization accentuated this tendency in two respects: it increased the geographic distances separating urban populations, and it gave the residents of the more privileged neighborhoods a set of tools for excluding racial and ethnic groups they considered undesirable. Early in the twentieth century, suburban residents discovered that zoning laws could be an effective instrument for preserving land values and maintaining social class and racial segregation, and over the next few decades virtually all wealthy and middle-class suburbs adopted zoning restrictions. Patterns of segregation were also enforced by developers, who routinely imposed deed restrictions forbidding property owners from selling to blacks and other groups they deemed to be a threat to property values. It took decades, but eventually deed restrictions were overturned by the courts. Zoning laws, however, have continued largely unchanged, and they remain as an effective strategy for regulating residential development.

For affluent people, the benefits of residential segregation have been substantial. Those living in suburbs with high property values and plenty of business investment have been able to pay lower taxes but at the same time enjoy higher levels of public services than the residents of poorer municipalities. In the past, central cities were disadvantaged in comparison to suburbs, and as a consequence they became "the receptacle for all the functions the suburbs [did] not care to support."[1] Originally, the strategies used to maintain residential segregation were aimed specifically at minorities, new immigrants, and the poor, most of whom remained clustered in

OUTTAKE

THERE IS A DEBATE ABOUT GATED COMMUNITIES

The proliferation of gated communities (perhaps more accurately called common interest developments or CIDs) is fragmenting the urban landscape into a mosaic of publicly governed municipalities and privatized spaces. A lively debate is being fought over the question: Is privatized government a good or a bad thing? Arguments on each side of the issue should be considered.

One of the points Evan McKenzie makes in his groundbreaking book, *Privatopia*, is that CIDs are private governments that sharply segregate affluent urban residents from those who rely upon public services. He maintains that CIDs facilitate a "gradual secession" of the affluent from the political and social life of cities, potentially making them "financially untenable for the many and socially unnecessary for the few." He points out that the homogeneous populations that make up most CIDs also undermine any sense of shared social responsibility. Sheryll Cashin echoes this sentiment when she notes that residents of CIDs "tend to view themselves as taxpayers rather than citizens, and they often perceive local property taxes as a fee for services they should receive rather than their contribution to services local government must provide to the community as a whole." This change in perspective has consequences: private security guards replace police, and walled-off recreation areas replace community centers and swimming pools.

Common interest developments have defenders, too. Robert H. Nelson argues that CIDs make it possible for residents to "protect their own neighborhood environment, and also provide a wider range of choice for new residents in search of a neighborhood physical and social environment corresponding to their own individual preferences." In his view, privately governed associations respect one of the most basic rights of human liberty, the right of free association. He maintains that homogeneity within individual neighborhoods is not necessarily a bad thing, since it is based upon the freedom to associate: "the special case of race aside, the right of a neighborhood association to discriminate among potential new unit owners should be protected as a basic matter of defending the right of freedom of association under the U.S. Constitution."

Gated communities, common interest developments, or whatever we wish to call them, are becoming the norm in America's metropolitan regions. They are here to stay. As a result, in the next few years the debate is likely to shift toward a middle ground, involving questions such as whether to compel neighborhood associations to respect constitutional rights and rules of procedural democracy. To this end, one scholar has proposed a bill of rights for private residential government. This might be an effective remedy for the rights of people living within CIDs, but it would not do much to reduce the spatial fragmentation of metropolitan areas.

Sources: Evan McKenzie, *Privatopia: Homeowner Associations and the Rise of Residential Private Government* (New Haven, Conn.: Yale University Press, 1994), p. 186; Sheryll D. Cashin, "Privatized Communities and the 'Secession of the Successful': Democracy and Fairness Beyond the Gate," *Fordham Urban Law Journal* 28 (2001): 1679; Robert H. Nelson, *Private Neighborhoods and the Transformation of Local Government* (Washington, D.C.: The Urban Institute Press, 2005), pp. 260–261, p. 400; Susan F. French, "The Constitution of a Private Residential Government Should Include a Bill of Rights," *Wake Forest Law Review* 27 (1992): 345–352.

decayed neighborhoods in central cities and, sometimes, in nearby older suburbs. But with the rise of multiethnic suburbs in the 1980s, the metropolitan turf wars have become more complicated. Recently, the differences between central cities and their surrounding suburbs have narrowed. In many American cities, affluent residents have been moving downtown, and a large number of suburbs have attracted poor people and waves of foreign immigrants. As a consequence, the fragmentation of metropolitan areas have taken on a finer grain that goes beyond the competition among separate governmental jurisdictions.

In a far-reaching development, the strategies for exclusion used in the past are being replaced by the privatization and walling off of residential developments. By creating privately governed common interest developments (CIDs), homeowners are able to escape many of the burdens of the public realm altogether. Gated communities have become ubiquitous in all urban areas in all regions of the country. Surrounded, as they often are, by a perimeter of walls, fences, or other barriers, they have the effect of segmenting urban populations to a finer degree than was possible through the policies imposed by suburban governments. The effect they exert on metropolitan politics and geographic patterns is still evolving, but certainly they possess the potential to create an urban landscape that is, in key respects, at least as fragmented as in the past.

HOW THE SUBURBS BECAME SEGREGATED

Many threads make up the story of how American suburbs became fragmented into a patchwork of segregated neighborhoods, subdivisions, and independent suburban jurisdictions. There is, to begin with, a cultural explanation: Americans long nurtured an antiurban bias that was reinforced by the generations of immigrants who poured into them in the nineteenth century and the massive demographic movements of the twentieth. There is an economic interpretation, too, that stresses the material benefits that the residents of suburban jurisdictions realized by gaining control of local tax and spending policies. A third explanation, which we treat in this section, traces the rise of the suburbs to the actions of developers who found residential segregation to be an effective marketing strategy for selling their product. Which came first: consumer preferences, or marketing? There may no definitive answer to this question, but it is worth posing nevertheless.

The present suburban pattern was firmly established in the years following World War II. The pent-up demand for housing coincided with new government policies to promote homeownership. Never before had it been so easy to secure a loan. In 1934, Congress created the Federal Housing Authority to ensure the home loans made by banks. The legislation was followed in 1944 by a law authorizing the Veterans Administration to make loans to returning veterans for no money down and for long amortization periods. These policies made it possible for millions of middle-class families to buy homes even if they had few savings—or none at all, in the case of returning veterans. Developers were quick to realize that an enormous market had been opened up, and they seized the opportunity. Within a few years, large development firms became the front-line agents that shaped the development of the suburban subdivisions that multiplied across the urban landscape. As one scholar observed:

> The plain fact is that . . . the main force in our process of urban development is the private developer. The primacy of the bulldozer in transforming rural land to urban uses, the capacity of the private company to build thousands of homes on quiet rolling hills is a predominant fact of American urban life.[2]

What the developers put in place during the suburban boom of the postwar years became the foundation for the pattern of settlement that still exists in America's urban areas.

To a considerable extent, racial and social segregation between cities and suburbs as well as among suburban jurisdictions was fated by the actions of developers who saw it as an effective or even necessary marketing strategy. The suburbs were promoted as ways to achieve instant social status, escape the problems of the cities, and live in a closely regulated social environment. Thus the suburbs became sharply differentiated from the cities, both in people's minds and in reality. Developers were careful to target narrowly defined segments of the population and to exclude others. This strategy worked particularly well for the developers of exclusive subdivisions, who found that the bigger the house and the higher the income of buyers, the more money they could make.

The families who made the suburban move exercised less choice about it than is commonly supposed. The availability of relatively inexpensive land in outlying areas encouraged real estate developers and builders to promote construction outside the cities. In their attempt to market the new subdivisions, developers virtually invented an iconic image of the American dream—the suburban house. As a result it may be said that the suburbs were created first by developers and only second by the choices made by buyers. Developers influenced the character of the suburbs by selecting the clientele that could best supply profits—chiefly the middle to upper classes—and by molding the tastes and preferences of these consumers. Realtors, developers, and financial institutions aggressively marketed the suburbs because new housing construction maximized their profitability.[3] To market the houses they built, these entrepreneurs promised not only a home but also an entire way of life. They were not merely the builders of houses; they were "community builders."[4]

One of the first and most influential of the community builders was Jessie Clyde Nichols. Born on a farm close to Kansas City, Kansas, Nichols attended the University of Kansas and later studied economics at Harvard. In 1900 Nichols took a trip to Europe, where he admired the beauty and grandeur of European cities. He saw no reason why cities in the United States could not be even more majestic than the cities of Europe. In 1905 Nichols began buying up land southwest of downtown Kansas City, where he intended to build and sell top-market residences.

Nichols was different from the typical small-time real estate operator, or "curbstoner," who bought a few small parcels of land on the edge of the city, divided them into lots, and hoped to make a speculative profit. Nichols believed in a scientific approach to land development. In a speech before a real estate convention in 1912, Nichols attracted national attention by criticizing those land developers who went for the fast sale and the quick profit. Instead, he advocated a long-term approach. He shocked his contemporaries by arguing that planning was not only compatible with private profit but could actually increase profits over the long run. As he later put it in a landmark article on suburban shopping centers, "good planning is good business."[5] Over the years Nichols became a persuasive advocate for planned suburban development. He was a leader in the National Association of Real Estate Boards (NAREB), and in 1935 he founded the Urban Land Institute (ULI), which is influential in the housing industry to this day. In his lifetime, he saw the private planning he pioneered become public policy through local subdivision regulations, zoning laws, and federal loan guarantee programs.

Nichols put his principles into practice by developing the Country Club District on the edge of Kansas City, considered by many at the time the most beautiful suburb in the nation. Nichols appealed to his wealthy clientele with extraordinary aesthetics—he modeled the suburb's shopping center, the first in the nation, on the architecture of Seville, Spain. Nichols also applied the latest in household technology, such as piped gas and electric service, in a period when servants were becoming less common. Nichols's suburban houses promised to provide a secure haven far from the stresses and tensions of city life. Husbands could go off to work in the city secure in the knowledge that their wives and children were safe in the idyllic environment of the Country Club District.

Nichols's projects were limited to the upper classes. To guarantee they would remain this way long after he had completed his work, Nichols devised the self-perpetuating deed restriction, which required owners to follow requirements laid down by the developer.[6] The deed restrictions specified minimum lot sizes, minimum cost for houses, setbacks from the street, and even the color and style of houses. And the deeds specified that the houses could be bought by and sold to whites only.[7] These restrictions became an important marketing tool because they promised exclusivity and secure property values.

Until the years after World War II, developments like those built by Nichols were available mainly to the upper middle class. By the late 1940s this began to change. In the late 1930s, Levitt & Sons succeeded as a medium-sized developer of plain tract housing for upper-middle-class families leaving New York City for Long Island, but the company's big break came during World War II, when it won contracts to build thousands of houses for the U.S. Navy around Norfolk, Virginia. It is here that the Levitts worked on the mass production techniques that revolutionized home building throughout the United States. Within a few years after the war, the firm founded by William J. Levitt, his father Abraham, and his brother Alfred became the largest home builder in the United States.

Unlike Nichols, William Levitt drifted into building houses. Caring little for school, Levitt dropped out of New York University after his third year because, as he put it in a *Time* magazine cover story, "I got itchy. I wanted to make money. I wanted a big car and a lot of clothes."[8] In 1936, after he passed through several jobs, Levitt and his father decided to build a house on a Long Island lot they had been unable to sell. They made a profit. From this small beginning, Levitt launched his extraordinary career.

The Levitts quietly began buying up land from Long Island farmers and producing inexpensive homes by using assembly-line methods. The basic process involved laying a concrete slab for a foundation, erecting preassembled walls, then tying the structure together with a roof trucked to the site. The Levitts broke down the complex process of building a house into 26 operations, and then assigned each step to a separate contractor. Because each contractor did the same job over and over again, it was possible to achieve incredible speed.[9] Levitt avoided unions and used piecework incentives to speed the process even more.[10] At the Levitt lumberyard, one man was able to cut parts for ten houses in one day.[11] By 1950 the firm was producing one house every 16 minutes.[12] By preassembling as many components as possible, Levitt reduced the amount of skilled labor necessary on the job site, and by purchasing directly from the manufacturers, he eliminated middlemen's fees. Overall, Levitt was able to build a typical house for about $6,000, an affordable amount even for some working-class families.[13]

Between 1947 and 1951, the Levitts converted 4,000 acres of potato farms in Hempstead, Long Island, into "the biggest private housing project in American history."[14] Ultimately housing 82,000 residents, Levittown, as it came to be known, became a huge success. Because of the huge pent-up demand for inexpensive housing following World War II, in the first years people lined up and camped out for days waiting to purchase one of the homes. The basic Cape Cod model sold for $7,990. With federal guarantees for the loan and no down payment required for veterans, an ex-GI could buy a Levitt house for only $56 a month.[15]

Like Nichols, Levitt believed that tight controls over buyers and their behavior were the best way to guarantee rising real estate values. Restrictive covenants required the grass to be cut each week (if not done, one of Levitt's men would cut it and send a bill) and disallowed fences (but allowed hedges). Laundry could not be hung out on a clothesline. In addition, the covenants barred tenants or homeowners from selling to or even allowing their property to be used by blacks. The standard lease for the first homes in Levittown, in which the tenant had an option to buy, contained this language: "The tenant agrees not to permit the premises to be used or occupied by any person other than members of the Caucasian race. But the employment and maintenance of other than Caucasian domestic servants shall be permitted."[16] Levitt argued that economic realities required him to recognize that "most whites prefer not to live in mixed communities,"[17] but clearly he was motivated by more than mere economics; he evicted two tenants who had allowed black children to play in their homes.[18] In 1960 not a single black family lived in Levittown,[19] and even 30 years later only about one-fourth of 1 percent of its residents were African American.[20]

In the mid-1950s, Levitt decided to build two more Levittowns, one in Pennsylvania and one in New Jersey. Opened in October 1958 and finished in 1965, Levittown, New Jersey, provided several new features. Fearing that an unfavorable image of sterile uniformity would damage sales, the company offered several house styles and floor plans. The idea of mixing styles was offered by William Levitt's wife and implemented by him over the objections of his executives.[21] Levitt did not offer changes from a standardized model to provide more aesthetically pleasing suburban residential areas.

His motives were strictly economic; in order to sell houses, he needed to ensure that the houses would continue to appeal to the aspiring middle class.

Levitt attracted purchasers by other means as well. Long-term financing with low monthly payments was made possible through the firm. He also offered his clientele a preselected community. His firm attempted to exclude people who did not conform to certain middle-class attributes. Prospective customers were screened, for example, by clothing and appearance. All homes were expressly designed for families with young children. Advertisements stressed that it was a planned community with schools, churches, swimming pools, and parks. In all of these respects, the Levitt company carefully selected the residents of its communities.

Levitt's fortunes began to change in 1968 when he sold his development company to the International Telephone and Telegraph Corporation (ITT) for $60 million in ITT stock. The stock, which he used as collateral for loans, plunged in value. Because of a clause in his sales contract, Levitt was forbidden to renew his building activities for ten years, except in cities where ITT had no interest. Levitt invested $20 million in a project in Iran, but the new government took it over after the 1979 revolution. In 1987, at the age of 80, Levitt was forced to declare bankruptcy and was evicted from his New York City offices.[22]

The careers of Nichols and Levitt demonstrate the power of private developers in shaping the suburbs. Developers were more concerned with molding consumer tastes through marketing than anticipating what buyers might want. Segregation on the basis of incomes and lifestyles was a natural result of the logic of marketing, which required developers to project an upbeat, reassuring message. These observations hold for contemporary suburbs as well. Whether a developer builds luxury single-family homes, townhouses for young middle-class home buyers, condominiums for singles, or a gated community, the character of the community that results will reflect the developers' advertising strategy. Buyers can choose their environment before they move, but once they have decided where they are going to live, they "are very largely prisoners of that environment with but little opportunity of changing it."[23]

SELLING THE AMERICAN DREAM

In the two decades after World War II, the suburban home, complete with a patio, barbecue grill, and a tree in the yard, assumed sacred status in the American dream. The suburban house was more than a physical structure; it also pointed the way to the promised land of middle-class success. Most advertisements in the 1950s played on themes of social status and exclusivity. The idea of escaping the riffraff of the city was often made explicit. Advertisements also made thinly veiled references to blacks; one developer, for example, urged potential buyers to "get out of the jungle" of the city.[24] But no theme was worked more often than the appeal to instant success and status:

> Babylon—An early American Waterside Village—Recreated! For the person who has reached that position in life where they desire complete comfort and relaxation.[25]

Birchwood Park, a Long Island suburb, promised that

When you settle at East Hempstead you are "on the right side of the tracks" in more ways than one. It's the hub of Long Island's most desirable residential section.

A developer advertising in the same real estate section labeled one of his home models "The Cadillac—Split Level Plus. . . . A most worthy addition to the 'Blue-bloods of Distinctive Homes.'" For "living on a higher plane," said the builder, "you must get a 'Cadillac'!!"[26] Not to be outdone, another developer warned that his homes were not built for the "man in the street":

> The Cedar Hill Ranch Home, frankly, wasn't designed for the man in the street. There are many homes costing less that ably satisfy his needs. The size and appointments of Cedar Hill were fashioned for the family who considers anything less than the best inadequate. . . . Yes, Cedar Hill was definitely designed for the family accustomed to finer things.[27]

Starting in the late 1960s, some developers began to promote projects designed for clientele groups other than young family-centered couples. Around many cities, and especially in Florida, Arizona, and Southern California, developers began to construct condominiums and apartments for the growing market of retired and older adults. Naturally, suitable images were required to sell these projects. The following are typical:

> Jefferson Village: The first totally-electric condominium community for people 52 or over. Now that the children have moved out, is your house too large for you? Then consider the comfort of living in a full country apartment, provided for by a full staff of electric servants.[28]

Or,

> Retirement: Where you live it determines how you live it. The "second lifetime" of retirement can be a delight or a delusion. It often depends on where you decide to live it.[29]

A dramatic rise in the number of singles and childless couples in 1970s brought about a shift in marketing strategies. Anyone who has seen television ads for beer would surely anticipate that developers would soon turn to sex and companionship as an advertising standby:

> Your move—make it to Woodhollow—pick of the young professionals . . . great word association: Woodhollow and Young Professionals. Lawyers . . . nurses . . . teachers . . . engineers . . . anyone with success in mind.[30]

And,

> [F]or smart young pace setters who like being together . . . for professionals who enjoy being adult and young at the same time. It's Cypress Village, where you share much more in common with your neighbors.[31]

Here, the promise to fulfill "needs" for "a special kind of excitement" seems almost poignant, as if the developer is actually offering a dating service:

> Today's young people are constantly seeking to fill their needs, whether working, playing or relaxing with a special kind of excitement. The Village gives you the opportunity to fill these needs.[32]

And still other developers thought all veiled references should be cast to the winds, in favor of a direct approach:

> A play pen for kids. Big Kids. It's our clubhouse. Top of the knoll. Sort of an adult playground. The kind of place you go with that certain someone. It's roomy and comfortable. A lounge for relaxing . . . cocktails and snapping logs in the fireplace. The games we play are rated M.[33]

Over time, changing demographics brought a new look to the suburbs. In the 1950s and 1960s, virtually all suburbs were built for the standard-issue American family. Home buyers who did not fit that profile were looked on with suspicion. The remaking of the suburbs to account for new lifestyles required a reconsideration of the notion that all attached or multiunit dwellings were unfit for the suburbs. The makeover required a succession of new marketing campaigns, each containing a somewhat altered version of the American dream.

THE IMPERATIVE OF RACIAL SEGREGATION

The rise of the twentieth-century American suburb went hand-in-hand with a cultural imperative of racial segregation. The precedents for segregation enforced by social custom, law, and the policies of the housing industry were established very early, and by the time these practices were abandoned in the late 1970s, a metropolitan land use pattern of racial segregation had become basically fixed. Those patterns are now changing, but slowly and unevenly.

Beginning in the early twentieth century, restrictive covenants became the main instrument used by the real estate industry to enforce segregation. When a buyer purchased a house, the deed might come with a printed covenant that restricted its subsequent sale. Typically, blacks were the chief target, although sometimes Jews and "consumptives" (anyone with tuberculosis) might also be named. Restrictive covenants became, in effect, governmental policy when the supreme courts of 14 states upheld their legality and ruled they could be enforced in the courts.[34] It is estimated that restrictive covenants applied to homes sold in half of the subdivisions built in the United States before 1948, when the U.S. Supreme Court ruled they could not be enforced in courts of law.[35]

The National Association of Real Estate Boards (NAREB) was established in 1908 to represent the interests of builders and real estate agents. From the beginning, the association set out to convince potential home buyers that real estate was a good investment. Builders and real estate agents accepted as a fundamental law of economics the principle that the value of property was connected to the homogeneity of neighborhoods. Based on this premise, the NAREB "racialized" land use in urban areas by promoting the idea that whites and blacks must be strictly segregated.[36] From 1924 until 1950, Article 34 of the Realtors' national code (circulated to realtors everywhere by the NAREB) read, "A Realtor should never be instrumental in introducing into a neighborhood a character of property or occupancy, members of any race or nationality, or any individual whose presence will clearly be detrimental to property values in the neighborhood."[37]

In addition, most local real estate boards were guided by written codes of ethics prohibiting members from introducing "detrimental" minorities into white neighborhoods. The textbooks and training materials used in real estate training courses took care to point out that real estate agents were ethically bound to promote homogeneous neighborhoods. The leading textbook used in such courses in the 1940s compared some ethnic groups to termites eating away at sound structures:

> The tendency of certain racial and cultural groups to stick together, making it almost impossible to assimilate them in the normal social organism, is too well known to need much comment. But in some cases the result is less detrimental than in others. The Germans, for example, are a clean and thrifty people. . . . Unfortunately this cannot be said of all the other nations which have sent their immigrants to our country. Some of them have brought standards and customs far below our own levels. . . . Like termites, they undermine the structure of any neighborhood into which they creep.[38]

Any real estate agent found breaking the code by selling to members of the wrong groups was subject to expulsion from the local real estate board and loss of license. Even brokers who were not affiliated with the national association felt compelled to accept the Realtors' guidelines because most of their business depended on referrals.

In 1948, in the case of *Shelly v. Kraemer*, the U.S. Supreme Court ruled that racially restrictive covenants could not be enforced in the courts.[39] Even so, as we have seen in the case of Levittown, covenants continued to be written, at least in some developments. They were enforced by a pressure exerted by realtors, developers, homeowner associations, and neighbors. Banks refused to make loans to blacks trying to buy in white neighborhoods; in any case, realtors refused to show them the homes. The suburbs did not begin opening up to blacks until Congress passed the 1968 Housing Act, which barred racial discrimination in the sale and rental of housing.

But old patterns of settlement have been difficult to change even without overt discrimination. The emergence of the common interest development (CID) proved remarkably efficient in preserving the social-class uniformity of residential developments. When home buyers purchase a home in a CID, they automatically agree to abide by a list of restrictions on the use of their property. They also pay fees for their share in the cost and maintenance of services and amenities held "in common" (thus the term "common interest") with other residents. The "community" of homeowners is legally bound by a variety of covenants, contracts, and restrictions (CC&Rs). Such rules can be used to enforce the homogeneity of neighborhoods even more effectively than restrictive covenants, with one principal exception—they cannot be used explicitly to sort out buyers on the basis of race, ethnicity, or gender.

The number of CIDs, which include cooperative apartments, condominiums, and single-family housing developments, exploded from fewer than 500 in 1964 to 10,000 by 1970 and to 150,000 by 1992, when 32 million Americans lived within them.[40] CIDs were concentrated especially in the Sunbelt, with California, Florida, and Texas leading the way. All through the Sunbelt, retired people moved in big numbers into gated communities. By 2005, 54.6 million people lived in 274,000 developments governed by homeowner associations.[41] In many metropolitan areas, they have become so common that new home buyers who do not want to live in one will find their housing options to be severely limited. Since 2000, 80 percent of all homes built in the United States are governed by homeowner associations that administer privately provided amenities.[42]

CIDs provided the institutional means for developers to become "community builders" in the purest sense. The CC&Rs that home buyers agreed to were drawn up by the developer before the first resident moved in. Developers could point to the CC&Rs to reassure home buyers that the future of their investment was secured against unwanted change. The CID mechanism also solved a pressing problem that immediately threatened developers' profits. By the late 1950s, suburbia had become synonymous with low-density tract housing, an equation that reflected the developers' success in marketing the suburbs as an escape from the cities. But by the 1960s, this version of the suburban dream began to yield lower profits. Builders found that the market for single houses constructed on individual lots was diminishing. Huge demographic and income groups, such as retirees and young singles and married couples without children, remained as vast untapped markets.

The problem for developers was that by the 1960s the constantly rising price of suburban land meant that they could build homes affordable for the middle class only if they could achieve much higher densities. Accordingly, the housing industry initiated a campaign to market a revised version of the suburban dream that would include row houses and apartment buildings, which previously had been associated with inner-city neighborhoods. By the late 1960s, the American Society of Planning Officials, the Urban Land Institute, developers, and the Federal Housing Administration (FHA) became sudden critics of the "gridiron" housing tracts and large-lot, low-density development they had promoted for so long. The CID idea anchored a campaign to convince local governments and consumers that higher-density development was compatible with the maintenance of property values and exclusion.[43]

In a report published in 1963, the Urban Land Institute pointed out that CIDs could achieve exclusion better than any alternative form of development: "Existing as private or semi-private areas they may exclude undesirable elements or troublemakers drifting in."[44] The FHA agreed to insure loans for condominiums in multiunit buildings in 1961. Two years later, the FHA released its first manual explicitly encouraging developers to build planned units that would be governed by homeowner associations. In 1964 the FHA and the Urban Land Institute copublished a 400-page volume describing the history of CIDs and setting forth detailed directions on how to establish CC&Rs and the homeowner associations to enforce them.[45] Since the early 1970s, the two biggest secondary mortgage purchasers, the Federal National Mortgage Association and the Federal Home Loan Corporation, have insisted on formulating and reviewing guidelines for residential associations before purchasing the loans on properties that will be governed by them. In only two decades, the institutional pressures applied by the housing industry and the federal government changed the face of the suburbs.

In popular parlance, CIDs are generally referred to as "gated communities," though this term is imprecise because many privatized developments are not actually physically gated. For developers, gates and walls are often used as a marketing tool; these features allow them to play up themes of security, seclusion, and exclusivity.[46]

Developers establish the rules and regulations and set up the homeowners' association even before the first property is sold. In this way, they are able to promise to buyers that all residents will follow closely prescribed norms of behavior and decorum. The covenants and restrictions enforced by residents' associations may dictate minimum and maximum ages of residents, hours and frequency of visitors, color of paint on a house, style and color of draperies hung in windows, size of pets and number of children (if either is allowed), parking rules, patios and landscaping—the list can be staggering in length and detail. Many CID residents no doubt find such regulations comforting. For others, the restrictions become intolerable, as evidenced by the high number of lawsuits filed against community associations.

Gated communities are planned as remarkably homogeneous environments. Some of them are developed and marketed to appeal to people on the basis of particular shared interests or life conditions. For example, communities exist exclusively for retirees, golfers, singles, and even nudists. Green Valley, Nevada, a massive gated community just outside Las Vegas, is segmented not only by different architectural styles, but by the cost and size of houses.[47] Each of these "villages" (as the developer calls them) carries the accoutrements of community: a name (Silver Springs or Valle Verde, for example), a community center, a school, a recreational center, and sometimes a park.[48] The separation between this private city and the outside world is, in effect, embellished by a finer-grained separation within.

After Congress passed the Housing Act of 1968, it has been illegal to discriminate on the basis of race in the selling or rental of housing. To some degree, the intensified social-class segregation facilitated by gated communities acts as a partially effective substitute. The median income for African American is 61 percent of the average earnings for non-Hispanic white families.[49] Any attempt to remedy economic segregation would be politically and legally unacceptable. But the consequence of the enduring racial inequalities is that the patterns of segregation inherited from the past will change very, very slowly.

WALLING OFF THE SUBURBS: INCORPORATION

The high degree of segregation imposed by the practices of developers and their allies in the federal government was reinforced by the policies of suburban governments. Throughout the twentieth century the number of independent suburbs multiplied and as a result, urban areas became increasingly fragmented into a multitude of governmental jurisdictions. The first steps in the direction of metropolitan fragmentation were taken earlier, but for a variety of reasons, until the 1920s the number of suburbs outside the big cities remained relatively small. Some of the people who moved beyond city boundaries in the post–Civil War era sought annexation rather than separation because public services were otherwise too expensive or hard to get. At other times, suburban residents were coerced into joining the city. From the turn of the century to the 1920s, for example, Los Angeles used its monopoly over water supply to force consolidation on neighboring communities, including Hollywood, Venice, Lordsburg, Sawtelle, Watts, Eagle Rock, Hyde Park, Tujunga, and Barnes City. But the formation of the Metropolitan Water District in 1927 ended Los Angeles's monopoly over water.[50] Subsequently, through an agreement among local governments called the Lakewood Plan, suburbs were able to obtain municipal services by contracting with the county government.[51] Almost overnight, the number of suburbs outside Los Angeles began to multiply.

On occasion, simple economic self-interest supplied a sufficient motive to incorporate a new suburb. E. J. "Lucky" Baldwin was a notorious gambler and entrepreneur in California in the early twentieth century. He got his nickname by making a fortune gambling on mining stocks,[52] and he was the defendant in a number of seduction and paternity suits that culminated in spectacular trials. Baldwin wanted to build a racetrack, but he knew he would be opposed by Southern California's foes of sin, led by the Anti-Saloon League. Accordingly, Baldwin decided to form his own suburb, called Arcadia. As the name implied, he intended the town to be his personal utopia. He imported his own employees as residents and handed out free watermelons on Election Day. Not surprisingly, they approved incorporation unanimously and elected a city council composed of Baldwin and his employees. Baldwin realized his dream when Santa Anita raceway opened on December 7, 1907.[53]

Suburban governments sometimes provided industrialists with havens from taxes and regulation. Efforts to incorporate were almost always successful when they were led by industry.[54] In 1907 meatpacking companies incorporated National City on the northern border of East St. Louis, Illinois, to avoid being taxed by East St. Louis. A few years later, Monsanto Chemical Company created the city of Sauget on East St. Louis's border for the same purpose. In the 1950s a group of industrialists tried to form a separate suburban jurisdiction in Los Angeles County in order to avoid having to pay for the services of a growing suburban population. When they found that the area did not include the 500 residents required for incorporation, they redrew the boundaries to include 169 patients of a mental sanitarium, which put them over the top. Appropriately, they named their new town "Industry."[55]

But for most suburbs, the motive driving the desire to incorporate was less nakedly entrepreneurial. Put simply, the people who had left the city wanted to wash their hands of it. The only effective way to ensure they could never be annexed by the city they had fled was to form a separate governmental jurisdiction. Incorporation was a way for suburban residents to gain control over taxes and services, and it provided a means of keeping out the people who still lived in the city. At the turn of the century, residents of Oak Park on the border of Chicago feared that the Slavic population might spill over from neighboring Austin. Their motive for incorporating, according to one author, was that "Slavic persons with little aversion for alcohol were rapidly settling the Austin area, and the native American Protestant population of Oak Park feared the immoral influences that might accompany these foreigners."[56] Between 1899 and 1902, Austin joined the city of Chicago, but Oak Park formed a separate suburban government.

At the edges of all the big cities, municipalities proceeded rapidly to incorporate. In 1890 Cook County, whose principal city is Chicago, had 55 governments; by 1920 it had 109. Similarly, the number of general-purpose governments in the New York City area grew from 127 in 1900 to 204 by 1920. There were 91 incorporated municipalities in the Pittsburgh area in 1890 but 107 in 1920.[57] During the 1920s new suburbs were formed by the score.

Political separation, however, was not always easy to accomplish. Local governments are not mentioned in the U.S. Constitution; legally, they are creatures of the states. In the early part of the nineteenth century, the incorporation of a local government was viewed as a privilege bestowed by state legislatures. In their fights to persuade state legislators to allow them to incorporate their own governments, people who had moved beyond the limits of the industrial cities claimed that smaller governments were closer to the people and were therefore the best possible expressions of democracy.[58]

Gradually, state legislatures made it so much easier for groups of citizens to create new towns and cities that incorporation shifted from a privilege to a right.[59] Eventually in all the states, any group of sufficient size that had migrated beyond the boundaries of the city could, if a majority of them approved, form a separate local government. "By the early twentieth century suburbanites had begun carving up the metropolis, and the states had handed them the knife."[60] By 1930 every state legislature in the country had adopted liberalized incorporation laws that put the decision of whether suburban residents would or would not be annexed by the central city firmly into the hands of those who had already fled the city.

Suburban residents have pursued incorporation with great enthusiasm. According to the census of 2002, there were 19,431 municipalities in the United States.[61] The pace has slowed, but the number of special-purpose districts has continued to grow rapidly (in 2002 there were more than 35,000). St. Louis County, Missouri, has 92 municipalities; DuPage County, outside Chicago, has 38. The proponents of incorporation have been motivated by a variety of concerns. In June 2005, 94 percent of the affluent residents of Sandy Springs, Florida, voted to support incorporation to achieve smaller government so that "Sandy Springs can control its own destiny," or as another put it, "My major thing, let's make the decisions here rather than downtown."[62]

Mostly, the residents of Sandy Springs were upset that some of their tax money supported services supplied to less affluent people living in their home county. A simple desire for government closer to home combines with bare-knuckled economic self-interest in most incorporation proposals. The principle most often cited in these battles is the desire to gain control over tax revenues and land use decisions. In 2005 a resident supporting the incorporation of the Village of the Falls in Dade County, Florida (outside Miami) said, "We want to be able to have a say how our tax dollars are spent," and, he added, "we want to control zoning of our neighborhood to maintain and improve our quality of life."[63]

Control over land use decisions is important because these policies are directly connected to local economic growth. In the most affluent communities, residents may wish to gain control so that they keep out malls, big-box stores, and other development they deem to be undesirable. The residents of most suburbs, however, are more likely to desire exactly the opposite. The fragmentation of urban areas into multitudes of independent governments has created an intense competition for economic growth. All but the most affluent suburban governments simply cannot raise revenues sufficient for providing adequate services unless they attract business; if they cannot do so, homeowners end up paying extremely high property taxes even while receiving inferior services. By the mid-1950s local governments were fighting hard for the first generation of shopping centers, which later would morph into enclosed malls. Local officials encouraged development through grants to private firms, abatement of local taxes, and the provision of infrastructure such as access roads. In the process, local officials sometimes took money on the side; a culture of corruption pervaded the land use process in many places.[64]

The competition for growth is especially intense in the 28 states that have authorized local sales taxes. Receipts from sales taxes can generate 40 percent or more of local revenues. Accordingly, local officials go to great lengths to land a mall, big-box store, and smaller retailers. The competition is fierce; in the words of a vice president of the Utah Taxpayers Association, "It's kind of a Cold War mentality. Basically what you have is cities competing against each other for sales tax dollars."[65] Ventura, California, provides an excellent example of what local officials are willing to do. To ensure the continued viability of the Buenaventura Mall, the city agreed to a $12.6 million subsidy package that obliged it to rebate 80 percent of the sales tax revenues that would be realized by an expansion and makeover of the mall. When a neighboring municipality, Oxnard, proposed a plan to share sales tax revenues among local governments, a Ventura city official summarily rejected the offer: "Now because their shopping center deteriorated . . . they want to share. I haven't seen any movement from them wanting to share Wal-Mart and all those stores along the . . . Freeway."[66] Battles motivated by attitudes exactly like that are playing out in metropolitan areas across the country.

WALLING OFF THE SUBURBS: ZONING

Zoning is probably the most powerful tool that municipalities can use to control land use. It may be used for many purposes, but without a doubt its origins are rooted in the desire to make it difficult or impossible for less affluent people to settle nearby. The nation's first zoning law was enacted in New York City on July 25, 1916. By the end of the 1920s, 768 municipalities with 60 percent of the nation's urban population had enacted zoning ordinances.[67] Quick adoption was made possible when real estate interests discovered what a useful tool zoning could be for protecting valuable land from uses deemed less desirable. As promoters of New York's ordinance explained it to audiences around the nation, "The small homeowner and the little shopkeeper were now protected against destructive uses next door. Land in the lower Fifth Avenue section, which had been a drag on the market when zoning arrived, was now undergoing so successful a residential improvement that rents were on the rise. 'Blighted districts are no longer produced in New York City.'"[68] The main claim made for zoning was that it kept land values high by segregating "better" from "inferior" land uses. In state after state, real estate groups and politicians lobbied for state laws enabling cities to zone their property.

New York City's zoning ordinance arose from the fear that fashionable sections of Fifth Avenue might be invaded by loft buildings from the garment district on the West Side. Indeed, abundant evidence indicated that such an invasion was likely to occur. From 1850 to 1900, New York's population increased from 661,000 to 3,437,000. Such growth rewarded speculators and entrepreneurs who had been discerning enough to predict the path of the city's expansion. But it was bothersome, too, for the upper-class residents who had repeatedly established themselves at the city's periphery, only to be pushed out again by encroaching waves of immigrants and businesses.

By the turn of the century, the upper class had established a mansion district and an exclusive shopping area on upper Fifth Avenue. The wealthy residents of the area felt threatened by the teeming masses only a few blocks away. The garment district, characterized by tall loft buildings in which thousands of poorly paid immigrant garment workers and carters worked, threatened to destroy the exclusive shopping district. A way—a legal way—had to be found to protect Fifth Avenue, which was often described (by the rich) as the cultural fulcrum of New York, "a unique place" in "the traditions of this city and in the imagination of its citizens," "probably the most important thoroughfare in this city, perhaps any city in the New World," an area with a "history and associations rich in memories," "the common pride, of all citizens, rich and poor alike, their chief promenading avenue, and their principal shopping thoroughfare."[69] The Fifth Avenue Association, which employed lawyers to invent this kind of rhetoric, pleaded in 1916 that Fifth Avenue was a special area that should be protected from encroachment. Fifty-four years later, the rationale behind zoning had changed little: "We moved out here . . . to escape the city. I don't want the city following me here," explained a Long Island resident.[70]

Between 1913 and 1916, the Fifth Avenue Association, composed of wealthy retail merchants and landowners, lobbied to exclude tall loft buildings from their district. At first they tried to limit the height of buildings, but soon they hit on a more ambitious scheme. In 1916 the Buildings Heights Commission, first appointed in 1913 to investigate the problems of tall buildings in New York City, proposed carving Manhattan into distinct zoned areas to ensure a "place for everything and everything in its place."[71] According to the commission, "the purpose of zoning was to stabilize and protect lawful investment and not to injure assessed valuations or existing uses."[72]

New York's law specified five zones based on different uses and values of land. In the zoning pecking order, residential uses assumed first place, even though commercial and industrial land was often more valuable. Next in the hierarchy were commercial business districts, differentiated on the basis of building height (the higher the buildings, the lower the place in the zoning hierarchy). Warehouses and industries were allotted last place.

New York City officials set out to publicize their law, in part to ensure it would be widely adopted before courts could challenge its constitutionality. "By the spring of 1918 New York had become a Mecca for pilgrimages of citizens and officials" who wanted to enact a similar ordinance. Within a year after passage of the legislation, more than 20 cities had initiated "one of the most remarkable legislative campaigns in American history."[73] Zoning was literally mass produced; most cities copied the

New York ordinance and adopted it with few changes. Zoning soon became the chief weapon used by urban real estate interests to protect land prices. By 1924 the federal government had given zoning its seal of approval. A committee of the Department of Commerce drafted the Standard State Zoning Enabling Act, which served as a model zoning law for all the nation's cities.

In 1926 the U.S. Supreme Court reviewed a case from Ohio, *Village of Euclid v. Ambler Realty Co.*, and in a landmark decision it declared that zoning was a proper use of the police power of municipal authority.[74] One interesting facet of the case revealed how zoning would be used in the future. Ambler Realty had purchased property in the village of Euclid in hopes it would become valuable as commercial property. In 1922 the village zoned Ambler's property as residential, which had the effect of instantly lowering its market value. In bringing suit against the village, Ambler argued that Euclid's zoning law had lowered its property values without due process of law. In its decision, the Court set forth a classic statement in defense of restrictive zoning, arguing that the presence of apartment, commercial, and industrial buildings undermined residential neighborhoods. There was an assumed hierarchy of uses, which the Court itself enunciated:

> With particular reference to apartment houses, it is pointed out that the development of detached house sections is greatly retarded by the coming of apartment houses . . . the coming of one apartment house is followed by others, interfering by their height and bulk with the free circulation of air and monopolizing the rays of the sun which otherwise would fall upon the smaller homes, and bringing, as their necessary accompaniments, the disturbing noises incident to increased traffic and business, and the occupation, by means of moving and parked automobiles, of larger portions of the streets, thus detracting from their safety and depriving children of the quiet and open spaces and play, enjoyed by those in more favored localities—until, finally the residential character of the neighborhood and its desirability as a place of detached residences is utterly destroyed.[75]

In its decision, the Court ruled that separating residential from other land uses was a legitimate use of the city's police power to promote the order, safety, and well-being of its citizens.

Zoning became popular at the same time that well-to-do suburbs proliferated around the large cities—Beverly Hills, Glendale, and a multitude of other communities outside Los Angeles; Cleveland Heights, Shaker Heights, and Garfield Heights outside Cleveland; and Oak Park, Elmwood Park, and Park Ridge outside Chicago. It is not difficult to understand why such communities liked the zoning concept. The possibility that the poor might disperse throughout metropolitan areas threatened people living in exclusive neighborhoods, both in central cities and in suburbs. From its inception, zoning became the legal means to ensure what informal social class barriers or the housing market might not have been able to achieve—the exclusion of the inner-city Great Unwashed.

To accomplish this separation, restrictive residential zoning attempted to exclude apartments, to set minimum lot sizes, or to stop new construction altogether. Apartments in the suburbs represented the possibility of class, lifestyle, or racial changes. The residential character of a tree-lined, curved-street subdivision with individual homes set well back seemed to be threatened by apartment buildings. "We don't want this kind of trash in our neighborhood" was an attitude applied even to luxury apartments. Apartments symbolized the coming to suburbia of city problems:

> The apartment in general, and the high-rise apartment in particular, are seen as harbingers of urbanization, and their visibly higher densities appear to undermine the rationale for the development of the suburbs, which includes a reaction against the city and everything for which its stands. This is particularly significant, since the association is strong in suburbia between the visual characteristics of the city and what are perceived to be its social characteristics.[76]

The residents of many suburban communities became deeply concerned when apartment projects were proposed. For example, an executive living in Westport, an exclusive suburb in Connecticut, exclaimed, "Thank god we still have a system that rewards accomplishment, and that we can live in places where we want to live, without having apartments and the scum of the city pushed on us."[77] Most suburbs banned the building of apartments entirely. In the 1970s over 99 percent of undeveloped land zoned residential in the New York region excluded apartments.[78] Although this did not mean apartments could not be constructed, it did require apartment builders to secure zoning variances, which maximized the chances for opposition.[79]

Suburban governments also attempted, in effect, to regulate the social class and incomes of people who occupied single-family homes. Subdivision regulations and building codes made developers go through a costly review process that artificially increased the cost of new houses and gave local residents an opportunity to oppose new developments. But the most common device for raising the minimum cost of new construction was (and is) large-lot zoning. Sometimes the regulations requiring large lots also specified minimum floor-space requirements, the use of particular building materials, and minimum street setbacks. These kinds of regulations raised the cost for the home buyer and thus helped protect an exclusive area.

Large-lot zoning is a device to keep out people with lower incomes. In some upper-class communities, this means keeping out the middle class; in some middle-class communities, it means excluding the working class. A defender of 4-acre lot minimums in Greenwich, Connecticut, said that large-lot zoning is "just economics. It's like going into Tiffany and demanding a ring for $12.50. Tiffany doesn't have rings for $12.50. Well, Greenwich is like Tiffany." A New Jersey legislator defended large-lot zoning as a means of making sure "that you can't buy a Cadillac at Chevrolet prices." An official of St. Louis County, where 90,000 acres were zoned for 3-acre lots in 1965, indicated that his suburban county welcomed anyone "who had the economic capacity [to enjoy] the quality of life that we think our county represents . . . be they black or white."[80]

Exclusionary zoning often makes room for industrial and commercial investment that will provide more in taxes than it consumes in services. Of course, affluent communities want nothing except certain kinds of industry—industry that does not produce bothersome pollution and traffic. Sy Schulman, a Westchester County (New York) planning commissioner, wryly noted that the ideal industry "is a new campus-type headquarters that smells like Chanel No. 5, sounds like a Stradivarius, has the visual attributes of Sophia Loren, employs only executives with no children and produces items that can be transported away in white station wagons once a month."[81] Because the demand for such clean industry exceeds the supply, there is a fierce competition for it. As with other aspects of suburban development, it is the wealthier suburbs that usually win.

THE CHALLENGE TO EXCLUSIONARY ZONING

As a tool for creating and perpetuating residential exclusion and privilege, zoning went largely uncontested in the federal and state courts for more than half a century.[82] But in the 1970s it was challenged in the federal courts on the ground that it violated the equal protection clause of the Fourteenth Amendment to the U.S. Constitution. Lawton, Oklahoma, southwest of Oklahoma City, had attempted to use its zoning ordinance to exclude apartments, but in 1971 the federal appellate court for its circuit ruled that municipalities could not enact zoning ordinances that had the effect of excluding minorities unless they could show a nondiscriminatory intent concerning their land use objectives.[83] In April 1971 another case gave even more hope to proponents of residential integration. The U.S. Court of Appeals for the Second Circuit rejected an attempt by the city officials of Lackawanna, New York, to block the building of a black housing subdivision in a white neighborhood.[84] Clearly, suburban municipalities were under the gun to show that their zoning ordinances were not enacted simply to keep out blacks.

In a case from Black Jack, Missouri, the courts imposed a tougher standard yet, one that made it appear that exclusionary zoning might be eliminated entirely. In September 1974 a federal appeals court ruled that the city's new zoning ordinance forbidding the construction of multiunit housing had a discriminatory *effect* even if it did not have a discriminatory intent, and therefore it violated the U.S. Constitution. In June 1975 the U.S. Supreme Court refused to review the circuit court's decision, thereby upholding it. The effect of the Black Jack decision had an enormous potential: If left to stand, local governments everywhere would find their land use practices subject to challenge.

Just two years later, however, the Supreme Court backed away from this strict constitutional standard. In reviewing the zoning ordinance of Arlington Heights, Illinois, which barred a federally subsidized townhouse project from being built—a restriction identical to Black Jack's—the Court declared that the effect of zoning laws could not be used as the only argument against them; rather, they had to be shown to have been enacted with the intent to discriminate: "Disproportionate impact is not irrelevant, but it is not the sole touchstone of an invidious racial discrimination."[85] The Supreme Court had already made it much more difficult for litigants to challenge zoning ordinances by requiring them to show a "distinct and palpable injury."[86] By 1977, then, the courts had gotten out of the business of reviewing local zoning laws, except in the rare case when a community was extremely blatant in applying them against blacks or other minorities.

The courts have consistently held that discrimination on the basis of income or class is not prohibited by the U.S. Constitution. If suburbs can show that their zoning laws are designed to protect the tax base and the exclusive residential character of the community, even though these discriminate against poor people, the laws will not be declared unconstitutional. In 1971, for example, the Supreme Court upheld an amendment to the California constitution, passed in 1950, which required that low-rent housing could not be built without prior approval by a referendum of the voters of the city. Although clearly biased against those seeking low-income housing, the Court ruled that discrimination on the basis of income was not unconstitutional under the equal protection clause of the Fourteenth Amendment.[87] In the intervening years, that court ruling has stood the test of time.

Since the federal courts have been unwilling to use the U.S. Constitution to break down the walls of suburban exclusion, this has left the state governments as the main avenue of redress for those wanting to challenge local zoning laws. But two well-publicized and highly controversial cases from Mount Laurel, New Jersey, reveal the formidable hurdles that stand in the way of change. In 1970 Mount Laurel, located not far from Camden and Philadelphia, was a mostly rural community. The area contained a small African American community that had been there since before the Civil War. Quakers had made Mount Laurel a sanctuary for runaway slaves on the Underground Railroad, and their descendants still resided in the area. Many of them lived in small shacks and converted chicken coops, and when these were condemned by the city of Mount Laurel, the residents realized they would be forced to move to the slums of Camden. They formed an action committee and applied for federal funds to build a subsidized housing project, but in 1970 the local planning and zoning board turned down the committee's proposal.

The residents then turned to the courts. They found three idealistic lawyers working for the Camden Region Legal Services who agreed to pursue a case to strike down Mount Laurel's zoning laws, which allowed only single-family homes and specified big lots, large building sizes (a minimum of four bedrooms), and substantial setbacks from the street. In 1972 a trial court found that Mount Laurel's zoning laws violated language in the New Jersey constitution that guaranteed equal protection of the law for all persons. Further, the court ruled that not only Mount Laurel but all of New Jersey's 567 municipalities had an obligation to provide land uses that would meet regional housing needs. The U.S. Supreme Court subsequently refused to hear an appeal of this decision.

A few years later, in 1982, the new chief justice of the New Jersey supreme court heard six cases showing that the city of Mount Laurel was ignoring the original trial court's decision. He combined the cases into one proceeding, and in 1983 the court issued a pathbreaking unanimous decision, widely known as Mount Laurel II. The court noted that the town of Mount Laurel had made no real attempt to comply with the original judicial directive; it had simply rezoned 33 of its 14,176 acres, and not one of the 515 low-income housing units required to meet the court's decision had been built.[88] To compel compliance with its original decision, Mount Laurel II required that New Jersey municipalities rezone land for low-income housing, if necessary, and make low-income housing attractive to developers through such devices as tax incentives and subsidies. Second, to encourage builders to pursue lawsuits against exclusionary zoning, the court established "builder's remedies," which allowed developers of low- and moderate-income housing to sue cities that tried to keep them out.

As a result of Mount Laurel II, New Jersey's suburban municipalities were besieged with lawsuits, and politicians were increasingly pressured to do something about the situation. Republican governor Thomas H. Kean, who won office in 1981, came out strongly against what he called an "undesirable intrusion on the home rule principle." In a 1984 interview, Kean stated, "I don't believe that every municipality has got to be a carbon copy of another. That's a socialistic country, a Communistic country, a dictatorship."[89] Kean advocated an amendment to the New Jersey constitution that would place local zoning policy beyond review by state courts. Meanwhile, he signed legislation that moved exclusionary zoning cases out of the courts and into arbitration before a nine-member Council on Affordable Housing (COAH), which was appointed by the governor.[90] Cities and towns were given a grace period to achieve their "fair share" regional housing goals.

In actuality, most communities were let off the hook completely. Municipalities were allowed, for example, to allocate up to 25 percent of their "fair share" to elderly people, and any city was allowed to transfer up to half of its fair-share obligation to another city in the region (if the receiving city approved), along with the funds to help the receiving town pay to build the housing. Older central cities were put in the position of competing against one another for subsidies from suburbs so they could obtain funds to meet the pressing housing needs of their low-income residents. What had begun as an effort to open up the suburbs ended up doing exactly the opposite.

Despite all of the political thunder and lightning, the payoff from the long, drawn-out Mount Laurel process was meager. Most New Jersey municipalities did nothing at all. In Mount Laurel, only 12 families had moved into low-cost mobile homes by the late 1980s, 12 more had put down deposits on similar units, and 20 low-cost subsidized condominiums had been completed. This was the grand total of low-income housing after 17 years and millions of dollars of litigation, and protracted political uproar.[91]

The New Jersey case illustrates the difficulty of changing local land use practices by using the courts when a political consensus is lacking. Mount Laurel represents the clash between two deeply held American values: equal protection of the law and local home rule. Americans are reluctant to support policies that force local governments to give up their autonomy. In an era when the federal government has cut housing subsidies drastically, even if local zoning laws could be successfully challenged, it is doubtful much low-income housing would be built in the suburbs. If the New Jersey experience offers a lesson, it is that exclusionary zoning is here to stay.

THE NEW FACE OF ENCLAVE POLITICS

Since the suburban boom following World War II there have been working-class, middle-class, and upper-class suburbs—for example, Levittown was a middle-class bastion on Long Island, but it remained worlds apart from the wealthier enclaves only a few miles away. In the last few years, many suburbs—especially those built between

1945 and 1970—have been undergoing rapid change. Middle- and working-class suburban homes built during this period tended to be small tract homes or bungalows that lacked the amenities and conveniences expected today.[92] These older subdivisions tend to be located in suburbs with low housing prices and a low level of public services, and many of them have become a new kind of urban slum, but much more isolated from jobs and transportation networks than slums located in the urban core. A large proportion of them are located in inner suburbs located close to the central cities, but others are sprinkled among more affluent suburbs further out.[93]

Poor people and recent immigrants find it easier to find housing in older suburbs because of low market demand for less desirable housing. For example, the 1950s-era suburbs of Long Island, including Levittown, are attracting thousands of immigrants from the Middle East, Central and Latin America, and Asia.[94] Some families crowd illegally into homes, and their children flood into local schools that lack the resources to educate them properly. They are hidden from the larger society in part because they are walled off into municipalities that have few resources—and therefore they are unable to make effective claims on the political system. As one scholar has asked, "Suburbs are now becoming—albeit not always willingly—multiclass, multiethnic, and multiracial. . . . Can older suburbs accommodate these new ethnic groups, or will outmoded, decentralized government structures and prejudice keep them hidden *baja del agua*—underwater?"[95]

The tendency to push marginalized groups "underwater" is reinforced by the rise of privatized enclaves of like-minded people trying to sever all contact with central cities and even with nearby neighborhoods.[96] Some gated communities built in the 1980s and 1990s seem like fortresses built to keep the menacing hordes at bay. The emphasis on security in some of these developments is akin to a state of war. Leisure World, a California retirement community, is surrounded by 6-foot walls topped with barbed wire. Quayside, a planned community in Florida, blends the atmosphere of a Norman Rockwell small town of the 1920s with the latest in high-tech security; laser beams sweep the perimeter, computers check the coded entry cards of the residents and store exits and entries from the property in a permanent data file, and television cameras continuously monitor the living and recreation areas. Such trappings of security constantly remind the inhabitants that the world beyond their walls is dangerous, so that "'being inside' becomes a powerful symbol for being protected, buttressed, coddled, while 'being outside' evokes exposure, isolation, and vulnerability."[97] In case all that did not make them feel secure enough, in 2006 a Texas developer was marketing a new subdivision as a "sex-offender free" development; prospective buyers would have to pass a criminal background check.[98]

In Southern California, fortress enclaves have become a ubiquitous feature of suburban development. In search of high-tech security, architects for the affluent "are borrowing design features from overseas embassies and military command posts," building hardened walls, secret passages and doors, and installing a dazzling array of sophisticated electronic surveillance devices.[99] There is such a heavy demand for gated communities in the Los Angeles suburbs that they are quickly replacing all other kinds of development. There is significant danger that the residents of gated communities will substantially secede from the public realm of democratic politics, where difficult decisions are made about the larger community of citizens that make up urban regions. In such a case, the urban crisis of the twentieth century, which divided cities from the suburbs, will be replaced by a new kind of urban crisis, one that not only pits suburb against suburb, but also enclave against enclave.

NOTES

1. Robert C. Wood, *Suburbia: Its People and Their Politics* (Boston: Houghton Mifflin, 1958), p. 106.
2. Robert C. Wood, "Suburban Politics and Policies: Retrospect and Prospect," *Publius, The Journal of Federalism* (Winter 1975): 51.
3. See Mark Gottdiener, *Planned Sprawl: Private and Public Interests in Suburbia* (Beverly Hills, Calif.: Sage, 1977).
4. The term is taken from Mark Weiss, *The Rise of the Community Builders* (New York: Columbia University Press, 1987).
5. J. C. Nichols, "The Planning and Control of Outlying Shopping Center," *Journal of Land and Public Utility Economics* 2 (January 1926): 22. By concentrating in one location and using leasing policy to determine store "mix," "Nichols created the idea of the planned regional shopping center," Kenneth T. Jackson, *Crabgrass Frontier: The Suburbanization of the United States* (New York: Oxford University Press, 1985), p. 258.
6. Gwendolyn Wright, *Building the Dream: A Social History of Housing in America* (Cambridge, Mass.: MIT Press, 1981), p. 202.
7. Mark H. Rose, "'There Is Less Smoke in the District,' J. C. Nichols, Urban Change and Technological Systems," *Journal of the West* (January 1986): 48. Rose adds, "As late as 1917, no more than five Jewish families resided in the district, the result of resales."
8. "Up from the Potato Fields," *Time*, July 3, 1950, p. 70.
9. Ibid.
10. "The Most House for the Money," *Fortune* (October 1952): 156.
11. Jackson, *Crabgrass Frontier*, p. 234.
12. Wright, *Building the Dream*, p. 252.
13. "Up from the Potato Fields," p. 68.
14. Jackson, *Crabgrass Frontier*, p. 234.
15. "Up from the Potato Fields," p. 68.
16. Bruce Lambert, "Levittown Anniversary Stirs Memories of Bias," *New York Times*, December 28, 1997, 14.
17. Quoted in Herbert Gans, *The Levittowners: Ways of Life and Politics in a Suburban Community* (New York: Pantheon Books, 1967), p. 372.
18. Lambert, "Levittown Anniversary," p. 14.
19. Jackson, *Crabgrass Frontier*, p. 241.
20. Lambert, "Levittown Anniversary," p. 14.
21. Gans, *The Levittowners*, pp. 8–9.
22. Joe R. Feagin and Robert Parker, *Building American Cities: The Urban Real Estate Game*, 2nd ed. (Upper Saddle River, N.J.: Prentice Hall, 1990), p. 211.
23. Robert Goldston, *Suburbia: Civic Denial* (New York: Macmillan, 1970), p. 68.
24. Ibid.
25. *New York Times*, March 22, 1953. See also the next advertisement in the same day's newspaper.
26. Ibid.
27. *New York Times*, October 26, 1952; emphasis in the original.
28. *New York Times*, May 26, 1968.
29. Ibid.

30. *St. Louis Post-Dispatch*, April 16, 1972.

31. *St. Louis Post-Dispatch*, August 18, 1974.

32. *St. Louis Post-Dispatch*, July 5, 1970.

33. Ibid.

34. Kevin Fox Gotham, *Race, Real Estate, and Uneven Development: The Kansas City Experience, 1900–2000* (Albany: State University of New York Press, 2002), p. 38.

35. Ibid.

36. Ibid., pp. 34–37.

37. National Association of Real Estate Boards, *Code of Ethics* (1924), art. 34 (Washington, D.C.: Author).

38. Harry Grant Atkinson and L. E. Frailey, *Fundamentals of Real Estate Practice* (Upper Saddle River, N.J.: Prentice Hall, 1946), p. 34, quoted in Evan McKenzie, *Privatopia: Homeowner Associations and the Rise of Residential Private Government* (New Haven, Conn.: Yale University Press, 1994), pp. 61–62.

39. *Shelly v. Kraemer*, 334 U.S. 1 (1948). The Court had struck down racial zoning some 30 years earlier in *Buchanan v. Warley*, 245 U.S. 60 (1917).

40. McKenzie, *Privatopia*, p. 11.

41. Community Associations Institute, Association Information Services, *CtreeseAIS@aol.com* (2006).

42. Ibid.

43. McKenzie, *Privatopia*, pp. 158–164.

44. Ibid., p. 158.

45. Ibid., pp. 163–164.

46. Dennis R. Judd, "The Rise of the New Walled Cities," in *Spatial Practices*, ed. Helen Liggett and David C. Perry (Thousand Oaks, Calif.: Sage, 1995), pp. 144–166.

47. David Guterson, "No Place Like Home: On the Manicured Streets of a Master-planned Community," *Harper's* (November 1992): 55–64.

48. Ibid., pp. 60–61.

49. U.S. Bureau of the Census, *The 2009 Statistical Abstract of the United States*, Table 669 (*http://www.census/gov/compendia/statab*).

50. Gary J. Miller, *Cities by Contract: The Politics of Municipal Incorporation* (Cambridge, Mass.: MIT Press, 1981), p. 12.

51. Ibid.

52. C. B. Glasscock, *Lucky Baldwin: The Story of an Unconventional Success* (Indianapolis, Ind.: Bobbs-Merrill, 1933), p. 140.

53. Jon C. Teaford, *City and Suburb: The Political Fragmentation of Metropolitan America, 1850–1970* (Baltimore: Johns Hopkins University Press, 1979), pp. 18–19.

54. Charles Hoch, "City Limits: Municipal Boundary Formation and Class Segregation," in *Marxism and the Metropolis: New Perspectives in Urban Political Economy*, 2nd ed., ed. William K. Tabb and Larry Sawers (New York: Oxford University Press, 1984), pp. 101–119.

55. Miller, *Cities by Contract*, pp. 49–50. Another good example of an industrial suburb is Teterboro, New Jersey, which in 1977 had only 24 residents but employed 24,000 nonresidents. Michael N. Danielson and Jameson W. Doig, *New York: The Politics of Urban Regional Development* (Berkeley: University of California Press, 1982), p. 92.

56. Teaford, *City and Suburb*, p. 18.

57. Data cited in Wood, *Suburbia*, p. 69; and in National Municipal League, Committee on Metropolitan Government, *The Government of Metropolitan Areas in the United States*, prepared by Paul Studenski with the assistance of the Committee on Metropolitan Government (New York: National Municipal League, 1930), p. 26.

58. See Anwar Syed, *The Political Theory of American Local Government* (Clinton, Mass.: Random House, 1966).

59. Teaford, *City and Suburb*, p. 6.

60. Ibid., p. 31.

61. U.S. Bureau of the Census, *Census 2000* (*http://www.census.gov/cens2000*).

62. Jon C. Teaford, *The American Suburb: The Basics* (New York: Routledge, 2008).

63. Quoted in ibid., p. 132.

64. Dolores Hayden, *Building Suburbia: Green Fields and Urban Growth, 1820–2000* (New York: Pantheon Books), p. 168.

65. Quoted in Teaford, *City and Suburb*, p. 115.

66. Quoted in ibid., p. 112.

67. Seymour I. Toll, *Zoned America* (New York: Grossman, 1969), p. 193.

68. Ibid., p. 197.

69. Ibid., p. 159.

70. Quoted in Michael N. Danielson, *The Politics of Exclusion* (New York: Columbia University Press, 1976), p. 54.

71. Toll, *Zoned America*, p. 183.

72. Ibid., pp. 182–183.

73. Ibid., p. 187.

74. *Police power* refers to the implied powers of government to adopt and enforce laws necessary for preserving and protecting the immediate health and welfare of citizens. The meaning of this, of course, is subject to a wide variety of interpretations.

75. *Village of Euclid v. Ambler Realty Co.*, 272 U.S. 365, 47 S.Ct. 114, 71 L. Ed. 303 (1926).

76. Danielson, *The Politics of Exclusion*, pp. 53–54.

77. "The End of the Exurban Dream," *New York Times*, December 13, 1976.

78. Danielson, *The Politics of Exclusion*, p. 53.

79. Because of the fears concerning apartment developments, the planning process involving their construction was complicated, requiring petitions for zoning variances, public hearings, and lengthy review proceedings. For an excellent account of these complexities, see Daniel R. Mandelker, *The Zoning Dilemma: A Legal Strategy for Urban Change* (Indianapolis, Ind.: Bobbs-Merrill, 1971).

80. Quoted in Danielson, *The Politics of Exclusion*, p. 60.

81. Quoted in Merrill Folson, "Westchester Finds Influx of Business a Worry," *New York Times*, April 18, 1967; cited in Danielson and Doig, *New York*, p. 90.

82. A detailed discussion of the legal status of zoning is not included in this section. For further information, the following sources are especially useful: Danielson, *The Politics of Exclusion*; Richard F. Babcock, *The Zoning Game* (Madison: University of Wisconsin Press, 1969); Richard F. Babcock and Fred P. Bosselman, *Exclusionary Zoning: Land Use Regulation and Housing in the 1970s* (New York: Praeger, 1973); Daniel R. Mandelker, *Managing Our Urban Environment* (Indianapolis, Ind.: Bobbs-Merrill, 1971); Randall W. Scott, ed., *Management and Control of Growth*, vol. 1 (New York: Urban Land Institute, 1975); and David Listokin, ed., *Land Use Controls Present Problems and Future Reform* (New Brunswick, N.J.: Center for Urban Policy Research, Rutgers University, 1975).

83. *Dailey v. City of Lawton*, 425 F.2d 1037 (1970).

84. *Kennedy Park Homes v. City of Lackawanna*, 436 F.2d 108 (1971).

85. Quoted in *St. Louis Globe-Democrat*, January 11, 1977.

86. In 1975 the Supreme Court made it more difficult to challenge exclusionary zoning in federal courts by "refusing standing"—dismissing a case on the grounds that the plaintiffs had no right to sue. Those who want to challenge an exclusionary ordinance must prove "distinct and palpable injury"; a suit cannot be based on general injury to those who do not live in the town but want to live there; see *Warth v. Seldin*, 442 U.S. 490 (1975).

87. See *James v. Valtierra*, 91 S.Ct. 133 (1971), and *Shaffer v. Valtierra*, 402 U.S. 137 (1971).

88. Joseph F. Sullivan, "Restless Seeker for Justice," *New York Times*, January 22, 1983; Robert Hanley, "After 7 Years, Town Remains Under Fire for Its Zoning Code," *New York Times*, January 22, 1983; Anthony DePalma, "N.J. Housing Woes Are All Over the Map," *New York Times*, April 17, 1983.

89. Robert Hanley, "Some Jersey Towns, Yielding to Courts, Let in Modest Homes," *New York Times*, February 29, 1984.
90. 1985 J.J. Sess. Law Serv. 222 (West).
91. Anthony DePalma, "Subsidized Housing Hurt in Ailing Market," *New York Times*, May 15, 1990.
92. Ibid., pp. 42–43.
93. Ibid.
94. Rosalyn Baxandall and Elizabeth Ewen, *Picture Windows: How the Suburbs Happened* (New York: Perseus Books, 2000), 239.
95. Ibid., p. 250.
96. Peter O. Muller, *Contemporary Suburban America* (Upper Saddle River, N.J.: Prentice Hall, 1981), p. 180.
97. Trevor Boddy, "Underground and Overhead: Building the Analogous City," in *Variations on a Theme Park: The New American City and the End of Public Space,* ed. Michael Sorkin (New York: Noonday Press, 1992), p. 139.
98. Betsy Blaney, "Texas Developers to Build Sex Offender-free Subdivision," *Chicago Tribune,* June 15, 2005, p. 34.
99. Mike Davis, "Fortress Los Angeles: The Militarization of Urban Space," in *Variations on a Theme Park: The New American City and the End of Public Space,* ed. Michael Sorkin (New York: Noonday Press, 1992), p. 173.

GOVERNING THE FRAGMENTED METROPOLIS

URBAN SPRAWL AND THE NEW URBAN FORM

Population movement from the urban core is a feature of urban development all over the world. With transportation breakthroughs such as automated rail systems and the automobile, urban areas in the advanced Western countries have been spreading out for at least a century.[1] But what distinguishes the urban pattern in the United States most clearly from that of other Western nations is not the extent of sprawl, but the fragmentation of metropolitan areas into a multitude of separate governments. In Europe and in most other nations, there are fewer suburbs because cities tend to encompass a large part of their metropolitan areas. In addition, national and regional governments finance and administer crucial services that are, in the United States, provided by municipalities and special districts. American suburbs are different from the European model because they are autonomous entities that make taxation, spending, and land use decisions without any meaningful oversight from higher levels of government. They operate independently, and there are a lot of them. In 2002 there were 87,849 local governments in the United States.[2] Statistics like these have led to a consensus that the "degree of governmental fragmentation in the United States is unique among the urban-industrial societies."[3]

The sprawled metropolis has spawned a set of chronic and sometimes vexing problems. Concerns intensify when the costs of commuting rise. In 2008 the cost of a gallon of gasoline peaked to over $4 in the United States, although it was still cheap compared to the nearly $10 that people in the United Kingdom paid, or the $7 price in France. However much gasoline prices may rise or fall, however, other problems remain. Commuters experience traffic congestion and gridlock almost every day. The public has become concerned about such issues as air pollution, the loss of open space and farmland, and polluted water. Urban sprawl has blossomed as an important public policy issue. Growth control measures appeared on ballots in many places in the 1970s, and the movement to control the pace and location of development has continued to pick up steam. People want the freedom to move where they please, but they are not happy when their neighborhoods seem threatened by a steady stream of newcomers.

The solutions offered for sprawl and the problems of regional governance may be grouped under three labels: the New Regionalism, Smart Growth, and the New Urbanism. Each of these movements offers its own distinct bundle of remedies. The New Regionalism is the latest expression of a reform movement that goes back to the early twentieth century. Founded on the premise that the uncontrolled movement of people to the suburbs creates blighted communities at the metropolitan core, the New Regionalists argue that only metropolitan-wide cooperation among governments can control land use, taxation, and other policies that promote unplanned sprawl. The Smart Growth movement emerged in the late 1980s around a collection of proposals designed to achieve "balanced" regional growth through improved transportation, community, and environmental planning. The New Urbanism movement became formally organized in the early 1990s, energized by the idea that better urban design and architecture were the necessary ingredients for achieving healthy neighborhoods and communities. Each of these movements confronts a formidable obstacle: the new urban form.

OUTTAKE

THE COSTS OF SPRAWL ARE HOTLY DEBATED

The urban specialist Neal Peirce calls Americans "the champion land hogs of history" because the country's urban areas are growing in land area at a rate four to eight times faster than the growth of the national population. The cost of sprawl, he said, is "frightening" because it brings "despair in the inner cities, environmental degradation, undermining of old neighborhoods and suburbs."

Peirce and other enemies of urban sprawl are able to marshal a great deal of convincing evidence to demonstrate its negative effects. They cite studies showing it is more expensive to supply most infrastructure—new highways, streets, and bridges; schools; sewer and water systems; street lighting; gas, electric, and telephone hookups; libraries and parks—to low-density areas than to high-density areas. They offer considerable evidence that sprawl has helped cause the decline of the central cities and the abandonment of neighborhoods in the cities and older suburbs. Evidence also indicates that the governmental fragmentation accompanying sprawl may slow the economic growth of regions.

The critics of sprawl also argue that sprawl can be blamed for numerous environmental problems. Thousands of acres of farmland, wetlands, and open space disappear each year. Runoff from highways, parking lots, and lawns pollutes streams and rivers; auto and truck traffic spews ozone-depleting and greenhouse gases into the atmosphere. Excess energy consumption and air pollution are implicated in global environmental problems. Urban residents in the United States consumed about four times as much gasoline per capita as did

(continued on next page)

urban residents in Europe in 1990. Urban sprawl was the basic reason for this difference. In the late 1980s, annual consumption in sprawled-out Houston was 567 gallons per person, compared to 335 gallons in New York City, where high population density facilitated the use of mass transit. (In Manhattan, gasoline consumption was only 90 gallons per person.)

But it should not be supposed there is only one point of view about urban sprawl. In fact, it is a hotly contested issue. Fred Siegel, a prominent scholar and writer, has argued that sprawl is a logical outcome of prosperity and the pursuit of the American dream, "an expression of the upward mobility and growth in home-ownership generated by our past half-century of economic success." Expanding on this theme, he argues that for people on the lower end of the economic scale, escape from poor neighborhoods and finally the city has been a key strategy for achieving a better life.

Strong evidence can be cited in support of this view. People moving within metropolitan areas tend to move from high-density to low-density neighborhoods, and these neighborhoods generally have more and better amenities. Perhaps for this reason, about two-thirds of the people living in urban areas prefer low-density neighborhoods. These are generally newer developments located at some distance from central cities. As their incomes go up, families tend to move to larger and newer homes. Today, one in seven newly constructed homes exceeds 3,000 square feet, a size reserved only for the wealthy in the past.

The two perspectives on urban sprawl seem to suggest a contradiction between freedom to choose, on one hand, and regulation and planning, on the other. This is why attempts to control sprawl run into consistent political opposition.

Sources: Neal Peirce, "The Senselessness of Urban Sprawl," *National Journal,* September 25, 1993, p. 2326; Burchell et al., *The Costs of Sprawl Revisited* (Washington, D.C.: National Academy Press, 1998; Arthur C. Nelson and Kathryn A. Foster, "Metropolitan Governance Structure and Income Growth," *Journal of Urban Affairs* 21, no. 3 (1999): 309–324; Peter G. Newman and Jeffrey R. Kenworthy, "Gasoline Consumption and Cities," *Journal of the American Planning Association* (Winter 1989): 26–27; Fred Siegel, "Is Regional Government the Answer?" *The Public Interest* (Fall 1999): 86.

THE NEW URBAN FORM

Urban sprawl is here to stay, in large part because the basic organization of urban areas has changed fundamentally in recent decades. The old urban form, which found a big city surrounded by rank on rank of spreading suburbs, is giving way to a new metropolitan form characterized by many nodes of activity.[4] In recent decades, the suburbs have gradually been transformed from wholly dependent satellites of cities, places where people lived but not where they worked, to self-sufficient enclaves. Although suburban development historically had been primarily a residential movement, since at least 1948 jobs began to decentralize even faster than population.[5] Retailing moved out at a slower pace than did manufacturing and wholesaling because retailing is directly dependent on a nearby critical mass of buyers. By the early 1960s, however, such a critical mass had been established, and before long regional shopping malls began to spring up to cater to the shopping and entertainment needs of suburban consumers.[6] Suburban residents no longer needed to go downtown, and a historic link between cities and suburbs was severed.

The suburbanization of manufacturing employment was made possible by technical innovations that freed factories from a dependence on rail connections.

Electrification made single-story plants on suburban land more economical than multistory buildings that housed belt-driven machinery powered by water or steam. In addition, manufacturers left cities because they viewed them as hotbeds of union organizing and unrest.[7] Through accelerated depreciation of assets, which allowed manufacturers to take tax deductions when they abandoned inner-city factories, and investment tax credits, which allowed manufacturers to take tax credits for new plant and equipment, the federal government subsidized the flight of industrial jobs to the suburbs (and Sunbelt).[8] By 1970 a majority of the manufacturing jobs in metropolitan areas were located in the suburbs.

The service sector was the last to suburbanize. Central business districts offered advantages to firms desiring face-to-face relations with clients and benefiting from the concentration of business services in downtowns. However, advances in communications made proximity less of an advantage than before. Routine service employment, the so-called back-office functions such as copying and secretarial services, were the first to leave expensive downtown office space. In 1975, for the first time, the amount of office construction in the suburbs exceeded the volume of office construction in central cities. Higher-level and higher-paid corporate services, however, such as legal assistance, corporate consulting, accounting services, and investment services, continued to locate in the downtowns of large cities, partly for prestige reasons. Although many corporations were still headquartered in central cities, many had moved out to the suburbs, in whole or in part. Some suburbs had developed into cities complete with their own office complexes that duplicated many of the characteristics of central business districts.

The effect of these developments was that the suburbs became more independent of their core cities than in the past. Cross-commuting became common; by 1980 twice as many people commuted from suburb to suburb as commuted from suburb to central city.[9] The historic urban form, in which a city is surrounded by dependent suburbs, began to break down and be replaced by the "polynucleated metropolis," characterized by several nodes of concentrated land use that combine residential, retail, recreational, light industry, and service firms. The new urban form has sometimes been called *exurbanization* or even *counterurbanization*,[10] plus a variety of odd and often confusing labels such as "urban villages, technohubs, suburban downtowns, suburban activity centers, major diversified centers, urban cores, galactic city, pepperoni-pizza cities, a city of realms, superburbia, disurb, service cities, perimeter cities, and even peripheral centers."[11] What these entities have in common is that they are springing up at the outer boundary of urban regions, often near freeway interchanges or airports.

A significant number of the new suburbs are large—in fact, some have grown larger than several of the older central cities, which have been losing population for half a century. Two researchers coined the term "boomburbs" as a way of accounting for booming suburbs that have grown by at least double-digit rates for every decade since 1970, and finally reaching a population of at least 100,000 population by the census of 2000.[12] They discovered that 54 cities met this standard, and that 12 of them contained more than 200,000 people. The total number of boomburbs might seem small, but they are clearly the fastest-growing cities just below the size of biggest cities in the nation, and they hold one-quarter of all residents living in small- and medium-sized places.[13] The census of 2000 showed that 15 boomburbs had joined the ranks of the 100 largest U.S. cities.

Despite their significant impact on urban areas, most boomburbs have attracted little attention, probably because they tend to lack the physical form and identity that might make them stand out. They generally lack tall buildings and heavily favor the automobile over pedestrians; office workers tend to be clustered in sharply defined office parks, and a large proportion of shopping is done in strip malls and mall clusters. Perhaps the most surprising fact about boomburbs is that they defy the suburban stereotype by attracting diverse populations: 45 of the 54 contain a higher proportion of Hispanic residents, and 42 have a higher proportion of Asians, than does the national population.[14]

Boomburbs are, in essence, fully developed cities, with a mixture of office, retail, residential, and sometimes light industry. They differ markedly with one another, but few, if any, fit the stereotype of the exclusive suburb, or of the one-dimensional bedroom suburb. High-rise office and condominium towers are beginning to sprout in some of them, and new housing construction tends to favor townhouse and condominium construction as much as free-standing homes. Their growth makes it clear, if it was not already, that urban sprawl is woven into the fabric of urban regions. A variety of problems may be associated with sprawl, but they are not likely to be solved by trying to dismantle the new urban form.

THE CONCERNS ABOUT SPRAWL

The term *urban sprawl* is often used loosely to refer to low-density residential development at the periphery of urban areas. One leading study published in 1974 defined it as residential density of two dwellings per acre, but a late 1980s study and another conducted by the Environmental Protection Agency in the early 1990s defined it as residential density of three dwellings per acre or less.[15] By such a definition, sprawl is rare in Europe and Asia, where land is scarcer than in the United States and land use controls are the norm. In such contexts, urban areas may be expanding outward, but not in such a way as to create the social and political dynamic that characterizes sprawl in the United States: low-density development at the edge of metropolitan regions that consumes huge tracts of land and entails the abandonment of older areas at the urban core.

When people move farther out, they generally are moving to lower-density suburbs. The result is that land is gobbled up at a rate all out of proportion to the population growth of urban regions—indeed, sprawl occurs even in metropolitan areas with steady-state or declining populations. For example, although the New York region's population grew by only 5 percent between 1964 and 1989, the amount of developed land increased by 61 percent.[16] Similarly, from 1950 to 1995 the population of the St. Louis region increased by just 35 percent, but the area of developed land exploded by more than ten times that much, by 355 percent.[17] The St. Louis region has been growing slowly, so its expanding size has little to do with population growth. Instead, people have been moving progressively outward. From 1986 to 2001, St. Charles County attracted 73,000 people from St. Louis County, which is adjacent to the city, but it attracted only 5,500 people from outside the region. St. Charles County is now filling up, and its growth is now outpaced by

Warren County, which lies even farther out in the St. Louis metropolitan area.[18] This kind of movement within urban regions is why nearly all of them continued to sprawl in the 1990s, regardless of their growth rates.[19]

Why does land disappear so fast even in slow-growth urban regions? First, families have become smaller in recent decades because of the increasing number of single-parent families, childless and unmarried couples, and singles. The smaller size of the typical suburban family requires more dwellings for a given population size and makes many of the single-family houses built only a couple of decades ago obsolete. Second, although average family sizes have been declining, the size of homes has steadily increased in step with a desire for more luxuries and amenities. And third, when people move within metropolitan areas, they tend to leave higher-density neighborhoods nearer the urban core for lower-density subdivisions farther out; only a small percentage move in the other direction. In a study conducted in the early 1990s, more than two-thirds of the survey respondents said that they preferred to live in low-density, single-family neighborhoods than in denser neighborhoods closer to the central city.[20]

But despite the widespread preference for low-density living, many suburban residents have discovered a downside. Commuters experience some of the negative effects of sprawl every day, firsthand and close up. In some urban areas, highway congestion has increased to the point that the daily commute has ceased to be merely annoying. In November 1999 *USA Today,* in a special report on national gridlock, offered up one horror story after another. The average commuter's daily experience seemed to be summed up by a Chicago driver's description of a bottleneck called "the Hillside Strangler": "It's not even a traffic jam. It's my enemy. It's my daytime bad dream."[21] In 2001 the knot of off-ramps that made up the Strangler was finally eliminated, but many other gridlocked spots remained. A study conducted in 2005 ranked Chicago second in the nation as the most congested (behind Los Angeles). The report estimated that in 2003 Chicago-area commuters spent 58 hours in traffic jams each year, an increase of 55 hours from just three years earlier. The authors concluded that the term "rush hour" had become virtually meaningless.[22]

If commuters think that urban highways have become more crowded in the last few years, they are right. In the 1970s there were 61 yards of roadway per vehicle in the United States, but by 1986 this space had shrunk by more than one-third, to 39 yards.[23] The number of vehicles on the roads has increased dramatically. Trucks by the dozen fill rearview mirrors because they have substantially eclipsed trains for the movement of goods. The number of licensed drivers jumped 65 percent between 1970 and 1997, but registered vehicles increased even more, by 87 percent. Demographic changes accounted for the higher traffic volumes. Although the U.S. population rose by only 32 percent between 1970 and 1997, the number of women in the workplace jumped by 240 percent.[24] As more women entered the workforce and recreational vehicles joined the family car in the garage, two- and three-car families became the norm. At the same time, cross-commuting gradually replaced trips to the metropolitan center. Even by 1980, before sprawl reached its current dimensions, over 40 percent of all work trips were suburb to suburb, and only 20 percent were from suburb to the central city in the average metropolitan region.[25] Reverse commuting—travel by central-city residents to jobs in edge cities or elsewhere in the suburbs—also increased.[26] Longer commutes combined with poor gas mileage drove up the costs of getting to work. In 2000 some residents of sprawled-out metropolitan areas such as Houston and Atlanta spent more for transportation than for housing.[27]

A growing popular and media concern about sprawl became evident by the mid-1990s, when many suburban residents came to regard sprawl as a form of urban blight brought too close to home. In May 1995 *Newsweek* magazine devoted a cover story to the problems of urban sprawl in New York, Memphis, Miami, Los Angeles, San Francisco, and Washington, D.C. In all of these regions, said the *Newsweek* reporters, sprawl had created "blighted metropolitan landscapes" of strip malls, traffic, and monotonous sameness. In reference to California, they observed, "No wonder they're so sterile—sterility is designed into them!" They wrote about "the new American phenomenon, the suburban slum," with aging tract housing interspersed with strip development.[28]

Four years later, in its July 19, 1999, issue, *Newsweek* featured sprawl again, this time declaring it had become an urgent public issue, part of a "livability" agenda being promoted by affluent suburban residents, suburban politicians, and Vice President Al Gore. The key elements of this agenda, according to *Newsweek*, included "the triple evils of sprawl: air pollution, traffic congestion, and visual blight."[29] In the fall of 1999, as part of its continuing Challenge to Sprawl Campaign, the Sierra Club released its annual ratings of how effectively the states were regulating sprawl.[30] News stories about the report were carried in national and numerous local newspapers, often as feature stories.

Even the conservative *Wall Street Journal* chimed in when it profiled the battle between community groups and developers in the suburbs surrounding Colorado Springs, Colorado. According to the *Journal,* the conflicts in Colorado Springs merely illustrated similar battles occurring in all of the rapidly growing metropolitan areas of the Rocky Mountain West, such as Denver, Salt Lake City, and Boise. Always an advocate of an unfettered market, the *Journal* nevertheless noted the efforts of Boulder, Colorado, to slow growth by adopting new regulations.[31] A couple of months later, in January 2000, the *Journal* reported that campaigns against sprawl had inspired a political revolution that was toppling pro-growth politicians.[32] Apparently trying to change public sentiment in its urban area, the *St. Louis Post-Dispatch* ran one of a series of articles on sprawl under the headline "Urban Sprawl Is a Hot Topic." The paper seemed puzzled by the attitude of its readers, observing, "But Missouri's attitude seems to be: 'What, us worry?'"[33]

Some politicians joined the media by making sprawl a big issue. In 1999 *Governing,* a magazine widely read by state and local public officials, devoted two issues and several other articles to the topic of urban sprawl.[34] In January 1997 Democratic governor Parris Glendening of Maryland promised to fight for an initiative to curb sprawl, and the next year the Republican governor of New Jersey, Christie Todd Whitman (appointed in 2001 to head the Environmental Protection Agency by President Bush), shepherded an even stronger bill through her legislature. In the latter half of the 1990s, more than half the nation's governors took on issues related to sprawl.

In fact, a growth-control movement had been picking up steam for some time. Leaders of the movement advocated such measures as caps on the pace of new construction, impact fees (imposed on developers as a way of paying some of the public costs of growth), and linkage fees (which require developers to help pay for costs linked to development such as affordable housing, schools, and day care). Growth controls spread rapidly in the 1970s; by 1975 they were in effect in over 300 jurisdictions across the country.[35] Between 1971 and 1986, more than 150 growth control measures appeared on local ballots; 50 measures appeared on ballots in 1986 alone, with three-quarters of them winning.[36] More than a decade later, in 1998, voters passed 70 percent of the 240 local no-growth measures placed on ballots.[37]

Interestingly, growth regulations were pushed hardest in politically conservative areas of Southern California. In 1986, over the objections of Mayor Tom Bradley, Los Angeles voters passed Proposition U, which effectively ended most new office construction in residential neighborhoods on the West Side and in the San Fernando Valley.[38] In the same election, voters in Newport Beach in Orange County, a bastion of conservatism, defeated plans for a $400 million mixed-use complex overlooking the harbor. The no-growth forces won even though they were outspent in the campaign by $500,000 to $10,000.[39]

Growth control was especially popular in wealthier cities. Ventura County, California, provides an example of the kinds of regulations commonly adopted. In November 1998, there was overwhelmingly approval of several local initiatives creating urban growth boundaries, which were designed to limit new development at the edges of the county's cities and towns. The new rules specified that land outside the boundaries of specified cities could not be rezoned for development until 2020. To ensure their wishes could not be overridden by public officials, these laws even took the power to rezone land protected from development out of the hands of the county's board of supervisors.[40] In the same month, New Jersey voters approved $1 billion to protect about half of the state's undeveloped open land from urban development.[41] More than 2,000 miles away, in November 2002, Nevada voters approved a conservation bond issue to protect open lands from unplanned sprawl. The impetus for the measure came from unbridled growth; in only 30 years the state's population had soared from less than a half million people to more than 2 million; by 2000, only 21 percent of Nevada residents were natives. The newcomers were trying to keep the Las Vegas and Reno urban areas from becoming as crowded as the places they had left.[42]

In the new century, antisprawl politics began to go well beyond measures to regulate growth. All kinds of initiatives perceived as promoting sprawl began to go down in defeat. In 2004 a statewide initiative passed that sharply curbed Oregon's aggressive land use laws, but three years later voters reversed that decision when it got tagged as promoting sprawl and taxpayer-funded bailouts for careless developers. Transportation measures that become labeled as promoting sprawl tend to go down in crushing defeat almost everywhere. For example, voters in the Virginia suburbs of Washington, D.C., fearful of a new stream of movement from the city, defeated Governor Mark Warner's 2002 proposal for a sales tax to finance new highway and transit construction.[43]

Despite voters' concerns, sprawl has not made it onto the national agenda because there are so many other concerns that crowd it out, such as the state of the economy, national security, health care reform, battles over social issues, and environmental regulation. In January 1999 Vice President Al Gore announced a proposal (never adopted) by the Clinton administration to spend $9.5 billion to preserve open space, build roads and public transit, and encourage local communities to plan new schools.[44] At one point, Gore promised to make urban sprawl a central issue in the 2000 presidential campaign. Calling it his "livability agenda," Gore said the sprawl issue would appeal to people caught in "tidal flows of traffic" who spent too much time trying to get to work and back, at the cost to their family life. According to Gore, "There have been races for governor and mayor all over this country where the voters have made it very clear that this is an issue about which they feel passionately, and I plan in the next 13 months to take this issue to the voters of America."[45] When challenged on the question of whether such a complex issue could be turned into a hot political item, Gore answered, "Give me time."

In fact, the issue played no role at all in the campaign. For his part, Republican presidential candidate George W. Bush refused to talk about it, saying it should be left to state and local governments.[46] In the 2004 presidential campaign, neither candidate mentioned the issue; neither did the candidates in the 2008 campaign for the White House. A very modest, though indirect, effort to address the issue appeared with the passage of the American Recovery and Reinvestment Act, signed into law by President Barack Obama on February 17, 2009. It reserved $12 billion for mass transit improvements, though not for expansion of existing systems.[47]

It is clear that urban sprawl cannot be curbed without far-reaching changes in public policies and governance arrangements. There is an obvious tension, however, between governmental regulation and the deeply held cultural values of individualism and free enterprise that define American politics. Leaders of three movements—the New Regionalism, Smart Growth, and the New Urbanism—have attempted to negotiate the treacherous terrain between personal autonomy and planning. Advocates of the New Regionalism tend to come down on the side of reform and regulation. Smart Growth advocates favor planning and regulation, but most of them shy away from large-scale solutions and believe that local governments must take the lead. For their part, the New Urbanists favor changes in land use regulations that will facilitate development on a "human scale," but most of all they rely upon private developers to make their dream of community come true. We will discuss these three movements, in turn.

THE NEW REGIONALISM

For almost a century, advocates of regional governance have decried the political fragmentation of the modern metropolis. If people would only give up their parochial attachment to many governments, they could gain—so the reformers claimed—a more efficient and competent governmental structure with the capacity to administer better services. In the 1990s the crusade for metropolitan reform took a new turn, under the rubric of the New Regionalism. The main concerns of the New Regionalism can be summarized as a conviction that "flight creates blight."[48] Proponents argue that governmental fragmentation divides metropolitan areas into a multitude of fiscal fiefdoms, with better-off cities able to provide superior services because they have access to good tax sources while poor cities struggle to fund even barely adequate services. Several urban scholars have argued that such inequality undermines the economic health of metropolitan regions, and not just of the disadvantaged governments within them, because metropolitan economies are composed of highly interdependent activities that are undermined by poorly trained workforces, inadequate transportation systems, and poor urban service systems. The regional economy is, in effect, a commons whose workings are determined by the quality of the linkages between workers and jobs, firms, and households.[49] For the New Regionalists, governmental fragmentation interferes with these connections and therefore undermines regional prosperity.

It should be recognized that the New Regionalism has roots in a long-standing movement for metropolitan reform (what we may call the *Old Regionalism*), even though the rationale for reform has changed. One of the things the New Regionalism shares with the earlier reform movement is a frustration that their proposals are often rejected. Time after time proposals for metropolitan government have been met with overwhelming and hostile opposition from local officials and from voters. Much of the reason is that few people think of themselves as regional citizens; instead, they identify with a particular town or city.[50] Referring to people living in the St. Louis area, E. Terrence Jones has observed, "They desire governments that are comfortable, like that old sweater in the closet [that] feels so snug when you put it on each winter."[51]

In its purest form, the Old Regionalism was founded on the idea that a single, consolidated government should exercise all public authority within a metropolitan area. The reformers believed only a few officials should be elected, with a sharp distinction drawn between politics (basically, campaign and elections) and public administration.[52] They compared the proliferation of municipalities within urban regions to wards in the cities—to reformers, wards were nothing but hotbeds of parochial politics, with their representatives lacking the capacity or the perspective to attend to the overall problems of the city. Likewise, they said, the multitude of governments in urban regions made it impossible to achieve efficiency and economy in the delivery of services. Thus, writing in 1912, one reformer said, "Here [in metropolitan Boston] are thirty-eight towns and cities as intimately related to everything that concerns daily life as the wards of an American city, but with no power or means . . . of constructing, or improving public works or of taking public action that is for the metropolitan district as a whole."[53]

Almost 20 years later, an influential reformer picked up the same themes when he described what he saw as the parochialism and chaos arising from the fragmentation of local government: "They [the many governments] tend to divert attention of the inhabitants from the fact that they are members of one large community and lead them to act as members of separate units. They result in great variation in municipal regulations . . . and in standards of services, in sectional treatment of problems which are essentially metropolitan."[54] The reformers pressing for single-government urban regions agreed on the solution: "Only a government with community-wide jurisdiction can plan and provide the services, physical facilities, guidance, and controls necessary to relate functional plans with real plans. None of the metropolitan areas has such a government today."[55]

The reformers of the Old Regionalism were convinced that truth and virtue were on their side. Such confidence fueled the bitter disappointment they felt when voters repeatedly rejected their proposals in metropolitan areas all across the country, campaign after campaign, decade after decade. Between 1921 and 1979, reformers went to voters 83 times in various metropolitan areas in an attempt to gain approval of city–county consolidations. They succeeded just 17 times, and only 2 of those successes came in metropolitan areas of 250,000 or more (Nashville–Davidson County, Tennessee, 1962, and Jacksonville–Duval County, Florida, 1967). (The consolidation of Indianapolis with Marion County, Indiana, in 1969 was imposed by the state legislature and not by a popular referendum.)[56]

Many other reform attempts were made to consolidate governments by creating two-tier systems (a metropolitan district with specific service responsibilities, but with municipalities and counties continuing to possess important powers). The most notable success came with the creation of Metropolitan Dade County (Miami) in 1957. Under this reform, the county assumed many of the responsibilities (such as fire and police protection, traffic control, parks and recreation, health and welfare programs, air pollution control, and some other activities) formerly assumed by municipal governments.

Most of the ambitious schemes to impose metropolitan governments went down in flames because both suburban and central-city voters wanted to preserve control over local powers and services. The experience in the St. Louis metropolitan area was typical, except there the reformers tried, and failed, more times than anywhere else: in 1926, 1930, 1959, 1962, 1989, and 1990. In 1926 the voters in St. Louis County defeated a proposal to consolidate the city of St. Louis with the county. Four years later, the county's voters vetoed a somewhat less ambitious proposal that would have placed the city and county under a regional government, except for a few services and public functions.[57]

In 1959 the reformers gave it another try. This time they proposed a Greater St. Louis City–County District that would have assumed responsibility for forging a regional plan and for promoting economic development; managing regional mass transit and traffic control on major streets and highways; administering all sewage facilities; and supervising all police training, communications, and civil defense. Municipalities would have been left with the responsibility of regulating local street traffic and providing police and fire protection and garbage pickup. Local officials in the county reacted with a furious campaign of opposition, and voters soundly defeated the plan.[58] But even before tempers cooled from this attempt, reformers were at it again. This time, in 1962, the "borough plan" would have placed the city and county under a single government and divided the county into 22 boroughs, each exercising some limited powers. This plan would have eliminated all existing municipalities. The plan was defeated by a 4-to-1 landslide, an even more lopsided margin than in 1959.

But the battle for reform was not over. In 1989 an elected board of freeholders placed a consolidation plan before the voters of St. Louis County (language in the Missouri constitution empowered such a board of "freeholders"—property owners—to make such proposals). In addition to reducing the number of municipalities in the county from 90 to 37, the plan would have transferred most land use, zoning, and building inspections to the county and also created a county commission to oversee fire and emergency services. It quickly became obvious that opposition to reform had not died in the nearly three decades that had passed since the previous reform try. An acrimonious campaign ensued, and both sides readied for the scheduled June 20, 1989, vote. Before Election Day, however, the U.S. Supreme Court declared the board of freeholders illegal because it denied equal protection of the law to non-property holders.[59]

The successive generations of reformers in St. Louis showed remarkable resolve because they felt truth and righteousness were on their side. It was not difficult for them to demonstrate that tax burdens and service levels varied wildly among municipalities. It was also easy to show that the city of St. Louis was in economic decline and had been since the 1920s. A pattern of racial and social-class segregation between the city and county, and between cities within the county, was a defining feature of the St. Louis region, and the zoning ordinances of the many municipalities demonstrably helped establish and preserve such segregation. But St. Louis's citizens did not necessarily interpret such information as a bad thing. Even if they had, it is doubtful that any reform cause could have overcome the deep attachment people felt to their local communities.

Some of the things reformers of the Old Regionalism saw as problems—such as varying taxing levels and service provisions—others saw as solutions. Most suburban residents had long felt this way, and in the 1980s they began to find support for their point of view in academic quarters. In September 1988, just a few months before the vote on the freeholders' plan, the influential Advisory Commission on Intergovernmental Relations proclaimed that urban residents benefited when they were given the ability to shop around for different bundles of taxes, services, and amenities offered by municipalities.[60] This and similar studies undermined the metropolitan reform movement. It became possible for the defenders of local autonomy to cite scholarly approval for the view that they were doing nothing but exercising their free choice to live wherever they wished rather than appearing to defend parochial self-interest.

The advocates of "big box" reform that encompasses the entire metropolitan area were given new hope by the 2001 merger uniting the city of Louisville with Jefferson County, Tennessee. Reformers thought that the merger might break a long-standing logjam; a successful city–county consolidation had not been accomplished since the partial merger between Indianapolis and Marion County in 1969. Immediately, calls for similar action were raised in Albuquerque, Buffalo, Cleveland, Memphis, Milwaukee, and San Antonio.

The Louisville–Jefferson County merger was preceded by an interlocal compact that paved the way to its political feasibility. In 1985 the city threatened to annex new territory. If the annexations were successful, the county would have lost much of its revenue base. After years of bickering, in 1988 the city and county agreed to divide occupational tax collections and to establish a centralized planning and development agency, which was charged with the task of reducing the competition among local governments for economic development. Even before the compact, voters had already become accustomed to a cooperative agreement in which the city and county jointly ran a water and sewer authority, park, zoo, library system, and a consolidated metropolitan school district. Thus, by the time the merger vote was held, it did not seem threatening to political elites, the business community, or to much of the electorate.

As a means of accomplishing a merger of taxes, services, and governmental administration, Louisville was officially absorbed into Jefferson County. Suburban voters gained a lot from the new arrangement. The fact that approximately two-thirds of the voters and metro council seats came from the former suburbs tilted political power in favor of affluent suburbanites at the expense of blue-collar inner-city residents, particularly African Americans. The realignment of political power should have come as no surprise; in other metropolitan regions inner-city political leaders had steadfastly opposed consolidation proposals precisely for this reason. But suburban voters may have gained little else but more influence. The main selling point for the merger—that services would become more efficient through streamlined administration—has not been realized to any measurable degree.[61] Neither has the merger resulted in a more equitable distribution of services than before.[62]

At this point is it hard to say if the Louisville example will spread because the political conditions that made reform possible in Louisville may be hard to find elsewhere. However, the advocates of metropolitan reform keep trying, though perhaps less often than in the past. In November 2004, a proposal to merge Des Moines with its surrounding county, Polk (Public Measure Letter A), failed miserably, by margins of almost two to one in both the city and county.[63] The results made it clear that Louisville's success will be hard to duplicate.

Recognizing this reality, most New Regionalist advocates have pushed for less ambitious schemes meant to promote more effective land use planning, equitable taxing arrangements, and high-quality service provision. To accomplish any of these goals, the almost complete control that municipalities exercise over these policies must be challenged. The Minnesota legislature has entertained perhaps more proposals than any other state for curbing the tendency toward polarization among jurisdictions. Bills have been considered that would require all municipalities to accept a "fair share" of affordable housing, pool their tax bases, give up local land use decisions to a regional planning authority, and regionalize critical public services. The years of controversy in Minnesota reveal how hard it is to accomplish this kind of reform even in a state where the political reformers have had political clout.

In 1967 the Minnesota legislature approved the creation of a Metropolitan Council for the Minneapolis urban region. Four years later, in what advocates called the "Minnesota Miracle" because of the unlikely compromises that made it possible, the state legislature approved a plan to partially equalize local revenues by requiring cities and towns in some parts of the state to participate in tax-sharing plans.[64] Local governments surrounding Minneapolis participated in a regional tax-sharing pool that required each city to place the taxes gained from an increase in the value of commercial industrial growth into a common pool. This tax-sharing arrangement helped curb beggar-thy-neighbor policies, such as tax abatements and direct subsidies, that municipalities had typically used to persuade shopping centers and other businesses to locate within their boundaries. In the original legislation, as amended in 1971, the Metropolitan Council was also given the authority to review the master plans of local communities, but with no authority to penalize local governments that did not cooperate. As a result of these and several pieces of legislation that followed in the 1990s, advocates of the New Regionalism came to regard Minnesota as a touchstone example of reform.

As long as the reformers stuck to the modest tax-sharing and planning arrangements that voters had become accustomed to, the new regime provoked little controversy. However, in 1993 the Democratic-controlled Minnesota legislature passed a fair-share housing bill, which was promptly vetoed by Republican governor Arne Carlson. In its original form, the legislation would have allowed the Metropolitan

Council to penalize local communities that used their zoning and regulatory powers to stop affordable housing (these communities would lose funds from a local revenue-sharing pool and would be barred from using tax abatements or tax increment financing for development). Even after all the penalties were removed in an attempt to placate the governor and his allies, Carlson still exercised his veto. As it happens, the governor would not have had to take such action after the 1994 elections because Republicans gained seats in the state House and Senate, and this doomed all fair-share housing legislation.

In 1994 a coalition of struggling suburbs joined representatives from Minneapolis and St. Paul to successfully push a Metropolitan Reorganization Act through the legislature, which Governor Carlson agreed to sign. The Metropolitan Council for the Twin Cities suddenly became a $600 million regional government that operated sewers and transit and supervised the regional airport.[65] In the same year, the legislature also took a step toward regional land use planning when it passed the Metropolitan Land Use Reform Act. The legislation did little—it only protected farmers from public assessments and tax increases that often forced them to sell to developers—but it provided a framework for the future. That future has not been realized, however, in large part because of the passionate opposition ignited by proposals that would curb the autonomy of local governments and the activities of developers.

In 1995 a bill was introduced in the legislature that would have pooled all municipal taxes collected on homes valued above $150,000. The legislation was defeated. Another much weaker tax-sharing bill on residential property, this one completely voluntary, became the lightning rod for a vicious partisan battle. Jesse "The Body" Ventura, the pro wrestler who became Minnesota's governor in 1998, attacked Myron Orfield, the Democratic state representative who had introduced the legislation. Ventura's rhetoric harkened back to the communist-hunting days of the 1950s: "Representative Myron 'the Communist' Orfield, his latest wealth-sharing strategy, I mean this guy really needs to go to China. I mean I think he'd be most happy there. . . . Oh Myron, Myron, Myron. You never realized the communists folded for a reason. You didn't figure it out, did you Myron?"[66] The tax-sharing legislation went down in defeat.

Despite its limitations, New Regionalists consider the tax-sharing plan in the Minneapolis region to be the best example of its kind. They point to Portland, Oregon, as the "best practices" example of far-reaching land use reform. The Portland, Oregon, metropolitan region has the most rigidly enforced growth boundary in the United States. Because it is drawn around a rapidly growing city, the boundary is easy to see both from the air and from the ground—on one side are townhouse developments and subdivisions; on the other, cows graze, grapevines leaf out, and wheat fields ripen. The growth boundary came about as a result of legislation passed by the Oregon state legislature in 1973 that required all local governments in the state to prepare a comprehensive land use plan and submit it to the State Land Conservation and Development Commission for approval. On the basis of the Commission's report, the legislature subsequently empowered an elected regional authority, the Metropolitan Service District, to establish and enforce a growth boundary in the Portland region. Portlanders soon labeled the new entity Metro, and in 1992 the name was made official when voters gave the entity expanded powers.[67]

In most states and metropolitan areas, an effective means of coordinating regional growth would be unthinkable because business organizations, developers, and local governments possess the power to stop the necessary state legislation. The political culture of Oregon explains why it is the exception. Environmental organizations and farmers supplied critical support for drawing a growth boundary around the state's largest city, Portland. Over time, the coalition supporting Portland's boundary has broadened its appeal with the argument that planned growth actually helps promote local prosperity.[68] After losing three attempts to overturn the growth boundary (in 1976, 1978, and 1982), businesses and developers seemed to become accustomed to the boundary because they "know what the rules are."[69] However, in 2004 a coalition led by developers managed to persuade the voters to approve Measure 37, a statewide initiative requiring local governments to compensate land owners who could make an argument that they lost economic value because of land use restrictions. Three years later, however, when the voters came to understand that the new law had given developers a way to tap into the public purse through a blizzard of lawsuits, they revoked the previous law by approving Measure 49, by an overwhelming majority.[70]

Since its adoption, growth beyond the boundary tends to occur in clusters, in and around smaller cities and towns within commuting distance of Portland. The subdivisions that normally spread across the landscape at the edges of urban areas are notably absent. The state government's willingness to override municipal governments is the key to preserving this kind of pattern. Historically, municipalities in all states have vigorously resisted attempts to control their land use decisions, and most state legislatures and administrative agencies have been reluctant to step into the fray. Oregon is exceptional in its attitude that "We've had some problems with them [municipalities] and had to whip them into line."[71]

Although state legislatures and suburban voters across the country have resisted schemes to achieve metropolitan-wide planning or tax-sharing, as in Minneapolis, and growth boundaries, as in Portland, they have embraced more modest arrangements when, as a practical matter, it has seemed in their interest to do so. Cooperative agreements exist among local governments almost everywhere in the United States. These agreements have typically arisen when an urban county has agreed to collect taxes to provide services for small municipalities. They have also evolved as interlocal agreements among two or more governments as a way of providing common services or sharing tax collection and assessments, data processing, and the like. For the most part they are mundane, boring, everyday administrative undertakings—the exact opposite of the bitterly contested fights over metropolitan reform.

Some examples of cooperation within metropolitan areas reveal both the accomplishments and the limitations of piecemeal reform. In the 1940s voters agreed to a new charter for St. Louis County (then the principal suburban county in the St. Louis region) that allowed the county to expand its service and administrative responsibilities. The county soon adopted a building code, and in the next few years it began to conduct electrical inspections of new construction in unincorporated areas; it also contracted with municipalities for this service. By 1964 the county was running 32 parks and an extensive library system. Following a charter revision in 1954, the county formed its own police department. Over the years, the county police have contracted with numerous cities for police enforcement. In 1971 voters approved another charter amendment, this one giving the county control over waste disposal and authorizing it to set minimum training and educational standards for firefighters. Today, the county also administers 911 emergency services, runs a system of health clinics, builds roads and coordinates transportation, and operates a system of jails and courts.[72]

Similarly, urban counties elsewhere have taken on new responsibilities. By the mid-1980s, DuPage County, west of Chicago, ran an extensive parks system and coordinated municipal services for those cities that volunteered to participate. Through a regional planning commission, it provided planning expertise and advice to cities and applied for federal grants on behalf of municipalities and special districts.[73] Oakland County, Michigan, north of Detroit, also slowly expanded its responsibilities, finally running an airport, providing contracted services to municipalities, and running a public library system and emergency services. Over time it has become, in effect, a regional government that coordinates public works projects.[74] By the early 1970s, Orange County, California, had evolved into an administrative structure sufficient to provoke repeated protests from local officials. Like other urban counties, it had grown less through big reform than by a gradual accumulation of responsibilities.

Urban areas have also been able to overcome many of the effects of governmental fragmentation through special districts. In 2002 there were 87,900 local governments in the United States; of these, fewer than one in four—19,431—were municipalities.[75] The fastest-growing form of local government is the special district—an authority granted taxing and spending powers so it can undertake designated responsibilities such as administering sewer systems, running toll tunnels and bridges, and providing mass transit services. Special districts are generally run more like private corporations than like governments, and most of them are virtually invisible.[76] Most of them come into existence to supply services to new developments (they are often organized, in fact, by developers for the purpose of providing public services to new subdivisions, malls, or other developments), but others are truly metropolitan in scope.

Urban counties, interlocal agreements, and special districts have facilitated improved service delivery while preserving municipal autonomy. Without them, governmental fragmentation would give rise to irresolvable problems; precisely because they exist, fragmentation can be sustained. But the proliferation of intergovernmental agreements and special districts creates an incredible level of complexity that undermines democratic governance. They are generally out of the public eye and are run like private corporations that are not responsible to voters.[77] Rather than acting as an antidote to sprawl, they facilitate it by providing a flexible means by which developers and urban residents can obtain the public infrastructure and services for new development at the urban edge. Because of the success of such cooperation efforts, the pressures for bigger, more ambitious schemes—such as metropolitan reform—are reduced. In effect, local government officials and citizens have found a way to solve the problems of regional governance without throwing out the baby with the bathwater.

SMART GROWTH

Smart Growth is a term coined in 1997 by Governor Parris Glendening of Maryland to describe the policies he proposed to build public infrastructure in designated growth areas while at the same time protecting other areas from development.[78] Because of its positive connotations, in the next few years the term became a popular label for a diverse collection of land use policies and environment regulations. Although it has generally been difficult to tell the difference between the New Regionalism and Smart Growth, those who use the latter term tend to find it useful because it is extremely ambiguous and malleable. Groups ranging from the Sierra Club and the National Trust for Land Preservation to the National Association of Home Builders claim to promote Smart Growth. If it is possible to identify the central message of the Smart Growth movement, it is that planned development is the answer to urban sprawl: Growth must occur, but it should be balanced growth, or "quality development," that improves blighted areas; promotes environmental quality; lowers energy consumption through better transportation systems and improved urban design; assesses the cost and need for new public infrastructure; and preserves agricultural, rural, and open space.[79]

Although the rhetoric of the Smart Growth movement often stresses that urban development must be seen in a metropolitan perspective, the term is also often used to promote more narrow objectives, namely to promote development that keeps poorer people or minorities from moving into a community. Thus, there is a split at the heart of the Smart Growth movement, although it is rarely acknowledged. On the one hand, citizens' and environmental groups marching under the Smart Growth banner may agree to the assertion, as stated in a study sponsored by the Bank of America, that "we continue to abandon people and investments in older communities as development leap-frogs out to fringe areas to accommodate another generation of low-density living."[80] In fact, however, the fate of older communities is rarely of any concern to affluent suburban residents; they care whether their new communities can avoid the problems associated with urban sprawl and new residential development.

The tensions within the Smart Growth movement can be seen in a controversy that broke out in November 1999 in Loudoun County, Virginia, when developer John Andrews ran into furious opposition to his plans to subdivide a cornfield into 69 one-acre lots. He intended to build an upscale housing development so he anticipated no problems, especially in a county dominated by Republican voters. But in the November elections, a new group calling itself Voters to Stop Sprawl swept all eight seats on the county's board of supervisors. Reading the tea leaves, the planning commission of the tiny town of Hamilton, which held zoning jurisdiction over the new development, did the unthinkable. It voted against it.

This revolt of the affluent against the affluent grew its roots in the same fertile soil found on the margins of every metropolitan area in America. Located 16 miles from Washington, D.C., until the 1980s Loudoun County was dotted with farms and horse barns. By the turn of the century, its population had quadrupled, and even though the new residents were prosperous, they brought with them traffic congestion, overcrowded schools, and new subdivisions. Explaining the sudden success of the revolt against sprawl, the newly elected Republican chair of the county board observed, "This wasn't a Republican or a Democrat thing. They [the new county board] did everything out there that the Republican Party should have done, but failed to do."[81]

Even in Loudoun County, Smart Growth carried different meanings. In the part of the county that was already developing, the major issues included the costs of infrastructure and the quality and aesthetics of new development. In the sections of the county that were still mostly rural, the preservation of open space and the character of the landscape dominated the discussion.[82] Opposition to new growth in Loudoun County has also been provoked by the spread of gated communities that fragment space into small, protected enclaves. These developments come with a variety of names meant to signify social standing: Brambleton, Forest Manor, Forest Run, Belle Terra. These developments leave older residents living in "scraps of communities . . . where people live in the old-fashioned way: in a house, on a road open to other roads, forming a place that anyone might pass through on the way to somewhere else."[83]

The issues raised in Loudoun County highlight a desire by affluent suburbanites to regulate development so that the problems associated with metropolitan development can be kept from their front door. Smart Growth appeals so broadly across the political spectrum precisely because it means so many different things to so many people. Often it seemingly brings together an unlikely alliance of conservatives and environmentalists, but just as often it drives them apart. It all depends upon the particular issue at hand. As a result, the application of Smart Growth principles across the United States is extremely uneven and likely to remain so.

Most communities are unlikely to adopt policies that fit the Smart Growth model, but others are aggressive in trying to direct growth to protect the environment. Planning requirements that add up to the usual definition of Smart Growth are metropolitan in scope and necessarily include such policies as greenbelts and urban development corridors. In Boulder, Colorado, the city and county have taken steps to reduce growth by designating a greenbelt around the city, establishing scenic areas, and refusing to supply public infrastructure or improvements except in areas approved for growth.[84] Montgomery County, Maryland, has designated three corridors that distinguish between existing communities, fringe growth areas, and rural and agricultural areas, and a timed growth plan has been recommended that would control the rate of development in each area.[85] Several metropolitan areas have adopted the idea of corridors, or "tiers," and land use specialists of the American Bar Association are pushing it.[86]

But even the relatively modest policies supported by various participants in the Smart Growth movement have run up against a sizable backlash. In part the battle lines have been drawn along an ideological fault line that pits those in favor of increased governmental authority against those dedicated to limiting the powers of government. In the St. Louis region, for instance, Republicans in suburban St. Charles County have objected to the term *urban sprawl*, asserting they are simply exercising their "urban choice" when they moved to the suburbs. In this formulation, sprawl is equated with freedom.

One critic, Fred Siegel, has argued that sprawl "is not some malignancy to be summarily excised, but, rather, part and parcel of prosperity."[87] Siegel claims that fragmented government offers abundant advantages. It enables people who live in badly governed central cities to escape to other jurisdictions that provide an array of alternative places to live, shop, and conduct business. Most of all, he believes that fragmented government avoids the heavy hand of a single, powerful regional government that restricts choice.[88]

An even more biting critique has been leveled by Robert Bruegmann, who challenges the empirical evidence that sprawl, if defined as low-density development, has even been occurring. His data show that much of suburban development of recent years has actually been of relatively high density. His description of Los Angeles's urban pattern makes it clear why this may be so: "From the air, virtually the entire Los Angeles basin appears as a dense carpet of buildings, with most houses packed together on lots that are considerably smaller than their counterparts in eastern cities. In addition, and in sharp contrast to many eastern cities, there are few vacant lots."[89] Bruegmann also presents evidence showing that the pace of decentralization is slowing down, having reached its peak in the 1960s and declining since. In the past, the suburban ideal was the freestanding house on a large lot. But row houses and small lots have now become the norm, and empty spaces left unfilled by past development are being filled. Thus, in the Chicago region nearly one-fourth of recent new housing units are row houses, and similar practices have come to cities in the South and West as well.[90]

From such evidence Bruegmann draws the conclusion that antisprawl campaigns and the Smart Growth movement are misguided because they are aimed at fixing problems that are already being solved by the housing market and by consumer choice: "every individual has some role in determining how the city looks and functions. If I shop at a suburban Wal-Mart rather than a downtown department store or choose to live in an apartment near the old downtown rather than in a single-family house on five acres in exurbia, these choices have an urban form. If my choices are echoed by those of many other people, they can have a profound effect."[91] In other words, says Bruegmann, people's choices, not public policy, mainly determine the shape of the metropolis.

Whatever the merits of the arguments made by the contenders in the sprawl debate, the outcome will be decided less by ideology than by practical politics. The policies associated with Smart Growth gain support to the degree that suburban residents are persuaded that planned growth is likely to improve the quality of their lives. Their judgments are more likely based on personal experience than on the kinds of abstract evidence offered by scholars. One problem is that the evidence is generally in dispute.

Several studies have shown that the costs of public infrastructure are higher when urban development is left unregulated.[92] When infrastructure such as highways, sewers, water lines, and utilities are supplied in areas with low-density development, costs are much higher than in high-density areas. Infrastructure costs are also driven up when the existing public facilities in older areas are abandoned. A Smart Growth advocate has pointed out that in the 20 years between 1970 and 1990, a Maryland county spent $500 million to close 60 schools while opening 60 more, just to keep the schools located in areas where people had moved. He also cited a study estimating that by 2020 Maryland residents would spend $10 billion on new roads, sewers, and water systems in newly developed areas. From this evidence, he concluded that regional planning was necessary to stop the twin processes of abandonment and new investment.[93]

For most suburban residents, the argument that sprawl drives up the cost of infrastructure is not likely to carry much weight, especially because those costs are widely distributed, hard to measure, and paid, in large part, by the states and the federal government. Because financing is so complex, it is difficult to document the argument that people in older areas help subsidize the cost of new development.[94] It is even less likely that suburban residents will suddenly be struck with remorse by the thought that by moving out, they have contributed to the decay of older cities and neighborhoods. Possibly, however, suburban residents may pay some attention if an effective case can be made that decay at the urban center threatens the economic viability of the regions they live within. Accordingly, this argument has gained much currency in debates over urban sprawl.

Some analysts have turned the familiar refrain that sprawl brings "despair to the inner cities"[95] on its head by claiming it may ultimately bring despair to the suburbs as well. Of 13 studies conducted between 1989 and 1996, all but one showed that central-city economic performance was associated with the economic performance of suburbs and of metropolitan areas; in addition, studies showed a relationship between greater interjurisdictional inequality and regional economic performance.[96] However, no connection was shown between the degree of concentrated poverty within metropolitan areas and the economic health of suburbs.

Aside from the rather technical nature of such studies, it is hard to imagine most suburban residents will buy into abstract arguments about how their own fate is linked to that of their poorer neighbors. Self-interest tends to be immediate—a lower tax bill, a better school, rising property values—but concern for others tends to be more abstract. For this reason, attempts to implement fair-share housing and tax equalization are likely to become intensely partisan issues wherever they are proposed. Even so, some measures will prove more popular. The revolt against uncontrolled growth in Loudoun County, Virginia, was prompted by a concern that unchecked development was ruining the environment that people had moved to the suburbs to enjoy. Perhaps it is the sheer ugliness of sprawl that provokes intense reaction from affluent suburban residents—a feeling that paradise is being lost. For them, a recent movement called the New Urbanism may have special appeal because it offers benefits with practically no costs.

THE NEW URBANISM

Advocates of the New Urbanism promote Smart Growth principles such as regional land use planning, but their passion is focused especially upon how new patterns of land use, urban design, and architecture can be used to revive local community and reduce reliance on the automobile. Thus, the charter for the New Urbanism, adopted in the first membership meeting in 2000, argues that "individual architectural projects should be seamlessly linked to their surroundings," asserts that "the economic health and harmonious evolution of neighborhoods, districts, and corridors can be improved through graphic design codes," and makes the case that "civic buildings and public gathering places require important sites to reinforce community identity and the culture of democracy."[97]

The New Urbanism is energized by a diagnosis of a terrible disease—"blighted metropolitan landscapes," "banal places with the souls of shopping malls, affording nowhere to mingle except traffic jams, nowhere to walk except in the health club."[98] The proposed antidote is made up of transportation networks designed to reduce reliance on the automobile and carefully designed urban environments with harmonious streetscapes and pleasing design features (such as buildings with dormers, gables, and porticos) that integrate home, business, recreation, and community life. By fostering a sense of community in the suburbs, advocates of the New Urbanism hope to calm the restlessness that makes people constantly move on to the next subdivision in their search for a suburban Eden.

The alleged disease of the American suburb has long been the subject of commentary. The writer James Howard Kunstler begins his book *The Geography of Nowhere* with this vivid summary:

> Eighty percent of everything ever built in America has been built in the last fifty years, and most of it is depressing, brutal, ugly, unhealthy, and spiritually degrading—the jive-plastic commuter tract home wastelands, the Potemkin village shopping plazas with their vast parking lagoons, the Lego-block hotel complexes, the "gourmet mansardic" junk-food joints, the Orwellian office "parks" featuring buildings sheathed in the same reflective glass as the sunglasses worn by chain-gang guards, the particle-board garden apartments rising up in every little meadow and cornfield, the freeway loops around every big and little city with their clusters of discount merchandise marts, the whole destructive, wasteful, toxic, agoraphobia-inducing spectacle that politicians call "growth."[99]

In Kunstler's account, suburban residents have learned to live "in places where nothing relates to anything else," a landscape in which daily activities—home, work, shopping, recreation—are pulled apart into large-scale segregated developments accessible only by automobiles: "The houses are all in their respective income pods, the shopping is miles away from the houses," and schools, malls, and office parks are also set apart, together with their seas of cars glistening on massive parking lots.[100] This version of suburbia might present the image and possibility of open space, but in actuality (in this narrative) human beings are forced to sit in their cars, gridlocked, or find themselves in the embrace of a gated community, school, or shopping mall.

Like clear-cutting a forest, a parking lot, mall, or a housing subdivision can be most efficiently built by means of industrial methods; the first step is a bulldozer that removes everything for the sake of progress. Such methods link efficiency and wastefulness in an intimate dance. Urged on by advertising, constant changes in product lines and styles, and the proliferation of disposable packaging, "most consumer goods are destined for a one-night stand."[101] Applied to land and places, such a consumer habit has far-reaching social consequences—"cycling of people through places," a mobility and rootlessness that replaces community with the hope of renewal that comes from moving, "a kind of magic that keeps expectations high."[102] If the new place disappoints, the answer will be found in another move, and still another one after that.

Together with transportation systems that favor the automobile, the zoning regulations adopted by local governments keep in place the land use patterns that bother advocates of the New Urbanism. Virtually all suburban jurisdictions follow a standard planning regime that separates residential, commercial, and industrial development in big chunks. The effect is to make neighborhoods less walkable, because corner stores, strip malls, and barber and beauty shops, and so forth, are rigorously zoned out of large residential subdivisions, thereby forcing people to drive a long way for basic services. Zoning practices, thus substantially, dictate transportation patterns: suburban residents really have no choice but to take to the highway.

Can suburban environments be designed to discourage this constant restlessness? The founders of the New Urbanism think they can do it by designing neighborhoods that nurture community, transportation systems that get people out of their cars, and urban environments built to human scale. The Congress for the New Urbanism, organized in 1994, announces in its founding charter that it "views divestment in central cities, the spread of placeless sprawl, increasing separation by race and income, environmental deterioration, loss of agricultural lands and wilderness, and the erosion of society's built heritage as one interrelated community-building challenge."[103] Although the Congress goes to some pains to point out that "we recognize that physical solutions by themselves will not solve social and economic problems," the approach of the New Urbanism is almost entirely oriented to the physical redesign of urban space. The 27 principles endorsed by the Congress emphasize "the neighborhood, the district, and the corridor as the essential elements of development." These principles stand in opposition to the style of urban development that has relied on the bulldozing of vast spaces for single uses such as subdivisions, shopping centers, and office parks. Such segmentation has created an urban pattern that favors cars over human beings, forcing people to spend time on the highway that might be spent at home or in a community setting.

Three leaders of the New Urbanist movement have distilled these precepts into a simple refrain:

No more housing subdivisions!
No more shopping centers!
No more office parks!
No more highways!
Neighborhoods or nothing![104]

In place of monotonous subdivisions of look-alike houses, "the goal of the New Urbanism is to promote diverse and livable communities with a greater variety of housing types, land uses, and building densities—in other words, to develop and maintain a melting pot of neighborhood homes serving a wide range of household family sizes, cultures, and incomes."[105]

To replace the shopping centers, the New Urbanists urge the building of pedestrian-friendly shopping areas on streets and squares, within walking distance of nearby residences. Office parks are to be banned because they segregate work from home and shopping; like shopping centers, they entail the proliferation of huge parking lots and maximize reliance on the automobile.[106] The New Urbanists recognize "automobiles are a fact of modern life," but they urge that the grid of high-speed streets and highways intersecting urban areas be replaced by highway corridors clearly separated from neighborhoods. Within neighborhoods, they want to slow traffic by narrowing streets and creating traffic circles and other "traffic calming" devices. They also promote the idea that bicycle paths and sidewalks should be built along all streets and that mass transit must be made convenient.[107]

New Urbanist environments would be delightful places to live; people would be walking and bicycling to a café or restaurant, stopping to visit with their neighbors, walking to work. Unfortunately, such environments are unlikely to be realized very often in any complete form. For residents to be able to walk and bicycle to shop, work, and play, densities would have to be as high as those achieved in the downtowns of major cities. Such densities cannot be achieved without high-rise living. However, many New Urbanist developments are composed of relatively low-density town-houses or single-family homes located in gated communities, making it certain that the spatial integration of activities sought by the New Urbanism cannot be achieved except when a housing project is inserted into a densely packed city. This goes against the grain of the New Urbanism, which markets itself as an antidote to sprawl and amorphous suburban development.

Unless New Urbanist developments change the overall character of metropolitan areas they cannot have the impact that their designers envision. They may even directly contribute to the urban sprawl that they were supposed to help reduce. The urban scholar Dolores Hayden describes her experience when she visited Celebration, the Disney Company's New Urbanism development near Orlando and Disney World: "After an hour and a half stuck on crowded freeways within Orlando, I spotted the white three-rail fence that wrapped the exterior of the development, an imitation of the rural fences used on the old horse farms and ranches of central Florida."[108] In one deft touch Hayden has captured two elements of many New Urbanist developments: particular projects do not (and cannot) change the geography of urban regions, and they are prone to nostalgic reconstructions that do not necessarily fit into the urban environment. Both of these elements are apparent in New Town, a New Urbanist development in St. Charles, Missouri, a distant satellite suburb (or perhaps Edge City) of St. Louis. The two-story antebellum porches and pillars of New Town are meant to echo a past—but is it Missouri's? A more consequential problem is that it is not located near any mass transit; clearly, it is built for commuters. A critic observed, "You see these new developments and they look like something out of a magazine from the Urban Land Institute. They say they're sustainable development but they're in the middle of a friggin' desert. They're not connected to any public transportation. You still have to drive to get there."[109]

Urban residents may be tired of freeway congestion and gridlock, and they may sometimes revolt against the ugliness of large-scale development—especially when it is in their backyard—but unless it tackles such issues, the New Urbanism is likely to become little more than a recipe for design features that developers can use to market their developments. In Celebration, all houses have front porches, a touch from the past designed to encourage people to visit with their neighbors (although, as it happens, it is too hot in Florida for this to work). The houses also have other design features meant to signify a happy, wholesome suburban life—gables, neo-Victorian trim, picket fences. One suspects that Celebration is much like the Frontier Village or Main

Street in Disneyland, California—"authentic reproductions" based on an idealized version of the real thing. If affluent home buyers come to prefer the design features of the New Urbanism, developers will be happy to accommodate them. Many of the architectural touches of the New Urbanism—stone and copper facades, porches, elaborate door lintels and balconies—cost money, and thus they serve as markers more of social class than of community. They add to the real estate markup.

To serve as an effective remedy for urban sprawl, the New Urbanism must gain support from a coalition of political interests capable of achieving regional planning. Only in that manner can the many goals of the New Urbanism become feasible. The task is formidable. Are suburban residents ready to give up their single-family homes, lawns, and multiple cars? Do they really care about community? Are they willing to share tax bases or support other measures to reduce disparities within urban regions? Judging from history, the answers to these questions are not likely to be positive.

AN UNLIKELY REVOLUTION

Attempts to implement regional government always will come up against a formidable set of constraints that doom most proposals. Americans are attached to their local governments. Racial and social class differences among jurisdictions continue to reinforce the tendency to separation, as does the fact that affluent residents benefit from fragmentation through lower taxes and higher service levels. State governments become involved in issues of local governance only reluctantly.[110]

For all of these reasons, municipalities and their citizens tend to guard their land use and other local powers jealously. Except for Portland, Oregon, no regional body in the United States holds the authority to regularly countermand local land use regulations. Because resistance to regional land use planning has been so difficult to overcome, states and regions have opted instead for land trust programs that replace regulations with attempts to preserve farmland and open space. From 1988 to 1998, 4.7 million acres of open space were protected from development, an increase of 135 percent. Several states have attempted to curb sprawl by buying up open space. In 1998 voters in New Jersey agreed to spend $98 million in state and local taxes and issue $1 billion in bonds to protect land from the developers. In the same year, the Florida legislature established a $3 billion bond program and Illinois committed $160 million for the acquisition of open space. New York's governor launched a task force to study ways to favor redevelopment over new development, and Connecticut's governor set a goal of tripling the amount of land preserved from sprawl.[111] In May 2000 Congress authorized $42 billion to be spent over 15 years to preserve land from development.[112]

Does such activity indicate that an antisprawl revolution is around the corner? New Jersey's experience with land trusts suggests otherwise. In 1998 Governor Christie Todd Whitman announced that New Jersey's program—with its goal of acquiring more than a million acres of open space—could serve as a national model. But in the end, New Jersey was reluctant to place environmental concerns ahead of economic development. In 2000, when Merrill Lynch announced it would leave the state unless it was granted permission to build in a rural area, politicians quickly caved. An assistant in the governor's policy office explained, "They wanted a suburban-style campus, so it was either here or Pennsylvania."[113] Even in the unlikely event that politics elsewhere might be different, land trusts can do little more than preserve islands of open space in the stream of development.

Suburban residents are caught in a bind, and the way out is likely to be painful. On the one hand, they are fed up with gridlock and the bulldozer, but on the other they tend to oppose regional solutions, even when these might be the most effective means of reigning in sprawl. As the urban historian, Jon C. Teaford, has observed, "change appears to be the ultimate enemy," change that might threaten "the charm of New England towns and the rural atmosphere of equestrian retreats."[114] Change might come in the form of tear-down mansions, affordable housing projects, or big-box stores. The control of land use decisions by their local governments appear to give suburban residents a means for forestalling change, and so they are reinforced in their resolve to preserve municipal autonomy. The multitude of separate municipalities in every urban region makes it difficult to achieve metropolitan-wide solutions, but only rarely are suburbanites likely to sacrifice local autonomy on behalf of an abstract ideal.

NOTES

1. For a comparative analysis of suburban development in advanced industrial countries, see Donald N. Rothblatt and Daniel J. Garr, *Surburbia: An International Assessment* (New York: St. Martin's Press, 1986), and Christopher M. Law, *The Uncertain Future of the Urban Core* (London: Routledge, 1988).
2. U.S. Bureau of the Census, *2002 Census of Governments, Preliminary Report No. 1* (Washington, D.C.: U.S. Government Printing Office, 2002), p. 5, Table A.
3. Kenneth Newton, "American Urban Politics: Social Class, Political Structure, and Public Goods," in *Readings in Urban Politics: Past, Present and Future*, 2nd ed., ed. Harlan Hahn and Charles H. Levine (New York: Longman, 1984).
4. Jon C. Teaford, *Post-Suburbia: Government and Politics in the Edge Cities* (Baltimore: Johns Hopkins University Press, 1997), p. 1.
5. James Heilbrun, *Urban Economics and Public Policy*, 2nd ed. (New York: St. Martin's Press, 1981), p. 48.
6. Peter O. Muller, *Contemporary Suburban America* (Upper Saddle River, N.J.: Prentice Hall, 1981), p. 123.
7. David M. Gordon, "Capitalist Development and the History of American Cities," in *Marxism and the Metropolis: New Perspectives in Urban Political Economy*, 2nd ed., ed. William K. Tabb and Larry Sawers (New York: Oxford University Press, 1984), p. 41.
8. George E. Peterson, "Federal Tax Policy and Urban Development," in *Central City Economic Development*, ed. Benjamin Chinitz (Cambridge, Mass.: Abt Books, 1979), pp. 67–78.
9. Robert Cervero, "Unlocking Suburban Gridlock," *Journal of the American Planning Association* 52, no. 4 (Autumn 1986): 389.
10. Brian J. L. Berry, *The Open Housing Question: Race and Housing in Chicago, 1966–1976* (Cambridge, Mass.: Ballinger, 1979).
11. Joel Garreau, *Edge City: Life on the New Frontier* (Garden City, N.Y.: Doubleday, 1991), p. 6.
12. Robert E. Lang and Jennifer B. LeFurgy, *Boomburbs: The Rise of America's Accidental Cities* (Washington, D.C.: Brookings Institution Press, 2007).

13. Ibid.
14. Ibid., pp. 56–57.
15. Office of Technology Assessment, Congress of the United States, *The Technological Reshaping of Metropolitan America*, OTA-ETI-643 (Washington, D.C.: U.S. Government Printing Office, 1995).
16. Anthony Downs, *The Costs of Sprawl: Environmental and Economic Costs of Alternative Development Patterns of Metropolitan America* (Washington, D.C.: Real Estate Research Corporation, 1974), p. 2.
17. Neal Peirce and Curtis Johnson, "St. Louis: Exploded Galaxy?" *St. Louis Post-Dispatch,* March 16, 1997, p. 6B.
18. Martha T. Moore, "Cool Climates, Hot Suburbs, Mixed Blessings," *USA Today,* November 11, 2003, p. 18A.
19. Russ Lopez and H. Patricia Hynes, "Sprawl in the 1990s: Measurement, Distribution, and Trends," *Urban Affairs Review* 38, no. 3 (January 2003): 325–352.
20. Office of Technology Assessment, *Technological Reshaping,* Chapter 8.
21. Scott Bowles, "National Gridlock," *USA Today,* November 23, 1999, p. 2A.
22. Texas Transportation Institute, Texas A&M University, *The Urban Mobility Report* (Lubbock, TX, 2006).
23. Wald, "How Dreams of Clean Air Get Stuck in Traffic."
24. Bowles, "National Gridlock," p. 2A.
25. Robert Cervero, "Unlocking Suburban Gridlock," *Journal of the American Planning Association* (August 1986): 389.
26. H. V. Savitch and Ronald K. Vogel, *Regional Politics: America in a Post-City Age* (Thousand Oaks, Calif.: Sage, 1996), p. 18.
27. Janet Frankston, "Suburban Sprawl's Sticker Shock," *Chicago Tribune,* January 5, 2003, Section 16, pp. 1–2.
28. Jerry Adler, "Bye, Bye Suburban Dream," *Newsweek,* May 15, 1995, pp. 40–45.
29. Daniel Pederson, Vern E. Smith, and Jerry Adler, "Sprawling, Sprawling . . . ," *Newsweek,* July 19, 1999, pp. 23–27.
30. Ibid.
31. Vicki Lee Parker, "Western Cities Grapple with Rapid Growth," *Wall Street Journal,* September 22, 1999, p. B16.
32. John J. Fialka, "Campaign Against Sprawl Overruns a County in Virginia, and Soon Perhaps Much of Nation," *Wall Street Journal,* January 4, 2000, p. A24.
33. Bill Lambrecht, "Urban Sprawl Is a Hot Topic," *St. Louis Post-Dispatch,* February 7, 1999, p. A6.
34. *Governing: The Magazine of States and Localities,* January 1999 and August 1999 issues.
35. D'vera Cohn, "Big Is No Longer Beautiful for Many U.S. Communities," *Santa Barbara News-Press,* March 4, 1979, cited in John R. Logan and Harvey L. Molotch, *Urban Fortunes: The Political Economy of Place* (Berkeley: University of California Press, 1987), p. 159.
36. Mark Baldassare, "Suburban Support for No-Growth Policies: Implications for the Growth Revolt," *Journal of Urban Affairs* 12, no. 2 (1990): 198.
37. Sierra Club, *Solving Sprawl: The Sierra Club Rates the States* (Washington, D.C.: Sierra Club, 1999), p. 2.
38. Robert Reinhold, "Growth in Los Angeles Poses Threat to Bradley," *New York Times,* September 22, 1987.
39. Charles Lockwood and Christopher B. Leinberger, "Los Angeles Comes of Age," *Atlantic Monthly* (January 1988): 48.
40. William Booth, "For Voters, the Target Is Sprawl," *Washington Post National,* December 7, 1998, pp. 30–31.
41. Ibid., p. 31.
42. Martin Griffith, "Alarmed by Growth, Nevadans Go 'Green,'" *Chicago Tribune,* December 19, 2002, p. 39.

43. See *http://www.nosprawltax.org/*, and a *Washington Post* editorial at *http://www.ppionline.org/ppi_ci.cfm?knlgAreaID=141&subsecID=299&contentID=252266*.

44. Terence Samuel, "Gore Pushes a Plan to Help Curb Problems Related to Urban Sprawl," *St. Louis Post-Dispatch,* January 12, 1999, p. A8.

45. Terence Samuel, "Al Gore Makes Sprawl Central to His Campaign," *St. Louis Post-Dispatch,* October 12, 1999 (*http://www.postnet.com*).

46. Fialka, "Campaign Against Sprawl," p. A24.

47. Ibid.

48. Fred Siegel, "Is Regional Government the Answer?" *The Public Interest* (Fall 1999): 88.

49. William R. Barnes and Larry C. Ledebur, *The New Regional Economies* (Thousand Oaks, Calif.: Sage, 1998).

50. E. Terrence Jones and Elaine Hays, "Metropolitan Citizens of St. Louis," paper prepared for a poster session at the annual meeting of the American Political Science Association, September 1, 2001; reprinted in Dick Simpson, *Inside Urban Politics: Voices from America's Cities and Suburbs* (New York: Longman, 2004), pp. 286–292.

51. E. Terrence Jones, *Fragmented by Design: Why St. Louis Has So Many Governments* (St. Louis: Palmerston and Reed Publishing, 2000), Foreword.

52. G. Ross Stephens and Nelson Wikstrom, *Metropolitan Government and Governance: Theoretical Perspectives, Empirical Analysis, and the Future* (New York: Oxford University Press, 2000), pp. 31–32.

53. Quoted in ibid., p. 33.

54. Paul Studenski, *The Government of Metropolitan Areas in the United States* (New York: National Municipal League, 1930), p. 29.

55. Victor Jones, "Local Government Organization in Metropolitan Areas: Its Relation to Urban Redevelopment," in *The Future of Cities and Urban Redevelopment*, ed. Coleman Woodbury (Chicago: University of Chicago Press, 1953), pp. 604–605.

56. Vincent Marando, "City–County Consolidation: Reform, Regionalism, Referenda, and Requiem," *Western Political Quarterly* 32, no. 4 (December 1979): 409–422.

57. Teaford, *Post-Suburbia*, p. 110.

58. Ibid., pp. 110–112.

59. Ibid., p. 195.

60. Ibid., p. 194.

61. The source for this discussion of the Louisville merger is H. V. Savitch and Ronald K. Vogel, "Suburbs Without a City: Power and City–County Consolidation," *Urban Affairs Review* 39, no. 6 (July 2004): 758–790; also see Alan Greenblatt, "Anatomy of a Merger," *Governing* 16, no. 3 (December 2002): 2025.

62. Hank V. Savitch, Lin Ye, and Ron Vogel, "Promise versus Performance: The Louisville-Jefferson County Merger," paper delivered at the annual meeting of the Urban Affairs Association, Seattle, Washington, April 2007.

63. Hank V. Savitch, Ronald K. Vogel, and Lin Ye, "Beyond the Rhetoric: Lessons from Louisville's Consolidation," *American Review of Public Administration,* vol. 1, 2009.

64. See the Minnesota Historical Society, "Public Education: The Minnesota Miracle" (*http://www.mnhs.org/library/tips/history_topics/18public.html*).

65. Myron Orfield, *Metropolitics: A Regional Agenda for Community and Stability* (Washington, D.C.: Brookings Institution Press, and Cambridge, Mass.: Lincoln Institute of Land Policy, 1997), p. 13.

66. Quoted in ibid., p. 149.

67. Paul G. Lewis, *Shaping Suburbia: How Political Institutions Organize Urban Development* (Pittsburgh: University of Pittsburgh Press, 1996), pp. 105–107.

68. Christopher Leo, "Regional Growth Management Regime: The Case of Portland, Oregon," *Journal of Urban Affairs* 20, no. 4 (1998): 363–394.

69. Lewis, *Shaping Suburbia*, p. 115.

70. For a discussion on Measure 37 and 49, see *http://www.oregon.gov/LCD/MEASURE49/index.shtml*.

71. John DeGrove, *Land, Growth, and Politics* (Chicago: APA Planners' Press, 1984), pp. 249–250.

72. Teaford, *Post-Suburbia,* pp. 136–138.

73. Ibid., pp. 145–146.

74. Ibid., p. 152.

75. U.S. Bureau of the Census, *2002 Census of Governments,* Report GC02-1P (Washington, D.C.: U.S. Government Printing Office, 2002).

76. Nancy Burns, *The Formation of American Local Governments: Private Values in Public Institutions* (New York: Oxford University Press, 1994).

77. Gerald E. Frug, "Beyond Regional Government," *Harvard Law Review* 115, no. 7 (May 2002): 1785.

78. Elizabeth Gearing, "Smart Growth or Smart Growth Machine? The Smart Growth Movement and Its Implications," in *Up Against the Sprawl,* ed. Jennifer Wolch, Manuel Pastor Jr., and Peter Dreier (Minneapolis: University of Minnesota Press, 2004), p. 280.

79. Robert H. Freilich, *From Sprawl to Smart Growth: Successful Legal, Planning, and Environmental Systems* (Washington, D.C.: American Bar Association, 1999), p. 323.

80. Bank of America, "Beyond Sprawl: New Patterns of Growth to Fit the New California" (*http:// www.seafirst.com/community/comm_env_urban1.html*).

81. Fialka, "Campaign Against Sprawl," p. A24.

82. Ibid.

83. Stephanie McCrummen, "Subdivisions Impose Social Divide," *Washington Post,* May 1, 2005 (*http://www.washingtonpost.com*).

84. Ibid., pp. 195–196.

85. Ibid., pp. 131–132.

86. Ibid.

87. Siegel, "Is Regional Government the Answer?", p. 85.

88. Ibid., pp. 85–98.

89. Robert Bruegmann, *Sprawl: A Compact History* (Chicago: University of Chicago Press, 2005), p. 68.

90. Ibid., pp. 63–65.

91. Ibid., p. 225.

92. For a comprehensive review, see Office of Technology Assessment, *Technological Reshaping,* Chapter 8.

93. Edward T. McMahon, "Stopping Sprawl by Growing Smarter," *Planning Commissioners Journal* 26 (Spring 1997): 4–7.

94. Office of Technology Assessment, *Technological Reshaping.*

95. Peirce and Johnson, "St. Louis: Exploded Galaxy?" *St. Louis Post-Dispatch,* March 16, 1997, p. 6B.

96. Rosalind Greenstein and Wim Wiewel, eds., *Urban-Suburban Interdependencies* (Cambridge, Mass.: Lincoln Institute of Land Policy, 2000), pp. 25–28.

97. Congress for the New Urbanism, *Charter of the New Urbanism* (New York: McGraw-Hill, 2000).

98. Adler, "Bye, Bye Suburban Dream."

99. James Howard Kunstler, *The Geography of Nowhere* (New York: Touchstone, 1993), p. 10.

100. Ibid., p. 118.

101. John A. Jakle and David Wilson, *Derelict Landscapes: The Wasting of America's Built Environment* (Savage, Md.: Rowman and Littlefield, 1992), p. 182.

102. Ibid., p. 40.

103. Congress for the New Urbanism, *Charter of the New Urbanism.*

104. Andres Duany, Elizabeth Plater-Zyberk, and Jeff Speck, *Suburban Nation: The Rise of Sprawl and the Decline of the American Dream* (New York: North Point Press, 2000), p. 243.

105. Marc A. Weiss, in Congress for the New Urbanism, *Charter of the New Urbanism,* p. 91.

106. Elizabeth Moule, in ibid., pp. 105–108.

107. Douglas Farr, in ibid., pp. 141–146.

108. Dolores Hayden, *Building Surburbia: Green Fields and Urban Growth* (New York: Pantheon Books, 2003), p. 206.

109. Chad Garrison, "Brave New Town," *Riverfront Times*, June 1–7, 2006, p. 19.
110. For an excellent discussion of all these points, see Donald F. Norris, "Prospects for Regional Governance Under the New Regionalism: Economic Imperatives Versus Political Impediments," *Journal of Urban Affairs* 23, no. 5 (2001): 562–566.
111. Terence Samuel, "Suburban Communities Grab Up Land to Keep Developers at Bay," *St. Louis Post-Dispatch*, May 14, 2000, p. A8.
112. Ibid.
113. Iver Peterson, "In New Jersey, Sprawl Keeps Outflanking Its Foes," *New York Times*, March 17, 2000, pp. A1, A19.
114. Jon C. Teaford, *The American Suburb: The Basics* (New York: Routledge, 2008).

CITY FINANCES AND THE DYNAMICS OF GROWTH

WHY CITY BUDGETS MATTER

Few activities can put a person asleep faster than reading a city budget. Everyday services such as police protection, maintenance of water and sewer pipes, and 911 emergency phone services are virtually hidden from view because they are ubiquitous and expected aspects of our daily lives. Only occasionally do the everyday operations of urban government hit a nerve. The economic crisis of 2008 and 2009 became such an occasion because it forced states and lower-level governments to reconsider even their most fundamental responsibilities. In response to the economic downturn, by February 2009 83 percent of cities had cut expenditures and services.[1] By December, Philadelphia had closed 11 of its 54 libraries and announced that 67 of its 81 pools would not open in the summer. Beginning January 1, San Diego eliminated all six of the centers it had established to help citizens with city services, and cut the number of new police recruits by half. Seattle reduced spending on youth violence and homeless services. The hardest-hit cities began cutting even essential services; for example, Pontiac, Michigan, closed eight public schools and reduced the number of police officers from 200 to only 73. The impact of such measures were magnified by budget cuts being imposed by state governments, which were feeling the same pressures. In March, 2009, 34 states were cutting a wide range of social-services programs.[2] Such measures seemed especially painful because they came when social problems were becoming visibly worse. In Fresno, California and a few other cities across the nation, tent cities began popping up to house people who were newly unemployed, and now without a home. These settlements recalled images of the hundreds of shantytowns that dotted the landscape during the Great Depression.[3]

By raising taxes and cutting services, states and cities were making the recession worse and, in effect, canceling out some of the economic stimulus efforts undertaken by the federal government. This is part of the reason why aid to state and local governments was included in the $787 billion stimulus package passed by Congress on February 13, 2009. The American Recovery and Reinvestment Act sent $79 billion of fiscal assistance directly to the states. Of immediate relevance to the cities, it also authorized $144 billion for infrastructure projects undertaken by state and local governments and $41 billion for school districts. It was the largest amount of federal money set aside for states and cities since the Great Society legislation of the 1960s.

The stimulus package provided a greater influx of federal money than at any time since the 1930s, but it did not restructure the intergovernmental system. Whether the new arrangements prove to be temporary or not depends upon whether they last beyond the economic crisis that precipitated them, but even if they do, there is no prospect that the basic intergovernmental system of government finance will be altered. In the United States, cities do not rely on the national government for a significant share of their revenues. Mostly, they must rely on their own sources to generate the revenues necessary to finance their services, and the stimulus package does not change that basic fact. The federal dollars were designated for infrastructure projects; cities were not allowed to use them to solve current budgetary problems.

Cities in the United States, unlike their counterparts in other countries, receive little support from national government. Because cities must generate almost all of their own revenues, they devote a lot of attention to policies designed to improve their competitive position vis-à-vis other places. Although this time it involved public dollars rather than private investment, the stimulus package of 2009 revealed just how the competition among governmental jurisdictions works. When Congress authorized $144 billion for infrastructure projects, it set off a race that pitted states against states, states against cities, and cities against one another. Like every other public official in the country, Frank C. Ortis, the mayor of Pembroke Pines, Florida, declared, "We have a wish list."[4] In his case, the wish was to repair sewer lines. But it was clear that the federal money would not stretch far enough to fund all the wish lists across the country. States and cities scrambled to make the case that their projects were especially urgent, and that they fit the "shovel ready" criteria laid down by the Obama administration.

The stimulus package established a battleground among jurisdictions. The sudden availability of federal dollars made it newsworthy, but in fact this kind of interjurisdictional competition is a central feature of the American intergovernmental system at all times. For cities, the battleground extends into metropolitan areas as well, as cities vie with one another for malls, big-box stores, office parks, and many other kinds of development. Depending upon one's point of view, this is a positive, dynamic feature of the U.S. system, or it is a waste of public dollars when governments offer subsidies just to influence the location of activities that would go on anyway. At bottom, the system is sustained by the fiscal needs of governments that make it up, and it is one of the reasons why city budgets are intensely political, and why they matter.

OUTTAKE

HUNDREDS OF LITTLE HOOVERS MAKE
THE ECONOMIC CRISIS WORSE

Many historians and economists have commented on the blunder by President Herbert Hoover and the Republican Congress in 1932, when they increased taxes and cut spending in an attempt to balance the federal budget. The nation was already locked into a serious depression, and their actions took money out of the economy at a time when it was desperately needed. During the economic crisis of 2008 and 2009, states and cities acted, in effect, like hundreds of "little Hoovers" by also raising taxes and cutting services, actions that would surely work against federal efforts to stimulate the economy. As pointed out by the economist Paul Krugman, they had little choice because a fundamental characteristic of the intergovernmental system requires them to balance their budgets, thus making it impossible for them to see their way through.

It is also not easy for states and local governments to weather the downturn by drastically cutting budgets because most of the services they provide are essential to the immediate health and welfare of their citizens. They are the front-line providers of education and medical care, and they play a vital role in environmental regulation and in the building of basic infrastructure like roads, bridges, and mass transit. But during the economic downturn states and local governments became so desperate that they were forced to reconsider even these priorities. In December, 2008, California put a freeze on educational expenditures and infrastructure expenditures, including emergency repairs to schools, and Maine put $50 million in highway repairs on hold. Athens-Clarke County, Georgia, put off a bond issue to build an overdue sewage treatment plant. Seattle cut spending for youth violence programs and housing for the homeless. Cities across the country laid off or cut employees' salaries. In all these ways, state and local governments acted like little Hoovers.

Krugman wants to change the intergovernmental system so that it stops working at cross-purposes by nationalizing Medicaid, basic educational costs, and infrastructure. He asks some provocative questions: "As a nation, we don't believe our fellow citizens should go without essential health care. Why, then does a large share of funding come from state governments, which are forced to cut the program precisely when it's needed most? Similarly, "Why . . . is basic education mainly paid for by local governments, which are forced to neglect the next generation every time the economy hits a rough patch? And why should investment in infrastructure, which will serve the nation for decades, be at the mercy of short-run fluctuations in local budgets?"

Most people see strengths as well as weaknesses in America's intergovernmental system. For this reason, fundamental changes like those suggested by Krugman are not likely to come soon, but he is right when he says that economic crises raise issues about the way that the United States finances its governmental activities.

Sources: Paul Krugman, "Fifty Herbert Hoovers," *New York Times*, December 28, 2008 (*http://www .nytimes.com/2008/opinion/29krugman.html*); also Mary Williams Walsh, "Under Strain, Cities Are Cutting Back Projects," *New York Times*, September 30, 2008 (*http://www.nytimes.com/2008/10/ 01business/01muni.html*).

CITIES IN THE U.S. FEDERAL SYSTEM

Cities in the United States operate within a very peculiar system of governments, at least when compared with the practices in most of the world. For example, in most Western nations, much of the basic infrastructure and many of the services provided to citizens originate from central governments. By contrast, cities in the United States derived only about 4 percent of their revenues from the national government in 2002, compared to 14 percent in Japan (in 2003) and one-half or much more in Western European countries.[5] In addition, most cities outside the United States do not have to rely on private lenders to raise money for capital projects; those are generally financed by national governments. The U.S. arrangement is very unusual: "By not providing capital resources to subnational governments from the central government, the United States stands apart from almost every other advanced capitalist state, even other federal states."[6] Their place in the U.S. intergovernmental system basically limits their freedom to maneuver.

Municipal governments are located at the bottom of a three-tiered federal system of governance. At the top, the federal government enjoys the greatest freedom to impose taxes and go into debt. At its discretion, it may make states and cities implement policies that are costly (such as drunk driving, education testing, and antipollution laws), but it does not necessarily provide the money for such "unfunded mandates." The federal government has access to the best, most flexible sources of revenue: the personal income tax, payroll taxes (for social security), and corporate income taxes. States are next in line. They also collect personal income taxes (but at a lower rate), and they also impose sales and receipts taxes. A large share of the states' revenues comes from intergovernmental transfers from the federal government—funds to help pay for welfare, medical and social services, pollution control measures, transportation infrastructure, security, and so on. Intergovernmental transfers are here to stay basically because members of Congress succeed in their careers by delivering programs for the folks back home (which is called pork barrel funding if it is in somebody else's state). The states are not allowed to run deficits year-to-year, and they pass this restriction on to their cities. City governments in 99 out of the 100 largest cities in the country are, by law, required to balance their budgets.[7] Compared to the states, cities receive a small share of intergovernmental transfers. A consequence of being at the bottom of the federal system is that cities have fewer sources of revenue and operate under more stringent budget rules than governments at any other level.

Local governments may be at the bottom in powers, but not in responsibilities. As shown in Table 12.1, in 2002 local governments employed 13.2 million workers, with the largest employers being school districts, municipalities, and counties. This was more than four times the 2.7 million people who worked for the federal government and more than six times as many federal workers when postal workers and civilian military personnel are excluded. Local governments also employed more than twice as many workers as the states.[8] Even so, the federal government collected $1.8 trillion in revenue in fiscal year 2002, three times as much as the $597 billion in own-source revenue collected by cities. One notable fact is that although local governments collect less revenue and spend less money, they hire far more workers than any other

Table 12.1   Federal, State, and Local Government Employment
and Revenues, 2002

Employment (in Thousands)	
Federal civilian	2,690
Federal less U.S. Postal Service and Department of Defense	1,179
State	5,072
Local	13,277
Counties	2,729
Municipalities	2,972
Townships	488
School districts	6,367
Special districts	721
Revenues (Own Source; in Billions of Dollars)	
Federal	$1,800
State	726
Local	597

Note: The revenue figures do not include intergovernmental transfers or borrowing.

Sources: U.S. Bureau of the Census, *2002 Census of Governments*, vol. 3, no. 2, *Public Employment* (Washington, D.C.: U.S. Government Printing Office, 2002), Tables 1 and 3; state and local revenue data from U.S. Bureau of the Census, *2002 Census of Governments*, vol. 4, no. 5, *Compendium of Government Finances* (Washington, D.C.: U.S. Government Printing Office, 2002), Table 4; national revenue data from U.S. Bureau of the Census, *Statistical Abstract of the United States, 2003* (Washington, D.C.: U.S. Government Printing Office, 2003), Table 475.

level of government. This is because the services that local governments provide, such as education, police, fire, and sanitation, are extremely labor intensive.

The states impose restrictions on how local governments may finance their operations. But there is another strict limitation as well: All local governments must constantly calculate whether their level of taxation is so high that it might drive investors and residents into other jurisdictions. Thus property taxes cannot creep up past a certain level, and the cities allowed by their states to impose earnings or corporate income taxes must consider whether these might injure the local business climate. The constant worry about how local finances and policies will affect local economic performance is actually created by the U.S. intergovernmental system. The ability of a city to collect revenues is directly related to local economic conditions. If property values are falling, so will property tax collections; if retail sales are down, sales taxes fall; if fewer people use facilities in the city, user fees will drop.

The budgetary policies of the federal or state government filter down to local governments. In December 2002, in the midst of a recession, state budget deficits reached levels not seen since World War II or, in some cases, since the Great Depression of the 1930s. Because the deficits had reached 13 to 18 percent of state expenditures, states took steps to slash spending. Because a substantial portion of state spending flows to local governments—for education, pollution control, and infrastructure such as roads, bridges, water and sewer lines, health clinics, and so on—the cities expected to receive less aid than before. Compounding the problem, the federal government also began to withhold funds. Previously, for example, the White House had promised to send money to cities to assist in the enhanced security costs associated with homeland security and had also promised to defray some of the costs borne by school districts for new educational testing requirements imposed by Congress. Neither was forthcoming. When Congress passed the economic stimulus package in February 2009, it was the first time in a long time that the national government provided substantial new resources to help the cities.

WHERE THE MONEY COMES FROM

The sources for the revenues that cities collect are dictated by two basic considerations: what state laws allow, and what the local officials feel they can impose without harming their ability to compete for investors and middle-class residents.[9] Nearly all cities are allowed by their states to impose property taxes, probably because this tax has such a long history. Twenty-eight states allow their cities to impose taxes on retail sales, but only 8 percent of cities (most of them in Ohio and Pennsylvania) are able to impose income taxes.[10] Most of them are also allowed to charge user fees for such facilities as public parking, museums and zoos, ice rinks, and swimming pools, and in the same spirit, most cities are permitted to collect taxes that target visitors, such as hotel/motel and entertainment taxes. Cities also rely on a continuous flow of intergovernmental revenues, a small amount from the federal government (e.g., for pollution control and law enforcement), but most of it from the states or passed through the states from the federal government (especially important are road construction and maintenance, corrections, and public safety). It is difficult to find a pattern that fits all cities.

The revenue source that saved the cities from the worst fiscal effects of the urban crisis came in the form of federal aid in the 1960s and beyond. Between 1965 and 1974, intergovernmental transfers to all cities rose 370 percent, more than twice the 153 percent increase in municipal expenditures.[11] As shown in Figure 12.1, in 1978 direct federal aid to cities peaked at 26 percent of cities' own-source revenue. The Reagan administration effectively ended the special relationship that had been forged between the federal government and cities under previous Democratic administrations. By 1992 federal aid bottomed out at 4.5 percent of city revenues, climbed slightly to 6.4 percent by 1997, and fell to 4 percent by 2002.[12]

Since the era of significant federal aid ended, cities have been very resourceful in finding ways to raise revenue. The creativity of local officials has been checked mainly by two considerations. First, when taxes reach a high enough level, taxpayers are prone to rebel, as evidenced by the taxpayer revolts against property taxes that swept the country in the 1970s. Second, local officials are always aware that an excessive level of taxation may chase businesses and middle-class taxpayers away. This

Figure 12.1   Direct Aid to Cities as a Percentage of Own-Source Revenue, 1965–2002

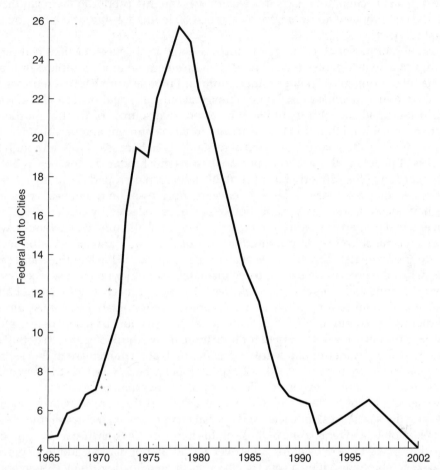

Sources: Helen F. Ladd and John Yinger, *America's Ailing Cities: Fiscal Health and the Design of Urban Policy,* updated ed. (Baltimore: Johns Hopkins University Press, 1989), p. 270. Updated using U.S. Bureau of the Census, *2000 Census of Governments,* vol. 4, *Government Finances of Municipal and Townships Governments,* Report GC 97 (Washington, D.C.: U.S. Government Printing Office, September 2000); U.S. Bureau of the Census, *2002 Census of Governments,* vol. 4, no. 5, *Compendium of Government Finances,* 2002, Table 2 (*http:// www.census.gov/prod/2005pubs/gc024x5.pdf*).

checks and balances system does work perfectly, of course, but it does impose some general rules of the game.

The property tax was once the principal source of revenue used by local governments. The most important and widely used form of property tax is the ad valorem real property tax, a levy imposed as a percentage of the value of land and its improvements. From colonial times through the early years of the republic, real property was taken to be the best indicator of both wealth and the ability to pay taxes. Indeed, this was generally true. Most of the wealth of the era was tied to the land, and fortunes were made in land speculation. A person's wealth was roughly proportional to landholdings. The real property tax, therefore, was relied on to finance state and local governmental services.[13]

Taxation of personal (or nonreal) property—that is, assets other than real estate and improvements—evolved steadily as the cities became more complex. As trade and manufacturing grew in importance, more and more wealth became represented in bank accounts, merchandise, patent rights, machinery, capital stock, and corporate assets. Cities (and states) began to levy taxes on such sources of wealth in order to maintain a reliable relationship between individual tax burdens and personal wealth. Such assets were often hard to find and assess, however. Because of this, although the numbers of people with significant personal assets mushroomed after the Civil War, the proportion of the property tax attributable to personal property actually fell.[14]

Because they are distasteful to residents and businesses, in recent years property taxes have steadily fallen as a proportion of revenues collected by cities. In 1902 personal and real property taxes accounted for 73 percent of all municipal revenues, with license and franchise fees accounting for most of the rest. These taxes continued to provide approximately three-fourths of all local receipts until the late 1930s and early 1940s, when the proportion began to decline in favor of other revenue sources, especially new municipal sales and income taxes.[15] By 1962 property taxes yielded barely 50 percent of municipal revenues in the 72 largest metropolitan areas (even though the property tax continued to generate almost all the revenue for school districts). By fiscal 1975 property taxes accounted for little more than a third (35 percent) of the revenues in the largest metropolitan areas, despite a 130 percent increase in the average per capita levy since the early 1960s.[16] In 2002 property taxes raised just 17 percent of the share of own-source revenues collected by local governments.[17]

Other sources of revenue had increased much faster than property taxes, including especially sales taxes, user fees, and special charges for such entertainment costs as hotels, motels, and rental cars. Because of this trend, by 1996 reliance on the property tax had dropped to 19 percent for cities over 400,000 in population, and to 15 percent by 2002. In some big cities, property taxes accounted for less than 10 percent of the budget. Property taxes have remained more important for other local governments than for cities, accounting for 25 percent of the taxes collected by them, and nearly all of the revenues (97 percent) collected by school districts.[18]

Only in rapidly growing cities of the Sunbelt has the property tax been used as an important source of revenue growth since the 1960s. This was possible because of the sharply escalating value of property in those cities. In Phoenix, the value of taxable property rose 251 percent from 1965 to 1973; in Newark it increased only 2 percent and in Detroit 14 percent during the same period.[19] However, these differences disappeared during the recession of 2008–2009, when property values fell even faster in the Sunbelt than elsewhere. But changing property values in the industrial cities were only part of the problem. Antiquated assessment procedures in many cities fail to keep the assessed valuations of property in line with their market values both in periods of inflation and deflation.[20]

The property tax has a number of weaknesses, which has prompted cities to search for alternatives. The 2008–2009 recession revealed that it was as hazardous for cities to rely on property taxes as it was for homebuyers to rely on rising property values. Foreclosure rates rose faster and property values plummeted faster in some metropolitan areas of the Sunbelt than anywhere else, with real estate values falling by more than 40 percent in Florida, Arizona, and California. Property tax revenues were predicted to fall by 10 percent in California over a three-year period, but it would be even worse if property tax assessments actually kept up with changes in the value of real estate. Santa Clara County, which had experienced a 7 percent increase in property tax revenues the year before, was bracing for a 2 percent reduction by June 2009, and the assessor expected to review almost half the properties in the county before the next year.[21] Across the nation, a tax revolt began brewing because home-owners who saw their property values fall expected their tax bills to fall as well, but this often did not happen. Tax assessors offices were inundated with appeals.[22]

The property tax has another drawback because of the high proportion of tax-exempt property. According to one study, almost one-third of all real property in the United States is subject to some kind of exemption.[23] In 1982 in just 23 states and the District of Columbia, there was $15 billion in exempt property for religious institu-tions, $22 billion for educational institutions, $15 billion for charitable institutions, and $128 billion for government property.[24] In recent decades, the proportion of tax-exempt property has increased. Many cities have provided tax relief for the homes owned by elderly or poor people ("circuit breaker" laws). States and cities have tried to attract or retain businesses and investors by forgiving or reducing their property taxes. Many states have exempted various forms of business property, such as machines and inventory, from taxation without consulting local governments.[25]

The burden of tax-exempt property falls most heavily on those cities that are least able to afford it because central cities have twice as much exempt property located in them as their surrounding suburbs.[26] In 1985 more than 51 percent of the real prop-erty in Boston was tax exempt, up from 41 percent in 1972.[27] A 1983 article traced a 3.2-mile route through Boston where a walker would not set foot on a single parcel of taxable property.[28] Cities must provide services for these properties, including police and fire protection, but the owners pay no taxes. The situation in New York so incensed one taxpayer that he sued the city tax commission over the "subsidy of religion," going all the way to the U.S. Supreme Court before finally losing the case.[29]

Taxpayers' revolts that started in the 1970s forced governments to reduce their reliance on property taxes. During that period, at least 14 state legislatures enacted laws that limited property tax rates or spending by local governments.[30] Even more far reaching were the citizen initiatives. The first widely publicized of these was Proposition 13 in California, which was passed by popular referendum in June 1978. From March to November 1978, 16 states held initiatives or referenda to limit taxes or spending, although not all were binding on public officials.[31] Thirteen of the citizen initiatives passed. More such proposals were approved after 1978. Since that time, public officials have tended to regard any proposal to raise property taxes as the third rail of politics. This, more than any other factor, accounts for the declining importance of the property tax for cities.

Although they are used by a few cities, earnings taxes have proven to be less popular even than property taxes. One method cities have used to deal with this problem is to levy earnings taxes to be paid by anyone working within the city. Although Charleston, South Carolina, is reported to have collected a tax on income prior to the Civil War, the modern municipal income tax movement began in Philadelphia in 1939. That levy, a flat-rate payroll tax on all earnings of persons who lived or worked in the city, was adopted to relieve financial pressures during the Great Depression. The big advantage of the income tax is that it enables cities to tax nonresident commuters. Research demonstrates that the export ratio (proportion of taxes paid by nonresidents) is higher for local income taxes than for sales taxes or property taxes.[32] In 2002 it was levied by about 8 percent of municipalities of 50,000 or more.[33] Nearly all cities in Ohio, Pennsylvania, and Kentucky could impose it, plus the larger cities in some other states, such as New York City, Kansas City, and St. Louis, but 90 percent of the cities that collect income taxes are in Pennsylvania and Ohio.[34] More cities would probably use it, but few states allow them to, and there is a nagging fear that it makes cities less competitive within their metropolitan regions because people and businesses can easily move to escape the tax.

Sales taxes, user fees, and fees for permits and special services have been the taxes of choice since the 1970s. As of 2002, twenty-eight states allowed their cities to impose retail sales taxes, which added up to nearly 58 percent of cities with over 50,000 in population.[35] Sales taxes have been useful because they are highly flexible. Taxes on retail sales taxes can yield big revenues even when they are adjusted by tiny increments, and a substantial portion of the tax is paid by people not living within the city's boundaries. This is especially valuable for cities with large retailing centers serving a regional market, such as malls and big-box stores. Cities will go to great lengths to land big retailers, as revealed at the April, 2009, meeting of the International Council of Shopping Centers held in Las Vegas. Economic development specialists and city officials from across the nation flocked to the convention to schmooze with developers and representatives of chain store retail outlets. For local officials, the stakes were both economic and symbolic: "Mom-and-pop stores may provide local flavor, but chain stores are societal benchmarks. Mayors hear it from their constituents all the time: 'Why don't we have a Trader Joe's? Why don't we have a Bass Pro Shops? What are we, some kind of backwater?'"[36]

With the fiscal bottom line and the reputation of local public officials riding on the outcome, the competition among jurisdictions for retail is extremely intense. Accordingly, governments try to outbid one another by offering subsidies to developers and retaining consultants to help them make deals. Businesses are skilled at shopping around, and they reap rewards for their efforts: in 1995 and 1996, state and local corporate subsidies added up to almost $49 billion.[37] To put such numbers in perspective, it may be helpful to consider a 1998 study, which reported that the combination of federal, state, and local incentives offered to influence the location of business cost "every working man and woman in America the equivalent of two weekly paychecks" a year.[38]

However attractive they may be, reliance on sales taxes can be hazardous. Stores that move in can move out just as easily, making subsidies appear to be a poor deal for local governments. In the recession that began in 2008, the take from retail taxes dropped sharply because of declining sales and store closings. Officials in cities that relied heavily on sales taxes reported greater declines in revenues than those relying more on property taxes or on a mixture of property, sales, and income taxes. Those with many sources of revenue did the best.[39]

During economic downturns, city officials are prompted to find ingenious ways to extract money from taxpayers. Since 2000, two episodes have prompted such bursts of creativity. The terrorist attacks of September 11, 2001, changed the cities' economic fortunes very quickly. Travel and tourism plummeted, along with the stock market and retail sales. By March 2002 sales taxes had declined to 97 percent of earlier estimates, and income and tourist taxes had fallen to 90 percent.[40] Cities were squeezed between falling revenues and sharp increases in costs for law enforcement and security. As a result, they began making deep cuts in expenditures. They had barely recovered from those budgetary problems when the economy plunged into recession in 2008.

To create an illusion that they are not raising taxes at all, cities have imposed an astonishing variety of user and special-services fees. The trend began in earnest in the early 1990s. In 1991, 73 percent of cities increased user fees and 40 percent adopted new user fees for at least one city service.[41] Fees for parking, museums, botanical gardens, zoos, aquariums, planetariums, ice rinks, and swimming pools were increased, and many of the institutions and programs supporting these services were expected to be self-supporting. In many cities, garbage collection became a private service for which each household pays instead of being a public service paid for out of general tax revenues.

In response to mounting budget deficits in 2003, states and cities all over the nation redoubled their efforts to raise revenues by imposing new fees or hiking those already on the books. New York's mayor, Michael Bloomberg, a Republican, increased fees by $139 million, but he also proposed lowering the city's income tax rate. Literally dozens of fees were involved, including a 33 percent increase in subway and bus fares, a 7 percent jump in tuition for public colleges, increases in parking fines, and higher fees to obtain a marriage license and birth certificate or to place a cell phone call from within the city. Fees had already been hiked for the use of public tennis courts and baseball diamonds. In California, a long list of new fees increased the costs of college tuition, car licenses, hunting and fishing licenses, admission to museums and parks, and even tuberculosis (a proposed $50 fee for anyone testing negative and $400 for positive).

The economic meltdown that began in 2008 prompted city officials to become more inventive than ever before. Winter Haven, Florida now levies a fee to cover the services provided by police and firefighters when they respond to auto accidents. Londonderry, New Hampshire, charges a $25 fine for any dog owner who fails to renew a dog license on time. Cities have learned that they can reap a steady revenue stream by hiring private companies to install and monitor cameras at intersections to recall traffic violations. One mayor has floated the idea of a "streetlight user fee" of $4.25 to pay for the city's cost of operating streetlights. Honolulu, Hawaii, is considering raising its fees for zoo parking by 500 percent.[42] The real problem that arises from raising money through fees rather than taxes is that they are extremely regressive in nature: the fee costs the same regardless of the income of the person paying it. Over the last few years, less regressive forms of taxation (which is what fees are, in reality) have remained steady or even dropped.[43] In this way, the fiscal policies of local governments goes a long way toward canceling efforts by the federal government to erect a social safety net for poor and the working class families.

WHERE THE MONEY GOES

Collectively, local governments in the United States spend huge sums of money. In 2005, for example, they spent $1.14 trillion; cities accounted for about one-third of this total. The leading municipal budget by far is New York City, with $52.9 billion in planned expenditures and appropriations for the 2007 fiscal year. The next two largest cities, Los Angeles and Chicago, planned to spend $5.7 billion and $6.7 billion, respectively.[44]

City spending is driven by powerful forces that are largely beyond the control of local officials and voters. City governments are not sovereign entities. Higher levels of government (state and federal) allocate responsibilities—generally called *mandates*—to city governments within the intergovernmental system. Equally important, no matter how dire their budgetary situation may be, cities must provide a minimum level of services necessary for maintaining the physical well-being of city residents and the viability of a city: public health, police and fire protection, education, water distribution, sewage collection, parks, highways, museums, and libraries.

The relative distribution of municipal expenditures among various services and responsibilities for 2002 is shown in Table 12.2. Most cities spend their money on a variety of basic services that most citizens take for granted, such as education, highways, parks and recreation, sewage and waste disposal, and police and fire protection. However, the biggest cities tend to devote a larger proportion of their budgets to social programs such as housing and community development, health and hospitals, and public welfare; indeed, the six cities with more than one million residents allocated a combined 14.5 percent for public welfare—more than twice the proportion spent by cities with populations of 400,000 to one million people. It should be noted that most cities, even most big cities, do not run the schools within their boundaries; normally, education is financed through independent school districts. The exceptions include some older cities, such as New York, Boston, San Francisco, and Baltimore, which built schools before it had become the usual practice to finance education through special districts, and Chicago, which took over its schools in 2000.

Except for education, many of the social services the cities provide would be considered by most people as redistributive in nature, in the sense that they disproportionately benefit lower-income residents. However, failure to treat the problems of the poor can reverberate through the urban community and affect everyone. Public hospitals and health clinics, for example, are used mostly by people without health insurance. In the absence of public health facilities, many families would quickly become reduced to desperation and penury in an attempt to find health services. Considered on its own merits, this would be a social disaster, but in addition, rates of

Table 12.2   Direct Expenditures for Selected Services in Largest U.S. Cities (Based on 2002 Population)

	Cities of 1,000,000 Population	Cities of 400,000 to 999,999 Population
Expenditures		
Education	22.4%	18.5%
Community development and housing	6.6	4.9
Public welfare	14.5	6.8
Health and hospitals	11.1	9.0
Police protection	11.9	12.7
Fire protection	4.7	6.5
Corrections	2.5	2.0
Highways	4.6	6.1
Parks and recreation	3.0	6.9
Sewerage	5.3	8.2
Waste management	2.7	3.1
Governmental administration	3.6	7.0
Interest on debt	7.0	8.2

Note: General expenditures only.

Source: Recalculated using U.S. Bureau of the Census, *Statistical Abstract of the United States, 2006*, [2006], Table 448 (online data book: *http://www.census.gov/compendia/statab/*).

communicable and contagious diseases such as tuberculosis and AIDS would spread more quickly.

Homelessness is another social problem that most cities attempt to treat with a more complex and compassionate manner than mere law enforcement. Virtually all large cities have a population of homeless people wandering downtown streets. Law enforcement can manage but cannot solve the problem. In January 2003 Chicago's mayor, Richard M. Daley, announced an effort to end homelessness in the city by 2013 by closing homeless shelters and using the money to fund permanent housing and social services. The mayor's proposal, which was drafted by nonprofit organizations working with city administrators, was motivated, in part, by the expense and intractability of the problem. It cost $1,200 a month to provide temporary shelter for a family of three—money that could, instead, be devoted to rental of permanent housing and social services.[45]

Public health services account for a large chunk of the budgets of large cities and they are too important to abandon. Cities and counties engage in restaurant inspections and move quickly when cases of food poisoning break out. Health clinics offer free flu shots and screening for diseases. There are constant reminders of the importance of such services. In the summer of 2002, an epidemic of the West Nile virus, which is carried by birds, spread throughout the Midwest, with a heavy outbreak in

Illinois. The state of Illinois and Chicago authorities moved fast in an attempt to track the disease. Local governments throughout the Chicago area sprayed ponds and rivers where mosquitoes might breed, and plans were in place to initiate an aggressive campaign of eradication at the start of the mosquito-breeding season in the spring of 2003. But such measures do not reveal how critical public health services are to the urban population. A flu pandemic would overwhelm the public health systems of most cities.

Although smaller cities spend about the same proportion on health and hospitals, they spend less on other social services. Big cities take on more responsibilities for a variety of reasons: Their citizens demand more and better services (for example, well-trained police officers and firefighters), they pay higher salaries to their public employees, and they experience the high service costs made necessary by high-density populations, aging buildings and infrastructure, and high rates of poverty and unemployment. Because they take on more, they spend more; on average, the cities with populations exceeding a million people spend about twice as much for each citizen as the average U.S. city and many times more than most small cities.

City expenditures rose sharply in the second half of the twentieth century, not only in total amount but also relative to the economy as a whole, increasing from 5 percent of the gross national product (GNP) in 1949–1950 to a high of 9 percent in 1975–1976. But after the recession of 1974–1975, the brakes were applied to municipal budgets. The six biggest cities lost almost 10 percent in spending power from 1975 to 1980, when inflation is taken into account. After adjusting for inflation, cities of all sizes, on the average, did not increase spending at all over the same years. Since 1980 spending has declined slightly (after adjustment for inflation) for cities of all sizes.

The ability of cities to maintain expenditure levels is closely related to local economic vitality. As shown in Table 12.3, some cities in the Frostbelt were forced to make deep cuts in their budgets in the 20-year period from 1975 to 1996. Measured in constant 1996 dollars (to account for inflation), Baltimore's budget shrank by 36 percent, Cleveland's by 16 percent, and St. Louis's by 27 percent. Of the Frostbelt cities shown in Table 12.3, only New York and Chicago were able to increase their budgets. The contrast with Sunbelt cities is striking. Of the five shown, four increased their budgets substantially; indeed, Phoenix more than doubled its spending. It is true that the populations of several Frostbelt cities fell during this period at the same time that Sunbelt cities grew rapidly. However, city expenditures are not related one to one with population; if anything, older cities bear a bigger burden because of old infrastructure and serious social problems.

The economic vitality of cities varies tremendously, and the differences are particularly sharp between central cities and their suburbs. In a 1960 sample of 62 cities, the per-capita income of central-city residents was 105 percent that of people living in the suburbs; in other words, people living in central cities earned, on the average, slightly more than suburban residents. Clearly, many affluent people still lived in the cities, even after more than a decade of suburban flight. By 1989 the income ratio had fallen drastically; by then, city residents made just 84 percent as much as the residents of suburbs. In 1989 the poverty rate in central cities was 18 percent, but in the metropolitan areas outside central cities it was only 8 percent.[46]

Table 12.3 Total Expenditures for Selected Cities in Frostbelt and Sunbelt, 1975–1996 (in Millions of 1996 Dollars[a])

	Fiscal Year 1975 Expenditures	Fiscal Year 1996 Expenditures	Percentage Change 1975–1996	Percentage Change 1991–1996
Frostbelt Cities				
Baltimore	$2,811	$1,802	−36%	0%
Chicago	2,880	3,890	35	12
Cleveland	764	644	−16	2
New York	34,292	38,753	13	2
St. Louis	670	487	−27	−14
Sunbelt Cities				
Dallas	$614	$1,197	95%	32%
Denver	934	1,716	84	48
New Orleans	661	652	0	−15
Phoenix	567	1,221	115	6
San Jose	376	790	100	5

[a]Adjustments for inflation are calculated using GNP Price Index for state and local government purchases, U.S. Bureau of Economic Analysis, *Survey of Current Business, Dec. 1999*, p. 141, Table 3.

Sources: U.S. Bureau of the Census, *City Government Finances: 1975–76*, GF 76, no. 4 (Washington, D.C.: U.S. Government Printing Office, 1977), Table 5; U.S. Bureau of the Census, *Statistical Abstract of the United States, 1995* (Washington, D.C.: U.S. Government Printing Office, 1995), Table 493; and U.S. Bureau of the Census, *Statistical Abstract of the United States, 1999* (Washington, D.C.: U.S. Government Printing Office, 1999), p. 335, Table 531.

High rates of poverty boost the cost and the need for city services. Central cities and older suburbs, therefore, are particularly vulnerable to fiscal stress. Poverty and unemployment are basically national problems, but they are concentrated in central cities and older suburbs, a result of historical patterns of population movements and of exclusionary policies that keep poor people out of wealthier suburban jurisdictions. The governments of central cities and older suburbs are in no position to reduce poverty and unemployment, but they are disproportionately saddled with these problems.

Poverty boosts public spending not only for welfare and social services but also for a broad range of other services. Central-city governments spend money on lead paint poisoning prevention (a problem prevalent in older homes), rat control, and housing demolition. Courts have ordered cities to provide shelter for the homeless at a significant expense to local governments. In 1987, for example, New York City, as required by court order, spent $274 million to provide emergency shelter to its homeless population.[47] Poverty also drives up the cost of many services. Street cleanliness is more difficult to maintain in ghetto neighborhoods, where the streets are used heavily for recreation but infrequently repaired. Costs of fire protection are higher than elsewhere because of deteriorating housing, the high density of building, old and outdated wiring, and a concentration of flammable materials.

Almost all older cities have experienced significant population losses due to the flight of the middle class to the suburbs. As a city's population falls, the cost of providing infrastructure and basic services, such as police and fire, does not decline correspondingly.[48] Cities still have the same sewer and water lines—often old and in need of frequent repair—and the same miles of streets to plow and patrol. Once the middle class has fled, however, there are fewer taxpayers to pay for these services, and the taxpayers who are left make less taxable income and own less valuable property than those in surrounding jurisdictions.

Another factor that drives up the cost of city services is the panoply of expensive mandates forced on cities by higher levels of government. Cities are not mentioned in the U.S. Constitution; legally, city governments are the creatures of the states. Although many cities have home rule charters that allow them to govern themselves internally within broad guidelines, municipal corporations are not fully sovereign. The scope of a city's service responsibilities is beyond its control. State and federal governments can, and frequently do, order cities to provide particular services or meet minimum standards of service provision, and cities only rarely receive more money to cover the costs of the mandated standards and services.

Beginning in the mid-1960s, unfunded federal mandates imposed on cities have proliferated. In the case of concurrent powers shared by the federal and state governments, Congress has the power to preempt (override) state and local laws. According to the Supremacy Clause (Article VI) of the Constitution, when there is a conflict between a national law and a state (or local) law, the national law prevails. After 1965 Congress frequently used its powers of preemption to force city governments to address pressing problems without members of Congress having to take the politically unpopular action of appropriating money. Thus Congress has been able to take credit for solving problems while foisting the costs of these solutions onto lower levels of government.

The Supreme Court upheld federal preemption in the 1985 *Garcia* decision.[49] In *Garcia*, the Court upheld the constitutionality of the 1974 amendments to the Fair Labor Standards Act, which applied minimum wage and overtime pay provisions to public transit workers in San Antonio. This decision made it clear that state and local governments are not protected from federal preemption statutes by the Tenth Amendment (which reserves powers not granted to the federal government to the states). Their only protection comes from political pressures they can put on Congress. In 1986 the U.S. Department of Labor estimated that the cost to state and local governments of complying with the new labor standards exceeded $1.1 billion.[50]

Federal mandates to preserve environmental quality have been enormously expensive. The Clean Air Act of 1990, for example, required 100 cities to install antipollution devices on their garbage incinerators at an estimated average cost of $20 million per incinerator.[51] The U.S. Environmental Protection Agency estimated that the total cost of environmental mandates for local governments increased from $7.7 billion in 1972 to $19.2 billion in 1987.

In March 1995 Congress passed, and President Clinton signed, the Unfunded Mandates Reform Act, which required Congress to weigh the costs and benefits of new rules costing over $50 million and to help pay the costs if state and local governments were forced to implement them, but this legislation came rather late in the day for most cities. In any case, it has been ignored. In 2002 President Bush promised to defray the increased cost of security borne by cities because of the war on terrorism. As of April 2003, no aid was forthcoming, and the amount proposed was considered inadequate by local officials. During the Bush administration, mandates (though they are rarely called that) have become commonplace as a way of passing legislation without paying for the resulting programs. The No Child Left Behind Act, which took effect in 2002, makes federal aid of any kind to school districts dependent upon the ability of students in those districts to pass standardized tests. Though the federal government promised to pay for some of the costs of the testing, by 2005 it was $25 billion behind in reimbursements.[52] Legislation that cost state and local governments money has been passed in several other areas as well.

A variety of economic and political forces beyond the control of local officials impact local government expenditures. Economic downturns, concentrated poverty, unfunded mandates, and terrorist threats impose unpredictable costs. As one fiscal expert observed,

> A city's fiscal health . . . depends on economic, social, and institutional factors that are largely outside the city's control. Poor fiscal health is not caused by poor management, corruption, or profligate spending, and a city government's ability to alter the city's fiscal health is severely limited.[53]

The economic downturn that began in 2008 brought that lesson home.

CITIES FOR SALE: THE MUNICIPAL BOND MARKET

If cities relied on taxation alone, they would never have been able to build the permanent infrastructure on which all city life depends. From the mid-nineteenth century to the present, cities have issued municipal bonds to private investors as a way of borrowing money.[54] Cities are authorized by state legislation to issue long-term bonds to pay for capital improvements, such as schools, highways, bridges, and hospitals, that will benefit city residents over a long period. Cities in most states can borrow short term, using tax anticipation notes (TANs) repaid in 30 to 120 days, to cover temporary budget shortages or to time their entry into the long-term bond market. Unlike the federal government, cities cannot use bond funds to cover long-term operating deficits.

Given the continuing need to build and maintain public infrastructure, access to the municipal bond market is essential for the well-being of cities. Cities depend directly on the willingness of private-sector individuals and institutions to buy their bonds. The municipal bond market is a significant sector of the economy. Borrowing typically represents 20 to 25 percent of all state and local spending. In 2002 the total long-term debt amortized by bond issues for all local governments amounted to $399 billion, but local governments also had incurred significant "outstanding" debts that have to be paid through their own budgets.[55]

The most important fact about municipal bonds is that they are tax exempt. Because the interest income derived from municipal bonds is not subject to taxation, investors are willing to buy municipal bonds at a lower interest rate than they would pay for corporate bonds. In effect, the federal government provides cities with a subsidy by exempting municipal bonds from taxation. In 1988 the Supreme Court ruled that state and local governments had no constitutional right to borrow at tax-exempt rates; Congress has the power to take away this subsidy to state and local governments.[56]

Municipal bonds are purchased by commercial banks, casualty insurance companies, pension funds, and, increasingly, wealthy individual investors, who find the federal tax exemption especially attractive.[57] The federal subsidy to cities through the bond market is relatively inefficient because only part of it, in the form of lower interest rates paid to investors, goes to cities. The rest of the federal subsidy is siphoned off to investors who avoid paying federal taxes by buying the tax-exempt municipal bonds. Legislation has been proposed, but never passed, to allow municipalities to float bonds at normal interest rates in exchange for a direct subsidy by the federal government.[58] In this way, the subsidy would go entirely to cities and not, indirectly, to investors.

Cities issue two types of long-term bonds: general obligation bonds and revenue bonds. General obligation bonds pledge the "full faith and credit" of the city's taxing powers behind the bonds, generally require approval by voters or a representative body, and are used to build public infrastructure like bridges and parks. Revenue bonds are not guaranteed by the issuing government and therefore do not require voter or legislative approval; anticipated future revenues from the facilities that are constructed with the bond monies are committed to pay back the bonds.

Revenue bonds are usually issued by public authorities established by state-enabling legislation. Run by appointed boards, authorities are free from democratic controls.[59] However, when revenues are not sufficient to pay bond premiums (and they often are not), local governments generally must make up the difference. Sports stadiums (such as the Superdome in New Orleans) often lose millions of dollars a year, and taxpayers pay these debts.

By 2002 there were more than 35,000 special authorities in the United States and they had issued $215 billion in new long-term debt.[60] Almost any facility that can charge user fees—sports stadiums, convention centers, museums, aquariums—is financed through revenue bonds. Local government borrowing through revenue bonds has risen sharply since the 1970s. Until the 1970s general obligation bonds represented about 60 percent of outstanding local long-term debt.[61] By 2002, however, nonguaranteed revenue-bond debt represented 60 percent of all outstanding debt issued by city governments and special authorities.[62]

Revenue bonds permit cities to use their tax-exempt borrowing privileges to support private programs and activities. In the late 1970s, cities began issuing mortgage revenue bonds to subsidize interest rates for middle-income home buyers, although in 1980 Congress restricted this practice with the passage of the Mortgage Subsidy Act. In an attempt to stimulate economic growth, in the 1970s and 1980s cities increasingly issued industrial revenue bonds to subsidize a broad assortment of businesses, including Kmart, McDonald's, liquor stores, and law offices. Critics charged that the tax-exempt borrowing was being used for private purposes that did not serve any public interest. Examples of flagrant abuses abounded. Chester County, Pennsylvania, for example, issued revenue bonds for an adult bookstore and topless go-go bar in downtown Philadelphia. Congress, noting the hemorrhage of federal tax revenues, restricted the use of revenue bonds by passing the Tax Equity and Fiscal Responsibility Act of 1982 and the Deficit Reduction Act of 1984.[63] The Tax Reform Act of 1986 placed state-by-state limits on what it termed governmentally subsidized "private-activity bonds."[64]

Besides being used for questionable private purposes, municipal bonds have been subject to a number of other abuses. Even before the economic crisis of 2008–2009, some local governments got into trouble by borrowing money and putting it into risky investments, hoping to make substantial profits. Unwilling to raise taxes, in 1993 Orange County, California, attempted to maintain services by putting the proceeds of bond sales into risky investments called *derivatives* that were essentially gambling on the direction of interest rates. When interest rates plunged, Orange County lost $1.6 billion. In April 1994 Orange County became the largest local government in history to file for federal bankruptcy protection under Chapter 9. More than 180 other governments lost money in similar high-risk investment pools in the same period.

Until the recent recession, however, such episodes were the exception rather than the rule. But the 2008–2009 downturn, and the fiscal issues it brought to cities, exposed serious deficiencies in the way the municipal bond market was run. In fact, the tip of the iceberg had been sighted years before. In the early 1990s, the municipal bond market had been rocked by charges that underwriters, in order to obtain lucrative government bond business, kicked back profits to public officials in the form of campaign contributions.[65] In April 1994 the Securities and Exchange Commission (SEC) enacted Rule G–37, which barred campaign contributions by municipal bankers. To get around this ban, municipal finance companies provided funding for lavish receptions at the 1996 Democratic and Republican conventions where bond underwriters could mingle with top state and local officials. At the Republican convention in San Diego, this included golf and tennis parties, a fishing expedition, and a luncheon honoring House Speaker Newt Gingrich.[66] A 1996 lawsuit alleged that underwriters overcharged municipalities for escrow accounts by as much as $1 billion.[67] Such abuses have led to repeated demands that the municipal bond industry be more closely regulated.[68]

More serious issues emerged during the 2008–2009 downturn, when hundreds of municipalities encountered problems with their bond investments. Like individuals, local government officials usually rely on experts in the financial industry to advise them on investments. One such advisor was David Rubin, who founded one of the leading consulting firms for municipal bonds, CDR Financial Products in Beverly Hills, California. Since the early 1990s Rubin has toured the country drumming up business, advising local government officials to refinance debt with risky interest-rate provisions (much like the ARMs offered to homeowners) and invest in high-yielding but risky derivatives of the same kind that devastated stock markets in 2008. Rubin made campaign contributions even these appeared to violate an SEC ban. Some of his bonds ran up unusually high fees.[69] In Tennessee, Morgan Keegan was one of several firms invited by the state to run a seminar for local officials in late 2008. By then the company had already cornered the market in municipal bonds within the state; since 2001 it had sold $2 billion in bonds to 38 towns and counties. Because

Morgan Keegan, like other financial firms, made higher commissions on derivative bonds rather than fixed-rate bonds, it took care to steer the clients into them. Right at the time that cities and towns in Tennessee began to see municipal revenues fall, the interest rates they paid on the bonds soared.[70]

News broke in January 2009 that three federal agencies and several state attorneys general had been gathering evidence on price-fixing and collusion among municipal bond brokers. The sums involved were vast: states and cities bought $400 billion in bonds each year. Brokers, banks, and other firms divided up the spoils by secretly parceling out the business by fixing bids, which allowed them to reap higher fees. A system of campaign contributions and suspicious payments to governmental officials helped keep the system in place. An antitrust lawyer representing state and local governments referred to it as "one of the longest-running, most economically pervasive antitrust conspiracies ever to be uncovered in the U.S."[71] Federal officials suggested that Congress adopt new regulations, but as late as April 2009 Congress had not taken up the matter. However, it is certain that federal and state agencies will continue their investigations, and more is bound to come to light.

Cities are at the mercy of the bond market because the cost of borrowing is basically determined by their bond ratings. A bond rating purports to represent the relative credit quality of the issuing municipality and thus determines the rate of interest a city must pay. A high rating means a lower interest rate, on the theory there is less risk for the investor. When a city's bond rating is lowered due to fiscal problems, a bond may be more difficult to sell, and the additional interest paid over the amortized life of the bond can amount to millions of dollars.

Bond ratings are published by several national rating firms, including Moody's Investors Service, Standard and Poor's Corporation, and Fitch's Investor Service. Cities pay to have their bonds rated, but they have no choice but to seek a rating if they want to be able to market their bonds. Although the purpose of the rating is to assess risk, in fact municipal bond ratings are totally unrelated to the likelihood of default. (Default may not mean the loan was not repaid; a payment may simply not have not been paid on time.) The discrepancy in the interest rates between the highest and lowest investment grade bonds is inexplicable on the basis of relative risk.[72] From 1929 to 1933, when 77 percent of all municipal defaults of the twentieth century occurred, the highest rated bonds recorded the highest incidence of default.[73]

Major cities simply do not fail to pay their debts. True, from the first recorded default in 1838 (Mobile, Alabama) through 1969 more than 6,000 bond defaults were recorded by local governments. Fewer than a third of these, however, involved incorporated municipalities (cities); most of the rest were special districts that provided particular services such as irrigation. Seventy-five percent of all such failures occurred between 1930 and 1939. Less than 10 percent occurred after the depression.[74] During the worst period for municipal bonds, 1929 through 1937, only 8 percent of all cities and 20 percent of their bonded debt were ever in default.[75] Almost all of the debts were eventually paid.

From World War II through early 1970, a total of 431 state and local units defaulted on their obligations. The total principal involved was $450 million, approximately

0.4 percent of the outstanding state and local debt. Three special authorities, the West Virginia Turnpike Commission, the Calumet Skyway Toll Bridge, and the Chesapeake Bay Bridge and Tunnel Commission, accounted for over 74 percent of this amount (virtually all local governments are considered municipal in the bond market). Only 2 of 24 major default situations ($1 million or more) were related to general obligation bonds.[76] Of 114 defaults by cities during the 1960s, almost all were temporary or technical defaults. Only 34 involved general obligation bonds, and in all these cases the cities had populations under 5,000 and the amount in default was less than $1 million.[77]

An analysis of cases filed in federal district courts between 1938 and 1971 reveals that nine cities took advantage of federal municipal bankruptcy legislation. With one exception (Saluda, North Carolina), all the cases came from small, rather obscure cities in Texas (Ranger, Talco, Benevides) or Florida (Manatee, Medley, Center Hill, Webster, Wanchula). Only in the case of Benevides (population 2,500) were general obligation bonds of post–World War II origin involved. In all other cases, the defaulted debt was of prewar origin, related to revenue bonds, or unrelated to bonds altogether.[78]

In the rare cases when a city defaulted on its obligations, it has invariably involved only a technical failure to pay on time, and the failure has been temporary. Bondholders have always recovered their money. On December 15, 1978, Cleveland became the first major city to default, even in a technical sense, since 1933. On that day, the city failed to make payments on $14 million in short-term notes; the city renewed payments a few months later and officially ended default in 1980.[79] No city has defaulted as a consequence of the 2008–2009 downturn, and it is doubtful that a state would allow that to happen. There would appear to be little justification for the differential rating of city bonds except to give business to rating services and make money for investors.

THE FISCAL BASIS OF METROPOLITAN COMPETITION

The fact that local governments must finance, through taxing and borrowing, nearly all their own activities forces them to place a high priority on promoting local economic development. Municipalities are constantly engaged in a range of activities designed to give them an edge in the competitive struggle for survival. The dividing line between the public and private sectors is often blurred. In exchange for subsidies, some cities have taken profit-sharing positions in development projects. In the case of popular Quincy Market development in downtown Boston, for example, the city provided $12 million—almost 30 percent of the total cost of the project—and gave the Rouse Corporation a 99-year lease on the property. In exchange, the city was guaranteed a minimum annual cash payment plus a portion of income from store rents above that minimum.

However, it is important to recognize that the biggest development and infrastructure projects are not financed directly by municipalities, but by independent special-purpose authorities. Using only their own fiscal resources, cities could not have financed the incredible level of public investment that has been poured into new development and infrastructure projects in recent decades. For example, more than

$2 billion was spent annually in the first half of the 1990s on sports facilities and convention centers alone.[80] In addition, billions of public dollars have been spent on urban entertainment and cultural districts, renovated waterfronts, aquariums, marketplaces, festival malls, and the other elements of the tourism/entertainment complex. Municipal governments could not possibly have raised such resources, although they have been essential to the task. Cities have been involved in complicated deal making, offering to provide public infrastructure and amenities, to rezone or assemble parcels of land through the power of eminent domain, to reduce or forgive taxes, or to subsidize private development.[81] But the latter role—the fiscal one—has more often been assumed by new public/private authorities created for the purpose.

Beginning in the 1980s, a generation of visionary mayors accepted the fact that they would have to find ways to regenerate their own economies. These "messiah mayors" preached a gospel of self-help for cities in desperate need of new ideas and directions. As noted by the historian Jon Teaford, "if nothing else the messiah mayors . . . boosted the spirits of many urban dwellers and made them proud of their cities."[82] But much more was involved than cheerleading. These mayors also pioneered in the creation of institutions capable of financing and administering projects considered important for promoting the economic viability of the city. Thus, sports authorities were created for the purpose of building sports stadiums, mall authorities were incorporated to build and administer mall and entertainment complexes, and development corporations came into being to implement local development projects. These special-purpose authorities—institutions created to accomplish a specific public purpose—were essentially public development insitutions run like a private corporation, established specifically to receive a combination of public subsidies and private investment funds.[83] They were granted the authority to earmark taxes, charge user fees, issue bonds, establish trust funds, and use other mechanisms for bringing public and private money together to finance big undertakings.[84]

This institutional device gave municipal officials a way out of the straitjacket of debt limitations imposed on municipal governments because they were now able to offload the costs of development onto institutions that were capable of generating their own resources. These public/private institutions were generally established through enabling legislation passed by state legislatures, and they were run by boards appointed by a governor and mayor, the mayor alone, or some combination of public officials. They were not bound by the rules that frustrated public initiatives by general-purpose governments. They could make decisions without worrying about what voters thought. Because they were run much like private corporations, they were able to protect their information and books from public scrutiny, but at the same time, because they pursued public objectives, they could act just like governments and generate revenue, receive funds from other governments, and borrow money and sell tax-free bonds.

The sprawling McCormick Place convention center and the renovated Navy Pier entertainment complex in Chicago provide an example. Both are administered by the Metropolitan Pier and Exposition Authority, which is governed by a board appointed by the mayor of Chicago and the governor of Illinois. The state of Illinois designates $98 million annually, derived from revenues from taxes (mainly a tax on cigarette sales) to pay off previous bonds for construction and remodeling.[85] Not only has Illinois paid for the world's largest convention center complex (which is undergoing another expansion), in 2000 the Pier and Exposition Authority floated a $108 million tax-exempt bond issue to build and own the Hyatt Regency McCormick Place Hotel.[86]

It is a mistake to describe special authorities as mere mechanisms for financing and administrating large undertakings. They are also political in nature and are always on the lookout for ways to promote their own projects and enhance their fiscal and administrative capacity. In the case of the professional football and baseball stadiums in Baltimore, an agency of the state government, the Maryland Stadium Authority, financed the two stadiums through proceeds from a sports lottery offered through the Maryland State Lottery.[87] The campaign to build the sports stadium was guided by this new agency, which commissioned studies to show a powerfully positive impact on Baltimore's economy. When another state agency followed with its own studies, it reduced the estimated impact, but independent studies sharply contested even these estimates as unrealistic, concluding that stadium development brought virtually no measurable economic benefit.[88]

The political nature of special authorities is illustrated in the case of the Denver Metropolitan Stadium District, which the Colorado legislature created in 1990 as a means of pushing forward plans for a new baseball stadium. The bill establishing the district did not contain financing mechanisms, because any that would have been proposed would have ignited controversy. Instead, the task of lining up political support for a new stadium was left to the seven-member stadium district board. Securing financing was more a political than a fiscal exercise. In close collaboration with the city of Denver, the board ran an astute campaign that kept voters in the metropolitan counties outside Denver in the dark about whether the stadium might be built close to or within their own jurisdictions. The uncertainties about location carried the day. In August 1990 voters in the six-county district passed a sales tax levy to build the stadium; large majorities in the city and an adjacent county overcame a losing margin elsewhere.[89] Just as many voters had suspected, the fix had been in all along, and the stadium was built in downtown Denver.

Special-purpose authorities have sprung up to administer the many components that make up the tourism/entertainment complex in cities. In addition to the special authorities established to finance and administer particular facilities such as convention centers, festival malls, and sports stadiums, redevelopment corporations have proliferated to refurbish business districts, revitalize neighborhoods, and provide amenities desired by local residents and visitors. Many of these authorities administer tax increment finance (TIF) districts, which raise their revenues by marketing bonds to investors based on the taxes that are expected to be collected when the land is redeveloped (a new mall, for example, will generate new sales tax revenue, which would be used to make payments on the bonds). A bond issue provides a TIF district with the funds to make public improvements that may be necessary for luring developers. In 2002 there were more than 130 TIFs in the city of Chicago, and 217 in suburban Cook County.[90]

The proliferation of special-purpose authorities throughout metropolitan areas has removed more and more of the most important public policies from general-purpose municipalities. Although municipalities are run democratically—with mayors, city councils, and other elected officials—special-purpose authorities operate out of the public eye. Some of the most expensive and sometimes controversial undertakings have been assigned to special-purpose authorities. Convention centers and stadiums are built with public money, but with little or no public input. An absence of public accountability always raises troubling questions. In the 1950s urban renewal authorities regularly abused their powers. Transportation authorities rammed highways through urban neighborhoods. Then, as now, the application of governmental authority without adequate public accountability led to abuses. The fiscal politics of metropolitan competition tempts governments to build now, and ask questions later. In the complex institutional environment of today's metropolitan areas, it is a lesson worth remembering.

FISCAL POLITICS AND FEDERALISM

Countless activities financed by cities are essential to the health and well-being of citizens. In a nation in which nearly 40 percent of citizens lack health insurance, they are frontline providers of health services provided through public hospitals and clinics, not only for the poor but also for families of the underinsured middle class. They provide essential housing services, even if most of this takes the form of contributing to or maintaining homeless shelters. And nearly all larger cities provide some public welfare, normally emergency aid for people who do not qualify for other benefits. During cold and heat emergencies, cities are expected to assist in providing immediate help. Between July 17 and 20, 1995, the city of Chicago was hit by a heat wave in which temperatures reached 106 degrees. City officials were not only unprepared, they did not feel it was in their purview to respond except through normal emergency services. By the time the heat wave had run its course, the number of excess deaths attributed to the heat wave reached 739. Realizing a repeat of such a disaster would become a public relations nightmare as well as a social catastrophe, the city subsequently (but quietly) put into place an emergency plan to mobilize its personnel and resources if a similar disaster struck.[91] The tragic events of that summer revealed a simple truth: cities simply cannot opt out of their responsibilities. Thus, when cities face budgetary shortfalls, they walk a tightrope; there is only so much they can cut.

Cities are also constrained by developmental politics to improve the local bottom line. Infrastructure projects may be put off for a while, but the logic that compels them to compete is too overwhelming to put off major projects for long. Every individual city must promote growth in order to nurture the local economy and the fiscal health of the city itself. Paul Peterson, a leading scholar of urban politics, has taken the position that because economic or market standing is fundamentally important to cities and their citizens, they should do nothing that might compromise the possibility of achieving economic success.[92] This position may provoke disagreement, but urban leaders act as if they know it is true. This makes them play a delicate game in which they try to balance the restless search for new revenue against the climate that lures new investment, and keeps middle-class residents and businesses from moving elsewhere. It is a game made all the more dicey because most of the rules are set by other governments, and by the institutions of the private economy.

NOTES

1. Chris Hoene, "Fiscal Outlook for Cities Worsens in 2009," *Research Brief on America's Cities*, by National League of Cities, Issue 2009-1 (Washington, D.C.: National League of Cities, 2009) (*http://www.nlc.org*).
2. Legislative News, *Governing*, April 9, 2009 (*www.governing.com/legis.html*).
3. Jesse McKinley, "Cities Deal with a Surge in Shantytowns," *New York Times*, March 25, 2009 (*www.nytimes.com/2009/03/26/us.26tents.html*).
4. Monica Davey, "States and Localities Angle for Stimulus Cash," *New York Times*, February 15, 2009 (*http://www.nytimes.com/2009/02/16/us/politics/16stimulus.html*).
5. U.S. Bureau of the Census, *2002 Census of Governments*, vol. 4, no. 5, *Compendium of Government Finances*, 2002, Table 4 (*http://www.census.gov/prod/2005pubs/gc024x5.pdf*). For national government transfers as a proportion of local revenue in Japan, see Japanese Ministry of Internal Affairs and Communications, White Paper on Local Public Finance, 2005 (*http://www.soumu.go.jp/iken/zaisei/17data/jyoukyou_e.pdf*).
6. Thomas H. Boast, "A Political Economy of Urban Capital Finance in the United States" (Ph.D. diss., Cornell University, 1977), p. 114.
7. Carol W. Lewis, "Budgetary Balance: The Norm, Concept, and Practice in Large U.S. Cities," *Public Administration Review* 54 (November/December 1994): 517–518.
8. U.S. Bureau of the Census, *2002 Census of Governments*, vol. 3, *Public Employment*, 2002, Tables 1 and 3 (*http://www.census.gov/prod/2004pubs/gc023x2.pdf*); *2002 Census of Governments*, vol. 4, no. 5, *Compendium of Government Finances*, 2002, Table 4; U.S. Bureau of the Census, *Statistical Abstract of the United States, 2003* (Washington, D.C.: U.S. Government Printing Office), p. 322, Table 475.
9. Any summary of revenue sources for all cities is misleading and therefore not presented in this chapter. Cities simply vary too much for such summaries to be meaningful; earnings taxes can be collected by a few cities, but not most; sales taxes are allowed by 28 states, and so forth.
10. Michael A. Pagano, *City Fiscal Conditions in 2002: A Research Report on America's Cities* (Washington, D.C.: National League of Cities, 2002), p. 3.
11. Eric A. Anderson, "Changing Municipal Finances," *Urban Data Services Reports* 7, no. 12 (Washington, D.C.: International City Manager Association, December 1975), p. 2.
12. U.S. Bureau of the Census, *2002 Census of Governments*, vol. 4, no. 5, *Compendium of Government Finances*, 2002, Table 2.
13. Refer to Richard T. Ely, *Taxation in American States and Cities* (New York: Crowell, 1888), pp. 109–113; and Sumner Benson, "A History of the General Property Tax," in *The American Property Tax: Its History, Administration, and Economic Impact*, ed. C. G. Benson, S. Benson, H. McClelland, and P. Thompson (Claremont, Calif.: College Press, 1965), p. 24.
14. E. R. A. Seligman, *Essays in Taxation*, 9th ed. (New York: Macmillan, 1923), p. 24.
15. U.S. Bureau of the Census, *Historical Statistics of the United States: Colonial Times to 1970*, Bicentennial ed., pt. 2 (Washington, D.C.: U.S. Government Printing Office, 1975), p. 1133.
16. Calculated from the data in U.S. Bureau of the Census, *Local Government Finances in Selected Metropolitan Areas and Large Counties: 1969–70*, GF 70, no. 6 (Washington, D.C.: U.S. Government Printing Office, 1970), p. 7; U.S. Bureau of the Census, *Local Government Finances in Selected Metropolitan Areas and Large Counties: 1974–75*, GF 75, no. 6 (Washington, D.C.: U.S. Government Printing Office, 1976), p. 7.
17. U.S. Bureau of the Census, *2002 Census of Governments*, vol. 4, no. 4, *Finances of Municipal and Township Governments*, 2002, Table 1 (*http://www.census.gov/prod/2005pubs/gc024x4.pdf*).

18. Ibid; also *2002 Census of Governments,* vol. 4, no. 5, *Compendium of Government Finances,* 2002, Table 4.

19. George Peterson, "Finance," in *The Urban Predicament,* ed. William Gorham and Nathan Glazer (Washington, D.C.: The Urban Institute, 1976), p. 52.

20. Ibid., p. 53.

21. Karen de Sa, "Santa Clara County Assessor Warns of Dramatic Plunge in Home Values, Lowered Taxes to Result," *MercuryNews.com* (*http://www.mercurynews.com/ci_12068004?source*).

22. Patrik Jonsson, "As Home Values Fall, Property Tax Revolt Brews," *The Christian Science Monitor,* April 2, 2009 (*http://features.csmonitor.com/economyrebuild/2009/04/02*).

23. Alfred Balk, *The Free List—Property Without Taxes* (New York: Russell Sage Foundation, 1971), pp. 10–12.

24. J. Richard Aronson and John L. Hilley, *Financing State and Local Governments,* 4th ed. (Washington, D.C.: Brookings Institution Press, 1986), p. 136.

25. Helen F. Ladd and John Yinger, *America's Ailing Cities: Fiscal Health and the Design of Urban Policy,* updated ed. (Baltimore: Johns Hopkins University Press, 1989), pp. 129–130, 180. See also Michael Wolkoff, "Municipal Tax Abatement: A Two-Edged Sword," *New York Case Studies in Public Management* 4 (Albany, N.Y.: Rockefeller Institute of Government, 1984).

26. Gregory H. Wassall, *Tax-Exempt Property: A Case Study of Hartford, Connecticut* (Hartford, Conn.: John C. Lincoln Institute, 1974), p. 27.

27. Todd Swanstrom, *Capital Cities: Challenges and Opportunities* (Albany, N.Y.: Rockefeller Institute of Government), p. 17.

28. Michael J. Barrett, "The Out-of-Towners," *Boston Globe Magazine,* August 7, 1983.

29. *Walz v. Tax Commission of the City of New York,* 397 U.S. 664 (1970). See also Boris I. Bittker, "Churches, Taxes and the Constitution," *Yale Law Review* 78 (July 1969): 1285–1310.

30. John L. Mikesell, "The Season of Tax Revolt," in *Fiscal Retrenchment and Urban Policy,* ed. John P. Blair and David Nachmias (Beverly Hills, Calif.: Sage, 1979), p. 109.

31. Ibid.

32. Ladd and Yinger, *America's Ailing Cities,* p. 54. Surprisingly, local sales taxes have an even worse export ratio than property taxes.

33. Pagano, *City Fiscal Conditions in 2002,* p. 3.

34. Ibid.

35. Michael A. Pagano, *City Fiscal Conditions in 2002: A Research Report on America's Cities* (Washington, D.C.: National League of Cities, 2002), p. 3.

36. Christopher Swope, "The Retail Chase: Cities will do almost anything to land the store of their dreams," *Governing,* April 2007, p. 28.

37. Kenneth Thomas, *Competing for Capital; Europe and North America in a Global Era* (Georgetown University Press, 2000), as cited in Rachel Weber, "What Makes a Good Economic Development Deal?" in Richard M. McGahey and Jennifer S. Vey, ed., Retooling for Growth: Rebuilding a 21st Century Economy in America's Older Industrial Areas (Washington, D.C.: Brookings Institution Press, 2008), p. 284.

38. Donald Bartlett and James Steele, "Corporate Welfare," *Time,* November 9, 1998, as quoted in ibid., p. 284.

39. Christiana McFarland, "State of America's Cities Survey: Local Retail Slowdown," Research Brief on America's Cities, by National League of Cities, Issue 2009-2 (*http://www.nlc.org*).

40. Ibid., p. 20.

41. Michael A. Pagano, *City Fiscal Conditions in 1991: A Research Report of the National League of Cities* (Washington, D.C.: National League of Cities, 1991), p. 24.

42. David Segal, "Cities Turn to Fees to Fill Budget Gaps," *New York Times,* April 10, 2009 (*http://www.nytimes.com/2009/04/11/busines/11fees.html*).

43. Michael Powell and Christine Haughney, "Wary of Taxes, Officials Boost Fees; Tactic Hurts Poor and Working Class, Critics Say," *Washington Post,* April 7, 2003, p. A3.

44. City of New York, "Adopted Budget Fiscal Year 2007: Expense Revenue Contract" (*http://www.nyc.gov/html/omb/pdf/erc7_06.pdf*); City of Los Angeles, "Budget for the Fiscal Year 2006–2007," p. 26 (*http://www.lacity.org/cao/bud2006-07/Proposed_Budget_2006–07.pdf*); for Chicago, 2007 Line Item Budget—Budget Summaries, Summary F (*http://www.ci.chi.il.us/webportal/COCWebPortal/COC_EDITORIAL/03_Summary_Tablels.pdf*).

45. Gary Washburn, "City Maps Long-term Homeless Program," *Chicago Tribune*, January 22, 2003, p. 3.

46. Larry C. Ledebur and William R. Barnes, *City Distress: Metropolitan Disparities and Economic Growth* (Washington, D.C.: National League of Cities, 1991), pp. 2, 6. Figures based on the 85 largest metropolitan areas.

47. Jonathan Kozol, *Rachel and Her Children: Homeless Families in America* (New York: Crown, 1988), p. 14.

48. Roy Bahl, Jorge Martinez, and Loren Williams, "The Fiscal Conditions of U.S. Cities at the Beginning of the 1990s," Urban Institute Conference on Big City Governance and Fiscal Choices, Los Angeles, June 1991, pp. 5–6.

49. *Garcia v. San Antonio Metropolitan Transit Authority,* 469 U.S. 528 (1985).

50. Employment Standards Administration, *Minimum Wage and Maximum Hours Standards Under the Fair Labor Standards Act* (Washington, D.C.: U.S. Environmental Protection Agency, 1986), pp. 110–111; U.S. Congress, House Committee on Education and Labor, *Report to Accompany H.R. 3530,* 99th Cong., 1st sess., 1985. H. Rept. 99–331, p. 30; both cited in Joseph F. Zimmerman, "Federally Induced State and Local Governmental Costs," paper delivered at the annual meeting of the American Political Science Association, Washington, D.C., August 29–September 1, 1991, p. 14.

51. Todd Sloane, "Clean Air Act Likely to Burn Many Municipalities," *City and State*, November 19, 1990, p. 2, cited in Zimmerman, "Federally Induced State and Local Government Costs," p. 12.

52. Alan Greenblatt, "The Washington Offensive," *Governing* 19, no. 1 (January 2005): 27.

53. Ladd and Yinger, *America's Ailing Cities,* p. 291.

54. Bonds issued not only by cities but also by states and all local governments are referred to as municipal bonds, a cause of endless confusion.

55. U.S. Bureau of the Census, *2002 Census of Governments,* vol. 4, no. 5, *Compendium of Government Finances,* 2002, Table 13.

56. *South Carolina v. Baker,* 108 S.Ct. 1935 (1988).

57. Alberta Sbragia, "Finance Capital and the City," in *Cities in Stress: A New Look at the Urban Crisis,* ed. M. Gottdiener (Beverly Hills, Calif.: Sage, 1986), p. 210.

58. See Robert Huefner, *Taxable Alternatives to Municipal Bonds, Research Report No. 53* (Boston: Federal Reserve Bank of Boston, 1972); and *Building a Broader Market: Report of the Twentieth Century Fund Task Force on the Municipal Bond Market,* with a background paper by Ronald W. Forbes and John E. Peterson (New York: McGraw-Hill, 1976).

59. For insightful discussions of the powerful role of local authorities, see Ann Marie Hauck Walsh, *The Public's Business: The Politics and Practices of Government Corporations* (Cambridge, Mass.: MIT Press, 1978); and Alberta M. Sbragia, *Debt Wish: Entrepreneurial Cities, U.S. Federalism, and Economic Development* (Pittsburgh: University of Pittsburgh Press, 1996).

60. U.S. Bureau of the Census, *2002 Census of Governments,* vol. 4, no. 2, *Finances of Special District Governments,* 2002, Table 10 (*http://www.census.gov/prod/2005pubs/gc024x2.pdf*).

61. Elaine B. Sharp, "The Politics and Economics of the New City Debt," *American Political Science Review* 80, no. 4 (December 1986): 1271–1288.

62. U.S. Bureau of the Census, *Statistical Abstract of the United States* (Washington, D.C.: U.S. Government Printing Office, 1992), p. 285.

63. Thomas A. Pascarella and Richard D. Raymond, "Buying Bonds for Business: An Evaluation of the Industrial Revenue Bond Program," *Urban Affairs Quarterly* 18 (September 1982): 73–89.

64. Daphne A. Kenyon and Dennis Zimmerman, "Private-Activity Bonds and the Volume Cap in 1990," *Intergovernmental Perspective* 17, no. 3 (Summer 1991): 35–37.

65. For citations on municipal bond corruption, see Sbragia, *Debt Wish*, pp. 224–225.

66. Leslie Wayne, "Ban on Political Contributions Considered for Bond Lawyers," *New York Times*, August 5, 1996, p. D2.

67. Peter Truell, "Municipal Bond Dealers Face Scrutiny," *New York Times*, December 17, 1996, p. D1; Michael R. Lissack, "A Giant Shell Game Snares Taxpayers," *Albany Times Union*, August 1, 1996, p. A11.

68. "Shine the Light on Muni Deals," *BusinessWeek*, August 26, 1996.

69. Mary Williams, "Bond Advice Leaves Pain in Its Wake," *New York Times*, February 16, 2009 (*http://www.nytimes.com/2009/02/17/business/17muni.html*).

70. Don Van Natta Jr., "Firm Acted as Tutor in Selling Towns Risky Deals," *New York Times*, April 7, 2009 (*http://www.nytimes.com/2009/04/08/us/08bond.html*).

71. Mary Williams Walsh, "Nationwide Inquiry on Bids for Municipal Bonds," *New York Times*, January 8, 2009 (*http://www.nytimes.com/2009/01/09/business/09insure.html*).

72. Thomas Geis, "Municipal Credit and Bond Rating System," paper delivered at the Municipal Officers Association Meeting, Denver, May 31, 1972, pp. 5–6.

73. Ibid.

74. U.S. Advisory Commission on Intergovernmental Relations, *City Financial Emergencies* (Washington, D.C: U.S. Government Printing Office, 1971), p. 10.

75. Ibid., p. 12.

76. Ibid., p. 16.

77. Ibid., p. 17.

78. Ibid., pp. 81–82.

79. Todd Swanstrom, *The Crisis of Growth Politics: Cleveland, Kucinich, and the Challenge of Urban Populism* (Philadelphia: Temple University Press, 1985), Chapter 7.

80. Peter Eisenger, "The Politics of Bread and Circuses," *Urban Affairs Review* 35, no. 3 (January 2000): 316–333.

81. For a detailed account of these complex processes, see Bernard J. Frieden and Lynne B. Sagalyn, *Downtown Inc.* (Cambridge, Mass.: MIT Press, 1989).

82. Jon Teaford, *The Rough Road to Renaissance: Urban Revitalization in America, 1940–1985* (Baltimore: Johns Hopkins University Press, 1990), p. 307.

83. These arrangements are described in Peter K. Eisenger, *The Rise of the Entrepreneurial State: State and Local Economic Development Policy in the United States* (Madison: University of Wisconsin Press, 1988).

84. James Leigland, "Public Infrastructure and Special Purposed Governments: Who Pays and How?" in *Building the Public City: The Politics, Governance, and Finance of Public Infrastructure*, ed. David C. Perry (Thousand Oaks, Calif.: Sage, 1995), p. 139.

85. State of Illinois, Compliance Audit Report (1998 and 1999; *http://www.state.il.us/auditor*).

86. William Fulton, "Paying the Bill," *Governing* 15, no. 11 (August 2002): 60.

87. Donald F. Norris, "If We Build It, They Will Come! Tourism-Based Economic Development in Baltimore," in Judd, *The Infrastructure of Play*, p. 162.

88. Ibid., p. 151.

89. Susan E. Clarke and Martin Saiz, "From Waterhole to World City: Place Luck and Public Agendas in Denver," in Judd, *The Infrastructure of Play*, pp. 183–184.

90. Rachel Weber, "Equity and Entrepreneurialism: The Impact of Tax Increment Financing on School Finance," *Urban Affairs Review* 38, no. 5 (2003): 619–644.

91. Eric Klinenberg, *Heat Wave: A Social Autopsy of Disaster in Chicago* (Chicago: University of Chicago Press, 2002), p. 9.

92. Paul Peterson, *City Limits* (Chicago: University of Chicago Press, 1981), p. 22.

THE FALL AND RISE
OF THE INNER CITIES

AN URBAN RENAISSANCE

By the beginning of the twenty-first century, it became clear that most central cities were on the rebound. Downtown business districts and entertainment/tourist districts drew people from throughout metropolitan areas and elsewhere. City neighborhoods also seemed to be undergoing a renaissance. An informal *New York Times* survey of nine cities (Boston, Chicago, Houston, Los Angeles, Miami, New York, San Antonio, San Diego, and Washington, D.C.) conducted in 2000 found that as a result of the declining crime rates of the 1990s, businesses and new residents began pouring into neighborhoods previously considered off limits. Displacement of poorer residents was no doubt occurring, but the quality of life for long-term residents had improved.[1] Within a few years, it became apparent that inner-city revitalization in many places had reached a critical threshold, so that it was unlikely to be reversed even in the circumstance of an economic crisis like the one that begun to unfold in 2008. However, a few cities where the downtown comeback has been shaky, such as Detroit, may reach a tipping point from which they cannot recover.[2]

Most American central cities experienced at least some degree of downtown development and neighborhood gentrification, a process wherein affluent professionals and young people were moving into neighborhoods previously occupied by the working class or poor. From 1990 to 2000, downtown populations increased in 18 of 24 cities studied by the Fannie Mae Foundation and the Brookings Institution.[3] Although the number of new downtown residents was quite small in some cities, even modest growth represented a historic turnaround. Some cities that had been losing population for a half century gained in the 1990s, and even the few that continued to lose population did so at a reduced rate.[4] The recovery was uneven. Some cities were still in fragile condition, but for most, the signs were pointing in the right direction.

The revival of downtowns can be traced to two major developments, both of them tied to the processes of globalization. First, downtowns were becoming the centers of businesses connected to a new global economy centered around electronic trade and commerce, telecommunications, finance, marketing, and corporate services. Cities that have tied themselves most closely to the global economy of high-level services have done the best, especially in downtown areas, but even smaller places have followed the trend.[5] Second, tourism/entertainment, culture, and urban amenities were becoming clustered in and near downtown areas. Jobs are connected to amenities; the affluent residents who live downtown want to commute less but also prefer to live in an environment with exciting street life, nightlife, culture, and entertainment. With their historic architecture, public monuments, redeveloped waterfronts, and older neighborhoods, cities are uniquely positioned to provide an exciting urban culture. For the first time in decades, cities seem to be indispensable to the future of their metropolitan regions.

OUTTAKE

BALTIMORE'S REVITALIZATION IS DEBATED

Called the "Cinderella city of the 1980s," Baltimore is one of the nation's best-known examples of a downtown development strategy that emphasizes tourism and entertainment. Because of its size and proximity to New York City and Washington, D.C., Baltimore was not likely to attract a concentration of global corporations, so it focused singularly on tourism and entertainment. In its heyday Baltimore's inner harbor was a thriving center of commerce, but by the 1960s it was an eyesore composed of rotting, rat-infested piers, abandoned buildings, and desolate parking lots, perched on a harbor that smelled, in the writer H. L. Mencken's words, "like a million polecats." The audacious idea was to transform this blighted mess into a national tourist attraction.

The linchpin of the plan to redevelop the Inner Harbor was Harborplace, anchored by two translucent pavilions enclosing a festival mall designed by the developer James Rouse. Rouse intended to create "a warm and human place, with diversity of choice, full of festival and delight." Completed in 1980, Harborplace succeeded beyond anyone's expectations, attracting 18 million visitors the first year, earning $42 million, and creating 2,300 jobs. In 1981 the National Aquarium was completed, giving the Inner Harbor a distinct and highly visible tourist attraction. By 1992 more than 15 million visitors had toured the aquarium's exhibits, including a 64-foot glass pyramid housing a reproduction of a South American rain forest.

The success of the Inner Harbor development and other projects in the downtown unleashed a surge of private investment in downtown Baltimore. Between 1980 and 1986, the number of visitors and the amount of money they spent tripled; to accommodate the increased demand, the number of hotel rooms also tripled. The city's job development programs succeeded in placing 1,300 persons in jobs at Harborplace in just six years, and more than 40 percent of the Harborplace workforce was drawn from minorities. By 1990 the Inner Harbor and nearby projects had created an estimated thirty thousand new jobs directly and indirectly; later a study estimated that visitors to Baltimore spent $847 million in just one year, 1998, which supported a visitor-related payroll of $266 million and generated $81 million in state and local taxes.

The energizing force behind Baltimore's redevelopment was Donald Schaefer, who served four terms as the city's mayor from 1971 to 1987. The city's renaissance made him into a national political figure. In 1984 he was hailed as "The Best Mayor in America." In November 1986, Schaefer rode the wave of positive publicity about Baltimore's redevelopment into the Maryland governor's mansion. But the drumbeat of good news about the city's downtown revival overlooked the conditions in the city's deteriorating neighborhoods. Kurt Schmoke, who succeeded Schaefer as Baltimore's first black mayor in 1987, observed, "If you were revisiting Baltimore today after a 20-year absence, you would find us much prettier and much poorer."

In actuality there are two Baltimores, one inhabited by suburban workers and visitors, the other by poor people who live in the slums. Revitalization in the downtown and at the harbor did not stop the hemorrhaging of the city's population, which fell by 135,000 people from 1980 to 2000, to 651,000. Despite a continued recovery, by 2007 the city population had fallen further, to 637,000. Meanwhile, the suburbs continued to grow, and the suburbs continued to attract more and better jobs: In 1950 the city's residents made slightly more than the residents of surrounding suburbs, but by 2000 they made half as much.

This profile raises important questions about Baltimore's version of downtown revitalization: Have public dollars been wisely spent? Is development that focuses on tourism and entertainment misguided? There are opposing answers to these questions. According to one critic, the glitter of Inner Harbor hides the problems in the rest of the city:

> [T]he Inner Harbor functions as a sophisticated mask. It invites us to participate in a spectacle, to enjoy a festive circus that celebrates the coming together of people and commodities. Like any mask, it can beguile and distract in engaging ways, but at some point we want to know what lies behind it. If the mask cracks or is violently torn off, the terrible face of Baltimore's impoverishment may appear.

But there is an opposing view. Tangible benefits have accrued because of Baltimore's strategy, including the creation of jobs, an improving tax base (but not enough to offset losses in other parts of the city), and the physical reconstruction of an important part of the city. Without the downtown redevelopment, nothing else would have been happening in the rest of Baltimore anyway. Finally, no city is in a position to overcome the large-scale social factors that have brought about the move to the suburbs and the decay of the inner cities.

Will the real Baltimore please stand up?

Sources: Neal R. Peirce, Robert Guskind, and John Gardner, "Politics Is Not the Only Thing That Is Changing America's Big Cities," *National Journal* 22 (November 26, 1983): 2480; Tony Hiss, "Annals of Place: Reinventing Baltimore," *New Yorker,* April 29, 1991, p. 62; Christoper Corbett, "What's Doing in Baltimore," *New York Times,* February 23, 1992; Bernard L. Berkowitz, "Rejoinder to Downtown Redevelopment as an Urban Growth Strategy: A Critical Appraisal of the Baltimore Renaissance," *Journal of Urban Affairs* 9, no. 2 (1987): 129; Donald F. Norris, "If We Build It, They Will Come! Tourism-Based Economic Development in Baltimore," in *The Infrastructure of Play,* ed. Dennis R. Judd (Armonk, N.Y.: M. E. Sharpe, 2003), pp. 150–151; Richard C. Hula, "The Two Baltimores," in *Leadership and Urban Regeneration: Cities in North America and Europe,* ed. Dennis Judd and Michael Parkinson (Thousand Oaks, Calif.: Sage, 1990); David Harvey, *Spaces of Capital: Towards a Critical Geography* (New York: Routledge, 2001), pp. 143–144.

THE DECLINE OF DOWNTOWN

The distribution of economic activities in the nation has changed fundamentally over the past 100 years. In the late nineteenth and early twentieth centuries, cities prospered as centers of manufacturing production. Railroad connections made it possible to transport raw materials into industrial cities and ship the finished products to markets around the world. Large factories, by employing the new energy sources of steam and electricity, reaped the benefits of economies of scale as the new techniques of mass production were perfected. These factories required thousands of workers. As the center of the nation's economic production, cities, with their concentrations of immigrant workers, burst at the seams.

By the mid-nineteenth century the term *downtown* came into common usage to differentiate the commercial district at the southern end of Manhattan from "uptown," the mostly residential areas a few blocks north. Through the years "downtown" came to refer to the central commercial areas of cities everywhere. Downtown was where street railways converged, where the buildings were tall, where retailing and professional businesses were closely packed, and where crowds of people jostled one another on the streets. Downtown was busy and crowded; restaurants were packed full at lunchtime. Writers in the popular press and in novels were fascinated by downtown because it seemed to be a microcosm representing the tremendous energy and anarchy of the American economy and social system.[6]

Downtowns became steadily more densely crowded in the first decades of the twentieth century. They were extremely compact, covering one square mile in Chicago by the end of the 1920s, and less than a square mile in St. Louis, Los Angeles, Boston, and Detroit, and even less area in most other cities.[7] Nearly all banks, public utilities, law firms, advertising agencies, accounting firms, and the head offices of large industrial corporations were clustered downtown, as were virtually all department stores and most other large retailing establishments.[8] Taller and taller buildings allowed the downtowns to grow up rather than out. The specialized nature of these buildings, devoted as they were strictly to commerce and professional activities, replaced the smaller buildings that had provided spaces for a mixture of commercial, professional, and residential uses. As a result, by the 1920s the phrase "central business district" gained currency. Although generally used interchangeably with "downtown," the phrase accurately reflected the sharply defined separation between different land uses that became a hallmark of urban development.[9]

By the twentieth century, downtown had become "an idealized public place and thus a powerful symbol" of American culture—a place where people of all backgrounds mingled, a "turf common to all."[10] But even in the 1920s, at a time when downtowns were livelier than ever before, they began to lose their status as centers of goods production, wholesale trade, and retail sales. Chain retailers began opening stores closer to their customers in the suburbs, a step signaling the gradual deconcentration of retailing. Small business districts began to sprout up that competed with downtown, a process aided by the automobile. Bigger troubles came with the depression of the 1930s. Businesses closed their doors; older buildings fell into disrepair and decay.[11]

The Great Depression laid bare a truth that had escaped much notice in the prosperous decades of the 1920s. Within metropolitan areas, a spatial restructuring had been taking place for a long time. Manufacturing was beginning a slow exodus to the suburbs. The development of highways and truck transportation enabled factories to move to the periphery of metropolitan areas and beyond, especially to locations with convenient connections to interstate highways. Modern mass production requires large amounts of inexpensive land for one-story assembly-line production methods. With the range of commuting made possible by the automobile, factories could locate at a distance from residential centers and still be accessible to workers.

Shopping districts had also begun to compete with downtowns. In the 1950s cities were still the centers of retail trade. The large downtown department stores offered the best selection and prices, and middle-class shoppers took mass transit downtown to shop. But over the next decade suburban development and the automobile killed downtown shopping. By the 1960s suburban shopping centers had begun to eclipse central business districts. With big parking lots and freeway interchanges nearby, the shopping centers and their later incarnation, the malls, were more convenient for shoppers, who had by now completely abandoned mass transit for the automobile.

These trends were accelerated by the civil rights protests, racial violence, and riots of the 1960s. When downtowns became stigmatized as threatening and dangerous places, the white women shoppers who drove retail sales escaped to the quiet atmosphere of shopping centers far away from the much-publicized turmoil.[12] Suburban developers seized the opportunity to create an ambiance that contrasted sharply with city streets. In 1956 the first enclosed, climate-controlled mall, Southdale, opened in the Minneapolis suburb of Edina. By making shopping comfortable all year round, it was an instant success.[13] Mall owners created a leisurely environment conducive to consumption, including common hours for stores, directories and uniform signs, and benches and landscaping. By comparison, downtown shopping seemed chaotic and inconvenient, and sometimes even menacing. By 1974, 15,000 shopping centers had captured more than 44 percent of the nation's retail sales.[14] Downtown department stores began to close for good. Hudson's, a longtime landmark in Detroit, finally closed its doors in 1981.[15]

What was left of inner-city economies crashed in the 1970s. The events of the next two decades introduced a new tongue-twister into the English language, *deindustrialization*, a word invented to refer to the rapid restructuring of urban economies. Technological advances in production processes, such as the use of robots for assembly, made it possible to produce goods with far fewer workers than in the past. Between 1970 and 1988, although the volume of production increased, the nation's manufacturing employment remained stable at 19 million jobs. Deindustrialization also occurred because factories left urban regions; indeed, many left the United States entirely. Manufacturers also moved out of older metropolitan areas to such places as the Caribbean, Latin America, and Asia, where wages were much lower and environmental regulations were lax.[16] Metropolitan areas that had grown up around manufacturing slid into a sharp, sometimes shocking decline, with unemployment rates rising, in some cases, to 20 percent of the workforce. The situation for inner cities seemed even more precarious. Having absorbed one blow after the other, and now facing this final calamity, it was not clear that downtowns had any future whatsoever.

GLOBALIZATION AND THE DOWNTOWN RENAISSANCE

Though it was difficult to see at first, the dark clouds of deindustrialization had a silver lining. The loss of manufacturing was accompanied by a rapid rise in the number of service jobs. From 1975 to 1990, 30 million new jobs were created in service industries, so by the end of the 1980s, 84 million people were employed in services, as compared to 25 million in goods production.[17] Almost 80 percent of employment growth in the 1980s came in the form of service jobs.[18]At the same time that factory workers found their jobs disappearing, new opportunities opened up for educated white-collar workers. As shown in Table 13.1, in seven northeastern and midwestern metropolitan areas, the percentage of jobs in the manufacturing sector fell from 32 to 12 percent in the 40 years from 1960 to 2000. The largest gains came in services, which grew from 15 percent of local employment to 36 percent over the same period. Wholesale/retail and finance, insurance, and real estate remained about the same. The changing profile of employment in urban economies reflected the large-scale changes ushered in by globalization. And the new services economy pointed the way toward a strategy for reviving the inner cities and their downtowns.

It took some time, but by the mid-1970s, civic leaders finally came to the conclusion that central cities could not compete head to head with suburbs for manufacturing, retailing, and wholesaling. Those sectors had already become highly decentralized, and it was unlikely that this pattern could be changed. If central cities were going to come back, they would have to chart a new direction. Service-sector jobs in finance, corporate employment, and tourism pointed the way. A generation of "messiah mayors" preaching a gospel of self-help for their downtowns led the way in experimenting with new methods of fostering local development by using public funds to leverage private investment in office towers, malls, and tourist and entertainment facilities.[19] Cities offered property tax breaks, often over many years; used eminent domain to assemble land for new development; and created tax increment finance districts (TIFs) and business improvement districts (BIDs) as a way of improving the environment for investment.

Table 13.1   Change in Job Categories in Seven Northeastern and Midwestern Metropolitan Areas, 1960–2000

	Percentage Employed in Each Category				
	1960	**1970**	**1980**	**1990**	**2000**
Manufacturing	32%	26%	21%	14%	12%
Transportation, communications, and public utilities	8	7	6	5	5
Wholesale and retail trade	21	21	21	22	20
Finance, insurance, and real estate	7	7	8	9	8
Services	15	19	24	31	36
Government	13	16	17	16	14

Source: U.S. Department of Labor, Bureau of Labor Statistics, *Earnings and Employment* (Washington, D.C.: U.S. Government Printing Office, 1960, 1970, 1980, 1990, and 2000).

TIFs, BIDs, and other development authorities were extremely important because they were able to raise large amounts of capital for public improvements and direct subsidies to businesses by issuing tax-free bonds to investors. The bonds are paid off (over 30 or 40 years) by the increased volume of taxes expected from future development. Other special authorities, such as convention and visitors' bureaus, mall authorities, sports authorities, museum districts, and the like, financed public improvements or new facilities by charging users fees (admission to events, for example), issuing bonds (to be paid by users fees), and gaining access to designated taxes. Through such mechanisms, large amounts of money were raised for the remaking of downtown areas.

A downtown renaissance began to take shape. In addition to new office buildings and refurbished business districts, by the mid-1980s many mayors could brag about their "trophy collection," which (when complete) included at least one luxury hotel (preferably one with a multistory atrium), a new sports stadium (usually domed), a downtown shopping mall, a redeveloped waterfront, and a new convention center.[20] These facilities constituted the infrastructure necessary for cities to become centers of corporate white-collar employment, entertainment, culture, and a burgeoning tourism and convention trade.

The data in Table 13.2 show that downtown populations increased in cities in all regions of the nation, from the old industrial heartland to the Sunbelt. Some cities

Table 13.2   Downtowns That Grew in the 1990s (18 Selected Cities)

City	1990 Downtown	2000 Downtown	Population Change	Percentage Change
Atlanta	19,763	24,731	4,968	25%
Baltimore	28,597	30,067	1,470	5
Boston	75,823	79,251	3,428	4.5
Chicago	27,760	42,039	14,279	51
Cleveland	7,261	9,599	2,338	32
Colorado Springs	13,412	14,377	965	7
Des Moines	4,190	4,204	14	0.03
Denver	2,794	4,230	1,436	51
Detroit	5,970	6,141	171	3
Houston	7,029	11,882	4,853	69
Los Angeles	34,655	36,630	1,975	6
Memphis	7,606	8,994	1,388	18
Milwaukee	10,973	11,243	270	2.5
Norfolk, VA	2,390	2,881	491	20.5
Philadelphia	74,655	78,349	3,694	5
Portland, OR	9,528	12,902	3,374	35
San Diego	15,417	17,894	2,477	16
Seattle	9,824	16,443	6,619	67

Sources: Adapted from Rebecca R. Sohmer and Robert E. Lang, *Downtown Rebound* (Washington, D.C.: Brookings Institution Press, Fannie Mae Foundation, 2001), pp. 2–3; also see Rebecca R. Sohmer and Robert E. Lang, "Downtown Rebound," in *Redefining Urban & Suburban America: Evidence from Census 2000,* ed. Bruce Katz and Robert E. Lang (Washington, D.C.: Brookings Institution Press, 2003), pp. 63–74.

(such as Atlanta, Baltimore, Boston, Chicago, Los Angeles, and Philadelphia) built on a downtown population base that was already substantial in 1990 (ranging from 19,763 in Atlanta to 75,823 in Boston). Other cities (such as Cleveland, Denver, Detroit, Houston, Memphis, and Norfolk) attracted new residents to downtown populations that were small in 1990 (in all cases about 7,500 or less). The total number of people who moved into the downtown areas of these cities during the 1990s tended to be small, but the newcomers nevertheless brought dramatic effects. New condominium and apartment towers sprung up; restaurants, bars, and personal service businesses opened. The decades-long flight from the urban core seemed to have come to an end.

The economic sectors that led the revitalization of downtown comprised the components of a new globalized economy that revolved around high-level corporate and professional services, telecommunications, and technology. Globalization has been facilitated by technologies that make information exchange nearly instantaneous and by the ability of corporations to manage operations in many places at once. Since the 1980s corporations have been growing larger through mergers and buyouts. Large firms are able to coordinate activities on a global scale—the movement of capital investment, the location of factories, and the distribution and marketing of products. The innovations required by modern corporations in product design, advertising, the adoption of new technologies, and corporate organization are made possible by frequent coordination among highly specialized professionals, most of whom do not work within a single organization. As a consequence, corporations prefer to locate in close proximity to other firms.

The skyscrapers that sprout from the downtowns of American cities are the physical manifestation of the clustering of economic activities in central cities. In the global era, corporations have located in downtowns and in edge cities and in office parks located in the suburbs. However, downtown areas have continued to attract the firms that benefit most from intense concentration. The management and control functions of corporations are disproportionately centralized in a network of cities that occupy strategic places in a global economy. In many cities across the United States, downtowns have been revitalized for the simple reason that many business concerns find it advantageous to be located next to one another. Especially (but not exclusively) in larger cities, high-level professional operations and information industries have become clustered into "strategic nodes with a hyperconcentration of activities"[21] supporting layer upon layer of highly educated, technologically sophisticated professionals offering specialized services—corporate managers, management consultants, legal experts, accountants, computer specialists, financial analysts, media and public relations consultants, and the like.

Corporate headquarters cluster most densely in a few global cities such as New York, Paris, London, Chicago, Los Angeles, Miami, Hong Kong, Sydney, and Tokyo.[22] Sitting atop the new urban hierarchy created by globalization, these cities house corporations that manage production and distribution networks around the world. The largest corporations, especially international banks, stock and commodity exchanges, and media empires, are located in global cities. Second-level cities, such as Montreal and Hamburg, may lay claim to a few international firms, but for the most part they house national and regional corporate systems. Further down the hierarchy, medium-sized cities such as Atlanta, Cleveland, and St. Louis are mainly the hubs of regional corporate networks. Down the pyramid further still are cities that depend on quite specialized activities such as an auto plant (Smyrna, Tennessee), a cluster of electronics software firms (San Jose, California), or a meatpacking plant (Beardstown, Illinois). In these ways even small places are tied to the global economy. Those that are not slip into irrreversible decline.[23]

The professionals who locate near or in downtown areas demand a high level of urban amenities, and this expectation has filtered down to include most urban dwellers. By the end of the 1990s, the successful downtowns and neighborhoods offered a unique "urban culture," a special mix of job opportunities and amenities that could not be found anywhere else: restaurants, blues and jazz clubs, art galleries, theaters and performance halls, and also the elements necessary for an exciting nightlife, such as bars, dance clubs, after-hours clubs, and coffee shops.[24] These cultural activities have great economic consequence for cities; without them, jobs directly connected to the global economy would go elsewhere because young professionals will not stay for long in dull places. In this way, economics and culture have become inseparable.

THE NEW URBAN CULTURE

The movement to downtowns has been driven by affluent young professionals known by a number of slang terms such as *yuppies* (young urban professionals), *dinks* (dual-income, no kids), and *jingles* (singles with joint living arrangements). White populations in the 24 downtowns studied by Fannie Mae and the Brookings Institution increased by 7.5 percent in the 1990s, a faster population growth than for blacks (6 percent) and Latinos (4.8 percent). By contrast, in neighborhoods outside downtown areas, white populations fell by 10.5 percent while black populations held almost steady (growing by 2.4 percent) and Latino populations virtually exploded (growing by 43 percent).[25]

There are two distinct tiers of service employment in the global economy. The upper tier includes jobs in business and financial services (white-collar professionals such as lawyers, accountants, investment brokers, and computer and communications specialists). The lower tier is composed of employment in food, retail, and personal services (such as those provided in restaurants, stores, Laundromats, and barbershops). The bifurcated labor force is reflected in the urban landscape. Affluent people live in downtown areas with high property values; outside of the downtown, there is a patchwork of gentrifying neighborhoods, some of them located near or even within poverty-stricken areas. What makes this patchwork pattern possible is the nature of the new development. The affluent middle class often live within condominium towers or gated communities, well protected from nearby blight.[26]

The professionals who have flocked into downtown and gentrifying neighborhoods, have driven up the cost of housing, sometimes to fantastic levels. New condominium towers and townhouse developments have become signifiers of urban regeneration, as have the renovation of old factory and warehouse buildings (some of them long abandoned) for retail and housing. The deteriorated neighborhoods located at and near the urban center have attracted a sometimes odd mixture of affluent yuppies, and artists and people with unconventional lifestyles who prefer an urbane over an orderly environment. Two characteristics have made these neighborhoods especially attractive—the presence of historic and architecturally significant buildings such as old Victorians and row houses, and their location near the central business district and amenities such as waterfronts, museums, parks, performing arts venues, sports stadiums, and nightlife.

The term *gentrification* has come into common usage as a shorthand way of referring to this process. The gentrification story line goes something like this: affluent newcomers drive up demand, bringing sharp increases in land values; as a result less affluent, minority, and older residents are forced to move. Property taxes escalate when land values rise; dilapidated property becomes subject to new standards of maintenance; and neighborhood institutions such as churches and schools close because families with children tend to be replaced by singles and childless couples.

Some gentrified neighborhoods are mainly residential, but more frequently they are composed of a mixture of housing, retail, and services establishments (especially hair salons, health clubs, cleaners, and coffeehouses). Within the neighborhood or close by are restaurants, exclusive shopping districts, parks, and cultural facilities. The character of gentrified neighborhoods is determined by work and lifestyle: "In their limited free time, yuppies and dinks tend to emphasize convenience over cost in making lifestyle decisions. A Chicago bank vice president in her early thirties explained that the time factor determines most of her dining decisions. To cook at home requires planning: one must first go to the store and shop, and when she gets home at eight o'clock it is too late to start. 'So we pick up the telephone, call a bunch of local restaurants and ask about the waiting times.'"[27]

A leading urban scholar, Richard Florida, has identified the rise of "the creative class" to explain the recent emphasis on tourism, culture, and entertainment. This class, which is composed of highly educated professionals with rarified intellectual, analytic, artistic, and creative skills, frequently regard lifestyle as more important than a particular job in choosing a place to live.[28] The members of this class demand social interaction, culture, nightlife, diversity, and authenticity, which became defined as "historic buildings, established neighborhoods, a unique music scene or specific cultural attributes. It comes from the mix—from urban grit alongside renovated buildings, from the commingling of young and old, long-time neighborhood characters and yuppies, fashion models and 'bag ladies.'"[29] Florida indicates that the creative class tends to reject the "canned experiences" associated with tourist enclaves. Instead, the creative class has become the basis for a new political movement that demands a high level of urban amenities, both public and private, in the downtowns and neighborhoods they frequent.[30] The result is a revival of the downtown and of inner-city neighborhoods after decades of decline.

TOURISM AND ENTERTAINMENT

Tourism, entertainment, and culture are crucial to downtown revival. The reasons are not difficult to uncover. Travel and tourism is the world's largest industry (measured by value added to investment).[31] Travelers and tourists spend huge amounts of money on lodging, food, entertainment and culture, transportation, souvenirs, and other services and products. Worldwide, about one-tenth of all jobs are generated by travel and tourism.[32] To remake themselves into places that tourists want to visit, cities have invested heavily in tourism facilities and the reconstruction of downtown environments. Indeed, the rebuilding of downtown areas to make them friendly for visitors has been so massive that this period of city-building can be compared to the building of the industrial city a century ago, when cities invested in mass transit systems, paved streets, sewer and water systems, and parks. The only other period of city-building on such a scale occurred in the 1950s and 1960s, with the urban renewal clearance projects.[33] In the latest phase, cities have built an expensive infrastructure essential to tourism and entertainment. Any city that does not have the full complement of facilities is at a disadvantage.

In Chicago, as in many cities, the leading industry is now tourism and entertainment. The number of tourists increased from 32 million in 1993 to 43 million in 1997, a product of indefatigable promotion and a huge investment in the infrastructure of tourism.[34] Chicago has built the world's largest convention center, an entertainment district on an old pier (Navy Pier), and has one of the world's most beautiful park systems, which runs for miles along the Lake Michigan lakefront. The city is host to several extraordinary museums and other attractions (such as the John G. Shedd Aquarium and the Adler Planetarium), maintains elaborate floral and garden displays along Michigan Avenue and on many other streets, and hosts dozens of events each year in the parks. Grant Park, which stretches between the downtown Loop and Lake Michigan, is the most visited park in the United States, attracting more visitors than even the Grand Canyon.[35] Chicago has a complex economy, but it would be in trouble without tourism.

In older cities, tourist entertainment venues have often been constructed on sites that were once devoted to manufacturing, warehousing, retailing, or harbor activities. These developments try to project a contrived, nostalgic, and idealized version of city life, and they do so by utilizing architectural features that define the historic city. For instance, South Street Seaport in New York strives to create an ambience evoked by "authentic reproductions" of a working harbor[36]—in effect, an urban miniversion of Disneyland (in Anaheim, California), with its Main Street, U.S.A., and Frontier Village. The examples abound: the Wharf and Ghirardelli Square in San Francisco and the renovated Union Stations everywhere (while the actual train stations are out of sight and sound).

Making older cities attractive to tourists was not an easy task. In the wake of the riots of the 1960s, downtowns became stigmatized as violent, dangerous places. Where crime, poverty, and urban decay made parts of a city inhospitable to visitors, specialized areas were built that were, in effect, tourist reservations. Such "tourist bubbles" made it possible for the tourist, who was unfamiliar with the local landscape, to move inside "secured, protected and normalized environments."[37] The aim was to create an illusory world within an otherwise alien or even hostile setting. But when crime rates began to fall in the 1990s and downtown office construction and gentrification took off, street life and urban culture became the objects of fascination and consumption for visitors. Where they have succeeded, cities have become, at least for some purposes, the true centers of their metropolitan regions, the home of activities, culture, and a lifestyle not easily imitated in the suburbs.[38] From coast to coast, in cities as different as Boston, San Francisco, Chicago, New York City, and Portland,

Oregon, visitors wandered and mingled freely with local residents. In fact, except in convention centers, it became harder to distinguish visitors from everyone else. The "localization of leisure turned cities into entertainment destinations not only for out-of-town visitors but also for suburban commuters and the growing number of affluent downtown residents."[39] Increasingly, local residents have become "as if tourists," acting like tourists even when they stay home.[40]

The infrastructure that makes central-city tourism possible includes convention centers, sports stadiums, festival malls and urban entertainment districts, cultural venues such as performing arts centers and museums, and, in a few cities, gaming casinos.[41] Especially in the case of convention centers and sports stadiums, public funding has often become a contentious issue, with proponents playing up the benefits associated with city marketing and economic growth, and opponents countering with charges that public support for such facilities is a case of misplaced priorities. But for mayors and other public officials, the economic benefits of city image-making, whether it involves expanding a convention center, building a new sports stadium, or improving a museum, is beyond dispute.

Convention Centers

Until the 1960s few cities had built the huge convention centers that are so prevalent in and near downtown areas today. For the most part, town halls doubled as assembly facilities, if any were needed. In the 1920s some cities built the first generation of meetings and exhibition halls; St. Louis, for example, built the St. Louis Arena in 1929 to accommodate an agricultural exhibit. During the Great Depression, the federal government, through the Public Works Administration, financed large public assembly and exhibition facilities in a number of cities. This generation of halls often contained one or more auditoriums as well as exhibition space under one roof, and in many cities these structures were not replaced until the 1980s or 1990s. These all-purpose facilities were expensive to operate and virtually always lost money, but they had the effect of attracting, and even helping to create, an array of traveling shows and exhibitions. The benefits to the local economy and to their own fortunes were soon comprehended by civic boosters, who then pushed for larger and better facilities.

In the 1950s a few cities began constructing a second generation of meeting halls in the form of convention centers built specifically for professional meetings and trade shows. The proliferation of convention centers began in the 1960s and accelerated in the 1970s as air travel, growing affluence, and greater specialization in the job market gave rise to more meetings, exhibitions, and consumer shows (such as autos, boats, and electronics), and conventions. In the 1980s cities began a virtual arms race for the convention trade, with even small towns joining the competition. More than 70 percent of the convention centers existing in 1998 had opened since 1970.[42] But the race had just begun. In the ten years from 1993 to 2003, capital spending for convention centers doubled, to $2.3 billion annually, and in the 13 years from 1990 to 2003 convention-center space increased by 51 percent. At least 40 cities were planning to build new facilities or expand the old ones. All this activity meant that the cost of each facility went up but the business would have to be divided among many contenders.[43]

All convention centers require annual subsidies for the payment of construction bonds and for operating costs, but escalating construction, maintenance, and promotion costs have not deterred cities from investing in larger and more elaborate convention facilities. Much is at stake. In 2002 there were nearly 23,000 associations and 6.5 million total private business establishments in the United States.[44] The 23,000-plus associations in the nation spent $32 billion for meetings in 1992, and corporations spent an additional $29 billion on off-premises meetings and conventions.[45] Tourism-related organizations alone had 1.4 million members in 1998, and the meetings industry produced $81 billion in economic output.[46] The average attendance at new exhibitions nearly quadrupled from 1990 to 1997.[47] Although only from 4 to 5 percent of meetings are held in convention centers,[48] the size of the meetings and convention business has been large enough to prompt hundreds of cities to build or expand their existing convention centers. Forty-one convention centers were being built or renovated in 2000, and 66 were slated for expansion or renovation.[49]

As more cities build and expand their facilities, the competition among cities has become extraordinarily intense. The top 15 cities in North America accounted for almost half of all conventions with exhibitions in 2000. But as shown in Table 13.3, even the city convention center that attracted the largest number of

Table 13.3 Top 16 North American Cities by Number of Exhibitions Hosted, 2000

City	Percentage Share
Orlando	4.7%
Toronto	4.6
Las Vegas	4.4
Chicago	3.7
New Orleans	3.4
Atlanta	3.2
Dallas	2.9
New York	2.6
San Diego	2.5
Washington, D.C.	2.5
Nashville	2.2
Denver	2.0
San Francisco	1.9
Anaheim	1.7
San Antonio	1.7
Boston	1.6

Source: Center for Exhibition Industry Research (CEIR), Press Release, February 27, 2002.

exhibitions—Orlando, Florida—accounted for just a 4.7 percent share. The 10th city on the list shown, Washington, D.C., attracted 2.5 percent of all exhibitions, and the city in 16th place, Boston, pulled 1.6 percent of the nation's exhibitions. As the number of cities competing for conventions increases, it becomes difficult for a particular city to increase its share of the nation's convention business. There is also a great deal of volatility because meeting planners are presented with a constantly growing range of options.

A convention facility is necessary for a city to enter the race, but obviously a lot of other factors determine a city's ability to compete successfully for meetings. In Orlando's case, obviously, nearby Disney World is the entire story. For other cities, such a singular magnet is rarely, if ever, available. Large cities, with their abundance of entertainment, cultural, and commercial attractions, remain the primary drawing cards for national and international conventions. Las Vegas has its own attractions because it has concentrated so exclusively upon entertainment. The publisher of *Tradeshow Week*, Adam Schaffer, commented that "Las Vegas is almost a nation unto itself. Everybody wants to go to Vegas—they want to go to a show, shop, etc., be entertained."[50] Of course visitors want the same in every city, so it is not sufficient to merely build a convention center and hotel. Cities must also construct an infrastructure and provide the amenities that meeting planners and their clients will find attractive.

By the 1980s virtually every major city in the United States had formed a convention and visitors bureau, and throughout that decade these increased rapidly in size. Convention bureaus construct lists of international, national, regional, and local associations that regularly sponsor or organize conventions. The bureaus send them promotional literature and frequently attend the meetings of these organizations, where they may stage rather elaborate promotional presentations or exhibits. Cities often invite representatives of the tourist industry and of important business and professional groups for a complimentary visit. In May 2003, for instance, the St. Louis Convention and Visitors Bureau hosted 4,000 professionals who were attending a meeting of the Travel Industry Association of America's Press Tour and Pow-Wow. The booths in the convention center were filled with representatives of rental and RV companies, hotels and hotel chains, airlines, and bus and cruise lines. States and cities set up booths as well.[51]

Despite such efforts, the St. Louis convention center failed to increase attendance significantly from 2000 to 2004. Meanwhile, the Renaissance Hotel, which had been built using funds from the city's empowerment zone, lost an estimated $2.4 million in 2004. Its low occupancy rate of 50 percent had already prompted Moody's Investment Service to put its bonds on a watch list.[52] St. Louis's experience was duplicated in many cities: a $5.3 million loss for Seattle's center and a $5 million loss for San Jose's in 2003. In a bid to get more business, convention center managers began offering special deals to lure more conventions, but these bargains virtually guaranteed that operating losses would be locked in. The Hawaii, Seattle, Columbus, Indianapolis, and Nashville centers have offered free rent for specified periods (through 2010 for Hawaii's). Dallas has offered a half-rent bargain, plus rebates for hotel use and discounts on airfare, shuttle service, and exhibit setup costs.[53]

Sports Stadiums

Civic boosters consider professional sports franchises pivotal to the economic revitalization of central cities and often have used sports facilities as an anchor for development.[54]
Cities compete vigorously for sports teams by helping finance the construction of stadiums and allowing owners to keep parking and concession fees and other revenues.
Because teams sometimes move or can threaten to, sports cartels and team owners have
usually been able to persuade cities to meet their demands. In the 1990s approximately
$10 billion in public funds were devoted to the building of sports facilities in urban
areas for major league professional teams.[55] Although earlier studies seemed to make a
convincing case that sports stadiums did not bring measurable benefits to local
economies, recent research shows that in many contexts they do.[56] One study indicated
that stadiums located in the downtown areas of six cities made a positive contribution
to the regional economy. A study of the Gund Arena and Jacobs Field in Cleveland
found that these facilities contributed to the economic redevelopment of downtown.[57]

It is important to add that the economic impacts are only part of a complex picture.
Sports teams have long been central to the civic and cultural life of American cities.
Oddly, the assumption that a team expresses a city's essence, spirit, and sense of community has not been much eroded since teams became highly mobile. Part of the reason
for this is that local boosters consider professional sports teams an absolutely essential
signifier of "big league" status. Sports teams carry a substantial emotional charge, so
their worth is rarely, if ever, calculated in simple economic terms. Through the national
and international publicity accompanying network broadcasts of games and playoffs,
professional sports teams are a powerful vehicle for conveying a city's image.

Professional sports is a big business. In 2006 five National League Franchises
were worth more than $1 billion, with the Washington Redskins leading the list at
$1.4 billion, and the New England Patriots at $1.78 billion. The Minnesota Vikings,
valued at $720 million, was last on the NFL list. The New York Yankees, the most valu-
able team in baseball, was also worth more than $1 billion.[58] National Basketball
Association (NBA) and professional hockey franchises could be bought for smaller
sums, making it possible, in some cases, for someone with an extra $100 to $200 million
available to bid for a team.[59] In Denver, Colorado, the four major professional sports
teams were valued at a total of $1.3 billion in 2002, which came out to more than
$500 per person in the metropolitan area.[60]

Sports teams are profitable, despite the claims of owners and the leagues that
many of them lose money. In 2002 baseball commissioner Bud Selig testified to Congress that major-league baseball generated an operating loss of $200 million that year,
but *Forbes* magazine produced figures showing a $75 million profit.[61] The escalation
of team values all through the previous decade made it a dubious claim that baseball
owners lost money. The lucrative media contracts for most baseball teams also made
the claim suspect.[62]

For decades, professional sports teams were so closely identified with their cities
of origin that moving would have been unthinkable. In baseball, this link was first
broken in 1953, when the Boston Braves relocated to Milwaukee. The baseball franchise relocation game began in earnest in 1957, when owner Walter O'Malley moved

the Brooklyn Dodgers to Los Angeles. O'Malley fought for years to find the land for a new stadium in Brooklyn to replace the decrepit Ebbets Field, which had opened in 1913. But he was repeatedly thwarted by Robert Moses, who, as head of New York's Bridge and Tunnel Authority, its Park Commission, Construction Commission, and Slum Clearance Committee, controlled the land needed for a new park.[63] To lure the Dodgers out of New York, Los Angeles agreed to renovate its minor-league stadium at Chavez Ravine and give the stadium to O'Malley. As the clincher, they offered him 300 acres of downtown Los Angeles real estate.[64] Considering the obstacles put in his way in Brooklyn, it would have been difficult for O'Malley to refuse the deal.

It did not take long for other owners to follow O'Malley's lead. Threats to move became potent weapons for prying more subsidies out of cities. Between 1953 and 1982, there were 78 franchise relocations in the four major professional sports: 11 in baseball, 40 in basketball, 14 in hockey, and 13 in football.[65] In just six years, from 1980 to 1986, more than half the cities with major-league sports franchises were confronted with demands for increased subsidies, with relocation an implied if not always explicit threat hanging over negotiations.[66] From 1980 to June 1992, an incredible amount of activity involved baseball and football teams. During this period, 20 cities sought baseball teams and 24 cities tried to attract football teams, an interesting statistic considering that there were, at that time, a total of 28 major-league baseball and 28 professional football franchises (two new expansion football franchises were added in 1993, with several cities competing for them). Eleven cities had completed or were building stadiums, and 28 more considered building or had plans to build stadiums. As shown in Table 13.4, new sports facilities were completed in the downtowns of 30 North American cities from 1990 to 2002. These were often the high-profile flagship projects of more comprehensive efforts at downtown development.[67] This impressive list includes cities from coast to coast and three cities in Canada. Approximately 50 minor-league and collegiate sports facilities also were completed in the 1990s.[68]

Table 13.4   North American Cities with New Downtown Sports Facilities, 1990–2002

Atlanta	Detroit	St. Louis
Baltimore	Houston	St. Paul
Boston	Indianapolis	Salt Lake City
Buffalo	Los Angeles	San Francisco
Charlotte	Miami	San Jose
Cincinnati	Montreal	Seattle
Cleveland	Nashville	Tampa
Columbus	New Orleans	Toronto
Dallas	Phoenix	Vancouver
Denver	Pittsburgh	Washington, D.C.

Source: Tim Chapin, "Beyond the Entrepreneurial City: Municipal Capitalism in San Diego," *Journal of Urban Affairs* 24, no. 5 (2003): 568.

Except for baseball, where teams move less frequently, moves have become an ever-present possibility for many cities, in part because they pay off for the owners. In the 1990s, for example, the Quebec Nordiques (a hockey team) moved from a small market to Denver, Colorado, and renamed themselves the Avalanche. In 1995, in their first season, they won the Stanley Cup for the first time. In 1996, when the NFL Cleveland Browns became the Baltimore Ravens, they signed a stadium deal that increased revenues substantially enough to allow them to pay big signing bonuses to key players. In 2001 they won the Super Bowl. Perhaps even more dramatically, the perennially losing Rams left Los Angeles (actually Anaheim) for St. Louis in 1995. An extraordinary stadium deal was the lure, and after four more losing seasons, the team won Super Bowl XXXIV in 2000.[69]

Because cities are desperate to get and keep a professional sports team, owners realize that public subsidies are theirs for the asking. From 1953 to 1986, 67 of the 94 stadiums used by professional sports teams were publicly owned.[70] Beginning in the early 1980s, the two most important new revenue sources for sports teams came from network broadcasting and local and state subsidies.[71] By the end of the 1980s, it had become a rare exception when an owner agreed to build a stadium with private dollars. Owners came to expect other subsidies as well, in the form of guaranteed attendance minimums, the construction of luxury boxes, and control of stadium merchandising.

As teams became more and more footloose, cities found themselves at a disadvantage. In an attempt to improve their poor bargaining positions, some cities built stadiums even when they did not have teams. In the 1980s Indianapolis built a football stadium, then persuaded the owner of the Baltimore Colts, Robert Irsay, to move. After the Maryland legislature passed an eminent domain law to make it possible for Baltimore to seize the Colts for public use, Irsay moved the team in the middle of the night. But probably the most famous case is the $139 million domed stadium built by St. Petersburg, Florida, in 1988 in the hopes of attracting a major-league baseball team. Called "heaven's waiting room," boosters justified the Florida Suncoast Dome as a way of changing the city's image as a conservative retirement community.[72] For years, the stadium remained the site of tractor pulls and concerts. In the 1990s St. Petersburg tried to lure several major-league baseball teams, including the Seattle Mariners, the San Francisco Giants, and a National League expansion team. When Florida won a baseball team in 1991, it was awarded to Miami. In October 1993 an expansion team of the NFL was awarded to Jacksonville; St. Petersburg's stadium was built expressly for baseball and would not have been suitable for football. St. Louis, which also put in a bid for one of the NFL expansion teams, lost out. St. Louis undertook the construction of a domed stadium anyway, many months before the negotiations that eventually brought the Los Angeles Rams to the city in 1995.

Stadiums require generous land, infrastructure, and direct public subsidies because almost all of them (but not usually the teams playing in them) lose money. Annual operating deficits are generally considerable; the New Orleans Superdome lost about $3 million a year during the 1980s, for example, compared to the annual $1 million loss for the Silverdome in Pontiac, Michigan. In its first year, the Florida Suncoast Dome lost $1.3 million, plus $7.7 million in debt payments.[73] Modern domed stadiums cost so much to build that they can rarely schedule enough events or charge enough for them to avoid operating deficits; the only one in the country without deficits in 2004 was the Metrodome in Minneapolis, which did not require a tax subsidy.[74] Toronto ended up paying $400 million for its domed stadium; St. Louis's domed stadium, completed in 1995, cost $301 million.[75] The costs have only escalated since. In September 2008 the Indianapolis Colts played their first football game in the Lucas Oil Stadium, built at the cost of $720 million. In the New York area, three teams were looking forward to playing in new stadiums. Work was proceeding on a $1.3 billion stadium for the Yankees, while just a few miles away, one costing $1.6 billion was being built for the Jets and Giants; both opened in 2009.[76]

It is undoubtedly true, as civic boosters argue, that the most important benefits of a major sports franchise are intangible and therefore impossible to measure solely in economic terms. However, as teams became more mobile and owners asked for more, such arguments began to wear thin. In December 1996 the owners of the Seattle Mariners baseball team put the team up for sale, even though the city had earlier bought land and made plans to construct a new ballpark. Just a few months earlier, Seattle's football team, the Seahawks, had threatened to leave town, and it too demanded a new stadium. Together, the two stadiums were estimated to cost $760 million. A group called Citizens for More Important Things initiated a campaign opposing public subsidies behind this slogan: "Just say no to welfare for the wealthy."

From 2000 to 2006, public funds supplied 54 percent of the construction cost for new major league baseball stadiums and 55 percent of the costs for football stadiums.[77] These subsidies often provoked opposition, but there are other sources of dissatisfaction, too. Fans of the Mets, the Yankees, the Giants, and the Jets expressed outrage at the escalating price of tickets in the stadiums. At the three stadiums in New York, ticket prices in the new stadiums went up by two times or more. Season tickets for the best seats that had cost $1,000 each in the old Yankee stadium jumped to $2,500 when it opened in 2009.[78] In August 2008 the Giants announced that they would charge from $1,000 to $20,000 for personal seat licenses, which only entitled the holders to then buy season tickets. "Here I am, buying a stadium for John Mara," a Giants ticket holder complained; "This is a greedy ploy with the only benefits going to them."[79]

Events in St. Louis provide a prominent example of the difficulties sometimes encountered by team owners who are seeking public funds. In 2000 the baseball Cardinals launched an effort to persuade the state legislature and the city to build a new stadium to replace Busch Stadium, which had been constructed in 1965 with private funds (though public money was used to build an adjacent parking facility and to make public improvements). After going to the legislature three times and coming back emptyhanded, the Cardinals began an effort to piece together a package combining private funding and public subsidies from the city and other sources. Already the city's voters had passed a referendum requiring a vote on any public funding proposal of more than $1 million for stadiums. One day before the new law was to take effect, the Land Clearance and Redevelopment Authority, whose board members and chief administrator are appointed by the mayor of St. Louis, approved the elimination of a 5 percent tax that had always been assessed on the team's ticket sales. St. Louis County was also expected to commit $45 million and the state of Missouri $40 million in public infrastructure, such as highway and street improvements.[80]

Ticket prices have increased sharply to help pay for the new stadiums, and as a consequence, professional sports attendance has become more stratified by income and class. For example, the new Cardinals stadium in St. Louis which opened in 2008, has twice the number of club seats as in the old Busch Stadium, and prices almost doubled. There were fewer luxury boxes, but they cost more. All other ticket prices rose, as well. Virtually all new stadiums have incorporated a larger number of premium and luxury seats as a means of increasing revenues.[81]

Malls, Entertainment, and Lifestyle Complexes

Enclosed malls have become a weapon that cities use in the regional competition for recreational shopping and tourism. Cities typically have heavily subsidized the construction of downtown malls. To support mall development, they have devoted Community Development Block Grant and Urban Development Action Grant funds, floated bonds to finance site acquisition and loans to developers, offered property tax abatements, created tax increment districts, built utilities tunnels, constructed sewer lines and water mains, and rerouted and repaved streets. Civic leaders are eager to support mall development because it promises to bring a special form of "entertainment" retailing downtown. Boston's early success set the tone for such expectations.

On August 26, 1976, Boston's mayor, Kevin White, presided over opening-day ceremonies for Quincy Market in downtown Boston. The brainchild of developer James Rouse, who made a fortune developing suburban shopping malls, Quincy Market was housed in three 150-year-old market buildings that were creatively renovated, at a cost of more than $40 million, into a collection of boutiques, gourmet food shops, and restaurants.[82] Few expected Quincy Market—located as it was in the center of a declining central city with inadequate parking and no big-ticket items to sell—to succeed. Indeed, six weeks before opening day, the retail complex was less than 50 percent leased. To hide the empty stores, Rouse came up with the idea of leasing pushcarts to artists and craftspeople for $50 a day, plus a percentage of the sales.

By 11 o'clock on opening day, only a modest crowd had gathered for the ceremonies. After the speeches were over, Mayor White cut the ribbon, and developer Rouse and a company of kilted highland bagpipers led the crowd inside for a champagne reception. At lunchtime, the crowd swelled as curious workers poured out of nearby office buildings. By midafternoon, it was clear that opening day would be a huge success, with police estimating the crowd at 100,000.

People never stopped coming to Quincy Market. In its second year of operation, the market drew 12 million visitors—more than Disneyland that year. Newspapers reported the market's "instant acceptance" by the public, which delighted in the colorful sights, sounds, and smells of the food and imaginatively displayed merchandise and the festival air created by a liberal sprinkling of pushcarts, magicians, acrobats, and puppeteers. The banks that financed the project were originally highly skeptical; they calculated that Quincy Market would have to produce retail sales comparable to the most successful suburban shopping malls ($150 per square foot) to justify its unusually high development costs. Quincy Market shocked the experts by producing sales of $233 per square foot in its first year, with the pushcarts doing best of all. The opening of Quincy Market was hailed by the media as a sign of an urban renaissance. It seemed to disprove the conventional wisdom that the downtowns of American cities were doomed to obsolescence and decline.

Initially, malls were important not only because they helped reverse the long-term decline of downtown retailing but also because they provided a means of creating defended space in the midst of urban crime and decay. Malls built by the developers John Portman and James Rouse and their imitators became such common features of American downtowns that it was hard to recall how recently they had been constructed. The malls increasingly engulfed and centralized activities that were formerly spread through the urban community at large. Such complexes were easily criticized as "fortified cells of affluence,"[83] but there can be little doubt that as locations for tourism and entertainment, these spaces were extremely successful.

Since opening his first mall in Boston, Rouse has designed festival malls for cities all across the country. What made Rouse's developments so distinctive and newsworthy was the artful combining of play and shopping. His formula was to create a carnival atmosphere, accomplished through a mixture of specialty shops, clothing stores, restaurants, and food stands, with musicians, jugglers, acrobats, and mimes to entertain shoppers. There soon were Rouse malls at the Gallery of Market Street East in Philadelphia, Grand Avenue in Milwaukee, Pike Street Market in Seattle, Horton Plaza in San Diego, Trolley Square in Salt Lake City, Union Station in St. Louis, Harborplace in Baltimore, South Street Seaport in New York, and on and on.

Many of the enclosed malls began modestly and then accreted block by block over many years, with tubes and skyways connecting the various components. In Minneapolis, a sprawling mall complex has grown by eating away the interiors of the downtown buildings, leaving their historic facades intact. In Kansas City, the Crown Center inexorably spread from its beginnings as a luxury hotel; by the mid-1990s, it occupied several city blocks. In Montreal and Dallas, veritable underground cities have been formed through a network of tunnels. The mall's assault on Atlanta has been much more direct; the huge Peachtree complex has been built on the rubble of the historic downtown.

Because they are an aspect of leisure and tourism, the kinds of malls built in downtown areas do not necessarily compete head-to-head with suburban malls. Rather, they rely on a style of shopping that combines entertainment with consumption. The malls' mix of gift and souvenir shops, specialty food stores, bars, and fast-food or franchise restaurants mimic tourist villages such as Jackson Hole, Wyoming, and Estes Park, Colorado. In the West Edmonton Mall in Alberta, Canada, for example, leisure facilities take up about 10 percent of the total floor space, but their presence is essential to an ambience of leisure that permeates the entire mall.[84] The West Edmonton Mall copies Disney World in the theming of particular areas, such as an imitation Parisian street, Bourbon Street in New Orleans, Hollywood, and Polynesia. The combination of shopping and leisure in this way encourages a "shop 'til you drop" atmosphere.

In these environments, out-of-town visitors mingle with local residents because in them, local consumers are prompted to act as if they are, in effect, in a dreamscape far removed from the city outside. The similarity between Disney theme parks and these environments is not accidental. Thirteen years before James Rouse opened Quincy Market in Boston, he asserted that Walt Disney was the most influential urban planner ever. And so he was. Malls and entertainment complexes establish the atmosphere and the context that potentially make every city, whatever its past function or present condition, a tourist attraction.

Sprawling indoor complexes connected by pedestrian bridges and tubes have proliferated in American cities,[85] especially where the surrounding environment may seem threatening. Perhaps the most comprehensive complexes have been built in Atlanta and Detroit, where a large proportion of downtown office workers commute to the sealed realms of the Peachtree Center in Atlanta and the Renaissance Center in Detroit. In both of these structures, workers drive into parking garages and then enter a city-within-a-city where they can work, shop, eat lunch, and find a variety of diversions after work. They never have to set foot in the rest of the city.

Architect John Portman pioneered the first bubble city when he opened the Peachtree Plaza in downtown Atlanta in 1967. The Peachtree complex dates back to the original cylindrical towers that distinguished Portman's first atrium hotel, which opened in downtown Atlanta in 1967. It was an instant hit with architectural critics, the media, and the public. The hotel lobbies and vaulted atriums that made up the complex were dazzling, filled with flowing water and pools, ascending ranks of balconies vanishing toward a skylight, corridors rigged with lights and mirrors, glass elevators outlined in lights.

By the late 1980s, Peachtree Plaza had swallowed up Atlanta's historic downtown. Sixteen buildings clustered around the aluminum cylinder that housed the Marriott Hotel, anchoring a constantly expanding, enclosed downtown business district. Atlanta moved indoors, its city streets left almost deserted, especially at night. Shops, hotels and their lobbies, offices, food courts, and atriums are connected by a maze of escalators, skytubes, and arcades forming glassed-in skyways that isolate inhabitants from the streets below. Pedestrians can gain access to the center only through a few grand porticos, usually the entrance to a hotel lobby. The effect is to sharply separate the city-within-a-city from the public street outside.

Portman later built several other complexes, lesser in scale but aspiring to a similar sense of grandeur, in several other cities—the Renaissance Center in Detroit, the Hyatt at Embarcadero Center in San Francisco, the Bonaventure Hotel in Los Angeles, and the Marriott Marquis in Times Square, New York City. In most cities, the Portman-like complexes do not swallow up an entire downtown. However, urban entertainment complexes have sprung up that enclose a large amount of space and house several related activities. These complexes commonly house one or more malls, but they also spread out to portions of the surrounding city. Because they offer a way to build a defended space even in a seemingly hostile environment, entertainment centers provide even the most dilapidated cities with a strategy for revitalizing the urban core.

New York City's Times Square and San Francisco's Yerba Buena Center both anchor urban entertainment centers, but such centers have sprung up elsewhere as well, usually in historic areas and often in connection with revitalized waterfronts. Contained within these districts are restaurants, coffeehouses, sports bars, jazz clubs, dinner theaters, and other entertainment venues, plus an array of corporate retail tenants offering an assortment of clothes, shoes, electronic goods, jewelry, and the like.[86]

The degree to which space is segmented in cities varies significantly; indeed, it is safe to say that Atlanta and Detroit occupy one end of a spectrum. In recent years

Boston, San Francisco, Seattle, Portland (Oregon), and Chicago—in fact, most cities—have opened up and become more accessible to visitors and local residents. Cities have invested heavily in amenities such as street plantings, pedestrian malls, parks, and riverfronts. Local residents and visitors fill busy streets that only a couple of decades ago were quiet and forbidding. Tourists visit enclaves such as South Street Seaport in New York and Ghirardelli Square in San Francisco, but they also spill out into nearby streets and neighborhoods. This trend will continue to unfold as long as crime rates in city centers remain relatively low.

Casino Gaming

Until the 1980s few casinos existed in any major city in the world, but in less than two decades, casino gaming spread rapidly. Since the mid-1980s, gaming casinos have become established as a component of tourism promotion in many cities throughout the world—notably in Adelaide, Perth, Sydney, and Brisbane; in Montreal, Winnipeg, and Windsor; in Christchurch and Auckland; in Amsterdam and Rotterdam; and in several cities on the Mediterranean, such as Athens, Istanbul, and Cairo.[87] But in the United States, gaming has become established in only a very few cities.

Atlantic City, New Jersey, broke Nevada's monopoly over gaming in 1978, but it took until 1992 for New Orleans to open the first casino in a major U.S. city. In 1990 Iowa became the first state to approve riverboat gaming. After the opening of the first boat in Iowa in April 1991, six riverboats generated $12 million in state income taxes within eight months, prompting neighboring states to begin steps to join the competition.[88] In 1992 riverboats began operating in Illinois, two near St. Louis (one in East St. Louis, Illinois, directly across from St. Louis and the Gateway Arch). Mississippi began operating boats in 1993. Missouri, Louisiana, and Indiana all approved riverboat gaming soon after, with operations beginning in 1994.[89] Within a year, Kansas City and St. Louis, Missouri, joined the list.

Since then, however, the spread of gaming in U.S. cities has nearly come to a full stop. This may seem surprising because of the obvious potential for gaming to make a significant contribution to the local economy, and because at the state level and in nonurban areas it has established a strong presence. As a means of promoting economic development on Indian reservations, in 1988 Congress passed the Indian Gaming Regulatory Act. The legislation permitted tribes to negotiate with states to run gaming operations and required the states to negotiate with the tribes that wanted to open casinos. Since then, casinos have been opened on Indian lands in 22 states. In addition, all through the 1970s and 1980s, states adopted lotteries either through legislative action or referenda; by 1994, some 38 states ran lotteries. Following the spread of state lotteries, gambling became legitimated as a source of tax revenues. By 1996, 26 states allowed or had approved casino gaming in some form, but most gaming occurred on Indian-owned land.[90]

There are three major reasons why gaming has encountered resistance. A national movement organized by the religious right to oppose gaming has enjoyed success because it taps into a widespread concern about the social and moral effects of gambling. Although the majority of Americans have come to accept gambling as a legitimate activity over the past 30 years,[91] a Harris Poll conducted in 1992 still found that 51 percent of the public opposed casino gaming in their own state, and 56 percent opposed it in their own communities.[92] The media find gambling a convenient topic, much like crime, for "controversy" and "analysis." For example, in its April 1, 1996, issue *Time* magazine carried a feature story that documented a national backlash against gaming. Proposals to allow gaming typically are accompanied by a considerable amount of controversy. In 1992 Colorado voters soundly defeated a constitutional amendment that would have allowed gaming to spread past the three communities named in an earlier referendum. In Missouri, three contentious voter referendums were required before the industry, with strong support from public officials, was able to secure approval for full casino operations.

Industry projections of the potential contributions of gaming to local treasuries often make it appear that gaming would constitute a magic elixir for urban economies. But this appeal has fallen short because gaming has frequently become so controversial. In 1996 ten state legislatures refused to pass laws to legalize casinos or slot machines,[93] and Congress passed legislation to initiate a two-year study of gaming. When completed in 1999, the study urged states and localities to be cautious about pursuing gaming. But because local officials are engaged in a restless search for new ways of stimulating local economies, the idea that gaming may help is difficult to resist. In 2002 the mayor of Chicago, Richard M. Daley, mentioned the possibility that Chicago might seek approval for a casino license. This trial balloon was quickly shot down. However, to help solve the budget problems created by the 2008–2009 recession, in May 2009 the Illinois legislature approved an expansion of video poker games throughout the state. Faced with mounting fiscal problems, it would not be surprising if Mayor Daley followed this example by reviving his idea for a downtown casino.

The Politics of Tourism

Critics often note that many of the facilities of tourism and entertainment do not pay for themselves. Public officials and civic boosters do not, on the whole, care much if they do. This apparently cavalier attitude toward taxpayers' money can be explained by noting the general irrelevance—to city officials and civic boosters—of cost–benefit analyses of tourism infrastructure. The attitudes of public officials toward development projects have "little do with the . . . profitability . . . of a project" and far more to do with the vision officials share about the overall direction a city is taking.[94] The intense interurban competition dictates that cities must compete; to do so they must be as generous as their competitors in providing subsidies, and they must try to adopt every new variation that comes along. The competition imposes a logic of its own that is hard to resist.

Public officials may be proceeding on the basis of blind faith, but they feel they have little choice. It is true that abject, even humiliating failure is possible, as the attempt by Flint, Michigan, to become a tourist city makes clear. In the 1970s, after the closing of its General Motors plant devastated the local economy, public officials in Flint launched an effort at regeneration behind the motto "Our New Spark Will Surprise You." The city committed $13 million in subsidies to the construction of a luxury hotel, the Hyatt Regency. Within a year, it closed its doors. Approximately $100 million in public money was used to build AutoWorld, a museum that contained, among other items, the "world's largest car engine" and a scale model that portrayed downtown Flint in its more prosperous days. AutoWorld closed within six months. Still more public subsidies were committed to the construction of the doomed Water Street Pavilion, a theme park/festival market built by the renowned mall developer James Rouse. But few, if any, mayors would find it useful to be deterred by Flint's fiasco, which was wryly recorded in Michael Moore's popular movie *Roger and Me*.[95]

Virtually all cities of consequential size must take some steps to promote tourism, recreation, and culture. Now that the basic infrastructure is in place in many cities, public support for the arts and culture has become common. Every one of the nation's 50 largest cities provides public support for the arts. Some smaller cities also offer subsidies. From the big cities (New York, with the Kennedy and Lincoln Centers and more recently, the Ford Center on 42nd Street) to villages (Riverhead, a hamlet outside New York City on Long Island, which is building an arts and historic district), from the downtowns in need of a boost (Newark, with its $180 million New Jersey Center, opened in October 1997) to the already prosperous (San Francisco, with a newly renovated opera house and several other performance halls), the development of local culture has become a leading formula for urban revival.[96] The text for a major exhibit in 1998 sponsored by the National Building Museum in Washington, D.C., noted that culture has replaced both the urban renewal bulldozer and the preservation movements that followed in its destructive wake as the main focus for downtown revitalization.

Collectively, cities of all sizes support an almost unimaginable variety of events that carry the signature of local culture and community. Jazz and blues festivals, strawberry and garlic festivals, jumping frogs and gold rush days, rodeos and fireworks—such activities help define and sometimes knit together local communities.[97] These activities usually take place in or near the new tourism/entertainment infrastructure (in smaller towns, this may mean at local parks, bandstands, waterfronts, or baseball diamonds). Every city must go through debates about how much of the public purse should be devoted to these activities, but few cities can afford to forgo public subsidies altogether.

OLD AND NEW DOWNTOWNS

Many writers have decried the disappearance of the old downtowns and neighborhoods that give older cities their identities and distinctive character. In 1961, when she published her classic work *The Death and Life of Great American Cities*, Jane Jacobs instantly became the best-known and most influential voice for this perspective. Writing in defense of her beloved Greenwich Village in the Lower East Side of New York, Jacobs attacked the master planning and large-scale development characteristic of the urban renewal era. Jacobs counterposed the virtues of small blocks, crowded streets, mixed uses, and what she called the "heart-of-the-day ballet" of street life with the "monotony and repetition of sameness" of planned environments.[98]

To Jacobs, a "marvelous order" was hidden beneath the surface of disorder on busy city streets, a disorder that was necessary "for maintaining the safety of the

streets and the freedom of the city."[99] Through their constant presence, people running the businesses fronting the sidewalk—storekeepers, barkeepers, shoe repairers,
the owners of cleaners and barbershops, and their regular customers as well—kept
their eyes on the comings and goings just outside the windows. In this way the
sidewalk ballet made room for everyone, but at the same time public safety and
order was attended to, without anyone planning it or even thinking about it. Here is
a description of Jacobs's street when she got back to her home on Hudson Street:

> When I get home from work, the ballet is reaching its crescendo. This is the time of roller
> skates and stilts and tricycles, and games in the lee of the stoop with bottletops and plastic
> cowboys; this is the time of bundles and packages, zigzagging from the drug store to the
> fruit stand back over to the butchers.[100]

Much more recently, in his study of New Haven, Connecticut, Douglas Rae has decried the "end of urbanism," which he defines as the "patterns of private conduct and
decision-making that by and large make the successful governance of cities possible."[101] In the age of urbanism, the life of the city was focused on downtown streets and
the densely settled neighborhoods surrounding them. Echoing Jacobs, Rae writes of the
"dense fabric of tiny stores" that were "only partly in the business of selling groceries:
they were also governing sidewalks and the people who walked them."[102] This "sidewalk republic" made it unnecessary for formal government to intervene in people's
lives because informal social networks were adequate for supplying most basic needs.

What brought about the demise of urbanism? In Rae's account, the coming of the
automobile, suburbanization and policies that encouraged it, the decline of industrial
employment, racial strife, and globalization (which replaced locally oriented businesses
with national corporations) all contributed.[103] Taken together, these factors (and others)
led to the decentering of residential and economic activities. The urban renewal and
highway projects, though intended to save the core, only made things worse through
the wholesale clearance of historic buildings, business streets, and neighborhoods.

The recent revival of downtowns and the gentrification of nearby neighborhoods
should not be taken as evidence that the world that Jacobs, Rae, and others[104] write
about is being resurrected. It would be more accurate to conclude that the old downtowns died for good, and have now been replaced by something else. Metropolitan
regions continue to flow outward. Other nodes of activity—suburban business districts, malls, corporate campuses, edge cities—continue to develop. The downtowns
of central cities will never be the singular center of activity that they were in the past.

In key respects the new downtowns are also less diverse than they once were. In
central business districts the dense collection of small shops has long been replaced
by big buildings and, in the larger cities, by skyscrapers. Chain stores and outlets,
such as Starbucks, the Gap, and Victoria's Secret, are outlets for national and international corporations. Cineplexes have replaced small theaters; chain supermarkets
have replaced many of the specialized shops that separately sold meat, vegetables,
candy, and ice cream.[105] Many business establishments have moved out of the downtowns entirely, such as large appliance stores and automobile dealerships. Shopkeepers
no longer keep their eyes on the street, if they can see it at all, and corporate
minimum-wage employees do not have an interest in it.

Residential use is what drives the revival of many downtowns today. In Manhattan, old commercial space has been in great demand because the buildings are being turned into condominiums. In Philadelphia, office space has stayed about the same since 1990, but new residential towers have popped up all over the downtown.[106] In St. Louis, many old warehouse and office buildings might have been torn down if not for condominium conversions; indeed, a downtown retail mall built as recently as the 1980s is being converted into a luxury condominium complex. The urban scholar Richard Florida reports that in his research on the "creative class," focus groups and interview respondents named diversity as one of the most essential qualities they sought when making a choice about where to live; his research subjects also said they wanted to live in places that felt "authentic," with "real buildings, real people, real history."[107]

It is important to make a distinction between the true downtowns and the "uptown" gentrified neighborhoods that surround them. They are not the same. Today, most downtown neighborhoods contain mostly high-income residents. But neighborhoods not far away, such as Wicker Park in Chicago, may be made up of new condominium towers filled with affluent people or they may be composed of renovated, architecturally significant buildings populated by a mélange of artists, musicians, and students, as well as affluent professionals.[108] Greenwich Village shares much in common with Wicker Park, but neither is much like Chicago's Loop or the Miracle Mile on Michigan Avenue, with its rows of high-end chain stores and nearby condominium towers. Any generalizations about the character of the new downtowns and neighborhoods must, to some degree, gloss over the fantastic differences in the urban environment from one neighborhood to the next, or even from block to block.

Is the diversity the "creative class" seeks merely an impoverished version of what city downtowns and neighborhoods once offered? It is hard to say. A century ago, the New Haven neighborhoods that Rae studied contained people of all social classes, incomes, and ethnic backgrounds.[109] Similarly, a diverse array of people live in some of the trendiest of today's inner-city neighborhoods. Superficially, these neighborhoods may bear a striking resemblance to the past when their historic buildings become occupied by small restaurants, bars and taverns, music venues, art galleries, and shops, plus some sprinkling of chain stores and themed environments. But the people walking the streets and the businesses they patronize are, in fact, completely unique to the twenty-first century. People of the creative class can put aside any anxiety about whether the environment they live in is authentic. It surely is, but not because nostalgia for a lost world makes it so.

NOTES

1. New York Times News Service, "City Neighborhoods Are Undergoing a Renaissance as Crime Rates Drop," *St. Louis Post-Dispatch*, May 29, 2000, p. A-12.
2. Richard Florida, "How the Crash Will Reshape America," *The Atlantic*, March 2009, p. 52.
3. Rebecca R. Sohmer and Robert E. Lang, *Downtown Rebound* (Washington, D.C.: Brookings Institution Press and Fannie Mae Foundation), pp. 1–4.
4. Patrick A. Simmons and Robert E. Lang, "The Urban Turnaround," in *Redefining Urban & Suburban America: Evidence from Census 2000*, ed. Bruce Katz and Robert E. Lang (Washington, D.C.: Brookings Institution Press, 2004), pp. 56–58.
5. Mark Abrahamson, *Global Cities* (New York: Oxford University Press, 2004).

6. Robert M. Fogelson, *Downtown: Its Rise and Fall, 1880–1950* (New Haven, Conn.: Yale University Press, 2001). My discussion of the history of downtown borrows heavily from Fogelson's excellent book, which should become a standard reference work on every urban scholar's bookshelf.

7. Ibid., pp. 186–187.

8. Ibid., pp. 197–198.

9. Ibid., pp. 183–185.

10. Alison Isenberg, *Downtown America: A History of the Place and the People Who Made It* (Chicago: University of Chicago Press, 2004), pp. 5–6.

11. Ibid., pp. 218–219.

12. Isenberg, *Downtown America*, p. 219.

13. Ibid., p. 65.

14. Ibid., p. 69.

15. Kenneth T. Jackson, *Crabgrass Frontier: The Suburbanization of the United States* (New York: Oxford University Press, 1985), p. 261.

16. Barry Bluestone and Bennett Harrison, *The Deindustrialization of America* (New York: Basic Books, 1982).

17. U.S. Bureau of the Census, *Statistical Abstract of the United States, 1992*, 112th ed. (Washington, D.C.: U.S. Government Printing Office, 1992), p. 397.

18. Robert B. Reich, *The Work of Nations* (New York: Random House, Vintage Books, 1991), p. 86.

19. Jon C. Teaford, *The Rough Road to Renaissance: Urban Revitalization in America, 1940–1985* (Baltimore: Johns Hopkins University Press, 1990), p. 307.

20. Bernard J. Frieden and Lynn B. Sagalyn, *Downtown, Inc.: How America Builds Cities* (Cambridge, Mass.: MIT Press, 1989), p. 43.

21. Saskia Sassen, *Cities in a World Economy* (Thousand Oaks, Calif.: Pine Forge Press, 2001).

22. The concept of the global city is somewhat imprecise. Some scholars would question whether Chicago, Miami, and Los Angeles are global cities in the same sense as New York, London, and Tokyo, which clearly contain a much denser concentration of financial and media firms and corporations with true international reach. The two books to consult regarding this debate are Saskia Sassen, *The Global City: New York, London, Tokyo*, 2nd ed. (Princeton, N.J.: Princeton University Press, 2001), and Janet L. Abu-Lughod, *New York, Los Angeles, Chicago: America's Global Cities* (Minneapolis: University of Minnesota Press, 1999).

23. Norman J. Glickman, "Cities and the International Division of Labor," in *The Capitalist City*, ed. Michael Peter Smith and Joe R. Feagin (Cambridge, Mass.: Basil Blackwell 1987), pp. 66–86.

24. Richard Florida, *The Rise of the Creative Class and How It's Transforming Work, Leisure, Community and Everyday Life* (New York: Basic Books, 2002), p. 225.

25. Ibid.

26. Abrahamson, *Global Cities*, p. 33.

27. Quoted in ibid., p. 33; from Susan Stephenson, "DINKS Dine Out," *Restaurants and Institutions* 107 (April 1, 1997): 78.

28. Florida, *The Rise of the Creative Class*, p. 224.

29. Ibid., p. 228.

30. Terry Nichols Clark, Richard Lloyd, Kenneth K. Wong, and Pushpam Jain, "Amenities Drive Urban Growth," *Journal of Urban Affairs* 24, no. 5 (1993): 493–516.

31. World Travel & Tourism Council (WTTC) website (*http://www.wttc.org*).

32. Ibid.

33. Norman Fainstein, Susan S. Fainstein, Richard Child Hill, Dennis Judd, and Michael Peter Smith, *Restructuring the City: The Political Economy of Urban Redevelopment* (New York: Longman, 1983).

34. Clark, Lloyd, Wong, and Jain, "Amenities Drive Urban Growth," p. 504.

35. Ibid, p. 505.

36. Christine Boyer, "Cities for Sale: Merchandising History at South Street Seaport," in *Variations on a Theme Park: The New American City and the End of Public Space*, ed. Michael Sorkin (New York: Hill and Wang, 1992), pp. 189–190.

37. G. J. Ashworth and J. E. Tunbridge, *The Tourist-Historic City* (London and New York: Belhaven Press, 1990), p. 153.

38. For an expanded discussion, see Dennis R. Judd, "Visitors and the Spatial Ecology of the City," in *Cities and Visitors*, ed. Lily M. Hoffman, Susan S. Fainstein, and Dennis R. Judd (New York: Blackwell, 2003), pp. 22–38.

39. John Hannigan, *Fantasy City: Pleasure and Profit in the Postmodern Metropolis* (New York: Routledge, 1998).

40. Richard Lloyd, *Neo-Bohemia: Art and Commerce in the Postindustrial City* (New York: Routledge, 2006), p. 126; also "Neo-Bohemia: Art and Neighborhood Redevelopment in Chicago," *Journal of Urban Affairs* 24, no. 5 (2002): 517–532.

41. See also Dennis R. Judd, "Constructing the Tourist Bubble," *The Tourist City*, ed. Dennis R. Judd and Susan S. Fainstein (New Haven, Conn.: Yale University Press, 1999).

42. David H. Laslo, "Proliferating Convention Centers: The Political Economy of Regenerating Cities and the St. Louis Convention Center Expansion" (Ph.D. diss., University of Missouri–St. Louis, May 1999).

43. All data from Heywood Sanders, *Space Available: The Realities of Convention Centers as Economic Development Strategy* (Washington, D.C.: Brookings Institution Press, January 2005), p. 1.

44. *Encyclopedia of Associations*, 38th ed., *National Organizations of the United States*, vol. 1–3 (New York: Author, 2002).

45. George G. Fenich, "The Dollars and Sense of Convention Centers" (Ph.D. diss., Rutgers University, 1992), p. 34.

46. Laslo, "Proliferating Convention Centers," p. 67.

47. *Tradeshow Week Data Book, 1998* (New York: Bill Communications, 1998), p. 6.

48. "State of the Industry 1993," *Successful Meetings* (July 1993): 32–33.

49. *Convene Magazine* website (*http://www.pcma.org/convene*).

50. Associated Press, "Las Vegas Still the King of Convention Cities," April 26, 2006 (*http://www.msnbc.msn.com/id/12498996*).

51. Joe Pollack, "Visitors Fly Under Media Radar," *St. Louis Journalism Review* (June 2003): 5.

52. Sanders, *Space Available*, p. 25.

53. Ibid., p. 22.

54. Robyne S. Turner and Mark S. Rosentraub, "Tourism, Sports and the Centrality of Cities," *Journal of Urban Affairs* 24, no. 5 (2003): 489.

55. Charles Santo, "The Economic Impact of Sports Stadiums: Recasting the Analysis in Context," *Journal of Urban Affairs* 27, no. 2 (2005): 177.

56. Ibid., pp. 177–191. Some leading studies are Robert A. Baade, "Professional Sports as Catalysts for Metropolitan Economic Development," *Journal of Urban Affairs* 18 (1996): 1–17; Mark Rosentraub, David Swinderll, M. Przybylski, and D. R. Mullins, "Sports and Downtown Development Strategy: If You Build It, Will Jobs Come?" *Journal of Urban Affairs* 16 (1994): 211–239; John Zipp, "The Economic Impact of the Baseball Strike of 1994," *Urban Affairs Review* 32, no. 2 (November 1996): 157–185; Dan Coates and B. Humphries, "The Growth Effects of Sports Franchises, Stadia, and Arenas," *Journal of Policy Analysis and Management* 18, no. 4 (1999): 601–624; Robert Noll and A. Zimbalist, eds., *Sports, Jobs, and Taxes: The Economic Impact of Sports Teams and Stadiums* (Washington, D.C.: Brookings Institution Press, 1997); and Phillip A. Miller, "The Economic Impact of Sports Stadium Construction: The Case of the Construction Industry in St. Louis, MO," *Journal of Urban Affairs* 24, no. 2 (2002): 159–173. Some smaller teams have been able to turn minor-league teams into profitable investments for the public by resorting to public ownership—see Joseph W. Meder and J. Wesley Leckrone, "Hardball; Local Government's Foray into Sports Franchise Ownership," *Journal of Urban Affairs* 24, no. 3 (2002): 353–368. This option is not open with the major sports because the sports cartels are able to exclude all teams that do not meet their regulations, which includes private ownership.

57. Z. Austrian and Mark S. Rosentraub, "Cleveland's Getway to the Future," in Noll and Zimbalist, *Sports, Jobs, and Taxes,* pp. 355–384.

58. Associated Press, "Forbes: Five NFL Franchises Worth over $1 Billion Each (*http:/sports.espn .go.com/nfl/news/story/?id*).

59. Kurt Badenhausen, Cecily Fluke, Lesley Kump, and Michael K. Ozanian, "Double Play," *Forbes,* April 15, 2002 (*http://www.forbes.com*).

60. Davide Dukcevich, "America's Most Valuable Fans," *Forbes,* February 1, 2002 (*http://www .forbes.com*).

61. Michael Ozanian, "Is Baseball Really Broke?" *Forbes,* April 3, 2002 (*http://www.forbes.com*).

62. Infoplease.com; keywords Sports—Business/Ballparks/Arenas. Comparisons among the professional sports are difficult to make. The National Football League has a fully nationalized media arrangement with teams sharing in revenues (which has promoted equity among the teams). By contrast, major-league baseball teams sign their own contracts with mostly local or regional media outlets, with limited revenue sharing among the teams. Thus in 2002 major-league baseball's four-year media contract was estimated at almost $1.8 million, but this figure is a tiny proportion of all media revenues collected by the individual teams.

63. For a closely textured and entertaining account of the battle between O'Malley and Moses, see Michael Shapiro, *The Last Good Season: Brooklyn, The Dodgers, and Their Final Pennant Race Together* (New York: Doubleday, 2003).

64. Neil J. Sullivan, *The Dodgers Move West* (New York: Oxford University Press, 1987).

65. Arthur T. Johnson, "The Sports Franchise Relocation Issue and Public Policy Responses," in *Government and Sport: The Public Policy Issues,* ed. Arthur T. Johnson and James H. Frey (Totowa, N.J.: Rowman and Allanheld, 1985), p. 232.

66. Arthur T. Johnson, "Economic and Policy Implications of Hosting Sports Franchises: Some Lessons from Baltimore," *Urban Affairs Quarterly* 21, no. 3 (March 1986): 411.

67. Tim Chapin, "Beyond the Entrepreneurial City: Municipal Capitalism in San Diego," *Journal of Urban Affairs* 24, no. 5 (1993): 567–568.

68. F. Jossi, "Take Me Out to the Ballgame," *Planning* 64, no. 5 (1998): 4–9.

69. Jacob Luft, "Relocation Celebrations: NFL, NHL Franchises Find Success in New Cities," January 26, 2001; CNNSI.com-Statitudes: "NFL, NHL Teams Benefit from Moving On."

70. Robert A. Baade and Robert E. Dye, "Sports Stadiums and Area Development: A Critical Review," *Economic Development Quarterly* 2 (1988): 265–275; Robert A. Baade, "Professional Sports and Economic Development," *Journal of Urban Affairs* 18, no. 1 (1996): 1–18.

71. Charles C. Eichner, *Playing the Field: Why Sports Teams Move and Cities Fight to Keep Them* (Baltimore: Johns Hopkins University Press, 1993), pp. 12–13.

72. Ronald Smothers, "No Hits, No Runs, One Error: The Dome," *New York Times,* June 15, 1991.

73. Eichner, *Playing the Field,* p. 67.

74. See the websites *http://www.gophersports.com/pdf4/40448.pdf* and *http://www.msfc.com/about/dfm.*

75. Donald Phares and Mark S. Rosentraub, "Reviving the Glory of Days Past: St. Louis's Blitz to Save Its Image, Identity, and Teams," in *Major League Losers: The Real Cost of Sports and Who's Paying for It,* ed. Mark S. Rosentraub (New York: Basic Books, 1997).

76. Richard Sandomir, "New Stadiums: Prices, and Outrage, Escalate," *New York Times,* August 28, 2008 (*http://www.nytimes.com/2008/08/26/sports/26tickets.html*).

77. Josh Goodman, "Skybox Skeptics," *Governing* 19, no. 6 (March 2006), pp. 41–42.

78. Sandomir, "New Stadiums."

79. Ibid.

80. Heather Cole, "Cardinals, City Sing Stadium Deal," *St. Louis Business Journal,* November 8, 2002, p. 1.

81. Ibid., p. C7.

82. This account of Quincy Market is based on Frieden and Sagalyn, *Downtown, Inc.,* pp. 1–7, 175.

83. Mike Davis, "Fortress Los Angeles: The Militarization of Urban Space," in *Variations on a Theme Park*, ed. Michael Sorkin (New York: Noonday Press, 1992), p. 155.

84. Myriam Jansen-Verbeke, "Leisure + Shopping = Tourism Product Mix," in *Marketing Tourism Places*, ed. Gregory Ashworth and Brian Goodall (London and New York: Routledge, 1990), p. 132.

85. Sharon Zukin, *Landscapes of Power: From Detroit to Disney World* (Berkeley: University of California Press, 1991).

86. The Urban Land Institute, *Developing Urban Entertainment Centers* (Washington, D.C.: Urban Land Institute, 1998).

87. William R. Eadington, "The Emergence of Casino Gaming as a Major Factor in Tourism Markets: Policy Issues and Considerations," in *Change in Tourism: People, Places, Processes*, ed. Richard Butler and Douglas Pearce (London and New York: Routledge, 1995), pp. 159–186.

88. Fred Faust, "It Wasn't in the Cards," *St. Louis Post-Dispatch*, April 10, 1994, pp. 1–5E.

89. *Company Analysis* (New York: Donaldson, Lufkin and Jenrette Securities Corporation, June 23, 1993), p. 12.

90. Eadington, "The Emergence of Casino Gaming," p. 4.

91. *Company Analysis*, p. 6.

92. Robert Goodman, *Legalized Gambling as a Strategy for Economic Development* (Northampton, Mass.: United States Gambling Study), p. 34.

93. Ellen Perlman, "The Gambling Glut," *Governing: The Magazine of States and Localities* 9, no. 8 (May 1996): 49–56.

94. Michael A. Pagano and Ann Bowman, *Cityscapes and Capital: The Politics of Urban Development* (Baltimore: Johns Hopkins University Press, 1995), p. 74.

95. Michael Moore, *Roger and Me*, A Dog Eat Dog Films Production (Warner Bros. Pictures, 1989).

96. Bruce Weber, "Cities Are Fostering the Arts as a Way to Save Downtown," *New York Times*, November 18, 1997, p. A1.

97. Dennis R. Judd, William Winter, William Barnes, and Emily Stern, *Tourism and Entertainment as a Local Economic Development Strategy: The Report of a NLC Survey* (Washington, D.C.: National League of Cities: A Research Report, 2000), p. 8.

98. Jane Jacobs, *The Death and Life of Great American Cities* (New York: Vintage, 1961), pp. 51, 223.

99. Ibid., p. 50.

100. Ibid., p. 52.

101. Douglas Rae, *City: Urbanism and Its End* (New Haven, Conn.: Yale University Press, 2003), p. xiii.

102. Ibid.

103. Ibid., p. xiv.

104. Two other excellent books dealing with these themes are Ray Suarez, *The Old Neighborhood: What We Lost in the Great Suburban Migration: 1966–1999* (New York: Free Press, 1999); and Michael Shapiro, *The Last Good Season: Brooklyn, the Dodgers, and the Final Pennant Race Together* (New York: Doubleday, 2003).

105. For details on New Haven's experience, see Rae, *City: Urbanism and Its End*, pp. 234–243.

106. Alan Ehrenhalt, "Extreme Makeover," *Governing* 20, no. 7 (July 2006): 29.

107. Florida, *The Rise of the Creative Class*, pp. 227–229.

108. Lloyd, *Neo-Bohemia*.

109. Rae, *City: Urbanism and Its End*.

CHAPTER 14

GOVERNANCE IN THE GLOBAL ERA

A DELICATE BALANCING ACT

Sometimes it may seem that urban officials are obsessed with issues of economic vitality and competition. But it is important to keep in mind that this priority does not take place in a vacuum. Other political issues are forcing themselves into the political arena. Racial and ethnic conflicts have long served as fault lines in the politics of America's cities, and sometimes they have become so urgent that they displace almost all other issues. In the 1960s, for example, race riots forced racial discrimination onto the national political agenda, and managing the political fallout became a nearly full-time occupation for public leaders, especially in the central cities. In recent decades, the volume of foreign immigration has reached such proportions that it can only be compared to the immigration flows of the nineteenth and early twentieth centuries. The cities have become the places where the tensions arising from such a large-scale social change must be negotiated. In such a context, governance becomes an urgent and difficult task. Can city governments keep the peace among the contending groups?

The peace has not always been preserved. The history of American cities is peppered with violent clashes. White mobs attacked blacks in New York City in 1863, East St. Louis in 1917, Chicago in 1919, Tulsa in 1920, and on many other occasions. Blacks rioted in Detroit in 1944 and again in the 1960s. More recent social disorders reveal that racial tensions still exist. Riots erupted in black neighborhoods in Cuban-dominated Miami four times in the 1980s, beginning with the Liberty City disorders in May 1980. Each of the riots was associated with the killing of a black man by Latino or non-Latino white police officers.[1] In 1991 rioting erupted in Washington, D.C., when a black female police officer attempted to arrest some Latino men and again when police shot a Salvadoran immigrant. Ethnic tensions reached a breaking point in the Crown Heights neighborhood in Brooklyn in 1991 and 1992, culminating in a boycott by the

African American community of a Korean greengrocer and violent street confrontations between African Americans and Hasidic Jews.

The most serious riot of the twentieth century occurred in Los Angeles in 1992, with 53 people dead, 2,383 injuries, 16,291 arrests, more than 5,500 fires, and over $700 million in property damage. Unlike previous riots, it was multiethnic, involving blacks, Latinos, and Asians.[2] During the riots, 30 percent of the approximately 4,000 businesses destroyed were Latino owned,[3] but looters and arsonists especially singled out Korean-owned businesses.[4] In subsequent years, it might have seemed that racial and ethnic tensions had subsided, but in April 2000 fears of rioting ran rampant in Miami the day after federal agents seized Elian Gonzalez from relatives in Miami and returned him to his father in Cuba. Cuban American leaders called for calm, fearful that rioting might break out. This incident revealed that the social fabric is held together by tenuous bonds in America's cities.

Maintaining social order without the use of force is the challenge of urban *governance.* City governments are designed as mechanisms not only for promoting economic vitality and providing services, but also for managing social and political tensions. They do this best by incorporating into the democratic process the various political interests that make up a city. The legitimacy of local government requires that citizens perceive it as sufficiently representative and responsive to their needs. If citizens become convinced that their participation makes no difference, they will demonstrate their alienation from the political system by withholding their vote, refusing to participate in the civic life of organizational politics, and—occasionally—by resorting to violence to vent their frustrations.

Cities are contested arenas within which groups jostle for political influence and advantage. In recent decades, the struggles for power have given rise to two distinct and potentially conflicting political movements. The first, the fight for political incorporation, drew its strength from the conviction that particular groups and sectors of society had been denied adequate representation at all levels of the political system in America. The fight for incorporation originated in neighborhood protests of the 1950s against urban renewal and highway building. Neighborhood organizations began to press on several fronts, including demands for representation in city government, improved services, and community control of schools and police. Their continued existence was ensured by the civil rights movement and the federal programs of the 1960s. The War on Poverty, Model Cities, and other programs contained citizen participation requirements, and federal funds flowed into neighborhood organizations or equivalent institutions such as community action and Model Cities agencies.

The result was a profound transformation in city politics. The civil rights and community organizing activities helped mobilize the black electorate. Within a few years, African American mayors and other public officials were taking the reins of city governments. Neighborhood organizations and community action agencies were transformed into community development corporations (CDCs). The 3,600 CDCs in the United States provide major services in virtually all large cities and in smaller ones, and in some cities they play a major political role as well.[5]

The drive for political incorporation has now embraced immigrant groups, though very unevenly. Latinos have become influential in the politics of the many cities where they have moved in large numbers, as have Asians. But the changing complexion of politics has highlighted the difficulty of forging and maintaining multiethnic coalitions. The expectation that blacks and Latinos would make common cause because both groups are disadvantaged has not been realized. In Denver, despite the fact that Latino and black leaders have forged a good working relationship, a coherent political agenda has not emerged, aside from the benefits that automatically inhere in incorporation itself (such as access to public office and to public employment). Even within the Latino community, "there is little consensus on a Latino political agenda . . . much less one that would reflect the shared concerns of blacks and Latinos over poverty, affordable housing, safety, health care, and neighborhood well-being."[6] *Minority* is a problematic term that papers over significant differences; the challenge is to forge alliances over issues that attract support from across ethnic groups.[7]

A second political movement has also changed city politics. Concerned about crime and disorder, in the 1980s white working-class and middle-class voters were mobilized by Republican and conservative candidates. This was a revolutionary development; for as long as anyone remembered the central cities had been the special preserve for Democratic, liberal politicians. A new generation of conservative mayors promised to cut taxes by holding down spending. To bring order to the streets, they promised to get tough with criminals, panhandlers, and homeless people. Further, they promised to use local government to restart the engine of private investment. This three-part agenda appealed to a broad alliance of voters, but it brought with it the danger that racial and ethnic antagonisms might be reignited.

In fact, however, there has been a remarkable degree of convergence between these two seemingly antagonistic political movements. Unlike their counterparts at the national level, urban conservatives, reflecting the complex makeup of their constituencies, have generally taken moderate positions on such explosive social issues as affirmative action hiring and multicultural curriculums in the schools. Likewise,

OUTTAKE

HAVE THE BENEFITS OF MINORITY INFLUENCE IN CITIES MADE A DIFFERENCE?

The first blacks elected as mayors of major American cities—Richard Hatcher in Gary, Indiana, and Carl Stokes in Cleveland (both elected in 1967)—successfully pushed for more spending for health, education, housing, and job training programs, and for increases in federal grants. Studies showed that in the next several years, cities with black mayors and council members had a higher proportion of social welfare expenditures. These findings seemed to apply to Latino officeholders as well. A study that measured the degree of incorporation of blacks and Latinos into the politics of ten California cities in the early 1980s found that "political incorporation was responsible for dramatic changes in bureaucratic decision

(continued on next page)

rules in many policy areas" such as local-government hiring and contracting procedures. The study also found that incorporation increased voter turnout and the mobilization of new leaders. Significant gains were achieved in integrating municipal labor forces, school administrators, and teachers, and neighborhood programs were initiated in many cities. Old racial barriers fell. Many observers interpreted these findings as a sign that more progress was yet to come, including initiatives in neighborhoods and social programs that might bring broad benefits to disadvantaged minorities.

Such expectations were dashed. Coleman Young and Andrew Young presided over conventional downtown-growth politics in Detroit and Atlanta. Wilson Goode campaigned for the mayoralty of Philadelphia in 1983 on a platform that promised to streamline city bureaucracies, build a convention center, improve the port, and promote economic development. A comprehensive study in 1983 found that black urban officials expressed attitudes and followed policies not distinctly different from white urban leaders regarding levels of city taxation and indebtedness.

In the intervening years, blacks and Latinos have been elected to office in cities of all sizes and in all parts of the nation. As Latino and Asian populations increased, the biracial politics of an earlier time has given way to a complex multiethnic politics. To assemble winning electoral coalitions, it has become necessary to downplay racial issues and find issues that cut across many groups. Issues have changed as well; like whites, minority groups are stratified along class lines. Middle-class blacks, Asians, and Latinos are more open to moderate and conservative ideas than in the past. As a consequence, the gains of the first generation of minority mayors have been preserved, but demands on behalf of the poor have been moderated.

Has minority incorporation into the political system paid off? From one perspective, office-holding itself is "symbolic but terribly important." In addition to the symbolic benefits of incorporation, the material benefits have also been substantial; the gains in public employment have contributed not only to middle-class economic progress but also to significant changes in police behavior in minority communities. Another frequently expressed view is that minority incorporation should have been economically beneficial for the minority middle class as well as for the poor. Perhaps this kind of expectation is unrealistic: "The painful truth is that many of the forces shaping the conditions under which the mass of low-income minority people live are not under the control of city governments."

Sources: E. Nelson Jr. and Philip J. Meranto, *Electing Black Mayors: Political Action in the Black Community* (Columbus: Ohio State University Press, 1977); Charles H. Levine, *Racial Conflict and the American Mayor: Power, Polarization, and Performance* (Lexington, Mass.: D. C. Heath, 1972); Albert K. Karnig and Susan Welch, *Black Representatives and Urban Policy* (Chicago: University of Chicago Press, 1980); Rufus P. Browning, Dale Rogers Marshall, and David H. Tabb, *Protest Is Not Enough: The Struggle of Blacks and Hispanics for Equality in Urban Politics* (Berkeley: University California Press, 1984), p. 252; Terry Nicholls Clark and Lorna Crowley Ferguson, *City Money* (New York: Columbia University Press, 1983), pp. 144–148; Rufus P. Browning, Dale Rogers Marshall, and David H. Tabb, *Racial Politics in American Cities*, 3rd ed. (New York: Longman, 2002), pp. 374–377.

self-styled progressive mayors who emphasize issues of social justice tend to move to the center and join their more conservative counterparts in pursuing policies that promote economic growth and downtown development. At the local level, partisan and ideological differences break down, and often do not matter at all. Especially in larger cities that contain a multitude of groups and interests, urban officials become engaged in the practical task of responding to the political demands of a complex local polity.

THE INCORPORATION OF BLACKS AND LATINOS INTO CITY POLITICS

Between 1956 and 1972, nearly 4 million people were displaced in cities as a result of two federal programs: urban renewal and interstate highways. Up to one-fifth of the entire population of New Haven, Connecticut, was displaced by public projects over roughly the same period.[8] The uncompensated costs equaled 20 to 30 percent of the annual income of families forced to move, a fact that prompted a noted researcher to call it "an injustice on a massive scale."[9] Of course, the costs of displacement were borne not only by individuals; the social networks and community ties making up the neighborhoods torn apart by clearance were irretrievably broken.

In the 1960s community organizers won significant victories against urban renewal and highway projects. The Embarcadero and Central Freeway projects in San Francisco were stopped in their tracks by well-organized groups. Community leaders also mobilized people to sit down in front of bulldozers trying to clear land for urban renewal; in the end the city was forced to come up with an acceptable relocation plan.[10] The numerous protests across the country brought about changes in federal relocation guidelines. By 1970, 400 communities were fighting against highway plans.[11]

But to exert lasting impact, minority and neighborhood leaders had to go beyond protest and become part of the fabric of local politics. Federal programs provided the avenue. In his 1964 state of the union message, President Lyndon Johnson called for an "unconditional war on poverty," and that summer Congress passed the Economic Opportunity Act, which authorized the establishment of community action agencies (CAAs) funded by the federal government and "developed, conducted, and administered with the maximum feasible participation of residents of the areas and members of the groups served."[12] Two years later, Congress approved the Model Cities program, which also contained requirements for citizen participation. Participation requirements provided a way for federal administrators to bypass local Democratic Party organizations, which had long ignored the needs of African American communities. By giving grants directly to community action and Model Cities agencies, the federal government was able to build direct ties with African American voters, thus improving the electoral prospects for the Democratic presidential ticket.[13]

Within a year and a half of the passage of the Economic Opportunity Act, more than a thousand CAAs were operating in cities around the country. Most of the CAAs received and administered federal funds quietly. About 10 percent of them went further, however, when their staffs organized against such institutions as local housing agencies, welfare offices, school boards, and mayors' offices. These activities nurtured activists and encouraged new neighborhood organizations to form. One study of Cincinnati found a high correlation between War on Poverty involvement in neighborhoods and the development of neighborhood organizations. The Neighborhood Services program, launched in 1967, even paid the salaries of part-time staff working for community organizations. During the first two years of the War on Poverty, 20 new neighborhood organizations formed in Cincinnati, twice as many as there had been in the previous decade.[14] Thus the War on Poverty aided community organizing in low-income neighborhoods, which previously had lacked the financial resources and connections to organize themselves.

Predictably, community leaders came up against bitter opposition. Mayors were incensed that the federal government was funding their political opponents. Referring to the War on Poverty, San Francisco's mayor John Shelley said, "I have a very definite feeling this program is headed in a direction we don't want . . . it has the potential for setting up a great political organization. Not mine. Because I have had nothing to say about it."[15] The mayors responded by pressuring Congress to give them more control over the program. In 1967 Congress passed an amendment to the appropriations bill for community action agencies that stipulated all future grants be routed through state or local governments. The amendment also gave public officials the right to appoint the members of CAAs and lifted the requirement that all board members had to come from the community served by the CAA.

Although this amendment gave city hall leverage over the community action agencies and, indirectly, over the nonprofit organizations and neighborhood organizations receiving funds from the CAAs, there was no turning back the clock. The complexion of city politics had already changed too much. Even though local elected officials were able to reassert some influence over many of the federal programs flowing into the cities, community groups continued to flex their muscles. Many federal programs still allocated funds directly to such groups. Federal, state, and local governments contracted with community groups to provide social services such as job training, day care, and housing. The impact of the community organizing movement reverberated through city politics. Neighborhood organizations became a permanent feature of local politics in cities large and small. They were essential for recruiting new political leadership and helped prepare the way for the first generation of African American mayors.

Until 1967 not a single African American had ever been elected mayor of a major American city. In that year, Richard Hatcher was elected mayor of Gary, Indiana, and Carl Stokes became the mayor of Cleveland. In the intervening years, the number of black mayors of major cities (over 50,000 population) increased steadily, reaching 28 in 1988 and 38 five years later.[16] As shown in Figure 14.1, the number of African American elected officials in the United States increased from 1,469 in 1970 to 9,101 by 2001; 454 of them were mayors.[17] The vast majority of these officials were elected to positions in local governments, with large numbers in education, the judicial system, and law enforcement.

With the election of Kurt Schmoke as the first black mayor of Baltimore in 1987, every city of more than 100,000 people that had a majority black population had elected an African American mayor. At different points in the 1980s, African American candidates won the mayor's office in four of the five largest cities in the country, even though African American voters were in the minority in those cities (David Dinkins in New York, Tom Bradley in Los Angeles, Harold Washington in Chicago, and Wilson Goode in Philadelphia), and in the 1990s African Americans won in several cities where they constituted a minority of voters, including St. Louis, Denver, Kansas City, and Seattle.

Figure 14.1 Black Elected Officials,[a] 1970–2001, and Latino Elected Officials,[b]
1985–2005

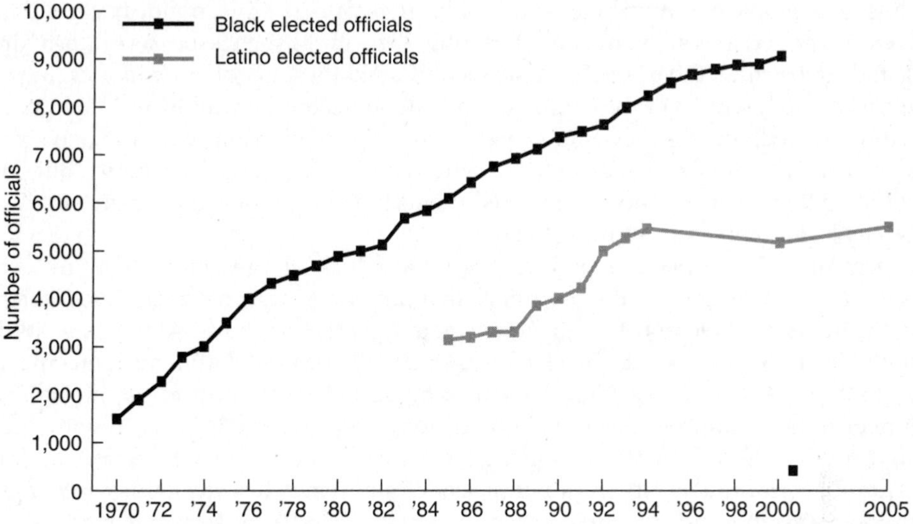

[a]Includes Congress.
[b]Does not include Congress.

Sources: National Association of Latino Elected and Appointed Officials (Washington, D.C.: Author, *National Roster of Hispanic Elected Officials,* annual); National Association of Latino Elected and Appointed Officials, "NALEO At-A-Glance" (*http://www.naelo.org/ataglance.html*); Joint Center for Political and Economic Studies, *Black Elected Officials: A Statistical Summary* (Washington, D.C.), p. 250, Table 399; Joint Center for Political and Economic Studies, *Black Elected Officials: A Statistical Summary, 2001* (Washington, D.C.: Author), p. 13.

The biracial nature of politics in American cities changed rapidly beginning in the 1980s, when Latinos began entering political office in large numbers. As shown in Figure 14.1, the number of Latino elected officials at all government levels in the United States grew from 3,147 in 1985 to 5,459 in 1994 before dropping off slightly to 5,041 in 2005.[18] Latino mayors won office in Denver, Miami, San Antonio, and numerous smaller cities. Federico Peña's election in Denver in 1983 was considered a breakthrough because he was the first Latino to be elected mayor of a large American city without a Latino majority. At the time, Latinos constituted just 18 percent of the city's population, with blacks making up another 12 percent.[19] Peña and the former mayor of San Antonio, Henry Cisneros, were appointed to President Bill Clinton's cabinet in 1993.

Minority mayors have been forced to negotiate the difficult terrain of coalition politics. In the vast majority of the cases where African Americans or Latinos have become mayors in big cities, their respective groups have not constituted a majority of either the overall population or of the voters. Even in those cases where blacks or Latinos have made up an electoral majority, minority candidates have almost always had to win a significant proportion of the votes cast outside of minority neighborhoods to assemble a winning electoral coalition. Because of this, minority candidates have been forced to walk a fine line. The more they stress such issues as minority hiring and contracting, the more they risk alienating white supporters. Minority mayors have found that whatever the composition of their electoral coalition, they are unable to do very much unless they forge a good working relationship with the one group that can bring about prosperity in the downtown—the business community. But once in office, if they seem to ignore their constituents in the neighborhoods, minority mayors may harm their chances for reelection.

A comparison of electoral politics in the nation's two largest cities, New York and Los Angeles, sheds light on the conditions that can undermine interracial and interethnic coalitions. By 1990 non-Latino whites made up less than half—43 percent—of the population of New York City. Blacks accounted for 25 percent, Latinos 24 percent, and Asians 8 percent.[20] With a large Jewish population (accounting for about half the number of non-Latino whites) that was historically sensitive to discrimination and supportive of the civil rights movement, New York City seemed to be an ideal setting for forging a multiracial and multiethnic coalition. In fact, however, this context produced an unstable and fractious politics that first elected a conservative white ethnic politician as mayor (Ed Koch elected and reelected in 1977, 1981, and 1985), then a one-term African American mayor (David Dinkins, 1989), followed by a Republican conservative (Rudolph Giuliani, 1993 and 1997). By contrast, Los Angeles, which is also racially and ethnically diverse, elected an African American mayor, Tom Bradley, in 1973, and then kept him in office for five consecutive terms. Blacks accounted for just 14 percent of the population of Los Angeles in 1990. Much can be learned about the nature of coalition politics by an examination of the Bradley years.

Tom Bradley, the son of Texas sharecroppers, moved to Los Angeles with his family at the age of seven. An exceptional student and athlete, he attended the University of California, Los Angeles, and then took a job with the Los Angeles Police Department. Moving his family to a largely white neighborhood, he organized a new community relations unit on the West Side, where he formed close personal contacts with Jewish merchants and civic leaders. Studying at night, he obtained a law degree and quit the force to practice law. Bradley became active in reform Democratic politics at a time when cooperation was being forged among upwardly mobile African Americans, Jews, and liberals—all of them largely excluded from the regular Democratic Party.

In 1969 the reform Democrats ran Bradley as a mayoral candidate against the conservative incumbent, Sam Yorty. In the racially polarized atmosphere, which was still influenced by the Watts riot of four years before, Yorty won an overwhelming majority of white votes and received particularly strong support from upper-middle-class homeowners in the San Fernando Valley. When he ran against Yorty four years later, Bradley broadened his appeal by expressing his support for policies to stimulate the revitalization of the downtown and by promising to keep taxes low. This time, Bradley was able to pull enough white and Latino votes to defeat Yorty. Bradley's electoral coalition included African Americans of all income levels, higher-income and especially

Jewish white liberals, and Latinos. In subsequent elections, Bradley gradually incorporated Asian Americans into his coalition as well. Bradley succeeded largely because he was able to symbolize different things to different people: "Whites saw Bradley as a symbol of racial harmony, while blacks saw him as a symbol of racial assertion."[21]

Bradley's success was predicated on a long history of collaboration between white liberals and the upwardly mobile black middle class. Both groups had been systematically excluded from governance prior to Bradley's victory, and therefore they did not view each other as competitors but as allies in ousting the Yorty regime. After his initial victory, Bradley also reached out to businesses, making the downtown banks and corporations key elements of his regime. As a result, Bradley always had a massive campaign chest at his command when he ran for reelection.

Many of the conditions that allowed an African American to become the mayor of Los Angeles were absent in New York, despite the fact that blacks were already well entrenched in New York City's government by the mid-1960s.[22] By the time blacks entered New York City's political system, liberals and Jews had already established themselves by successfully electing a liberal Republican, John Lindsay, as mayor for two terms (1966–1973). Although New York's blacks, Jews, and white liberals could clearly cooperate, their leaders viewed one another with suspicion. These tensions came to a head in 1968, when the African American community attempted an experiment in community control in the Ocean Hill–Brownsville schools in Brooklyn. The school board's attempt to transfer 19 teachers, some of them Jewish, out of the district resulted in a bitter citywide strike by the teachers' union, which divided blacks and Jews in ways that are still being felt in New York today. The same sort of conflicts and suspicions have characterized the political relationships between African Americans and Latinos, 90 percent of whom identify themselves as white (the other 10 percent mostly come from the Caribbean).[23] Conflicts among these groups allowed Ed Koch to assemble a conservative coalition with Jews and Catholics at its center, which became the basis of his mayoral victories in 1977, 1981, and 1985.[24]

In 1989 New York elected a black mayor, David Dinkins. Having come up through the regular Democratic Party, Dinkins possessed a dignified, nonconfrontational style that was nonthreatening to whites, although without doubt blacks made up the heart of his electoral coalition. In the early stages of the mayoral contest, Koch miscalculated by attacking Jesse Jackson, who had made a run for the presidency the year before, for expressing support for the Palestine Liberation Organization (PLO). Koch commented that Jews "would have to be crazy" to vote for Jackson. An African American newspaper, *Amsterdam News*, replied bitterly by reminding Koch that "he is mayor of the city; not just of New York Jewry."[25] In an atmosphere of growing racial tension, many white voters felt Dinkins would be better able to keep the peace, and he defeated Koch in the 1989 multicandidate Democratic primary by a 51 to 41 percent margin.

Dinkins lasted one term and was defeated by a self-styled conservative, Rudolph Giuliani, in 1993. Giuliani, a former prosecutor and a Republican, quickly set out to terminate affirmative action programs, slash spending for welfare and housing, cut health services, and beef up the police forces.[26] Crime control became the leitmotif of his administration, and he became nationally prominent for his advocacy of the "broken windows" theory, based on the premise that if small crimes were punished, larger ones would be deterred. While in office, Giuliani made a point to snub African American leaders and groups. In 2001, when he was forced to leave office because of term limits, he was succeeded by Republican Michael Bloomberg, who with his own money spent $99 per vote to narrowly defeat the Democratic candidate.[27]

New York's racial politics became divisive only in part because white voters became concerned about crime and social disorder. The city also had become racially and ethnically diverse to the point that the various groups began to resent any benefits conferred on another group.[28] The Latino population had grown very rapidly since the mid-1960s and felt that blacks had secured a disproportionate share of municipal offices and perks. But even Latinos were divided among West Indians, Dominicans, Puerto Ricans, and Jamaicans. Asian voters also fought for a place in politics. This fractious politics has contributed to racial polarization, improving the prospects for any mayoral candidate who focuses on controlling crime and promoting downtown development—two issues that appeal quite broadly.

White candidates in other cities, most notably Los Angeles, have likewise been able to play a game of divide and conquer; indeed, racial resentments have been the key ingredient in the rise of several conservative mayors. But such cases are not necessarily typical. Overt hostilities are not the norm, and there are many examples of successful coalitions across racial and ethnic lines. Denver provides a good example. Federico Peña became the city's first Mexican American mayor in 1983 by cobbling together a coalition of educated white professionals connected to Denver's high-tech economy and Latino and African American voters. Peña stressed downtown and neighborhood development but also initiated affirmative action hiring in all public agencies and appointed a large number of minorities to boards and commissions. His African American successor in 1991, Wellington Webb, embellished Peña's programs by emphasizing infrastructure improvements throughout the city and by establishing a revolving fund for affordable housing.[29] Denver's experience shows it is possible for minority candidates to emerge from a "unite and govern" rather a "divide and conquer" politics.

The Rewards of Political Incorporation

The ability to elect a mayor is only the first step toward exercising political power. To actually derive substantial benefits, it is also necessary for minorities to seek political incorporation, which can be defined as possessing "an equal or leading role in a dominant coalition that is strongly committed to minority interests."[30] Incorporation entails the ability to influence a city council and the various bureaucracies that deliver important services; otherwise, a mayor can become isolated, unable to deliver on the campaign promises made. In Chicago, for example, Harold Washington, who was mayor from 1983 to 1987, found himself tied down in the so-called council wars during his entire first term. The city council—still dominated by white ethnic politicians left over from the Daley organization—overrode Washington's policy proposals. Department administrators and city workers routinely ignored problems in the African American neighborhoods; instead, they followed orders from aldermen and precinct captains hostile to Washington. Blacks in Chicago had succeeded in electing a mayor, but until Washington's second term, they did not change Chicago's government very much.

To govern effectively and deliver benefits to supporters, a mayor must assemble a broad and comprehensive governing coalition. In American cities, authority is fragmented and dispersed.[31] The mayor's office is a center of power, but many other centers of power can act as veto points to frustrate mayoral leadership. To produce significant results that can be used to run for reelection, mayors need cooperation from institutions well beyond the city council, including labor unions, the media, independent authorities (such as school boards), the courts, and state and federal officials. To be effective while in office, a mayor must seek support from many sectors.

Most African American mayors have supported a pro-growth downtown development agenda.[32] Atlanta's experience shows why. In 1973 Maynard Jackson was elected the first African American mayor of Atlanta with strong support from the black community and from neighborhood activists in both black and white neighborhoods. Jackson came into office with a strong social reform program, explicitly rejecting what he termed "slavish, unquestioning adherence to downtown dicta."[33] What set Jackson apart from previous mayors was that he insisted business elites "come to city hall to meet in his office and to ask for his support, rather than simply to inform him of their needs and assume his compliance."[34]

To undertake complex projects that he could take credit for when seeking reelection, however, Jackson needed the support of the business community, and, over time, he was pulled toward accommodation with the downtown business elite. He supported all the major redevelopment projects favored by downtown business, including construction of the Metro Atlanta Rapid Transit Authority (MARTA) system, which mainly connected downtown to the Atlanta airport. Jackson's successor, civil rights activist Andrew Young, continued Jackson's unqualified support of downtown development. Commenting on his partnership with business, Young said, "Politics doesn't control the world. Money does."[35]

Jackson and Young were able to increase African American public employment, government contracts for minority-owned firms, and African American representation on the police force, but the booming downtown and suburbs did little to help blacks trapped in inner-city low-income neighborhoods. They were left behind.[36] From 1980 to 1985, predominantly white areas in the Atlanta region experienced job growth 14 times greater than predominantly black areas. Between 1970 and 1982, the percentage of central-city households living in poverty doubled. Atlanta's housing and job markets remained highly segregated. After 1980, applications to higher education, especially among Atlanta's black males, fell rapidly. A 1989 study by the *Atlanta Constitution* found that one black man in six had been imprisoned.[37]

The administration of Mayor Tom Bradley, who was elected in 1973 with the support of a broad electoral coalition, also illustrates the extreme importance that all mayors attach to economic growth. Early on, Bradley stressed the need to make Los Angeles a "world class" city. He courted Japanese investors, who poured more than $3 billion into Los Angeles real estate in 1988 alone. Before Bradley, there was almost no downtown in Los Angeles; in 1975 only 5 buildings were above 13 stories. By 1990 there were over 50 such buildings—many of them visible in the dramatic footage that opened the television series *L.A. Law.*[38]

To subsidize downtown development, Los Angeles created a huge 255-block tax increment finance (TIF) district. The TIF allowed the city to float bonds to provide public improvements and services to stimulate private investment. But because the city was required to use all the additional taxes from the downtown redevelopment to retire the bonds or to support further development, the new taxes could not be used for projects or services elsewhere in the city.[39] The downtown office complex experienced a boom, but the high-level professional jobs generated by corporate investment were taken either by suburban residents or by professionals who moved into gentrified neighborhoods close to the downtown. The overall effect was to displace lower-income residents, drive up the cost of housing, and segment urban space into enclaves. Finally recognizing the depth of the housing crisis, in 1991 Mayor Bradley began to push for "linkage" fees that would require developers to allocate funds for low-income housing in exchange for approval of downtown building projects. But it was too little, too late.

The 1992 riots showed how impossible it was for Bradley to satisfy all of the contending interests in the city's politics. His policies had mainly aided real estate developers and expanded opportunities for white-collar professionals, including some who were black and Latino. Redevelopment did not benefit the poor. According to the 1990 census, the poverty rate in South Central Los Angeles, where the riots started, was 33 percent. The area was seething with tensions between newly arrived Central American immigrants and longtime African American residents. The riots exposed the depth of the racial and ethnic tensions in the city.

Bradley did not even succeed in satisfying affluent white voters. When development spread from downtown to the affluent West Side, Bradley began to encounter stiff opposition from environmentalists who objected to increased air pollution and traffic congestion. Unable to keep up with new development, the sewage system broke down in 1987, dumping millions of gallons of raw sewage into Santa Monica Bay. Bradley proposed a cap on new sewer construction to slow the pace of new development. The next year, however, Bradley infuriated environmentalists by reversing his long-standing opposition to oil drilling in the Pacific Palisades, an area on the ocean floor extending several miles out from Los Angeles. Under siege from residents in low- as well as high-income neighborhoods, Bradley chose not to run for a sixth term in 1993.

Whatever the circumstances they face, minority mayors and city councils must try to deliver on their election-year promises. Public employment is their most important resource. Studies have consistently shown that when blacks are politically incorporated—that is, when they win the mayor's office and infiltrate the institutions of local government—minority employment in city government increases.[40] From 1973 to 1991, Mayor Bradley managed to increase the jobs held by blacks, Latinos, and Asians in municipal government from 36 to 50 percent. Minorities are often concentrated in lower-level jobs, but in Los Angeles during this period minority representation in top-level city jobs increased as well.[41]

Minority mayors have also frequently enacted preferential procurement programs requiring that a minimum percentage of city contracts be given to minority business enterprises (MBEs). In 1973, at a time when blacks accounted for a majority of Atlanta's population, black-owned firms received only one-tenth of 1 percent of the city's contracts. By 1988, as a result of preferential procurement, minority firms were awarded 35 percent of the city's contracts. Such programs have been damaged, however, by evidence that some MBEs have acted as mere fronts for nonminority firms doing most of the work.[42] Moreover, like many affirmative action programs, preferential procurement generally has benefited higher-income and better educated people within the minority community. Atlanta's first black mayor, Maynard Jackson, boasted that the minority set-asides for Atlanta's airport expansion created 21 African American millionaires; however, benefits to the low-income community were more difficult to identify.[43]

The U.S. Supreme Court has made it harder for cities and states to use preferential procurement programs. In *City of Richmond v. J. A. Croson Co.* (1989), the Court ruled that Richmond's program requiring that 30 percent of contracts be set aside for MBEs violated the equal protection clause of the Fourteenth Amendment.[44] To withstand the "strict scrutiny" standard of constitutionality, cities must document past discrimination by city government and demonstrate that race-neutral alternatives will not solve the problem. This ruling makes preferential procurement difficult but not impossible to implement.[45]

Police reform is another important policy benefit flowing from political incorporation. Police brutality and inadequate police protection have long been two of the most frequently expressed grievances in minority communities around the country. For many years, the police department of Los Angeles was loathed in minority communities. Under the city's governmental structure, the LAPD operated well beyond the influence of elected officials. Appointed by an independent Police Commission, the chief of police had a free hand in running the department. The LAPD had always prided itself on its tough law-and-order approach to law enforcement, and the chief liked to brag about the department's state-of-the-art high-tech weaponry. In Los Angeles, policing relied on helicopters equipped with infrared cameras for night vision and 30-million-candlepower spotlights, called Nightsuns, that could turn night into day. Street numbers painted on rooftops gave police helicopters a navigable street grid from the air (now replaced by satellite navigation). Synchronization with patrol cars was facilitated by a communications system conceptualized by Hughes Aircraft and refined by NASA's Jet Propulsion Laboratory.[46] In low-income neighborhoods, this strategy meant the LAPD acted more like an occupying army than as an instrument for preserving public safety.

From 1978 to 1992, Chief Daryl Gates ran the LAPD as his own personal fiefdom. Under operation HAMMER, patrol officers and elite tactical squads descended on South Central Los Angeles, arresting thousands of minority youths in each sweep. Young men were brought in for a wide range of infractions, from selling drugs to suspected gang activity to charges of loitering and jaywalking. In the absence of other charges, resisting arrest became a favorite police option. By 1990 as many as 50,000 suspects had been arrested in these sweeps, which is astounding considering only about 100,000 African American youths lived in all of Los Angeles.[47] The LAPD had a practice of using a dangerous chokehold to control people in custody. In 1982, after frequent use of the chokehold resulted in a rash of deaths among young black men, Chief Gates made the inflammatory statement that the problem could be traced to the anatomy of blacks rather than to police practices: "We may be finding that in some Blacks when [the carotid chokehold] is applied the veins or arteries do not open up as fast as they do on normal people."[48] The beating of Rodney King, which set off the 1992 riots, came as no surprise to blacks in Los Angeles.

Mayor Bradley, who had the advantage of being a former cop, succeeded in bringing the LAPD under some degree of civilian control, but only after 20 years of fierce political battles. The LAPD's share of the city's budget fell from 23 percent in 1972–1973 to 18 percent in 1987–1988. Between 1980 and 1988, minority representation in the LAPD increased from 20 to 32 percent, but the numbers of minorties in leadership positions still lagged. Most importantly, in June 1992, shortly after the riots, the voters approved Proposition F. Strongly supported by Bradley, Proposition F limited the terms of police chiefs and removed their civil service protection. Having campaigned vigorously against Proposition F, Chief Gates resigned and was succeeded by an African American, Willie Williams, who pledged to implement community-based policing.[49]

What the Los Angeles case shows is that even under adverse conditions, when minorities are incorporated into the political system, they are able to bring about important changes. In Los Angeles, the black community considered it essential that more African American police officers be hired and the police department be brought under greater civilian control.[50] Racism and police brutality still occur within integrated police forces, but changing the composition of the force is a first step toward reform.

An increasing number of racial and ethnic groups have recently sought incorporation into city politics. When these groups must cooperate to gain access to the political system, they are often able to put aside their differences and support a candidate. But these alliances are hard to keep together. A study of 41 cities with at least 10 percent blacks and 10 percent Latinos found that, generally, black and Latino municipal employment was associated with the incorporation of both groups into local political systems. The same research showed, however, that as the African American population increased, the Latino share of municipal employment fell.[51] Tensions arise because it is difficult to satisfy both groups with the limited jobs and other resources available. In New York City, the failure of blacks and Latinos to forge a stable electoral coalition facilitated the election of conservative mayors Ed Koch and Rudolph Giuliani. Similarly, after Bradley retired in Los Angeles, his black and Latino coalition fell apart, which paved the road to the mayor's office for Republican conservative Richard Riordan.

However, the main weakness of the racial and ethnic coalitions has not been their instability but their failure to deliver much-needed social programs. In the 1960s and 1970s, when federal grants were flowing into cities, the first generation of minority mayors was able to fund programs that benefited the poor. Since the withdrawal of federal funds, mayors have found it difficult to find the necessary resources to fund housing, health, jobs, recreation, and other initiatives. Minority mayors emphasize economic development as much as they do not because they have given up on the goal of providing benefits to their constituents, but because they see no other way to raise the resources necessary to deliver on their promises. In short, they pursue trickle-down policies based on the logic that "private economic development in the city produces jobs in the private sector and tax money that may be used for jobs and purchases in the public sector. Through the various affirmative action devices . . . a certain proportion of these jobs and purchases may be channeled to the black community."[52] But on the whole, these jobs have been marginal to the goal of general economic advancement for blacks and Latinos.[53] One reason for this is that public jobs cannot be the answer. Public-sector jobs can supply employment to no more than 6 to 8 percent of the black population of central cities—even assuming no jobs would go to other groups.[54] In any case, a large proportion of public jobs, minority business contracts, and other benefits have gone to middle- and upper-income people and even to suburban residents.[55]

To expect substantial economic gains from political participation is probably unrealistic, however. Incorporation of any group cannot result in the overturning of the basic economic arrangements that preserve inequality. As noted by one scholar, "There is no precedent for expecting political participation to produce revolutionary outcomes for any group in American urban politics specifically or American politics in general."[56] Still, considerable progress has been made. Minority regimes have been quite successful in altering hiring policies and reining in the police. These are important accomplishments.

However, studies provide little evidence that the incorporation of blacks and Latinos into political systems has led to significantly different taxing, spending, and service delivery policies. For the most part, African American mayors have not significantly altered development trends favoring downtown areas over the neighborhoods. The incorporation of African Americans and Latinos has had the effect of making people feel better about local politics, however. Survey research shows that blacks living in cities with a black mayor expressed more trust in and paid more attention to political affairs, and they participated more in politics.[57] Participation by Latinos has increased in the cities where Latinos have become incorporated into local power structures.[58] Regardless of its objective limitations, minority incorporation has increased the legitimacy of city governments among a substantial portion of the urban population.

NEIGHBORHOOD ORGANIZATIONS AND POLITICAL INCORPORATION

Neighborhood activists have taken the lead in challenging the assumption that cities should focus primarily on local economic growth. Big downtown projects pushed by mayors and business elites—convention centers, sports stadiums, subsidized mall and entertainment districts—are regularly questioned because of the presence of neighborhood organizations. The incorporation of neighborhoods into city politics has created a political dynamic in which neighborhood organizations and their leaders articulate issues of equity and social justice and provide social services whereas city hall and downtown business tend to promote an ideology of growth.

Neighborhood organizations have become an important means of delivering urban services, and they often do so for city governments. A 1990 survey of 161 cities with populations of over 100,000 people found that 60 percent of them had active systems of neighborhood councils, with 70 percent of these being officially recognized by city government.[59] By the early 1990s, New York City had instituted a system of moderate decentralization wherein 59 community planning boards appointed by elected officials exercised advisory powers over land use and city services.[60] St. Paul has one of the most extensive systems of neighborhood control in the country. Seventeen district councils, each elected by district residents, possessed substantial powers over zoning, the distribution of goods and services, and capital expenditures.[61] A 1991 survey of 133 cities with populations over 100,000 found that 64 percent had formed housing advocacy coalitions,[62] which work with governments, nonprofit organizations, and developers to build housing for low- and moderate-income families. The degree to which neighborhood organizations are incorporated into local government structures varies greatly from city to city, but these organizations play some role virtually everywhere. For example, in most cities, a substantial proportion of the federal government's block grant funds flow through neighborhood and nonprofit organizations.

In some cities, community organizations have helped to elect mayors and other public officials. In 1967 Kevin White was elected mayor of Boston in part because of support from neighborhood groups that opposed urban renewal. Once in office, he supported rent control and set up "Little City Halls" around the city to satisfy demands for more community control. Later, White lost neighborhood support when he reversed himself on rent control and supported unbridled downtown growth. In 1972 Neil Goldschmidt won the mayor's office in Portland, Oregon, with key backing from neighborhood activists. A veteran of the civil rights movement before being elected to the Portland City Council, Goldschmidt had worked with Legal Services, which provided legal assistance to antipoverty and community groups. In 1971 and 1972, Goldschmidt cast the only dissenting votes on the city council on major urban renewal projects. As mayor, he formalized neighborhood authority over selected land use decisions, and the city even provided professional staff to neighborhood associations so they could review planning proposals. Between 1974 and 1979, the number of neighborhood groups in Portland doubled to 60.[63]

Another early success for the neighborhood movement came in Cincinnati. This was notable because the city's reform-style governmental structure—with a city manager and at-large nonpartisan elections—seemed to discourage the decentralization of decision making. But in 1971 several neighborhood groups came together to propose a slate of council candidates. Enough members of the slate were elected to make up a majority of the new city council. Whereas the previous Republican council had emphasized downtown development, the new council stressed neighborhood revitalization. Soon Cincinnati instituted neighborhood planning and began providing direct assistance to neighborhood associations.[64] From 1969 to 1979, Hartford, Connecticut, operated under a city council whose members had strong roots in the neighborhoods. During these years, the city negotiated an equity partnership for neighborhood groups in major downtown developments, thus providing these organizations with a steady source of income and a stake in the downtown's success.[65] In 1981 Santa Monicans for Renters' Rights (SMRR) swept the city council elections in Santa Monica, California, and then implemented a rent control ordinance that reportedly saved renters $1.1 billion between 1987 and 1997.[66]

Such success stories should not be taken as typical, however. The politics of most cities continue to be focused on downtown development, and in many cities—especially Sunbelt cities like Phoenix, Las Vegas, and Houston—neighborhood groups have had relatively little success in organizing or in shaping city government policies. Commenting on Houston, one study called its neighborhood groups "largely invisible." During the 1970s and 1980s, Houston had only one organization representing poor neighborhoods, The Metropolitan Organization (TMO).[67] Although TMO won infrastructure improvements for poor neighborhoods, it failed to stop the Hardy Toll Road that, for the convenience of white suburban commuters, destroyed many units of moderate-income housing.[68] Denounced as radical, TMO has been excluded from the governing regime. Compared with cities like Boston and San Francisco, which have hundreds of community-based nonprofit housing developers, Houston had only five in the early 1990s. In 1988 Houston spent only 10 percent of its Community Development Block Grant (CDBG) on housing, compared to 75 percent in Boston and Santa Monica.

Neighborhood groups are often perceived as antibusiness and lacking in a broad program of economic revitalization. The belief that the main purpose of government should be to facilitate the accumulation of private economic wealth is still the dominant ideology not only in cities but in American culture generally. In 1977 Dennis Kucinich was elected mayor of Cleveland with strong support from neighborhood groups and minority voters. He carried this confrontational approach into the mayor's office, engaging, for example, in a bitter fight with corporations and banks over tax abatements for downtown properties. In retaliation, the banks pushed Cleveland into default by refusing to refinance the city's debt. Perceived as antibusiness, Kucinich was defeated by Republican George Voinovich after only two years in office.[69]

Mayors cannot govern effectively in the face of widespread business opposition. Somehow, they must bridge the chasm between downtown and neighborhood interests. Ray Flynn of Boston was one of the nation's most successful mayors in bridging this gap. First elected in 1983, Flynn left office nine years later to become ambassador to the Vatican. Growing up in South Boston, Flynn's father was an immigrant longshore worker, and his mother cleaned downtown office buildings. After serving 15 years on the city council, Flynn mounted a surprisingly strong campaign in the 1983 mayoral race by building on his support from tenants' groups and neighborhood organizations. He stirred up his poor, largely Roman Catholic followers by pitting them against the Yankee blue bloods and downtown Republicans and promised to implement linkage policies to force developers to help the neighborhoods.

Once in office, Flynn recognized the importance of forging a governing coalition. Largely abandoning the confrontational rhetoric that had gotten him elected, he called for an alliance with business based on a program that would pursue downtown development and neighborhood revitalization at the same time. Boston's booming downtown office market allowed developers to make profits even while paying linkage fees. By walking a tightrope between downtown and the neighborhoods, Flynn was able to accomplish an impressive agenda of reform. He strengthened the city's rent control laws and enacted regulations to limit the conversion of rental units into condominiums. Flynn enacted a housing policy that required developers of projects with ten or more units to set aside 10 percent of the units for low- and moderate-income families. To deal with redlining, Flynn enacted a "linked deposit" policy in which the city would deposit its funds only with banks that demonstrated a commitment to Boston's neighborhoods. The city contributed funds to Boston's nonprofit housing developers and also gave crucial support to one of the most successful comprehensive neighborhood revitalization projects in the country, the so-called Dudley Street Neighborhood Initiative (DSNI). With one-third of the land vacant, DSNI was blocked from assembling desirable parcels by an incredible jigsaw puzzle of private owners. In an unprecedented move, the city gave DSNI, a community-based organization, the power of eminent domain so it could force owners to sell their properties.[70]

How successful was Flynn in improving the lives of neighborhood residents? By 1993 linkage had raised about $70 million and helped build 10,000 affordable housing units, and by the end of Flynn's second term, community-based housing corporations had built or rehabilitated another 5,000 units. The banks agreed to commit $400 million to a community reinvestment plan for low- and moderate-income neighborhoods. Through Neighborhood Councils and other innovations, the Flynn administration granted residents more power over land use decisions. Nevertheless, only so much could be accomplished purely through local efforts.[71] Innovative local housing policies could not compensate for cuts in federal housing assistance imposed by the Reagan administration. And there was relatively little the Flynn administration could do about the income inequality arising in Boston from the combination of a booming corporate services sector and a rapidly declining industrial base.

Community Development Corporations

Beginning in the late 1960s, neighborhood organizations across the country began to spin off community development corporations (CDCs) to deliver services and rehabilitate housing in their neighborhoods. CDCs are nonprofit corporations run by boards composed of area residents, formed for the purpose of delivering services and building infrastructure in neighborhoods or in somewhat larger areas. Federal, state, and city governments contract with CDCs to administer services such as job training, day care, homeless shelters, health clinics, and meals-on-wheels. They also administer funds to rehabilitate housing or fix up playgrounds and other neighborhood facilities. To varying degrees, CDCs have become incorporated into local governmental structures, although they exercise considerable autonomy in deciding how to spend the funds they receive. Because they nurture their own constituencies, in many cities they have become influential political organizations.

The CDC movement began in the 1960s as a variation on the community action agencies funded by the federal government (many CDCs evolved from community action agencies). They were supposed to arise from and represent the neighborhoods where they were located. By seeking funding from many sources, they would establish their independence and thereby be able to represent the neighborhoods. It was expected that, over time, they would evolve into agencies that delivered important social and community services.

The CDC idea was planted when Senator Robert Kennedy toured the Bedford–Stuyvesant section of Brooklyn on a chilly afternoon in 1966. After seeing unemployed men lounging on street corners, children playing without coats in 30-degree cold, and mounds of uncollected garbage, Kennedy attended a meeting with community activists. Angry residents took out their frustrations on the surprised senator. A prominent black politician from the area told Kennedy: "I'm weary of study, Senator. Weary of speeches, weary of promises that aren't kept. . . . The Negro people are angry, Senator."[72] Appalled by the urban decay and the bitterness expressed by the residents, Kennedy vowed to devise a comprehensive strategy that would involve the residents themselves in revitalizing their neighborhood. The result was the Bedford–Stuyvesant Restoration Corporation (BSRC). Public funds were the key to leveraging private investment. The recipient of $33 million in federal dollars between 1968 and 1974, BSRC succeeded in attracting retail stores and rehabilitating thousands of housing units.

By the mid-1970s an estimated 200 CDCs had been established in the country, and in the next few years they sprang up almost everywhere. A 1989 survey of 133 cities with populations of more than 100,000 found CDCs active in 95 percent of them.[73] According to a national survey, by 1994 the number of CDCs in the United States had grown to over 2,000.[74] CDCs were much more common on the West Coast and in the Northeast than in the South and the mountain states.[75] With a median staff size of seven, most CDCs were quite small, often employing from one to five people. Ninety percent of CDCs were engaged in housing production, 23 percent were involved in business development, and 66 percent were focused on advocacy and community building.[76]

Over the years, a network has evolved to support the work of CDCs. National institutions developed by the Ford Foundation and the Enterprise Foundation (the latter established by the developer James Rouse)[77] market federal low-income housing tax credits (LIHTCs) to wealthy investors, who are enticed by the tax write-offs. The investments are then bundled together and allocated to CDCs, which rehabilitate housing units and sell them to individual buyers (who generally qualify for below-market interest loans). The LIHTC program has become the main federal support for low-income housing, with nonprofits receiving in 1994 over one-quarter of the subsidies. Foundation support for CDCs expanded from $74 million in 1987 to $179 million in 1991.[78] Housing advocacy coalitions have formed in 85 cities as conduits for low-income tax credits, foundation grants, and local, state, and federal housing funds. By pooling funds from many sources, the advocacy coalitions work with CDCs (and sometimes independently) to build affordable housing.

CDCs receive assistance from private banks, which were goaded into helping by the requirements of the Community Reinvestment Act (CRA) of 1977. Congress passed the CRA in response to intense pressure applied by neighborhood groups, which sent activists from cities around the country to pack the halls of Congress. The protesters argued that banks were engaging in redlining—the practice of drawing a red line around certain areas and refusing to grant mortgage loans within those boundaries. The CRA outlaws redlining, specifically stating that "regulated financial institutions have continuing and affirmative obligations to help meet the credit needs of the local communities in which they are chartered."[79] It is almost impossible to define the "affirmative obligations" of banks, and federal regulators have tended to side with the banks, very rarely ruling against them.

Nevertheless, the CRA has given advocacy agencies and CDCs leverage with the banks. Under the CRA, a community group can file a formal protest with a relevant federal regulator if it thinks a bank is failing to meet the credit needs of the community. During the time when the protest is under consideration, the bank is forbidden to engage in certain actions, such as buying another bank or opening up a new branch. To avoid such disruptions and to steer clear of negative publicity, banks are usually willing to cut a deal with neighborhood activists. According to one study, by 1992 approximately $18 billion in new investment commitments had been negotiated with private lenders by over 300 neighborhood groups in 70 cities across the country.[80] Much of this money has been used by CDCs to build or rehabilitate housing.

Some CDCs have become significant players in local politics. The New Community Corporation (NCC) of Newark, New Jersey, is one of the country's oldest and most successful CDCs. Formed after the 1968 riots in Newark, by the mid-1990s the NCC had become the city's largest employer, providing jobs for 1,426 people. The NCC's job training centers placed 1,100 graduates each year, operated 2,500 housing units, ran seven day-care centers enrolling 500 children, and operated a nursing home, a credit union, a domestic violence shelter, a supermarket, and a restaurant. Until the late 1990s, when some corporate offices once again began moving into Newark, the NCC filled the vacuum left by the absence of big employers.

Mayors often find CDCs troublesome, but they must work with them. With the exception of a period of cooperation under Mayor Harold Washington, CDCs in Chicago have been viewed as rivals who might threaten the power and patronage of the Democratic Party's organization. By contrast, Pittsburgh has brought CDCs directly into its governance structure. In most cities, the city council, mayor's office, or an administrative agency of the city government determines how block grants and city funds will be spent, and CDCs compete for a piece of the pie. In Pittsburgh, an unusual arrangement exists in which the Partnership for Neighborhood Development, which is composed of representatives of CDCs, foundations, business, and city government, makes the allocation decisions. As a result, 80 percent of the city's capital budget between 1978 and 1987 went to neighborhoods, compared with only 20 percent at the peak of neighborhood investment in Chicago.[81]

CDCs have steadily increased their capacity, especially in the area of low-income housing. In 1994, for example, they produced an estimated 30,000 to 40,000 units of low- and moderate-income housing. Proponents of CDCs argue that they do more than rehabilitate housing—they rehabilitate communities. At their best, CDCs are expressions of grassroots democracy, run by local residents and not by remote planners in city hall or Washington, D.C. CDCs form grassroots lobbying efforts to press for funding from governments, foundations, and private corporations. The main argument for CDCs is that they knit together the fabric of local community by empowering the residents to solve their own problems.

The problem with the CDC model is that poverty, inequality, and neighborhood decline are brought about by factors well beyond the influence of individual neighborhoods. CDC development is uneven in different regions of the country and within cities. Neighborhoods that are well organized are represented by CDCs, but as one would expect, neighborhoods with the highest poverty levels are generally those that are the least organized. Even the most successful CDCs cannot address the root causes of poverty, inequality, and urban decline. Critics maintain that these causes can only be addressed by challenges to the national political system. As CDCs have been pulled into delivering services and developing housing, they have largely given up their advocacy mission.[82] When CDCs rely on corporations, foundations, and governments for funding for their continued existence, they hesitate to confront these same institutions.[83]

Whatever their limitations, CDCs have become an essential part of the institutional fabric in neighborhoods all across the country. They help mobilize citizens, supply critical services, and bring additional public and private resources into communities. CDCs have been able to garner substantial resources from private corporations and foundations, but they are still largely creatures of public funding. A 1992 study of 130 CDCs found that 78 percent received federal funds and that such funding represented about twice the resources derived from any other public or private source.[84] The biggest danger to CDCs is that federal support could be withdrawn at any time.

THE CONSERVATIVE REACTION

In the 1990s the national conservative movement began to put down roots in local politics, energized in considerable measure by racial, ethnic, and class divisions within the cities. Within a few years, self-styled conservative white mayors replaced prominent African American mayors in several cities. In 1993 Rudolph Giuliani, a white former district attorney, defeated New York's first black mayor, David Dinkins; that same year in Los Angeles, white millionaire financier Richard Riordan defeated Mike Woo, an Asian American who tried unsuccessfully to reconstruct Tom Bradley's coalition. A year earlier, Bret Schundler had become the first Republican in 75 years to be elected mayor of Jersey City, New Jersey, and Republican Stephen Goldsmith became mayor of Indianapolis. Elsewhere, African American mayors were defeated by Democrats who advocated distinctly downtown-oriented agendas. Richard M. Daley, the son of Democratic machine boss Richard J. Daley, twice defeated African American opponents, and Edward Rendell replaced Philadelphia's first black mayor, Wilson Goode.

The conservative reaction was provoked by resentments about minority political demands, especially in the areas of affirmative action and busing; opposition by downtown business elites to higher taxes and programs with a social welfare dimension, such as linkage policies; and widespread anxiety about crime and disorder. The conservative mayors also promised a renewed focus on downtown development and amenities. Coming into office with this mix of issues, conservative mayors faced the challenge of delivering tangible benefits to their core constituencies without provoking unacceptable levels of racial and ethnic animosity.

The first generation of conservative mayors came into office during a period of high tension. In the wake of the Los Angeles riots of 1992, issues connected to social disorder, drugs, and crime reverberated all through the American political system. By playing on such themes, Republican Rudolph Giuliani was able to overcome a six-to-one Democratic advantage in party registration in the 1993 mayoral race in New York City. Whereas Giuliani received 78 percent of the white vote, the African American incumbent, David Dinkins, carried 95 percent of the African American vote. Giuliani's campaign slogan, "Taking Back the City," played on a law-and-order theme and racial antagonisms. Latinos played a crucial role in the election. Giuliani had lost by a narrow margin in 1989, when he received 34 percent of the Latino vote. In the 1993 election, Giuliani put a prominent Latino politician, Herman Badillo, on his ticket for the office of city comptroller. This time, Giuliani got 39 percent of the Latino vote. He also benefited from an unusually high voter turnout in the borough of Staten Island, a turnout stimulated by a ballot initiative calling for secession from New York City. Racial tensions provided the main motivation for the controversial proposal to secede.[85]

Latino voters also supplied the swing vote in the 1993 Los Angeles mayoral race. A Republican, Richard Riordan, carried only 14 percent of the African American vote that year, but he defeated a Democratic candidate, Mike Woo. Riordan won the election by persuading 67 percent of white voters and 43 percent of Latino voters to support him. To achieve the necessary name recognition, Riordan poured $6 million of his own money into the campaign. Riordan had acquired his fortune by financing leveraged buyouts through junk bonds and by speculating in downtown Los Angeles real estate. He had been a frequent contributor to Tom Bradley's campaigns, and by portraying himself as a pragmatic manager "tough enough to turn L.A. around," he was able to win 31 percent of the votes cast by previous Bradley supporters.[86] In April 1997 Riordan won reelection with 61 percent of the vote; he improved his support among Latino voters but lost the black vote by a three-to-one ratio.

The conservative mayors have fought hard to reverse policies perceived as unfairly benefiting blacks. At the time Giuliani was elected, 38 percent of New York City's municipal jobs went to blacks, even though they constituted only 29 percent of the city's population.[87] On taking office, Giuliani repealed the city's affirmative action policies in hiring and contracting, and he began to reduce city payrolls. Within two years, the city's workforce had been trimmed by 17,000 workers.

Concerns about law and order also contributed to the conservative turn in city politics. Crime became a highly charged symbolic issue, "a shorthand signal, to crucial numbers of white voters, of broader issues of social disorder, tapping powerful ideas about authority, status, morality, self-control, and race."[88] Some voters perceived black mayors as being soft on crime because they sometimes advocated more spending on social services and supported civilian review boards to monitor police conduct.[89] Conservatives vowed to "get tough" with criminals. As a former federal prosecutor, Giuliani was ideally situated to portray himself as a law-and-order candidate.

Giuliani delivered on his promises by cutting budgets for almost every city agency except the police and fire departments. He hired William Bratton as his police commissioner. Bratton instituted three controversial policing strategies. First, officers were allocated to hot spots identified from daily computer mappings of shootings and drug sales. Second, police began to crack down on minor offenses such as drinking in public, urinating on the street, and hassling motorists by demanding money for cleaning their windshields. This strategy was derived from the so-called broken windows theory of urban decline. Stated broadly, the theory suggested that small signs of decay, such as broken windows and trash on empty lots, serve as signs that a neighborhood is dangerous and in decline. As applied to crime control, it meant that small offenses would be punished. Third, officers were encouraged to frisk people who were stopped for minor violations, such as playing loud music or drinking in public, in order to get guns off the street.

The new policing strategies appeared to work when New York's crime rate dropped dramatically. The number of murders fell nearly 60 percent, from a high of 2,262 in 1990 to 983 by 1996. Formerly regarded as one of the most dangerous cities in the country, for the first six months of 1996 New York City ranked 144th out of the largest 189 cities in per capita total crime.[90] Although the media attributed the decline to the new policing strategies, in fact the crime rate had begun to drop in the last year of the Dinkins administration, and the fall in the city's crime rate followed a national trend. Nevertheless, Giuliani made the improved crime statistics a major plank in his successful 1997 reelection campaign. In Giuliani's second term, crime continued to fall (again, in parallel with a national trend). There were 672 murders committed in the city in 2000.[91]

In addition to exploiting racially charged issues, conservative mayors also claimed to possess the magic formula for bringing prosperity to the local economy. The formula was made up of a combination of cuts in spending and aggressive policies to stimulate investment. Conservatives had initially developed their analysis of the urban condition in response to New York City's fiscal crisis of 1975. When the banks refused to underwrite any more of its loans in April of that year, the city suddenly found it impossible to borrow the money it needed to meet payroll obligations and redeem outstanding notes. Conservatives blamed the crisis on a habit of profligate spending. The writer Ken Auletta said the prominent conservative William F. Buckley had been right when he ran for mayor in 1965. As Auletta put it: "We [in New York City] have conducted a noble experiment in local socialism and income redistribution, one clear result of which has been to redistribute much of our tax base and many jobs right out of the city."[92]

Ed Koch won the mayoral race in 1977 by emphasizing just such an analysis of the causes of New York's fiscal crisis. Soon after entering city hall, Koch asserted that "the main job of municipal government is to create a climate in which private business can expand in the city to provide jobs and profit. It's not the function of government to create jobs on the public payroll."[93] In subsequent years, Koch provided billions of dollars of incentives for businesses at the same time he laid off 60,000 city workers. His policies appealed to homeowners in Brooklyn and Queens, who were sick of high taxes, and to real estate developers and to Wall Street firms, who expressed their gratitude in the form of generous campaign contributions.

In the 1990s conservatives continued to attack their opponents as representatives of special interests whose free-spending policies would bankrupt cities. At the same time, they maintained that all problems could ultimately be solved if the private sector were unleashed. The rhetoric of fiscal crisis became a useful way of withdrawing the city from a variety of programs and services with a social content.[94] Mayor Giuliani cut city payrolls and services, reduced income taxes and property taxes on condominiums and co-ops, and slashed the commercial rent tax and the hotel tax on the grounds that reduced taxes would stimulate private investment. His counterpart across the country, Los Angeles mayor Richard Riordan, took a similar approach. "Economic development is the whole future of the city," Riordan said during his first year in office.[95] Working to reduce the regulatory burden on developers, Riordan pushed generous business subsidies. In one case, he put together a $70 million subsidy package to convince Dreamworks SKG to build its new studio in Los Angeles.[96]

Privatization, which was often identified as part of the conservative agenda of the 1980s, became popular with mayors across the political spectrum. The term meant that to reduce costs, city governments should contract out such services as garbage collection and even education (in the form of charter schools). As a way of cutting costs and improving quality, privatization is long standing and noncontroversial. In the city-building era at the beginning of the twentieth century, cities contracted for streetcar, telephone, and utilities services, and many also contracted with private firms for water supply. The city of San Francisco contracted out garbage collection to private companies as early as 1932.[97] Partial privatization, which involves contracting out publicly funded services, often saves city governments money. One of the earliest scholarly evaluations concluded that Scottsdale, Arizona, by contracting for fire protection from a private firm, paid about half of what it would have had to pay if it had provided the service itself.[98] A 1982 survey of 1,780 cities found that the average city contracts approximately 26 percent of its services, in whole or part, to private firms.[99]

In the 1980s, however, privatization became a strategy not only to make government more efficient but also to reduce the size and scope of government altogether. E. S. Savas, called the "the godfather of privatization," served as assistant secretary of Housing and Urban Development (HUD) during the Reagan administration. In his books, Savas stressed that privatization was a tool not only to make a better government but to make a more limited government—"limited in its size, scope, and power relative to society's other institutions."[100] Savas later became an adviser to the Giuliani administration, which used privatization mainly as a threat to squeeze concessions out of municipal unions.

Among mayors, Indianapolis mayor Stephen Goldsmith became one of the most ardent proponents of privatization. Elected in 1992, during his first 18 months in office Goldsmith privatized 14 services, sold off the municipal golf course, and slashed the city payroll from 5,700 to 4,200, giving Indianapolis the lowest number of employees per capita of any of the nation's 50 largest cities.[101] When Goldsmith attempted to contract with neighborhood groups and churches to maintain local parks, however, he found little interest, and his proposal to privatize two troubled public housing projects was vehemently opposed by the residents themselves.[102] Called a "populist Republican," Goldsmith won support by allocating city resources to neighborhood organizations in distressed inner-city neighborhoods, but critics argued that this only crippled the ability of the city to regulate some of its key services.[103]

It is difficult to assess the political significance of the conservative mayors, in part because policies at the urban level rarely can be neatly put into an ideological box. In fact, mayors respond to the constituencies that elect them, and to the overall demographic profiles of their cities. All mayors realize that they must appeal to a diverse array of racial and ethnic groups. For this reason, conservative mayors rarely toe the line in observing the national Republican platform. For example, in the 1990s and beyond both Giuliani and Riordan bucked the national Republican agenda and opposed legislation that would deny government benefits to immigrants who had not yet become citizens. Giuliani's stance cost him dearly in his bid for the presidency in 2008.

A CONVERGENCE OF STYLES

Though it may sometimes appear that a vast gulf divides the different groups that make up the urban electorate, in recent years there has been a notable convergence in governance styles. Conservative and liberal mayors alike must emphasize issues of economic growth. For their part, the conservative mayors must also recognize political realities. This means they must avoid taking inflammatory positions on social issues, and it also means that whatever their preferences, they must learn to work with neighborhood leaders and organizations. Mayors must be careful not to rock the boat in those cities where community development corporations have forged close working relationships with city councils and with city planners and administrators. As a consequence, mayors devoted to fiscal austerity and law-and-order policies often preside over city administrations that work actively with neighborhood organizations and CDCs.

The nature of a city's economy and its political culture powerfully shape a mayor's municipal agenda. The key to the long-term success of any mayor depends upon both an economic and a political logic. On the one hand, a mayor must pursue policies that promote local prosperity. To do this, a mayor must provide a high level of services and amenities to middle-class voters, and nurture a favorable business climate for business. At the same time, other constituencies must remain satisfied enough, or at least not excessively alienated. Economic growth will not solve all problems, and sometimes it foments tensions. In most cities today, the reality is that blacks, Latinos, Asians, women, and, in some cases, gays and lesbians have become incorporated into local political structures, and their influence must be recognized. For this reason, except in cities with a divisive political culture or a racially charged atmosphere, mayors tend to be more pragmatic than ideological. Mayors of all political stripes find themselves caught between an economic logic that leads them to use public resources to promote economic growth and a political logic that requires them to cultivate broad electoral support.

The election of Barack Obama to the presidency in 2008 changed the political atmosphere within which officials at all levels operate. He is a centrist figure, and has spoken often of the importance of reducing the importance of race in U.S. politics. The economic crisis of 2008–2009 fixated public attention on other priorities. But racial and ethnic differences are a fundamental feature of American society, and especially of politics within urban areas. It need not be highly contentious, but the mayor of a city with a complex ethnic and racial makeup cannot afford to ignore its presence.

NOTES

1. Christopher L. Warren, John G. Corbett, and John F. Stack Jr., "Hispanic Ascendancy and Tripartite Politics in Miami," in *Racial Politics in American Cities*, ed. Rufus P. Browning, Dale Rogers Marshall, and David H. Tabb (New York: Longman, 1990), p. 166.

2. James H. Johnson Jr., Cloyzelle K. Jones, Walter C. Farrell Jr., and Melvin L. Oliver, "The Los Angeles Rebellion: A Retrospective View," *Economic Development Quarterly* 6, no. 4 (November 1992): 356–372.

3. Jack Miles, "Blacks vs. Brown," *Atlantic* (October 1992): 41–68; see also Mike Davis, "In L.A., Burning All Illusions," *Nation* (June 1, 1992): 743–746.

4. Tim Rutten, "A New Kind of Riot," *New York Review of Books* (June 11, 1992): 52–54.

5. National Congress for Community Economic Development website (*http://www.ncced.org/aboutUs/faqs.html*).

6. Rodney E. Hero and Susan E. Clarke, "Latinos, Blacks, and Multiethnic Politics in Denver: Realigning Power and Influence in the Struggle for Democracy," in *Racial Politics in American Cities*, 3rd ed., ed. Rufus P. Browning, Dale Rogers Marshall, and David H. Tabb (New York: Longman, 2002), p. 327.

7. Raphael Sonenshein, "The Prospects for Multiracial Coalitions: Lessons from America's Three Largest Cities," in Browning, Marshall, and Tabb, *Racial Politics in American Cities*, 3rd ed., pp. 333–356.

8. Susan S. Fainstein et al., *Restructuring the City: The Political Economy of Urban Redevelopment*, rev. ed. (New York: Longman, 1986), p. 49.

9. Anthony Downs, *Urban Problems and Prospects* (Chicago: Markham, 1970), Chapter 8.

10. Chester Hartman et al., *Yerba Buena: Land Grab and Community Resistance in San Francisco* (San Francisco: Glide, 1974), p. 128.

11. Quoted in Harry C. Boyte, *The Backyard Revolution: Understanding the New Citizen Movement* (Philadelphia: Temple University Press, 1980), p. 11.

12. Economic Opportunity Act of 1964, Public Law 88–452, title II.

13. Frances Fox Piven and Richard A. Cloward, *Regulating the Poor: The Functions of Public Welfare*, rev. ed. (New York: Vintage Books, 1993), Chapter 9.

14. John Clayton Thomas, *Between Citizen and City: Neighborhood Organizations and Urban Politics in Cincinnati* (Lawrence: University Press of Kansas, 1986), pp. 33, 69.

15. Quoted in Piven and Cloward, *Regulating the Poor*, pp. 271–272.

16. U.S. Bureau of the Census, *Statistical Abstract of the United States: 1995* (Washington, D.C.: U.S. Government Printing Office, 1995), p. 287.

17. Joint Center for Political and Economic Studies, *Black Elected Officials: A Statistical Summary, 2001* (Washington, D.C.: Author, 2001), p. 8.

18. National Association of Latino Elected and Appointed Officials (Washington, D.C.: Author, *National Roster of Hispanic Elected Officials*, annual).

19. Hero and Clarke, "Latinos, Blacks, and Multiethnic Politics in Denver," p. 316.

20. John Mollenkopf, *A Phoenix in the Ashes: The Rise and the Fall of the Koch Coalition in New York City Politics* (Princeton, N.J.: Princeton University Press, 1992), p. 12.

21. Raphael J. Sonenshein, *Politics in Black and White: Race and Power in Los Angeles* (Princeton, N.J.: Princeton University Press, 1993), p. 63.

22. Patrick D. Joyce, "A Reversal of Fortunes: Black Empowerment, Political Machines, and City Jobs in New York City and Chicago," *Urban Affairs Review* 32, no. 3 (1997): 291–318.

23. Charles P. Henry, "Urban Politics and Incorporation: The Case of Blacks, Latinos, and Asians in Three Cities," in *Blacks, Latinos, and Asians in Urban America: Status and Prospects for Politics and Activism*, ed. James Jennings (Westport, Conn.: Praeger, 1994), p. 18.

24. Our account of Koch is based on Mollenkopf, *A Phoenix in the Ashes*.

25. Quotes in ibid., pp. 171–172.

26. John Mollenkopf, "New York: Still the Great Anomaly," in Browning, Marshall, and Tabb, *Racial Politics in American Cities*, p. 120.

27. Ibid.

28. Ibid.

29. Hero and Clarke, "Latinos, Blacks and Multiethnic Politics in Denver," p. 317.

30. Rufus P. Browning, Dale Rogers Marshall, and David H. Tabb, "Minority Mobilization in Ten Cities: Failures and Successes," in *Racial Politics in American Cities*, 2nd ed., ed. Rufus P. Browning, Dale Rogers Marshall, and David H. Tabb (New York: Longman, 1995), p. 9.

31. Barbara Ferman, *Governing the Ungovernable City: Political Skill, Leadership, and the Modern Mayor* (Philadelphia: Temple University Press, 1985), Chapter 1; Clarence N. Stone, *Regime Politics: Governing Atlanta 1946–1988* (Lawrence: University Press of Kansas, 1989), Chapter 1. Urban regime theory stresses that cities are not governed by elected officials but by "informal arrangements by which public bodies and private interests function together in order to be able to make and carry out governing decisions." Ibid., p. 6.

32. See Adolph Reed, "The Black Urban Regime: Structural Origins and Constraints," *Comparative Urban and Community Research* 1, no. 1 (1987): 138–189; and "Demobilization in the New Black Political Regime: Ideological Capitulation and Radical Failure in the Postsegregation Era," in *The Bubbling Cauldron: Race, Ethnicity, and the Urban Crisis*, ed. Michael Peter Smith and Joe R. Feagin (Minneapolis: University of Minnesota Press, 1995), pp. 182–208.

33. Maynard Jackson, quoted in Stone, *Regime Politics*, p. 87.

34. Adolph Reed Jr., "A Critique of Neo-Progressivism in Theorizing About Local Development Policy: A Case from Atlanta," in *The Politics of Urban Development*, ed. Clarence N. Stone and Heywood T. Sanders (Lawrence: University Press of Kansas, 1987), p. 206.

35. Quoted in Stone, *Regime Politics*, p. 136.

36. The evaluation of black progress in Atlanta that follows is based on Gary Orfield and Carole Ashkinaze, *The Closing Door: Conservative Policy and Black Opportunity* (Chicago: University of Chicago Press, 1991).

37. Cited in ibid., p. 151.

38. William Julius Wilson, *The Truly Disadvantaged: The Inner City, the Underclass, and Public Policy* (Chicago: University of Chicago Press, 1987), p. 135.

39. Sonenshein, *Politics in Black and White*, p. 168.

40. Rufus P. Browning, Dale Rogers Marshall, and David H. Tabb, *Protest Is Not Enough: The Struggle of Blacks and Hispanics for Equality in Urban Politics* (Berkeley: University of California Press, 1984), pp. 171–174; Peter K. Eisinger, "Black Mayors and the Politics of Racial Economic Advancement," in *Urban Politics: Past, Present, and Future*, 2nd ed., ed. Harlan Hahn and Charles H. Levine (New York: Longman, 1984), pp. 249–260; Kenneth R. Mladenka, "Blacks and Hispanics in Urban Politics," *American Political Science Review* 83, no. 1 (March 1989): 165–191. Mladenka concludes that minority mayors have little impact on policy outcomes, but minority council majorities do.

41. Sonenshein, *Politics in Black and White*, p. 152.

42. Timothy Bates and Darrell Williams, "Preferential Procurement Programs and Minority-Owned Businesses," *Journal of Urban Affairs* 17, no. 1 (1995): 1.

43. Stone, *Regime Politics*, p. 145.

44. *City of Richmond v. J. A. Croson Co.*, 109 S.Ct. 706 (1989).

45. Mitchell F. Rice, "State and Local Government Set-Aside Programs, Disparity Studies, and Minority Business Development in the Post-*Croson* Era," *Journal of Urban Affairs* 15, no. 6 (1993): 529–553.

46. Mike Davis, *City of Quartz: Excavating the Future in Los Angeles* (London: Verso, 1990), pp. 251–253.

47. Ibid., p. 277.

48. Ibid., p. 272.

49. Sonenshein, *Politics in Black and White*, pp. 155–161.

50. Albert Karnig and Susan Welch, *Black Representation and Urban Policy* (Chicago: University of Chicago Press, 1980); Eisinger, "Black Mayors"; Browning, Marshall, and Tabb, *Protest Is Not*

Enough; Mladenka, "Blacks and Hispanics in Urban Politics"; Grace Hall Saltzstein, "Black Mayors and Police Policies," *Journal of Politics* 51, no. 3 (August 1989): 525–544.

51. Paula D. McClain and Albert Karnig, "Black and Hispanic Socioeconomic and Political Competition," *American Political Science Review* 84, no. 2 (June 1990): 535–545; Paula D. McClain, "The Changing Dynamics of Urban Politics: Black and Hispanic Municipal Employment—Is There Competition?" *Journal of Politics* 55, no. 2 (May 1993): 399–414.

52. Eisinger, "Black Mayors," p. 257.

53. See the detailed case studies of 12 cities in Browning, Marshall, and Tabb, *Racial Politics in American Cities*, 3rd ed.

54. Eisinger, "Black Mayors," p. 258.

55. Wilson, *The Truly Disadvantaged*, p. 115.

56. Perry, in Browning, Marshall, and Tabb, *Racial Politics in America*, 3rd ed., p. 251.

57. Lawrence Bobo and Franklin D. Gilliam Jr., "Race, Sociopolitical Participation, and Black Empowerment," *American Political Science Review* 84, no. 2 (June 1990): 377–393.

58. See Browning, Marshall, and Tabb, *Racial Politics in American Cities*, 3rd ed.

59. Carmine Scavo, "The Use of Regulative Mechanisms by Large U.S. Cities," *Journal of Urban Affairs* 15, no. 1 (1993): 100.

60. Robert F. Pecorella, *Community Power in a Postreform City* (Armonk, N.Y.: M. E. Sharpe, 1994).

61. Jeffrey M. Berry, Kent E. Portney, and Ken Thomson, *The Rebirth of Urban Democracy* (Washington, D.C.: Brookings Institution Press, 1993), p. 13.

62. Edward G. Goetz, *Shelter Burden: Local Politics and Progressive Housing Policy* (Philadelphia: Temple University Press, 1993), p. 52.

63. Carl Abbott, *Portland: Planning, Politics, and Growth in a Twentieth-Century City* (Lincoln: University of Nebraska Press, 1983), Chapters 8 and 9.

64. Thomas, *Between Citizen and City*, Chapter 6.

65. Pierre Clavel, *The Progressive City: Planning and Participation, 1969–1984* (New Brunswick, N.J.: Rutgers University Press, 1986), Chapter 2.

66. Stella M. Capek and John I. Gilderbloom, *Community Versus Commodity: Tenants and the American City* (Albany: State University of New York Press, 1992), p. 182.

67. Ibid., p. 212.

68. Joe R. Feagin, *Free Enterprise City: Houston in Political and Economic Perspective* (New Brunswick, N.J.: Rutgers University Press, 1988), pp. 279–280.

69. Todd Swanstrom, *The Crisis of Growth Politics: Cleveland, Kucinich, and the Challenge of Urban Populism* (Philadelphia: Temple University Press, 1985).

70. Peter Medoff and Holly Sklar, *Streets of Hope: The Fall and Rise of an Urban Neighborhood* (Boston: South End Press, 1994).

71. Peter Dreier and W. Dennis Keating, "The Limits of Localism: Progressive Housing Policies in Boston, 1984–1989," *Urban Affairs Quarterly* 26, no. 2 (December 1990): 191–216.

72. Quoted in Jack Newfield, *Robert Kennedy: A Memoir* (New York: E. P. Dutton, 1969), p. 94.

73. Goetz, *Shelter Burden*, p. 117.

74. National Congress of Community Economic Development (NCCED), *Tying It All Together: The Comprehensive Achievements of Community-Based Development Organizations* (Washington, D.C.: Author, 1995), pp. 1, 2.

75. U.S. Department of Housing and Urban Development (HUD), *Status and Prospects of the Nonprofit Housing Sector* (Washington, D.C.: Author, June 1995), p. 31.

76. NCCED, *Tying It All Together*, p. 9.

77. James Rouse died on April 9, 1996.

78. Reported in HUD, *Status and Prospects*, p. 46.

79. Community Reinvestment Act of 1977, 12 USC 2901.

80. Calvin Bradford, *Community Reinvestment Agreement Library* (Des Plaines, Ill.: Community Reinvestment Associates, 1992); as reported in *From Redlining to Reinvestment: Community Responses to Urban Disinvestment*, ed. Gregory D. Squires (Philadelphia: Temple University Press, 1992), p. 2.

81. Barbara Ferman, *Challenging the Growth Machine: Neighborhood Politics in Chicago and Pittsburgh* (Lawrence: University Press of Kansas, 1996), p. 99.

82. Randy Stoecker, "Empowering Redevelopment: Toward a Different CDC," *Shelterforce* (May/June 1996).

83. Robert Fisher, "Community Organizing in the Conservative '80s and Beyond," *Social Policy* 25, no. 1 (Fall 1994): 11–20.

84. Avis C. Vidal, *Rebuilding Communities: A National Study of Urban Community Development Corporations* (New York: New School for Social Research, 1992), p. 54.

85. Karen M. Kaufmann, "A Tale of Two Cities: The Impact of Intergroup Conflict on Mayoral Voting Behavior in Los Angeles and New York," paper delivered at the American Political Science Association Meeting, San Francisco, August 29–September 1, 1996, p. 18. Giuliani was reelected by a wide margin in 1997.

86. Ibid., p. 22.

87. Institute for Puerto Rican Policy, *The Giuliani Budget Cuts and People of Color: Disproportionate Employment Impact* (New York: Institute for Puerto Rican Policy, 1994), p.1; as reported in Michael Leo Owens, "Race, Place, and Government Employment," paper delivered at the New York State Political Science Association Meeting, Ithaca, New York, March 29–30, 1996, p. 12.

88. Thomas Byrne Edsall and Mary D. Edsall, *Chain Reaction: The Impact of Race, Rights, and Taxes on American Politics* (New York: Norton, 1991), p. 224. Emphasis on the word *signal* removed from the original.

89. Grace Hall Saltzstein, "Black Mayors and Police Policies," *Journal of Politics* 51, no. 3 (1989): 525–544.

90. Randy Kennedy, "FBI Reports New York Safer Than Most Cities," *New York Times,* January 6, 1997, p. B5.

91. University of Virginia Library, Geospatial and Statistical Data Center (*http://fisher.lib.virginia.edu/crime/crimes94.html*).

92. Quoted in William E. Simon, *A Time for Truth* (New York: Berkeley Books, 1978), p. 155.

93. Quoted in Martin Shefter, *Political Crisis/Fiscal Crisis: The Collapse and Revival of New York City* (New York: Basic Books, 1985), p. 175.

94. Ester R. Fuchs, *Mayors and Money: Fiscal Policy in New York and Chicago* (Chicago: University of Chicago Press, 1992).

95. Quoted in Laura Mecoy, "Ain't Too Proud to Beg: Is L.A.'s Businessman Mayor Good for L.A. Business?" *Los Angeles,* July 1996.

96. Ibid.

97. David F. Linowes, *Privatization: Toward More Effective Government. Report of the President's Commission on Privatization* (Urbana: University of Illinois Press, 1988), p. 2.

98. Roger S. Ahlbrandt Jr., *Municipal Fire Protection Services: Comparison of Alternative Organizational Forms* (Beverly Hills, Calif.: Sage, 1973).

99. Derived from *Rethinking Local Services: Examining Alternative Service Delivery Approaches* (Washington, D.C.: International City Management Association, 1984), Table B; as reported in E. S. Savas, *Privatization: The Key to Better Government* (Chatham, N.J.: Chatham House, 1987), p. 72.

100. Ibid., p. 288.

101. Nancy Hass, "Philadelphia Freedom: How Privatization Has Worked Wonders in the City of Brotherly Love and Beyond," *Financial World* 162, no. 16 (1993): 37.

102. William D. Eggers, "Righting City Hall," *National Review* 46, no. 16 (1994): 40.

103. Rob Gurwitt, "Indianapolis and the Republican Future," *Governing* 7, no. 5 (February 1994): 24–28.

CHAPTER 15

THE POLITICAL FAULT LINES OF THE GLOBAL ERA

URBAN POLITICS IN THE TWENTY-FIRST CENTURY

Globalization has intensified competition among cities, quickened the pace of immigration, and changed spatial relationships within metropolitan areas. Cities have fought hard for a share of the new global economy, and they have succeeded to a remarkable degree. The professional and service-sector employment connected to the global economy have contributed to the revival of central cities. In many cases, urban regions hit hard by the deindustrialization of the 1970s and 1980s have made stunning comebacks. Immigration has created tensions, but it also has made the suburbs more racially and ethnically diverse than they ever have been before. Metropolitan regions continue to sprawl outward, but the new urban form has decisively ended the bitter antagonisms that pitted city against suburb in the postwar era.

Not long ago, it would have been said that downtown revitalization and the opening of the suburbs to people of all income levels and ethnic backgrounds would have signaled the end of "the urban crisis," at least as it came to be defined in the second half of the twentieth century, as a crisis of racial segregation and conflict. Now the impact of these developments seems less certain. Although crime rates, residential segregation, and concentrated poverty have all declined, these trends are contradicted by other developments, including especially the sharp dichotomy between affluent service workers in the central city and the armies of low-income workers who commute there, and the proliferation of ethnic enclaves in the suburbs. Since 2000 the national poverty rate has been rising, and economic restructuring continues to lock many workers out of the labor market. The economic crisis of 2008–2009 is certain to make some of these problems worse, but the basic contours of urban politics will not be much changed.

THE ECONOMIC IMPERATIVE: A REPRISE

In recent decades, cities (as well as nations) have joined in a fierce competition for a share of the global economy. Local efforts have had some effect, as evidenced by the groves of skyscrapers and clusters of entertainment facilities that have sprouted in recent years in the larger cities that house the new economic activities that drive downtown development: finance, telecommunications, corporate and professional offices, tourism and leisure. Cities of all sizes and circumstances try to get their share. Just two months before Hurricane Katrina hit the city, the state of Louisiana agreed to give the New Orleans Saints $12.4 million to keep them from leaving.[1] Meanwhile, as we now know, the levees were in bad repair. For some people, this policy trade-off might be interpreted as a metaphor for the policy priorities of governmental officials everywhere.

Who reaps the benefits of the new global economy? The advantages for a cosmopolitan class that hold the best jobs can be observed in the urban lifestyle magazines published in all cities that aspire to a measure of stature. These magazines are similar from city to city because the target audience is unvarying: an affluent middle class made up disproportionately of empty nesters and younger singles or childless couples. Each month, columns written by a new breed of lifestyle writers and critics profile restaurants and entertainment spots, wine and cigar bars, shopping opportunities, and the other components of an urbane lifestyle. As a result, similar downtown environments have been reproduced over and over, even in cities that seem not to be "global," although the details may differ.

It is important to consider whether affluent urban residents live, work, and play in "Potemkin cities,"[2] where a thriving downtown and a tourist bubble hide urban problems, or in "boutique cities" like Seattle and Denver, where highly paid professionals are able to sustain a critical mass of expensive restaurants, international boutique and clothing stores, and neighborhoods with stratospheric housing prices.[3] In the past, African Americans in poor neighborhoods were often threatened by the urban renewal bulldozer. In the new century, ethnic minorities and new immigrants face a bulldozer with a friendlier face; after all, homeowners living in gentrifying neighborhoods can reap benefits from rising property values. But there is no use glossing over the fact that there are many losers: working-class residents and the poor are regularly shoved out by the gentrifying professional class. The politics of economic inequality plays out a little differently in the suburbs, but with equal force. The residents of older inner-ring suburbs often are displaced by gentrification, like their city cousins. Housing prices throughout metropolitan regions have been rising faster than average incomes since at least the mid-1990s, and in some areas long before.

What possible remedies are there for these problems? Judging by the policies they favor, for local political leaders the most important thing they can do is more of the same. Other issues may seem pressing, but none receive more care and feeding than businesses, investors, affluent homeowners, and others (such as tourists) who might help bring prosperity. At the same time, urban leaders go to great pains to persuade the citizenry that everyone benefits from these policies. Such public relations are a crucial task at all times, but especially when racial and ethnic groups may feel neglected, and when ugly social problems are hard to ignore.

THE POLITICS OF GOVERNANCE: A REPRISE

Despite its pivotal importance, the economic imperative sometimes must give way, or is balanced by, another imperative: the need to attend to the competing claims made by a complex mixture of groups. The flood tide of immigration set off by globalization has guaranteed that the task of governance will be as challenging as ever in the past. Though issues of race and ethnicity are constantly present and sometimes become contentious, it must be emphasized that there is no single or overriding interest that brings the various groups together. "Rainbow" coalitions that bring together African Americans with new immigrant groups have been rare, but tensions among the groups have been common.[4] Broad alliances within the central cities are rare enough; in the suburbs, they are made virtually impossible by governmental fragmentation. A particular group may exert influence in one community, but in the next they may be absent from the political scene altogether.

Racial and ethnic tensions still arise over two issues: police conduct and gentrification. Flashpoints for racial tension, including the possibility of disorders, still exist. Incidents involving the police precipitated virtually all of the riots of the 1960s.[5] Police conduct still stokes frequent controversies, and from time to time these have erupted into civil disorders. A quite typical incident occurred in early August 2006, in the Cabrini-Green public housing projects in Chicago, when police shot a 14-year-old boy who was brandishing a BB gun. In the wake of the shooting, demonstrators turned out to march around city hall. In cities all across the nation, such incidents occur frequently, and any one of them can ignite racial turmoil.

The gentrification of neighborhoods is also a source of tension. For more than forty years, the Humboldt Park neighborhood in Chicago has been home to the largest Puerto Rican population in the city, and one of the largest in the United States. Two steel sculptures of the Puerto Rican flag serve as a reminder that the neighborhood has a distinctive culture. But as white professionals and artists have flooded into the neighborhood and housing prices have rapidly increased, longtime residents have been displaced. In 2006 one store window displayed a "No Yuppies" sign, and verbal confrontations sometimes occured. As if to pour gasoline onto the flame (though inadvertently), one of the newcomers said, "I try to tell them before Puerto Ricans were there, there were European Jews. And before the Jews, the Polish community was here. Neighborhoods change."[6] Perhaps so, but not without resentment, resistance, and the myriad problems that displacement brings in its path.

Economic inequality is an issue shared in common by African Americans and the new immigrants. Since the turn of the twenty-first century, the number of people living in poverty has been steadily rising in the United States, from a low of 11.4 percent in 2000 to 12.5 percent in 2003. The poverty figures were much higher for children; by 2003, 17.6 percent of the population under the age of 18 was living in poverty households. The numbers of the medically uninsured also rose during this period, to 15.6 percent of the population.[7] Tax cuts enacted in 2001 and 2002 increased tax burdens for middle-income taxpayers while reducing them for upper-income households.[8] These tax policies were just the latest round in a series of policies that have been redistributing incomes and wealth upward in the United States since the 1980s.

In the past, poverty and inequality have been closely associated with social disorder, expressed in the form of crime, riots, and family disorganization and community breakdown. High levels of family and community pathology still exist in poverty communities, but this does not much matter to the members of the middle class as long as it does not touch them directly. The expressions of social disorder that touch them or that carry great symbolic weight—crime and urban rioting—have abated in the last decade. But this social peace may be fragile. In a survey conducted on the tenth anniversary of the Los Angeles riots of 1992, 50 percent of Los Angeles residents expressed the belief that riots were likely to break out in the next five years. Strikingly, this appraisal did not vary significantly among different ethnic and racial groups. These findings do not mean riots will occur, but they are not reassuring, either.[9]

The disorganized response to the devastation visited upon New Orleans by Hurricane Katrina in September 2005 cast a national spotlight on the racial inequalities still present in America's cities. Because they lived in the least desirable areas of the city—the lowest elevation—blacks were disproportionately affected by the flooding. The political vulnerability of African American residents was also revealed. When disaster struck, the Bush administration's response was built on the assumption that everyone in New Orleans had ample personal resources. It "assumed that people would evacuate New Orleans on their own, without giving much thought to who these people were, what resources they had, or where they would go. They acted as if everyone had an SUV full of gas and family or friends (or a second home) waiting to take them in somewhere else."[10] For some people, this gaffe might be interpreted as a metaphor for the racial divide that continues to haunt American society, and for the failure of government to effectively respond to it.

THE POLITICS OF DEFENDED SPACE: A REPRISE

The falling crime rates of the 1990s were directly related to the revival of street life and nightlife in central cities. In most American cities, people representing all income, ethnic, and racial groups mingle freely on streets and in tourist and entertainment venues. But at the same time the new downtowns and gentrified neighborhoods are as segregated as the suburbs, though on a smaller scale. Many affluent urban residents commute from subdivisions, gated communities, townhouse developments, or condominium complexes (or at the other end of the social scale, from ghettos and run-down neighborhoods) to high-rise downtown office buildings or suburban office parks, and they drive to enclosed malls or mall complexes for shopping and commute to tourist bubbles to enjoy themselves.[11] This lifestyle creates a situation in which some urban residents experience the urban environment as little more than a series of enclosures, each connected by a transportation corridor that is itself cut off from the rest of the city.

Evidence indicates that the construction of enclaves and some degree of residential integration are happening at the same time. In the 1990s Asians and Latinos settled in the suburbs in large numbers, but a large proportion of both groups now live in ethnic enclaves that are more separated from whites than before.[12] Residential segregation levels for Latinos and Asians increased slightly in the 1990s,[13] but these groups were less segregated in the suburbs than in the central cities.[14] Some suburbs are highly segregated, whereas others provide housing opportunities for minorities and immigrants, especially if they earn middle-class incomes.

It is difficult to read the spatial future of the suburbs from present patterns. There can be no doubt that suburbs have opened to minorities and to the poor. The immigration of Asians, Latinos, and other groups has made most metropolitan areas, including their suburbs, multiethnic rather than biracial. During the 1990s, for example, two parallel streams moved to Orange County, California, just outside Los Angeles: highly educated professionals and foreign-born immigrants. The two streams could hardly have been more different; high-income families making more than $150,000 per year jumped by 184 percent in the county, but at the same time the number of foreign-born immigrants increased by 48 percent.[15] Commenting on these trends, a noted demographer said the county could go into two directions, either a "mostly gated-community-type mentality" or "immigrants start integrating into middle-class areas, so you have a blended suburbia."[16]

In part, residential patterns may be a consequence of how recently minorities and immigrants have moved into the suburbs. Over time, they may become incorporated into the politics of suburbs just as they have become incorporated into the politics of central cities. Suburbs are highly variable. Oak Park and Cicero, both on the border of Chicago, have changed quickly in the last few years. Oak Park is a middle-class to upper-income suburb that also has a stock of affordable housing. Cicero is much different: Long a white working-class bastion known for rough-and-tumble, often corrupt politics, in a decade it has become a majority-Latino city. Suburbs of all types are similarly changing in metropolitan areas across the United States. Segregated enclaves are sure to continue, but they will not necessarily be the defining feature of suburban life.

Even if so, other forces are at work that may turn cities and urban areas into a constellation of enclaves. Soon after the terrorist attacks on September 11, 2001, the urban scholar Peter Marcuse predicted that the fear of terrorism would lead to the fortification and close surveillance of urban spaces. In addition to physical fortifications and increased barriers of access, he mentions metal detectors, fingerprint card entry, and other devices for controlling people's movement.[17] Marcuse asserts that the barricading of urban space will make any form of democratic expression and popular protest, such as rallies and marches, more difficult. The result would be that "the core of urban social and political life" would be undermined.[18]

In contradiction to this view, crowds still gather freely at public events on downtown streets and surveys have shown that by March 2002—less than a year after the terrorist attacks in the United States—public anxieties about the threat of terrorism were relatively low.[19] But these attitudes will persist only as long as further attacks do not occur, and as long as urban crime is kept from the districts inhabited by affluent people. Without doubt, cities are more open than they were in the troubled period of urban riots, intense racial animosity, and rising crime; at the same time, the privatization urban space goes in the opposite direction.

THE CAPACITY TO GOVERN

The slow and disorganized response to the devastation wrought on New Orleans by Hurricane Katrina in September 2005 raised questions about the capacity of America's governmental institutions to solve major problems. Governments at all levels were implicated in the Keystone Cops response. Mayor Ray Nagin seemed perplexed and overwhelmed. Many police officers failed to come to work; a few even joined in the looting of local stores. The city's hospitals virtually abandoned care for some patients for several days. Despite a history of close calls from hurricanes, the city had no disaster plan in place. At first the mayor told residents to stay, then he told them to leave.[20]

Even if the city had been better run, the disaster would have been too much for it to handle; clearly, higher levels of government were needed. But the bumbling response by local officials was more than matched by the federal government's incompetence. Mayor Nagin expressed his frustration: "I don't know whether it's the governor's problem. I don't know whether it's the president's problem. But somebody needs to get their ass on a plane and sit down, the two of them, and figure this out."[21] In fact, however, even in the aftermath it has not been figured out, and the complex intergovernmental system in the United States makes it difficult to do so.

The terrorist attacks of September 11, 2001, also raised the alarm about the capacity of governments to respond to large-scale disasters. In New York's case, the response was much more effective. The city's emergency response was extraordinary by any standard. Mayor Giuliani provided strong leadership—strong enough to make him a potential presidential contender. Days after the attack on the World Trade Center Twin Towers, President Bush promised $20 billion to the city. Most of this money was spent for emergency response, debris removal, and overtime labor costs. Nearly half the funds, those designated for rebuilding projects, including transportation improvements, had not been spent by 2006.[22]

What is the proper relationship between the federal government and the cities? Do cities possess the capacity to respond to all problems that may face them? Hurricane Katrina and the terrorist attacks offer a mixed message. With sufficient national attention and effective local leadership, the response can be impressive, as revealed by the massive response to Hurricane Gustav when it threatened New Orleans in September 2008. Nevertheless, it is clear that the fragmented system of government in the United States is not well equipped to respond to emergencies, a fact brought home by flooding on the Mississippi River near St. Louis in June 2008. Governments at all levels found it hard to respond to the imminent danger to dikes protecting small towns because the levees were "owned and maintained by all sorts of towns, agencies, even individual farmers."[23] The task of responding is at least equally difficult when it comes to smaller, incremental, less dramatic and more intractable problems, such as urban poverty, a shortage of affordable housing, gang violence, and inadequate education.

The political landscape of national politics has been fundamentally altered by the election of Barack Obama as President. He is a transformational figure in many ways, but it is too early to tell if the relationship between the national government and the cities will change very much. The American Recovery and Reinvestment Act, which was signed into law by President Obama on February 17, 2009, authorized $144 billion for infrastructure projects, and a substantial portion of those funds will be expended by local governments. The Obama administration also launched a $1 billion program to put 5,500 more police on the streets.[24] In striking contrast to the previous administration, officials in the White House are establishing relationships with local officials and their organizations. In February, the President appointed an "urban czar" to oversee and coordinate urban-related programs. These are small steps, but they seem to indicate that indifference to the cities may become less of a presence in federal–local relations than in the past.

NOTES

1. "Louisiana Forks Over $12.4M to Saints," *USA Today*, July 6, 2005, p. 15C.
2. According to historical accounts, General Potemkin constructed fake villages in preparation for a tour by Catherine II of the Crimea in 1787. The purpose was to fool her into thinking his conquests were of great value to the Russian empire.
3. Neal R. Peirce, "Business Basic: Rx for All Cities," *Washington Post*, March 5, 1999.
4. Reuel R. Rogers, "Minority Groups and Coalitional Politics," *Urban Affairs Review* 39, no. 3 (January 2004): 283–317.
5. *Report of the National Advisory Commission on Civil Disorders* (New York: Bantam Books, 1968).
6. Antonio Olivo, "Edge About 'Yuppies'," *Chicago Tribune*, June 12, 2006, pp. 1, 20.
7. CNN.com, "Census: More Americans Living in Poverty," August 31, 2004 (*http://www.cnn.com*).
8. Ibid.
9. Mara A. Marks, Matt A. Barreto, and Nathan D. Woods, "Race and Racial Attitudes a Decade After the 1992 Los Angeles Riots," *Urban Affairs Review* 40, no. 1 (2004): 3–18.
10. Peter Dreier, "Katrina and Power in America," *Urban Affairs Review* 41, no. 4 (March 2006), p. 535.
11. Dennis R. Judd, "Enclosure, Community, and Public Life," in *Research in Community Sociology: New Communities in a Changing World*, ed. Dan A. Chekki (Greenwich, Conn., and London: JAI Press, 1996), pp. 217–238.
12. John R. Logan, "The New Ethnic Enclaves in America's Suburbs," a report by the Lewis Mumford Center for Comparative Urban and Regional Research (Albany, N.Y.: 2002), pp. 1–2.
13. Ibid., p. 253.
14. William A. V. Clark and Sarah A. Blue, "Race, Class, and Segregation Patterns in U.S. Immigrant Gateway Cities," *Urban Affairs Review* 39, no. 6 (2004): 667–688.
15. Jim Hinch and Ronald Campbell, "Gated Enclaves One Future for Orange County," *Orange County Register*, May 15, 2002 (*http://www.ocregister.com*).
16. Ibid., quoting William Frey, a demographer in the Milken Institute of Los Angeles.
17. Peter Marcuse, "The 'War on Terrorism' and Life in Cities after September 11, 2001," in *Cities, War, and Terrorism: Towards an Urban Geopolitics*, ed. Stephen Graham (New York: Blackwell, 2005), p. 271.
18. Ibid., pp. 274–275.
19. Peter Eisenger, "The American City in the Age of Terror: A Preliminary Assessment of the Effects of September 11," *Urban Affairs Review* 40, no. 1 (2004): 115–130. The surveys summarized by Eisenger were reported in Christopher Hoene, Mark Balassare, and Christiana Brennan, *Homeland Security and America's Cities: Research Brief on America's Cities* (Washington, D.C.: National League of Cities, 2002); and Center for Urban Studies, *Michigan Statewide Survey* (Detroit, Mich.: Wayne State University, 2003).

20. Peter Dreier, "Katrina and Power in America," *Urban Affairs Review* 41, no. 4 (March 2006): 534–535.

21. Ibid., p. 528.

22. Steven D. Stehr, "The Political Economy of Urban Disaster Assistance," *Urban Affairs Review* 41, no. 4 (March 2006): 495.

23. Monica Davey, "Call for Change Ignored, Levees Remain Patchy," *New York Times*, June 23, 2008 (*http://www.nytimes.com/2008/06/22us/22midwest.html*).

24. National League of Cities, "NLC Applauds Announcement of COPS Hiring Recovery Program" (*http://www.nlc.org/PRESSROOM/PRESSRELEASEITEMS/*).

INDEX